GW00372326

Linked Local
Area Networks

LINKED LOCAL AREA NETWORKS

Second Edition

ALAN J. MAYNE

A Wiley-Interscience Publication

JOHN WILEY & SONS

New York · Chichester · Brisbane · Toronto · Singapore

Library of Congress Cataloging in Publication Data:

Mayne, Alan J. (Alan James), 1927–
 Linked local area networks.

 "A Wiley–Interscience publication."
 Bibliography: p.
 Includes index.
 1. Local area networks (Computer networks)
I. Title.
TK5105.7.M39 1985   001.64′404   85-6290
ISBN 0-471-80152-6

Printed in the United States of America

10 9 8 7 6 5 4 3 2 1

Preface

In the middle of 1983, John Wiley & Sons commissioned me to prepare the second edition of this book, whose first edition was published by The October Press Limited in England.

This book presents a general overview of computer networks and networking, and brings out the relations between different aspects of this subject area, as well as the connections with computing, office automation, and information technology in general. It emphasizes local area networks, but gives enough information about wide area networks to indicate how to link local area networks at different sites of the same organisation.

Although it is moderately technical in places, it does not require much specific knowledge in the reader, apart from a broad general appreciation of computing and telecommunications and their practical applications.

Organisations using integrated office, business, and information systems need to make increasing use of computer networks, especially local area networks, but also wide area networks that communicate between their premises at different locations. Therefore, nonspecialist users, as well as computer experts and other technologists, should gain a working understanding of the full potentialities and capabilities of networks. This book is thus intended especially for decision makers and managers as well as data processing and technical staff in organisations which might require computer networks and office automation.

To help provide them with the necessary background and understanding, this book is particularly addressed to those in organisations who need well authenticated and explicit guidance through the theory and practice as well as potential of networked computer facilities, which are linked locally or citywise or nationally or internationally. It should provide them with the most important general information, which will place them in a position to pursue their more detailed enquiries in greater depth.

The original four parts of the first edition of the book, on network systems and services, network technologies, network applications, and wider aspects of networks, have been retained with little alteration. In order to do full justice to the very rapid and extensive advances in computer networking that have been occurring since then, I have added Part Five, "Recent Developments," which contains six new chapters, and is organised similarly. This takes account of progress made up to and including early 1984.

Chapter 19, "Recent Developments in Network Systems and Services," is similar to Part One. Chapter 20, "Recent Developments in Network Technologies," and Chapter 21, "Recent Developments in Network Architectures Protocols and Standards," correspond to Part Two; Chapter 20 also covers in greater detail equipment inside networks and network testing, management and control systems, and Chapter 21 outlines the structures of several leading network architectures. Chapter 22, "Recent Developments in Network Applications," is like Part Three. Chapter 23, "Case Studies of Networks," describes over sixty examples of different types of computer networks in actual use, between them covering a wide range of applications and organisations. Chapter 24, "Current Network Problems and Prospects," updates Part Four.

In the rest of the book, I have added an extra section at the end of "Guide to Further Reading," to sum up the most recent literature on computer networks and allied fields. I have updated the Appendices and Indexes, although the Glossary has needed little change.

In the new material of the book, I have devoted relatively more attention to developments in North America, where most readers of the second edition are likely to live and work, but I have given much coverage also to progress in the UK, Europe, and Japan, especially.

I am most grateful to James T. Gaughan, Editor of the Wiley Interscience Division, for his helpful advice, and to my literary agent, Richard Gollner of Radala and Associates, for introducing me to John Wiley and Sons, Inc. I wish to express my thanks to both of them for their continuing encouragement for my work on a project that I have always found very interesting, but sometimes difficult because of the very fast and relentless expansion of its subject matter.

ALAN J. MAYNE

Milton Keynes, England
October 1985

Preface to the First Edition

At the beginning of 1979 I started to work in the field of computer networks when I was invited to join the INDRA Group at the Department of Computer Science, University College London. This Group, ably led by Professor Peter T. Kirstein, Head of the Department, has been carrying out some very important research on computer networks and several allied information technologies, for nearly ten years. From the outset it has played an important part in international discussions about research on networks and standards for networks.

In particular, it has been the leading British Group in the Arpanet, a well-known international network, sponsored by the USA's Defense Advanced Research Projects Agency, that links computers working for universities and defence projects on both sides of the Atlantic. As such, the Arpanet's participants, including members of the INDRA Group, have been notable pioneers of many aspects of the science, technology and art of computer networking. Starting with work on land-based wide area networks, members of the Arpanet later made important contributions to work on local area networks, especially the Cambridge Rings and Ethernets, packet radio networks, and satellite networks.

In due course the INDRA Group itself added electronic mail and message services, facsimile, office automation and videotex to its interests, and it established close cooperation with several other organisations, not only universities and defence establishments but also the Post Office Research Centre, later to become the British Telecom Research Laboratories, and the firms of Logica and GEC.

Because of this, and because INDRA receives a very extensive collection of literature on all aspects of computing, data communications and information technology, I was in an exceptionally good position to study computer networks further and to become aware of advances in this field very soon after they were made, indeed sometimes while they were still in progress.

In the middle of 1981 I met Stephen Pugsley, Head of Publishing of The October Press, who commissioned me to write first *The Videotex Revolution*, published in May 1982, and then the present book. I am very grateful to him for the invitation to write this book, to Peter Kirstein and other members of INDRA and several members of the British Telecom Research Laboratories for their encouragement and for the valuable information that they provided, to fellow-members of the OFIX Working Party on Local Area Networks for their useful discussions, and to all of them for their helpful advice.

I am grateful to Peter Kirstein and his colleagues for allowing me to use the computing facilities of his Department, including its version of the UNIX operating system, to word process most of the text of this book.

In addition, I am grateful to Keith Wolfenden, Professor of Information Processing in the Department of Computer Science, University College London, and to others, too numerous to mention individually, for their valuable discussions with me about information retrieval, data bases, and information services, subjects which are relevant to the theme of this book, as they constitute one of the most important applications of computer networks.

I have found the writing of this book specially interesting, not only for the reasons already mentioned, but also because I was able to introduce a wide variety of different subjects. I welcomed the chance to discuss, not only the network systems and technologies, but also their applications and impacts. This gave me a good opportunity to discuss briefly, near the end of this book, my ideas on how the human situation as a whole could be improved with the aid of computer networking and other information technologies, and to report on the Peace Network, one of several pioneering projects which could well make a valuable contribution to this major objective.

ALAN J. MAYNE

London, England
December 1982

Acknowledgments

The author and the publisher are grateful to the following copyright holders and their representatives, who have kindly given permission to reproduce the following figures and illustrations:

Barbara Howley, Administrator Copyrights and Permissions of The Institute of Electrical and Electronics Engineers, Inc., New York, for permission to reproduce, from Vol. **66,** No. 11 (November 1978) of *Proceedings of the IEEE*, its Special Issue on Packet Communication Networks: from "Principles and lessons in packet communications," by L. R. Kleinrock, Figure 1 as Figure 6.10; from "Issues in packet-network interconnection," by V. G. Cerf and P. T. Kirstein, Figures 1 to 7 as Figures 6.12, 9.7, 9.4 to 9.6, 6.13 and 6.14, and Figures 15 to 18 as Figures 17.1 to 17.4; from "General purpose satellite networks," by I. M. Jacobs, R. Binder and E. V. Hoversten, Figures 1, 4 and 8 as Figures 8.4, 10.1 and 10.2; from "Advances in packet radio technology," by R. E. Kahn, S. A. Gronemeyer, K. Burchfiel and R. C. Kunzelman, Figure 12 as Figure 8.3; from "An introduction to local area networks," by D. D. Clark, K. T. Pogran and D. P. Reed, Figures 2 and 10 as Figures 6.16 and 6.15; from "Economic analysis of integrated voice and data networks," by I. Gitman and H. Frank, Figures 13 and 14 as Figures 15.1 and 15.2.

Malcolm Stern, Editorial Director, Gower Publishing Company, Aldershot, Hampshire, for permission to reproduce, from its books edited by Alan Simpson, the following figures: from *Planning for the Office of the Future* (1981), Figure 4 on page 38, Figure 8 on page 8, and Figures 6 and 7 on page 83, as Figures 11.1, 11.2, 12.1, and 12.2; from *Planning for Electronic Mail* (1982), Figure 5 on page 94 and the figure on page 59, as Figures 6.5 and 13.1; from *Planning for Telecommunications* (1982), Figure 1 on page 111, Figure 3 on page 59, Figure 4 on page 60, and Figure 3 on page 27, as Figures 6.3, 6.4, 6.6 and 11.6.

Malcolm Stewart, Editor, Macmillan, London and Basingstoke, and the author, for permission to reproduce, as Figure 6.2, Figure 4.11 from page 66 of Robert Cole's book, *Computer Communications* (1982).

Dr Einar H. Frederiksson, Publisher, North Holland Publishing Company, Amsterdam, for permission to reproduce, as Figure 11.5, the figure on page 58 of *The Office of the Future* (1979), by R. P. Uhlig, D. J. Farber, and J. H. Blair.

Drew Selvar, Manager, Publishing Services Department, Pergamon Press, Inc., NY, USA, for permission to reproduce, as Figure 18.1, Figure 6.4 on page 83 in Chapter 6, "Future household communications-information systems," by E. Bryan Carne, in the book *Communication Technologies and Information Flow* (1981), edited by T. J. M. Burke and M. Lehman.

Rita Koshy, Assistant Permissions Editor, Prentice-Hall, Inc., NJ, USA, for permission to reproduce, as Figures 9.2 and 9.3, Figure 1-6 from page 13 and Figure 1-8 from page 22 of Andrew S. Tanenbaum's book, *Computer Networks* (1981).

Lydia Holland, PSS Marketing, British Telecom, for permission to reproduce, as Figure 5.1, the figure from page 8 of the brochure, *PSS—A Basic Guide* (1980), and, as Figure 5.2, the figure from the leaflet, *Euronet—The Technology* (1980).

J. R. Smart, Technical Marketing Executive, British Telecommunications Systems Ltd., for permission to reproduce, as Figures 4.5, 6.18 and 8.2, Figures 1, 3 and 12 of the *System X* (1982) brochure.

C. J. Hughes, Deputy Director of Research, British Telecom Research Laboratories, and G. Bonami, General Secretary of the Comité du Colloque International de Commutation, Paris, for permission to reproduce, as Figures 6.19 and 6.20, Figures 3 and 4 from page 348 of the paper by C. J. Hughes and J. W. Atkins, "Virtual circuit switching for multiservice operation," International Switching Symposium (Paris, May 1979).

PTT Telecommunicatie, The Netherlands PTT, for permission to reproduce, as Figure 5.2, the figure from page 101 of *Datanet 1*, papers collected from *Het PTT-Bedrijf*, Vol. **22**, No. 3 (Feb 1982).

Dr. Alan Cane, Editor of the Technical Page, *Financial Times,* and Joy Boyce, Manager Press Relations, International Computers Ltd., for permission to reproduce, as Figure 3.6, the figure from the article by Geoffrey Charlish, "Why ICL plus 19 equals progress," on page 18 of *Financial Times* (28 Jun 1982).

Bernard Dunkley, Managing Editor, IEE Professional Publications, Stevenage, Herts, and the author, for permission to reproduce, as Figure 14.1, the diagram on page 13 of the paper, "Viewdata as a control tool," by D. R. Hirst in *IEE Conference Publications* **208.**

Simon Middleboe, Editor of *Microprocessors and Microsystems*, and Butterworth Scientific Ltd., Guildford, Surrey, and the authors for permission to reproduce the following diagrams in Vol. **6,** No. 1 (Jan/Feb 1982): Figure 1, from page 21 of the article by D. Shepherd and P. Corcoran, "A gateway development system," as Figure 10.3, and Figure 2 from page 26 of the article by Simon Middleboe, "Local area networks," as Figure 6.1.

Derek Meakin, Managing Editor of *Windfall, The Apple computer users' magazine*, published by Database Publications Ltd., Stockport, for permission to reproduce, as Figure 3.1, the figure from pages 54 and 55 of the article "How Apples talk to other Apples—and the rest of the world," in Vol. **1,** No. 12 (June 1982), and, as Figure 3.7, the figure on page 25 of the article by P. J. Robinson, "Linking Apple II with its big brother," in Vol. **1,** No. 10 (April 1982).

Rollo Turner, Publications Manager, Online Publications Ltd. and the author, for permission to reproduce, as Figure 11.3, the figure from page 137 of the paper by Mark Fishburn, "High level protocols for office systems," in *Local Networks 82.*

Rollo Turner, Publications Manager, Online Publications Ltd., and Marketing Manager, London Online Inc., and the authors, for permission to reproduce, as Figures 20.1 and 20.2, the figures from pages 327 and 328 of the paper by J.

Warrior and Anil Husain, "Reliability in fiber optic ring networks," in *Local Networks—Distributed Office and Factory Systems—Proceedings of LocalNet '83* (New York).

The International Council for Computer Communication, and the Editor and author, for permission to reproduce, as Figures 16.1 and 16.2, Figures 1 and 2 from pages 590 and 592 of the paper by Barbara Huckle, "A proposal for improving access to heterogenous computer networks," in the Conference Proceedings, *ICCC 82*, edited by M. B. Williams.

P. Zanella, CERN, Geneva, and the author, for permission to reproduce, as Figures 4.1 and 9.1, Figure 37 on page 64 and Figure 38 on page 68 of V. Zacharov's paper "Computer systems and networks: Status and perspectives," *Proceedings 1980 of the CERN School of Computing*, Pub. CERN 81-03 (1981), pp. 8–77.

The author and the publisher are grateful to the following copyright holders and their representatives for permission to reproduce short extracts of text:

Dr Einar H. Fredriksson, Publisher, of the North Holland Publishing Company, for permission to reproduce, from page 58 of *The Office of the Future* (1981), edited by Ronald P. Uhlig et al, the second definition of office automation, quoted in Chapter 11, page 207.

Dr. Alan Cane, Editor of the Technical Page, *Financial Times*, for permission to reproduce the quotation in Chapter 11, pages 217–218 from the article by R. Raggett on page IX of *Financial Times Survey, The Electronic Office* (13 Apr 1982).

Wang Corporation for permission to reproduce from the beginning of their brochure, *Office Automation and the Six Technologies*, the first definition of office automation quoted in Chapter 11, page 207.

Sabine Kurjo, for permission to reproduce in the Epilogue a quotation from one of her papers about the Peace Network and for her half in checking and updating the Epilogue.

The author and the publisher are grateful to the following companies, who have kindly given permission to reproduce figures from their product brochures and leaflets:

Acorn Computers Ltd., for consisting and Orbis Computers Ltd., for permission to reproduce Figure 2.1 from Acorn's brochure, *The Cambridge Ring.*

CASE plc, for permission to reproduce Fig. 2.6 from their Grapevine brochure, and Figures 6.11 and 8.1 from its CASE DCX 816 and CASE 440/12 Intelligent Modem leaflets.

Datapoint (U.K.) Ltd., for permission to reproduce Figure 2.5 from its Datapoint ARC brochure.

Digital Microsystems Ltd., a subsidiary of Extel Group plc, for permission to reproduce Figure 3.5 from its Hi Net leaflet.

International Computers Ltd. for permission to reproduce Figures 19.1 and 22.1 from its brochures, *ICL Distributed Office Systems—Wordprocessing* and *ICL Information Systems.*

Keen Computers Ltd., for permission to reproduce Figure 3.3 from their Omninet leaflet.

Master Systems (Data Products) Ltd., for permission to reproduce Figure 2.4 from its MASTERNET brochure and Figures 6.7 to 6.9 from its MASTER SWITCH brochure, Master Systems C11 7502 leaflet, and Master Systems T7 3270 leaflet.

Micom Systems, Inc. and Micom-Borer Ltd., for permission to reproduce Figures 19.2 and 20.3 from its Instanet brochure.

Micro-Writer Ltd., for permission to reproduce Figure 7.4 from its Micro-Writer brochure.

Modcomp Computer Services, Inc., for permission to reproduce Figure 12.3 from Modcomp Software Product Bulletin 807.

Nestar Inc., and Nestar Systems Ltd. (formerly Zynar Ltd.), for permission to reproduce Figure 3.2 from its brochure *Linking People and Information through Personal Computers.*

Network Systems Corp., for permission to reproduce Figure 2.3 from its Hyperchannel document.

Office Technology Ltd., for permission to reproduce Figure 11.4 from its I.M.P. Office System Controller brochure.

Plessey Communications Ltd., for permission to reproduce Figure 6.17 from its Plessey IDX brochure.

Plessey Controls Ltd., for permission to reproduce Figures 20.4 and 20.5 from its 8600 Series and 8687 Telex/Packet Gateway brochures.

Prime Computer (UK) Ltd., for permission to reproduce Figures 2.2 to 2.4 from its PRIMENET Product Bulletin and PRIMENET Communications Hardware Bulletin.

Siemens AG, for permission to reproduce Figures 7.1 to 7.3 from its Text Terminal T4200 Model 40, Facsimile Terminal HF1048, and Facsimile Terminal HF2060 leaflets.

Thame Systems Ltd., for permission to reproduce Figure 2.2 from *Thame Systems Product News.*

U-Microcomputers Ltd., for permission to reproduce Figure 3.4 from its U-Net leaflet.

Contents

area network operating systems • File transfer • Media conversion •
Remote running of computer programs • Telesoftware • Integrated
distributed computing systems • References

Chapter 14   Other Applications of Networks

Public services and utilities • Electronic publishing • Computer con-
ferencing and teleconferencing • Networks for education and training
• Community information services • Home information systems •
Medical applications of networks • Industrial applications of networks
• Miscellaneous applications of networks • References

PART FOUR   WIDER ASPECTS OF NETWORKS

Chapter 15   Network Costs and Economics

Operating costs of local area networks • Operating costs of wide area
networks • Costs and revenues of network services • Tariffs and pricing strategies • Demand and market for network systems and services
• References

Chapter 16   Impact of Networks

Human interfaces with networks • The economic impact of networking
• Impact of networks on public awareness • The social impact of networks • Security in networks • Telecommunications regulations and
networks • Legal aspects of networks • Political impact of networks •
References

Chapter 17   Network Problems and Issues

Network design • Congestion and flow control • Routing • Addressing • Transmission errors • Reliability • Deadlocks • Network protocol problems and issues • Network operating problems and issues •
Regulatory problems and issues • Economic problems and issues • Human and social problems and issues • References

Chapter 18   Future Prospects of Networks

Lessons to be learnt from past experience of networking • Future prospects for network technologies • Future prospects for interconnection
of local network systems • Future prospects for network services •
"Intelligent" computer networks • Future economic impacts and po-

Linked Local
Area Networks

Introduction

This book provides a moderately detailed user-oriented survey of the different aspects of computer networks, which use telecommunications to link computers and other information processing devices that are situated in different places. Although it describes all kinds of computer networks, it is devoted especially to those types of network that are most likely to meet the needs of specific organizations. Thus it provides an extensive treatment of "local area networks," where the machines to be connected are on the same site or in the same neighbourhood. It also considers at some length various systems that link different local area networks, even when they are separated by very long distances. Because of this, the wide area network infrastructure is discussed, as well as the local networking environment.

In their simplest form, computer networks allow users of computer terminals to have direct access to local or remote computers; more generally, they provide for "distributed computing systems," whereby users can reach several computers at once, and for communication between different computers. With recent developments in information technology, it is now also possible for local area networks and other computer networks to bring together into the same system devices performing different functions of office automation, such as word processing, electronic publishing, telefacsimile, electronic mail, and information retrieval, as well as data processing itself.

Sophisticated, well integrated, "work stations" are now available, that allow users a variety of information display and data input devices, whose capabilities go far beyond those of simple terminals, yet these devices can easily be attached to computer networks. Thus many network systems provide extensive facilities for response and interaction by their users.

Like several other information technologies, such as "videotex," which uses modified television sets or visual display terminals to present computer-based information in user-accessible visual forms, networking has begun to have increasingly important impacts on many aspects in many parts of the world. Combining ideas and techniques from computing, telecommunications and electronics, its effects on human life throughout the planet seem likely to be very important by the year 2000. Thus this book considers some of the far-reaching implications and issues of computer networking, as well as its practical aspects.

1

AIMS OF THE BOOK

This book aims to give intelligent users of information technology a moderately detailed picture of the available computer network systems, services, technologies and applications. It deals mostly with local area networks, both those that are self-contained and those that are linked together, but it also provides a general appreciation of wide area networks and personal computer networks. In addition, it discusses the impact of networking on all aspects of human life and it explores some possible future developments. It aims to provide very up-to-date information, and describes many recent and proposed advances.

Throughout, the book considers mainly what facilities computer network systems can provide and what services and functions they can perform, on behalf of their users. Thus it is primarily user-oriented, catering both for those who have to use, select or install computer networks inside their own organisations, and for executives, managers and other users who require a general idea of their capabilities and possibilities. It presents the most important and basic general principles, and indicates what is actually and potentially possible with the available technologies. In some respects, its coverage is complementary to that of other recent books on computer networks, as it treats extensively certain topics that are not discussed in detail there; it treats in less detail several other aspects that some of them present in depth. It is largely complementary to my book *The Videotex Revolution*, also to be published by John Wiley & Sons.

Readers of the book do not need to have expert knowledge of computing, telecommunications and information technology; they require only a broad general appreciation of their principles, uses and capabilities. Those technical details, that users do not have to know in order to operate their network systems effectively, are either omitted or only mentioned briefly.

As the book is intended to be a preliminary, though broadly-based and fairly comprehensive, guide to users of computer networks, especially to users of local area networks, it provides extensive references to further relevant literature and information sources, to enable them to obtain the additional information and practical know-how that they need. In order to use these references most effectively, readers should first consult the Guide to Further Reading, immediately after this Introduction, that lists and describes briefly some important books, conference proceedings, periodicals and information sources on computer networks, and explains the notation used for the references. Lists of relevant references are placed at the end of each chapter, and there is also a Supplementary Bibliography at the end of the book.

SOME IMPORTANT DEFINITIONS

The definitions given below, and used throughout the book, as far as possible represent generally agreed terminology. Definitions, that refer only to very specific aspects of networking, or to technologies that are allied to it but not part of it, are given in appropriate chapters and in the glossary at the end of the book.

"Computer networks," sometimes called "computer-communication networks," use telecommunications to link together physically separated computers, input/output terminals, and other information-processing devices; in addition, at least one of the computers in a network controls the communications between its different components.

"Local area networks" (LANs) are computer networks that are either contained inside a single building or site or are situated within a compact area whose longest dimension is not more than a mile or two. "Wide area networks" (WANs) cover larger regions, usually much larger regions, typically having distances between their components ranging from a few miles to hundreds or even thousands of miles; thus their coverage is very often national, and quite often multinational or international. "Linked local area networks"(LLANs), which are specially considered by this book, are groups of local area networks that are placed inside a wide area network infrastructure in such a way that they can communicate with each other effectively, in a well integrated way, over large distances.

In their earliest and simplest form, computer networks transmitted their data via "public switched telephone networks" (PSTNs), which were originally designed as networks of telephone lines and telephone exchanges to link together large numbers of telephones. More recently, as the data traffic sent over computer networks became progressively more extensive, "data networks" were developed, that were specially designed to convey data as opposed to voice signals, even though they still often used transmission via PSTNs. Data networks are at present either ''circuit-switched,'' "message-switched" or "packet-switched." For a "circuit-switched" data network, a given data message is sent between a given origin and a given destination, only when a specific circuit, following a specific route, has been assigned to it for the duration of its transmission, as for telephone calls. For a "packet-switched" data network, data are conveyed in carefully formatted packets that are automatically sent by the network between their correct origins and their correct destinations. For a "message-switched" data network, whole messages instead of packets are sent as units.

The "structure" of a network is its general configuration, specifying its components, including "nodes" and "links," and the geometrical relations between them. Each "node" is a point in the network, through which at least one link passes; each "link" is a connection between two neighbouring nodes,usually defined in a given direction, though sometimes viewed as the pair of paths, in both directions, between these nodes. "Peripheral nodes" or "devices" are nodes acting as origins and/or destinations of data messages, and are thus points at the edge of the network. "Interior nodes" or "switching nodes" route the data messages or packets appropriately, by switching them from the links down which they have just travelled to the correct links for them to enter; they are thus points inside the network, and not at its edge. A "gateway" is a direct interconnection between two different networks, and can be viewed either as a switching node, belonging to both networks, or as a special pair of "switching links," one end of which is in one network and the other end of which is in the other network.

The "architecture" of a computer network precisely defines the functions that the network and its parts should perform, together with the ways in which the network should be organised. In particular, the architecture specifies the levels of different functions in the network, ranging from data transmission at the lowest levels to user applications at the highest level. The "protocols" of the network are the procedures and techniques, used to control the exchange of data between different parts of the network, by implementing the functions in accordance with the architecture. Thus each protocol operates at a level, determined by its defined function in relation to the architecture.

In order to achieve the maximum possible "compatibility" inside a network, so that its different devices communicate effectively with each other, and also between networks, so that the same or similar protocols can be used across network boundaries, considerable efforts have been made to "standardise" the most important types of protocol, largely through the efforts of national and international "standards bodies."

EVOLUTION OF NETWORKS

Computer networking started in the mid-1960s, when both "time sharing" services and data networks became available.

"Time-shared" computing systems were developed, linking clusters of terminals to a single mainframe computer, so that each terminal had a share of access to the computer's central processing unit. Some of these systems had both terminals and computers on the same site, but it was not long before time shared systems, linking terminals to remote computers by telephone lines, became commercially available. At this stage, it also became possible for a terminal user to select the remote computer of his choice by dialling the right telephone number.

Circuit-switched data communications networks, using the public switched telephone networks and also private lines, arose at about the same time. For example, the British Post Office introduced the first of several of its Datel services, both inside the UK and internationally, in 1965.

Packet switching was first proposed in 1965, and the Arpanet, the first packet-switched data network, began to be developed in 1968. Tymnet, the first public packet-switched network, was started in the USA in 1969, to be followed by Telenet in 1975. From 1976 on, experimental public packet-switched services began to be developed in several countries; for example, The Experimental Packet-Switched Service (EPSS) became operational in 1976 and was established fully in 1977. National and international packet-switching services are now becoming more and more widely available, using a variety of techniques, including broadband transmission lines, coaxial cables, and, more recently, satellites and fibre optics.

In the late 1970s, the development of local area networks was pioneered by Cambridge University, which originated the "Cambridge ring," and by Xerox Corporation, which developed Ethernet in the USA, in collaboration with DEC and Intel. The number of commercially available LAN systems, and the variety of devices that can be attached to them, are both increasing rapidly, and the performance characteristics of the best available systems are also improving steadily.

At about the same time, the extensive development and usage of personal computers began in the USA, and both local area and wide area personal computer networks were introduced. The number of commercially available personal computer network systems, and the number of different models of personal computers that can be networked, have both expanded steadily during the early 1980s. Much of this development has occurred together with videotex systems and telesoftware systems for personal computers.

Just as computer networking was originally a convergence between computing technology and telecommunications technology, today it is using and has started to integrate several more information technologies, including: office automation and information processing on the applications side; satellite communications, laser technology and fibre optics on the transmission side; and new input/output, display and storage techniques and devices.

There has been increasing emphasis on integrated LANs, combining a variety of organisational functions and services in a unified way, connected by means of a WAN infrastructure that is moving more and more towards the concept of "integrated services digital network" (ISDN), incorporating a variety of data, image and voice traffic inside the same system. In this way, increasingly effective and comprehensive LLAN systems are coming into operation.

NETWORK SYSTEMS AND SERVICES

Because they have to be handled by users who are often not familiar with computer systems, the network systems need to be reasonably user-friendly and easy to operate, even though they often have complicated and intricate designs and procedures "behind the scenes." Thus simplicity of operation is very important, although the more sophisticated network systems also allow more advanced, but more efficient, alternative operating procedures to be available as options.

Local area networks (LANs) usually cater for a single organisation, such as a business occupying offices at one site, or a university or college computing service. Following the pioneering work of the late 1970s on experimental LANs, using the ring and linear (bus) configurations, many LANs of both types are now becoming commercially available, and some of them are now also able to provide linked LAN (LLAN) services, which are specially useful for companies and other organisations have premises at several widely separated locations. A notable feature of LANs is the wide variety of devices that can be attached to them, catering for a whole range of office and information processing services.

Another class of network system, which may fairly soon become of considerable if not great importance, is based on the use of a personal computer or other small computer system, acting simultaneously as a terminal, a processor, and a network node. Although micronets or personal computer networks (PCNs) of this sort can often be viewed as LANs, they are treated as a somewhat different type of network in this book, because of appreciable differences in the functions that they perform and in the relative importance of these functions. Typically, PCNs are clusters of personal computers, usually arranged in a ring or bus configuration, together with a few shared devices, including fairly extensive file storage and a high quality printer. PCNs can also operate in a WAN mode, for example when personal computers are used as intelligent, terminals to remote minicomputers, mainframes, or videotex systems, and again when personal computers, at widely separated places, communicate with each other over a WAN.

As already pointed out, wide area networks (WANs) include public switched telephone networks, circuit-switched data networks, and packet-switched data networks. Hitherto, most WANs have used a single transmission medium, such as telephone lines or broadband cables. As a result of recent technological advances, more and more WANs are being installed as "mixed-media" networks, using a combination of transmission technologies, such as land lines and satellites, and "multi-media communications" networks, handling data, text, graphics and voice simultaneously.

Linked local area networks (LLANs) combine both LANs and WANs, by using WANs to interconnect their constituent LANs, together with gateways to interface the LANs to the WANs. LLANs also need to use "interworking" protocols that enable effective and reliable communications to be set up between devices on different LANs as well as devices on the same LAN.

Whereas organisations, using only LANs, operate network services that are entirely self-contained, most organisations require at least some access to WANs and to the infrastructure of network services that they provide. In many countries, the infrastructure is provided by a (usually national and public-operated) postal, telegraph, telephone and telecommunications authority, called a "PTT" for short. In some other countries, such as the USA, there is no PTT and the WAN network services are provided by several private companies, but there is also a national body (e.g., the FCC in the USA) that coordinates national telecommunications regulations. International WAN services are being provided increasingly by national PTTs, in mutual collaboration, but private international WAN services have been operated by several American common carriers for some years.

NETWORK TECHNOLOGIES

Computer networking brings together various technologies concerned with electronics, telecommunications, computing and information processing.

A considerable variety of network architecture has been devised. The "star" network, linking a cluster of terminals to a central computer, has been used in both LANs, and WANs. However, LANs usually have either a "ring" configuration, with all their devices attached to nodes in a loop of cable, or a "bus" configuration, where their devices are attached to nodes on a single line of cable. WANs tend to use fairly general configurations of nodes, including peripheral (device) nodes and switching nodes. WANs are linked to neighbouring LANs and WANs by special gateways, which are nodes or node-pairs that act as interfaces between them.

Although the earliest computer networks used very simple terminals, to provide users with access to local or remote computers, more sophisticated, "intelligent," forms of network terminals were later developed, to be used predominantly by business users and information providers, and having additional capabilities. A whole range of devices that can be attached to networks is now available for users, including: graphics displays, sometimes in colour, word processors, a variety of printers and computers, even voice input and output devices. Multi-purpose terminals, with a considerable range of facilities, including local computing, word processing and data storage, are beginning to appear on the market. Memory devices and file stores that can be attached include: floppy disk drives, "hard" (fixed) magnetic disks, magnetic tapes, video storage and, very recently, optical storage.

Transmission technologies, used in telecommunications, include: telephone lines, high bandwidth transmission lines, coaxial cables, fibre optics, lasers, radio waves, and satellite communications.

Standardisation is becoming increasingly necessary, to avoid a chaotic proliferation of mutually incompatible network systems; on the whole, it seems to have been making good progress during recent years. Standard protocols are being developed, that provide operating rules for the interchange of information and for communication, both for data networks themselves and for the wide variety of applications that these networks support.

Technologies and techniques are also required for network control and for the improvement of network performance. To be fully effective, network control, to keep the network in full working order as continuously as possible, requires network measurements and regular monitoring of network performance. The performance and other characteristics of network behaviour can be investigated both empirically and with the aid of mathematical models of networks and network traffic and protocols. Predictions of network performance can then be made by means of a judicious combination of analytical and simulation techniques applied to the models. Network design can be improved by devising appropriate performance and operating criteria, using models and empirical data to predict the performance of propose modifications or new features, and learning from practical experience of networks.

NETWORK USERS

In principle, computer networks can be used by almost any organisation, after a relatively small amount of preliminary demonstration and training, as their terminals and work stations can be made simple to operate if the network operating systems are well designed. However, many network systems also provide more sophisticated facilities for those who are skilled in computing and information processing.

Broadly speaking, most of the network users are likely to be organisations and those individuals inside organisations who are assigned to the tasks of network operation. Here, the chief classes of user are those members of the organisation who use it for various information processing functions and services required by the organisation, and network specialists who will be involved in the selection, installation and development of network systems. Most of these organisations will use LANs, which will increasingly often also belong to wider LLAN systems. A few organisations, will continue to use WAN systems only.

Some of these organisations,such as libraries and information services, community services, charities, voluntary bodies, societies, departments of local and national government, and intergovernmental bodies, will also cater for members of the public, who have various information problems that can be solved with the aid of computer networking.

With the development of videotex systems and personal computer systems, not only is an extra dimension being added to the network services available to organisational users, but members of the public can make direct use of computer networks in their homes for several purposes.

NETWORK APPLICATIONS

Perhaps the single most important application of computer networking, and certainly one of the most rapidly expanding, is its use for integrated office and business systems, in conjunction with other forms of office automation. These systems can operate at a local level, using LANs to carry out various office functions at a single site; they can also operate on behalf of organisations with several premises, using WANs to link their different LANs. Functions that can be supported by these systems include word processing and text processing, electronic mail and message services, and management information systems, as well as ordinary computing and data processing.

In addition, computer networks can support various financial transaction services for companies and other organisations. Similar transaction services for citizens are less well advanced, but electronic banking, credit card, shopping and travel booking facilities are beginning to operate or are being planned.

Computer networks have already been able to improve greatly the operation of data bases, information retrieval facilities, and other information services. Data bases made available in this way include those provided by private and public videotex systems, to provide useful information on a wide variety of subjects, and very large specialist data bases accessed by "ordinary" online retrieval services. One of the most significant developments is the provision of "third party data base" facilities, which allow a network's own data bases to be supplemented by a large number of other computer data bases, which can be linked to it through network "gateways."

There are many other actual and potential applications of networking, covering most aspects of human life. These include the use of network for: distributed computing and data processing, telesoftware, education and training, electronic publishing, message services, computer conferencing, community information services, and home information systems.

WIDER ASPECTS OF NETWORKS

Both local area and wide area networks have a variety of impacts on different aspects of human life, including economic and financial, social, legal and political aspects. They are beginning to transform people's lives, especially in many office and business work places, and they are beginning to have far-reaching effects on public awareness, education and financial transactions, for example.

As most network operators incur considerable expenses, they must levy appreciable, sometimes fairly high, charges for their services; thus the costs of network systems have to be considered, and appropriate tariffs and pricing strategies have to be derived. Some attention must also be devoted to marketing, in order to obtain the customers who can pay for these services; effective marketing in turn requires an adequate understanding of actual and potential demand for networking, from organisational, business and other users. All these factors should be taken into account while assessing the economic viability of networks.

Networking has already started to have an increasing economic impact, which will become much larger within a few years, when its costs become low enough to attract a large number of users. Network-based transaction services will improve and transform the effectiveness of various financial and trading operations. Business and industry will become more effective as a result of network information and transaction services. The increasing use of network and other information and telecommunication facilities will progressively reduce the demand for transport, thus removing a major source of costs. When networking and other information services become cheap enough, they could be made more widely available, while many other services are being cut back because they are too "costly." Last but not least, greatly improved overall economic and financial planning will become possible as a result of much better economic data, obtained much more promptly.

Like all major technological innovations, networking could have bad effects as well as good ones, and all these effects need to be explored and discussed in good time, so that individuals and organisations, businesses and public authorities can all act responsibly to ensure that it is used for the benefit of mankind. Networking, like other information technologies, could have led to "Big Brother" in 1984, if wrongly applied, hence the need for adequate legislation and public regulations for certain aspects of its use. On the one hand, freedom of information and communication needs to be ensured as far as possible; on the other hand, undue invasions of privacy and confidences must be avoided.

The social impacts of networking and other information technologies that use it, such as videotex, could be very wide. For example, they will help to make people more aware of the world around them, and they could contribute to more effective education for citizenship and better training for jobs and constructive uses of leisure. Citizens will be able to cooperate and communicate better with each other and with public officials, and they will be able to participate more directly in democratic discussions and in political dialogues.

As with earlier inventions, such as the motor car and television, the general impact of these technologies on indivdual life styles is bound to be very great. There is a potential for more isolated, home-bound lives on the one hand, but also for more social interaction and communication and mutual cooperation on the other. It seems likely that patterns of living will become much less centralised, much more at the local level. Individuals could have much greater opportunities, not only for becoming better informed and well educated, but also for developing their full potentialities and for having their good ideas taken further by others who are interested.

Guide to Further Reading

One of the aims of this book is to give both intelligent users of computer networks, and those involved in their selection, installation and operation, a reasonably comprehensive introductory picture of those aspects of computer networking that they need to know about. Inevitably, the book will not meet all their requirements, and, sooner or later, they will have to read further literature about those topics which they need to explore in greater depth.

They can approach this in at least four ways. Firstly, they can study literature about computer networks that gives a broad general perspective of the subject or that is likely to contain individual articles about them. Secondly, they can follow up some of the literature references cited in those chapters of this book in which they are especially interested or which cover those aspects of the computer networks with which they are most concerned. Thirdly, they can contact directly the computer network services and experts on computer networks. Fourthly, they can seek the advice of libraries and information services.

The first seven sections of this "Guide to Further Reading" cater for those who wish to follow the first approach. The first section lists some "key references" that provide reviews of the computer networking "state of the art"; most of them are reasonably up-to-date at the time of writing. But it should be borne in mind that the state of knowledge about computer networks, and indeed computer networking technology itself, are both evolving very rapidly! Thus new key books or new editions of the existing ones will fairly soon take the place of those cited there. The second section lists some other books and conference proceedings on computer networks that provide a fairly general coverage. The third section lists some books and conference proceedings that are more specialised and technical. The fourth section lists some books and conference proceedings on office automation and other application areas and technologies that are allied to computer networking. The fifth section lists some of the periodicals that are fairly likely to have some important articles on computer networks, although, inevitably, this list provides only a selection of those that are relevant. The sixth section lists some bibliographies on computer networking.

The seventh section of this "Guide" lists some of the most important new and more recent books, periodicals, and conference proceedings on computer networks. Most of these have been published since the first edition was written.

For the benefit of those readers, who wish to follow the second approach of reading and studying some of the literature references given at the ends of the chapters of this book, the eighth section of the "Guide" explains the notation used for literature references in the book.

Those readers, who wish to contact the computer network services and computer networking experts directly, should use the directories of computer services and network system suppliers near the end of this book. They give fairly extensive lists of computer networking organisations and companies in the USA and UK, and mention a few in other parts of the world.

Those readers who wish to follow the fourth approach can contact appropriate libraries and information services. Suitable libraries include the British Library Science Reference Library, libraries at universities and polytechnics, and some of the larger public reference libraries. Suitable on-line information services include BLAISE and INSPEC in the UK and several bibliographic data bases in the USA.

SOME KEY REFERENCES ON COMPUTER NETWORKS

One of the most comprehensive general discussions of computer networks is given in the two books *Communications Networks for Computers,* by D. W. Davies and D. L. A. Barber (1973) Wiley, New York and Chichester, and *Computer Networks and Their Protocols*, by D. W. Davies, D. L. A. Barber, W. L. Price and C. M. Solomonides (1979) Wiley.

A good introductory book, covering much of this ground in less detail, is *Computer Communications,* by Robert Cole (1982) Macmillan, London and Basingstoke, England, which is useful for those working in the commercial computing field, although written mainly for computer science students.

D. R. McGlynn (1978) *Distributed Data Processing and Data Communications*, Wiley, gives an extensive survey of networking, including details of many aspects of importance to users.

Bennet P. Lientz (1981) *An Introduction to Distributed Systems*, Addison-Wesley, Reading, MA, USA, and London, is a very important user-oriented book. It is a practical guide to the steps and methods, used in analysing, designing, implementing and managing distributed systems. It deals with their whole life cycle, including definition of user requirements and control, operations, maintenance, and system upgrading and replacement. Other topics covered include data communications, computer networks, system architecture, and the new technologies of office automation.

Some of James Martin's books, written at a less technical level, give good overviews of networking and allied fields:

Telecommunications and the Computer (1976, 2nd. ed.) Prentice-Hall, Englewood Cliffs, NJ, USA.
Future Developments in Telecommunications (1977, 2nd. ed.) Prentice-Hall.
Design and Strategy for Distributed Data Processing (1981) Prentice-Hall.
Computer Networks and Distributed Processing (1981) Prentice-Hall.

and, at a more popular level and also discussing the impacts of computing and information technology,

The Telematic Society—A Challenge for Tomorrow (1981) Prentice-Hall, which is an updated version of *The Wired Society* (1978) Prentice-Hall.

Key conference proceedings on computer networks include the following:

Business Telecomms—The New Regime (1981) Online Publications, Northwood Hills, Middlesex, and *Business Telecommunications* (1980), Online Publications, contain useful sets of papers on some of the electronic communications tools and their applications to business.
Local Networks and Distributed Office Systems, 1981 and *Local Networks and Distributed Office Systems, 1982,* Online Publications, give valuable selections of both user-oriented and technical papers. For convenience, they will be referred to as *Local Networks 81* and *Local Networks 82,* respectively.
Ed. J. Salz (1981) *Computer Communications—Increasing Benefits for Society,* North Holland, Amsterdam and New York, presents a comprehensive survey of the state of the art and some of the future directions of computer networking.
Ed. J. Csaba, T. Szentiványi and K. Tarnay (1981) COMNET *81—Networks from the User's Point of View*, North Holland, analyses experiences of running and using teleprocessing and computer networks already in operation, with special reference to the problems (and their solutions) of using computers from remote terminals.
Ed. Madeline M. Henderson and Marcia J. MacNaughton (1980) *Electronic Communication: Technology and Impacts*, Westview Press, USA, includes sections on computer conferencing and social and policy issues.
Useful collections of papers are given, for example, in Ed. W. W Chu (1979) *Advances in Computer Communications and Networking*, Artech House, Dedham, MA, USA, which reprints over fifty key papers on most aspects of networking, and in the November 1978 special issue of the *Proceedings of the IEEE* on packet communication networks.

Finally, this section lists three important reference books for network users:

M. Corby, E. Donohue and M. Hamer (1981) *Telecomms Users' Handbook,* Telecommunications Users Press, due to have a second edition in 1985.

K. Sherman (1981) *Data Communications—A Users Guide,* Reston Publishing Company, Reston, VA, USA.

S. J. Aries (1981) *Dictionary of Telecommunications,* Butterworths, London.

SOME OTHER GENERAL BOOKS ON COMPUTER NETWORKS

There are several other general books, collected papers and conference proceedings on computer networks that are also useful, including the following:

Ed. M. D. Abrams, R. P. Blanc and I. W. Cotton (1978) *Computer Networks: A Tutorial,* IEEE Press, Los Alamitos, CA, USA, a collection of papers on many aspects of networks.

Ed. N. Abramson, F. F. Kuo (1973) *Computer Networks,* Prentice-Hall, a collection of general papers and papers on network models.

J. E. Bingham and G. W. P. Davies (1980) *Planning for Data Communications,* Macmillan.

Ed. R. P. Blanc and I. W. Cotton (1976) *Computer Networking,* IEEE Press, a collection of earlier papers on many aspects of networks.

G. M. Boot (1981) *The Distributed System Environment,* McGraw-Hill, New York and London, especially Chapter 2 on user experience and Chapter 4 on distributed systems and network architectures.

D. N. Chorafas (1981) *Computer Networks for Distributed Information Systems,* Petrocelli, New York and Princeton, NK, USA.

D. N. Chorafas (1981) *Data Communications for Distributed Information Systems,* Petrocelli.

Ed. R. R. Korfhage (1978) *Computer Networks and Communications,* AFIPS Press, Montvale, NJ, USA, a collection of papers.

Ed. J. M. McQuillan and V. G. Cerf (1978) *A Practical View of Computer Network Protocols,* IEEE, Long Beach, CA, USA.

SOME MORE SPECIALISED AND TECHNICAL BOOKS ON COMPUTER NETWORKS

Besides the books by Davies et al (1979) and McQuillan and Cerf (1978) already mentioned, there are two recent, specially comprehensive, books on computer network protocols and communications protocols:

A. S. Tanenbaum (1981) *Computer Networks,* Prentice-Hall, a very comprehensive review of protocols used by PTT's, commercial organisations, and Arpanet, with very extensive bibliographies.

Ed. F. F. Kuo (1981) *Protocols & Techniques for Data Communication Networks,* Prentice-Hall.

J. Pužman and R. Pořízek (1980) *Communication Control in Computer Networks,* Wiley.

Network theory, models and design are discussed extensively by:

M. Schwartz (1977) *Computer-Communication Network Design and Analysis*, Prentice-Hall.

R. L. Sharma, P. J. T. de Sousa and A. D. Inglé (1982) *Network Systems—Modeling, Analysis and Design*, Van Nostrand Reinhold, New York and London.

Models for local area networks are presented in:

C. Tropper (1981) *Local Computer Network Technologies*, Academic Press, New York and London.

Local area networks have been covered by quite a number of conference proceedings. Besides the key works *Local Networks 81* and *Local Networks 82*, already mentioned, two other useful proceedings are:

Update Local Area Networks (1979) Proceedings of the Local Area Communications Network Symposium, Boston, May 1979.

Ed. A. West and P. Janson (1981) *Local Networks for Computer Communications*, North Holland.

Other important aspects of networking are discussed in:

Ed. K. G. Beauchamp (1979) *Interlinking of Computer Networks*, Reidel, Dordrecht, The Netherlands, London and Boston, USA, conference proceedings.

CASE (1982) *Pocket Book of Computer Communications*, Computer and Systems Engineering plc, Watford, Hertfordshire.

D. R. Doll (1978) *Data Communications: Practical Networks and Systems Design*, Wiley, with good coverage of terminal networks.

J. Martin (1978) *Communication Satellite Systems*, Prentice-Hall.

Ed. Skwirzinski (1981) *New Concepts in Multi-User Communication*, Sijthoff and Noordhoff, The Netherlands, mathematical and technical.

C. Weitzman (1980) *Distributed Micro/Minicomputer Systems—Structure, Implementation and Application*, Prentice-Hall, especially Chapter 6 on application examples and case studies.

SOME BOOKS ON OFFICE AUTOMATION AND ALLIED TECHNOLOGIES

A key work on information technology in general, covering networking, office automation, and allied technologies, and suitable for both users and specialists, is:

P. Zorkoczy (1982) *Information Technology: An Introduction*, Pitman, London.

Gower Publishing Company, Aldershot, Hampshire, is publishing several books on office automation and other user-oriented aspects of information technology, including applications of computer networks. Most of these are in their series, *The Office of the Future,* whose books include: *Planning for the Office of the Future* (1981), *Planning for Electronic Mail* (1982), *Planning for Word Processing* (1982), and *Planning for Telecommunications* (1982). They have also published:

D. Jarrett (1982) *The Electronic Office—A Management Guide to the Office of the Future.*

Another important work on office automation is:

R. P. Uhlig, D. J. Farber and J. H. Bair (1979) *The Office of the Future,* North Holland.

The following list gives a sample of other useful books on various allied technologies and applications of computing and information technology.

Ed. G. Cantraine and J. Destine (1981) *New Systems and Services in Telecommunications,* North Holland, a conference proceedings including papers on satellite telecommunications, data and picture broadcasting and distribution, teleconferencing, Teletex, and videotex.

Ed. W. Kaizer (1978) *Electronic Text Communication* (in English and German), Springer, Berlin and Heidelberg, Germany, and New York, conference proceedings.

A. J. Mayne (1986) *The Videotex Revolution* (second edition), Wiley, New York and Chichester, England, a comprehensive survey of videotex, both viewdata and teletext, with extensive bibliography, reference lists and indexes.

C. J. Sippl and F. Dahl (1981) *Video/Computers: How to Select, Mix, and Operate Personal Computers and Home Video Systems,* Prentice-Hall.

Ed. R. P. Uhlig (1981) *Computer Message Systems,* North Holland, perhaps the most complete survey yet published on electronic mail and message systems, covering all aspects.

PERIODICALS COVERING COMPUTER NETWORKING AND RELATED FIELDS

The *Financial Times* occasionally has supplements on computing, office automation and other aspects on information technology, of which the most recent is its *Supplement, The Electronic Office* (13 April 1982). Its Technical Page has news items on all kinds of technology, including especially computing, telecommunications, electronics, and information technology.

The weekly computer press, including especially *Computer Weekly* and *Computing,* has a considerable number of news items and articles, and occasionally supplements, on computer networks and allied technologies, as well as on the computer systems and techniques that are used with networks. *Electronics Weekly* and *New Scientist* also have some relevant articles and sometimes news items.

Relevant monthlies that are user-oriented, though sometimes fairly technical, include: *Business Information Technology, Byte, CS & M (Communications & Systems Management, Computer* (especially the September 1979 issue), *Communications International, Computer Management, Datamation, Data Processing Magazine, IEEE Spectrum, Infomatics, Office Systems, Personal Computer World, Practical Computing, What's New in Computing,* and *Wireless World.*

British and American specialist and technical periodicals, some monthly and some quarterly, specialising in computer networks or having many relevant articles, include: *Computer Communications, Computer Communications Review, Computer Networks, Data Communications, IEEE Communications Magazine, IEEE Transactions on Communications* (especially the January 1977 and April 1980 special issues on computer networks and the January 1982 issue on communications in the automated office), *The LOCALNetter™ Newsletter, NetLink,* and for policy issues, *Telecommunications Policy. Data Communications* and *IEEE Communications Magazine* are especially useful to data communications and network users as well as professionals.

Other periodicals, having some relevant articles, include: *ACM Computing Surveys, Bell Systems Telephone Journal, Communications of the ACM, Computer Bulletin, Computer Journal, Computer Technology Review, Computers and Digital Techniques, dp International* (both the quarterly magazine and the annual review), *Electronics and Power, IBM Systems Journal,* several periodicals in the *IEEE Transactions* group, *Information Processing & Management, Journal of the ACM, Proceedings of the IEEE* (especially the November 1978 issue mentioned earlier), and *Proceedings of the Institution of Electrical Engineers.*

Series of conferences, whose proceedings are normally published, and which give extensive coverage to computer networking and telecommunications, include: the Data Communications Symposia, the Berkeley Workshops on Distributed Data Management and Computer Networks, Distributed Computing Systems (DCS) Conferences, IEEE Compcon, International Conferences on Communications (ICC), International Conferences on Computer Communications (ICCC), National Computer Conferences (NCC), National Telecommunications Conference (NTC), Spring Joint Computer Conferences (SJCC), and some of the EUROCOMP and Online Conferences. Other conferences on computing, telecommunications, etc. often have some relevant papers on computer networks.

BIBLIOGRAPHIES ON COMPUTER NETWORKS

Extensive bibliographies on computer networks and computer networking are provided by several of the key references, listed earlier in this Guide, including the books by Davies et al, Pužman and Pořízek, and Tanenbaum, both of which list hundreds of items.

Other useful bibliographies include:

H. A. Freeman and K. J. Thurber (1980) "Updated bibliography on local computer networks," *Computer Communication Review,* **10** (3) 10–18.

A. J. Hinchley (1978) "An annotated bibliography of future networks," *Future Networks, Infotech State of the Art Report, 1978,* Infotech, Maidenhead, Berkshire, 207–230. Contains key references on various aspects, including impact and possible future.

P. T. Kirstein (1979) "Some international developments in data services," *Interlinking of Computer Networks,* 3–30.

J. F. Shoch (1979) "An annotated bibliography of local computer networks," *Xerox PARC Technical Report* SSL-79-5.

H. M. Wood et al. (1976) *Annotated Bibliography of the Literature on Resource-Sharing Computer Networks,* NBS Special Publication **384**, National Bureau of Standards, Washington, D.C. which has over a thousand critically annotated items.

There is also the useful, though unpublished, *An Annotated Bibliography of Computer Networks,* by Adrian V. Stokes which is more up-to-date but especially valuable for references to earlier literature.

The best sources of abstracts of relevant literature, especially technical articles, on computer networks, are *Electrical Engineering and Electronics Abstracts,* and *Computing and Control Abstracts,* both published by INSPEC, and available as an online information source as well as in printed form.

GUIDE TO THE MOST RECENT LITERATURE ON COMPUTER NETWORKS

The books *The Data Ring Main—An Introduction to Local Area Networks*, by D. C. Flint (1983) Wiley Heyden, Chichester and New York, *Local Area Networks—Issues, Products, and Developments,* by V. E. Cheong and R. A. Hirschheim (1983) Wiley-Interscience, New York, *Local Networks—An Introduction*, by William Stallings (1984) Macmillan, New York, and Collier Macmillan, London, *Introduction to Local Area Computer Networks*, by K. C. E. Gee (1983) Macmillan, London and Basingstoke, England, *Local Networking: Analysis Implementation and Global Interconnection*, by M. L. Rothberg (1985), Data Communications, Brooklyn, NY, *Local Area Networks: A User's Guide for Business Professionals*, by J. H. Green (1984), Scott, Foreman & Co., Glenview, IL, and *A Manager's Guide to Local Area Networks*, by F. Derfler, Jr. and W. Skillings (1983) Prentice-Hall, Englewood Cliffs, NJ, are all good introductions to many aspects of local area networks. The conference proceedings *Local Computer Networks*, edited by P. Ravasio, G. Hopkins and N. Naffah (1982) North-Holland, Amsterdam, includes papers on advanced current research on local area networks.

The books *Computer Communications, Vol. 1, Principles*, edited by W. Chou

(1983) Prentice-Hall, Englewood Cliffs, NJ, and *Data Communications, Networks and Distributed Processing,* by U. D. Black (1983) Reston Publishing Company, Reston, VA, cover extensively various parts of wide area networking.

The book *Telecommunications and Networking,* by U. W. Pooch, W. H. Greene and G. G. Moss (1982) Little, Brown, Boston, MA, is user-oriented but also fairly detailed. Shorter books, with a practical approach, include *A Practical Guide to Computer Communications and Networking,* by R. J. Deasington (1982) Ellis Horwood, Chichester, and Halsted Wiley, New York, and *Reviewing Your Data Transmission Network,* by P. R. D. Scott (1983) NCC Publications, Manchester, England. *Basic Guide to Data Communications,* edited by R. Sarch (1985), Data Communications, Brooklyn, NY, is a collection of 59 articles from *Data Communications;* it caters both for experts needing to know the current state of the art and for newcomers. *Business Data Communications: Basic Concepts, Security and Design,* by J. Fitzgerald (1984), Wiley, is oriented to network managers and network users.

The book Telecommunications Primer, by G. Langley (1983) Pitman, London, is a useful introduction to telecommunications and networking in general.

Recent books on the theory and mathematical modelling of computer networks include: *Performance Models of Distributed Systems,* by E. Gelenbe (1983) Addison-Wesley, London and Reading, MA, the conference proceedings *Performance Models of Data Communication Systems and Their Applications,* edited by G. Pujolle (1981), North-Holland, Amsterdam and *Principles of Computer Communication Network Design,* by J. Seidler (1983) Ellis Horwood and Halsted Wiley. Now there is so much literature on computer networks, with so many new books and periodicals continuing to appear, that this Guide has inevitably omitted some important titles. Another important guide of this sort, which should fill in many of the gaps, is the recent article "Reference books that track data communications," *Data Communications,* **14** (1) 137–147 (Jan 1985).

Key conference proceedings on computer networks include the following three, which contain many of the important references cited in Part Five: *Local Networks—Distributed Office & Factory Systems—Proceedings of LocalNet '83 (New York)* (1983) Online Inc., New York, and Online Publications, Pinner, England, *Local Networks—Strategy Systems—Proceedings of LocalNet '83 (Europe)* (1983) Online Publications, and *Business Telecom—Proceedings of the International Conference, London, 1983* (1983) Online Publications. In Part Five, I refer to them by their respective shortened names: *LocalNet 83 (New York), LocalNet 83 (Europe),* and *Business Telecom 83.* Further important conference proceedings are often published.

The December 1983 issue of *Proceedings of the IEEE,* Vol. **71,** No. 12, edited by H. C. Folts and Richard Des Jardins, is a special issue on open systems interconnection—new standards architecture and protocols for distributed information systems, which contains some recent key papers on these topics.

Important, mostly new, periodicals, relevant to computer networking and its applications, and not mentioned in the first edition, include: *British Telecommunications Engineering* (formerly *Post Office Electrical Engineers Journal), Com-*

munications Management, IEEE Journal on Selected Areas in Communications, Information Services & Use, Japan Telecommunications News, and *Which Office System?*

Important additional periodicals on computing, which contain articles on computer networks, include: *Computer News, Dec User, ICL Technical Journal,* and *Which Computer?*

Many other important books, conference proceedings, and periodicals, mostly of rather more specialist interest, are named in the relevant parts of Chapters 19 through 24 and in the reference lists at the ends of these chapters, also in the Supplementary Bibliography.

Quite a number of them, especially of those that are applications-oriented, are described in the useful catalogue *Publications Catalogue 84,* Online Publications, Pinner Green House, Ash Hill Drive, Pinner, Middlesex, HA5 2AE, England, and *Learned Information Catalogue 1983/84—Publications in Library and Information Science,* Learned Information, Besselsleigh Road, Abingdon, Oxford OX13 6LG, England. Note that orders for titles in the Online catalogue, placed in North America or South America, should be sent to Taylor and Francis Inc., 242 Cherry Street, Philadelphia, PA 19106.

Other publishers, whose catalogues are worth consulting for new books on computing and computer networks, include Addison-Wesley, McGraw-Hill, Prentice-Hall, and Wiley.

Data Communications Buyers' Guide 1984 (1983) McGraw Hill, New York, contains product indexes for a wide variety of computing and computer networking equipment and services, together with a directory of vendors. A new edition of this guide may have appeared by the time this book is in print.

NOTATION USED FOR LITERATURE REFERENCES

Most of the references, cited in this book, are either to specific articles or papers in books, conference proceedings, or journals, or to specific books by one or two authors. In these cases, the author's name (or authors' names) come(s) first, followed by the year (or more specific date) of publication between brackets, followed by the title of the article between inverted commas or other specified indication (if the item is not a whole book), followed by the underlined title of the book or conference proceedings or periodical, perhaps followed by the volume number and issue number (if in a periodical), followed by a page number(s) if the item is an article, and by details of the publisher if the item is a book of conference proceedings. Citation of such items in the text is by author name(s), followed by date of publication. If the cited "author" is an editor, the author's name is preceded by "Ed.". The following examples illustrate the reference formats that are used.

1. Robert Cole's book is listed as: R. Cole (1982) *Computer Communications,* Macmillan, London and Basingstoke, England.

    It is cited as (Cole, 1982), if the reference to the author is indirect, or as Cole (1982), if the reference to the author is direct.

2. Peter T. Kirstein's article in *Interlinking of Computer Networks* is listed as:
   P. T. Kirstein (1979) *Interlinking of Computer Networks,* 3–30.
   It is cited as (Kirstein, 1979) or Kirstein (1979).

3. The article by Wilkes and Wheeler in *Update Local Area Networks* is listed
   as: M. V. Wilkes and D. J. Wheeler (1979) "The Cambridge Digital Communication Ring," *Update Local Area Networks,* 47–60.
   It is cited as (Wilkes and Wheeler, 1979) or Wilkes and Wheeler (1979).

4. The book by Abrams and two others is listed as: Ed. M. D. Abrams, R. P.
   Blanc and I. W. Cotton (1978) *Computer Networks: A Tutorial,* IEEE Press,
   Los Alamitos, CA.
   It is cited as (Abrams et al, 1979) or Abrams et al (1979).

5. The article by Takuji Watanabe in the December 1980 issue (Volume **4,**
   No. 4) of *Telecommunications Policy* is listed as: T. Watanabe (Dec 1980)
   "Visual communication technology—Priorities for the 1980s," *Telecom-
   munications Policy,* **4**(4) 287–294.
   It is cited as (Watanabe, 1980) or Watanabe (1980).

6. The article by Chris Barnard in the issue of *Computing* for 9 July 1981 is
   listed as: C. Barnard (9 Jul 1981) "Zynar wants to net shaky dpm with
   micros," *Computing,* 22–23.
   It is cited as (Barnard, 1981) or Barnard (1981).
   These procedures are slightly modified when the same author has more
   than one reference listed in the same chapter.

7. Kenneth J. Thurber has three 1982 articles in the reference list for Chapter
   2. They are listed as:
   K. J. Thurber (1982a) "Open networks for mixed supplier terminal and
   minicomputer equipment," *Local Networks 82,* 61–70.
   K. J. Thurber (1982b) (Apr 1982) *The LOCALNetter™ Designer's Handbook,* Architecture Technology Corporation, Minneapolis, MN.
   K. J. Thurber (1982c) (ongoing) *The LOCALNetter™ Newsletter,* Architecture Technology Corporation, Minneapolis, MN.
   They are cited as (Thurber, 1982a) or Thurber (1982a), (Thurber, 1982b)
   or Thurber (1982b), and (Thurber, 1982c) or Thurber (1982c), if cited separately, and as (Thurber, 1982a to 1982c) or as Thurber (1982a to 1982c),
   if cited together.
   A simultaneous citation of references by several different authors separates the individual citations by semi-colons. For example, a simultaneous
   citation of examples 1 and 4 is cited as (Cole, 1981; Abrams et al, 1978).
   Where there is no named author, listing and citation are either by the
   title of the document, or by the name of the publishing organisation.

The references in a chapter are listed alphabetically, with author names and/or
organisation names and/or title intermixed. The alphabetical ordering of a reference is determined by the surname of the first author listed or, if there is no named
author, by the full title of the reference or the full name of the publishing organisation.

PART ONE

NETWORK SYSTEMS AND SERVICES

Chapter 1

General Principles of Networking

This chapter explains the most important general principles that are used in most forms of computer networks, including local area networks, personal computer networks, wide area networks, and linked local area networks. It considers only those principles that are widely used, leaving presentations of the more specialist facilities and procedures to the relevant chapters.

Firstly, there are brief discussions of the purposes and user requirements of networking. This chapter then considers in turn user interfaces to computer networks, network architecture, devices and other equipment linked to networks, data transmission, network standards and protocols, network control and performance.

PURPOSES OF NETWORKING

By bringing together the already rapidly expanding technologies of computing and telecommunications, *computer networking* is adding to both of these technologies capabilities that neither of them would have separately.

On the one hand, it makes possible a form of computing that is *distributed* in several ways. For example, several users at different locations can access the same computing system. The same user can carry out a data processing job, different parts of which are carried out by different computers in a network. A group of linked users can use their own computers or "intelligent" terminals for some purposes, but also use commonly held file stores, printers or processors for others. Users can not only access a very wide variety of computer data bases, sometimes over very long distances, but often extract and transform for their own purposes selected subsets of the information that these data bases contain.

On the other hand, computer networking adds an extra dimension to the scope of telecommunications in the ordinary sense. It provides several communications media and channels, for numerical data, text, formulae, diagrams, graphics and images, as well as voice; indeed, in its most advanced form, it can handle multimedia messages, using *all* these modes of message content. To telephone communications and broadcasting, it has added data communications, telex, tele-facsimile, and more recently Teletex (a sophisticated form of communicating word-processing), videotex (the communication of information from computers to user-friendly displays), and electronic mail and message services.

But the potentialities of computer networking go farther still, because totally new applications of *integrated information* processing are emerging, that require *both* computing and telecommunications for their fulfilment. These include the whole realm of office automation that is now evolving rapidly, financial transaction services that are coming more and more to the public attention, electronic publishing, integrated information services, and a variety of ways in which geographically separated people will be able to communicate, exchange ideas, and interact with each other.

Thus computer networking has already established itself as a vitally important area of practical application, and will rapidly become much more important during the next few years. Not only will it perform many valuable functions is business and industry, but it will also be used increasingly widely by more and more members of the public.

USER REQUIREMENTS

If computer networking is to become a widely used and well-integrated set of techniques, for large groups of people, whether executives, managers, professionals, office workers, or citizens, one of the first requirements that it must fulfill is *user-friendliness. In other words, it should positively invite* the user to come and try it; no longer should it put up a barrier, and convey a feeling of inaccessibility, together with a uneasy sense that it can be practised only by a few "esoteric wizards" who seem to use ultra-obscure, jargon-ridden language.

That this is a real challenge is evident not only from the very genuine technical, not to mention human, political and social, difficulties of computer networking, those problems tend to be very much harder than those of computing alone or telecommunications alone! It also requires considerable, if not great, advances over the low degree of user-friendliness all too often present in many areas of "ordinary" telecommunications and "ordinary" computing. Which reader of this book will *not* have come across the exasperating difficulties, under too many circumstances, of trying to make even commonplace telephone calls? Which computer user will *not* have experienced the ham-handed ways in which manuals of even highly popular computer systems quite often do not explain sufficiently clearly and accurately what the user should do in certain types of situation? Worse still, they sometimes forget to mention these contingencies at all!

Thus one vitally important ingredient of user-friendliness is that the basic concepts of computer networking be explained as simply as possible, given the circumstances, in as easy and clear a language as possible, with all necessary technical terms properly defined where they arise, preferably with illustrative examples. Indeed, this is one of the objectives of the present book!

A closely related ingredient is that, for any specific function of computer networking that a user needs to carry out with a specific system, either on the job or as a member of the public, there should be a clear but comprehensive statement of the whole sequence of steps that need to be carried out. This statement should neither be too long and complicated to be offputting nor too short and concise to be unreadable, and it should include at least one *example*!

Another important requirement of a computer networking system or service is that it should provide its users with a range of functions and facilities that are appropriate for their needs. Thus, for a business system, there is a fairly well defined group of requirements for office automation and integrated information systems, even now, and these will doubtless develop further! For private users, there are not only requirements for simple individual or household functions, such as electronic mail and financial transactions, but also the need to contribute to information, education and entertainment. In assessing this sort of requirement, it should be realised that it is *not* static, but rather that it is evolving rapidly. Not only that; users may well increasingly demand their own say in the new facilities to be offered by the computer-information-communication networks of the future.

Last but not least are the ergonomic requirements of networking, that the equipment used shall provide a pleasant environment and interface for the user, that is neither tiring nor, in the long run, a health hazard or source of stress.

USER INTERFACES

A typical user interface to a computer network, whether it is a terminal or a more elaborate work station, includes both a display and a keyboard; these are two of the most basic means of communication between the network and its users.

Displays are usually obtained through specially designed visual display units (VDUs), not unlike television sets, that can present a combination of text and graphics information, usually in black and white or black and green, although colour displays are also available. A display not only conveys the most important messages from the computer network and computing systems themselves; it can also show messages from other users and generally provides an immediate visual record of information input through its associated keyboard.

Keyboards allow users to input text of their own choice to the network and to the system. This next includes their instructions to the system, messages that they want to send to other users, information that they wish to file, and programs that they decide to run. Typically, terminals have a keyboard that is alphanumeric, containing keys for digits, letters of the alphabet (now usually though not always in both upper and lower case), punctuation marks, and special symbols. Many terminals also have cursor control keys, controlling the movement of the cursor, a small symbol, appearing on a display, that indicates where the next keyboard input will be shown.

Visual information for users is often provided also by printers, that capture on paper what may otherwise be fleeting images on display screens. Output on paper is usually an extra advantage, as printed page images typically contain much more text than VDU displays and are often more readable. Some printers can also provide graphics output, occasionally in colour too, and plotters are available which can provide high quality graphical forms on paper.

Voice channels are being provided on some data networks and communication networks. This is sometimes done by integrating telephone communications with data communications and text communications. In addition, special devices for voice input and voice output are becoming available; for example, the former can allow the recognition of up to several dozen different spoken sounds, while the latter implement various forms of computer speech.

NETWORK STRUCTURES

The first basic principle of network structure is that a computer network can be subdivided into several computing and information processing devices, all linked together by a common communications subsystem, sometimes called the "subnet" (See Figure 1.1). The essential requirement is that, regardless of the diversity of the different devices, the subnet should nevertheless be able to establish effective communication and interchange of information between all of them.

The subnet may itself have a variety of configurations, of which some of the most common are illustrated in Figure 1.2. These configurations include: the *star* network, where there is one central node, usually attached to a central computer; the *loop* or *ring* network, where all the nodes are strung round a single loop of wire or cable; the *bus* network, where all the nodes occur in linear sequence, from one end of a long line, the "bus," to the other; the *mesh* network, where there is a rich interconnection between many different nodes, indeed sometimes between all pairs of nodes; the *radio* network, where there is no configuration of specific paths between different nodes, but where they are all in effective "wireless" radio contact with each other.

There are also important distinctions to be made between local area network (LAN) configurations, sited within a compact geographical area, and wide area network (WAN) configurations, the distances between whose nodes range from less than a mile to thousands of miles. Usually, the LANs have ring or bus configurations, while the WANs are usually meshes; star networks, though now less usual than before, can appear as either LANs or WANs.

The other basic principle of network architecture is that different types of network may be interconnected with each other, in such a may that any pair of nodes, accessible to each other via a path through several consecutive interconnected networks, can communicate effectively with each other. More specifically, neigh-

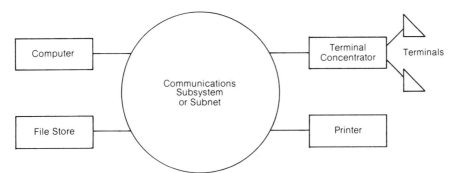

Fig. 1.1. Example of a computer network, sharing attached devices, subnet and interfaces between devices and subnet   SOURCE: Based on author's drawing

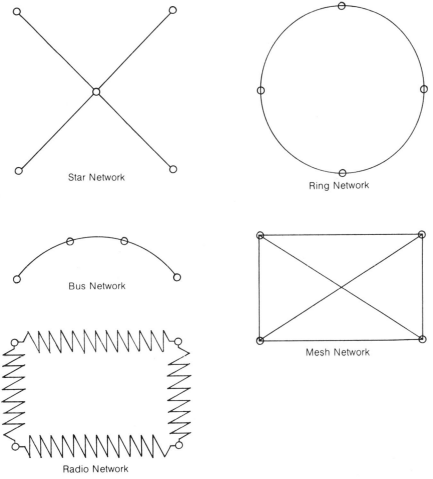

Fig. 1.2. Some typical computer network configurations   SOURCE: Based on author's drawing

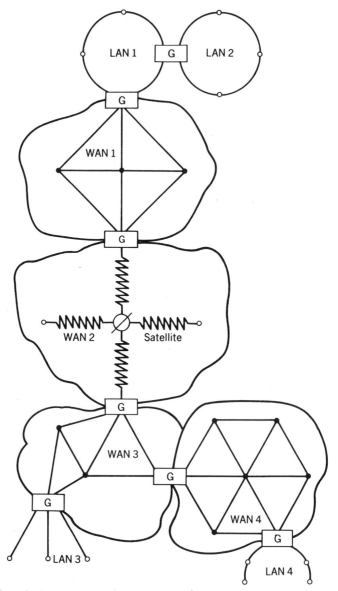

Fig. 1.3. Example of network configuration, showing interconnected WANs, including a satellite WAN, linking separated LANs   SOURCE: Based on author's drawing

bouring networks are joined to each other by "gateways," which can be viewed either as single nodes, belonging to two or more networks, or as a configuration of neighbouring, mutually linked, nodes, belonging to the different networks that are being brought together there. Figure 1.3 shows a typical configuration of interconnected networks of various types; for example, it shows not only interconnected neighbouring WANs but, very important, the linkages between different LANs, separated from each other by intervening WANs.

EQUIPMENT LINKED TO NETWORKS

In the early days of computer networks, there were usually only two kinds of device attached to them, computers and terminals. The situation is very different now, when just about every information or communications device under the sun can be linked to a network.

User interfaces, that can be connected to networks, include "ordinary" terminals, that are usually VDUs, graphics terminals and plotters, that specialise in more or less sophisticated types of visual display, word processors, a wide variety of printers, voice input devices and voice output devices. Sometimes, clusters of devices are joined to a network through a multiplexer, rather than each of these devices being connected directly.

Any sort of computer can now be interfaced with a network, ranging from the smallest microcomputer, through personal computers and minicomputers, to mainframes and distributed array processors.

Rapidly becoming more important, with the onset of office automation and other technological advances, are the multi-purpose work stations and integrated work stations, which combine several functions in a single device in a more or less unified way. Typically, devices of this sort can act as terminals, displays, word processors, computers, *and* data communicators, all at once.

Another very important class of devices, that can be attached to networks, are the file stores and mass memories. These can hold from about a hundred thousand to many million characters of information. They range from floppy disks and "hard" magnetic disks of various shapes and sizes, through magentic tapes and video storage, to the optical information stores, which can already hold very large amounts of information very compactly and promise to have very much better performance within only a few years from now.

DATA TRANSMISSION

Originally, computer networks relied entirely on telephone lines for the long distance communication of information across them. Today, with the advance of technology, the range of possible data transmission media is quite considerable. High bandwidth transmission lines and coaxial cables are providing channels for data transmission, over both short and long distances, that are far more ample and reliable than those available on telephone lines. Recently, fibre optics cables have begun to develop steadily, and will soon be able to provide local and even medium-distance channels of even higher capacity, at costs that are still reasonable.

"Wireless" data communications of several types are coming into their own. Radio waves have not only provided the basis for more or less local "packet radio" services; they are also used in satellite communications sytems, and information, "piggybacked" on broadcast television systems, is used in several teletext systems. Recently, advances in electro-optical technology have allowed the development of communications system using laser light.

NETWORK ARCHITECTURES STANDARDS AND PROTOCOLS

The architecture of a computer network precisely defines the functions that the network and its components should perform, and the ways in which the network should be organised. The main purpose of the architecture is to ensure that the design and user requirements of the network are met as far as possible, by arranging that the different parts of the network cooperate effectively and by enabling the network system as a whole to evolve according to its aims. In effect, the architecture is an "organisation chart" of the network. It is defined in terms of the relations between the different parts of the network; these relations include both protocols and interfaces.

Network protocols are essential, both for providing the basic rules of formatting and handling information that is to be communicated from one part of a network to another, and for helping to overcome problems of mutual "incompatibility" between different devices that are connected to a network, or, more generally, a system of interconnected networks. Very closely related to the design of protocols is the formulation of suitably agreed network standards, which is actively promoted by various national and international standards bodies, together with the specialist working parties that they have set up to consider and discuss new protocols.

In accordance with the principles of network architecture, the functions of a network, and therefore the protocols that implement them, operate at different layers and levels, of which seven are now generally recognised. At the lowest level, there is the physical intercommunication system, then, going progressively higher, there are link protocols, covering data transmission over links, and network protocols, primarily concerned with communication and routing across networks. At a middle level, there are transport protocols, looking after reliable end-to-end transmission of a message from one device, over a network or sequence of networks, to another. Higher still are the session protocols, responsible for handling connections between individual processes in computers and devices that communicate with each other, and presentation protocols, performing generally useful transformations and conversions of the data to be exchanged. At the top level, there are application protocols, covering a range of user-oriented functions, such as transfer of information between data bases, distributed computing, and electronic mail and message services.

NETWORK CONTROL AND PERFORMANCE

In order that a computer network may be adequately controlled, it is important to obtain a good idea of its actual performance. This may be achieved empirically, partly by making network measurements at various times and places, partly by more systematic monitoring of important parts of the network. Various sorts of control, including flow control and congestion control, help to keep the information traffic across the network in reasonable order, and prevent it from getting out of hand.

In order to obtain a full idea of network performance, it is necessary to supplement empirical studies of network behaviour by theoretical studies. These use mathematical models to throw light on the performance of part or whole of a network, and the resulting calculations on the models are carried out, using a judicious combination of analytical and simulation methods. In this way, using also the results of empirical studies, more or less accurate predictions can be made of how a network will behave if certain changes are made to its physical characteristics, to its configuration, and to its traffic. Such predictions can be used both to improve the day-to-day operation of a network, and to make valuable suggestions for the improvement of its architectural design and of the protocols that it uses.

Chapter 2

Local Area Networks

A wide range of local area network (LAN) systems has now been developed, well over 50 of these systems are now available commercially, and more of them are being introduced almost every month. This chapter surveys a representative selection of them, without making any claim to be comprehensive. The systems discussed here are designed for use by businesses and other large or fairly large organisations; those systems, that are based on personal computer networks and "micronets", and generally suitable for small organisations, are described in Chapter 3. The most recent developments are presented in Chapter 19.

The present chapter begins by reviewing briefly some of the available LAN technologies, which are also considered in more detail in Part 2, especially in Chapters 6, 8 and 9. It outlines the chief characteristics of two of the most important classes of LANs, namely the Cambridge Rings and the Ethernets.

The rest of the chapter describes some important examples of the nearly 200 commercially available LAN systems, which are surveyed briefly in Thurber (1982a) and more fully in Thurber (1982b), with perriodical updates of information in Thurber (1982c). It starts with ring-based and Ethernet-like systems, then proceeds to broadband systems, and after that to some integrated LAN systems, providing a very wide range of services for business offices and other organisations; finally, it considers briefly some miscellaneous LANs.

It should be noted that the claims made by the manufacturers and vendors of these and other network systems and products should be evaluated very carefully by prospective users, in relation to the specific needs and existing equipment and methods of their organisations, in relation to the estimated costs and previous operating experience of the systems and products, and in relation to the likely evolution of computing and information technologies during the next few years.

REVIEW AND CLASSIFICATION OF LOCAL AREA NETWORK TECHNOLOGIES

A considerable variety of LAN technologies is available, these technologies have been surveyed and compared by Cotton (1979), for example, who gives over thirty literature references. They can be classified in four ways:

1. By *configuration* or *topology*, for example: star, ring, bus, mesh (fully connected), as shown in Figure 1.2.
2. By *medium*, the method by which data are transported within the network, for example: twisted pair wires, cable, radio; digital baseband signalling, using only one frequency; digital broadband systems, using several frequencies shared by a channel; modulated signalling.
3. By *sharing technique*, the way in which many users are allocated bandwidth in the network, for example: dedicated (non-shared), time or frequency division multiplexing, statistical multiplexing, contention.
4. By *user services* and *protocols*, which can be provided by intelligent devices, attached to the network or its interfaces, regardless of the internal network transmission techniques.

Any sharing technique can be used with any technology (Clark et al, 1978), who describe a number of interesting combinations.

Some of the arguments for and against some of the most common variants of some of the technologies are now summarised; for further details, see Cotton (1979).

Local non-switched networks, using dedicated lines, are most suitable where only relatively few users need interconnection or where most users need to communicate only with one other user, as in the original time-sharing computer systems.

Local circuit switching can be achieved, either through a public telephone exchange or through a branch exchange on the user's premises. Any user can be dialled conveniently, and costs are fairly small for low speeds, up to about 1200 bits/second.

Local message-switched networks tend to have reliability problems, especially when based on central switches, but can be attractive.

Local packet-switched networks are very feasible, though sometimes more expensive than other approaches. Most of the LAN systems, described in this chapter, indeed in this book, are in this category.

Ring networks very efficiently share available transmission bandwidth, and can be implemented at high data rates with very simple transmission facilities; despite initial misgivings about their possible unreliability, they have turned out to be very reliable in practice.

Ethernets and other similar bus networks are suitable for serving many users at a single site, where no pair of stations is more than a few miles apart. They can provide gateway access to other networks. They are also very reliable and have good performance.

Cable bus systems allow many different services, such as data, voice and television traffic, to be supported on the same cable. Continuous high-bandwidth users, such as computer-computer and television traffic, and bursty low-speed users, such as interactive terminals, can both be accommodated well.

Markov (1981) introduces a taxonomy of LANs that is in some respects like that of Cotton (1979); for example, they both classify according to configuration and medium, while Markov's classification by application is not unlike Cotton's by user service and protocol. However, Markov also classifies by size, distinguishing between LANs that are small (two to 64 nodes), medium (64 to 512 nodes), and large (at least 512 nodes), and by method of controlling access to the network.

Datapoint (1982a) has introduced a concept of "local network generation." Thus *first generation* LANs offer users device-oriented point-to-point data transfer capabilities to a set of stand-alone devices of many types. *Second generation* LANs have common file formats, multiple access to files without conflict, limited hybrid operation with shared-logic and processor-based work stations, and facilities for linking geographically separated LANs. *Third generation* LANs offer resource sharing through the entire network, easy access to all resources, geographical independence allowing worldwide networks, simplified programming, and provision of full support of all functions of the network on non-intelligent terminals. *Fourth generation* LANs merge voice, data, text and messages into global network systems.

Flint (1982) has classified LANs according to the most powerful kinds of devices that they can support. The more effective these devices are, the more sophisticated is the corresponding network and the higher is its internal speed. At the lowest end of the range are the "terminal support networks," with internal speeds of 20 to 300 Kbits/sec. Then there are the "micronets," described in Chapter 3, with data rates of 100 Kbits/sec to 1.5 Mbits/sec; they are cheap but can usually handle only one type of microcomputer or personal computer. "Minicomputer networks" are faster (2 to 10 Mbits/sec) but considerably more expensive. Most of the "integrated office networks" on the market have similar speeds, are based on minicomputers *and* telephones, and attempt to meet all the communication needs of the "office of the future"; but they are expensive, and also not fully proven, as they have been introduced so recently. At the top end of the range, "mainframe networks" are very fast (50 to 500 Mbits/sec), but seem unlikely to be relevant to the LAN systems that will be used by most organisations.

Yeomans (1982) has introduced a classification of LANs by key functional requirement. "Micronets," describe in Chapter 3, have the key functional requirement of being able to support low cost, but in many cases intelligent, terminals and work stations. They have data rates up to 1Mbits/sec, use existing interfaces such as the RS232C, have some limited gateway facilities, and can support up to 200 attached devices. "Datanets" have the key functional requirement of interconnection between devices handling text, data, graphics and images. They have data rates up to 20 Mbits/sec, new (but standard) interfaces, and gateways to other datanets and to WANs, and can support up to 5,000 attached devices. "Voice/ datanets" have the key functional requirement of full integration of text, data, graphics and images with real-time voice. They have data rates up to 100 Mbits/

sec, interfaces for both voice and data handling, and gateways to voice networks and to datanets (both LANs and WANs), and can support up to 10,000 attached devices.

Davis (1982) has briefly compared the baseband and broadband approaches. Baseband, including networks like Ethernets, has the advantages of an accepted standard, and a cheap, easy, passive connection; its limitations are shorter distances, up to only about a mile and a half, and no real-time voice or television. Broadband has the benefits of much longer range, up to about thirty miles, and provision for voice, data and television channels; it has the disadvantages of no standards, expensive modem connection, and the need for "retuning" when adding further connections.

Metcalfe (1981) provides a strategic overview of LANs, providing a background with respect to which some of the key issues about LANs may be considered.

CAMBRIDGE RINGS

Cotton (1979) points out that several ring networks were developed in the USA in the late 1970s, for example at the University of California at Irvine, Ohio State University, and the Bell Telephone Laboratories, and he gives references to further information about them. One of the best known types of ring system, and probably the most used in the UK, is the class of *Cambridge Rings*, the original prototypes of which were developed at Cambridge University, and have been described by Wilkes and Wheeler (1979) and Hopper and Wheeler (1982), for example; see also the Acorn (1981) brochure for a shorter, user-oriented summary.

A Cambridge ring has *ring stations* placed round it, each of which is connected to a device; see Figure 2.1. The attached devices may be of almost any type, including mainframes, minicomputers, microcomputers, terminal concentrators, file stores, and gateways to other networks. It is used for equipment sharing, handling of files in common stores, and other forms of distributed computing. The stations are up to about 300 yards apart.

The ring transmits addressed data packets from one station to another, at a data rate of about 10 Mbits/sec, which can adequately handle data flows to and from the attached devices. Besides the device stations, there is a *monitor station*, that exercises overall control of the ring, and an *error logging station*.

Ring costs are kept low, by using elegant hardware design, based on custom logic arrays, together with standard twisted pair cabling.

High reliability is achieved by providing three powerful independent levels of error detection within the ring, together with a node design that ensures correct operation of the ring, whatever happens to its stations. The ring is continuously monitored for errors, and each fault is quickly located; this scheme is also used to detect ring breaks. Eight years' experience at Cambridge University has shown the successful and reliable operation of the ring in practice.

The ring is highly versatile, because of the considerable variety of devices that can be attached to its stations, and because of its internetworking potentialities.

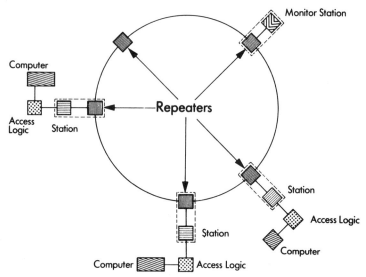

Fig. 2.1. Cambridge Ring structure SOURCE: Acorn Computers Ltd. Brochure, *The Cambridge Ring*

In view of these advantages, it is not surprising that Cambridge Rings are already used widely in the UK, not only by university computer centres and departments, but also as the basis for several commercially available designs, including the Logica VTS POLYNET, the SEEL TRANSRING, the Orbis Ring, and the Toltec Data-Ring (Cole, 1982).

For example, Logica VTS is experimenting with, and operating, distributed office systems based on Cambridge Ring technology (Sweetman, 1981); it may well announce some significant new ring systems and products in the office automation, site networking and process control areas by the end of 1982 (Cole, 1982). POLYNET connects up to 254 nodes, using twisted pair telephone grade cable, operating at 10 Mbits/sec with distances up to 100 metres between nodes (Thurber, 1982a). It can use DMA interfaces, offering point-to-point data rates of 1 Mbits/sec, and a program interrupt interface with data rates of 100 to 300 Kbits/sec. Currently, interfaces exist for DEC PDP 11 minicomputers, LSI 11 microcomputers, and Intel MultiBus systems.

The SEEL TRANSRING 2000 series, which is based on the Cambridge ring design, is a range of modules, which can be connected to provide a cost-effective high bandwidth communication network, linking computers from a variety of manufacturers (SEEL, 1981).

Racal-Milgo's PLANET (Private Local Area NETwork) uses a twin coaxial cable ring main (Williams, 1982). Theoretically, data can go round the ring at 10 Mbits/sec, but, in practice, equipment connected to the ring slows this down to a practical maximum of about 3.5 Mbits/sec. Computers, word processors and printers, of different manufacturers, can all be attached to the ring. It is said to be possible for it to communicate with several devices simultaneously and to provide conference facilities.

SILK

The Swiss company Hasler developed SILK (System for Integrated Local Communications) as a modern communications system, aiming to open new dimensions of communications in the private and local sector (SILK, 1981; Jackson et al, 1981). It is a digital loop system for both voice and data traffic, carrying such diverse services as data transmission, telegraphy and telephony, and allowing 1050 linked devices. It uses relatively short address-coded packets, circulating in one direction on an optical fibre ring circuit with transmission rate 16.9 Mbits/sec and total user data transfer rate up to 10 Mbits/sec. Reliability is increased by using secondary and even tertiary ring channels, which can be operated in the event of failures of local ring sections.

Experimental SILK networks have been set up at several sites (SILK, 1981). A system for experimental office communication has been set up at the Heinrich-Hertz-Institute in Berlin, where a SILK narrowband network is integrated with a digital broadband network, using optical fibre channels of 140 Mbits/sec, 280 Mbits/sec and 560 Mbits/sec, and an analogue broadband network for switching video telephone signals. Communication services here comprise telephony, facsimile, all forms of data transmission, video telephony, colour television, and stereo sound, with SILK covering the data and telephony services.

At the SILK news distribution system at *Deutsche Welle (Voice of Germany)*, the texts of messages are stored, and connected participants can exchange information. Processors, archives, display units and printers are connected to the system.

At ZDF (Zweites Deutsches Fernsehen), a SILK network is used as a television studio remote control system.

ETHERNET AND SIMILAR BUS NETWORKS

One of the best known and earliest introduced types of bus network is the Ethernet, developed at the Xerox Corportion's Palo Alto Research Centre in the USA. It is a baseband network, and also uses the *contention* principle, where messages are broadcast to all stations in the medium, in this case the bus, and where any messages that overlap with each other in time are cancelled, then retransmitted after random intervals.

The Ethernet is described in moderate detail by Shoch et al (1982) and by Metcalfe and Boggs (1976) and more briefly by Cotton (1979). Its early version was called Experimental Ethernet, and its current version is called Ethernet Specification (Shoch et al, 1982). In its configuration, several independent terminals are connected through an interface to a transceiver, which is in turn connected to the bus transmission medium, typically a coaxial cable, with data rate of about 10 Mbits/sec. Stations can be attached to the cable at any point, and the cable can be extended from any of its points in any direction by using repeaters. Each station has an interface, designed according to the type of device attached to the station, and a controller responsible for retransmitting colliding or unacknowledged packets. Current designs of Ethernets combine the interface and controller in a special buffered device between the station and the transceiver.

Xerox now operates many individual Ethernets, interconnected by gateways, throughout the USA, serving thousands of users. Performance characteristics have been found to be very good, even under very heavy loads of data traffic. Several years ago, Xerox formed an alliance with Digital Equipment Corporation (DEC) and Intel to market its Ethernet Specification products.

Quite a number of companies, both in the USA and in the UK, are now selling LANs and LAN products, based on the Ethernet technology. These include: Ungermann-Bass Inc. in the USA and its British agent Thame System Ltd.; Geac Computer Corporation Ltd. of Canada, with offices also in the USA, UK, and West Germany; 3Com in the USA and its British agent the Sintrom Group; Sension Scientific Ltd. in the UK.

Ungermann-Bass is not only using Ethernet systems but is also introducing broadband products, which offer voice, video and data channels (Davidson, 1981; Davis, 1982; Thame Systems Ltd., 1982; Thurber, 1982a; Whiteley, 1981). The Ungermann-Bass Net/One networking system already embodies the Ethernet standard, which has been adopted by many manufacturers. It can be interfaced with systems from many manufacturers, and has protocols to suit users' evolving requirments; it has full development and network management tools. Ultra-reliable and flexible operation is claimed. It will be possible to upgrade existing Net/One products to broadband systems, and mixed Ethernet and broadband systems are envisaged, to which both existing and new users could be connected. Figure 2.2 shows a typical example of a Net/One configuration. Already, over a hundred Net/One systems are operating worldwide.

Geac's LAN system (Geac, 1982) uses the Ungermann-Bass Net/One architecture, whose simple coaxial cable bus can have up to 255 connections to intelligent nodes, with each node having ports for up to 24 devices. It can be used in offices, factories, warehouses, government departments, universities, etc. It supports free point-to-point communication between computer systems, terminals, printers, word processors, and a wide variety of other digital devices. It has extensive gateway facilities, allowing any of its terminals to access external time-sharing systems, public packet-switched networks, telex, videotex services, and other public and private computer networks. 3Com offers a range of Ethernet equipment, including: the 3C300 UNIBUS Ethernet Controller, which can connect any PDP 11 or VAX minicomputer to Ethernet; the 3C200 Q-bus Ethernet Controller, which can connect LSI 11 microcomputers to Ethernet; the 3C100 Transceiver and associated equipment (3Com, 1981).

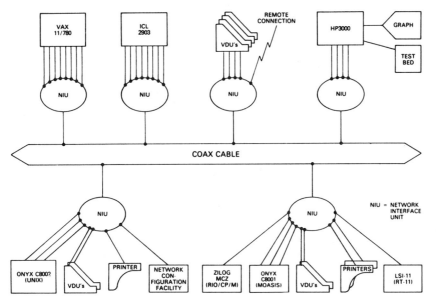

Fig. 2.2. Example of an Ungermann-Bass Net/One™ configuration SOURCE: Thame Systems Ltd. *Product News*

Sension Scientific Limited offers a full range of Ethernet products and provides Ethernet LANs, using a single robust coaxial cable for interconnection over a range of up to about a mile (Sension Scientific, 1982). Application areas for which it can be used include: electronic offices, data collection systems, terminal switching, distributed processing, high speed computer interconnection, and interconnection of microprocessor systems.

LOCALNET

Sytek Inc. in the USA, whose British agent is Network Technology Limited, has developed LocalNet as a low cost, high performance LAN, based on a synergistic combination of analog, digital and data communications technologies (Network Technology, 1982; Thurber, 1982a; Biba, 1981a and 1981b). It uses industry standard broadband cable television distribution facilities, allowing over 20,000 users to be supported simultaneously. A wide variety of user equipments can be interconnected, with end-to-end data security, flexibility of configuration, and ease of installation.

System 20, the first group of products in the LocalNet family, was designed to meet the immediate and near-future needs of a variety of users, in government, finance, industry, education, etc. It is implemented as a modular growth-oriented family of network products. It is claimed to be cost-effective, reliable, and compatible with a broad range of devices and interface standards. As it occupies only a relatively small part of the cable bandwidth, its services can coexist with other broadband services, such as high-speed data links, voice and video.

LocalNet extensions and improvements provide substantially increased capabilities for network interconnection, user device interfaces, security and privacy, and network management and control.

HYPERBUS AND HYPERCHANNEL

Network Systems Corporation's Hyperbus is a digital communications exchange for the interconnection of terminals, minicomputers and front-end processors (Network Systems, 1982a; Binney, 1981; Thurber, 1982a; Waldron, 1982). It uses a hierarchical bus structure, with a baseband coaxial cable having data rate of 6.3 Mbits/sec. It has been designed to meet the growing demand for a high speed digital communications network, allowing the maximum performance of computer terminals, graphics subsystems and other digital communications equipment. It can accommodate a wide variety of applications and protocols, and it can thus provide local networking capability for terminals, office equipment, process control and distributed minicomputers.

Network Systems' Hyperchannel is intended to allow virtually any computer to "talk to" any other computer, at very high data rates, up to 50 Mbits/sec, and distances of thousands of feet (Network Systems, 1982b and 1982c; Thornton et al, 1975; Binney, 1981; Thurber, 1982a). Its configuration is shown diagrammatically in Figure 2.3.

As its data throughput is much higher than that of ring networks and Ethernets, it can carry out such tasks as high speed bulk file transfer, centralised data base processing, and real-time front-end and back-end processing. The Hyperchannel Link Adapter allows high speed data transfer between geographically separated computer centres, at rates up to 44.7 Mbit/sec, using a microwave transmission facility or special high-speed telephone lines. The Satellite Link Subsystem permits high speed satellite communication between computer centres in any part of the world.

Hyperchannel also offers 3270 terminal support to IBM MVS/370 users (Network Systems, 1982d), and its NETEX software system that allows wider and easier communications between different types of computer than was previously possible (Network Systems, 1982e).

Rather than seeking roughly equal treatment among all stations, as is typical of the Ethernets and rings, the Hyperchannel provides a priority scheme, to ensure that the data communications needs of high priority devices are totally satisfied before any traffic is carried for low priority devices. This approach seems to be better suited to the applications for which it was designed, and to be quite effective for moderate numbers of nodes.

Hyperchannel is now installed at over a hundred sites, most of which are large

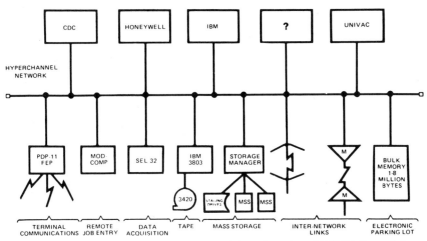

Fig. 2.3. Typical Network Systems' HYPERCHANNEL configuration   SOURCE: Network Systems Corp. Hyperchannel document

computer centres with several central processors and many types of peripheral equipment. Its users include: university computer centres, communications suppliers, large oil companies and manufacturers, and airlines.

MASTERNET

The MASTERNET Electronic Office System, including the MASTERNET LAN, is marketed by Master Systems (Data Products) Limited, and provides a completely integrated information systems architecture, well suited to the needs of a business or other organisation (Master Systems, 1983). It uses a duplicated ring configuration, with data transfer rates of 10 Mbits/sec. Its multi-function work stations provide user-friendly access to any required information source, as well as local computing power if that is required. Its network transfers information reliably between its interconnected in-house processing devices. Its gateways provide connections to a wider variety of external data bases and computer networks. Figure 2.4 shows a tyical MASTERNET system configuration, including links to other MASTERNET networks and outside information and computing services.

MASTERNET supports a wide range of applications, including file handling, information retrieval, access to outside data bases and information services including viewdata services, word processing, electronic mail, and personal computing. MASTERNET has also been designed to provide an integrated data, image and voice processing system, so that it has facilities for short voice messages and for voice annotation of text. It thus provides: fast access to management information, of whatever type and wherever it is held; facilities for rapid document preparation; improved communications and document transmission; more computing power at

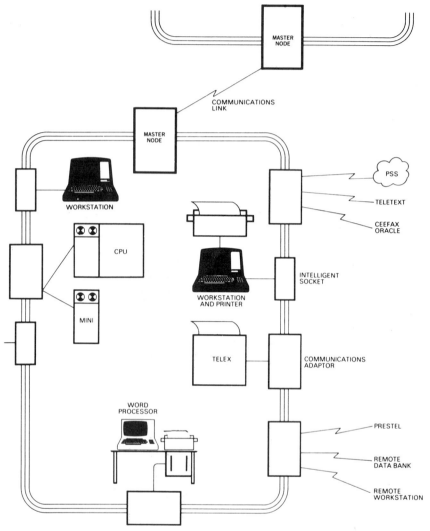

Fig. 2.4. MASTERNET system configuration   SOURCE: MASTERNET Brochure, Master Systems (Data Products) Ltd.

the work station; and, as a result, higher productivity. Brooks (1981) and Master Systems (1982) describe an earlier version of MASTERNET, the XIBUS Electronic Office System, using the XINET LAN.

ARC AND ARCNET

Late in 1980, Datapoint Corporation introduced ARC (Attached Resource Computer) and ARCNET as a third generation LAN, based on its Resource Management System (Datapoint, 1982a and 1982b; Thurber, 1982a). In 1981, it announced a combination of the ARC coaxial cable information pathways with the ISX (Information Switching Exchange), to form an even more powerful fourth generation LAN (Datapoint, 1982a and 1982c).

These ARC LANs are designed to serve the full range of business and office information processing needs, offering sophisticated operating systems and software utilities, data processing with compatible file structures, and a high quality laser printing system. Data storage devices, tape drives, printers and other peripherals are all shared and accessible throughout the network, regardless of their physical locations in it. ARC supports the operation of inexpensive work stations with full function capabilities, at a cost much lower than using intelligent processors. Figure 2.5 shows a typical ARC network configuration.

Applications provided include: user-friendly word processing, easy-to-use colour graphics, speedy electronic mail and message service, and computer-based voice communications management.

ARC networks are flexible and integrated, being adapted to users whose requirements for network systems grow as their organisations expand. The functions of ARC LANs all work together, and separate ARC LANs at different locations can easily be linked together by leased lines or other public telecommunications services.

WANGNET

Wang Laboratories' WangNet uses a broadband technique, and a "branching tree" configuration, to provide an integrated LAN supporting a wide range of services (Wang, 1981a; Stahlman, 1982). Remote WangNet also allows geographically separated Wang systems to communicate with each other (Wang, 1981b).

WangNet uses a dual coaxial cable link, with one 350 MHz cable to transmit information and another to receive it. These cable pairs link different nodes on the network, and it is also possible for one cable pair to branch off another at a given node, thus allowing a tree-like topology. For each cable, the WangNet bandwidth is divided into three bands: the Wang Band for communications between Wang systems, the Interconnect Band for applications using standard protocols, and the Utility Band for cable television applications such as video conferencing and security. Transmission rates vary from 300 to 64,000 bits/sec for non-Wang devices and up to 12 Mbits/sec between Wang systems. Communications with non-Wang systems and devices can be incorporated within WangNet.

WangNet is an advanced resource-sharing network, with a comprehensive range of services and applications. It integrates text, data video, telecommunications, electronic mail, file handling, photo-composition, graphics, and many other functions. As such, it is a powerful aid to productivity and decision making inside an organisation. Remote WangNet also supports various applications, including remote interactive data processing and long distance file transfer and document transmission.

Integration

The Cornerstone of the Integrated Electronic Office™

The ARC local network supports the needs of the "office of the future" today. What you see here is a fourth generation ARC network which serves the needs of a large user organization. Each department uses multiple capabilities of the network. And all departments have full access to the system's functions -- word processing, electronic message service, laser printing, facsimile capabilities, and other resources -- regardless of their physical locations.

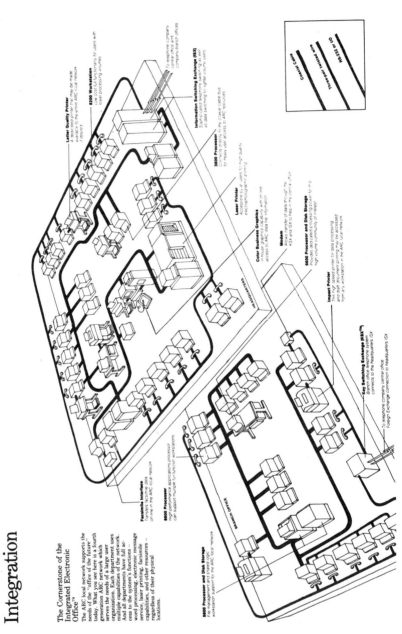

Fig. 2.5. Datapoint ARC network configuration   SOURCE: Datapoint Corporation ARC Brochure

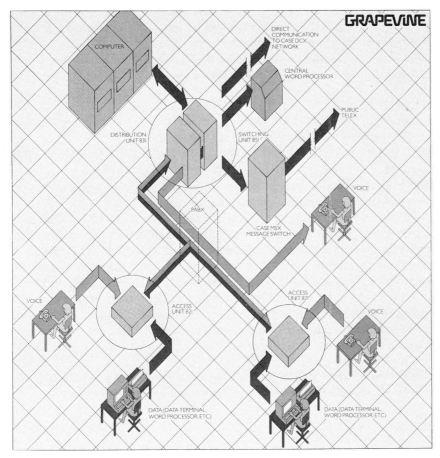

Fig. 2.6. CASE Grapevine configuration   SOURCE: CASE Grapevine Brochure

Courtesy of CASE (Computer And Systems Engineering plc)

OTHER LOCAL AREA NETWORK SYSTEMS

Thurber (1982a) describes briefly six of the LAN systems that have been discussed earlier in this chapter, together with the following three, that are not further detailed here: Amdax CallNet, Control Data LCN (Loosely Coupled Network), and Protean Associates PRONET, another ring network. As already mentioned, Thurber (1982b, 1982c) goes into much more detail about LAN systems and products that are available commercially, especially in the USA.

Hopkins (1981) describes recent developments in the MITRENET, a LAN system developed near Boston, USA, some years ago.

The Hawker Siddeley MULTILINK LAN connects together computers, terminals, and any other devices that have an RS232 interface; any two devices then communicate with each other as if directly linked (Hawker Siddeley, 1982). Each device is connected via a MULTILINK station, a self-contained unit with its own Z80A processor, which can perform any special action that is required. The network is fast enough to carry twelve simultaneous two-way transmissions, each at 19.2 Kbits/sec, the maximum speed of an RS232 interface. The network is low cost, simple to instal, and device-independent; its total length can be up to 250 miles.

ICL offers Netskil, its "total" LAN service, that includes consultancy. It also offers Microlan, a 1 Mbits/sec LAN for direct work station connection, which is described briefly by Charlish (1982) and in Chapter 3.

Kemp and Reynolds (1982) describe ICL's network architecture, IPA, which is based on the ISO Reference Model (see Chapter 9).

IBM has not yet implemented any full-scale LAN system or product, Chapter 19 mentions the LAN products that it intends to introduce.

CASE has developed Grapevine, its own low cost version of a LAN, which uses internal telephone system wiring (CASE, 1982; Cane (1982)). At any existing telephone location within a building, both the telephone handset line and the data terminal line are plugged into an 821 access unit, which in turn plugged into a British Telecom wall socket. The 821 sends data down the telephone lines, via the PABX (branch exchange) to the distribution/switching unit. Data traffic is then switched according to the resource chosen by the user, which can be computer, word processor or communications; speech is sent back to the PABX for normal voice transmission. Grapevine has a carrier system and a switching system. A typical configuration is shown in Figure 2.6.

Other systems, using PABXs for local networking, are considered briefly in the section on network exchanges in Chapter 6 and also in Chapter 19.

REFERENCES

Acorn (1981) *The Acorn Econet*, Acorn Computers Ltd., Brochure.

K. J. Biba (1981a) "Packet communication networks for broadband coaxial cable," *Local Networks 81*, 611–625.

K. J. Biba (1981b) "LocalNet: A digital communication network for broadband coaxial cable," *Proceedings 1981 IEEE Spring COMPCON*, San Francisco.

P. Binney (1981) "How HYPERbus and HYPERchannel fit into a two-bus local network architecture," *Local Networks 81, 611–625*.

Richard Brooks (11 Oct 1981) "ITT taps into British office of the future," *The Sunday Times*, p. 72.

A. Cane (4 June 1982) "Grapevine—The low cost solution for the local area network," *Financial Times*, 31.

CASE (1982) *GRAPEVINE*, Computer Systems and Engineering plc, Brochure.

G. Charlish (28 June 1982) "Why ICL plus 19 equals progress," *Financial Times*, 18.

M. Cole (1982) "The Cambridge ring—European Developments," *Local Networks 82*, 54–50.

I. W. Cotton (1979) "Techniques for local area computer networks," *Update Local Area Networks*, 25–44.

D. D. Clark, K. T. Pogran and D. P. Reed (Nov. 1978) "An introduction to local area networks," *Proceedings of the IEEE*, **66** (11) 1497–1517.

Datapoint (1981a) *ARC*, Datapoint Corporation, Brochure.

Datapoint (1981b) *Join the Intelligent Bus Route to . . . ARC*, Datapoint Corporation, Brochure.

Datapoint (1981c) *The Integrated Electronic Office—Productivity for the '80s*, Datapoint Corporation, Brochure.

John M. Davidson (1981) "Interconnection services and Net/One," Paper, 10 pages.

R. Davis (Feb 1982) "The networking controversy," *Communications International*.

D. Flint (1982) "The local area network as the backbone of new business systems," *Local Networks 82*, 15–32.

Geac (1982) *Local Area Networking with Full External Access*, Geac Computers Ltd., Leaflet.

Hawker Siddeley (1982) *MULTILINK—Universal Local Area Network*, Hawker Siddeley Dynamics Engineering, Ltd., Leaflet.

G. T. Hopkins (1981) "Recent developments on the MITRONET," *Local Networks 81*, 97–105.

A. J. Hopper and D. J. Wheeler (1982) *Local Area Networks: The Cambridge Ring*, Addison-Wesley, London and Reading, MA.

J. Kemp and R. Reynolds (May 1982) "IPA—A processing architecture based on the ISO Network Reference Model," *Microprocessors and Microsystems*, **6** (4) 171–176.

J. D. Marlow (1981) "Taxonomy of local computer networks," *Local Networks 81*, 143–156.

Master Systems (1982) *XIBUS—The Fully Integrated Office Electronic System*, Master Systems (Data Products) Ltd., Brochure.

Master Systems (1983) *MASTERNET—The Invisible Network for Master Systems*, Master Systems (Data Products) Ltd., Brochure.

R. M. Metcalfe (1981) "A strategic overview of local computer networks," *Local Networks 81*, 1–9.

R. M. Metcalfe and D. R. Boggs (Jul 1976) "Ethernet: Distributed packet switching for local computer networks," *Communications of the ACM*, **19** (7) 395–404.

Network Systems (1982a) *Hyperbus—Preliminary Product Description*, Network Systems Corporation, Brochure.

Network Systems (1982b) *Network Systems—Connecting the Computer Industry*, Network Systems Corporation, Brochure.

Network Systems (1982c) *Hyperchannel—The Network Becomes the System*, Network Systems Corporation, Leaflet.

Network Systems (1982d) *Local Access from Remote Locations*, Network Systems Corporation, Leaflet.

Network Systems (1982e) *Communications in a Mixed Environment*, Network Systems Corporation, Leaflet.

Network Technology (1982) *Local/Net System 20 Overview*, Network Technology Ltd., Brochure.

SEEL (1981) *TRANSRING Local Area Network*, Scientific and Electronic Enterprises Ltd., Brochure and Leaflets.

Sension Scientific (1982) *Quick Guide to Ethernet* and other Leaflets, Sension Scientific Ltd.

J. F. Shoch, Y. K. Dalal, D. D. Redell and R. C. Crane (Aug 1982) "Evolution of the Ethernet local computer network," *Computer*, **15** (8) 10–26.

SILK (Spring 1981) *Hasler Review*, **14** (1). Special Issue on Hasler SILK.

M. Stahlman (Jan 1982) "Inside Wang's local net architecture," *Data Communications*, **11** (1) 85–90.

D. Sweetman (1981) "A distributed system built with a Cambridge Ring," *Local Networks 81*, 451–464.

Thame Systems (1982) "Ethernet and broadband networks," *Thame Systems Ltd., Product News*.

J. E. Thornton, G. S. Christensen and P. D. Jones (Nov 1975) "A new approach to network storage management," *Computer Design*, **14** (11) 81–85.

K. J. Thurber (1982a) "Open networks for mixed supplier terminal and minicomputer equipment," *Local Networks 82*, 61–70.

K. J. Thurber (1982b) *The LOCALNetter Designer's Handbook*, Architecture Technology Corporation, Minneapolis, MN.

K. J. Thurber (1982e) *The LOCALNetter Newsletter*, Architecture Technology Corporation, Minneapolis, MN.

M. Waldron (Sep 1982) "Hyperchannel spreads net," *Communications System & Management*, **1** (4) 37–39.

Wang (1981a) *WANGNET—The Corporate Communications Resource*, Wang Laboratories Inc., Brochure.

Wang (1981b) *Remote WangNet*, Wang Laboratories Inc., Brochure.

J. Whiteley (Apr 1981) "Soft net," *Systems International*.

M. V. Wilkes and D. J. Wheeler (1979) "The Cambridge Digital Communication Ring," *Update Local Area Networks*, 47–60.

E. Williams (15 Apr 1982) "Planet from Racal-Milgo as an office Spring offering," *Financial Times*, p. 12.

J. M. Yeomans (1982) "Micronets: Self contained, low cost and available now," *Local Networks 82*, 51–59.

3Com (1981) 3C Ethernet System Leaflets, 3Com Corporation.

Chapter 3

Personal Computer Networks and Micronets

Many, if not most, models of personal computer can now be provided with facilities for communicating with each other over local area networks, and for communicating with remote computers over telephone lines and even over wide area networks. Several LAN systems are now on the market, that were specifically designed to network clusters of personal computers and provide them with shared facilities such as large file stores and high quality, relatively expensive, printers. In addition, there are the micronets, already mentioned in Chapter 2, which are lower performance LANs for use with office systems, but cheap enough to be within the price range that can be afforded by many smaller businesses.

This chapter starts with a brief general review of networking facilities for personal computers. Then it describes some of the personal computer LAN systems now available. After that, it considers some of the micronet LAN systems, designed for office use and other business applications. Finally, it gives some examples of how personal computers and other microcomputers can be linked to remote computers and external network systems and services. The most recent developments are presented in Chapter 19.

Because I am more familiar with the Apple II personal computer system than with any other, I have chosen quite a number of my examples from networking systems designed to work with it. This should not be taken to imply that comparable facilities are not available, or will not soon be available, for other leading makes of microcomputer; indeed, several examples of such facilities are mentioned.

NETWORKING FACILITIES FOR PERSONAL COMPUTERS

Most personal computers can be interfaced to a wide variety of peripheral devices. Normally, these devices include keyboard, monitor or TV set display, printer and tape recorder, often also floppy disk drive and hard disk drive. For many models, networking facilities can also be provided usually by placing a communications card or other interface card inside the computer. There are at least three important types of networking that can be used: personal computer LANs, personal computer-to-external computer links, and communication between personal computers and various outside systems and services via telephone lines and WANs. Figure 3.1 shows some of the possible ways of implementing these types of networking for the Apple II personal computer.

Saal (1981) reviews some of the possibilities for personal computer LANs, and also discusses LANs in general and how they relate to personal computers. As he points out, personal computer networks allow the use of independent personal computer work stations, together with the possibility of sharing some of the devices and information on the network between different users.

Personal computer LANs now on the British market include: the Acorn Econet, which can link Acorn Atoms and BBC Microcomputers (Acorn, 1981); Nestar's Cluster/One, which can link Apples (Zynar, 1981a, 1981b, 1982a and 1982b); the Corvus Omninet and Miracle, which can also link Apples (Keen, 1981a and b); and the U-NET, which can be used with Apple II and and other personal computers (U-Microcomputers, 1981). These are described in the next few sections.

Clements and Daugherty (1981) propose a simple design for an ultra-low-cost network for personal computers, using a cable to link together the personal computers in the network, via their RS 232 interfaces; this approach has the advantage that RS 232 interfaces are already very widespread among personal computing equipment.

Personal computers can be used as intelligent terminals, accessing remote minicomputers and mainframes. This is usually done by placing communications cards inside them and using modems or acoustic couplers to link the communications cards with neighbouring telephone lines.

Personal computers can also be used as viewdata terminals, using suitable adaptors and local telephone lines (Mayne, 1986). They can be linked to other external services and WANs, either via telephone lines, using communications cards and modems or acoustic couplers, or via gateways from personal computer LANs.

Personal computer WANs have been operating for several years for users of various types of personal computer in the USA. In the UK, they are already available for users of Pets and TRS 80s, and may soon be provided for users of Apples and other personal computers (ACC, 1982; *Windfall*, 1982).

ECONET

One of the cheapest personal computer LANs is the Acorn Econet that links together up to 255 Acorn Atoms and/or BBC Microcomputers made by Acorn (Acorn, 1981). These computers can act as independent work stations, but are able to reach each other very quickly and access shared facilities such as floppy disk drives and printers. They can all communicate with each other independently, and any one of them can be set up as a master station, which is able to define priorities and to communicate with all the other computers at once or singly.

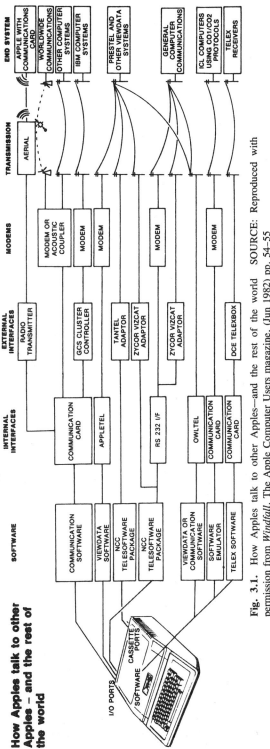

How Apples talk to other Apples – and the rest of the world

Fig. 3.1. How Apples talk to other Apples—and the rest of the world SOURCE: Reproduced with permission from *Windfall*, The Apple Computer Users magazine, (Jun 1982) pp. 54–55

Stations are connected to each other by a four-wire cable, along which there is a data transfer rate of up to 210 Kbits/sec. Stations may be separated by up to 1 km. Different Econets may be joined together by gateways.

The shared disk facility is provided by a station dedicated to running the "file server" program, which organises disk files for the network. The shared disk may hold both public files, accessible to all users, and private files, accessible only to the users that created them or to privileged users. Users are allowed to create and delete only their own files.

Econet has several advantages over time-sharing systems, including low cost, and better speed, reliability and flexibility. For example, a ten-computer network with a 400 Kb file station costs a few thousand dollars.

As Acorn also provides teletext and Prestel interfaces, an Econet, or any of its individual work stations, may be configured to receive any of the three public videotex systems-Ceefax, Oracle and Prestel-that are available in the UK.

CLUSTER/ONE

On a larger scale than Econet, but still fairly small by the standards of typical office LANs, the American company Nestar Systems Inc. has developed the Cluster/One Model A microcomputer LAN, which is marketed by Nestar Systems Ltd. (formerly Zynar Ltd.) in the UK (Zynar, 1981a, 1981b, 1982a and 1982b; Powers, 1981; Saal, 1981). It can support up to 65 Apple II and/or Apple III computers within a distance of about 300 metres of each other, together with a common hard disk store of 16.5 MB or 33 MB and a 20 MB cartridge tape back-up if required.

The Cluster/One is highly versatile, both in layout and in range of applications. Its configuration can be a bus, a daisy chain, a tree or a star; its design is modular, so that user organisations can add to it as quickly or as slowly as they like, as their needs evolve. As Figure 3.2 shows, a very varied set of devices, software systems, and applications can be accommodated within the same system, and there are facilities for linking with remote mainframes and minicomputers and Apples, as well as with other networks. It also has Notice Board and Electronic Mail facilities.

These links to remote sites are now being developed and promoted vigorously (Kennett, 1981). The #1,000 FTS file transfer server is designed to transfer files of any size automatically to another FTS on a remote Cluster/One or, on request, directly to or from a user station. Its hardware is based on the Owltel viewdata interface. Another communications device used is the buffered communications card. Servers to emulate IBM's 3780 and 3270 terminal protocols will help to improve mainframe links, later in 1982.

Costs are relatively low, although much higher than for an Econet, and they work out at a few thousand dollars per work station.

The Nestar in-house viewdata system, OverView, complements its LAN system and integrates naturally with it. Viewdata frames can be created in Prestel format, and be accessed by all users in the network or by closed user groups only, as required. Bulk updating of remote viewdata systems is supported. OverView work stations can also carry out the functions of normal work stations.

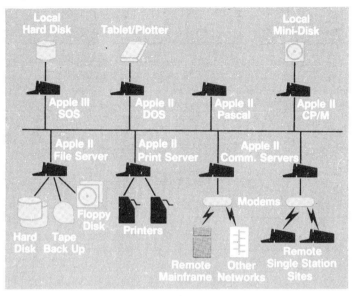

Fig. 3.2. Nestar Cluster/One network options   SOURCE: Nestar, Inc./Nestar Systems Ltd. Cluster/One Leaflet

To sum up Nestar's approach, it would like its customers to be able to integrate LAN and mainframe facilities, but it also believes that the addition for communications to personal computers can provide the basis for a powerful alternative to mainframes and minicomputers.

OMNINET AND MIRACLE

Corvus Systems in the USA has developed the Omninet personal computer LAN for linking up to 64 different microcomputers or peripherals into a fast, low cost network; this sytem has been marketed in the UK by Keen Computers Ltd. (Keen, 1981a). It is able to connect many popular personal computers and microcomputers, ranging from the Apple II to the LSI 11.

Figure 3.3 shows a typical configuration. The connecting bus is a simple twisted-pair cable, and a simple interface board is also used. The intelligent network interface, called a "transporter," contains processors and software that eliminate much of the complexity that might otherwise be needed in other parts of the system. The speed of the network is about 1 Mbits/sec. Each transporter manages the network for that node, and there is no need for any master network controller; it also performs certain high-level tasks that are often the responsibility of host computers in other networks. It implements the lowest four levels of the ISO Reference Model of Open Systems Interconnection; hence its name, as the transport layer is the top level that it handles.

Omninet itself links its personal computers to shared printers and also to shared

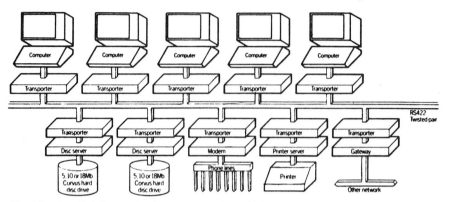

Fig. 3.3. A typical Corvus Omninet network   SOURCE: Keen Computers Ltd. Omninet Leaflet

hard disk drives, with capacities 5MB, 10 MB, and 18 MB, that have also been developed by Corvus. In addition, it can link to other networks and systems via modem and public switched telephone network, and also via gateways and neighboring WANs.

At an earlier stage, Corvus Systems had also developed the Miracle system, that could link several Apple II computers with shared Corvus hard disks, and was also marketed by Keen Computers Ltd. in the UK (Keen, 1981b). This system used up to eight Constellation host multiplexers, each linking up to eight microcomputers in a star configuration. It also provided a Mirror 100 MB videotape system as an inexpensive back-up to the Corvus hard disks. Many types of microcomputers could be connected, including Apple II and Apple III, TRS 80 I and II, Personal Machines 380Z, LSI 11, Cromemco, North Star, Superbrain, and Vector Graphic.

U-NET

U-Net is a cheap but quite powerful micronetwork system, using an Apple II personal computer or a U-NET Controller as a network controller and various other microcomputers as satellites (U-Microcomputers, 1981). The satellite computers can use the resources of the network host computer, with network controller, to communicate with each other and use certain shared facilities like disk drives, printers and real-time clock. The configuration for this system is shown in Figure 3.4.

Further development and improvement of the system is in hand; for example, active consideration is being given to the use of hard disks as storage devices for the system, together with compatibility with Pascal and CP/M as well as Basic software. Apple IIs, BBC Microcomputers, and other important types of personal computer can be used as satellites.

Although the U-NET was first developed for the educational area, for use of microcomputers in schools and colleges, it also has many applications in the business and scientific areas.

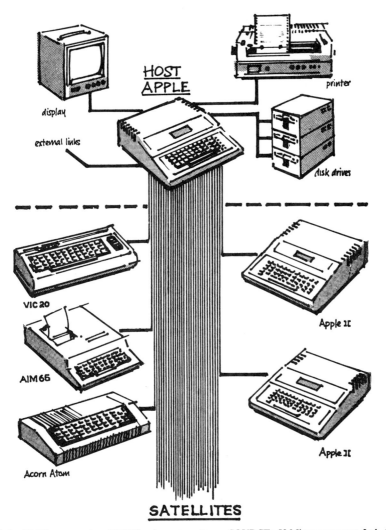

Fig. 3.4. U-Microcomputers U-NET micronet system   SOURCE: U-Microcomputers Ltd. U-Net Leaflet

MICRONETS

Several writers on LANs have pointed out that there is likely to be a considerable demand by smaller businesses and organisations for LANs with lower performance but also lower cost than the faster and more sophisticated LANs described in Chapter 2. The next part of the present chapter considers briefly some examples of these "micronets", which, strictly speaking, should in some respects be considered separately from personal computer LANs, although in other respects they may be rather similar.

One of the most useful general discussions of micronets has been provided by Yeomans (1982). His general classification of LANs, including micronets as an important category of LANs, at the "lower end" of the range, was summarised early in Chapter 2.

An important table in his paper summarises the key technical characteristic of 14 of the micronet systems that are available now; topology, cable type, transmission method, transmission rate, and terminal interfaces. Yeomans describes and reviews some of the commercially available micronets according to functional rather than technical characteristics. He points out that their users should be concerned that micronets do not restrict their freedom to expand their systems or interface to other networks.

Yeomans introduces the following classification of micronets:

1.   Those that allow communications between any pair of attached devices.

2.   Those that allow "simultaneous" communications to resources such as disk servers and printer servers, and thus require packet switching rather than circuit switching.

3.   Open versus closed systems. An *open system* is compatible with RS-232C, the only widely accepted communications standard at OSI Layer 1, the physical level. An *ajar* system has gateway compatibility, through a communications server, with other accepted standards. A *closed* system is designed for a particular supplier's equipment and protocols only, and is thus not guaranteed to interface with other systems.

Yeomans also considers some strategies for upgrading micronets. Firstly, increase the number of attached devices, but note that this number may in practice be well below the theoretical maximum. Secondly, provide internal gateways to other devices in or near the system. Thirdly, provide gateways to WANs and external systems.

Z-NET

Zilog's Z-Net II communications package allows many Zilog System 8000s to be connected together via a high-speed LAN system, with data rate 800 kbits/sec (Zilog, 1982). The 8000s in turn can be connected, for example, to PDP 11s and other non-Zilog machines using the UNIX operating system.

The higher level communication protocols used are an extended version of UNET, a UNIX-based package, developed by 3-COM Corporation, which has been designed to provide totally media-independent network communications for UNIX-based machines.

UNET provides the user with three modes of communication:

1.   Virtual terminal facility, allowing a user of one machine to log on to another of the machines linked to the network.

2. File transfer facility.
3. UNET Mail System, which can send messages to any user, storing the message in his mailbox if he is not logged on at the time.

The UNET facilities can be invoked either from a user's terminal or from within an application.

Charlish (1982a) has described the application of a Z-Net to a communications system inside a hotel, using coaxial cable strung round the building (Charlish, 1982a).

HINET

The HiNet Local Computer Network, developed by Digital Microsystems Inc. in the USA, now a subsidiary of the Extel Group, is a flexible micronet providing both high speed local processing and shared 21 MB hard disk storage (Digital Microsystems, 1981; Gamester, 1981). The system has a master computer, exercising overall control, and up to 32 satellite computers or user stations. HiNet uses standard ribbon cable for short distances, up to 200 feet, and dual twisted pair plus earth cable for longer distances. Figure 3.5 shows a typical configuration for a small business office.

Every work station in a HiNet is tailored to the needs of its user(s); any configuration is possible, from a straight VDU User Station to a full station with local local storage and one or more printers. HiNet has data protection security and data back-up facilities, rapid response, and control flexibility. It is easy to instal, and it uses the CP/M operating system.

HiNet can start simple, but develop as a user organisation's needs evolve. It provides simultaneous working of different application programs, and different users can access the same file at once. Its Master file stores all the applications programs and the data files for the network system.

MICROLAN

ICL is already marketing Microlan, a 1 Mbits-sec LAN for connecting work stations directly to the network itself and other network systems and services (Charlish, 1982b). A typical configuration is shown in Figure 3.6. Each work station is linked to the LAN through a suitable device, and the LAN also has interfaces to outside services, such as WANs, teletex and videotex. Thus a user works from an individual station, to communicate with his office via the LAN, with the rest of his department via a LAN interface, and to company subsidiaries via a PABX connected to the LAN.

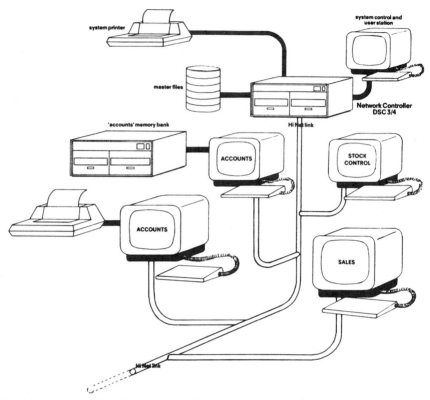

Fig. 3.5. Example of Digital Microsystems HiNet configuration   SOURCE: Digital Microsystems Ltd. HiNet Leaflet

APOLLO DOMAIN

Apollo Computer Inc. has developed the Domain (Distributed Operating Multi-Access Interactive Network) System, which provides every user with his own dedicated computer system, and links these computers by a ring network, with transmission rate of 12 Mbits/sec and with up to 1000 metres between nodes (Apollo Computer, 1981).

Each computing node is a powerful personal computer, based on a central processor build around twin Motorola 68000 microprocessors; each node can support up to 3.5 MB of error-correcting memory and is initialy provided with 512 KB of this memory.

Each work station has a high resolution display that can handle graphics output and be partitioned dynamically into several active windows, each showing the input or output for a series of processes running concurrently for the user. For example, a work station can be configured for engineering/graphics applications or as a "programmers workbench".

Extra peripherals, such as high speed line printers, plotters, magnetic tapes,

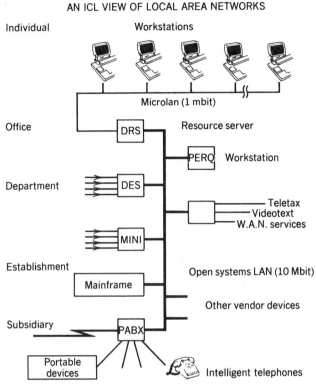

Fig. 3.6. AN ICL view of local area networks   SOURCE: *Financial Times* (28 Jun 1982) "An ICL view of local area networks," using diagram provided by ICL

and 300 MB disks, can be interfaced to a work station. There is also a Multibus interface to the proposed new IEEE communications standard, and access to WANs can be achieved through a special gateway interface.

PERSONAL COMPUTERS AS INTELLIGENT COMPUTER TERMINALS

Many models of personal computers can be linked to minicomputers and mainframes by attaching the right sort of equipment to them and running them with the right software. For example, this can be done by placing a communications card inside a personal computer and then linking it to a telephone line by means of a modem or acoustic coupler. In this way, personal computers can be operated effectively as remote intelligent terminals.

Several examples of how an Apple II computer as a remote terminal are now described briefly. The methods are likely to be similar for many other types of personal computer.

Apple-Com is an inexpensive software package that allows an Apple II to be turned into an intelligent PDP 11 terminal (Nicklin, 1982). It will run on an Apple System with 48 Kb memory and communications card and acoustic coupler or modem. Because it uses DEC's very versatile Peripheral Interchange Program (PIP), it allows files to be transferred from an Apple floppy disk to the PDP 11 and from the PDP 11 for storage on the Apple disk; files can also be created, viewed and deleted, and directories of files can be set up. Although Apple-Com was developed specifically for PDP 11s, it will work for any computer and operating system that supports PIP or PIP-type commands. This includes the DEC and CP/M operating systems and the many models of personal computer that can use CP/M.

Apple-Com has been found useful for the following applications at least:

1. It makes the Apple into a good time-sharing terminal, with ability to receive and store files.
2. Remote data input and validation, with downline data transfer during off-peak hours.
3. Daily business transactions can be processed locally on the Apple during a working day, and their details can then be sent to the central computer in a short transmission at the end of the day.
4. Business data can be distributed to remote sites.
5. Electronic mail.
6. Software distribution; the latest versions of a program can be sent to a remote site or transferred between two local computers.

The GCS Cluster Controler allows an Apple II to communicate directly with an IBM mainframe and thus provide facilities like those of an IBM 3270 terminal (Robinson, 1982). It will handle up to eight Apple IIs, giving each of them access to an IBM down a single line, using asychronous modems, which is attached to a port on the IBM 3705 teleprocessing monitor and is addressed by it as an IBM 3271. See Figure 3.7 for a typical configuration of Apples connected to an IBM host computer. The GCS controller will also support serial and parallel printers and many other synchronous devices. Each Apple requires a communications card and an 80-column display facility, together with driver software, provided by GCS.

Using Appleterm software and a special 80-column card and synchronous communications card, developed by Mike Dennis Associates, Apples can emulate ICL 7500 terminals and connect to any ICL mainframe computer that performs as an XBM primary (*Windfall*, 1982, P. 55). Input screens can be handled with ICL software as well as Apple software.

The Interlink software package, developed by General Microcomputer Systems, allows an Apple with a communications card, modem and disk drive to provide direct access to any time-sharing system, at speeds up to 1200 bits/sec (*Windfall*, 1982, p. 53.).

Owl Micro-Communications Ltd. has developed Owlterm, a Pascal communications program that turns an Apple II computer, with a Pascal system and

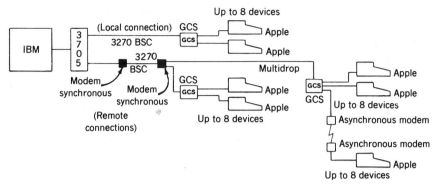

Fig. 3.7. Clusters of Apples connected to an IBM host computer SOURCE: Reproduced with permission from *Windfall*, the Apple Computer Users magazine, (April 1982) p. 25

language card, into an asynchronous (teletype compatible) terminal to a local computer, or through an acoustic coupler or modem, to remote computers (Owl Micro-Communications, 1982). Owlsync 2780/3780 provides an Apple II with IBM-compatible communications for Apple II.

In the USA, TAFT (Terminal Apple with File Transfer) has been developed as a short but useful program to turn Apples into simple CRT terminals and enable them, via their RS-232 interfaces, to transfer files to remote computers at a low cost (Gabriele, 1982). TAFT's most obvious commercial use would be as a data capture station, whereby it would collect and store data from various input devices, such as keyboards, graphic tablets and voice inputs, and then communicate this data to the organisation's central computer at the end of a working day.

PERSONAL COMPUTER LINKS OVER WIDE AREA NETWORKS

There is already quite a wide range of possibilities for linking personal computers over the public switched telephone network to various external computing and information services (ACC, 1982; *Windfall*, 1982). The previous section has already given some examples of how to connect personal computers to remote computers, using telephone lines.

Another very important application is the linking of personal computers to videotex systems (Mayne, 1986). A wide range of adaptors is already available, allowing personal computers, situated in the UK, to access Prestel.

The National Computing Centre has launched a new system, that will enable Apples to link directly to Prestel and to the increasing number of external data bases run on viewdata-compatible systems (*Windfall*, 1982, p. 52). This system allows Apple users to communicate with each other, via bulletin boards, and to download a variety of applications software from the Prestel data base into their own machines. The NCC system uses the MicroTantel adaptor and a special software disk.

Owl Micro-Communications Ltd. has introduced a new interface package, Owl-tel, which will allow Apple users to connect to Prestel and other networks (Owl Micro-Communications, 1982; *Windfall*, 1982, p. 54). It enables the Apple to receive viewdata signals at 1200 bits/sec for direct viewing, disk storage, printer output, or processing. In Prestel mode, it can reply to Prestel at 75 bits/sec, but it can also operate, for example for Apple-to-Apple communication, at speeds up to 1200 bits/sec for the public switched telephone network via a modem or with private networks via leased lines. By adding the APES professional editing system to Owltel's standard user-friendly editing instructions, an information provider can use Apple as a viewdata editing terminal.

In the USA, personal computers can easily communicate with information utilities and time-sharing networks such as The Source and Compuserve, that also provide electronic mail and other services. For example, an Atari 400 or Atari 800 personal computer can be interfaced in this way, using the Telelink I program cartridge, together with the Atari 850 interface model and a suitable modem (Flint, 1981).

REFERENCES

ACC Symposium (17 April 1982) "Your computer and the telephone," Symposium held by Amateur Computer Club (ACC), at Polytechnic of North London.

Acorn (1981) *The Acorn Econet*, Acorn Computer Ltd., Brochure.

Apollo Computer (1981) *Apollo Domain Architecture*, brochure, also leaflets on Domain, Apollo Computer Inc.

G. Charlish (1982a) (15 Mar 1982) "Local nets make hotel debut," *Financial Times*, 7.

G. Charlish (1982b) (28 Jun 1982) "Why ICL plus 19 equals progress," *Financial Times*, 18.

K. Clements and D. Daugherty (Oct 1981) "Ultra-low-cost network for personal computers," *Byte*, **6**(10), 50–66.

Digital Microsystems (1982) *HiNet Computer Network*, Digital Microsystems Ltd., Leaflet.

Digital Microsystems (1983) *HiNet—Travel the Network*, Digital Microsystems Ltd., Brochure.

G. Flint (Oct 1981) "Atari's Telelink 1", *Byte*, **6**(10), 86, 90.

T. Gabriele (Jun 1982) "TAFT: Terminal Apple with file transfer," *Byte*, 7(6) 410–432.

B. Gamester (8 Oct 1981) "US firm proves value of low-cost micro networks," *Computer Weekly*, 7.

Keen (1981a) *OMNINET* Keen Computers Ltd., Leaflet.

Keen (1981b) *Miracle*, Keen Computers Ltd., Leaflet.

D. Kennett (17 Jun 1982) "Links to remote sites for Zynar Ltd. network," *Computer Weekly*, 2.

A. J. Mayne (1986) *The Videotex Revolution*, second ed., Wiley, Chichester and New York.

Microprocessors and Microsystems (Jun 1982) "Z-Net II—A network for 16-bit micros," **6**(5) 256.

H. Nicklin (Jan 1982) "A cost effective terminal computer," *Windfall*, **1**(7) 47.

Owl Micro-Communications (1982) Owl Micro-Communications Ltd., miscellaneous leaflets.

I. E. Powers (1981) "NESTAR MODEL A: A low cost network for microcomputers," *Local Networks 81*, 65–72.

P. J. Robinson (Apr 1982) "Linking Apple II with its IBM big brother," *Windfall*, **1**(10) 24–25.

H. J. Saal (1981) "Local area networks—Possibilities for personal computers," *Byte*, **6**(10) 92–112.

U-Microcomputers (1981) *U-Net*, U-Microcomputers Ltd., Leaflet.

Windfall (Jun 1982) "Apples wing round the world," *Windfall,* **1**(12) 52–55, five short articles on different aspects of Apple II communications.

J. M. Yeomans (1982) "Micronets: Self-contained, low cost and available now," *Local Networks 82,* 51–59.

Zilog (1982) *Z-Net Communications Package for System 8000,* Zilog (UK) Ltd., Press Release.

Zynar (1981a) *Nestar's Cluster One Model A—Large system performance at 'personal' computer cost,* Zynar Ltd., Brochure.

Zynar (1981b) "Outline system description—Local microcomputer network system and back-end storage network," Zynar Ltd., Technical Information.

Zynar Ltd. (1981c) (Oct 1981) "OverView—In-house viewdata with a difference," *Zynar Ltd. Newsletter,* **1**(1) 4.

Zynar Ltd. (1982) *Cluster/One—Linking People and Information Through Personal Computers,* Zynar Ltd., brochure.

Note: Zynar Ltd. has now been renamed "Nestar Systems Ltd."

Chapter 4

Wide Area Networks

Wide area networks (WANs) cover a large physical area, that can be a whole country or even extend world wide, for example when run by multinational organisations. WANs thus cater for computer communications over distances much longer than those handled by LANs.

They can be used for communications between individual devices, separated by distances anything between a few yards and many thousands of miles. Besides connecting computers to more or less remote terminals, they can be used to link LAN's with network users and network computers in general. In particular, they can be used to bring together geographically separated LANs, including those belonging to single organisations with several different sites, into integrated *linked local area networks (LLANs)*.

This chapter describes briefly some of the wide area network *systems* actually in operation or now being installed. Chapter 5 gives some details of some of the network *services* that use these systems. Chapters 6, 8 and 9, respectively, discuss their structures, their transmission systems, and their architectures and protocols. It should be noted that WAN systems, unlike LAN systems, are comparatively rarely offered as commercial products, even though there are private WAN systems, used solely by large organisations and businesses, in addition to the public WAN systems. Further details are given in books on computer networks and data transmission, for example Cole (1982), Davies and Barber (1973), Davies et al (1979), and McGlynn (1978). Zacharov (1981, Subsection 7.3) gives brief introductory discussion that is fairly up-to-date. For reference information, see Corby et al (1982) and, much more briefly, CASE (undated).

There are several ways of classifying WAN systems. Firstly, they can be subdivided into those using telephone systems and lines and those using specially designed data networks.

Data networks can in turn be subdivided into those using circuit switching, message switching or packet switching. Cole (1982, Section 7.1) gives a useful discussion of these different types of switching and their advantages and disadvantages.

Data networks can also be classified by the transmission media that they use, including telephone lines, other land lines, coaxial cables, optical fibres, radio links, and satellite communications, or, as in *mixed media* data networks, a combination of these.

In addition, they can be classified according to the types of messages that they can handle, ranging from those that handle only data and text to *integrated* data networks that can handle most sorts of messages, including data, text, graphics, image, and voice, together with mixtures of these types.

This chapter begins by considering the uses of the public telephone system as a WAN. It then describes in turn circuit-switched, message-switched and packet-switched data networks, discussing some of their advantages and disadvantages. PRIMENET is presented as a notable example of LLAN system. After that, further consideration is given to broadcast packet-switched networks, including satellite networks, using radio transmission, and to mixed-media packet networks, such as the Arpanet and the network used by the UNIVERSE project, that are pioneering new networking techniques, both for WANs and for LANs. Finally it introduces System X, the integrated services digital network (ISDN) that is now being developed and gradually implemented by British Telecom. The most recent developments are presented in Chapter 19.

THE PUBLIC SWITCHED TELEPHONE NETWORK

The telephone system is probably still the most important medium for computer telecommunications and wide area networking. This is because it was the only medium available for this purpose in the early days of computer networking, and because the development of data networks is still sufficiently recent for only a minority of computer users yet to have adopted their systems and services.

In most countries, the telephone system is run by public authorities. However, in the USA, it is operated by several private companies that have been licensed by the Federal Communications Commission (FCC) to provide telephone services and other telecommunications services. These public authorities and licenced companies are usually called *PTTs* (*Public Telegraph and Telephone* authorities).

In the developed countries, the PTTs have established *Public Switched Telephone Networks (PSTNs)*, that are comprehensive networks of telephone lines and connections designed to carry speech traffic. These networks are mostly linked together into a larger, international network, forming in effect a worldwide PSTN.

Davies and Barber (1973, Chapter 2) give a very full account of data communication, using the PSTN, as it was about ten years ago. Kirstein (1976, pp. 81–82) reviews briefly the data facilities available there a few years later. Relatively little has changed since then, because most of the new data communications developments have taken place in data networks and especially in packet-switched data networks.

The PSTN provides a fully developed example of a circuit-switched network, and thus experience with it has provided useful guidance for the design and operation of circuit-switched data networks. Some of the equipment used by these data networks is similar to some of that used by the PSTN.

Just as a *call,* establishing a connection between two subscribers for the duration of their conversation, is set up when a telephone is used, so a call is set up when one device transmits data to another over the PSTN. When a call is set up, in either case, a temporary circuit is established between the two user devices, and this circuit ceases to operate when the call is finished and the devices are disconnected.

Originally, data communication over the PSTN was used to connect computers to their remote terminals. At a later stage, directly communicating computers also used this network. Currently, some public viewdata systems, such as Prestel, use telephone lines to link their users' television sets or terminals with their data base computers. Many LAN systems, especially the micronets and personal computer networks, provide interfaces whereby LANs can use the PSTN to access other network users including other LANs.

Despite its widespread use for this purpose, the telephone channel was not designed for digital data transmission, and, being analogue, is not very well adapted to it. In order to connect a digital device to a telephone line, it is thus necessary *either* to use a *modem* (*modulator-demodulator*), to translate electrical signals from digital to analogue and back again, or to use an *acoustic coupler,* that codes digital signals into sound patterns that are then fed into a telephone microphone and decodes them at a telephone receiver.

Due to the problems of data transmission over the PSTN, including the unreliabilities and delays of the system and the need to dial calls (even though autodiallers are now available), many large companies and other important user organisations have used *leased circuits* or *leased lines,* that give more convenient and reliable transmission, although these lines are often still part of the PSTN.

A telephone connection through a PSTN provides a channel of bandwidth about 3.5 kHz. Most data communication over the PSTN, whether switched or leased, has used single voice channels, even though some leased circuits have used groups of 12 to 60 telephone channels, corresponding to nominal bandwidths of 48 kHz or 240 kHz, respectively. In practice, a telephone circuit can, for example, accommodate 200 bits/sec, 300 bits/sec, 600 bits/sec, and 1200 bits/sec modems, including the 12 bits/sec modem, with 75 bits/sec return channel, in a Prestel receiver. For multiplexed leased lines, rates of 4800 bits/sec and 48 kbits/sec are also available.

DATA NETWORKS

For many years, a very simple and primitive international data network, the Telex network in the UK together with its counterparts in other countries, has been operated by the PTTs for telegraph communications, using teleprinters as terminals. However, its data rate, 50 bits/sec, was far too slow for effective computer data communications, so that at first the PSTN was used to handle these instead.

Originally, it was felt, especially by the PTTs themselves, that adaptation of the PSTN would be sufficient to meet all future needs for computer data transmission. This attitude grossly underestimated both the volume and practical importance of data communication requirements as they later developed.

By the mid-1960s, it was becoming clear that the future of telephony as well as data transmission was with digital systems, even apart from the fact that demand for data communications and computer networking was expanding very rapidly. It began to be realised that only specialised data networks could meet their requirements properly.

In 1968, the CCITT established a study group for new data networks; during the next few years, it formulated recommendations that formed the basis for the first public data networks, in the full sense of the term, and their interfaces with computers and terminals. Some of these recommendations, and later ones, are discussed in Chapters 9 and 21.

Besides the classifications of data networks already mentioned at the beginning of this chapter, it is also useful to subdivide them between (mostly public) switched data networks and private data networks using leased lines. Digital data services, using leased line data networks, have been used widely and successfully in the USA especially, and several of these now have international coverage. Kirstein (1976) gives a useful earlier survey of existing and planned public data networks. Figure 4.1 (Zacharov, 1981) shows a typical configuration for a wide area computer network; note that the terminals accessing the system are usually multiplexed through terminal concentrators rather than being directly connected.

Both public switched and private leased data networks have their advantages and disadvantages. The former can offer circuit switching, packet switching or both. They can achieve economies of engineering and scale. They have brought good business opportunities for the PTTs; in the long run, when enough terminals and LANs and other systems and devices have been connected, they can be expected to become very profitable. For users, they provide the potential for a wider range of access to other users than any private network can provide, although this potential can be fully realised only when protocols and other standards have been sufficiently developed.

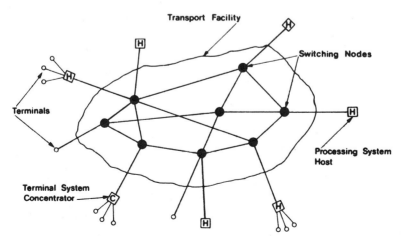

Fig. 4.1. A computer communications network   SOURCE: V. Zacharov "Computer systems and networks: Status and perspectives," Proceedings of the 1980 CERN School of Computing. Publication CERN 81-03 (1981), pp. 8–77. Reprinted with permission.

On the other hand, private networks can respond to individualised types of service requirements and offer facilities well tailored to meet these needs. Thus they can be especially suitable, both for multinationals and other large businesses and organisations, wishing to establish effective data communications and computer networking between their scattered and separated premises, and for large-scale worldwide computer time-sharing services meeting a wide variety of individual data processing needs. They can also provide useful supplementary services faster, at times when the provision of similar services by PTTs temporarily lags behind their demand.

Data networks in general already offer wideband circuits, even when using "ordinary" landlines; typical data rates that they have provided include 48, 50, 64 and 72 kbits/sec. With the more modern transmission technologies, which are outlined in Chapter 8, very much higher channel capacities, going up to millions of bits a second, have been implemented.

CIRCUIT-SWITCHED DATA NETWORKS

In a *circuit-switched* computer network, each computer has a private circuit to a local exchange, and the exchanges themselves form a WAN. Each time that communication needs to be established between a given pair of devices, a path must be found through the network, along which there are circuits available for connection when the call is set up. Because of this, a control system needs to be used, which sends its own messages to establish the circuits as and when required. Usually, this control system has its own sub-network, separate from the data network proper.

Circuit switching used to be favoured as a means of connecting computers, but has been largely replaced by packet switching, for new data networks, because of its disadvantages. It is still used by some WANs, including Caducée in France, EDS in West Germany, the Nordic Public Data Network in Scandinavia, and some of the earlier North American data networks. However, with the development of System X in the UK, circuit switching is being revived for data transmission. See the last section of this chapter.

Circuit switching has the following disadvantages. Its equipment is very expensive, yet the resulting circuits are not always reliable enough for computer communications. The resulting circuit can only be used by the two connected computers, while the call is in effect; all the links and switches, needed for the connection, must be available during the conversation, and the devices at both ends must be free to interact at the same time. Calls can take several seconds to set up, a very long time in computer terms.

It also has some advantages. As charges are made only for times of actual connection, its use could be favourable to those needing only occasional short calls. It is cost-effective when a single device is communicating for long periods at a time.

MESSAGE-SWITCHED DATA NETWORKS

A technique, that is entirely different from circuit switching, is *message switching,* described fully by Barber and Davies (1973, Chapter 8) for example, where the users and their devices exchange information by sending each other messages. This has the advantage that they need no longer take part in a simultaneous conversation, as copies of messages can be stored at intermediate nodes in the network, and forwarded when convenient (*store-and-forward technique*). Although there may still be some delay before a message reaches its destination, at least the user and his devices are no longer tied up while waiting for a connection to be made all the way to the message destination. Indeed, multiple destinations also become possible. Nor do repeated attempts have to be made to establish a call.

For both circuit switching and message switching, there can be congestion as the data traffic becomes increasingly heavy. In the former case, this is felt as an increasing time needed to set up a call, until the system is "saturated," with all circuits to the called party being engaged; under these circumstances, there is an indefinitely long delay before a call to that subscriber is eventually placed. In the latter case, there is an increasing delay in sending the message through the network to its destination; this time, "saturation" occurs when the storage and/or data links available are filled up, in which case the message may fail to get through and have to be retransmitted. However, it seems likely that, in most cases, a heavier loading is needed to cause saturation in message-switched networks than in circuit-switched networks.

One variant of message switching, namely "packet switching," is so important, and in some respects sufficiently different from, message switching in its original form, that it is treated by networkers as another mode of switching; it is thus considered separately in the next section of this chapter. From now on in this book, "message switching" is assumed to refer only to those variants of it that are distinct from packet switching.

In practice, the message-switched networks, in this sense, are largely those used for switching in telegraph and Telex networks. They are specially useful for many forms of administrative message traffic, where delays in forwarding are not critical.

In such systems, messages can be input, no matter what the current status of their destinations. Terminals of different codes and speeds can communicate with each other effectively. Stored messages can be retrieved and retransmitted in the event of errors and also in the event of failure to forward due to congestion further ahead in the network. Interconnection with the international Telex network is possible, so that users can easily access this worldwide message medium.

Several message switching systems, based on minicomputers, are now available as relatively "standard" products. For example, the Autex 1600 System (Chernikeeff Telecommunications, undated) is a Telex/telegraph message switching system, able to originate, send, distribute and receive messages from separate, possibly remote, terminals completely automatically, thus allowing effective office-to-office communication from one part of the world to another. Such systems are expected to bring about a considerable shift of administrative traffic from postal and telephone services during the next few years, and to make an important contribution to the development of electronic mail.

Message switching has several advantages over circuit switching. Because of its store and forward facility, a user can send a message when convenient, even if the receiver is not ready at that time, and computers and other devices can exchange information at different speeds. Messages can be broadcast, and better treatment can be given to messages of higher priority. Network equipment can be used more efficiently.

If very long messages are used, several disadvantages become evident; for example, such messages can hold up or even prevent the storage of other, possibly more important, messages, and are themselves more liable to loss due to lack of available space.

PACKET-SWITCHED DATA NETWORKS

Packet switching is a variant of message switching, where the "messages" that are used are much shorter than usual, and are required to have a length not exceeding a maximum that is laid down be the specific network system. Thus packet switching can be viewed as an extension and refinement of message switching in its original sense, as it divides "messages," as previously defined there, into sequences of "packets."

Just as each message contains information about its destination, in a message-switched system, so each packet starts with a "header" that includes destination data and other information required by the network, and that precedes its main body of data; it usually also has a "tail" that contains checking information. However, the packets are treated as separate units, and may therefore be transmitted by separate routes between their origin and their destination. As with message switching, each packet is stored and forwarded by the node(s) through which it passes along its path.

In order to avoid possible problems, a packet-switched network has to provide at least the following facilities:

1. Packet assembly and disassembly (PAD), together with sequencing, so that each message is split up into packets before being sent, and is re-assembled from its packets, in the right order, after they have arrived at its destination.

2. Storage or buffering at switching node(s) between the message's origin and its destination; these nodes may or may not differ for different packets in the message.

3. Control of errors and of other anomalies, such as lost and duplicate packets.

4. Routing of packets between their origins and destinations.

5. Flow control and congestion control, to provide a reasonable flow of packets through the network, and avoid a critical level of congestion that brings the danger of saturating the network.

These topics are beyond the scope of the present chapter, but they are considered in detail in Chapters 9, 10, 17, and 20.

Packet switching has several advantages over message switching. As already mentioned, message switching can encounter severe difficulties if the messages are long; these can usually be overcome by using the much shorter packets, whose smaller size makes it much easier to allocate and manage storage of transient data at the network nodes. Because messages are split into many packets, packets from several messages can be interleaved on one link, thus reducing the delays perceived by users. Many transmitters can send their data to one receiver, a single user can broadcast messages to many destinations. The total transmission times through the network are greatly reduced; whereas long messages are typically delayed for *minutes* in a message-switched network, packets usually reach their destination within a fairly small fraction of a second in packet-switched networks using only land lines. Packet switching is also more efficient and responsive than message switching, especially when data traffic is "bursty." With packet switching, any device can select the data rate appropriate to its traffic, whereas, with circuit switching, the communicating devices belong to mutually exclusive speed categories.

Packet switching has a few disadvantages. For example, it introduces further complexity in the system, and requires more elaborate and complicated protocols to handle the packet and carry out the translation processes between user messages and packet sequences. Each packet also has the "overheads," resulting from its need to have a header and, usually, a tail; this means that the proportion of transmitted data, that is user information, is somewhat lower than in other switching systems.

Nevertheless, it seems to be agreed by at least most experts on computer networks that packet switching is currently the best technique for transmitting and switching data across WANs. This is reflected by the fact that many if not most actual wide area data networks now in operation, and practically all the new ones that are now being installed, are packet-switched.

Some well-known examples of packet-switched networks are now mentioned. Further details are not given of most of them in the present chapter, because the computer network services that use them are described in the next chapter. However, PRIMENET is described in the next section, as an outstanding example of a network system that provides wide area communication and networking facilities between geographically separate LANs; in other words, it is an excellent example of a linked local area network (LLAN) system. Similarly, the Arpanet and its associated networks are described very briefly in the section after that, both because of their use of varied selection of transmission technologies, and because of their outstanding value as testing grounds for these technologies as they have been developed.

Packet-switched WANs have been operating since the early 70s. Perhaps the best known example, and one of the earliest, is the Arpanet. In the UK, the NPL (National Physical Laboratory) and EPSS (Experimental Packet Switching Service) networks did valuable pioneering work on the packet switching technique, before the establishment of the British Telecom's PSS (Packet Switching Service) network. In France, Cigale, Cyclades and RCP were important early networks, and Transpac is now the regular packet-switched network. In Spain, CTNE has been operating for some years. In several countries of Western Europe, after experience with the experimental EIN (European Informatics Network), Euronet has now been established. In the USA, Telenet and Tymnet are well-known packet-switched networks, which also developed Transatlantic network communications. Canada has used the Datapac data network. Another early international network, providing a packet-switched private line service, was Western Union's IDDS (International

Digital Service). More recently, British Telecom introduced IPSS (International Packet Switching Service).

Several private packet-switched networks have also been developed, including SITA (which also uses message switching) used by the airlines, SWIFT used by the banks, CERNET developed and used by the European Nuclear Research Centre (CERN), and several international networks set up by compuer companies for their clients, including CYBERNET, DECnet and PRIMENET, together with the networks set up by GEISCO, Honeywell, IBM, etc.

PRIMENET

PRIMENET has been developed by PRIME Computer to provide complete LAN and WAN communication services for all Prime computer systems (Prime Computer, 1980, 1981a to 1981c). Over geographically dispersed areas, it allows Prime computers to communicate with other Prime computers, computers from other manufacturers that support X.25 protocols, and terminals and computers attached to packet-switched networks (Figure 4.2). In LAN configurations, it enables Prime computers to be attached, through a high-bandwidth multi-point ring arrangement, to other Prime systems (Figures 4.3 and 4.4).

PRIMENET is the basis of Prime's approach to distributed computing and processing. It is a combination of hardware, communications software, and specific Prime products that support network communications, with various services and transmission techniques.

It consists of three software modules that let network designers operate and route network traffic efficiently, provide fast responses, and reduce transmission costs. The *program-to-program* module lets programs, stored in one or more computers, communicate with each other. The *program-to-terminal* module lets any program communicate with terminals attached to other systems or to a packet-switched network. The *program-to-file* module lets authorised users access any files in a network that they are entitled to reach.

The PRIMENET Node Controller allows up to 15 Prime systems to be con-

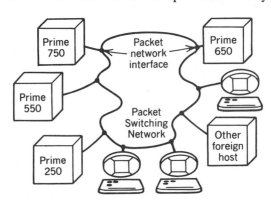

Fig. 4.2. PRIMENET communications through packet-switched networks SOURCE: Prime Computer, Inc., *PRIMENET Product Bulletin*

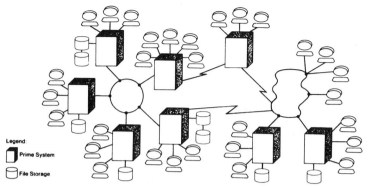

Fig. 4.3. A PRIMENET network using PNC ring connections, a packet-switched network, and dedicated synchronous lines   SOURCE: Prime Computer, Inc., *PRIMENET Product Bulletin*

nected with each other via a ring LAN. Systems can be added to or removed from the ring without affecting each other's performance.

In a WAN environment, PRIMENET can cater for many terminals, each accessing a central computing system, and, more generally, many terminals accessing several different computers, with centralised controls.

All PRIMENET facilities meet the X.25 protocol standards for computer-to-computer and computer-to-terminal communications. Any Prime system can easily communicate through a PRIMENET with any other X.25 system. For example, PRIMENET supports packet switching as implemented in the Telenet, Tymnet, Datapac, IPSS, PSS, Euronet, and Transpac networks; other networks are being added, to enable Prime computers to communicate easily with each other between continents and around the world.

Prime's Distributed Processing Terminal Executive (DPTX) allows Prime systems, as well as IBM systems, to communicate with IBM 3270 terminals. This means that users do not have to change application programs or access methods, available on an existing IBM network, when moving to a PRIMENET.

Using its RJE emulation packages, Prime systems can operate as mainframe terminals, over the PSTN, to remote mainframe computers, including CDC, Honeywell, ICL, IBM and Univac.

Using the PRIMOS operating system, together with PRIMENET, computers in the Prime 50 Series can be run, together with attached clusters of terminals, printers, magnetic tape drives, and large magnetic disk drives, to carry out a variety of office automation, data communication and data management tasks. Programming languages that are supported by this system include Basic, Cobol, Fortran, Pascal, PL/I and RPG II; a Source Debugger is also provided.

BROADCAST PACKET NETWORKS

Broadcast networks differ from other forms of networks by using a channel to which all the network users are connected, so that all the users in the network

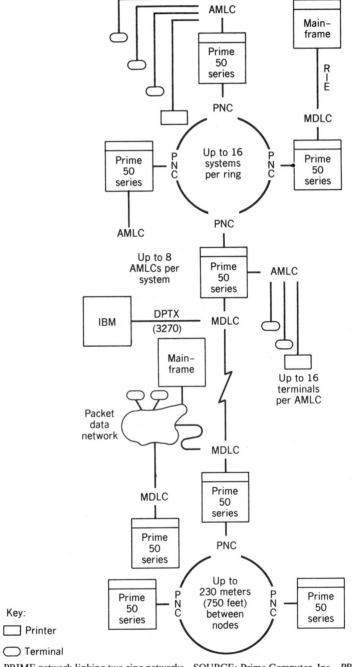

Fig. 4.4. PRIME network linking two ring networks SOURCE: Prime Computer, Inc., *PRIME Communications Hardware Product Bulletins*

receive any transmission made by a station on the channel. As already explained, broadcast networks include LANs of the Ethernet type and some other bus networks. The present section outlines of use of broadcast techniques in WANs.

The growing need for long-distance data transmission, together with the increasing costs and congestion of land-based communication links, has led to the consideration of using broadcast radio transmission for some wide area data networks. One of the first and best known radio nets was Alohanet, used for data communications between various places in the Hawaiian islands. Some of the special networking techniques developed there, including the use of broadcasting to all stations in the network, and arrangements for the retransmission of "colliding" messages, have been adapted for use by the satellite networks and the Ethernets.

The most important applications of radio transmission have occurred in the *satellite networks*. Any satellite network uses ground stations, acting as radio transmitters and receivers, together with a satellite in a geostationary orbit, about 22,500 miles above the Earth's surface. During a transmission, radio waves are sent by one of the stations to the satellite, and there bounced off so that they can be received by all the other stations in the network.

The use of communications satellites is now becoming widespread, not only for voice traffic and television transmissions but also for data communications. As for land-based data networks, so for data networks using satellites, packet switching is rapidly being adopted.

Experience with satellite networks so far has shown that they can be very effective and not particularly expensive, when used in a low data rate environment. One of their peculiarities is their long propagation delay, somewhat more than a quarter of a second for a round trip, which results because any satellite is so far above the Earth's surface that the time taken for the radio waves to travel across the network becomes noticeable. Existing satellite data communication is still at the experimental stage, and much more work needs to be done before its problems have bene solved and satellite data networks can become widely adopted for general applications. But the potential advantages are very great, due to the very large bandwidth of satellite channels.

MIXED-MEDIA PACKET NETWORKS

A *mixed-media* "network" combines several networking techniques and transmission methods; it is strictly speaking a group of separate networks, each using their own transmission medium and transmission technology, but interconnected with each other by suitably designed gateways, so that communication is possible between any pair of users or devices, anywhere in any of the networks.

Most of the mixed-media data networking so far done is still experimental, although mixed-media land lines, such as combinations of ordinary telephone lines, coaxial cables, and optical fibres, are by no means unknown in some of the networks providing regular services. Perhaps the best-known example of a mixed-media system is the Arpanet group of networks.

The Arpanet was established before 1970 by the Defense Advanced Research Projects Agency, a research sponsor acting on behalf of the United States Government, in order to link together computer centres, carrying out relevant research, so that they could share their available computing resources. At first, it was confined to centres in the USA, mostly in American universities, but later on, it added a Transpacific link to Hawaii, together with Transatlantic links to the UK, linking in several British universities via the elaborate Arpanet node configuration at University College London, and also to nodes in Norway and Germany.

One of the most notable features of the Arpanet has been that it has provided a focus for much of the most important research and development on computer networks, both LANs and WANs, and a forum for discussing many of the important problems and issues of networking. It has pioneered quite a number of networking techniques as well as several experimental networks and subnetworks. In particular, it has in effect become the world's first multi-media network, by adding to its overall internetworking configuration both Alohanet, the Hawaiian radio data network, and Satnet, the experimental satellite network used to implement its Transatlantic links.

Very recently, it has incorporated the mixed WAN-LAN configuration being developed in the UK by the UNIVERSE Project. UNIVERSE has been jointly sponsored by SERC (Science and Engineering Research Council), British Telecom, and several British companies, to experiment with various combinations of satellite networking and local area networking. It had earth stations at several sites, including University College London, Cambridge University, Loughborough University of Technology, the Rutherford-Appleton Laboratory, and the British Telecom Research Laboratories at Martlesham Heath. Each of these earth stations was connected to a LAN system with at least one ring network, that interworks with the satellite-based WAN. As University College London already had links with the Arpanet and with other British universities, these too became part of the resulting overall "very wide area" multi-media network system.

SYSTEM X AS AN INTEGRATED SERVICES DIGITAL NETWORK

System X is now being designed and gradually introduced, as British Telecom's future telecommunications network for the United Kingdom. It is well described, for example, in Chapter 1 of the *Telecomms Users Handbook* (Corby et al, 1982), in the British Telecom (1979) brochure, and in the paper by Harris (1979). Some of its facilities are also outlined by British Telecom (1980, p. 9). Moralee (1979) gives a useful discussion of the nature and background of System X, together with some of the earlier views that were expressed about it.

The idea for System X arose out of some original work carried out by British Telecommunications Research Limited in the early 1960s, which led to the formation in the late 1960s of a Joint Committee in which the Post Office, Plessey, GEC and STC participated. As a result, it has been conceived as a single system, that will carry signals for voice, vision and data in a unified way. The basic research on it has now been completed, and the British telecommunications industry has now begun its production. It will provide a wide range of services, not previously available to telephone users and in some cases not even to computer networks users.

It will use digital methods, as digital signals are handled much more easily than analogue signals, and as *all* types of messages can be reduced to a common digital foundation and framework. The use of digital transmission minimises the distortion and noise to which the telecommunication of messages is subject, and means that the distance travelled by a spoken message or any other message no longer affects the quality of its reception. These advantages will become even more marked when digital messages are transmitted by optical fibres, which British Telecom is planning to introduce into System X over the long-term future.

The System X electronic, digital, stored program control exchanges will provide completely compatible operation between all these different types of message, and will provide some additional benefits. As each new System X exchange is installed, it will allow increased use of digital transmission and switching inside the network, offering much better speed and quality of service within it. These exchanges will contain computers that will be able to switch circuits by using information embedded in encoded signals.

Figure 4.5 (British Telecom, 1979) is a schematic diagram of a typical System X configuration, and shows how its different types of exchanges are interconnected.

System X will provide a bandwidth of 64 kHz for its users' digital circuits, as compared with the bandwidth of about 3.5 kHz currently used by the analogue PSTN. Eventually, every telephone in the UK will be connected to a 64 kHz line, thus providing very greatscope for personal information services. This comparatively high bandwidth will have a large impact on computer communications services, especially, when System X becomes widely available, so that it will be of key importance to users of data transmission. Once it is operating widely enough, it will be easy to transmit data ovet the whole System X network.

If British Telecom is able to implement its plans of introducing System X within a reasonable time scale, the costs of telecommunications will fall and the quality will increase, with new services and facilities becoming possible. The first benefits that will come will be improved quality of speech transmission, fewer faults, and a much lower proportion of calls failing to get through. As it is developed, the services added will include:

1. Very fast push-button dialling
2. Short code dialling for numbers required often
3. Automatic repeated dialling
4. Dialling of engaged numbers until they become free automatically
5. Setting up a given call for a customer at a given time
6. Handling of incoming calls to allow outgoing calls at the same time and to permit a three-way message exchange
7. Three forms of automatic transfer and diversion of calls over a wide area

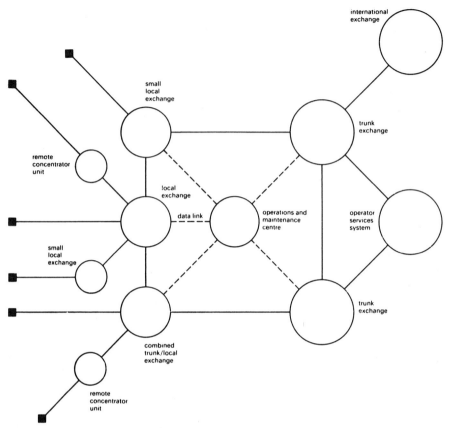

Fig. 4.5. Interconnection of System X exchanges   SOURCE: British Telecom, System X Brochure, p. 12

8. A facility for introducing a special short signal to notify a user engaged on a call that another user is to reach him

9. Barring of incoming and outgoing calls at a subscriber's request

10. More detailed telecommunications bills and accounts.

British Telecom plans to introduce System X gradually into the UK, where about 6,000 old-fashioned exchanges need replacing. It estimates that about two and a quarter million users will have been connected to System X by 1986, and about five million by 1990. In 1980, the installation of new switching equipment was started, linked by a skeleton digital network, overlaying and interworking with the existing telephone network. The penetration of System X into the British telecommunications system is expected to be significant by the mid-1980s, but its completion seems unlikely until well into the 1990s. But, as the programme for its introduction gathers momentum, the availability of its facilities should grow exponentially.

System X has: digital switching, digital transmission, stored program control with computers controlling operations within and between exchanges and re-routing calls if necessary, silent microelectronic chips including microprocessors, special channels for conveying control information, a series of interconnected modules fitting together in a carefully designed and well-integrated way, and modular software allowing new programs to be introduced without disrupting the system.

British Telecom is thus designing System X as an *integrated services digital network* (*ISDN*), designed to carry a very wide variety of information traffic in a unified way, using suitable digital codings of this information. Two of its leading researchers. Hughes and Atkins (1979), envisage that this increasing range of telecommunication services, now beginning to emerge, might be provided most effectively by a virtual-circuit-switched system, that promises the flexibility of providing "bandwidth on demand" and consistent with foreseeable trends in technology. Such a system would allow almost any new service to be introduced and operated efficiently, without the massive investment that would be involved if a separate network were to be set up. It would evolve out of an "existing" network, based on circuit-switched 64 kbits/sec digital voice-equivalent channels. Many of the papers in the conference proceedings, *Telecommunication Transmission—Into the Digital Era* (1981) develop further various aspects of the ISDN concept.

To sum up, System X is not only based on a new design of exchange, but is a key to a total system, an integrated services digital network, using a unified philosophy applied to a complete telecommunications service. It will provide a wide range of services and facilities, thereby reducing the need for in-house equipment and private circuits and leased lines. It has been well publicised, and the IDA Pilot Service is now operating an early version of it. This is gradually evolving into the full system.

REFERENCES

British Telecom (1979) *System X—The Complete Approach to Telecommunications*, Brochure

British Telecom (1980) *Telecom Research Laboratories*, Brochure.

CASE (undated) *Pocket Book of Computer Communications*, Computer and Systems Engineering plc, Watford, Herts, England.

Chernikeeff Telecommunications (undated) *Autex 1600—Automatic Telex and Telegraph Message Conveying and Switching Computer Systems*, Chernikeeff Telecommunications Ltd., Brochure.

R. Cole (1982) *Computer Communications*, Macmillan, London and Basingstoke.

M. Corby, E. F. Donohue and M. Hamer (1982) (1982/83 Edition) *Telecomms User Handbook*, Telecommunications Press, London.

D. W. Davies and D. L. A. Barber (1973) *Communication Networks for Computers*, Wiley, Chichester and New York.

D. W. Davies, D. L. A. Barber, W. L. Price and C. M. Solomonides (1979) *Computer Networks and Their Protocols*, Wiley, Chichester and New York.

I. R. F. Harris (May 1979) "An Introduction to System X," *International Switching Symposium*, Paris.

C. J. Hughes and J. W. Atkins (May 1979) "Virtual circuit switching for multiservice operation," *International Switching Symposium*, Paris.

P. T. Kirstein (Sep 1976) "Planned new public data networks," *Computer Networks*, **1**(2) 79–94.

D. R. McGlynn (1978) *Distributed Processing and Data Communications*, Wiley, New York and Chichester.

D. Moralee (June 1979) "British Telecommunication and the Information Age," *Electronics and Power*, **25**(6) 431–439.

Prime Computer (1980) *PRIMENET*, Prime Computer Inc., Product Bulletin.

Prime Computer (1981a) *Distributed Processing*, Prime Computer Inc., Brochure.

Prime Computer (1981b) (1981) *The 50 Series: The One System Solution*, Prime Computer Inc., Brochure.

Prime Computer (1981d) *PRIME Communications Hardware*, Prime Computer Inc., Product Bulletin.

Telecommunication Transmission — Into the Digital Era (1981) *IEE Conference Publication*, 193.

V. Zacharov (1981) "Computer systems and networks: Status and perspectives," *Proceedings 1980 CERN School of Computing*, Publ. CERN 81-03, 8–77.

Chapter 5

Network Services

This chapter describes briefly some of the data communication services available to users of wide area computer networks; it is concerned mainly with services available to users in the UK.

It considers in turn network services using the public switched telephone network, circuit-switched data networks, and packet-switched networks, both national and international. Several aspects of interest to network users are discussed, but consideration of the tariffs and other charges for these services is deferred until Chapter 15, on the economic aspects of computer networks. The most recent developments are presented in Chapter 19.

Special attention is given to the PSS, Euronet and IPSS packet-switched services, all of which are available to users in the UK; the first of these is intended for use between locations inside the UK and now also internationally, while the other two cover international communications between Great Britain and other countries.

Kelly (1981) gives a recent description of these and other public data network developments.

It should be noted that, for wide area communications, across appreciable distances of dozens, hundreds and even thousands of miles, an external infrastructure of network services is usually necessary; most of these services are provided by PTTs and other common carriers, although some private services are also available. The only exception to this is when a large organisation or a consortium of large organisations provides its own private communication channels between its geographically separated sites. This is in marked contrast to the situation with local area networks, where users generally provide their own network services, based on available LAN systems and products.

TELEPHONE NETWORK SERVICES

For quite a number of years, many countries have provided data communication services over the public switched telephone network (PSTN), using both dialled lines and privately leased lines. Typical data rates offered, in bits/sec, are: 75, 150, 200, 600, 1200 and 2400, using modems over public lines; 200, 600, 1200, 2400, 4800 and 48000, using modems over leased lines; 300 usually, 600 and 1200, sometimes, using acoustic couplers atttached to telephone sets. The basic applications supported by these services are mainly terminal-to-terminal and terminal-to-computer communications.

For example, early in the 1960s, the British Post Office recognised that it should provide its customers with facilities to allow them to exchange information with each other over the PSTN, both in the UK and overseas. The first of these public data transmission services, called "Datel Services," was introduced in 1964, followed by an international service, started in 1965. Datel services are now available from the UK to many European countries, the USA, Canada, Australia, and several other countries in various parts of the world.

This range of services includes: Datel 200, at 200 bits/sec; Datel 600, at 600 bits/sec; Datel 2412, at 2400 and 1200 bits/sec each way, with one model offering 150 bits/sec for one of the two ways in addition. More recently, a service with 1200 bits/sec to the user, and a return channel of 75 bits/sec from the user, has been provided by British Telecom for users of its Prestel viewdata service. These services, including Prestel, can all be used for communications between user terminals and remote computers.

Datel services operate, not only inside the UK, but also, as International Datel 2400, for example, between the UK and certain overseas countries, including most of Western Europe, the USA, and certain other parts of the world.

Although telephone dialling is normally used, to establish the connection manually, which typically takes of the order of 20 seconds, Datel 2412 provides an optional extra automatic calling unit, which enables computers and some terminals to reach remote stations automatically. Autodiallers are often also present in Prestel equipment.

In addition, Datel 2412 provides automatic answering, allowing an incoming call to be handled, and a modem to be connected to the line, without operator intervention.

CIRCUIT-SWITCHED DATA NETWORK SERVICES

The Telex services, provided by the national PTTs, are also interconnected so as to form an international Telex network, that can be viewed as a primitive data network, as it does not carry voice traffic and does not use the PSTN. However, this network uses analogue technology, not digital, as it was built long before modem digital technologies became available.

Because of its very low data rate, 50 bits/sec, Telex is not mentioned very much in this book. However, it should not be ignored, because it is *still* the only even remotely digital service available in many countries of the world, expecially in most of the developing countries. In addition, there *are* several ways of interfacing the Telex network with more sophisticated networks and of obtaining fairly effective, even though rather limited, interworking between them.

Several countries have introduced, or intend to introduce, circuit-switched data network services (Gibson, 1979). These include: The EDS network in West Germany; the Norwegian, Swedish and Nordic Data Networks in Scandinavia; ATT's leased-line digital service DDS and California's Datran in the USA; Data Route, Infodata and Infoswitch (also partly packet-switched) in Canada; DDX (also partly packet-switched) in Japan. Western Union's IDDS (International Digital Data Service) is a private line service provided on a circuit-switched network.

Kirstein (1976) describes briefly some of the services of this sort, that were available, or in the planning stage, about 10 years ago.

Although the national and international packet-switched data network services, to be described in the rest of this chapter, currently seem to be more important and more advanced, modern forms of circuit-switched services, using new technology, may well make a come-back.

In the UK, there are several projected developments of this sort inside the infrastructure of System X, which was described at the end of the last chapter as a new integrated network that is now being developed, although it will be about ten years before it is fully available. Some of these developments are outlined by Gibson (1979) and Ford and Davies (1978), for example.

System X will provide data switching systems from its basic switching equipment and electronic exchanges, so that the international CCITT recommendations for public data networks will be met, with additional development needed only for specialised data functions. British Telecom has formulated a strategy for the evolution and implementation of circuit-switched networks, based on these principles, taking into account the progressive penetration of digital transmission telephone systems throughout the UK and on the progress of its programme for the development of System X switching equipment.

In its basic circuit-switched network, expected to appear in the mid-1980s, the System X data exchanges will be linked by 2048 kbits/sec digital paths, of the type used in 30-channel PCM telephone systems. Signalling between its exchanges will be similar to that planned for the telephone system. It will provide synchronous circuits at 2400, 4800, 9600 and 4800 and 4800 bits/sec, so that one data channel will be provided in each 64 kbits/sec digital voice channel of a 2048 kbits/sec digital path. This will make easier the eventual achievement of an integrated services digital network (ISDN), whose evolution in connection with System X was mentioned at the end of the last chapter.

Extension of this circuit-switched network internationally is envisaged in due course, after the national system has been established. An important aspect of this will be the clear need for adequate interworking between circuit-switched and packet-switched data networks.

PSS

The UK's Packet Switching Service (PSS) was introduced by the British Post Office in 1980 (just before British Telecom took it over), as a completely new national network service, designed and equipped specifically for data transmission by computers and terminals throughout Britain. It is described fully in its brochures (British Post Office Telecommunications, 1980a and 1980b; British Telecom, 1981).

In November 1981, its name was changed to X-Switch Stream One, but it is perhaps still better known as PSS. Its network already covers a considerable part of the UK, including all its biggest cities.

It provides full duplex working, so that its terminals can both transmit and receive simultaneously, at any of the four line speeds, 2400, 4800, 9600 and 48000 bits/sec, that are currently offered.

Two kinds of equipment may be connected to the PSS network: packet devices and character devices. A *packet device* is able to handle data packets directly, and to conform with all three levels of the international standard network communications protocol X.25, that PSS and most other packet-switched networks use. A *character device* is unable to do this, and thus requires to communicate with the network via a *PAD (Packet Assembler/Disassembler)*. *Packet devices* include mainframe computers, *front-end processors*, which handle communications functions for computers, multiplexors, acting as gateways to private networks, and "intelligent" terminals. Character devices include teletypewriters and simple terminals and VDUs. Figure 5.1 shows diagrammatically the typical customers' connection to the PSS system (British Post Office Telecommunications, 1980b).

Packet devices, also known as *packet terminals*, are connected to the nearest PSS exchange by a Dataline. The four Dataline services available are Dataline 2400, Dataline 4800, Dataline 9600, and Dataline 48000, corresponding to the four different transmission rates already mentioned, and operating synchronously with full duplex working. Character terminals may be connected to a PAD, either by a Dataline or by dialling, using a Datel service and the PSTN. The Datalines available are Dataline 300, at 110 or 300 bits/sec, and Dataline 1200, at 1200 bits/sec, both asynchronous with full duplex. The Datel 200 service, at 110 or 300 bits/sec, and the Datel 600 service, at 1200/75 bits/sec, both asynchronous with full duplex, may also be used. Note that Datalines do not use a telephone but that Datels must use one.

Customers, not having a direct connection to PSS, but dialling in over the PSTN, share access to PADs. Each such user must have a Network User Identity (NUI), which is input each time a call is made, and may have more than one.

Packet terminals may communicate in three ways: *Datacalls*, that are analogous to telephone calls and carry messages while a channel to a given destination is occupied temporarily; *Permanent Datacalls*, intended for customers requiring continual transfer of data to and from a particular destination, and setting up a permanent channel there; *Minicalls*, for users who wish to send very short messages.

Some packet terminals are able to make and receive more than one call at a time, even if they have only one Dataline; in this case, each call is said to occur on a separate "logical channel." Packets from all the terminal's logical channels are interleaved over the link from the terminal, just as packets from many sources are interleaved over the PSS network.

Character terminals, unlike packet terminals, can support only one interconnection at a time, and may send Datacalls only. It it is connected to a PAD by a

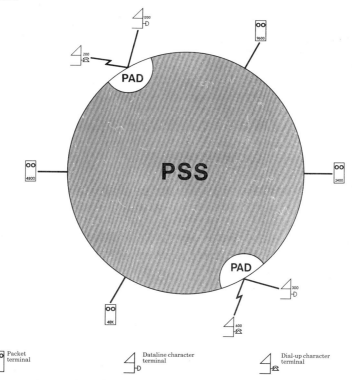

Fig. 5.1. Customers' connection to the PSS system   SOURCE: *PSS—A Basic Guide*, British Telecom, PSS Marketing Brochure, p. 8

Dataline, it may opt to be able to receive Minicalls also, and to have a *Direct Calling* facility, allowing it to establish Datacalls to a pre-arranged destination, without addressing procedures, as soon as it is online to PSS.

The *Closed User Group (CUG)* facility gives its members additional security and privacy over and above what PSS automatically provides for all its users. In effect, a CUG provides a private network operating within a public network. In its basic form, the CUG lets its members communicate freely with each other across PSS, but is excludes all other calls to or from the group. Forms of CUG with Incoming and/or Outgoing access with non-members are also possible. CUG integrity and security are not harmed even if a given terminal belongs to more than one CUG.

PSS's services for making international calls are described later in this chapter, in the Section on IPSS.

OTHER NATIONAL PACKET-SWITCHED NETWORK SERVICES

National packet-switched network services, operated by PTTs outside the UK, include: Common User in Australia, CTNE in Spain, Datanet 1 in The Netherlands,

Datapac and Infoswitch in Canada, DDX in Japan, Transpac in France. Infoswitch and DDX are also partly circuit-switched. Tymnet and Telenet were first established by private companies as public packet services, providing services inside the USA but later also internationally; other national packet services, based in the USA, include ITT's network service and Graphnet, a service specialising in the transmission of facsimile information. Several other nations are planning to introduce such services, for example Portugal (Mendes Madeira, 1982).

Kirstein (1976) summarises some of the characteristics of several of the experimental and operational national services being used in the mid-1970s; the earlier experimental services, including EPSS, have been closed, after serving the purposes for which they were intended.

The Netherlands PTT (1981, 1982) has provided detailed information about its packet-switched service Datanet 1; the latter of these publications not only discusses user aspects but gives extensive details of its architecture, technologies and operating techniques. Its facilities are in many ways similar to those offered by PSS, for example it offers the same four alternative data transmission rates. Figure 5.2 illustrates how it interconnects and relates with the telephone and Telex networks in Holland.

IPSS

IPSS is an international data communications service, that was opened by the British Post Office in December 1978 as one of the first public intercontinental data services to use packet switching (British Post Office Telecommunications, 1979a). It was designed and implemented to meet a wide variety of data communications requirements and applications.

As a result, it is highly flexible, and it is able to communicate with a wide range of terminals, operating at a variety of speeds, support various data communications applications, and provide high network reliability, with very low error rates.

From its outset, it has been operating services between the UK and the USA, via the three International Record Carriers (IRCs), ITT World Communications, RCA Global Communications and Western Union International (WUI), in particular providing links with the American packet-switched network services Tymnet and Telenet. However, British users wishing to access Tymnet via IPSS are now subject to certain restrictions; for example, an IPSS user wishing to access a given Tymnet user has to apply to British Telecom for permission to do so at least several days in advance, in order to be issued with an access code for that user.

Since it was established, IPSS has been extended to provide communications with packet-switched network services in several other countries, including Australia, Canada, Japan and Western Europe.

Under current British Telecom policies, IPSS is gradually being absorbed by PSS, so that, already, new customers, who wish to use international packet-

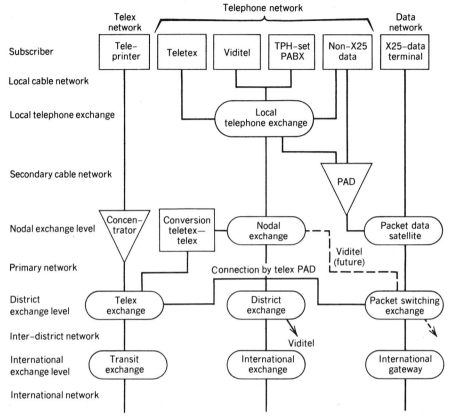

Fig. 5.2. Telecommunications in The Netherlands SOURCE: *Het PTT Bedrijf*, Vol. 22 (1982) (Edited by the Netherlands Postal and Telecommunications Service—The Hague) p. 101

switched services, should sign up for PSS instead. PSS is being linked to overseas networks as rapidly as possible.

For countries not yet connected to IPSS or PSS, a user of these services can contact a host facility in a country to which the service *is* available; this host can in turn make a separate call to the country with which the user wants to communicate.

EURONET

In December 1975, with the agreement of the Commission of the EEC, the nine EEC member countries' PTTs, accepted the responbility for providing a packet-switched network, Euronet, to meet their telecommunications needs. This network was implemented, to provide users in the European Community with access to scientific, technical, and socio-economic data, especially. It became operational in

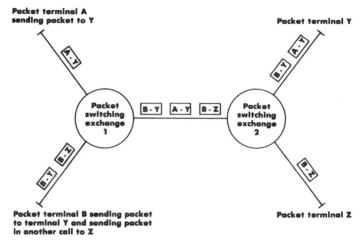

Fig. 5.3. Interleaving of packets in a packet-switched network   SOURCE: British Telecom International Euronet leaflet, packet interleaving diagram

1979. Eventually, it aims to integrate existing and future online information services there into a shared network, and its design will allow it to form the basis for a European public data network later on.

For a brief introductory description of Euronet, see the leaflets issued by British Telecom International (1980a to 1980c). Euronet offers a variety of special facilities, to enable users of different types of data terminals, even those operating at different speeds, to communicate with each other, and to gain the maximum benefit from the system. Each customer has a Network User Address (NUA) and also one Network User Identity (NUI) for each terminal installed at its NUA.

In common with PSS, IPSS and other packet-switched data services conforming to internationally agreed protocols and operating standards, Euronet supports two basic classes of terminal, Synchronous Packet-Mode, and Asynchronous Character-Mode. The former terminals must conform to the X.25 protocol and operate at one of the line rates 2400, 4800 and 9600 bits/sec; they automatically assemble the signals to be transmitted into packets, which are sent to a Packet Switch Exchange (PSE), where they are inter-leaved with other packet-base data traffic and forwarded to the appropriate destination (see Figure 5.3). The latter terminals must conform to the X.25 protocol and operate at line rates in the range 110 to 1200 bits/sec; most of the low-speed data terminals, commonly used for online information retrieval, satisfy these conditions. Connection of the terminals to the nearest PSE may be either via a Private Leased Circuit or via the PSTN.

One of the major benefits of Euronet is that it provides its users with access to Euronet DIANE (Direct Information Access Network for Europe), which is described briefly in the leaflet issued by British Post Office International Telecommunications (1979b). There is a regularly issued *Euronet DIANE Newsletter* to keep users of DIANE up-to-date with its developments. DIANE is an online information retrieval service, accessing many of the most important data bases in Western Europe, and it is described further in Chapter 12.

OTHER INTERNATIONAL PACKET-SWITCHED NETWORK SERVICES

Several international packet-switched network services are run by private companies. For example, Tymnet operates between the USA, Japan, Australia, and various West European countries, including the UK, although British Telecom and other European PTTs imposed some restrictions on its usage by "third party users" in their areas of jurisdiction. GEISCO operates worldwide time-sharing and distributed computing services that make its packet-switched service for the airlines of the world, which has been in use for quite a number of years, linking the computers and terminals of many of the airlines. However, its system has many of the characteristics of national packet-switched networks, and it has packet-switched nodes in the high-level part of its network.

Several other industries and sectors of the economy have shared-use networks linking their computers and very large numbers of their terminals, for example the SWIFT network service for banking, set up in 1976.

Although neither of them are operating now, it is worth mentioning briefly the two experimental international packet-switched network services DBA and EIN.

DBA (Database Access and Remote Computing Service) service was set up by the British Post Office, as a response to demand from British users to access important computer data bases in the USA. It became operational in February 1977, and it is described fully by Ford and Davies (1979) and also mentioned by Gibson (1979). It provided users of the Datel 200 service with direct access to the data bases and computing systems connected to Tymnet in the USA; in July 1977, it was extended to include access to Telenet in the USA. As a trial service, it was a great success, but is was discontinued some time· after the establishment of IPSS, and its users were invited to transfer to IPSS, via which their access to Tymnet and Telenet was now to be routed.

The Euronet Informatics Network (EIN) was operated in the late 1970s as an experimental service, though accessible only to a restricted group of users, with nodes in London, Paris, Zurich, Milan and Ispra. Its nodes were designed to have interfaces with the PSTN and the national data networks.

REFERENCES

British Post Office International Telecommunications (1979a) (Sep 1979) *IPSS—International Packet Switching Service—A Summary*, Leaflet.

British Post Office International Telecommunications (1979b) (Sep 1979) *Euronet DIANE*, Leaflet.

British Post Office Telecommunications (1980a) (Feb 1980) *PSS—The Public Data Service—An Introduction*. Brochure.

British Post Office Telecommunications (1980b) (Jun 1980) *PSS—The Public Data Service—A Basic Guide*, Brochure.

British Telecom (Mar 1981) *PSS—The Public Data Service—Facilities*, Brochure.

British Telecom International (1980a) (Sep 1980) *Euronet Customer Facilities*, Leaflet.

British Telecom International (1980b) (Sep 1980) *Euronet—Methods of Access*, Leaflet.

British Telecom International (1980c) (Sep 1980) *Euronet—The Technology*, Leaflet.

D. Casey (8 Apr 1982) "BT prepares four digital services," *Computing*, 17.

M. Corby, E. J. Donohue and M. Hamer (1982) (1982/1983) *Telecomms Users Handbook*, Telecommunications Press, London. (A new edition is due in 1985.)

M. L. Ford and F. W. Davies (1978) "International data networks—UK Post Office experience and plans."

M. E. Gibson (Mar 1979) "Future UK data communications servcies," *Computer Bulletin*, Series 2 (19) 8–9.

P. T. F. Kelly (1981) "Public data network developments," *dp International 1981*, 149–157.

P. T. Kirstein (Sep 1976) "Planned new public data networks," *Computer Networks*, **1** (2) 79–94.

A. Mendes Madeira (Feb 1982) "Planning Portuguese data switching," *Communications International*, **9** (2) 31, 34.

Netherlands PTT (1981) *Datanet 1—Packet Switching in the Netherlands*, Brochure.

Netherlands PTT (Feb 1982) *Datanet 1*, Papers collected from *Het PTT-Bedriif*, **22** (3) 87–150.

PART TWO

NETWORK TECHNOLOGIES

CHAPTER 6

Network Structures

The structure *or topology* of a network is its general arrangement, specifying the configuration of its components, including devices, nodes and links, and the geometrical relations between them.

A computer network consists of computers, terminals, work stations and other information processing devices, all of which are joined together by a common communications system, sometimes called a *subnet* (See Figure 1.1). The network structure thus determines the configurations of devices attached to the network and nodes with the subnet, together with the ways in which they are interconnected.

The *first basic principle of network structure* is that the subnet should be able to establish effective communication and exchange of information between all the devices attached to the network, regardless of the differences between them.

The *second basic principle of network structure* is that different types of network may be interconnected with each other, in such a way that any pair of devices or nodes, accessible to each other by a path through several consecutive linked networks, can communicate effectively with each other.

This chapter considers the basic structures used in local area networks, wide area networks, and interconnected networks: for each of these structures, it provides diagrams showing examples of typical network configurations, together with some explanatory text. Other examples of network configurations are given in the Figures in Chapters 1 to 4.

The subnet, and various parts of it, may have a variety of *configurations*, including the star, where one central node has links to a cluster of outlying nodes, the *ring* or *loop*, where a sequence of nodes is strung round a complete circuit of wire or cable, the *bus*, where all the nodes occur in linear sequence, from one end of a long cable or channel to the other, the *mesh*, where there are many connections between different nodes, in fact sometimes between all pairs of nodes, and the *radio* network, where there are no material connections, but where the network is in effect a fully-connected mesh, because any node can communicate by radio with any other node.

In addition to these basic structures, there are *compound structures*, whose configurations are obtained by joining together several configurations with basic struc-

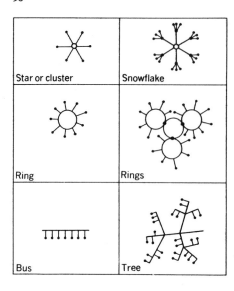

Fig. 6.1. There are quite a number of different network topologies SOURCE: *Microprocessors and Microsystems* (Jan/Feb 1982) 6 (1) p. 26

tures. For example, the *snowflake* is a star of stars, the *star ring* is a star whose central node is replaced by a ring, the *clustered ring* is a star of rings, and the *tree* is a structure of buses linked end-to-end in star-like fashion and/or linked end-to-end.

Figure 1.2 shows some basic structures, while Figure 6.1 gives examples of a basic configuration and a compound configuration for each of the star, ring and bus structures.

The chapter starts with a description of star networks, which are used for LANs and WANs linking terminals to computers, and which are now also used for some other LANs. It then proceeds to outline ring network and bus network structures, which are typical of most LANs. After that, there is a description of the structure and configurations of network exchanges, including digital PBXs and PABXs, and of some example of network nodes. The chapter then returns to network structures, briefly describing WAN structures, which are usually mesh-like. After that, it considers gateways between networks, and the structures of interconnected networks themselves, including especially the structures of linked local area networks. Finally, it gives some examples of structures proposed for the integrated data networks that are now being designed and developed. The most recent developments in network structures are presented in Chapter 20.

The treatment of exchanges in this chapter is moderately detailed, because it covers some of the other aspects, besides their structures and configurations, as this is the chapter in the book where they can most conveniently be considered. The most recent developments in network exchanges are presented in Chapter 19.

Most books on computer networks include brief general descriptions of network structures and configurations, although this is usually interleaved with discussions of other aspects of networks and not made the subject of separate chapters.

Tropper (1981) and Anderson (1979) give some useful examples of LAN configurations, for both ring and bus networks.

Baxter and Baugh (1982) give a brief overview of LAN structures, though again combined with a discussion of techniques for accessing LANs, which involve low level protocols and are thus considered in Chapter 9. The LAN structures that Baxter and Baugh describe are centralised and distributed rings and buses; the distributed structures are used in LANs of the usual sort, while the centralised structures are in effect LANs placed at the centre of star networks. They discuss some of the relative advantages and disadvantages of these different structures.

STAR NETWORKS

Cole (1982, Chapter 4) gives a good recent discussion of star networks, and an earlier description is given by McGlynn (1978, Chapter 2), for example.

Early interactive and time-sharing computing led to the requirement for networks of terminals linked to central computers, using character-oriented communications. This led to the adoption of the star network structure and topology for networks with asynchronous terminals. This structure applies, both for the case when the network is local, with the terminals being placed near the computer, and for the case when the terminals are remote from the computer and linked to it by telephone lines.

The simplest form of star network configuration is the cluster of terminals, each linked to the same central computer.

For a fairly large or large number of terminals, it is convenient to use *multiplexers* to bring together clusters of terminals in the same location, so that the network structure now becomes a *snowflake*, consisting of a cluster of multiplexers, forming a star, with each multiplexer linked to the central computer, and with each multiplexer in turn being the centre of a local cluster of terminals, itself forming a star.

More generally still, it is possible to use *cascaded* multiplexers, where some multiplexers are not connected directly to the central computer, but are instead linked to multiplexers that are nearer that computer.

Figure 6.2 shows a generalized asynchronous terminal network snowflake configuration that combines these principles. The star centered on the computer links

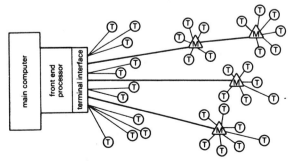

Fig. 6.2. Example of an asynchronous terminal network SOURCE: Robert Cole, *Computer Communications*, Macmillan, London and Basingstoke, England, p. 66, Fig. 4.11

a combination of multiplexers and terminals, the lines from which go into a *terminal interface*. Each of the multiplexers is the centre of a star of terminals, and one of the multiplexers links to a cascaded multiplexer. The terminal interface is connected to a *front end processor* (*FEP*), which acts as an intermediary between the interface and the computer, and relieves the computer of many of the tasks of organising and scheduling communications with the terminals.

Several star-like configurations have been used in LANs. For example, Closs and Lee (1980) describe a multi-star broadcast network for local communications. Here, the network stations are linked to star nodes by full duplex links, that can be cables and/or optical fibres. Each star node broadcasts a packet, sent by any one of its stations, to all the other stations attached to it. In this network, star nodes can be linked to form a rooted tree topology.

Rothauser et al (1980) describe meshed-star LANs, using block switches and buffered links. Saltzer and Pogran (1979) consider a star-shaped ring network, whose nature is outlined in the next section.

RING NETWORKS

Tropper, (1981, Chapter 2) gives some simple examples of ring network configurations.

Figure 6.3 shows a typical configuration for the Cambridge Ring, perhaps the best known design of ring network; each device is attached to the ring via an access box, a station, and a repeater, which is actually on the ring, and there is also a monitor station, which is on the ring and exercises overall control of the ring.

Sweetman (1981) describes the configuration of the Polynet, developed by Logica, that attaches office work stations, file servers and host minicomputers to a Cambridge Ring. Kirstein and Wilbur (1980) describe the configurations of the interconnected Cambridge Ring systems being developed at University College London.

Leslie et al (1981) show how the configuration of the original Cambridge Ring, at Cambridge University, was modified to handle voice communication as well as data communication. Most of the complex circuitry, which might have been placed in stations attached to individual telephones, is situated in a special processor attached to the ring, called a *dial server*. Each phone has a codec, a Z80 microcomputer, a ring station and a repeater. When a phone wishes to place a call, it first communicates with the dial server, which can then connect it to another phone on the ring, or to a file server, or to a phone on another ring, accessed via a gateway.

Figure 6.4 shows the configuration of a typical office LAN using a cable ring. Telephones, management work stations, and word processors are all connected to the ring through network interface units (NIUs), that also provide interfaces with various outside networks.

Saltzer and Pogran (1979) describe a special form of "star ring," where the loop between each pair of neighbouring repeaters goes through a "wire centre," so that the configuration looks like a daisy with many petals; it is said to have the advantage of making the ring easier to service and more reliable.

Closs and Lee propose "the multi-star broadcast network," an approach to LANs

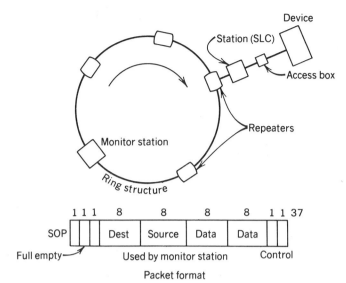

Fig. 6.3. Cambridge Ring configuration SOURCE: Ed. A. Simpson, *Planning for Telecommmuni-cations*, Gower Publishing Company, Aldershot, Hampshire, England, p. 111, Fig. 1

that combines the advantages of packet broadcasting and star networks. Its config-uration was described in the previous section.

BUS NETWORKS

Tropper (1981, Chapter 3) gives some simple examples of bus network configura-tion.

Metcalfe and Boggs (1976) describe the configuration of the original Ethernet, and Kellond (1982) gives examples of current Ethernet configurations, one of which is shown in Figure 6.5. In its simplest form, an Ethernet has a linear configuration, corresponding to a single bus. More generally, it uses several bus segments, with neighbouring segments being linked to each other by repeaters, and more distant segments, up to 1000 metres apart, being connected by remote repeaters joined to each other by short cables. Each station is attached to its neighbouring bus by a short connection ending with a tap.

Shoch (1979) shows how to use Ethernet as a voice network, as well as a data network, and gives examples of the configurations used for this purpose as well as for some other purposes.

Biba and Yeh (1979) describe the configuration and other characteristics of an-other design of bus network, the FordNet.

NETWORK EXCHANGES

Although used principally for telephony, some of the *private branch exchanges* (*PBXs*), including especially the *private automated branch exchanges* (*PABXs*), use

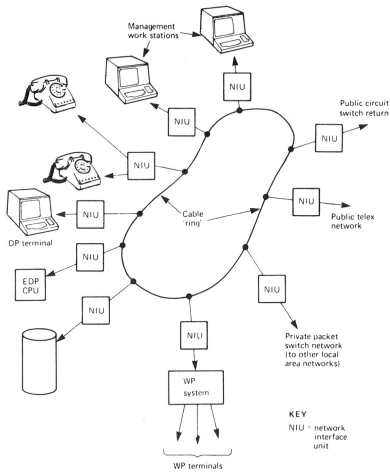

Fig. 6.4. Local area network with cable ring SOURCE: Ed. A. Simpson, *Planning for Telecommunications*, Gower Publishing Company, Aldershot, Hampshire, England, p. 59, Fig. 3

digital encoding and switching techniques, and can thus be used for data switching. There are also several *private digital exchanges* (*PDXs*) coming on the market. They are all beginning to be used extensively in LANs, as an alternative to ring and bus networks. As will be seen in the final section, network exchanges will also plan an important part in the WANs of the future.

The earlier state-of-the-art of PABXs is summarised by McGlynn (1978), who classifies them according to type of service, type of control, technology, type of switching cross-point, number of station lines,and number of trunk lines. *IEE Communications 82* (1982) includes several recent papers on PABXs and PDXs.

Figure 6.6 shows a typical configuration of a PDX used in an office environment. In effect, it acts as a local star network, with the PDX itself being the hub of the star. Not only telephones but also manager's work stations, word processors, and

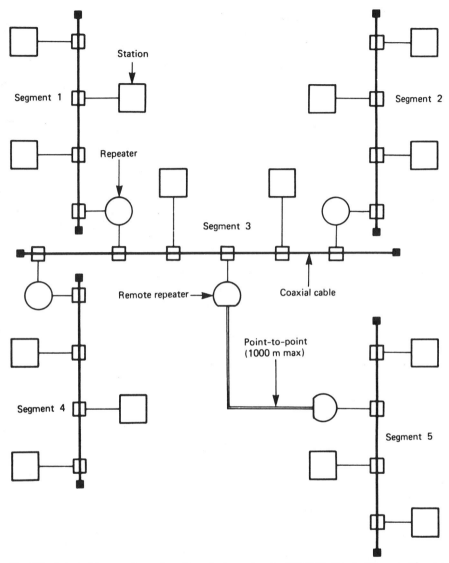

Fig. 6.5. A typical large scale configuration of a bus network   SOURCE: Ed. A. Simpson, *Planning for Electronic Mail*, Gower Publishing Company, Aldershot, Hampshire, England, p. 94, Fig. 5

computers with attached terminals can be connected. Other arms of the star link the system to the PSTN, the Telex network and, via leased lines, other PDXs.

Brown (1982) briefly reviews the application of PABXs to offices. He points out that telephone cabling, used with PABX equipment, can be set up to provide additional, non-voice, traffic, thus offering an alternative to special bus or ring cable, for linking terminals and other devices inside offices. Unfortunately, much existing PABX equipment does not have the capacity to handle such data traffic.

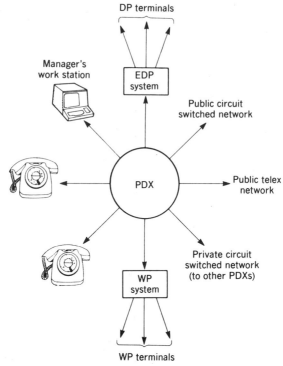

Fig. 6.6. Local area network with private digital exchange   SOURCE: Ed. A. Simpson, *Planning for Telecommunications*, Gower Publishing Company, Aldershot, Hampshire, England, p. 60, Fig. 4

Benstead (1982) presents the approach of a leading manufacturer, ITT, to the problem of integrating office communications by allowing existing PABX technology, that is relatively simple, to be used as a basis for the next stage of information transfer practice, bringing together voice, text and data communications.

Richer and Steiner (1981) have investigated the possible use of a computerised PBX as a switch in an office LAN. They conclude that, in the near future, there are various reasons for adding data traffic to office voice networks, and that the resulting combined network should be based on a star topology.

Van Kampen (1981) remarks that, in the past, local area communications in organisations have often been provided by PABXs and their associated cable networks. Conventional PABXs lack the flexibility and fully automated operation required for non-voice communications and functions, but "intelligent" PABXs can offer sophisticated communications services, complementary to those provided by LANs based on rings and buses.

Butscher (1981) described HMINET 2, a LAN which is connected as a PABX to the German public data network.

Several firms in the UK, including British Telecom, CASE, Gandalf, IBM, ITT, Mitel, Plessey, Pye, Master Systems, Reliance Systems, and Telephone Rentals, market PABXs suitable for the office environment. Some, though not all of them, offer digital PABXs and PDXs that can provide full text and data communications, as well as voice, facilities. National Computing Centre (1982) describes features and facilities of PABXs, currently approved for use in the UK, and provides guidance about their choice.

Charlish (1982) briefly describes ITT's use of PABXs to help integrate business systems using data, text and voice.

The CASE Data Concentrating Exchange (DCX) family is a typical example of a modern networking product that can be configured, both to provide effective switching and transmission facilities for in-house LANs for business, and to provide an interface between such a LAN and the outside world (Brown, 1982). CASE also markets the MSX-ST message switching exchange, designed for message-switched systems (CASE, 1982a).

The issue of *Electrical Communication*, Vol. 56 No. 2/3 (1981), describes the ITT 1240 Digital Exchange, which can be used for LANs as well as for automatic switching of voice channels. ITT Business Systems (1982) describes the "information transfer technology," centred on the PABX, that it uses to integrate data, voice and text communications both locally and over the PSTN.

The Plessey IBIS Integrated Business Information System, which can carry text, data and image information, in digital form, alongside normal voice communication, over standard twisted-pair telephone wiring, is based on a Plessey PDX (Plessey Communication Systems, 1982). It carries the digital information at speeds up to 64 kbits/sec, and it provides links to external communications channels, as well as providing full LAN services.

Master Systems (Data Products) Limited markets the PACX (Private Automatic Computer Exchange) produced by Gandalf. PACX is designed to connect many local or remote terminal users, with various requirements, to one or more computers; up to 1024 terminals and 512 computer ports can be handled at once, using line rates of up to 9·6 kbits/sec asynchronous and 19·2 kbits/sec synchronous (Gandalf, 1982; Master systems, 1982a and 1983). Figure 6.7 shows a typical computer network configuration, using a MASTER SWITCH PDX.

Camrass (1982) reviews developments in commercially available digital PABX systems in the USA and mentions some American suppliers.

NETWORK NODES

Network nodes include interfaces between various devices and the computer networks to which they are linked, and they also include *network switches*, that control the flow of data traffic between different links in a network. A good, reasonably up-to-date, introductory description of some aspects of network nodes is given by Cole (1982, Chapter 4 and also Chapter 10). Barber et al (1979, Chapter 2, "Packet Switching") also gives some examples of node configurations, including multiplexers, switches, and special node structures designed to counteract the effects of node failures in networks. Many of the PABXs and PDXs, described in the previous section, can be used as network nodes.

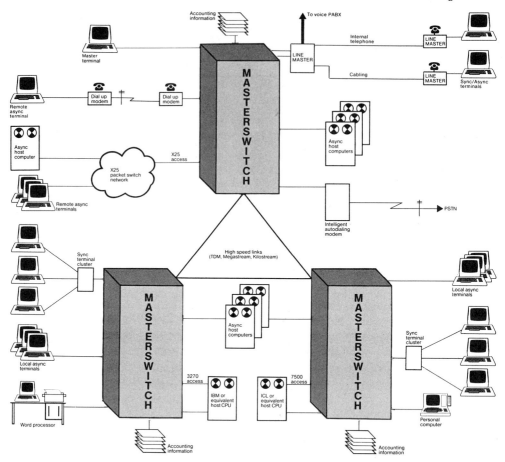

Fig. 6.7. Computer network configuration using a MASTER SWITCH Digital Exchange SOURCE: MASTER SWITCH Brochure, Master Systems (Data Products) Ltd.

Terminals and other local devices are usually interfaced to a network by modems, sometimes by acoustic couplers, if the network is the public switched telephone network (PSTN), by repeaters if it is a ring network, by taps if it is a bus network, and by PADs (packet assembler/disassemblers) if it is a packet-switched network like the PSS network. Some intelligent terminals and work stations can be linked directly to a packet-switched network.

A central computer is interfaced to the PSTN via a computer interface, consisting of a control device, attached to an input/output bus of the computer, and a UART or USRT, attached to the network link via a modem. A *UART (Universal Asynchronous Transmitter and Receiver)* is used for asynchronous communication, and a *USRT (Universal Synchronous Transmitter and Receiver)* is a similar device used for synchronous communication.

A *terminal multiplexer* is an interface between lines from the terminals, entering it via *ports*, and either an input/output bus to the central computer, if it is local, or a fast network link, if it is remote. A *remote multiplexer* shares the bandwidth of the fast communications channel, to which it is attached, with the slow terminal channels on its other side. For example, the CASE 814 Statistical Multiplexer allows up to eight separate 1200 bits/sec data links between two geographically remote locations to be carried on one telephone line (CASE, 1982b).

Terminal concentrators are similar to terminal multiplexers, except that they also provide facilities for storing some of the data traffic going through them, so that they can even out its flow. For example, the Master Systems C11 and T7 Network Access Modules allow a cluster of about a dozen ASCII VDU terminals, with data rates up to 9·6 kbits/sec, to operate as if they are display terminals to ICL and IBM host computers, respectively (Master Systems, 1982b and 1982c). Configurations of networks, using these nodes, are shown in Figures 6.8 and 6.9, respectively.

Circuit-switched networks have nodes that are exchanges, of the sort that were described in the previous section.

Packet-switched networks use nodes that are specially designed mini-computers, including the front end processors, already mentioned as host computer interfaces to networks, and switching nodes. A *switching* node contains a fair amount of buffers, providing storage space for various packets in transit through the node, together with programs that enable it to perform its functions. These functions include: routing of packets to their correct destinations, by assigning them to the correct links out of the node; management of the buffer space inside the nodes, so that it correctly carries out the required store-and-forward functions that are specified by the lower level network protocols; control of the bandwidth of the various data channels into and out of the node, again specified by protocols.

WIDE AREA NETWORK CONFIGURATIONS

WAN structures and configurations are very different from LAN structures and configurations, partly because they cater for communications over very much longer distances, and partly because of the very much lower rates of data transmission that they use in their links, measured in thousands rather than millions of bits per second.

As can be seen from Figure 6.10, WAN structures are usually meshlike, although they are generally not fully connected, as network paths between the more distant pairs of nodes pass through one or more intermediate nodes. This figure shows clearly the boundary between the subnet, connecting its nodes, are typically switching computers, by high-speed lines, and the attached devices and their connections. Note that host computers and terminal multiplexers or concentrators, for example are connected to their nearest nodes by high-speed lines. However, terminals are usually, though not always, connected to computers, multiplexers or concentrators, rather than directly to nodes; they are generally linked by low-speed lines.

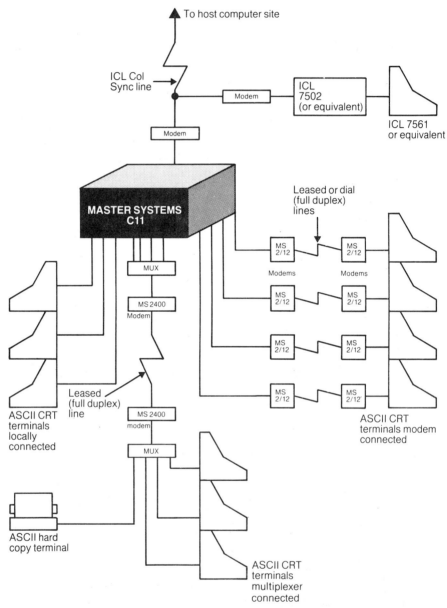

Fig. 6.8. Typical configuration of Master Systems C11 in 7502-based network   SOURCE: Master Systems (Data Products) Ltd. C11 7502 Leaflet

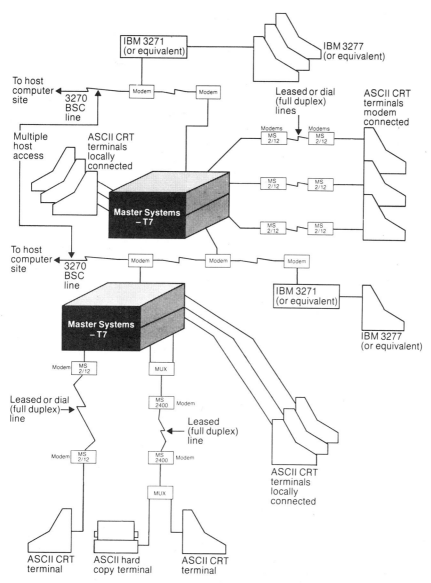

Fig. 6.9. Typical configuration of Master Systems T7 in 3270-based network   SOURCE: Master Systems (Data Products) Ltd. T7 3270 Leaflet

GATEWAYS AND INTERCONNECTED NETWORKS

In order to satisfy the second basic principle of network structure, stated at the beginning of this chapter, neighbouring networks need to be linked to each other through special interfaced nodes, known as *gateways*. Figure 1.3 shows a typical configuration of interconnected networks of varying types, showing the nature of

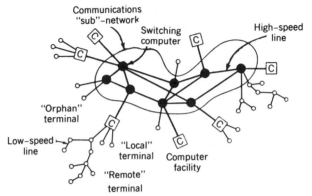

Fig. 6.10. The structure of a computer-communication network   SOURCE: Copyright © 1978 IEEE *Proceedings of the IEEE* (Nov 1978), 66 (11) p. 1321, Fig. 1

the structure of a "supernetwork," whose components consist of several types of LANs and WANs. In this example, all three types of internetwork interface and connection LAN-LAN, LAN-WAN and WAN-WAN, are present.

Figure 6.11 shows a configuration giving several examples of the use of an actual piece of commerically available equipment, the CASE DCX 816 Concentrator, as an interface between network and computer, as a terminal multiplexer, and as a gateway to an X25 network (CASE, 1982c).

In their very thorough discussion of all aspects of network interconnection, Cerf and Kirstein (1978) explain some of the principles of interconnection through gate-

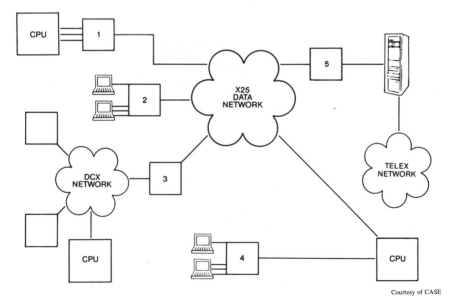

Courtesy of CASE

Fig. 6.11.   Network configuration using CASE DCX 816 PAD   SOURCE: CASE DCX 816 Leaflet

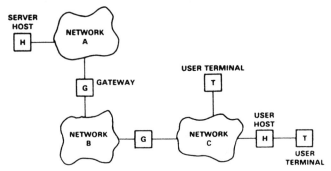

Fig. 6.12. Network concatenation   SOURCE: Copyright © 1978 IEEE *Proceedings of the IEEE* (Nov 1978), 66 (11) p. 1389, Fig. 1

ways and give examples of gateway configurations. Figure 6.12 shows a simple example of network concatenation, through a sequence of networks and intervening gateways. Figure 6.13 shows various gateway configurations, including half-gateways and gateways linking more than two networks at once, as well as the simple gateways between pairs of neighbouring networks. Figure 6.14 illustrates the use of gateways in connecting two national WANs via an international WAN.

Further aspects of gateways and half-gateways, especially the protocols by which they operate, are discussed towards the end of Chapter 9.

LINKED LOCAL AREA NETWORKS

A specially important example of network interconnection is the establishment of effective communications between widely separated local area networks, through intervening wide area networks, to form *linked local area networks (LLANs)*, which

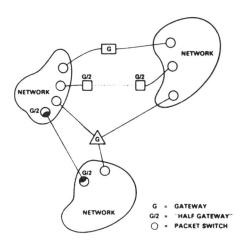

G   = GATEWAY
G/2 = ''HALF GATEWAY''
O   = PACKET SWITCH

Fig. 6.13. Various gateway configurations SOURCE: Copryright © 1978 IEEE *Proceedings of the IEEE* (Nov 1978), 66 (11) p. 1393, Fig. 6

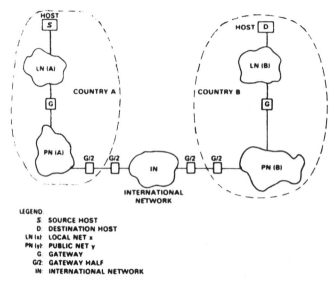

LEGEND:

       S: SOURCE HOST
      D: DESTINATION HOST
  LN (x): LOCAL NET x
  PN (y): PUBLIC NET y
      G: GATEWAY
   G/2: GATEWAY HALF
    IN: INTERNATIONAL NETWORK

Fig. 6.14. International packet-networking model   SOURCE: Copyright © 1978 IEEE *Proceedings of the IEEE* (Nov 1978), 66 (11) p. 1393, Fig. 7

are particularly useful for organisations having premises at several different locations.

In their introductory review of LANs, Clark and Pogran (1978) introduce the *subnetwork concept*, that provides for a mixture of LAN technologies within a uniform addressing and administrative structure. These subnetworks are linked by *bridges*, which have complexity between those of the repeaters, used in multi-segment bus networks like Ethernet, and gateways proper. Figure 6.15 illustrates

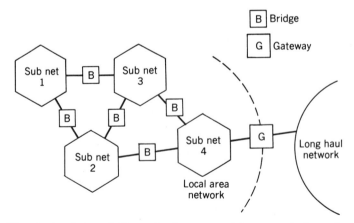

Fig. 6.15. The subnetwork concept. Here, a local area network is composed of a number of subnetworks, linked in some fashion by bridges   SOURCE: Copyright © 1978 IEEE *Proceedings of the IEEE* (Nov 1978), 66 (11) p. 1514, Fig. 10

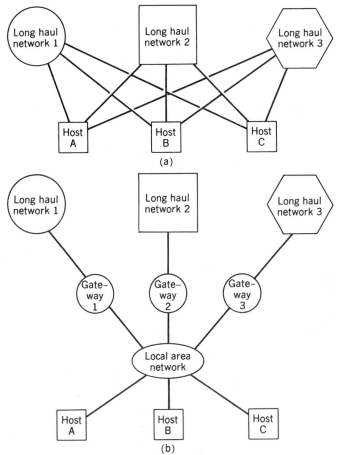

Fig. 6.16. The "M × N Problem" and a local area network as one solution to it SOURCE: Copyright © 1978 IEEE *Proceedings of the IEEE* (Nov 1978), 66 (11) p. 1499, Fig. 2

the subnetwork concept, showing the use of bridges to link subnetworks inside a LAN and a gateway to link that LAN with a neighbouring WAN. Figure 6.16 shows how to use a LAN to connect several neighbouring host computers with several distant WANs, without having to have separate links between each host-WAN pair.

Many, if not most, of the commercially available LAN systems, described in Chapter 2, and personal computer network and micronet systems, described in Chapter 3, can be linked over WANs to other LANs and/or remote mainframes. Several of the figures in those chapters give examples of configurations of this sort.

As already pointed out, data exchanges, such as the CASE DCX family, can be linked to LANs, for example Ethernets, to offer data communication facilities that neither can provide alone. A DCX network would allow large sites, supporting several interconnected services together with clusters of local terminals, to be interconnected, and, especially important, provide to small sites, which are more

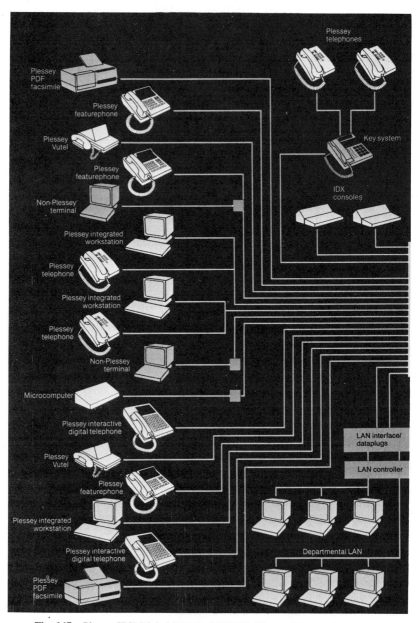

Fig. 6.17. Plessey IDX Digital PABX   SOURCE: Plessey IDX Brochure

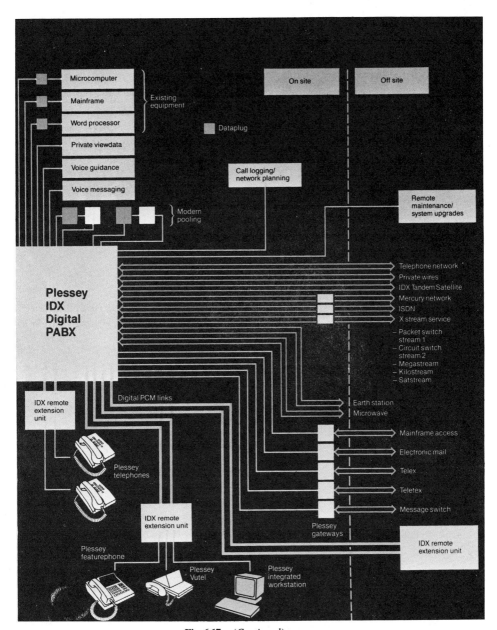

Fig. 6.17. (*Continued*)

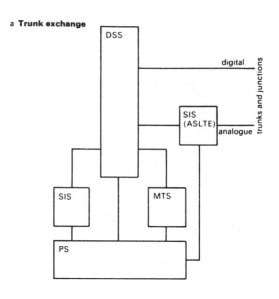

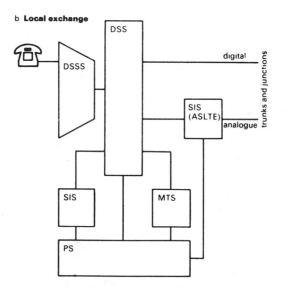

ASLTE analogue signalling line termination equipment
DSS digital switching subsystem
DSSS digital subscriber switching subsystem
MTS message transmission subsystem
PS processor subsystem
SIS signalling interworking subsystem

Fig. 6.18. System X system schematics SOURCE: British Telecom System X Brochure, p. 13

often used by most organisations, access to various centralised services for low cost terminals (Brown, 1982).

Brown points out that this approach not only integrates an effective WAN technology, such as DCX, with LANs, but also has the advantage that businesses with tight budgets can use DCX alone in the early stages of office automation but be able to instal a LAN later on, that is easy to integrate with that DCX.

Figure 6.17 shows clearly how the Plessey IDX can connect a local star network, to which various office work stations, word processors, terminals are attached, to a variety of channels to external networks, services and devices. These include the PSTN, leased lines, Telex, Teletex, other electronic mail services, and distant mainframes. Figure 6.6 also illustrates this principle.

As shown in Figure 6.7, the Gandalf PACX IV digital exchange can be linked to remote computers and remote terminals, via both the PSTN and X.25 networks such as the PSS network.

INTEGRATED DATA NETWORKS

Integrated data networks, which are designed to carry digital data, text, image and voice traffic in a unified way, have already been discussed at the end of Chapter 4. It was pointed out there that British Telecom is now developing System X as a new network of this sort.

The Systems X brochure (British Telecommunications Systems, 1980) shows in moderate detail the configurations of various subsystems used in System X. For example, Figure 6.18 shows typical configurations for a System X local exchange

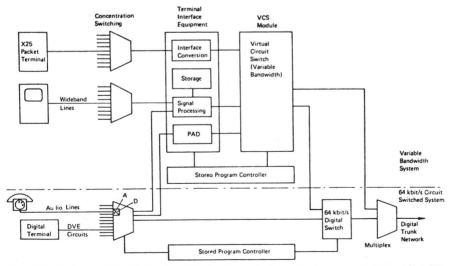

Fig. 6.19. Evolution of digital circuit-switched system to include virtual circuit switching   SOURCE: Hughes & Atkins paper, Fig. 3, *Proceedings of the International Switching Symposium*, Paris, May 1979

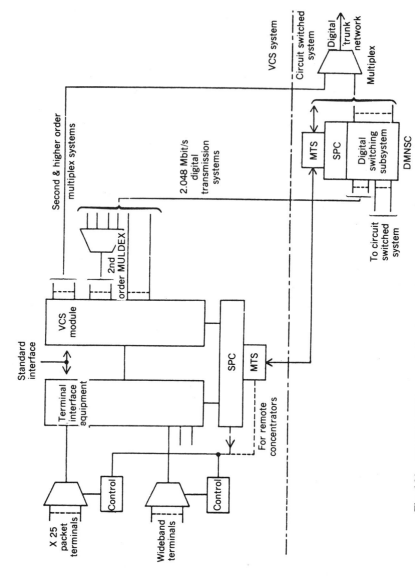

Fig. 6.20. Proposed VCS approach showing use of multiplex hierarchy SOURCE: Hughes & Atkins paper, Fig. 4, *Proceedings of the International Switching Symposium*, Paris, May 1979

and a system X trunk or tandem exchange, and illustrates how various subsystems and components are put together in a modular way.

Hughes and Atkins (1979) give examples of configurations for a variable bandwidth virtual-circuit switched system to be used in System X. Figure 6.19 shows how a digital circuit-switched system can evolve to include virtual-circuit switching, and Figure 6.20 shows a proposed hierarchical approach to virtual-circuit switching. Oliver (1982) and Smith (1982) give other examples of configurations to be used in the System X network.

REFERENCES

R. J. Anderson (May 1979) "Local data networks—Traditional concepts and methods," *Update Local Area Networks*, 127–147.

L. A. Baxter and C. R. Baugh (Jan 1982) "A comparison of architectural alternatives for local voice/ data communications," *IEEE Communications Magazine,* 20(1)44–51.

P. J. Benstead (1982) "The use of an existing PABX on the basis of an integrated office communication system," *Local Networks, 82,* 97–108.

K. J. Biba and J. W. Yeh (May 1979) "FordNet: A front-end approach to local computer networks," *Update Local Area Networks*, 199–215.

British Telecom (1981) "The role of British Telecom," pages 28–38 of Ed. A. Simpson, *Planning for the Office of the Future*, Gower Publishing Co., Aldershot, Hampshire, England.

British Telecommunications Systems (1980) *System X—The Complete Approach to Telecommunications*. British Telecommunications Systems, Ltd. Brochure.

D. Brown (1982) "Switching to the office of the future," pages 121–125 of Ed. A. Simpson, *Planning for Telecommunications*, Gower Publishing Co., Aldershot, Hampshire, England.

B. Butscher (1981) "HMINET 2—A local network connected to the German public data network," *Local Networks 81*, 419–433.

R. J. Camrass (1982) "Development in SPC PABX Systems," *Local Networks 82*, 87–95.

CASE (1982a) *MSX-XT*, Computer Systems And Engineering plc, Leaflet.

CASE (1982b) *814 Statistical Multiplexer*, Computer Systems And Engineering plc, Leaflet.

CASE (1982c) *DCX 816*, Computer Systems And Engineering plc, Leaflet.

V. G. Cerf and P. T. Kirstein (Nov 1978) "Issues in packet-network interconnection," *Proceedings of the IEEE*, 66(11) 1386–1408.

G. Charlish (1982) "When the total digital age dawns the twain will meet," *Financial Times*, 6.

D. D. Clark, K. T. Pogran and D. P. Reed (Nov 1978) "An introduction to local area networks," *Proceedings of the IEEE*, 66 (11) 1497–1517.

F. Closs and R. P. Lee (Aug 1980) "A multistar broadcast network for local-area communication," *Local Area Network Workshop*, 67–88.

R. Cole (1982) *Computer Communications*, Macmillan, London and Basingstoke, England.

D. W. Davies, D. L. A. Barber, W. L. Price and C. M. Solomonides (1979) *Computer Networks and Their Protocols*, Wiley, Chichester and New York.

Electrical Communication. Vol. S6 No. 2/3 (1981) Special Issue on ITT 1240 Digital Exchange.

Gandalf (1982) *PACX IV—Control over Computer Environments*, Gandalf Ditigal Communications Ltd., Leaflet.

C. J. Hughes and J. W. Atkins (May 1979) "Virtual circuit switching for multiservice operations," *International Switching Symposium, Paris*, 344–350.

IEE Communications 82 (May 1982) Proceedings, Communications Equipment and Systems Conference, Birmingham.

ITT Business Systems (1982) *Information Transfer Technology*, ITT Business Systems Ltd., Leaflet.

H. L. Jensen (1981) " A communication switch based on high performance local network systems," *Local Networks 81*, 157–174.

G. W. Kellond (1982) "Standard networking systems," pages 83–94 of Ed. A. Simpson, *Planning for Electronic Mail*, Gower Publishing Co., Aldershot, Hampshire, England.

P. T. Kirstein and S. R. Wilbur (Aug 1980) "University College London activities with the Cambridge ring," *Local Area Network Workshop*, 115–130.

I. M. Leslie, R. Banerjee and S. J. Love (1981) "Organization of voice communication on the Cambridge ring," *Local Networks 81*, 465–474.

D. R. McGlynn (1978) *Distributed Processing and Data Communications*, Wiley, New York and Chichester.

Master Systems (1982a) *Product Summary*, Master Systems (Data Products) Ltd., Brochure.

Master Systems (1982b) *Master Systems—C11 7502 Terminal Control Unit*, Master Systems (Data Products) Ltd., Leaflet.

Master Systems (1982c) *Master Systems—T7 3270 Terminal Control Unit*, Master Systems (Data Products) Ltd., Leaflet.

Master Systems (1983) *MASTERNET—The Invisible Network for Master Systems*, Master Systems (Data Products) Ltd., Brochure.

R. M. Metcalfe and D. R. Boggs (July 1976) "Ethernet: Distributed packet switching for local computer networks," *Communications of the ACM*, **19** (7) 395–404.

National Computing Centre (1982) *Choosing a PABX*, Manchester.

G. P. Oliver (1982) "The Integrated Services Digital Network," *IEE Conference Publications*, **209**, 8–13.

Plessey Communication Systems (1982) *Plessey IBIS Integrated Information System*, Plessey Communication Systems Ltd., Brochure.

Plessey Communications Systems (1984) *IDX*, Plessey Communications Systems, Ltd., Brochure.

I. Richer, M. Steiner and M. Sengoku (Dec 1981) "Office communications and the digital PBX," *Computer Networks*, **5** (6) 411–422.

E. H. Rothauser, P. A. Janson and H. R. Mueller (Aug 1980) "Meshed-star networks for local communication system," *Local Area Network Workshop*, 31–49.

J. H. Saltzer and K. T. Pogran (May 1979) "A star-shaped ring network with high maintainability," *Update Local Area Networks*, 179–190.

J. F. Shoch (Aug 1980) "Carrying voice traffic through an Ethernet local area network—A general overview," *Local Area Network Workshop*, 367–383.

M. Smith (1982) "A new network for digital data services," *IEE Conference Publications*, **209**, 177–187.

D. Sweetman (1981) "A distributed system built with a Cambridge Ring," *Local Networks 81*, 451–464.

Telecom Research Laboratories (1980) British Telecom Brochure.

C. Tropper (1981) *Local Computer Network Technologies*, Academic Press, New York and London.

H. van Kampen (1981) "Local area networks with intelligent PABX," *Local Networks 81*, 175–184.

Note: ITT Business Systems is now known as STC Business Systems.

Chapter 7

Equipment Linked to Networks

Most types of computers and other information processing devices can now be attached directly to local area networks and used as work stations for those networks. They can also be connected to wide area networks, either via gateways in the local area networks to which they belong, or, in the case of many terminals and computers, directly.

This chapter describes in turn the different types of equipment that can be linked to networks: terminals, graphics displays, word processors, printers, miscellaneous input/output devices, voice input and output devices, computers and multi-purpose work stations. It ends by considering some of the storage devices that can be used and accessed by computer networks, ranging from the small local store to the mass store, and based on magnetic, video and optical technologies. The most recent developments are presented in Chapter 20.

In each case, the emphasis is on what the devices can do, and only brief mention is given, in this chapter, of how they are connected to networks and operated in conjunction with them. Apart from a few illustrative examples of recent models, specific varieties of any given type of device are not usually detailed, but references are given to relevant literature about these devices, and the brochures and leaflets of their manufacturers may also be consulted.

TERMINALS

A large variety of terminals, which can be attached to both LANs and WANs, is now available. These range from the original teletype terminals, which had keyboard and printer alone, to modern terminals with keyboards and visual display units (VDUs) but no printer, and from "dumb" terminals, with no internal data processing facilities, to "intelligent" terminals, with at least some computing power. This section considers mainly "ordinary" terminals, with relatively little "intelligence," that are used for fairly routine operations, and that have basically alphanumeric output, whether as print or as display. The more sophisticated terminals are mostly considered in later sections, although a few examples are given at the end of this section.

McGlynn (1978) describes some of the available keyboard terminals and VDU terminals that were available a few years ago. He includes some of the terminals, using punched cards and paper tape, which used to be very popular but which are now becoming obsolete. The book by Pritchard (1974) discusses the choice of terminals that can be linked to online computer systems, although many further terminals have been developed since it was written.

Portable terminals, small and light enough to be moved easily by staff in the course of their duties, are now being introduced rapidly by industry (Cane, 1982a; John Bell Technical Systems, 1982).

ECC Publications (undated a) gives a guide to data communications and terminals in use today for small systems.

Mayne (1986, Chapter 6) surveys the different types of terminals specially designed for use with videotex. These range from the simple keypad, which has much fewer keys than usual, through adapted TV terminals and alphanumerical viewdata terminals, to sophisticated editing terminals and information provider terminals.

Churchill (1982a) mentions two recent examples of these terminals that will be especially useful to businessmen. The Plessey Prestel-viewdata terminal incorporates both voice and data communications in a compact desk-top unit. The Zycor Teledek 5000 is a portable terminal, contained in a briefcase, that can link into both private and public viewdata networks.

Computer (1982a) describes the versatile but inexpensive RCA VP-350 videotex terminal, which includes a modem for direct communications via the user's telephone. It is able to produce colour displays, with accompanying sound, on an attached colour TV set, and it has an expansion interface for connecting peripheral devices.

GRAPHICS DISPLAYS

"Ordinary" VDU terminals provide facilities only for alphanumeric display, showing only numbers, ordinary text (usually though not always in both upper and lower case), punctuation marks, and a few special symbols. However, several devices are available that can provide graphic displays as well.

Most personal computers have facilities for low resolution and moderate resolution graphics displays, often in colour, and this is true also of TV sets used as videotex terminals. Mayne (1986, Chapter 5) surveys the wide variety of visual displays available on different models of videotex terminals.

The versatile Microvitec Low-Complexity Colour Display (LCCD) terminal has been developed specially to provide high-quality colour resolution at optimal cost. It can be linked to many personal computers and is compatible with several viewdata adaptors (Microvitec, 1981).

Multi-purpose terminals range from "ordinary" videotex terminals, with such extras as cassette or floppy disk or hard disk magnetic memory and printers, to devices that can also act as computer terminals and/or stand-alone small computers in their own right.

The Text Terminal, developed at Queen Mary College, London, is an experiment in a possible office automation facility (Sturridge, 1980). It contains a powerful processor and sophisticated software, to allow the display to behave like several movable coloured pieces of paper.

High resolution colour graphics displays, using raster graphics to provide images that are considerably more detailed than those possible on TV sets or ordinary TV monitors, are also available, that can be used as terminals to computer networks. For example, several models are manufactured by the Ramtek Corporation (Ramtek, undated, 1981).

Charlish (1982a) reviews some recent developments in screen technology, and points out the current trends to more use of colour displays and graphic displays.

The book edited by Kazan (1981) contains three papers on different image display technologies, and gives many further references to relevant work. Of these, the paper by Judice and Slusky (1981) describes how to process images for two-level digital displays, and, especially on page 160, indicates applications for offices, small businesses and homes. Faughnan et al (1981) indicate some possible uses of cathodochromic materials in display systems, including computer terminals and projection displays, and Kaneko (1981) ends with a brief review of applications and conditions of use of liquid-crystal matrix displays.

WORD PROCESSORS

Word processing is a technique that allows text to be input, edited, and typed or printed electronically, in such a way that, at any time, the current version of the document being written is stored in memory in a named text file.

A *word processor* is a device, with a keyboard and a microprocessor, that is specially designed to perform word processing functions. Typically, it is like an electric typewriter, upgraded to perform these functions. The memory that is used to store text is usually a floppy disk.

A stand-alone word processor is a self-contained device that performs its word processing functions in isolation from other equipment. A communicating word processor has links with other word processors or with other devices including computers, either in the same LAN or across a WAN. Most word processors still have no independent data processing facilities, even though they contain a microprocessor, but the proportion of word processors, that are also able to do some computing and data processing, is rising steadily.

To an increasing extent, it is becoming possible to use personal computers and minicomputers as word processors, as the most important models of these computers already have a good selection of more or less sophisticated word processing software that can run on them. For example, the author's typescript of this book has been prepared with the aid of word processing packages, using a PDP 11 minicomputer with the UNIX operating system, and also using an Apple II personal computer.

Further information about word processing and reviews of the characteristics

and performance of specific models can be obtained from periodicals like *Word &
Information Processing* (formerly called *Word Processing Now*) and *Which Word
Processor. Practical Computing* and *Personal Computer World* include similar articles on personal computers, used as word processors, and on word processing
software packages. Computer Guides (1982) and ECC Publications (undated b)
provide guides to many of the available models.

The book by Simons (1981) provides a good general introduction to word
processing, and the book by Barton (1981) is a useful practical guide to business
users of word processors. The book by Townsend and Townsend (1981) explains
how to choose and use a word processor, while Diebold Europe SA (1978) gives
methods of evaluating word processors. Simpson (1982) contains a collection of
useful papers on word processing. Wharton (1981) reports briefly on some recent
developments in word processors and word processing.

More sophisticated word processors are used for example in Teletex terminals,
such as those provided by Philips (Tombs, 1981) and Siemens (Siemens, undated
a; see Figure 7.1), and those incorporated in multi-purpose work stations. An example of the latter is the I.M.P. work station, marketed by Office Technology
(1982a), which has all the usual word processing facilities and many additional
features to improve office productivity.

Word processing manufacturers are beginning to consider the possibility of using
word processors also as Prestel and viewdata terminals. For example, some of the
Wordplex word processors are able to do just that.

PRINTERS

A wide variety of printers have been used with computers of all kinds. They include: impact printers, non-impact printers (thermal, magnetic and electrostatic),
xerographic, ink jet, electronic, electrophoretic and laser printers, and not only
alphanumeric text and data printers but also plotters for printing graphics displays.
All these types of printer are described briefly by McGlynn (1978), for example,
and some of the more recent types are also reviewed by Charlish (1982b).

The available types of impact printers include dot matrix printers, adapted and
converted "golf-ball" typewriters, daisy wheel printers, and line printers. Dot matrix printers produce characters and sometimes also graphics symbols as configurations of closely spaced dots; they are often used as relatively inexpensive printers
for personal computers and other small computers, but the quality of their print is
usually only moderate. However, some dot matrix printers can be used for full
graphics output, being able to produce printed copies of VDU images for example;
a few models can even do this in full colour! Line printers are used by minicomputers and mainframes for fast, line at a time output, but are rather expensive.
Daisy wheel printers were originally used as high quality printers for word processors but can now also be attached to small computers; they have been rather
expensive, typically costing about £2,000, though some models are a good deal less

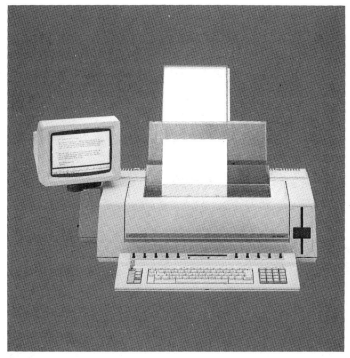

Fig. 7.1. Siemens Text Terminal T4200 Model 40 SOURCE: Siemens Text Terminal T4200 Model 40 Leaflet

than half that price, but they are also considerably faster than matrix printers and golf-ball typewriters.

Condon (1982) provides a practical guide for the evaluation of printers for office systems that are now on the market.

Zacharov (1981, pages 48–49) briefly describe the IBM 3800 laser printer, that uses an intensity modulated laser beam to produce an image of very high quality and definition, with very accurately placed characters and graphics. It is very fast and reliable but very expensive.

Computer typesetting is the use of computers to drive typesetting equipment especially phototypesetters, directly, or to prepare magnetic tapes or paper tapes or other stored representations of text which can later activate the typesetters. *Phototypesetters* project images of the text on to light-sensitive materials and prepare master copies of document pages in that way, in contrast to traditional methods of letter-press printing. In many respects, the principles of computer typesetting are similar to those of wordprocessing, although the documents that can be prepared with its aid can be far more elaborate and sophisticated, with a much wider range of type fonts and special characters. For example, the UNIX operating system, which runs on many minicomputers and is beginning to be implemented on personal computers, can be used for mathematical typesetting with suitable models of phototypesetters.

OTHER INPUT/OUTPUT DEVICES

Facsimile (*telefacsimile*) is a process where telecommunications is used to send copies of a document from one location to another; it is especially useful for documents containing tables, drawings and graphics, as well as text. Facsimile terminals on the market include the Siemens range and the Xerox Telecopiers. The Siemens models are the HF1048, shown in Figure 7.2, that is manually operated, the HF2050, that can receive facsimiles unattended, and the HF2060 shown in Figure 7.3, for more rapid transmission of large quantities of documents (Siemens, undated b); each of these models can both transmit a copy of an A4 document that is placed in its feed, and receive a copy of an A4 document. The Xerox Telecopier 495 can send and receive exact facsimiles of documents at high speed, in accordance with any of the CCITT facsimile standards (Groups 1 to 3).

Fig. 7.2. Siemens HF1048 Facsimile Terminal SOURCE: Siemens HF1048 Facsimile Terminal Leaflet

Fig. 7.3. Siemens HF2060 Facsimile Terminal SOURCE: Siemens HF2060 Facsimile Terminal
Leaflet

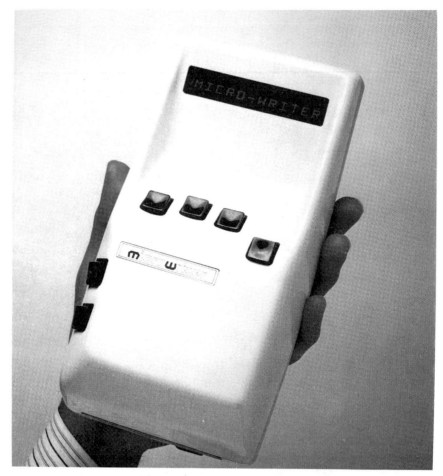

Fig. 7.4. Micro-Writer   SOURCE: Micro-Writer Ltd. Brochure

The Microwriter is a sort of pocket typewriter-plus-word processor, that has a five-finger-plus-control-keyboard, as shown in Figure 7.4 (Microwriter, 1982). The full range of characters can be typed by pressing the right combination of keys with the fingers, and it is claimed that the effective use of the keyboard can be learnt in about half an hour. The output can be displayed on the Microwriter itself, twelve characters at a time, or on an attached VDU or TV set sixteen lines at a time. The built-in memory can store 8,000 characters, i.e. about 1,500 words, and its contents can be transferred to or from ordinary audio tape cassette. When a piece of text has been edited, it can be typed by an attached printer at more than 500 words a minute; in normal office use, this printer can handle the output of up to fifteen Microwriters. With suitable modifications, the Microwriter could be used as a portable computer terminal, to transmit and receive a wide variety of information over the PSTN to and from remote locations.

The Tantus BIT PAD is an interesting example of a fairly new British input device to microcomputer systems (Tantus, 1981). It enables people to input data by selecting and pointing to the appropriate characters, symbols or words from a large flat pad. It is specially convenient, both because users can place their own tailor-made chart of symbols on the pad, and because it is very user-friendly.

Optical mark recognition (*OMR*) operates on somewhat similar principles, except that the user writes marks in the appropriate compartments, instead of just pointing to them. For such office operations as stock control, sales orders delivery schedules and quality control reports, it has much to offer (Charlish, 1982c).

Various machines are available also for *optical character recognition* (*OCR*), which has been used largely for automatic cheque reading, but also has other important business applications (Cane 1982b; Charlish, 1982c). For example, in offices handling a large amount of typing, it may be more cost effective to use typewriters and OCR for input to a word processing system, rather than provide each typist with a word processing work station. Although a start has been made on OCR of handwritten characters, at present they have to be written very carefully, in order to be recognised effectively.

For the last few years, there has been talk about the "smart" card, a plastic card, not unlike a credit card, with built-in memory and "intelligence," that is to be used for financial transactions. A "smart" card has now been developed by Philips, and has been used by trials in three French towns, with the cooperation of their banks (Charlish, 1982d). In these trials, shoppers intserted their cards into small customer terminals at the shops, working in conjunction with retailer terminals there, instead of paying by cheque.

Wilkens (1981) has pointed out that demands for new kinds of telecommunications services for information, learning and entertainment require many features in combination; for example, they need to use speech and still and moving patterns, as well as text and graphics. Recent developments in broadband transmission technologies helps to make it possible to design systems of this sort. He discusses some possibilities for such man-machine dialogues and machine-aided communications. Facilities for speech input and speech output are described briefly in the next two sections.

VOICE INPUT

Limited speech recognition facilities are already available, which typically can train the computer system to recognise between several dozen and about two hundred words when spoken by a given person (Cane 1982). These could be used, for example, to allow simple responses to be spoken instead of keyed into the system! Logica claims that its Logos device, a research tool to help the development of speech recognition systems, can learn about 2,000 words and recognise several hundred in one scan (Williams, 1982).

Voice recognition has enormous potential for simple office data entry tasks, such as input of numbers of specific commands (Kehoe, 1982). However, commercially viable systems for recognition of ordinary continuous speech seem unlikely to appear before the late 1980s.

VOICE OUTPUT

Devices for synthesising human speech are gradually improving and becoming cheaper. Thus they are likely to be widely used in business before very long, and their applications in the office include such tasks as data entry verification and checking, as well as "talking" electronic mail, catering for travelling executives especially (Kehoe, 1982).

British Telecom researchers believe that speech recognition and synthesis could be used for man-machine communications, using voice input and "voice" output over telephone lines (Williams, 1982).

Kurzweil Computer Products in the USA has developed a computer that can read books aloud, using an interesting combination of OCR and voice synthesis techniques (Restak, 1981, pages 124–125). Book pages are read, when placed face down on top of a scanner, and the speech output is more "natural" and less "mechanical" than usual for computer-generated speech.

Personal computers already offer a whole range of possibilities for audiovisual displays. Most of them have built-in facilities for generation of simple sounds, including musical notes which can be programmed in coordination with the generation of visual output on their screens. At some extra cost, add-on facilities are now available for generation of music of moderately high quality and for speech generation.

All the methods of voice input and output can in principle be combined with telecommunications, over both speech and data networks, as well as integrated digital networks.

COMPUTERS

In the early days of computer networking, mainframes and minicomputers were connected to terminals in time-sharing systems. Although this function of computers in networks is still important, many other functions have been added. In WANs, host computers have been used for a variety of purposes, not only for remote online operations and batch data processing, but also for enquiry/response, data collection, file management and message switching (McGlynn, 1978).

Zacharov (1981, pages 49–53) gives some examples of recent developments in computer hardware, including important improvements in their speed and reliability, due to modern VLSI technology. Several new designs of computers, including array processors, have been developed that use parallel processing. In some large computer systems, some of the peripheral functions are separated out, and *central filing machines* and *data base machines*, linked to large computers, are handling many of the information storage, filing and retrieval operations for such systems. In some of the LANs, *file servers* are performing similar functions.

At the other end of the scale, personal computers and other small computers can now play an integral part in the operation of LANs, and especially in personal computer networks, and they can be linked to WANs in various ways, for example they can be used as "intelligent" terminals to remote host computers. Computer Guides (1982) is a directory of available minicomputer systems and micro-computer systems.

Portable computers, with telecommunications facilities, can now be carried round by businessmen and other users, wherever they go, as long as they have access to a telephone. For example, the Navigator Management information system, marketed by Grid Systems Corporation in the USA, combines a briefcase-sized Compass personal computer with software packages and a network of support computers that can be reached via the PSTN (*Computer*, 1982b).

Recently, there has been growing interest in providing personal computers with adaptors, so that they can act as teletext and viewdata terminals, while continuing to perform their normal data processing functions. Sommer (1980) outlines some of the ways in which this can be done, and describes briefly some specific examples of these adaptors and of multi-purpose terminals.

MULTI-PURPOSE WORK STATIONS

Multi-purpose work stations are beginning to play an important part in LANs designed for use in offices and businesses.

A work station of this sort is able to operate in a self-contained mode, and it is usually driven by a minicomputer or microcomputer (West, 1981); it often also has gateways to outside networks. Its most important parts include a document production device, to capture key strokes and graphics, and a printer to type a variety of outputs. Through its keyboard and VDU, it may be commanded to print, create a hard copy, or send a message.

Management work stations will allow managers to enter data, retrieve selected information from data bases, and run programs, but they will also provide them with many new types of computer-based activities, that are often communications oriented (Agresta, 1981). Managers will have access to text files as well as data files, and be able to obtain and forward documents as well as mail and messages. They will be able to extract information from various sources and incorporate it in their own reports, which will contain graphs and charts produced by computer graphics.

Multi-function work stations are marketed by several companies that sell LAN systems. For example, the MASTERNET work station, marketed by Master Systems (Data Products) Ltd., offers facilities for creating, storing, retrieving and sending documents (Master Systems, 1983); it is a successor to the earlier Xionics work station (Master Systems, 1982; Xionics, 1982). It also has electronic mail, electronic appointments diary, and calculating facilities, and handles voice, so that spoken messages can be left for other users and spoken comments can be added to documents. It gives its users access to information held on computers within their organisation or outside it.

Office Technology (1981, 1982a) markets the I.M.P. Workstation and Principal Workstation, that provide sophisticated word processing facilities, together with electronic filing and communications, and various methods for input/output and processing of voice, text, data and graphics information. Thus they offer extensive support for administrators and managers. They can be linked to OSC Office System Controllers, that provide electronic filing for group and personal information, electronic mail between work stations, various other communications facilities, central printing, and extra processing capability for specialist tasks (Office Technology, 1982b).

Rediffusion Computers Limited's System Alpha range of "teleputers" are enhanced microcomputer systems that can provide full access to private viewdata systems (Rediffusion Computers, 1981). They have data storage, telecommunications, and various other office automation facilities.

Although not an office work station in the usual sense, the Technalogics Expandable Computer System (T.E.C.S.) is worth mentioning here. It can be operated, either as a videotex terminal, in teletext mode or Prestel mode, or as a microcomputer, which can run its own programs, in Basic and other high level languages, together with telesoftware from Oracle or Prestel (Sommers, 1980).

MAGNETIC STORAGE

Magnetic storage plays a very important part in computer networks, both for small scale storage for "intelligent" terminals, personal computers and other devices attached to them, and for large scale data storage in host computers, data bases and file servers.

Small scale magnetic storage is usually implemented by floppy disk drives, that contain easily removable and very portable floppy disks. There have been two sizes of floppy disk in common use, the $5\frac{1}{4}''$ disk, which holds about 100 KB to 500 KB of characters, and the $8''$ disk, which holds about 250 KB to 1 MB. More recently, smaller sizes of floppy disks have become increasingly popular, holding comparable amounts of information to those held by $5\frac{1}{4}''$ disks. One *KB* or *Kilobyte* is about a thousand characters, and one *MB* or *Megabyte* is about a million characters. Although individual disks cost only a few pounds each, sometimes only just over a pound each, disk drives and interfaces are fairly expensive, costing from about £100 upwards.

Hard disks and disk packs can be used for more extensive data storage, involving hundreds of Mb of information. The computer data bases of public and private online information systems are usually stored on hard disks.

Small computer systems and other "intelligent" work stations can be interfaced to a special form of hard disk, called a Winchester disk, that typically holds between about 5 MB and 40 MB of data, or to hard disks that can be backed up by removable disk packs each holding at least 5 MB. A drawback of hard disks is that they are fixed, and therefore cannot be used like large floppy disks, although disk packs can be used in this way.

Magnetic tapes can be used to back up hard disk storage in medium-sized to large computer systems, and typically each tape holds up to about 150 MB of data.

They have the advantage of being easily removable and compact to store, but they are less convenient to handle than disks.

Magnetic stores, including magnetic mass stores, are described in moderate detail by Chi (1982) and Zacharov (1981, pages 37–46). For example, the IBM 850 mass store, using a configuration of tape drives and 50 MB tape cartridges, can hold well over 200 GB of information, and the Xytek ATL 7110 automated tape library, now marketed by the Breagan Corporation in the USA, can hold about 1.4 TB of information (Miller, 1982).

Here, a *Gigabyte* (*GB*) is about a thousand MB, and a *Terabyte* (*TB*) is about a million MB. To give an idea of what these units of information mean, a medium-sized book contains of the order of one MB of information, and a large library contains a few TB.

For general discussions of mass stores, which may use principles other than magnetic storage, see for example the special issue of *Computer* for July 1982 (*Computer*, 1982c), the editorial for that issue (Miller, 1982), and Chi (1982). Charlish (1982e) also briefly reviews some of the possibilities. Optical and video mass storage are discussed in the next section.

VIDEO STORAGE AND OPTICAL INFORMATION STORAGE

In principle, optical information stores could become far more compact than any other type of storage device. Thus optical stores are becoming increasingly important as a means of storing extremely large data bases, with many millions of pages of information, within reasonably small spaces.

In practice, the most promising implementations of optical storage have been achieved through its integration with videodisk technology, especially through *videodisks*. Four types of videodisk are currently used, two of which use non-optical principles, namely the *CED* (*Capacitance Electronic Disk*) and the *VHD* (*Video High Density Disk*). The other two types use lasers to input data on to the disks and to read the resulting optical information patterns of them; they are the *reflective optical videodisk*, where reflected laser light is used, and the *transmissive optical videodisk*, where laser light is shone through the disk. For each type of disk, the information can be read off by using a videodisk player of corresponding type, that is attached to a TV set or monitor. Each videodisk is portable, being about a foot in diameter, and it is inexpensive, costing about £10 or less.

Interest in videodisks is expanding so rapidly that this field is already being covered by several periodicals, including the American newsletters and journals: *Optical Memory Newsletter, Video Systems, Videodisc/Videotex, Videodisc News, Videodisc Design/Production Group News*, and *Videoinfo*. For general reviews of the state of the art of videodisk technology, see Barrett (1981, 1982), Douglass (1982), Edelhart (1981), Heath (1981), Moberg and Laefsky (1982), Nugent and Christie (1982), Onosko (1982), Schubin (1981) and, very briefly, Zacharov (1981, pages 46–47).

Although the information is usually stored on videodisks as TV frames, because they were originally used to store films and TV programmes, the more sophisticated players now have facilities for selective viewing of still frames. Typically, a videodisk holds 54,000 frames per side, equivalent to half an hour's continuous viewing per side. Thus videodisks can now be used for educational purposes and for information retrieval for example, using programs that are operated either by the players themselves or by attached microcomputers.

Active research is now proceeding on videodisks that can store their data more compactly for purposes of archival information storage; see for example Kenville (1982), *Computer* (1982c, 1982d). Thus the Drexon™ optical disk can store 1250 MB of data, and "jukebox" systems, automatically handling hundreds of videodisks, and now being planned, may be able to handle a thousand times as much, well over one TB!

Barrett (1981) has made an extensive review of optical disk technology, and he has explored especially its implications for information retrieval. He includes comparative tables of performance and cost characteristics of optical disk and other mass data storage media. Horder (1981) provides similar information, and includes an extensive bibliography.

Videodisks can at present only be written once, although they can be read any number of times. In the *DRAW* (*direct read after write*) technology, it is possible for the writing and subsequent reading to be done by the same equipment. Although erasable optical disks may be achieved later in the 1980s, Copeland considers that the absence of erasability need not be a disadvantage, if the information handling operations are organised in the right way; indeed, for some applications, where archival information really *has* to be kept, it can be of positive benefit. He also considers that optical disk mass storage may eventually have several advantages, including reliability, over magnetic mass storage, although Chi (1982) believes that magnetic disk technology will provide powerful rivalry for a long time to come, as it too has potentials for improvement.

Another weakness of videodisks is that they have hitherto not been interfaced with computer systems very effectively, but research is being pursued in this area, which may soon make the videodisk a really effective computer peripheral.

Sippl and Dahl (1981) have explored some of the possibilities of integrating video technology, personal computing, and telecommunications, although they give more emphasis to video tapes than videodisks, because they can be connected to computers more easily. Both the developments that they envisage and the new possibilities for videodisks, that are now being researched, open up the possibility of a true convergence of video, computing and telecommunications, thus allowing linked local area networks to handle really large amounts of stored information, both on site and on a widely distributed basis.

Haskal and Chu (1977) describe the advantages and limitations of optical data storage in general, and review the status of research and development in the field at that time. They discuss some possibilities for very dense storage of information on optical media, together with some examples of recording systems.

Burns (1979a, 1979b) describes the *Slidestore*, an integrated approach to mass memory, that uses an alternative to videodisk technology. The information is held on 4″ × 4″ glass slides, each of which stores over 360 MB; the slides are contained in magazines of a hundred, and each mass store module has five magazines, so that it can holdover 180 GB of user information altogether.

REFERENCES

J. M. Agresta (1981) "Office of the future," pages 93–108 of Burke and Lehman (1981).

R. Barrett (1981) "Developments in optical disk technology and the implications for information storage and retrieval," *British Library R & D Report* **5623**.

R. Barrett (Apr 1982) "Prospects for the optical disc in the office of the future," *Reprographic Quarterly*, **14**(4) 140–143.

J. T. Barton (1981) *Word Processing*, Institute of Management Services, London.

John Bell Technical Systems (1982) *Portable Terminals: A Management and Buyer's Guide*, Two Volumes.

Ed. T. J. M. Burke and M. Lehman (1981) *Communication Technologies and Information Flow*, Pergamon Press, Oxford, England, and Elmsford, NY.

L. L. Burns (1979a) "The Slidestore—An integrated approach to mass memory," pages 393–397 of Ed. W. Waidelich (1979) *Laser 79: Opto-Electronics*, International Publishing Company, London.

L. L. Burns (1979b) "Slidestore—A laser mass memory for image storage," *SPIE*, **200**, 79–83.

A. Cane (1982a) (21 Oct 1982) "Horizons widen for the electronic notepad—opportunities for portable terminals," *Financial Times*, 13.

A. Cane (1982b) (13 April 1982) "New methods of input," *Financial Times Survey, The Electronic Office*, VIII.

G. Charlish (1982a) (13 April 1982) "Trend towards more colour and graphic display," *Financial Times Survey, The Electronic Office*, VI.

G. Charlish (1982b) (13 April 1982) "New printing systems are versatile and noiseless—Advent of the laser beam printer," *Financial Times Survey, The Electronic Office*, VI.

G. Charlish (1982c) (13 April 1982) "OCRs and OMRs are now moving into new territory," *Financial Times Survey, The Electronic Office*, XIII.

G. Charlish (1982d) (17 Aug 1982) "Philips first off the mark with the 'Smart' Card," *Financial Times*, 8.

G. Charlish (1982e) (13 April 1982) "Capacity of storage systems rising," *Financial Times Survey, The Electronic Office*, IV.

C. S. Chi (May 1982) "Advances in computer storage technology," *Computer*, **15**(5) 60–74.

D. Churchill (1982a) (13 Apr 1982) "New telephone terminals offer greater flexibility," *Financial Times Survey, The Electronic Office*, XII.

D. Churchill (1982b) (18 Jan 1982) "Discs and cassettes lead the way," *Financial Times Survey, Computers*, XVI.

Computer (1982a) (Jun 1982) "Videotex terminal includes phone and TV interfaces," **15**(6) 102.

Computer (1982b) (Jun 1982) "Business system is small personal briefcase-sized computer," **15**(6) 98.

Computer, Vol. **15**, No. 7 (1982c) (Jul 1982) Special issue on mass storage systems and evaluation of data control architectures.

Computer (1982d) (Jun 1982) "Optical memory disk stores 1250 M bytes," **15**(6) 100.

Computer Guides (Sep 1982) *Guide to Small Business Computer and Word Processing Systems*, 1983, Computer Guides Ltd., London.

M. A. Condon (1982) *Office System Printers*, NCC Publications, Manchester, England.

G. Copeland (Jul 1982) "What if mass storage were free?," *Computer*, **15**(7) 27–35.

Diebold Europe SA (1978) *Methodology to Evaluate WP Equipment*, NCC Publications, Manchester, England.

J. Douglas (1982) "Micro memories," *Science 82*, 40–45.

ECC Publications (1982a) *Guide to Data Communications and Terminals for Small Systems*, ECC Publications Ltd., London.

ECC Publications (1982b) *Guide to Word Processing Systems*, ECC Publications Ltd., London.

M. Edelhart (Nov/Dec 1981) "Optical disc—The omnibus medium," *Technology*, **1**(1) 42–57.

B. W. Faughnan, P. M. Heyman, I. Gorog and I. Shidlovsky (1981) "Cathodochromics: Their properties and uses in display systems," pages 87–155 of Kazan (1981).

H. Haskal and D. Chen (1977) "Optical data storage," pages 135–230 of ed. M. Ross (1977) *Laser Applications*, Vol **3**, Academic Press, New York and London.

T. Heath (Fall 1982) "Alternative videodisc systems," *Videodisc/Videotex*, **1**(4) 228–238.

A. Horder (2nd Ed., 1981) "Video discs—Their application to information storage and retrieval," *NRCd Publication No.* **17**.

C. N. Judice and P. D. Slusky (1981) "Processing images for bilevel digital displays," pages 157–229 of Kazan (1981).

E. Kaneko (1981) "Liquid-crystal matrix displays," pages 1–86 of Kazan (1981).

Ed. B. Kazan (1981) *Advances in Image Pickup and Display*, Vol. **4**, Academic Press, New York and London.

L. Kehoe (13 Apr 1982) "Voice synthesis systems of tomorrow," *Financial Times Survey, The Electronic Office*, XX.

R. F. Kenville (Jul 1982) "Optical disk data storage," *Computer*, **15**(7) 21–25.

D. R. McGlynn (1978) *Distributed Processing and Data Communications*, Wiley, New York and Chichester, Chapter 2, "Data Communication Hardware."

Master Systems (1982) *XIBUS—The Fully Integrated Electronic Office System*, Master Systems (Data Products) Ltd., Brochure.

Master Systems (1983) *MASTERNET—The Invisible Network For Master Systems*, Master Systems (Data Products) Ltd., Brochure.

A. J. Mayne (1986) *The Videotex Revolution*, second edition, Wiley, Chichester and New York.

Microvitec (1981) *Microvitec Puts Colour into Visual Displays*, Microvitec Ltd., Leaflet.

Microwriter (1982) *Write into Type*, Microwriter Ltd., Brochure.

S. W. Miller (Jul 1982) Guest Editor's Introduction to Computer (1982c), *Computer*, **15**(7) 16–19.

D. Moberg and I. M. Laefsky (Jun 1982) "Videodiscs and optical data storage," *Byte*, **7**(6) 142–160.

R. Nugent and K. Christie (Mar 1982) "Using videodisc technology," *Video Systems*, **8**(3) 16–20.

Office Technology (1981) *I.M.P. Workstation HPW.A—I.M.P. Principal Workstation HPW.B—User Interface for Information Processing*, Office Technology Ltd., Leaflet.

Office Technology (1982a) *The Most Helpful Wordprocessor is I.M.P. from OTL*, Office Technology Ltd., Leaflet.

Office Technology (1982b) *Office System Controllers OSC.A OSC.B OSC.C—User Interface for Information Processing*, Office Technology Ltd., Leaflet.

T. Onosko (Jan 1982) "Vision of the Future," *Creative Computing*, **8**(1) 84–94.

J. A. T. Pritchard (1974) *Selection and Use of Terminals in On-Line Systems*, NCC Publications, Manchester, England.

Ramtek (undated) *RAMTEK—The Display Company*, Ramtek Corp., Brochure.

Ramtek Corp. (1981) *The 6211 Colorgraphic Terminal*, Ramtek Corp., Leaflet.

Rank Xerox (undated) *Xerox Telecopier 495*, Rank Xerox (UK), Ltd. Leaflet.

Rediffusion Computers (1981) *System Alpha*, Rediffusion Computers Ltd., Leaflet.

R. M. Restak (1981) "Smart machines learn to see, talk, listen, even 'think' for us," pages 123–129 of Burke and Lehman (1981).

M. Schubin (1981) "Videodiscs as an information storage medium," *Videotex 81*, 303–307.

Siemens (undated a) *Text Terminal T4200 Model 40*, Siemens Ltd., Leaflet.

Siemens (undated b) *Correspondence Managed Electronically with Facsimile Equipment from Siemens*, Siemens Ltd., Brochure.

G. L. Simons (1981) *Introducing Word Processing*, NCC Publications, Manchester.

Ed. A. Simpson (1982) *Planning for Word Processing*, Gower Publishing Company, Aldershot, Hampshire.

C. J. Sippl and F. Dahl (1981) *Video/Computers—How to Select, Mix and Operate Personal Computers and Home Video Systems*, Prentice-Hall, Englewood Cliffs, NJ.

P. Sommer (1980) "Interfacing the individual to information services," *Practical Computing*, **3**(5) (May 1980) 76–79.

H. Sturridge (Jul 1980) "Through the screen, darkly," *Computer Management*, 33–36.

Tantus Microsystems (1981) *The BIT PAD Alternative to Keyboard Data Entry*, Tantus Microsystems, Leaflet.

D. Tombs (1981) "Teletex—The next major step in office automation," pages 69–75 of Ed. A. Simpson (1981) *Planning for the Office of the Future*, Gower Publishing Company, Aldershot, Hampshire, England.

K. Townsend and K. Townsend (1981) *Choosing and Using a Word Processor*, Gower Publishing Company, Aldershot, Hampshire, England.

W. J. Welch and P. A. Wilson (1982) *Facsimile Equipment—A Practical Evaluation Guide*, NCC Publications, Manchester, England.

J. M. West (1981) "Some new questions about office technology," pages 109–115 of Burke and Lehman (1981).

K. Wharton (1981) "Electronic office product developments," *Data Processing International 1981*, 133–136.

H. Wilkens (1981) "Systems for audiovisual and man-machine dialogue for a very large number of subscribers," *New Systems and Services in Telecommunications*, 341–345.

E. Williams (18 Jan 1982) "Robots that talk and listen," *Financial Times Survey, Computers*, XVII.

Xionics Ltd. (Mar 1982) *XIONICS*, Brochure.

V. Zacharov (1981) "Computer systems and networks: Status and perspectives," *Proceedings 1980 CERN School of Computing*, Publ. CERN 81-03, 8–77.

Note: It was announced in the computer press at the end of 1984 that Rediffusion Computers is to be renamed Rocc Computers.

Chapter 8

Transmission Technologies

The transmission technologies are concerned with the basic transmission systems that are needed for communication of data and information between people and machines, over distances ranging from a few yards, as with in-house local area networks, to thousands of miles, as with the larger wide area networks.

This first part of this chapter introduces some of the basic concepts of data transmission, including: modes of transmission, data rates, bandwidth, multiplexing, modulation, synchronisation, and switching.

The second part describes the technologies used for the physical transmission sytems: modems and codecs, telephone lines and channels, coaxial cables, optical fibres, lasers, radio waves and satellites.

The third part introduces some of the basic concepts of information theory, communication theory and data coding, together with their applications to: character codes, data compression, cryptography, error detection and correction codes, and variable bit-rate transmission.

The most recent developments in transmission technologies are presented in Chapter 20.

There is no one literature reference that covers all these aspects of data transmission with comparable amounts of detail, but there are several references that are useful for introductory further reading. CASE (undated) is a useful pocket guide to several of the practical aspects of data transmission, which Corby et al (1982) and Freeman (1981) describe in more detail, and which Scott (1982) also discusses. Cole (1981), Housley (1979) and McGlynn (1978) give good introductions to the basic concepts and some of the transmission technologies. Slana and Lehman (1982) and Zacharov (1981) provide useful summaries of quite a number of these technologies. Hamming (1980) gives an excellent introduction to the concepts of information theory and data coding, including especially error detection and correction codes, which are essential aids to reliable data transmission. The bibliography on local area networks, compiled by Shoch (1979), contains several relevant references.

Logica (1979) provides practical guidance on the evaluation and selection of data communications equipment, and includes a case study. ECC Publications (undated) is a guide to data communications and terminals for small systems.

DATA TRANSMISSION CONCEPTS

The basic concepts of data transmission are discussed at some length by Cole (1982, Chapters 1 to 3 and also Section 4.3), Freeman (1981, Chapters 1, 3, 8 and 11), McGlynn (1978, Chapter 6) and CASE (undated, pages 3–9, 18–19, 26–43). They are described in less detail by Corby et al (1982, Chapter 7), Tanenbaum (Sections 3.1 and 3.2) and Zacharov (1982, pages 59–62), for example.

The purpose of communication is to transfer information between a sender and a receiver through a suitable medium. *Data transmission* is the process of sending *digital information*, that is coded into discrete patterns, through a medium or sequence of media. In practice, the discrete data patterns are always patterns of bits, a *bit* being defined as the unit of information specifying a choice between two alternatives.

One basic problem, faced by any data transmission system, is that the signals carried by any physical transmission medium are represented by waveforms, which are always *analogue*, in the sense that their voltage or other degree of size varies continuously from one time to another. However, the data that are to be transmitted are represented in digital form, in contrast to speech which originates as sound waves, which are also analogue.

It can be shown mathematically that waveforms can be viewed as combinations of regularly varing *sine waves*, each of which is a simple periodically varying wave, having an *amplitude*, which is the maximum size (height) that it reaches during a period, a *frequency*, measured in *Hertz (Hz)*, which is the number of periods per second, and a *phase*, which is related to the times at which the height reaches its maximum.

A digital quantity can be represented by a waveform whose height takes only one of a few discrete values, for example a *square wave*, whose height takes only two different values. The problem is that square waves can be formed only approximately on actual transmission media; although the approximation is usually good enough in practice to avoid its misinterpretation, it is occasionally distorted sufficiently by *noise*, resulting from more or less random disturbances of the transmission medium, to lead to *errors* in transmitting individual bits. (Noise can of course also affect purely analogue transmission, for example when telephone speech becomes so distorted as to become incomprehensible.)

The different aspects of data transmission can now be defined. A *channel* is a path through a transmission medium, that carries data from a given sender to a given receiver, this data in turn being a *coded representation* of the information that is being exchanged. A *connection* is also a path through a transmission medium, that allows communication to occur between two given devices, and thus between people using those devices.

Note that a channel is always in one direction only, whereas a connection may be in either one direction or both, as defined by its *mode of operation*. In *simplex* mode, there is only one channel and the connection can operate in only one direction between the two communicating parties, so that they have to establish a new connection, using another channel, when they want to exchange their roles as transmitter and receiver and communicate in the reverse direction. In *half duplex* mode, both parties can send and receive information, but they cannot both send or both receive at the same time; there is still only one channel, but its direction can be reversed from time to time by switching, while maintaining the same connection. In *full duplex* mode, both parties can send and receive information at the same time, using two channels, with opposite directions, simultaneously in the same connection.

The *data rate* of a communications channel is the number of bits that is actually transmitted by it per second during normal operation. The *channel capacity* is the maximum data rate that can theoretically be maintained by the channel. In practice, the data rate is somewhat less than the channel capacity, due to the effects of noise and other factors. The average number of changes that occurs per second in the coded signals transmitted along the channel is measured in *bauds*.

Although baud rates are often confused with bit rates (data rates), it is important to realise that they have distinct definitions; they may or may not be the same, for specific communication channels (Zacharov, 1981, page 60). Bit rates can exceed baud rates; for example, the bit rate can be much greater than the baud rate of a given modem. Under some other circumstances, bit rates can be less then baud rates. In general, the relationship between bits and bauds depends on the data encoding scheme. When considering computer networks, it is more useful and meaningful to measure channels by bit rates rather than baud rates.

Another very important characteristic of a channel or of a transmission medium is its *bandwidth*, which is the difference between the highest frequency that it can transmit and the lowest frequency that it can transmit, i.e. the size of the range of frequencies that it can transmit, and which is thus measured in Hertz.

Channels are assigned to transmission media in different ways, according to their bandwidths. Typically, a low bandwidth medium carries only one channel at a time, while a high bandwidth channel is generally *multiplexed* so that it can carry several channels simultaneously. One of the most widely used forms of multiplexing is *frequency division multiplexing (FDM)*, where the frequency band of the medium is divided into sub-bands, one for each channel, in such a way that the sum of the bandwidths of the sub-channels is almost, though not quite, equal to the bandwidth of the medium. Anther form that is often used is *time division multiplexing (TDM)*, where successive time slots in the same frequency range are assigned to different channels, according to some specific rule. More generally, FDM and TDM can be combined, and other more complicated patterns of multiplexing can also be used. Digital multiplexing is discussed in detail by Davies and Barber (1973, Chapter 7).

Most transmission media convey electromagnetic signals around specific fundamental frequency called the *carrier frequency*, and the waveforms of the media consist of combinations of frequencies that are very near this frequency, so that the carrier frequency lies in the middle of the frequency band of the medium. Information is conveyed in the waveforms by *modulating* them in suitable ways, so that their shapes and frequency patterns are specifically related to the data that are being transmitted. For example, in digital transmission over analogue channels such as telephone lines, the waveforms are modulated into sequences of square waves or other rectangular patterns. In radio wave transmission or optical transmission, the carrier wave frequency is very high so that the analogue waveforms are themselves modulated on to the carrier wave and the digital patterns are then modulated on to these modulated waveforms. In *pulse code modulation (PCM)*, analogue signals, such as voice waveforms, are sampled at regular intervals, and the heights of the waves at those sampling instants are then converted into bit patterns representing their numerical values at those instants. Alternative ways of modulating continuous waveforms into digital form include *differential pulse code modulation* and *delta modulation*. The relation between bits, bauds and bandwidth depends on the modulation method. Modulation is discussed in the references listed earlier in this section, and also in some of the papers presented at the *Communications 82* (1982) Conference.

When data signals are transmitted, appropriate methods must be adopted to ensure that the receiving device knows where they begin and where they end. When *asynchronous transmission* is used, each data byte must be preceded by a *start bit* and followed by a *stop bit*. When *synchronous transmission* is used, bytes are transmitted continuously, with "idle" bytes "padded" between sequences of data bytes, and with each sequence of data bytes being preceded by at least two *SYNC bytes*.

In the latter case the receiver's clock is usually synchronised with the transmitter's clock by sending transmitter clock information down the channel with the data. A channel, that can carry clock information in this way, is called *synchronous*, or, preferably, *isochronous*. A channel that cannot carry such clock information is *asynchronous*, or, preferably, *anisochronous*.

Although synchronous terminals are usually used on isochronous channels, they can be used on anisochronous channels. Many asynchronous terminals can be used on isochronous as well as anisochronous channels.

Although it is discussed elsewhere in this book, brief reference should be made here to different forms of *switching*, i.e. ways of ensuring that transmitted messages reach their correct destinations.

In *circuit switching*, a special physical connection or "circuit" is set up, together with a *call* between the two communicating parties, such that the connection and the channel(s) between the parties are maintained, along the same route, for the duration of the call. In addition, the transmission passes straight through without a stop, so that there is no storing of any part of it at intermediate nodes.

In *message switching*, no "call" is established, but a message is stored at its originating node until its destination node is ready to receive it, and the connection is established at that time for the duration of the message.

In *packet switching*, similar "store-and-forward" principles are used, although from node to node rather than from origin to destination, and the message is also subdivided into much shorter *packets*, that are sent separately across the network. Two forms of packet switching may be distinguished: *virtual circuit* operation, where fixed routes are used for the duration of the message transmission, and the packets of the message are sent, in due relation to each other, through the appropriate protocols, and *datagram* operation, where the packets of a message are sent through as if they are independent entities, and where the receiver is responsible for reassembling them into the original message.

The different forms of modulation are in effect methods of coding the data that are sent so as to transmit them effectively in the specific media through which they pass. There are also other forms of coding that are related to the message content of the data and the protection of transmission against errors and against human interference; these forms of coding are handled by information theory and communication theory, and are considered at the end of this chapter.

MODEMS AND CODECS

Although digital signals are constructed and carried directly inside computers and other digital devices, and inside many forms of LAN, they cannot be conveyed through the transmission media of WANs without suitable modulation.

For transmission over telephone lines, this modulation is carried out by modems or acoustic couplers. A *modem (modulator-demodulator)* is a specially designed device for converting a digital signal from a computer or a terminal into representations of digital signals to be carried over the telephone line within the voice frequency band, typically about 400 Hz to 3000 Hz. The modem also performs the reverse function of converting the representations of digital signals on the line back into true digital signals at the other end.

An *acoustic coupler* is in some respects similar to a modem, but differs from it by producing the representations of digital signals in the form of patterns of *sound* pulses, at specified frequencies, that are fed into the microphone of the telephone for conversion into electrical waveforms there. At the other end, the receiver's acoustic coupler converts the coded sound signals from the earpiece of the telephone back into digital signals. (Care must be taken to shield acoustic couplers from excessive external noises!)

Scott (1980) explains the principles and practice of modern modem usage, and his book includes appendices on standards, terminology, and the wiring of modem connections. Modems are also described for example by CASE (undated, pages 53–59), Cole (1982, Chapter 3), Corby et al (Chapter 7), Freeman (1981, Chapter 8), and, more briefly, by Zacharov (1981, pages 59–62).

"Slow" modems typically operate at 300 bits/sec full duplex or 600/1200 bits/ sec in one direction and 75 bits/sec in the other, either simplex or half duplex or full duplex. In the former case, a teletype or slow VDU (110/300 bits/sec) may be connected to any computer in full duplex, by dialing through the PSTN. In the latter case, faster terminals can be connected, but a full duplex connection is possible only for a terminal connected to one particular computer by a leased line.

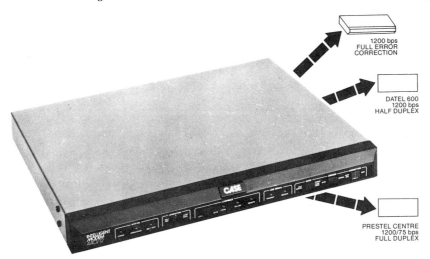

1200 bps
FULL ERROR
CORRECTION

DATEL 600
1200 bps
HALF DUPLEX

PRESTEL CENTRE
1200/75 bps
FULL DUPLEX

Courtesy of CASE

Fig. 8.1. CASE 440/12 Intelligent Modem SOURCE: CASE 440/12 Intelligent Modem leaflet

Viewdata modems, such as those used with Prestel, usually operate at 1200 bits/ sec from the computer to the terminal and 75 bits/sec in the reverse direction.

Synchronous connection can be provided using "fast" modems at higher data rates, namely 1200/2400, 4800 and 9600 bits/sec, but, again, a leased line is needed for full duplex, full speed operation. Very high data rates can be used for inter-computer communications, at data rates between 40.8 and 50 kbits/sec, over 48 kHz wide band circuits, using special configurations of special modems. Figure 8.1 shows an example of a modern modem, the CASE 440/12 Intelligent Modem.

The higher the speed of operation, the more complicated and costly is the modem. The complexity arises from the needs to compress the signal into the relatively narrow channels of the telephone system, to minimise the effects of line distortion and noise, and to prevent interference between adjacent lines and channels.

Codecs are used for converting *continuous* analogue signals into digital bit streams, for example when a dialed number, sent along a local telephone line, is converted into digital form at an exchange, and when a voice signal is converted into digital form by means of PCM or some comparable form of modulation. At the far end, a codec converts the digital form of signal back into an analogue signal.

Several papers on codecs were presented at the *Communications 82* (1982) Conference.

TELEPHONE LINES AND CHANNELS

The original forms of data communication all used telephone lines, and the majority of communications across WANs still use the PSTN. Data communications, using telephone lines and channels, is described for example by Cole (1982, Chapter 3), Corby et al (1982, in several chapters), Freeman (1982 Chapter 2), and more briefly by CASE (undated, pages 45 to 47 and 52), Tanenbaum (1981, Section 3.2), and Zacharov (1981, pages 54–55). Mayne (1986, Chapter 7) considers the special case of telephone communication between the Prestel computers and Prestel receivers.

In modern telephone systems, such as those in the UK, Europe and North America, physical "lines," made of copper exist only for very local connections, between telephones and their nearest exchanges. All other telephone channels are grouped together into *carrier systems*, of much greater bandwidth, using coaxial cables, microwave trasmission, or even satellite links. Figure 8.2 shows some examples of interconnections between the channels, including 32 kbits/sec and 2 Mbits/sec channels, that are being used by System X, the new integrated telephone and data network now being developed by British Telecom.

Most of the noise problems and resulting transmission errors arise at the relatively short local lines at each end of the connecting circuit. This arises partly because the telephone network was designed originally for voice transmission;

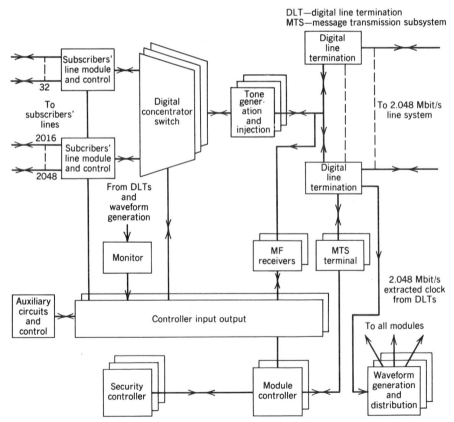

Fig. 8.2. System X concentrator module architecture SOURCE: British Telecom System X Brochure, pp. 18–19

channels that give the best voice quality happen to distort the square waves, used for data transmission, rather seriously. Thus communication equipment, using the PSTN, must be able to correct for transmission errors. The situation is somewhat better for leased lines.

In some countries, though not in the UK, the carriers are starting to provide networks especially designed for digital data transmission. For example, in the USA, AT&T's "DDS" service offers leased data channels. Its costs turn out to be much less than those of comparable 9600 bits/sec leased lines in the UK.

COAXIAL CABLES

Coaxial cables already play an essential part in providing long-distance telephone channels and other telecommunications channels. Modern coaxial cables can support data rates up to 140 Mbits/sec, which will carry the equivalent of well over 10,000 telephone (voice) channels; research is now being carried out on possible cables with 565 Mbits/sec transmission rate (British Telecom, 1980, page 26). These cables are thus suitable for high quality bulk transmission of data, text, image and voice at high speeds.

For a general description of telecommunications by coaxial cable systems, see for example Freeman (1981, Chapter 9). Zacharov (1981, p. 55) considers this topic briefly, and points out that it is very straightforward for local cable links to achieve transmission rates up to about 50 Mbits/sec for distances up to about 3 km.

Cables are used in many LANs, not only Ethernet, but also, for example, BIS (Segarra, 1981), Mitrenet (Hopkins, 1979) and Promisnet (Herzberg et al, 1979).

The Ferranti Videodata Systems announcement (Ferranti Computer Systems Ltd., 1980) describes an inexpensive coaxial cable system that can provide many hundreds of high speed and low speed data channels over a single cheap cable, to which many computer can be connected. Developed in 1978, it is now used by several industrial companies and by British Airways, and it could also be a useful component of office automation systems.

Coaxial cables have been used for several decades for *cable television (cable TV, CATV)*, which uses them as an alternative transmission medium to broadcast radio waves. CATV systems have been very popular in the USA and Canada, but they have not yet "taken off" in the UK, although there are signs that they may do so soon. The Americans have already used them fairly extensively for many experimental videotex systems and for several operational videotex systems (Mayne, 1986). They have also used them for wideband data communications systems (Wanner, 1978) and for two-way cable systems such as the Mitrix DCS system at MITRE (Smith, 1975).

OPTICAL FIBRES AND LASERS

Because light waves have enormously high frequencies, many times the frequencies of even the shortest microwaves, those transmission media that use them offer tremendous potentialities for data channels of very high capacity.

The chief optical communication system, now being developed, is based on transmission by laser light through *optical fibres*. An enormous amount of work has already been done to develop this technology, and the literature on it is already very extensive.

The conference proceedings edited by Ostrowsky (1979) gives an extensive review of the technologies of *fibre optics* and *integrated optics*, and it includes reviews of recent work on fibre optics in the UK (Midwinter, 1979) and Europe. This technology has been reviewed more recently in a special issue of *Electrical Communication*, Vol. **56**, No. 4 (1981), which includes papers on its uses for telecommunications.

Optical fibre communications are surveyed extensively by the book edited by Barnoski (1981a) and also by the special issue of *Proceedings of the IEEE*, Vol. **68**, No. 10 (Oct 1980). Ash et al (1976) review the nature and current status of integrated optics and indicated some ways of using it in optical communications systems.

Brief introductions to optical fibre communications are given, for example, by Freeman (1981, Chapter 14), March and Williamson (1981), and Zacharov (1981, pages 56–58). The proceedings of the *Communications 82* (1982) Conference contains some papers on recent developments in fibre optics.

Optical fibre communications is an *integrated optoelectronic* technology, as it uses optical fibres, lasers, electronic detectors and transistors in a single package, that provides fast and reliable data transmission (Bar-Chaim et al, 1981). For example, an optical fibre can link two multipleplexors, each of them connected to a cluster of electronic data channels.

Research is proceeding actively on the improvement of optical fibre communications; see, for example, British Telecom (1980, pages 29–33) and Midwinter (1979). Optical fibre communications systems with bandwidths of 8, 34 and 140 Mbits/sec are already operational in the UK, and future systems will also be designed for operation at 280 and 560 Mbits/sec.

As signals can now be sent several dozens of miles down optical fibres before they need regeneration, the range over which optical fibre communications systems can operate is steadily increasing.

Hanson (1981) provides a useful, user-oriented review of the use of fibre optics in LAN applications, aiming to bridge the gap between system requirements and technology, and to arrive at a reasonable understanding of the cost-performance trade-offs for this use of fibre optics.

Rawson (1979) and Rawson and Metcalfe (1978) consider some examples of the ways in which fibre optics can be used in LANs, and the sorts of LAN configurations and architectures that arise with its use. They describe their Fibernet experiment, carried out at Xerox PARC in Palo Alto, as an illustrative example.

Yamamoto (1982) introduces the concept of a *personal information processing and communications system (PICS)* using optoelectronics, and he describes the Research Information Processing System (RIPS) at the Japan Agency of Industrial Science and Technology, that partially implements this concept. Its large scale optoelectronic LAN serves nine research laboratories on neighbouring sites.

Barnoski (1981b) considers various applications of fibre optics to distribute information to several remote terminals, all linked together in a two-direction data distribution system. Such a system is of special relevance to short-range applications, such as transfer of informtion within aircraft, ships and other vehicles, as well as for LANs in offices and factories. Here, the maximum spacings between terminals would be a few hundred meters, and the data transmission rates would range from several Kbits/sec to several hundred Mbits/sec. Longer-range systems can also be designed, to set up a broadband LAN. All these applications use an optical fibre data bus, which is a single line carrying simultaneously the many different mixed signals that serve the individual terminals.

High bandwidth optical communications, sending laser light through air channels, are also beginning to be developed (Zacharov, 1982, page 56). This sort of optical link can be very simple, consisting of a light-emitting diode (LED), modulated electrically, and a receiving photodiode or an avalanche photodiode; it uses infra-red light, and its range is about 1 km, as it uses only low power. Higher powered systems, using externally modulated laser radiation, have ranges up to about 20 km. In both these cases, data transmission rates of about 10 Mbits/sec can be achieved, and the systems are quite cheap, portable, and easy to operate.

Gfeller et al (1978) describe a system of this sort that is placed inside a building, and is used to operate a LAN. LEDs and photodiodes are attached to terminals inside a room, and the paths of infra-red light between them are bounced off a "satellite" on the ceiling.

RADIO WAVES

Radio links have not only been used in various telephone systems, but they have also been adopted in certain LANs and in the satellite communications systems to be described in the next section.

Data transmission, using radio links, is described in detail by Freeman (1981, Chapters 4 to 6, 10 and 15) and outlined by Zacharov (1981, pages 55–56). Packet radio networks are described in detail by Kahn et al (1978) and more briefly by Shoch and Stewart (1979) and Tanenbaum (1981, Section 6.2). Hindin (1979) considers networks with mobile telephone channels. The proceedings of the *Communications 82 (1982)* Conference has about a dozen papers on radio transmission and radio sytems. The second part of the bibliography by Shoch (1979) lists many relevant literature references.

Although they are more liable to noise and although their transmission is always serial, digital radio channels are very widely used and very successful (Zacharov, 1981, page 56). As powerful techniques for their error control are now commercially available, their reliability can be made acceptable. Digital radio communication has the advantages of very high bandwidth, together with inexpensive, portable terminal equipment, and it can cover long distances. Its chief disadvantage is the shortage of available radio channels and the resulting need for extensive regulations governing their use.

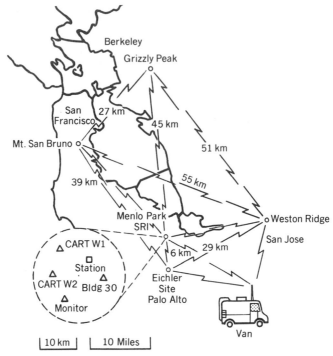

Fig. 8.3. Location of major elements of the packet radio test-bed during 1977   SOURCE: Copyright © 1978 IEEE, *Proceedings of the IEEE* (Nov 1978), 66 (11) p. 1489, Fig. 12

As the messages sent over a packet radio network are broadcast, many receivers can gain access to a radio transmission by single network station.

British Telecom (1980, pages 26–27) describes briefly some research into ways of improving the efficiency of digital data transmission by microwave, at transmission frequencies of 11, 19 and 30 Ghz.

The first computer network to use radio instead of wires for its communications was the ALOHA system at the University of Hawaii (Abramson, 1973; Kahn et al, 1978; Tanenbaum, 1981, Section 6.2.1). This system was set up to allow people at the University of Hawaii, which has seven sites on four islands, to reach the main computer centre at Oahu without using expensive and unreliable telephone lines.

Alohanet is part of the Arpanet system of computer networks. Also belonging to the Arpanet are two packet radio experimental networks, one of which is an experimental testbed network covering much of the San Francisco Bay Area (see Figure 8.3), and the other of which is a local distribution network in the Boston area, used for network station software development. The characteristics and techniques for operating these networks are described by Kahn et al (1978) and Kunzelman (1978).

Teletext, one of the two important forms of videotex, uses broadcasting techniques to transmit its pages of information. Its data signals are transmitted together with the signals for regular TV broadcasts, which can be sent either by high-frequency radio waves or over coaxial cables.

SATELLITE COMMUNICATIONS

Satellite communications, where microwave radio signals are bounced off a *communications satellite*, suspended about 22,500 miles above the equator of the Earth, provide the potential for data communications, using channels with very high capacities, as well as for telecommunications and television broadcasts between all parts of the world. Figure 8.4 is a schematic block diagram of a typical satellite communications system. The basic principles and applications of satellite communications have been described in some detail by Martin (1978) and have been outlined in the recent articles by Burdine (1981), Laurie (1981) and Marsh and Williamson (1981), and also by Freeman (1981, Chapter 7) and Zacharov (1981, pages 70–72). Tanenbaum (1981, Section 6.1) presents some of the technical aspects of satellite data transmission, especially its protocols.

Both Martin and Laurie argue that a single satellite could provide data channels, serving many thousands of users, at prices that they would find reasonable. For example, *Computing* (1982) outlines British Telecom's plans to connect its users to Satellite Business Systems' US network.

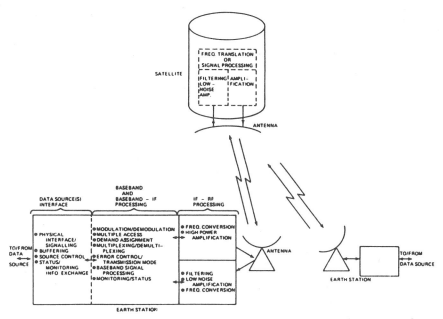

Fig. 8.4. Block diagram model of satellite communications system SOURCE: Copyright © 1978 IEEE, *Proceedings of the IEEE* (Nov 1978), 66 (11) p. 1450, Fig. 1

Clarke (1982) reviews some of the potentialities for using satellites as the basis for new telecommunications systems and services for the developing countries; his ideas are of special interest, as he originated the idea of communications satellites in 1945.

Satellite communications are discussed further in Parts C, E and J of the conference proceedings edited by Cantraine and Destine (1981) and in several papers of the proceedings of the *Communications 82* (1982) Conference.

Research on the use of satellites for digital data transmission has been proceeding for some years, for example in DARPA's Satnet project, that has set up and experimental computer network, using satellite telecommunications, that has provided transatlantic links between stations in the UK, West Germany, and Norway, on the one hand, and the rest of the Arpanet, in the USA, on the other. Jacobs et al (1978) give a detailed description of the satellite networking system used here and of its ongoing experimental programme.

More recently, the UNIVERSE project, was set up, being jointly sponsored and operated by the Science and Engineering Research Council (SERC), British Telecom, University College London, Cambridge University, Loughborough University of Technology, Logica and GEC. Under its "umbrella," important research has been carried out on the combined use of satellite data links and Cambridge Rings to provide an effective linked local area network.

Institution of Electrical Engineers (1981) describes the results of tests and experiments with the European OTS Satellite, which was launched in 1977 and has successfully conducted an extensive programme of satellite experiments, telecommunications tests, and radio propagation experiments.

Burren (1979) describes satellite communications systems in relation to the European Project Stella.

Commercial satellite data links are beginning to get under way too; having been used for some years in the USA, they may now become available in the UK too. For example, British Telecom plans to connect its users to Satellite Business Systems' US network (*Computing*, 1982).

INFORMATION THEORY AND COMMUNICATION THEORY

Information theory, otherwise known as *communication theory*, provides the theoretical concepts and mathematical tools for understanding the storage, transmission and coding of information, together with methods for handling transmission errors and achieving reliable transmission in the presence of noise.

The book by Hamming (1980) gives an excellent introduction to both information theory and coding. Other good books on information theory and its application to communications include those by Abramson (1963), Gallager (1968) and Guiasu (1977). Shorter expositions of some of its applications to data transmission are given by Cole (1981, Chapter 2) and Freeman (1981, Chapter 8), for example. The more technical paper by El Gamal and Cover (1980) gives a unified framework for *multiple user information networks*, where several users communicate with each other in the presence of arbitrary interference and noise.

Starting from the basic concept of *bit*, which is the amount of information contained in a choice between two alternatives, information theory builds up the concepts of *data rate* and *channel capacity*, and shows how to calculate the channel capacity, which is an upper bound to the rate at which information can be sent through the channel.

Information theory also describes how the *signal*, the information that the transmitter wishes to sent to the receiver, is distorted by *noise*, so that the received signal is a random transformation of the transmitted signal. It defines a *signal/noise ratio*, R, that measures how strong the signal is in relation to the noise that is disturbing it. A famous theorem by Shannon, the originator of information theory, states that the channel capacity C, in a noisy channel with frequency bandwidth B Hertz, is given by the equation

$$C = B \log (1 + R) \text{ bits/sec,}$$

where the logarithm is taken to the base two. This equation shows that the channel capacity can be greater than, equal to, or less than the bandwidth, according to the value of the signal/noise ratio.

DATA CODING

Data coding is the representation of pieces of information, that have specific functions or definitions or meanings, as appropriate patterns of bits, characters, or other suitable units of information. This section indicates some of the most important practical applications of data coding, and the next section considers its application to the achievement of reliable data transmission.

Data coding in general is described in several books on information theory and data coding, for example the books by Hamming (1980), McEliece (1977) and Abramson (1963).

One of its most important applications is to the specification of character codes, which are discussed by Davies and Barber (1973, Section 6.5) and CASE (undated, pages 9–18) and more briefly by Cole (1982, Section 4.1). *Character codes* represent individual characters as specific patterns of a given number of bits; *characters* are here defined to include: upper and lower case letters, the digits 0 to 9, punctuations marks, certain special symbols, and *control characters*, that have special functions in data transmission, both to local devices such as displays and printers, and over computer networks The best known character codes are: the American 7-bit ASCII code, the ISO 7-bit code IA5 (International Alphabet No. 5), that is almost identical to ASCII, but is usually encoded as 8 bits, including an extra *parity bit*, introduced for extra error checking, and the 8-bit EBCDIC code used by IBM. Because of this, it is natural to define a *byte* as 8 bits, so that a character is represented by a byte in a data stream, if any of these data codes are used.

CASE (undated) and Davies and Barber (1973) give full details of both IA5 and the EBCDIC codes; specifications of the ASCII code are given in manuals for specific computers and other devices which use it. Some older devices use other codes, which may have as few as 5 bits per character.

Data coding is used to provide various schemes for the modulation of data signals, which was mentioned near the beginning of this chapter. Davidson (1982) gives examples of coding methods that are used for the modulation of data transmitted by LANs, and he compares their performances.

Where network traffic is heavy, but large information files have to be transmitted nevertheless, there is a demand for *data compression*, a set of procedures whereby sequences of meaningful data are especially encoded so that their representation becomes more compact. For example, frequently occurring characters and symbols can be represented by fewer bits than characters and symbols that are used less often, as for example in *Huffman coding*, frequently occurring words can be abbreviated, and words can be systematically shortened according to their letter content. Data compression procedures must be devised so that it is easy to decode the encoded data streams at their destinations!

Data compression is discussed in the book by Davisson and Gray (1976) and more briefly by Tanenbaum (1981, Section 9.2). It was originally applied to text transmission, but has more recently been applied to image transmission, for example in telefacsimile; Jain (1981) reviews several of the available methods of image data compression.

Another application of data coding, that is in fact very ancient and much older than information theory, is the encoding of messages to make them secret during their transmission. *Cryptography* is the art, that now has become a science, of decoding these messages, when they are received by people for whom they are not intended, and also of encoding them so as to provide adequate protection against undesirable decoding. For example, the Data Encryption Standard (National Bureau of Standards, 1977) has already been widely used. The applications of cryptography to data security are discussed briefly in Chapters 16 and 24. Thus it is not further considered in the present chapter, except to mention that it is presented in detail in the book by Konheim (1981) and also by Davies (1979), Davies et al (1979, Chapter 9) and Tanenbaum (Section 9.1).

ERROR DETECTION AND CORRECTION CODES

Another very important application of data coding is the devising of *error detection and correction codes*, that transform a sequence of data so that it becomes much more resistant to the effects of noise, thereby making very reliable data transmission possible in the presence of noise. This can be applied bit-by-bit, so that a sequence of a given number of bits is followed by several, usually fewer, additional bits, so that errors in the sequence can be detected and corrected, as long as there are not too many of them; the additional bits are calculated from the message bits according to specific rules. These codes can also be applied byte-by-byte, for example in HDLC and in X25, Level 2, where two bytes of *CRC (cyclic reduncancy check)* are placed at the end of a data packet to perform this function.

It should be noted that it is *not* safe to assume that transmission errors occur in such a way that they affect different bits in a data stream independently; *bursts* of transmission errors can in fact be rather common. Codes shoud thus be designed to take due account of this factor.

Error detection and correction codes are described in quite a large number of books and papers, most of which are highly mathematical. The following references include information about practical aspects and applications of these codes. Hamming (1980) gives a good introductory treatment, and further details are available in the books by McWilliams and Eliece (1977), Peterson and Weldon (1972) and Wakerly (1978). Shorter treatments are given by Berlekamp (1980), Davies and Barber (1973), Freeman (1981, Chapter 8), Lin and Costello (1981), Slana and Lehman (1981), and Tanenbaum (1981, Section 3.5). Davies et al (1979, Section 6.6) describe the CRC code used in the HDLC and X25 Level 2 data link protocols.

VARIABLE BIT-RATE TRANSMISSION

Variable bit-rate (VBR) transmission allocates the data rate dynamically to a given communications channel, according to its instantaneous needs. This is possible when the channel is one of several channels sharing a transmission medium with high bandwidth.

Hughes and Atkins (1979) introduce the concept of a VBR system, and discuss some of the ways in which it might be activated by evolution from an existing circuit-switched network. Hughes et al (1981) develop these ideas further, specifying especially what telecommunications services can be carried in relation to the system's design parameters. They review various services and derive some general network performance requirements, that are used as a basis for assessing the transmission savings offered by dynamic multiplexing. These savings can be considerable for services that have peak data rates that are several times as high as their average data rates.

VBR transmission and VBR systems should be especially useful for integrated services digital networks, carrying a wide variety of traffic, and the studies by Hughes and his colleagues have been carried out in order to apply them to the design of one such network, British Telecom's System X.

REFERENCES

N. Abramson (1963) *Information Theory and Coding*, McGraw-Hill, New York and London.

N. Abramson (1973) "The Aloha System," pages 501–517 of Ed. N. Abramson and F. F. Kuo, *Computer-Communication Networks*, Prentice-Hall, Englewood Cliffs, NJ.

E. A. Ash et al (June 1976) "Integrated optical circuits for telecommunications," *Nature*, **261**(5559) 377–381.

Ed. M. K. Barnoski (1981a) (2nd. Ed., 1981) *Fundamentals of Optical Fiber Communications*, Academic Press, New York and London.

M. K. Barnoski (1981b) "Design considerations for multiterminal networks," pages 329–351 of Barnowski (1981a).

E. R. Berlekamp (May 1980) "The technology of error correcting codes." *Proceedings of the IEEE*, **68**(5) 564–593.

British Telecom (1980) *Telecom Research Laboratories*, Brochure.

B. H. Burdine (1981) "Satellite communications," pages 34–54 of Ed. T. J. M. Burke and M. Lehman (1981) *Communication Technologies and Information Flow*, Pergamon Press, Oxford, England, and Elmsford, NY.

J. W. Burren (1979) "Satellite communications systems and the European Project Stella," *Interlinking of Computer Networks*, 65–70.

Ed. G. Cantraine and J. Destine (1981) *New Systems and Services in Telecommunications*, N. Holland, Amsterdam.

CASE (undated) *Pocket Book of Computer Communications*, Computer and Systems Engineering plc. Watford, Herts, England.

N. Bar-Chaim, I. Ury and A. Yariv (May 1982) "Integrated optoelectronics," *IEEE Spectrum*, **19**(5) 38–45.

A. C. Clarke (Jun 1982) "New telecommunications for the developing world," *Interdisciplinary Science Reviews*, 7 (2) 102–111.

R. Cole (1982) *Computer Communication*, Macmillan, London and Basingstoke, England.

Communications 82 (Apr 1982) Proceedings of Communications Equipment, Birmingham, 20–22 April 1982, *IEE Conference Publication* No. **209**.

Computing (14 Jan 1982) "BT users to get US satellite network link," 7.

M. Corby, E. J. Donohue and M. Hamer (1982) *Telecommunications User's Handbook*, Telecommunications Press, London.

I. A. Davidson (1982) "An investigation of local area networks," *Communications 82*, 160–163.

D. W. Davies (1979) "Cryptography and Crypto-Systems," *Interlinking of Computer Networks*, 201–237.

D. W. Davies and D. L. A. Barber (1973) *Communication Networks for Computers*, Wiley, Chichester and New York.

D. W. Davies, D. L. A. Barber, W. L. Price and C. M. Solomonides (1979) *Computer Networks and Their Protocols*, Wiley, Chichester and New York.

L. D. Davisson and R. M. Gray (1976) *Data Compression*. Dowden, Hutchinson and Ross.

A. El Gamal and T. M. Cover (Dec 1980) "Multiple user information theory," *Proceedings of the IEEE*, **68** (12) 1466–1483.

Electrical Communication Vol. **56,** No. (1981) Special issue on Optical Fibre Technology.

Ferranti Computer Ssytems Ltd. (1980) *Ferranti Videodata Systems*, Announcement.

R. Freeman (2nd Ed., 1981) *Telecommunication Transmission Handbook*, Wiley, Chichester and New York.

I. T. Frisch (Oct. 1971) "Experiments on random access packet transmission on coaxial cable video transmission systems," *IEEE Transactions on Communications*, **COM-25**(10) 1199–1203.

R. G. Gallager (1968) *Information Theory and Reliable Communication*, Wiley, New York and Chichester.

F. R. Gfeller, H. R. Muller and P. Vettiger (Sep 1978) "Infrared Communication for in-house applications," *COMPCON Fall '78*, 132–138.

S. Giuasu (1977) *Information Theory with Applications*, McGraw-Hill, New York and London.

R. W. Hamming (1980) *Coding and Information Theory*, Prentice-Hall, Englewood Cliffs, NJ.

D. C. Hanson (1981) "Fibre optics in local area network applications," *Advances in Electronics and Electron Physics*, **57**, 145–229.

R. Y. Hertzberg, J. R. Schultz and J. F. Wanner (May 1979) "The Promis network," *Update Local Area Networks*, 87–111.

H. J. Hindin (24 May 1979) "Cellular system expands number of mobile-phone channels," *Electronics* **52** (11) 158–164.

G. T. Hopkins (May 1979) "Multimode communication on the MITRENET," *Update Local Area Networks*, 169–177.

T. Housley (1979) *Data Communications and Teleprocessing Systems*, Prentice-Hall, Englewood Cliffs, NJ.

C. J. Hughes and J. W. Atkins (1979) "Virtual circuit switching for multiservice operation," *International Switching Symbolism, Paris*, Paper 21B3.

C. J. Hughes, E. B. Holloway, D. J. Milham, J. W. Atkins and M. C. Davies (1981) "Service characterization modelling for variable bit-rate switching systems," *International Switching Symposium*, Paper 31.199.

Institution of Electrical Engineers (Apr 1981) *Results of Tests and Experiments with the European OTS Satellite, IEE Conference Publication* No. **199**.

I. M. Jacobs, R. Binder and E. V. Hoversten (Nov 1978) "General purpose satellite networks," *Proceedings of the IEEE*, **66**(11) 1488–1467.

A. K. Jain (Mar 1981) "Image data compression: A review," *Proceedings of the IEEE*, **69** (3) 349–389 (Mar 1981).

R. E. Kahn, S. E. Gronemeyer, J. Burchfiel and R. C. Kunzelman (Nov. 1978) "Advances in packet radio technology," *Proceedings of the IEEE*, **66**(11) 1488–1496.

A. G. Konheim (1981) *Cryptography*, Wiley, New York and Chichester.

R. C. Kunzelman (Jan 1978) "Overview of the ARPA packet radio experimental network," *Compcon Spring '78*, 157–160.

P. Laurie (Feb. 1981) "Satellite Communication," *Practical Computing*, **4**(2) 70–74.

S. Lin and D. J. Costello, Jr. (1981) "Coding for reliable data transmission and storage," Chapter 8 of Ed. F. F. Kuo (1981) *Protocols and Techniques for Data Communication Networks*, Prentice-Hall, Englewood Cliffs, NJ.

Logica (1979) *Selection of Data Communications Equipment*, NCC Publications, Manchester.

R. J. McEliece (1977) *The Theory of Information and Coding*, Addison-Wesley, Reading, MA.

D. R. McGlynn (1978) *Distributed Processing and Communications*, Wiley, New York and Chichester, Chapter 8, "Transmission Systems and Technologies."

J. McWilliams and N. J. A. Sloane (1977) *The Theory of Error Correcting Codes*, North Holland, Amsterdam.

P. Marsh and J. Williamson (23 Jul 1981) "Communications in the 1980s: Satellites and fibre optics," *New Scientist*, 213–218.

J. Martin (1978) *Communications Satellite Systems*, Prentice-Hall, Englewood Cliffs, NJ.

A. J. Mayne (1986) *The Videotex Revolution*, second ed., Wiley, Chichester and New York.

J. E. Midwinter (1979) "Recent work on optical fibre systems and components in the UK," pp. 371–382 of Ostrowsky (1979).

National Bureau of Standards (1977) "Data Encryption Standard," *Federal Information Processing Standards Publication*, **46**, Department of Commerce, Washington, DC.

Ed. D. B. Ostrowsky, *Fiber and Integrated Optics*, Plenum Press, New York.

W. W. Peterson and E. J. Weldon, Jr. (2nd Ed., 1972) *Error Correcting Codes*, MIT Press, Cambridge, MA, USA.

Proceedings of the IEEE, Vol. **68**, No. 10 (Oct 1980), Special Issue on Optical-Fiber Communications.

E. G. Rawson (May 1979) "Applications of fiber optics to local networks," *Update Local Area Networks*, 155–168.

E. G. Rawson and R. M. Metcalfe (Jul 1978) "Fibernet: Multimode optical fibers for local computer networks," *IEEE Transactions on Communications*, **COM-26**(7) 983–990.

P. R. D. Scott (1980) *Modems in Data Communications*, NCC Publications, Manchester.

P. R. D. Scott (1982) *Reviewing Your Data Transmission Network*, NCC Publications, Manchester.

G. Segarra (1981) "BIS—A broadband communications system,"*Local Networks 81*, 185–198.

J. F. Shoch (Oct 1979) "An Annotated Bibliography on Local Computer Networks," *IFIP Working Group 6.4 Working Paper* 79-1 and *Xerox PARC Technical Report* SSL-79-5.

J. F. Shoch and L. Stewart (Nov. 1979) "Internetwork communication via packet radio," *Proceedings of the 6th Data Communications Symposium*, Pacific Grove, CA.

M. F. Slana and H. R. Lehman (May 1981) "Data communication using the telecommunication network," *Computer*, **14**(5) 73–88.

E. K. Smith (Jan 1975) "Pilot two-way CATV systems," *IEEE Transactions on Communications*, **COM-23**(1) 111–120.

A. S. Tanenbaum (1981) *Computer Networks*, Prentice-Hall, Englewood Cliffs, NJ.

J. Wakerly (1978) *Error Detecting Codes, Self-Checking Circuits and Applications,* North Holland, Amsterdam.

J. F. Wanner (Dec. 1978) "Wideband communication system improves response time," *Computer Design*, **17**(12) 85–92.

T. Yamamoto (May 1982) "Information processing by optoelectronics," *IEEE Communications Magazine*, **20**(3) 4–11.

V. Zacharov (1981) "Computer systems and networks: Status and perspective," *Proceedings 1980 CERN School of Computing*, Publ. CERN 81-03, 8–77.

Chapter 9

Network Architectures, Standards and Protocols

This chapter discusses the ways in which networks are organised in order to meet the needs of their users reasonably effectively. It shows how the principles of these methods, the *network architectures*, are applied and implemented by operating rules and procedures, *the network protocols*, that are in many cases drafted according to recommended or agreed *standards*, with the aim of achieving mutual compatibility of different network systems as far as possible.

It starts by outlining some of the functions and requirements of computer networks. This provides the context for developing the principles of network architectures, the most important of these principles being that these different functions and requirements operate at different levels, each of which has a layer of architecture and a corresponding layer of protocol. Some specific examples of architectures are outlined, including the OSI Reference Model, which is probably the most important because it provides the basis for potentially very widely adopted, perhaps potentially universal, network standards; several other architectures, including the Arpanet architecture, IBM's SNA (Systems Network Architecture) and DEC's DNA (Digital Network Architecture) are also briefly mentioned. Reference is then made to the leading international and national bodies, concerned with the formulation of network standards and protocols.

The second part of the chapter is concerned with a representative selection of specific examples of protocols, starting with those at the lowest level and working up to the high level protocols; some of the basic principles of protocol operation are introduced during this exposition. As the lowest levels are concerned with transmission of data across a network and through its physical links, without much reference to the nature or uses of the data passing through, the lower level protocols are very dependent on the types of network with which they operate. Thus some of the different low level protocols, developed for rings, packet radio, bus networks, satellite networks, and wide area as well as local area networks, are considered in turn. At the intermediate level, transport protocols and gateway protocols are described, that are concerned with end-to-end transmission across a network, connection between networks, and transmission across a sequence of neighbouring networks. At the higher levels, terminal protocols, remote job entry protocols, file transfer protocols, and application protocols are presented in turn. Finally, there is a brief discussion of some possibilities for introducing free-form user-oriented protocols.

The number of different network protocols that have been devised must already number many dozen, if not several hundred, and the amount of work that has been done in their development, as well as the volume of literature describing them, is already vast. This chapter can therefore provide no more than a preliminary outline of network architectures, standards and protocols, and readers who wish to use or work with network protocols should then read some of the references listed at the end of this chapter. Even so, it is concerned mainly with what protocols are and what they do. Performance aspects are considered in Chapter 10, and some of the problems and issues that arise are discussed in Chapter 17, while indications of possible future developments are given in Chapter 18.

Chapter 21 presents the most recent developments in network architectures, standards, and protocols, as well as considering some relevant topics not discussed in detail in the present chapter.

Several books provide the useful starting points for further explorations of these subjects. These include: *Computer Networks and Their Protocols* (Davies et al, 1979), *Protocols & Techniques for Data Communications Networks* (Kuo, 1981), *A Practical View of Computer Network Protocols* (McQuillan and Cerf, 1978), *Computer Networks and Distributed Processing* (Martin, 1981a), *Design and Strategy for Distributed Data Processing*(Martin 1981b), *Communication Control in Computer Networks* (Puzman and Porizek, 1980), and *Computer Networks* (Tanenbaum, 1981a). Tanenbaum (1981a) gives an especially extensive description of protocols in different layers, and Martin (1981) also describes them in some detail.

Just published is the very useful book *Computer Network Architectures and Protocols* (Green, 1982), which is largely a revised and updated version of the April 1980 issue, Vol. **COM-28**, No. 4, of IEEE *Transactions on Communications*, a special issue on network architectures and protocols. The paper by Tobagi (1980) in this issue gives a valuable discussion of multiaccess protocols, the need for which arises whenever a scarce network resource is shared by many competing users, and which have been applied to local area networks, packet radio networks and satellite networks, as well as wide-area store-and-forward networks.

Several of the papers in the November 1978 issue, Vol. 66, No. 11, of *Proceedings of the IEEE*, a special issue on packet communication networks, are also very relevant, especially Cerf and Kirstein (1978), who include discussions of network architectures and of the use of protocols for the interconnection of networks, and Pouzin and Zimmermann (1978), who explain and discuss some general concepts of protocols. In addition, Clark et al (1978) provide a general discussion of the principles of low level and high level protocols for LANs, together with the principles of LAN-WAN interconnection, although they make little reference to specific LAN systems, apart from their presentation of one case study.

Vol. 12, No. 9 of *Computer* (Sep 1979) is a special issue on computer network protocols, most of whose papers are cited later in this chapter. Its editorial (Schneider, 1979) presents a hierarchical viewpoint on these protocols.

Short introductions to protocols are given in Chapters 8 and 9 of *Computer Communications* (Cole, 1982), and in the tutorial article by Tanenbaum (1981b), which also relates them to network architectures.

There are several important papers on protocols and architectures for local area networks in the Zurich Conference Proceedings, *Local Area Network Workshop* (1980); some of them are cited later in this chapter.

Thurber and Freeman (1980) and Shoch (1980) provide useful bibliographies of local area networks, which include references to LAN architectures, standards and protocols.

FUNCTIONS AND REQUIREMENTS OF COMPUTER NETWORKS

Some of the functions and requirements of computer networks have been discussed by Green (1980), at the beginning of his tutorial paper on network architectures and protocols, that is intended for readers who are unfamiliar with computer networks.

One of the basic functions of *any* computer network is to provide *access paths*, through which a user at one place can locate another user at another geographical location. For example, the pair of users might be a terminal user and an application program at a remote computer, another user or an application program querying or updating a distant file or data base, users exchanging messages, or programs interacting with each other, and so on. An *access path* is defined as the sequence of functions that allows one user to be physically connected to another, and also to *communicate* with that other user, despite transmission errors of various kinds and despite large differences in choices of speed, traffic pattern, format, etc., that are natural to these users as individuals.

The requirements for access paths, together with some of the ways in which they can be met, include the following:

1. Make sure that there is a path, between a user and the processor-based resources that he is trying to reach, that is a sequence of neighbouring links across at least one network.

2. Ensure that the path transmits bits of information, using modems for this purpose if it passes through any analogue channels.

3. Move individual messages, a function that is carried out by Data Link Control protocols, at the second level.

4. Make it economical to use the access path intermittently, because much if not most data traffic is "bursty," using techniques such as multiplexing, packet switching and fast circuit switching.

5. Send messages to the correct destination node and to the correct process in the device attached to that node, ensuring as far as possible that failed lines or stations en route are bypassed, by means of suitable addressing and routing procedures.

6. Store incoming messages from the network link until they can be serviced, and store outgoing messages until they can be carried by the transmission line.

7. Regulate the flow of outgoing data so that the buffers at receiving stations and intermediate nodes are not overflowed and so that the receiver does not have to wait unnecessarily long for further traffic, by using suitable flow control procedures.

8. Accommodate the timing patterns of the communications required by the conversing users, by means of suitable dialogue management procedures.

9. Accommodate the users' specific requirements and individualities, with respect to data format, character code, device control, access conventions, etc., through suitable protocol conversions.

It will be noticed that these requirements occur at successively higher levels, ranging from those oriented to physical transmission to those relating to specific human needs.

Largely corresponding to these needs, there is a set of network control functions, that activate and deactivate various parts of the access paths, provide some of the control parameters needed to operate them, and manage recovery in event of temporary breakdown. Network control can be more or less centralised, managed by one node or by only a few, or decentralised, shared by many nodes with no nodes dominant. The network control functions, required to form an access path through a network or sequence of networks, occur in layers closely related to the layers of requirements already mentioned. These functions are then implemented by specific network protocols at the appropriate levels.

PRINCIPLES OF NETWORK ARCHITECTURE USING LAYERS AND LEVELS OF PROTOCOLS

The *architecture* of a computer network precisely defines the functions that the network and its components should perform, together with the ways in which the network should be organised. The chief purpose of the architecture is to ensure that the design and user requirements of the network are met as far as possible, by arranging that the different parts of the network cooperate effectively and by enabling the network system as a whole to evolve according to its aims.

The discussion of the requirements and functions of networks, in the previous section, has shown that computer networks are almost always organised as a hierarchy of layers, with each layer performing a small set of closely related functions. Network architecture is thus defined in terms of the relations between the different parts of the network, at all layers of the network. These relations include both the *protocols*, which are the operating rules and procedures for conducting communications between different network users and devices, and which are defined for each of the different levels of the network, and the *interfaces*, which are the boundaries between adjacent layers of the network. The layers, interfaces and protocols in a network constitute its architecture.

These concepts can be illustrated by looking at the ISO Reference Model for Open Systems Interconnection, whose general layer structure is shown in the two parts of Figure 9.1. This pair of diagrams shows the seven layers of the ISO Model; starting from the bottom level and going up, they are as follows:

1. Physical Layer;
2. Data Link Layer;
3. Network Layer;
4. Transport Layer;
5. Session Layer;
6. Presentation Layer;
7. Application Layer.

Each layer can be viewed as a program or process, perhaps contained in a hardware device, that communicates with the corresponding process in another device. Figure 9.1 shows the relationships between the layers during communication between two host computers, through a path that includes an intermediate node, switch or *IMP (interface message processor)*. Here, the lower host layers of a host, at levels 1 to 3, think that they are communicating with the corresponding layers of the IMP, called *peers*. In contrast, the higher layers in a host, at levels 4 to 7, communicate directly with their peers in the other host.

As Figure 9.1 shows, data are in fact communicated from device to device, not horizontally at a given level, but vertically down through the layers of the transmitting machine and up through the layers of the receiving machine. There is *physical communication* at the lowest layer, Level 1, and inside the host and node de-

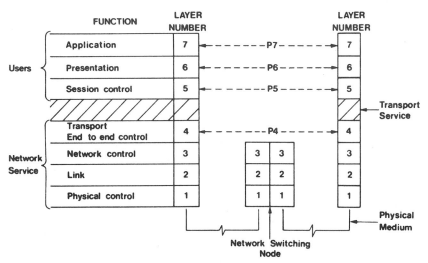

Fig. 9.1. The Open Systems Interconnection Model   SOURCE: V. Zacharov "Computer systems and networks: Status and perspectives." *Procedings 1980 CERN School of Computing.* Pub. CERN 81-03 (1981), pp. 8–77. Reprinted with permission

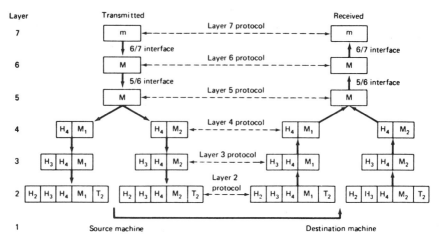

Fig. 9.2. Actual information flow supporting virtual communication in Layer 7   SOURCE: Andrew S. Tanebaum, COMPUTER NETWORKS, © 1981, p. 13. Reprinted by permission of Prentice-Hall, Englewood Cliffs, NJ

vices themselves, as opposed to the *virtual communication* used by the higher levels. During transmission, a given layer transforms the data, sent to it by the layer above, and adds to that date a *header* containing control information used by the protocol at its level, before passing the resulting message down to the layer below. Conversely, at the receiving device, the message moves up, with headers being stripped off as it proceeds. None of the headers for the layers below reaches a given layer.

Figure 9.2 gives an example of the actual information flow, supporting virtual communication at Level 7, together with the structures of the packets used at different levels. It shows how a message M, conceived as a unit by the top levels, is split into packets by the transport service, with headers H4, H3, H2, being added successively by layers 4, 3 and 2, and a tail T2 also being added by layer 2 for checking purposes. What is actually sent down the transmission line, physically, is a stream of data signals, representing the bytes or bits in the sequence of Level 2 packets that in turn represents the level 7 message M.

A given layer "knows nothing about" the header formats of protocols used by other layers, and has the task of transferring the data, reaching it from the layer above, to the receiving device. Thus each layer performs a well-defined set of functions, using only a specified set of services provided by the lower layers.

A major advantage of the use of layers in this way is that peer devices in any layer can change their protocol without affecting the other layers. For example, changes in a part of the network design, operating at a given level, do not require changes in those parts of the design concerned with other levels. This converts the design of the network as a whole from an unmanageable problem into several smaller, feasible problems, the design of the individual network layers.

Pouzin and Zimmermann (1978) describe briefly the basic structuring techniques used by most computer networks and distributed computing system architectures:

1. *Multiplexing*

In most cases, resources in networks and distributed systems must be shared between different activities; for example, in a packet-switched network, lines, nodes and node memories are shared between all users, and statistical multiplexing mechanisms dynamically allocate resources to activities when they need them.

2. *Switching*

Although most of the interactions are between pairs of entities, provision needs to be made for the action of an entity to be directed to a more general subset of the network entities, for example "all entities," as in *broadcast* switching, and "all entities with given characteristics," as in *associative* switching.

3. *Wrapping*

This concept has already been introduced when discussing the headers added to packets by successive layers of protocol. Figure 9.2 gives a clear illustration of what happens for an important specific example.

4. *Cascading*

Cascading forms a linear string of entities, each one interacting only with its neighbours; for example, in a packet-switched network, a cascade is found in the path between two devices, passing through a sequence of nodes, with all protocols between neighbours being identical except where network boundaries are crossed, at gateways.

5. *Assembly*

Protocols between entities are often related to the types of configuration in which they are geometrically placed. For example, there will be some differences in lower level protocols for star networks, ring networks, bus networks, and WANs (which typically have mesh configurations).

Note that an architectural model, such as the OSI Reference Model, suggests places where protocols, including standard protocols, could usefully be developed, for specific well-defined functions, but that it is not concerned with designing or formulating these protocols or their communication principles.

EXAMPLES OF NETWORK ARCHITECTURES

The best known model of network architecture is the *ISO Reference Model for Open Systems Interconnection (OSI Reference Model* or *ISO Reference Model* or *ISO Model* for short). This model was developed by the International Organization for Standardization (ISO) with the intention of providing a framework for the development of standard protocols performing various functions at all the levels of operation of computer networks. Other important examples of network architectures include *SNA (Systems Network Architecture)*, developed by IBM, *DNA (Digital Network Architecture)*, developed by DEC, and the architecture used by Arpanet. These are all architectures primarily designed for wide area networks; although large parts of them can also be used in local area networks, these networks need to specify additional protocols at the lower levels, as also do wide area networks using special transmission techniques such as packet radio and satellite communications.

The *OSI Reference Model* has been formulated in a paper in *Computer Networks* (ISO/TC97/SC16, 1981), prepared by a working party of the ISO, which introduces the general concepts of the model and of the layered architecture that it uses, and gives detailed descriptions of the seven layers of the model, as named in the previous section. Des Jardins (1981) gives a general overview of the model and its status, while Zimmermann (1980) outlines its history, and presents its principles, together with some indications of the initial set of protocols likely to be developed from it. Burkhardt and Schindler (1981) show that the OSI architecture has a very strong inner consistency, and explains the structuring principles by which it was derived. Schindler (1981) presents some personal views on OSI by an expert who was closely involved in its development; he deals with several of the central questions about open systems, how they arise, and how they might develop in the future.

Figure 9.3 shows the relations between the OSI, Arpanet, SNA and DNA architectures; it will be noticed that there are appreciable differences between their detailed subdivision of network functions into layers, although there is a broad similarity between them. Tanenbaum (1981b) gives brief descriptions of all four of these architectures. SNA is described further by Gray (1981) and McGlynn (1978), who gives fairly general expositions, and by Atkins (1980) and Hoberecht (1980), who consider specific aspects. DNA is described further by Wecker (1980).

Cerf and Kirstein (1978) discuss briefly several of the network architectures, including those of Arpanet, Tymnet, several of the PPTs, and, as an example of LAN architecture, Ethernet, which is also discussed by Boggs et al (1980). These are illustrated by Figures 9.4 to 9.7 respectively.

Layer	ISO	ARPANET	SNA	DECNET
7	Application	User	End user	Application
6	Presentation	Telnet, FTP	NAU services	Application
5	Session	(None)	Data flow control	(None)
4	Transport	Host-host	Transmission control	Network services
3	Network	Source to destination IMP	Path control	Transport
2	Data link	IMP-IMP	Data link control	Data link control
1	Physical	Physical	Physical	Physical

Fig. 9.3. Approximate correspondences between the various networks   SOURCE: Andrew S. Tanenbaum, COMPUTER NETWORKS, © 1981, p. 22. Reprinted by permission of Prentice-Hall, Inc., Englewood Cliffs, NJ

Application	RJE	Electronic mail	
Utility	Telnet	FTP	
End/end subscriber	NCP	TCP	NVP/NVCP
Network access	Permanent virtual circuit		Datagram
Intranet, end/end	Flow control, Sequencing Message reassembly		/////////
Intranet, node/node	Adaptive routing, Store and forward, Congestion control		
Link control	Non sequenced, multichannel error control		

Fig. 9.4. ARPANET protocol layering   SOURCE: Copyright © 1978 IEEE *Proceedings of the IEEE* (Nov 1978), 66 (11) p. 1391, Fig. 3

End/end subscriber	Terminal to host
Network access	Virtual circuit
Intranet end/end	/////////////////////
Intranet node/node	Frame disassembly, reassembly Routing, store/forward, congestion control
Link control	Frame-based error control retransmission, sequencing

Fig. 9.5. TYMNET protocol layering   SOURCE: Copyright © 1978 IEEE *Proceedings of the IEEE* (Nov 1978), 66 (11) p. 1391, Fig. 4

Utility	Terminal handling X.28, X.29
End/end subscriber	/////////////////////
Network access	X.25, permanent or temporary virtual circuits
Intranet end/end	Multiple virtual circuits, flow control
Intraned node/node	Routing, store/forward, Congestion control
Link control	HDLC or equivalent

Fig. 9.6. PTT protocol layering   SOURCE: Copyright © 1978 IEEE *Proceedings of the IEEE* (Nov 1978), 66 (11) p. 1392, Fig. 5

PROTOCOL LAYER	FUNCTIONS
6. APPLICATION	FUNDS TRANSFER, INFORMATION RETRIEVAL, ELECTRONIC MAIL, TEXT EDITING . . .
5. UTILITY	FILE TRANSFER, VIRTUAL TERMINAL SUPPORT
4. END/END SUBSCRIBER	INTERPROCESS COMMUNICATION (E.G. VIRTUAL CIRCUIT, DATAGRAM, REAL-TIME, BROADCAST)
3. NETWORK ACCESS	NETWORK ACCESS SERVICES (E.G. VIRTUAL CIRCUIT, DATAGRAM . . .)
2. INTRANET, END-TO-END	FLOW CONTROL, SEQUENCING
1. INTRANET, NODE-TO-NODE	CONGESTION CONTROL, ROUTING
0. LINK CONTROL	ERROR HANDLING, LINK FLOW CONTROL

APPLICATION	- - - - - - - - - - - - -		
UTILITY	FILE TRANSFER	VIRTUAL TERMINAL	DIRECTORY LOOK-UP, FILE ACESS
END-TO-END SUBSCRIBER	STREAM PROTOCOL		
	RELIABLE PACKET PROTOCOL		
NETWORK ACCESS	BROADCAST DATAGRAM (UNRELIABLE)		
▨			
▨			
LINK CONTROL			

Fig. 9.7. ETHERNET protocol layering   SOURCE: Copyright © 1978 IEEE *Proceedings of the IEEE* (Nov 1978), 66 (11) p. 1390, Fig. 2

Andrews (1980) reviews the sessions at the ICCC '78 Conference that were devoted to computer network architectures and operating experience of computer networks; he compares the basic concepts of several of the major architectures. He reports on circuit-switched and message-switched as packet-switched networks. Wecker (1979) has provided a general survey of network architectures.

Toda (1980) explains his philosophy for modelling higher level communications functions into a network architecture that he names *DCNA (Data Communication Network Architecture)*. He describes its logical structure, and proposes using it as a basis for defining higher level protocols, such as those for network management, message transfer, virtual terminal protocols and virtual file system protocols.

Schindler and Flasche (1981) discuss the essentials of the Presentation Layer of the OSI Model and the presentation service, that allows to work stations to communicate with each other, in a way that is independent of the particular equipment that they use. They explain the main alternative proposals and protocols for this service, that are now being considered by standardisation experts, and they point out the potential importance of its application to the integration of office automation.

Manufacturers' architectures, such as SNA and DNA, can be viewed as long-term plans, *independent* of any particular hardware and software products (Martin, 1981b, page 415).They are designed to support the widest reasonable range of the manufacturers' products, and are not necessarily compatible with the products of other manufacturers, apart from common carrier equipment, which they have to use. As many of the devices, that have to link with a network architecture, are mutually incompatible, using different codes, formats and application programs, there is a need for conversion procedures, and there is also a need for intercommunicating users and devices, to agree, before the start of their session, what resources, conversions and protocols they will need, to allow that session to work.

There are basically two approaches to networking and distributed computing. The first of these, typical of the earlier forms of networking, is for the computers and other devices in the system to use conventional software and straightforward data communication. Here, each message has a format, agreed between the communicating parties, with a header that indicates the message type and provides simple control information. Each application program, used as part of the network facilities, must keep to these specifications.

The second approach uses an architecture that hides the effect of distance, data format and incompatibility from the application programs. These programs, together with the user languages of the system, give commands that are formulated *as if* the system were not distributed. Here, the software does all the necessary conversions, data access and networking.

It is also possible to have networks and distributed systems that use a combination of these two approaches.

Several architectures have been developed specifically for LANs. Fishburn (1982) and DEC et al (1980) describe the protocols and architecture used with the original Xerox Ethernet system. Hunt and Ravasio (1980) discuss the Olivetti LAN system protocol architecture, which is based on the ISO Reference Model but has no Network Layer. Jacobsen (1981) considers LAN gateway and cluster controller architectures based on the ISO Model. Stack (1981) examines architectures for providing LAN interconnections with IBM mainframes.

NETWORKS STANDARDS BODIES

Standards for computing systems in general and computer networks in particular are becoming increasingly important. Inadequate standards and lack of standards in certain areas threatens the successful implementation of many business communications systems, especially those using office automation. Computer communications standards are needed to achieve a reasonable degree of integration between office systems, but none of their manufacturers seems able to provide a comprehensive enough approach to ensure full compatibility with other suppliers' equipment (Donnington, 1982).

Various international and national standards bodies are attempting to resolve these difficulties by providing appropriate standards for network architectures and protocols. These include the ISO (International Standards Organisation), CCITT (International Consultative Committee for Telegraphy and Telephony), ECMA (European Computer Manufacturers Association), internationally, and the BSI

(British Standards Institute), ANSI (American National Standards Institute), NBS (National Bureau of Standards), AFNOR (Association Francaise de Normalisation) and DIN (Deutsches Institut für Normung), nationally.

The CCITT has been especially successful in laying the foundations for public telephone and telex services and for basic data transmission services (CCITT Green Book, 1973), but further standards are needed for high level computer communications. It has already produced some important standards, including V.24, almost identical to the American RS232 and RS232C standards, which specifies the physical connections by most asynchronous terminals, and the X series of protocols. This has enabled the PTTs and common carriers to proceed with the establishment of both national and international data communication services to meet user demands. Kelly (1978) discusses some of the earlier CCITT work on standards.

The X protocols include: X.21, a Physical Layer protocol, which specifies the physical, electrical and prodecural interface between a computer and a node; X.25, the collective name for the protocols covering the lowest layers 1 to 3; the "XXX" set of protocols X.3, X.28 and X.29, involved in connecting ordinary terminals to packet-switched networks; X.75, which is used for inter-networking; X.121, which provides a numbering system for public computer networks, that is similar to the numbering system used by the PSTN. The X protocols are described, for example, in the X.25 Draft Recommendation (CCITT, 1980a), the CCITT Grey Book (1978, 1979) and the CCITT Orange Book (1977). Also of importance are the Draft Recommendations on the proposed new international Teletex service (CCITT, 1980b), which include a protocol in the Transport Layer.

On the other hand, the ISO has examined the "high level problem," and set up its ISO/TC97/SC16 Subcommittee for OSI (Open Systems Interconnection) in 1977, in view of the urgency of finding standards for linking heterogeneous computer networks (Zimmermann, 1980). "OSI" itself refers to standards for exchange of information between users, terminals, computers, other devices, networks and processes, that are "open" to each other for this purpose, through mutual use of the applicable standards (des Jardins, 1981). It implies mutual recognition and support of these standards, and *not* any particular systems implementation, technology, or means of interconnection.

Its first priority was to develop an architecture for OSI, which could serve as a standard to define standard protocols. As a result of its studies and discussions, it adopted its seven-layer Reference Model for OSI, already mentioned, whose text it published (ISO/TC97/SC16, 1981). It passed this on in July 1978 to its parent body ISO/TC97, along with recommendations to start officially, on this basis, a set of protocols standardisation projects to cover the most urgent needs. ISO/TC97 itself adopted these recommendations at the end of 1979, as the basis for later development of standards using OSI within ISO. CCITT's Group on "Layered Method for Public Data Network Services" also recommended use of the ISO Reference Model.

Standards bodies involved in OSI include ECMA, ANSI, BSI, AFNOR and DIN, as well as ISO and CCITT (des Jardins, 1981). ISO's seven-layer Reference Model is now generally accepted by these bodies and quite a number of other national standards bodies. CCITT Study Group VII, on "Public Data Networks," is developing a very similar model, to guide the development of applications and services, such as Teletex, telefax and videotex. It is to be hoped that ISO and CCITT will be able to cooperate continually to ensure a high degree of compatibility between the two.

Unfortunately, the ISO Model is liable to quite extensive differences of interpretation by implementers, so that full compatibility between commercially available systems is unlikely to be provided for some years (Donnington, 1982).

In the USA, the ICST (Institute for Computer Sciences and Technology) at the NBS has set up the Federal computer Network Protocol Standards Program (NBS, undated), which aims to make distributed computer networks possible, and to allow the interconnection of different devices, selected for favourable cost, performance and availability. The standards to be developed first will be those needed for general support of network users rather than for support of individual computing functions like graphics. They are intended to satisfy US Government requirements, while being as close as possible to other existing or planned protocols.

A series of protocols is being developed, within the overall framework of the ISO Model, for scheduled completion by the mid-1980s. This series includes protocols for: transport, session control, data transfer, terminal operation and connection, remote job entry, network interconnection, network interprocess communication, and distributed data processing. A command language is being developed, providing a set of commands for a user interface to the data transfer protocol. NBS has already produced several documents, not individually referenced here, providing further details of the work already done under this programme.

Also based in the USA, the IEEE Project 802 has been working actively on the development of a Local Network Standard. Clancy (1981) gives the earlier history of this project, reports on its status at the beginning of 1981, discusses its goals, and gives some details of the proposed structure of its standard. Sze (1982) reports on the status of the project about a year later. Its three Subcommittees cover High-Level Interface, Data Link and Media Access (DLMAC) and Physical; the latter two have subgroups dealing with more specific topics.

At the application level, the IEEE LAN standard is designed to support: file transfer, word processing, electronic mail, data base access, graphics, and digital voice within a LAN. It is also intended to support: file transfer, word processing, electronic mail, data base mass storage devices, printers, plotters, telephotocopiers, monitors and control equipment. Finally, it must support bridges and gateways to other LANs and to WANs. In order to do this, it was agreed that its architecture must conform to the ISO Model. It is designed to handle aggregate LAN data rates of 1, 5, 10, 15 and 20 Mbits/sec, and to allow the attachment of at least 200 devices to a LAN.

Project 802 began its standardisation efforts in the two bottom protocol layers, Physical and Data Link; it intends that its standard here should converge with the HDLC Data Link standard for WANs as far as possible, and be independent of network configuration, transmission rate and medium. It has divided the Data Link Layer into the Logical Link Control Sublayer, responsible for the usual link control and logical connection, and, below it, the Media Access Sublayer, concerned with a station's insertion of information into a link. Due to the existence of several important types of LANs, mostly with ring and bus topologies, Project 802 has recommended three allowed variants of its standard, to cater for these types, with one variant corresponding to Ethernet and similar bus networks.

Eldon (1981) proposes adding the IEEE Project 802 Standard to X.25, using this combination to provide a homogeneous gateway solution to the problem of linking and interfacing LANs with WANs. He has submitted his proposal for study by CCITT, ISO, ANSI and IEEE.

Heard (1981) reviews LAN standardisation activities in Europe, and points out that European awareness to the importance of LAN development and specification is growing fast. Users and suppliers both recognise the potential benefits of agreed standards for interconnection and interworking of systems via high performance communications networks. The European PTTs are anxious to improve the quality of LANs and to see how far WAN standards, especially X.25 and related protocols developed under the auspices of CCITT, can be adapted and applied to LANs.

CEC (Commission of the European Communities) has expressed a growing interest in LAN capabilities, watching technical and product developments with great interest, and encouraging various suppliers to propose the specification and implementation of LAN standards. It has sponsored various projects and subgroups, including a LAN sub-group, which are more directly concerned with increasing the level of awareness about systems based on LANs.

ECMA has formed a subgroup, within its TC24 Technical Committee, to examine the field of applications, architectures and standards, required for the most effective use of LANs. Its interest has been closely aligned with that of IEEE Project 802, described above, and it has given priority to specifying a standard for a bus network, using the CSMA/CD transmission technique. It aims to provide a basic framework for compatible linking devices to LANs. It has produced draft standards for: architecture and interconnection for four lowest LAN layers, a CSMA/CD data link protocol, a CSMA/CD Physical Layer protocol, and a CSMA/CD coaxial cable. It has proposed using applying transport service and protocol mechanisms directly above the link layer, with only a formal trace of the ISO Network Layer, to maintain conformity of architectures. It has also drafted a Transport Layer specification.

In the UK, direct coordination of LAN activities has started only relatively recently. In April 1981, the British Government established its FOCUS Committee on Information Technology Standards, serviced by the Department of Industry. FOCUS has set up and funded a LAN project team, composed of seconded experts, to examine fundamental LAN issues, including standardisation, and recommend further action. In addition, the British universities have brought together many interested parties, including both users and suppliers, to agree on interfaces and protocol specifications for the Cambridge Ring, which they are already using quite extensively. Several of these ring protocol specifications are nearly complete. In the absence of any other suitable forum, the universities' group, in collaboration with the Department of Industry and the FOCUS LAN team, has prepared a detailed programme for defining the required specifications. This group has discussed networks due to appear in the mid-1980s and formulated some interim specifications. Every effort will be made to achieve compatibility with the IEEE Project 802 Standard, now being developed, and other widely accepted LAN standards.

RING NETWORK PROTOCOLS

Tanenbaum (1981a, Section 7.2) and Tropper (1981) give useful introductions to some of the methods of passing data packets round a ring. Traffic in ring networks generally flows in one direction only, although bidirectional systems have been proposed. Thus each ring station receives messages from one of its neighbours and sends messages to its other neighbour. Messages circulate round the ring from their origin to their destination. According to the specific ring system used, messages may have fixed or variable length, and one or more messages may be allowed on the ring at a time.

Four basic types of ring, each with their corresponding access protocols, have been developed: token rings, contention rings, slotted rings, and register insertion rings.

The oldest, and still most popular, type of ring net is the *token ring*, where a special bit pattern, the *token*, circulates round the ring whenever all stations are idle. When a station wants to send a packet, it has to seize the token and remove it, before it can transmit. After it has finished transmitting its packet, it must regenerate the token. A ring interfaces can operate either in *listen mode*, during which it observes the traffic on the ring, and in *transmit mode*, during which it sends a packet.

The *contention ring* uses a token, but only when traffic is present. If there is no traffic, a station wishing to transmit just sends a packet, and then places a token in the ring, but it removes the token when the packet comes round again. If a station observes traffic on the ring, when it wishes to transmit, it waits for the token, seizes it, and then sends its own packet. Under high loads, no station will transmit unless it has seized the token, and the contention ring then acts like a token ring. When two stations decide to transmit simultaneously on an idle ring, a collision occurs and a special procedure is adopted.

In the *slotted ring*, fixed-length slots circulate round the ring, carrying an indication to the station of whether the next frame is occupied. For example, in the Cambridge Ring, the slot is a 37-bit packet, with one bit for start of packet, one bit giving an empty or full indication, one bit for use by the monitor station, one eight-bit byte for packet source number, one byte for packet destination number, two bytes of data, and finally a control bit and a status bit. When a station wishes to transmit, it waits for an empty slot, marks it as full, and places its data in the slot.

The *register insertion ring* is a more complicated variant of the slotted ring and has a special technique for preventing a station from monopolising the ring. A station's interface has a shift register, as well as an output buffer. Incoming packets pass through the shift register, being removed if addressed to the station, otherwise forwarded. The station's own packet is released into the ring when the status of its shift register indicates that it is possible to transmit.

Besides the basic protocols just described for the different types of ring, ring systems need additional protocols at various levels. At the lower levels, these are specific to the ring system; at higher levels and for interworking with WANs, application of the appropriate standard protocols, such as those developed within the framework of the ISO Model, is usually attempted.

As an illustrative example, consider the protocols used at various installations of the Cambridge Ring at British universities (Rubinstein et al, 1981; Dallas, 1981; Spratt, 1980 and 1981). At the lowest level, Cambridge University developed a Basic Block Protocol (BBP) for use on its ring; at a higher level, corresponding roughly to the Network Layer or Transport Layer, this was supplemented by a Byte Stream Protocol (BSP) above BBP. Although BBP and BSP have been found to work well on the whole, other universities have been experimenting with variants of these protocols and possible alternative protocols. University College London has implemented ring protocols that are designed to cater efficiently for both block and single character ring traffic. The University of Kent at Canterbury uses BBP and BSP, together with SSP (Single Shot Protocol) and TSBSP (a Transport Service BSP, which is similar to BSP), for its ring. It has also opted for use of the Network Independent Transport Service, developed by Study Group 3 of the PSS User Forum and now being implemented on ring X.25 connections to PSS, rather than applying X.25 and XXX protocols directly to the ring.

Andler et al (1980) propose architecture for a microprocessor-based communications device that performs functions, such as addressing and message fragmentation, that are usually located in communications systems software. The LAN with which this device is to be used is a token ring.

PACKET RADIO PROTOCOLS

Although packet radio networks are not LANs in the usual sense, their protocols are briefly considered in this part of the chapter, as one of them, the well-known ALOHA protocol, originally used in the Alohanet, the packet radio network linking the Hawaiian islands, has been used as the basis for the basic operation of the Ethernets and other bus networks.

The ALOHA protocol is an example of a "random access" technique, for use in broadcast networks; it is described briefly by Abramson (1973), Kleinrock and Tobagi (1975), Tanenbaum (1981a, Section 6.1) and Tropper (1981, pages 75–87) and in more detail by Abramson (1970). Roberts (1972) produced a variant of it, the slotted ALOHA protocol, that doubled the channel capacity of an ALOHA packet radio network.

Random access protocols are characterised by having no strict ordering of the nodes contending for access to the communications channel. Here, a station is free to broadcast its messages at times of its own choice, without being certain that no other station is trying to transmit at the same time. Because the network is broadcast, a station obtains the whole bandwidth of the network channel, once it gains access to that channel.

The price to be paid for this random access is that messages may be sent at the same time and thus collide, with the result that they are unusable. In the ALOHA protocol, stations that have just attempted to send messages, but have lost them in a collision, know that they have lost them, because the network is broadcast and they are able to listen to what happens. They then try to send them again after random time intervals, thus giving them a chance of being sent successfully next time.

The slotted ALOHA protocol uses similar principles, but also divides time up into discrete intervals, each corresponding to the time taken to transmit one packet. The beginning of a packet transmission can only occur at the start of one of these time slots.

Packet radio network protocols are discussed further by Kahn et al (1978) and Tobagi (1980), who also provide extensive references to further relevant literature.

BUS NETWORK PROTOCOLS

Luczak (1978) provides an extensive description of protocols and techniques for accessing the channels of bus networks,and divides them into three major categories: selection, random access (contention), and reservation, which are also described briefly by Tropper (1981, pages 74–80).

Selection techniques are the oldest access protocols, and arose in the control of access to multipoint communications lines and computer buses. Their basic principle is that each node must receive permission, before it can send its messages through the network. For *centralised selection,* a central channel controller grants this permission, while, for *distributed selection,* this control is distributed between the nodes.

Random access techniques have already been introduced, in the previous section, and were first used in packet radio networks. Their use in bus networks has been very widely adopted, chiefly because of the bursty nature of computer traffic. There, one of the most important types of random access techniques is *CSMA (carrier sense multiple access),* where the sending node listens to the channel before and perhaps during message transmission, and can sense whether other traffic is present (Tanenbaum, 1971a, Section 7.1; Kleinrock and Tobagi, 1975). If other traffic is sensed, transmission is delayed; otherwise, it proceeds, but there is a risk of packet collision, which occurs when two stations decide to send at the same time. The procedures for re-transmission after collision are similar to those used by the ALOHA protocols. There are several varieties of CSMA protocol; for example, Ethernets uses "1-persistent unslotted CSMA with interference collision detection."

In *reservation* techniques, a node transmits a message or packet during a time slot that has been reserved for its use. Reservation techniques may be *static,* for example *TDMA (time-division multiple access),* where each node is assigned a fixed number of slots per *frame* (repeated sequence of slots), and *dynamic,* where slots are assigned to nodes on a demand basis.

Tobagi and Ra (1980) discuss unidirectional and bidirectional broadcast system architectures for cable networks. Among other topics, they consider multiaccess protocols, also considered by Tobagi (1980), priority functions in distributed multiaccess systems, and a new efficient round-robin scheduling scheme, interrogating each station in turn.

Spaniol (1979) presents a new access protocol for LANs, which would include automatic reservations for packets whose first attempts at transmission have been unsuccessful due to collisions. Mok and Ward (1979) present a general approach to sharing a broadcast channel among multiple nodes and propose a protocol that combines the advantages of Ethernet, with its short message delays, and rings, with their high throughput.

As an illustrative example, the architecture and protocols for Ethernet are considered briefly. Metcalfe and Boggs (1976) give a general description of Ethernet, and explain its random access procedure. A notable feature of the retransmission procedure is that the average interval between retransmission attempts after collisions *increases* as the level of the traffic rises; this ensures that the network is not flooded with retries and collisions under heavy traffic conditions. Each Ethernet packet has a synchronisation bit, a destination address (8 bits), a source address (8 bits), up to 4000 bits of data, and finally 16 bits of checksum for data checking. DEC et al (1980) give a full specification of the Ethernet architecture and the earlier Ethernet protocols, and Boggs et al (1980) present PUP, the Ethernet inter-network architecture. Fishburn (1982) describes the protocols currently implemented by Ethernet, explains why they are necessary, and discusses the possibilities that they open up for users of automated office systems.

Quint et al (1981) describe the higher level protocols used by the Ethernet-like LAN at the IMAG Laboratories in France; basic network services provided there include: transport service, file transfer, remote printing, access to servers, mail service. These protocols provide a homogeneous set of tools for developing distributed software, and especially office systems applications.

Sommer (1981) describes an implementation of a transport protocol on SWAN (Single Wire Advanced Network), another Ethernet-like network.

Mark (1981) describes the protocols used by WELNET, a LAN using a 2 Mbits/sec data bus, acting as a broadcast channel. It has a three-level hierarchical protocol set, covering physical, data link and network levels.

SATELLITE NETWORK PROTOCOLS

Protocols for packet satellite networks are described in some detail by Binder (1981) and more briefly by Jacobs et al (1978), Tanenbaum (1981a, Chapter 6), and Tobagi (1978).

Satellite transmission uses broadcasting and also has the characteristic, unlike that of other networks, that there are very long round trip delays, slightly more than a quarter of a second, for packets passing between stations via the satellite. The reason for this is that communications satellites are placed in orbits about 22,500 miles above the Earth's surface. Bit error rates also tend to be higher than usual. For all these reasons, protocols for satellite networks are rather different from protocols for other kinds of network, and specially severe problems are liable to arise when interworking with other wise area networks.

For most satellite protocols, each station is synchronised, so that its transmissions may reach the satellite at times agreed by all stations. Nuspl et al (1977) survey the many techniques for achieving this global timing; at least for channel data rates below a few Mbits/sec, it is relatively simple and cheap to implement.

In the *fixed assignment TDMA* protocol, channel time is assigned to each station according to its expected traffic requirements. In its simplest form, time is divided into a succession of *frames* of equal length, and each frame is divided into *slots,* with one slot for each station. More complicated slot assignments and frame structues can be used if required, to cater for special patterns of traffic demand.

As for packet radio and bus networks, random access protocols have also been used widely in satellite networks. As the ALOHA and slotted ALOHA protocols were found to be inadequate, more refined random access protocols were developed, introducing principles such as reservation and priorities of demand.

The reservation-ALOHA protocol combines the fixed-assignment frame concept with a slotted ALOHA channel. For example, it can guarantee successive time slots to a station with a long queue of messages until the queue is cleared. *Roberts' reservation system,* like reservation-ALOHA, was designed to keep processing bandwidth requirements small and use the satellite channel relatively efficiently (Roberts, 1973). At any given time, the channel is either in a reservation state, during which reservations are being serviced, or in an ALOHA state, during which packets requesting reservation are sent. *R-TDMA (Reservation-TDMA)* uses fixed assignments to make reservations.

PODA (Priority-Oriented Demand Assignment) is a demand assignment protocol designed to satisfy efficiently the needs of a general-purpose network; it supports both block data (datagram) traffic and packet voice (stream) traffic, multiple delay classes, several message priorities, and variable message lengths. It integrates circuit-switched and packet-switched demand assignment techniques, and uses reservation schemes and both distributed and central control. For stream traffic, one reservation is used to set up the data stream, and packets are sent at regular intervals after that for the duration of the stream. The *FPODA* variant of the protocol is used when the total number of stations is small, and makes reservations by fixed assignments of one slot per station, as in R-TDMA. The *CPODA* variant is used for large numbers of stations, mixed stations, or situations with uncertain traffic needs, and makes reservations by random contention access, as in Roberts' protocol.

Several different protocols need to be considered for satellite telecommunications, due to the wide differences in network parameters, such as number of earth stations and traffic concentrations at stations, that are liable to occur. If traffic is high and steady at most or all stations, fixed capacity assignments tend to give the best performance. For bursty or variable station traffic, a demand assignment protocol significantly improves efficience and reduces delays. Except when very small messages are sent by many very bursty stations, an explicit reservation protocol is much better than random access reservation. In several respects, a protocol like PODA should be suitable for a wide range of traffic patterns and station configurations.

X.25 AND OTHER LOW LEVEL PROTOCOLS FOR WIDE AREA NETWORKS

As a very large amount of work has been done on low level protocols for WANs, covering layers 1 to 3 of the ISO Reference Model, this section provides only the barest outline of these protocols. The most detailed further information about them can be obtained in Tanenbaum (1981a, Chapters 3 to 5) and Davies et al (1979, Chapter 6 and also parts of Chapter 8). McGlynn (1978) provides a very useful description of the earlier low level protocols, especially those developed by computer manufacturers for their network systems. Martin (1981a, Chapter 8 and 22) and Tanenbaum (1981b, Sections 1 to 3) give useful summaries of low level protocols, while Cole (1982, Chapter 8) and Sloman (1978) provide good preliminary presentations of X.25. Several of the papers in *IEEE Transactions on Communications* (Apr 1980) provide details of important specific aspects of low level protocols; they will be cited later in this section.

The Physical Layer allows devices to send raw bit streams into a network, without reference to the groupings of the bits into larger units and to the meanings of these bits; these aspects are handled by protocols at higher levels. The Physical Layer covers physical interfaces between devices, rules for passing bits between them, and techniques for transmission along network links. It is described in detail by Tanenbaum (1981a, Chapter 3) and Bertine (1980), for example. They describe the layer itself, together with national and international standards developed for it. These standards include: RS-232-C for 25-pin and the newer RS-449 for 37-pin analogue terminal connectors, and CCITT's X.21 for digital circuit-switched networks. Folts (1980a) describes X.21.

Before the specific Data Link Layer and Network Layer protocols are considered, a brief outline is now given of some of the different types of these protocols together with some general principles of protocol operation.

Data link protocols may be subdivided into *asynchronous* protocols, transferring data at a variable rate, and *synchronous* protocols, transferring data at a fixed rate, with synchronised sender and receiver. Synchronous protocols may be *bit-oriented,* using bits as the unit of data, or *character-oriented (byte-oriented),* using characters or bytes as the unit of data.

When analysing and comparing data link protocols, relevant factors include: framing, synchronisation, transparency, line control, error control, acknowledgments, sequence control, time-out and retransmission.

Framing provides rules to determine the meaning of the bit stream or byte stream that is transmitted, for example which bits are characters, in bit-oriented protocols, and which bits or bytes belong to messages and which represent control data. For packet-switched networks, these rules specify packet formats, which, for level two packets, are typically header (containing control and addressing information), followed by data, followed by tail (checking information).

Synchronisation is a technique, used in synchronous protocols, to ensure that both sender and receiver are exchanging data in step with each other, with properly aligned bit, byte, packet and message transmission times.

Transparency is the ability to transmit data in the message that has the same bit pattern as control characters; this is achieved by applying bit-stuffing and other transformations to the bit patterns in the data part of the message, so that they are converted into bit sequences that can no longer be confused with the control bit sequences.

Line control determines which station transmits and which station receives a given message; inside a given packet, it is implemented by assigning data bytes or other data fields that specify the source and destination addresses of the packet.

Error control provides procedures for recovering from errors in transmission of the data, whenever they are detected. The error control fields at the end of a packet indicate the result of applying checks to the packet's data, using a suitable error detection code, this code being devised so that the probability that it fails to detect an erroneous packet is extremely small. Error control also activates retransmission of any packet that had to be cancelled because it was found to be erroneous.

Protocols make provision for *acknowledgment* of the safe receipt or otherwise of packets at their destinations. For data link protocols, the acknowledgments are sent on arrival of packets at the end of the link. For network protocols, they are sent when packets reach their destination mode. A *positive* acknowledgment is sent whenever a packet arrives, checked to be free of error, in the correct position in the message to which it belongs. A *negative* acknowledgment is sent, for example, when a packet arrives out of sequence, or when a packet arrives in sequence but is found to contain an error. It provides the sending node with a signal to retransmit a fresh copy of the missing packet.

For messages other than *datagrams* (single packets that are self-contained messages), almost all protocols require packets to be reconstituted into messages at their destination in the same order as the order in which they were sent. This requires *sequence control,* including the numbering of packets in sequence, together with negative acknowledgment, retransmission and other recovery procedures whenever packets are observed to arrive out of sequence. Receiver sequence control is applied at the node at the end of the link, for Level 2 packets handled by data link protocols, and at the destination node, for Level 3 packets handled by network protocols.

As already mentioned, a packet is *retransmitted* by a given node, when it receives a negative acknowledgment, indicating that it has not arrived, in its right position in the message, at its destination. Because there is a risk that acknowledgments themselves may be lost en route, retransmission of a packet is also activated after a *time-out* has occurred, i.e. if no acknowledgment of the packet has been received within a protocol-specified time interval after its transmission.

Edge and Hinchley (1978) provide a useful treatment of the efficiency of data link protocols and the factors that influence it. They consider especially the role of positive and negative acknowledgments and the time-out interval.

Network Layer protocols ensure that messages and the Level 3 packets that make them up, are routed correctly to their destinations. The two most important modes of operation that they use are the datagram mode, already mentioned, that delivers one-packet messages, and the *virtual circuit* mode, delivering the Level 3 packets of a message in the right order, and free of errors, along a route between successive nodes that is set up, by a *virtual call,* for the duration of the message transmission only.

Each Level 3 packet is transmitted inside a Level 2 packet, as part of the packet's data field. When a Level 2 packet reaches the end node of its link, that node then determines the Level 3 destination of any Level 3 packet embedded in it, and, if it finds one, removes it to the node's attached device, if that is its destination, otherwise transmits it via the next link along its route, inside a new Level 2 packet.

Other aspects of protocols, including congestion control, flow control, addressing and routing, together with deadlocks and other protocol problems, are discussed in Chapter 17. The modelling and performance of protocols are considered in Chapter 10 and at the end of Chapter 20.

McGlynn (1978) gives details of many of the earlier protocols in the Data Link Layer, including: the asynchronous Teletype and IBM 2740 protocols; IBM's synchronous character-oriented (Bi-Sync) Binary Synchronous Protocol; the synchronous bit-oriented protocols SDLC (IBM's Synchronous Data Link Control), ADDCP (Advanced Data Communications Control Protocol, established by ANSI), HDLC (High Level Data Link Control, formulated by ISO and incorporated in Level 2 of X.25), BDLC (Burroughs Data Link Control), BOLD (used by NCR as a subset of ADCCP), CDCCP (CDC's data link protocol); and the synchronous/asynchronous byte-oriented protocol DDCMP (DEC's Digital Data Communications Message Protocol). McGlynn also gives some details of X.25 itself.

Conard (1980) reviews character-oriented data link protocols, examining them from a historical viewpoint and giving several examples. Carlson (1980) gives a similar review of bit-oriented data link protocols. Although character-oriented protocols have been very useful in the past, and are still widely used in manufacturers' computer networks, they are now being superseded by the bit-oriented protocols, including X.25, that are being adopted as international standards.

X.25 is a comprehensive set of protocols that covers data communication at the lowest three layers of the ISO Model. It has been recommended as an international standard by CCITT and ISO, and it is rapidly being adopted as such by the PTTs and other public data carriers. It is being implemented by an increasing number of private as well as public packet-switched networks, and by many suppliers of network systems, computers, terminals and other devices. The Grey Book (1978) gives its original specification and CCITT (1980a) presents its draft revised specification. Folts (1979) gives a status report on X.25.

As defined, X.25 provides a standard procedure for a host computer, that it calls a *DTE (Data Terminating Equipment)* to access and use a node, that it calls a *DCE (Data Circuit Terminating Equipment* or *Data Communications Equipment)*. It enables this node to transfer data across a WAN to a remote DCE via the remote DTE attached to it. It *does not*, as such, assume that the WAN itself, between the DCE nodes so linked, uses X.25 or its variants for node-to-node transfer, although that is what the PTT networks propose to do. In principle, the WAN could use non-X.25 protocols across the network, and the X.25 user would be unaware of this.

At the Physical Level, it uses a protocol that is almost identical to X.21. At the Data Link Level, it uses a protocol that is essentially the same as HDLC. At the Network Level, it makes a virtual call to set up a virtual circuit for each multi-packet message that is sent across the network, and it closes the virtual call and removes the virtual circuit when that message has been transmitted. Its later versions also provide a datagram facility, together with a "fast select" facility that can include up to 128 bytes of user data inside call-establishment packets. Level 2 of X.25 is described in detail by Barber et al. (1979, Section 6.3) and more briefly by Cole (1982, Sections 8.2 and 8.3) and Tanenbaum (1981a, Section 4.3.2). Level 3 of X.25 is described in detail by Barber et al (1979, Section 6.4) and more briefly by Cole (1982, Sections 8.4 and 8.5) and Tanenbaum (1981a, Section 5.4.4). Sloman (1978) provides a detailed unified description of Levels 2 and 3 of X.25, while Schindler (1979) presents compact specification of X.25, written in a high level programming language. Folts (1980b) and Rybczynski (1980) discuss the improvements made to X.25 as a result of its revisions. Jacobsen and Thisted (1980) consider the relation of X.25 to other parts of the ISO Reference Model, with special reference to X.25's flow control principles.

TRANSPORT PROTOCOLS

The purposes of *transport protocols (host-to-host protocols)* are to provide reliable general-purpose communication between processes in host computers and other "intelligent" devices and to bridge the gap between the network transmission services, covered by the bottom three layers, and the user facilities, provided by the top three layers. The *transport service* of a network provides a universal communications interface, offering to implement and operate certain standard facilities, independent of the communications medium below. A transport service is thus the upper interface of a transport protocol.

Transport protocols and transport services are described in detail by Davies et al (1979, Sections 7.2 and 7.3), Tanenbaum (Chapter 8), Walden and McKenzie (1979), and Sunshine (1981b), and more briefly by Tanenbaum (1981b, Section 4).

A *transport station* is the implementation of a transport protocol in a specific software environment. Although it normally supports many processes simultaneously, most of its functions concern each connection independently. Its chief functions are to manage connection establishment and termination, flow control, buffering, multiplexing and addressing, so as to allow communication between any pair of users. It uses *virtual circuit primitives,* to carry out directly basic instructions such as CONNECT, LISTEN, CLOSE (a connection), SEND and RECEIVE.

Transport protocols also help to implement communication between users on different networks, interconnected by gateways. This aspect is considered in the next section.

Danthine and Magnee (1980) compare the features of transport layers in LANs and WANs, with special reference to their transport services and transport protocols.

Dallas (1980) sums up the proposals for a Network Independent Transport Service, defined by Study Group 3 of the PSS User Forum, and now being implemented on connections of various Cambridge Ring installations to PSS. He describes a realisation of this service for Cambridge Rings.

Fishburn (1982) outlines the Internet Transport Protocols for Ethernet, that have now been implemented by Xerox.

NETWORK INTERCONNECTION AND GATEWAY PROTOCOLS

The demand for network interconnection has arisen because computer network users have often needed to access computing resources on networks other than those to which they are directly connected. One purpose of linking networks together is to provide services of consistently high standard to all the users of the interconnected networks. There has thus been extensive interest in interconnection among network users,and a considerable amount of work has been done on it. Useful discussions of network interconnection has been given by Tanenbaum (1981a, Section 8.2), Postel (1980), Cerf and Kirstein (1978), Di Ciccio et al (1979), and Gien and Zimmermann (1979).

In order to provide adequate interconnection services, *either* suitable end-to-end internetwork transport protocols must be developed *or* the transport protocols of the individual networks must be made to interwork. In the latter case, *gateways* can be used, whose function is to convert or translate packets from one protocol to another.

The "obvious" approach is to set up gateways between pairs of networks at points where they interface; more generally, gateways can be set up between more than two networks all meeting at the same point. However, if separate protocol translator software had to be written for each such gateway between two or more networks, it would be a major task to write all that software.

An alternative, simpler approach is to set up an *interconnection network* between gateways, as shown in Figure 9.8. In this case, each of the interconnected networks has a link to its gateway, which is a node on the interconnection network. Thus a connection between a pair of networks now passes through at least two gateways, including the gateways to which they are directly attached. In addition, all, or at least most, of the networks would agree on a standard internetwork packet format and protocol, to be used *between* networks; as it would not need to be used inside networks, none of these networks would need to change its own protocols.

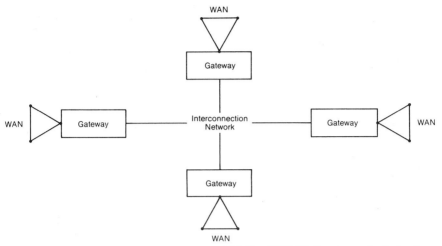

Fig. 9.8. Interconnection network linking several WANs   SOURCE: Based on author's drawing

For administrative and other non-technical reasons, it is often more convenient to use *half-gateways,* each of which is responsible only for converting packets to and from the internal format of the network to which it is attached. In this scheme, a gateway directly linking two networks would now consist of two half-gateways, one for each of the networks, which would also be connected to each other (Figure 9.9); alternatively, the gateways attached to an interconnection network can themselves be half-gateways.

The type of service, offered to the Transport Layer by the Network Layer, has a major influence on the design of the Transport Layer, as much for the internetwork case as for the intranetwork case. Two very different approaches to internetworking have arisen, according to whether the network layer offers a virtual circuit service or a pure datagram service to the Transport Layer. The CCITT internetwork protocol, X.75, is based on the former approach, while the Arpanet favours the latter for joining together its constituent networks.

X.75 is specified in the CCITT Grey Book (1979); in most respects, it is practically identical with X.25. It builds up an internetwork connection by chaining a series of intranetwork virtual circuits, ending at half-gateways, and virtual circuits

Fig. 9.9   Two linked half-gateways linking two WANs (note that WAN 1 operates half-gateway 1 and WAN 2 operates half-gateway 2)   SOURCE: Based on author's drawing

between neighbouring pairs of half-gateways. It is also possible to use X.75 for communication between private networks, attached to different public networks.

In the datagram approach to network interconnection, and end-to-end media-independent datagram passes from its source network to its destination network through intervening (half-)gateways and possibly also intervening network(s); as the different datagrams, belonging to a given message, may well travel different routes, possibly even passing through different sequences of gateways and networks, there is no guarantee that they will arrive in the right order at their destination. Thus a destination device must itself reconstruct the message from its component datagrams.

This approach is used by the Arpanet, as already mentioned, and also in the PUP (PARC Universal Packet) Internet Architecture, developed by Xerox to link Ethernet with the Arpanet and other networks (Boggs et al, 1980). The resulting internetwork system already serves about 1000 computers, on 25 networks of different types, linked by 20 gateways.

Jacobsen (1981) uses the ISO Reference Model as a tool to describe different network architectures, taking account of the types of network involved and the applications to be supported. He gives examples, based on the CCITT Teletex and ECMA transport layer specifications.

Eldon (1981) points out that the general office systems environment will in the future contain many LANs, that will need to be interconnected via public data networks. He warns that, despite progress in standardisation of WAN and LAN architectures and protocols, the competitive marketplace is leading to many incompatible network systems, supplied by different vendors. Via standard gateways, he considers that multiple LANs and WANs can be linked together with a minimum of difficulty; his proposal for a relevant standard has already been mentioned earlier in this chapter. He also quotes from several different definitions of "gateway."

Higginson and Kirstein (1981) discuss the use of network interconnection protocols, together with some of the problems arising, for electronic mail services, especially Teletex. They point out that CCITT (1980b) has recently formulated a set of Draft Recommendations for Teletex Standards, including S.70, a Network Independent Basic Transport Service.

TERMINAL PROTOCOLS AND REMOTE JOB ENTRY PROTOCOLS

Terminal protocols which belong to the Presentation Layer, provide basic services for uses of computer terminals, especially by providing these terminals with efficient and flexible access to computer networks and to the computing resources that are also linked to them. They are used, both for access to time-sharing services and for character-oriented communication between different computer processes.

Terminal protocols are described in moderate detail by Tanenbaum (1981a, Section 9.3), Magnee et al (1979), Day (1980 and 1981), and Jacobsen et al (1980), and more briefly by Tanenbaum (1981b, Section 6.3) and Davies et al (1979, Sections 7.4 and 8.5).

Terminal protocols have been devised to hide from computer networks the effects of incompatibilities between the many different models of computer terminals. To do this, two alternative approaches have been adopted.

A *parametric terminal protocol* attempts to express by sets of parameters the differences between terminals; in an actual terminal-computer session, the computer asks it to set the various terminal parameters to their requested values.

A *virtual terminal protocol* introduces the basic concept of a *network virtual terminal,* a hypothetical terminal that behaves in a standard way. By means of the terminal protocol, an interactive program, being used by a given terminal via a network, acts as if it were connected to a network virtual terminal.

The best known parametric terminal protocols are CCITT's XXX protocols, which have been designed to connect a wide variety of terminals, via *PADs (packet assembler/disassemblers),* to packet-switched networks using X.25. The XXX protocols are X.3, which defines the PAD parameters, X.28, which defines the terminal-PAD interface, and X.29, which defines the PAD-computer interface; they are specified in the CCITT Grey Book (1978) and described by Barber et al (1979, Section 8.5) and Martin (1981a, Chapter 23).

An important virtual terminal protocol is the Arpanet's Telnet protocol; the virtual terminal approach has also been used by the European Informatics Network (EIN), the Cyclades network in France, and the GMD network in Germany.

RJE protocols (remote job entry protocols) are also in the Presentation Layer, and enable network users to use one implementation of remote job entry software with a variety of batch user systems, including different models of computers made by different manufacturers. This application is perhaps the next most important network requirement, after support of interactive terminals, for users of contemporary data processing facilities.

RJE protocols are described by Day (1979 and 1981) and briefly by Barber et al (1979, Section 7.4). They have been proposed and implemented in several networks, including the Arpanet and the UCLA network in Los Angeles, that is connected to the Arpanet.

RJE protocols provide their users with basic functions such as commands for: user identification, job submission, retrieving output, determining job status, cancelling jobs if necessary, and controlling the transfer of jobs and their output across a network.

FILE TRANSFER PROTOCOLS

A *file transfer protocol* defines the set of rules and procedures for transferring files between the files systems of different computers. File transfer protocols are described by Day (1981) and also briefly by Tanenbaum (1981a, Section 9.4), Tanenbaum (1981b, Section 6.4) and Davies et al (1979, Section 7.4).

In heterogeneous networks, with different types of computers, the purpose of a file transfer protocol is to establish a *network virtual file system,* which allows a process in a computer to access data stored in a remote computer as if it were stored locally.

To do this, it has to carry out three functions:

1. *File transformation,* where the protocol attempts to provide standard, or at least compatible, representations of the data in a file, converting it into a form usable at its destination.

2. *File transfer,* enabling a user to open a file by a name of his choice, address data within it, and transfer data to and from it.

3. *File manipulation,* allowing a user to create, delete, rename, and perform other operations on remote files.

The Arpanet File Transfer Protocol (FTP) was defined early in 1973 and implemented soon after that; two other file transfer systems, RSEXEC and National Software Works, were developed by Arpanet users. DEC developed its Data Access Protocol (DAP) for use with its DECnet product.

Several European network groups have also work on file transfer protocols (Day, 1981; Gien, 1978), and their work seems to be more sensitive than the American work to general user needs. But a good deal more work needs to be done on file transfer protocols before they can be used really widely.

APPLICATION PROTOCOLS

The first six layers of the ISO Reference Model are the domain of network designers. The seventh layer, the Application Layer, is conceptually very different, as it is the domain of network users. Relatively little standardisation can occur here, as each user decides what applications he will carry out and what protocols he will use for them; there are few, if any, standard protocols for it.

However, the Application Layer is beginning to receive attention, and has become an active area of research. Tanenbaum (1981a, Chapter 10) reviews some of the work here. He points out that some issues are common to many applications, so that they can be discussed in general terms. These include distributed data bases, discussed in Chapter 12 of this book, and distributed computation and network operating systems, reviewed in Chapter 13.

USER-ORIENTED PROTOCOLS

Barber (1979 and 1980) has suggested a new approach to higher level protocols, that attempts to make them less complicated and more user-friendly. He questions whether the idea of layered protocols, which has been a very valuable aid for linking computers to networks, is really practicable for higher network functions, especially those involving users. Here, formidable complexities have to be faced, when seeking a general solution in terms of the OSI Reference Model, so that a more direct approach seems worth exploring, especially as it would quite possibly also make networks much more accessible to their users.

For example, for file transfer and file handling, he proposes the use of *free-form protocols,* where users would be allowed to introduce natural language control strings in place of the coded format characters often used to control data layouts. In this scheme, the originator of a file would thus be free to use any reasonable description of whatever file handling he wishes to do, as long as it is set out within universally agreed delimiters. He proposes a possible way of standardising a set of delimiters, that would allow commands, remarks and file handling instructions to be embedded in the files exchanged by computer systems over networks. This approach would allow the evolutionary development of complex file handling protocols, and it would make it easier to develop standards for new protocols for public data networks.

In an unpublished article (Mayne, 1979), I develop ideas that are in some ways similar to Barber's approach but which also generalise it, and I envisage that a very important class of high-level free-form *UOPs (user-oriented protocols)* could be developed and then agreed between specific groups of users, for example those interested in particular application areas. I outline a general framework for handling UOPs, and I give some illustrative examples of how these ideas might be implemented in practice.

UOPs can be developed in such a flexible way that there could be an almost unlimited range of applications, catering for a wide variety of user needs and choices. Here are five out of many possible examples:

1. Transfer of text files between users whose computers may have different character sets and codes.

2. Transfer of a text, typed at a terminal belonging to one computer, to another computer, operating a typesetter that prepares a high quality printed document, using extra characters and fonts not available on the terminal.

3. Facsimile transmission, where some reformatting and restyling of the picture image is required at the receiving end.

4. Transfer of structured files between users choosing formats that are different, but can be translated into each other explicitly by a program that can be called by a UOP; for example, transfer of a data base in one format, held in one computer, to another computer storing it in a second, related format.

5. Developing and running a program on one computer, that calls subprograms stored in other computers and perhaps also uses different programming languages.

REFERENCES

N. Abramson (1970) "The ALOHA System—Another alternative for computer communications," *Proceedings Fall Joint Computer Conference,* 281–285.

N. Abramson (1973) "The ALOHA system,"Abramson and Kuo (1973).

Ed. N. Abramson, F. F. Kuo (1973) *Computer Networks,* Prentice-Hall, Englewood Cliffs, NJ, USA.

S. Andler, D. Daniels and A. Spector (1980) "On enhancing local network communication devices," *Local Area Networks Workshop*, 207–221.

M.C. Andrews (Apr 1980) "Computer network architectures and operating experience of data networks at ICCC '78: Promise and practice," *Computer Networks*, **4**(2) 77–85.

J. D. Atkins (Apr 1980) "Path control: The transport network of SNA," *IEEE Transactions on Communications*, **COM-28**(4) 527–538.

D. L. A. Barber (15 Mar 1979) "*⟨"You don't know me, but ..."⟩*," *Computer Weekly*, 4.

D. L. A. Barber (1980) "A new approach to the evolution of complex protocols."

H. V. Bertine (Apr 1980) "Physical level protocols," *IEEE Transactions on Communications*, **COM-28**(4) 433–444.

R. Binder (1981) "Packet protocols for broadcast satellites," Chapter 5 of Kuo (1981).

D. R. Boggs, J. F. Shoch, E. A. Taft and R. M. Metcalfe (Apr 1980) "PUP: An internetwork architecture," *IEEE Transactions on Communications*, **COM-28**(4) 612–624.

H. J. Burkhardt and S. Schindler (May 1981) "Structuring principles of the communication architecture of open systems," *Computer Networks*, **5**(3) 157–166.

D. E. Carlson (Apr 1980) "Bit-oriented data link control procedures," *IEEE Transactions on Communications*, **COM-28**(4) 455–467.

CCITT (1980a) (Apr 1980) "Draft Revised CCITT Recommendation X.25," *Computer Communications Review*, **10**(1/2) 56–129.

CCITT (1980b) (Oct 1980) Draft Recommendations:
    S.60 "Terminal equipment for use with the Teletex service."
    S.61 "Character repertoire and coded character sets for the international Teletex service."
    S.62 "Control procedures for the Teletex service."
    S.70 "Network Independent Basic Transport Service."
    F.200 "Teletex Service."

CCITT Grey Book (1978) "CCITT Provisional Recommendations X.3, X.25, X.28 and X.29," ITU, Geneva, Switzerland.

CCITT Grey Book (1979) "CCITT Provisional Recommendations X.75 and X.121," ITU, Geneva, Switzerland.

CCITT Orange Book, Vol. VIII.2 (1977) "CCITT Recommendations X.1, X.2, X.25, X.92 and X.96, public data networks," ITU, Geneva, Switzerland.

V. G. Cerf and P. T. Kirstein (Nov 1978) "Issues in packet-network interconnection," *Proceedings of the IEEE*, **66**(11) 1386–1408.

G. J. Clancy, Jr, (1981) "A status report on the IEEE Project 802 Local Network Standard," *Local Networks 81*, 591–609.

D. D. Clark, K. T. Pogran and D. P. Reed (Nov 1978) "An introduction to local area networks," *Proceedings of the IEEE*, **66**(11) 1497–1517.

R. Cole (1982) *Computer Communications*, Macmillan, London and Basingstoke, England.

Computer, Vol. 12 (9) (Sep 1979) special issue on computer network protocols.

J. W. Conard (Apr 1980) "Character-oriented data link control protocols," *IEEE Transactions on Communications*, COM-28(4) 445–454.

I. N. Dallas (1980) "A Cambridge Ring local area network realisation of a transport server," *Local Area Networks Workshop*, 299–310.

A. A. S. Danthine and F. Magnee (1980) "Transport layer—Long haul vs local networks," *Local Area Networks Workshop*, 267–298.

D.W. Davies, D. L. A. Barber, W. L. Price and C. M. Solomonides (1979) *Computer Networks and Their Protocols*, Wiley, Chichester and New York.

J. D. Day (Sep 1979) "Resource sharing protocols," *Computer*, **12**(9) 47–56.

J. D. Day (Apr 1980) "Terminal protocols," *IEEE Transactions on Communications*, **COM-28**(4) 585–593.

J. D. Day (1981) "Terminal, file transfer, and remote job protocols for heterogenous computer networks," Chapter 3 of Kuo (1981).

DEC, Intel and Xerox (Sep 1980) *The Ethernet—Local Area Network Data Link Layer and Physical Layer Specifications Version 1.0.*

R. des Jardins (Apr 1981) "Overview and status of the ISO Reference Model of Open Systems Interconnection," *Computer Networks,* **5**(2) 77–80.

D. DiCiccio, C. A. Sunshine, J. A. Field and E. G. Manning (1979) "Alternatives for the interconnection of public packet switching data networks," *Proceedings Sixth Data Communication Symposium,* 120–125.

J. Donnington (1982) "The challenge of telecommunications," pp. 48–61 of Ed. A Simpson, *Planning for Telecommunications,* Gower Publishing Company, Aldershot, Hampshire, England.

S. W. Edge and A. J. Hinchley (Oct 1978) "A survey of end-to-end retransmission techniques," *Computer Communication Review,* **8**(4) 1–18.

W. J. Eldon (1980) "Gateways for interconnecting local area and long haul networks," *Local Area Networks Workshop,* 391–406.

M. A. Fishburn (1982) "High level protocols for office systems," *Local Networks 82,* 131–142.

H. C. Folts (Sep 1979) "Status report on the new standards for DTE/DCE interface protocols," *Computer,* **12**(9) 12–19.

H. C. Folts (1980a) (Apr 1980) "Procedures for circuit-switched service in synchronous public data networks," *IEEE Transactions on Communications,* **COM-28**(4) 489–496.

H. C. Folts (1980b) (Apr 1980) "X.25 transaction oriented features—Datagram and fast select," *IEEE Transactions on Communications,* **COM-28**(4) 496–500.

M. Gien (Sep 1978) "A File Transfer Protocol (FTP)," *Computer Networks,* **2**(3) 312–319.

M. Gien and H. Zimmerman (1979) "Design principles for network interconnection," *Proceedings Sixth Data Communication Symposium,* 109–120.

J. P. Gray (1981) "Synchronization in SNA networks," Chapter 8 of Kuo (1981).

P. E. Green, Jr (Apr 1980) "An introduction to network architectures and protocols," *IEEE Transactions on Communications,* **COM-28**(4) 413–424.

Ed. P.E. Green, Jr (1982) *Computer Network Architecture and Protocols,* Plenum Publishing Corporation, New York.

K. S. Heard (1982) "LAN standardization activities in Europe," *Local Networks 82,* 121–129.

P. L. Higginson and P. T. Kirstein (1981) "Network interconnection with provision for electronic mail services," *Local Networks 81,* 107–121.

V. L. Hoberecht (Apr 1980) "SNA function management," *IEEE Transactions on Communications,* **COM-28**(4) 594–603.

V. B. Hunt and P. C. Ravasio (1980) "Olivetti local network system protocol architecture," *Local Area Networks Workshop,* 245–265.

IEEE Transactions on Communications, Vol. **COM-28**(4) (Apr 1980) Special issue on computer network architectures and protocols.

ISO/TC97/SC16 (Apr 1981) "Data Processing—Open Systems Interconnection—Basic Reference Model," *Computer Networks,* **5**(2) 81–118.

I. M. Jacobs, R. Binder and E. V. Hoversten (Nov 1978) "General purpose satellite networks," *Proceedings of the IEEE,* **66**(11) 1448–1467.

T. Jacobsen (1980) "Gateway and cluster controller architectures based on the ISO Reference Model of Open Systems Interconnection," *Local Area Networks Workshop,* 407–417.

T. Jacobsen, P. Hogh and I. M. T. Hauser (Jan/Apr 1980) "Virtual terminal protocols—Transport service and session control," *Computer Communication Review,* **10**(1/2) 24–40.

T. Jacobsen and P. Thisted (Jan/Apr 1980) "CCITT Recommendation X.25 as part of the ISO Reference Model of Open Systems Interconnection," *Computer Communication Review,* **10**(1/2) 48–55.

R. E. Kahn,S. A. Gronemeyer, J. Burchfiel and C. Kunzelman (Nov 1978) "Advances in packet radio technology," *Proceedings of the IEEE*, **66**(11) 1468–1496.

P. T. F. Kelly (Nov 1978) "Public packet switched data networks, international plans and standards," *Proceedings of the IEEE*, **66**(11) 1539–1549.

L. R. Kleinrock and F. A. Tobagi (1975) "Random access techniques for data transmission over packet-switched radio channels," *Proceedings NCC*, 187–201.

Ed. F. F. Kuo (1981) *Protocols & Techniques for Data Communications Networks*, Prentice-Hall, Englewood Cliffs, NJ, USA (with bibliographies).

Local Area Networks Workshop (1980) Proceedings of the IFIP Working Group 6.4 Local Computer Networks Working Party 80/13 Conference, August 27–29 1980, Zurich, Switzerland.

E. C. Luczak (1978) "Global bus computer communication techniques," *Proceedings Computer Networking Symposium, National Bureau of Standards*, 58–67.

D. R. McGlynn (1978) *Distributed Processing and Data Communications*, Chapter 5 "Network Control Architecture."

Ed. J. M. McQuillan and V. G. Cerf (1978) *A Practical View of Computer Network Protocols*, IEEE, Long Beach, CA, USA.

F. Magnee, A. Endrizzi and J. Day (Nov 1979) "A survey of terminal protocols," *Computer Networks*, **3**(5) 299–314.

J. W. Mark (1981) "Protocol model for WELNET," *Local Networks 81*, 313–317.

J. Martin (1981a) *Computer Networks and Distributed Processing*, Prentice-Hall, Englewood Cliffs, NJ, especially Parts 2 and 3.

J. Martin (1981b) *Design and Strategy for Distributed Data Processing*, Prentice-Hall, Englewood Cliffs, NJ, especially Part 5, "Software and Network Strategy."

A. J. Mayne (Mar 1979) "Some possibilities for user-oriented protocols," unpublished paper.

R. M. Metcalfe and D. R. Boggs (Jul 1976) "Ethernet: Distributed packet switching for local computer networks," *Communications of the ACM*, **19**(7) 395–404.

A. N. Mok and S.A. Ward (Jun 1979) "Distributed broadcast channel access," *Computer Networks*, **3**(3) 327–335.

National Bureau of Standards (undated) *Federal Computer Network Protocol Standards Program: An Overview*, U.S. Department of Commerce, Washington, DC.

P. P. Nuspl, K. E. Brown, W. Steenaart and B. Ghicopoulos (1980) "Synchronization methods for TDMA," *Proceedings of the IEEE*, **65**(3) 434–444.

J. B. Postel (Apr 1980) "Internetwork protocol approaches," *IEEE Transactions on Communications*, **COM-28**(4) 604–611.

L. Pouzin and H. Zimmermann (Nov 1978) "A tutorial in protocols," *Proceedings of the IEEE*, **66**(11) 1346–1370 (with bibliography).

J. Puzman and R. Porizek (1980) *Communication Control in Computer Networks*, Wiley, New York and Chichester.

V. Quint, II. Pichy, X. Rousset de Pino, S. Sasynn, G. Sergeant and I. Vatton (1981) "Basic services for a local network," *Local Networks 81*, 277–288.

L. G. Roberts (1972) "Extensions of packet communication technology to a hand held personal terminal," *Proceedings Spring Joint Computer Conference*, 295–298.

L. G. Roberts (1972) "Dynamic allocation of satellite capacity through packet reservation," *Proceedings NCC*, 711–716.

M. J. Rubinstein, C. J. Kennington and G. T. Knight (1980) "Terminal support on the Cambridge Ring," *Local Networks 81*, 475–490.

A. Rybczynski (Apr 1980) "X.25 interface and end-to-end virtual circuit service characteristics," *IEEE Transactions on Communications*, **COM-28**(4) 500–510.

G. M. Schneider (Sep 1979) "Computer network protocols: A hierarchical viewpoint," *Computer*, **12**(9) 8–10.

S. Schindler (Dec 1979) "X.25 considered harmful?," *Computer,* **12**(12) 120–121.

S. Schindler (May 1981) "Open systems, today and tomorrow—A personal perspective," *Computer Networks,* **5**(3) 167–176.

S. Schindler and U. Flasche (1981) "Presentation service—The philosophy," *Local Networks 81,* 233–244.

J. F. Schoch (Apr 1980) *An annotated bibliography on local computer networks,* Xerox PARC Technical Report.

M. S. Sloman (Dec 1978) "X.25 explained," *Computer Communications,* **21**(6) 310–327.

R. Sommer (1981) "A real-time protocol for a sublocal network," *Local Networks 81,* 263–275.

O. Spaniol (Nov 1979) "Modelling of local computer networks," *Computer Networks,* **3**(5) 315–326.

E. B. Spratt (1980) "Operational experience with a Cambridge Ring local area network in a university environment," *Local Area Network Workshop,* 89–114.

E. B. Spratt (1981) "Development of the Cambridge Ring at the University of Kent," *Local Networks 81,* 503–518.

R. F. Sproull (Nov 1978) "High-level protocols," *Proceedings of the IEEE,* **66**(11) 1371–1386.

T. Stack (1981) "LAN protocol residency alternatives for IBM mainframe Open System Interconnection," *Local Networks 81,* 435–450.

C. A. Sunshine (1981a) "Protocols for local networks," *Local Networks 81,* 245–261.

C. A. Sunshine (1981b) "Transport protocols for computer networks," Chapter 2 of Kuo (1981).

D. T. W. Sze (1981) "IEEE LAN Project 802—Current status," *Local networks 82,* 109–120.

A. S. Tanenbaum (1981a) *Computer Networks,* Prentice-Hall, Englewood Cliff, NJ (with extensive bibliographies).

A. S. Tanenbaum (1981b) (Dec 1981) "Network Protocols," *ACM Computing Surveys,* **13**(4) 453–489 (with bibliography).

K. J. Thurber and H. A. Freeman (Apr 1980) "Updated bibliography on local computer networks," *Computer Architecture News,* **8**(1) 20–28.

F. A. Tobagi (Apr 1988) "Multiaccess protocols in packet communication systems," *IEEE Transactions on Communications,* **COM-28**(4) 468–488 (with bibliography).

F. A. Tobagi and R. Ra (1980) "Efficient round-robin and priority schemes for unidirectional broadcasting schemes," *Local Area Networks Workshop,* 131–149.

I. Toda (Apr 1980) "DCNA higher level protocols," *IEEE Transactions on Communications,* **COM-28**(4) 575–584.

C. Tropper (1981) *Local Computer Network Technologies,* Academic Press, New York and London.

Update Local Area Networks (May 1979) Proceedings of the Local Area Communications Network Symposium, Boston.

D. Walden and A. A. McKenzie (Sep 1979) "The evolution of host-to-host protocol technology," *Computer,* **12**(9) 29–38.

S. Wecker (Sep 1979) "Computer network architectures," *Computer,* **12**(9) 58–72.

S. Wecker (Apr 1980) "DNA: The Digital Network Architecture," *IEEE Transactions on Communications,* **COM-28**(4) 510–526.

H. Zimmermann (Apr 1980) "OSI Reference Model—The ISO Model of Architecture for Open Systems Interconnection," *IEEE Transactions on Communications,* **COM-28**(4) 425–432.

Chapter 10

Network Control and Performance

Effective network control is needed, to ensure that the performance of a computer network is of a consistently high standard and that user requirements are met, almost all the time. Due to system unreliabilities and human errors, it is unfortunately not possible to achieve 100% performance all the time, but contemporary network control technology usually allows this objective to be more or less nearly achieved.

For network performance and effective network control to be maintained, it is necessary firstly to obtain an adequate idea of how the network is actually performing and behaving, from day to day, hour to hour, and sometimes even second to second. A variety of network measurement, monitoring and control techniques and instruments have been developed for this purpose. Some of these techniques are outlined in the first part of this chapter.

Another very important aspect of network performance, which is useful for both network control and network design, is its prediction, which can only be carried out with the aid of theoretical studies, in addition to empirical data. Theoretical studies start from the formulation of mathematical models of the behaviour of whole networks or of important parts and components of them, and these are in turn based on "reasonable," though inevitably more or less simplified, assumptions. The performance predictions can then be made either by mathematical, analytical, numerical calculations or by simulation techniques or by a combination of these two approaches.

The second part of this chapter discusses briefly the mathematical and statistical methods and tools used by theoretical studies, and gives illustrative examples of the ways in which they have been applied by network experts. No attempt is made here to indicate the nature of the mathematics itself, and no formulae are quoted!

Recent developments in network control and performance, including the use of mathematical and statistical methods, are reviewed at the end of Chapter 20.

For general discussions of measurement and models, see for example Tobagi et al (1978), which has an extensive bibliography, and Gerla et al (1977).

The bibliography of papers on local area networks, compiled by Shoch (1980a), includes references to work on performance measurement and models.

Grubb and Cotton (1977) define several parameters that determine the quality of telecommunications services, and discuss their significance and their effects on networks.

NETWORK MEASUREMENTS

Computer network measurements are required both for long-term and for short-term purposes; Davies and Barber (1973, Section 11.5) give some examples of these applications and indicate the nature of the measurements needed.

Some measurements are required for network evaluation, network accounting, identification of trends in network uses, and planning for network growth and development. Here, the data can be analysed at leisure, and the methods of data collection do not depend very much on the types of measurment to be performed.

Some other kinds of information about network behaviour and performance are needed much more quickly, for such functions as control of data traffic, diagnosis of network faults, the detection of local malfunctions, and general network monitoring and testing, that is discussed in the next section. Here, reports are required very quickly about changes of state or abnormal conditions.

In order to inter-relate different measurements properly, it is necessary to record the times at which various events in the network occur. As will be seen, such a timing scheme is essential for network monitoring and control, but it is also very useful for performance measurement in general. One valuable measurement technique is *timestamping*, where time information is added to special packets, used for measurement, at various stages of their journeys.

Routine measurements can usefully be supplemented by specially designed measurement studies, which can provide valuable insight into the performance of computer networks as a whole, network protocols, host computers and other devices, and applications services provided for users. Measurements can be conducted, both at single sites and at several different sites jointly. Measurements of the throughput of data packets, and of the delays experienced by them as they cross the network and pass through its nodes, can be especially important. Other performance measures, that can be investigated by suitable tests, include: stability, robustness, reliability, protection against congestion, and "fairness" to different users.

Suitable measurement experiments can be devised, to estimate the effects of both artificial and live traffic on the performance of the network. More usually, these tests are applied to interactive traffic, passing through terminals, but tests of file transfers are also carried out often and form an important part of experimental measurement programmes.

Another very important function of the measurements, obtained from network experiments, is to provide a firm basis for the adequate empirical checking of the predictions made by theoretical models and by simulations. In order to make such cross-validation fully effective, it is necessary both to have adequate facilities for

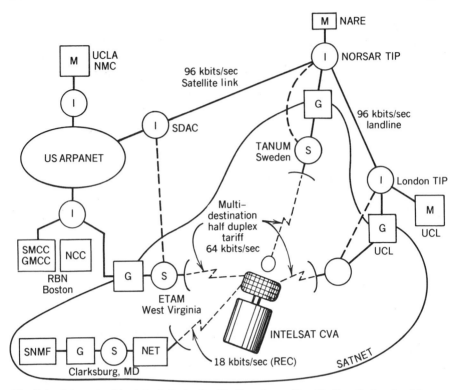

Fig. 10.1. Schematic of the Atlantic Packet Satellite Experiment. Key: H—Host; I—Interface Message Processor (IMP); T—Terminal Interface Message Processor (TIP); S—Satellite Interface Message Processor; G—Gateway Computer; M—Network Measurement Facility; UET—Unattended Earth Terminal (G/T 297); SNMF—Satellite Network Measurement Facility; NCC—Network Control Center; SMCC—Satellite Monitoring and Control Center; GMCC—Gateway Monitoring and Control Center; -- --Debugging Lines SOURCE: Copyright © 1978 IEEE *Proceedings of the IEEE* (Nov 1978), 66 (11) p. 1461 Fig. 4

measurement and to be able to perform the appropriate types of statistical and other analyses. For example, observations and statistical analyses need to be made of the distributions of message timings, the numbers of packets in messages, and the packet sizes, occurring in different types of data traffic. The characteristics of different packets and of the journeys that they made need to be examined similarly.

Extensive network measurements and experiments have been carried out on the Arpanet and on its constituent Satnet and packet radio networks (Kleinrock and Naylor, 1974; Kleinrock et al, 1976; Stokes et al, 1976; Gerla et al, 1977; Bennett and Hinchley, 1978; Jacobs et al, 1978; Kahn et al, 1978; Kleinrock and Gerla, 1978; McGlynn, 1977, Chapter 5; Tobagi et al, 1978; Chu et al, 1979). Figure 10.1 is a schematic diagram of the configuration used for the Atlantic Packet Satellite Experiment on the Arpanet and its attached satellite network Satnet.

The measurements have included: general studies of Arpanet performance and also experiments on network protocols, user traffic characteristics, the performance

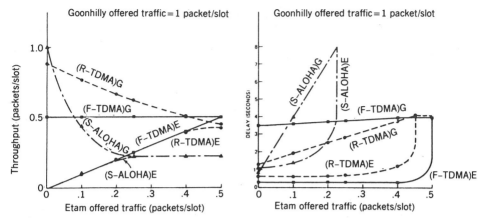

Fig. 10.2. Throughput and delay performance of different demand-assignment protocols under unbalanced load conditions   SOURCE: Copyright © 1978 IEEE *Proceedings of the IEEE* (Nov 1978), 66 (11) p. 1464, Fig. 8

of host-to-host connections, and the performance of node computers. The aims of the measurements included: performance evaluation and verification, study of user behaviour and characteristics, checking of network systems software, and provision of information relevant to network design. Figure 10.2 gives some illustrative examples of measured throughput and delays, for different protocols used in Satnet and for various levels of offered data traffic.

A variety of statistical data was collected, including *cumulative statistics* (*CUM-STATS*), about various events accumulated over given time periods, *trace statistics*, obtained from packets followed through their journeys, and *snapshot statistics*, providing instantaneous measurements of the queue lengths and buffer allocations of various devices and nodes. Artificial traffic was specially generated for some of the measurements, thereby supplementing the measurements made on user traffic. Many of the data were collected and analysed at the Arpanet's Network Measurement Center at UCLA (University of California, Los Angeles).

Other reports of network performance measurements have been made, for example, for: the Experimental Ethernet by Shoch (1980b) and Shoch and Hupp (1980); two Z-Net LANs by Belanger et al (1980); the CIGALE WAN in France by Grange and Mussard (1978); the Datapac WAN in Canada by Cohen et al (1978).

Abrams et al (1980) describe the network measurement system develped by the National Bureau of Standards in the USA.

NETWORK MONITORING AND CONTROL

Davies and Barber (1973, Section 11.5 and also page 306), Davies et al (1979, pages 67–68) and Tobagi et al (1978, page 1441) briefly discuss network monitoring, illustrating its principles of monitoring in the Arpanet.

The Arpanet makes especially extensive use of monitoring and performance reporting, because it is used for research into networks as well as for providing network services and communications facilities. The Arpanet monitoring and measurement system has three essential components: the IMP monitoring and reporting software, the "Network Control Center" at Boston (better viewed as a "network diagnostic centre," because the Arpanet's control is distributed, as Davies et al (1979, page 67) point out), and the network timing system.

The software, in the *IMPs* (*Interface Message Processors*) in the Arpanet nodes, allows the throughput of these nodes and the status of node-to-host and node-to-node connections to be monitored. Some of the data collected are used to update information carried by the nodes themselves, including routing tables, and some of them are sent on to the Network Control Center, to prepare the status reports that it compiles periodically.

This Center prepares summary statistics, for example on: traffic levels for each link in both directions, sizes and peak values of queues, use of buffers and standby equipment in nodes, together with availability, closures, repeated transmissions and error rates on links. It also builds up a comprehensive picture of the network situation at any given time, maintains a general log and display of the state of the Arpanet, and advises the Arpanet operators of any network failure. While it is not essential for the network's moment-to-moment operation, it is a valuable tool for the long-term "health" of the Arpanet.

Special monitoring facilities have also been provided for some of the networks associated with the Arpanet. Figure 10.1 shows the Satellite Monitoring and Control Center and the Gateway Monitoring and Control Center, used for Satnet in conjunction with the Arpanet, together with the Arpanet's own Network Control Center and four network measurement facilities; Jacobs et al (1978, pages 1460–1463) give details of this experimental and monitoring system. Kahn et al (1978, pp. 1494–1495) describe the network monitoring and control system used for PRNET, an experimental packet radio network in the San Francisco Bay area, that is attached to the Arpanet system.

Wilkinson (1977) describes the network control centre, that was used for the European Informatics Network (EIN), while it was in operation.

LANs usually have distributed control, although Cambridge Rings have special monitor stations that exercise overall network control. Control of WANs is generally distributed also. Private WANs usually have one operational diagnostic centre, coordinating all their maintenance operations. Public WANs have central diagnostic facilities, handling overall network system performance, supplemented by local centres that examine the performance and fault situation of links and nodes in their areas.

Monitoring requires not only the collection of adequate measurement data and performance statistics, but also the use of appropriate measurement instruments, called *network monitors*. A fairly wide variety of minicomputers has been used as monitors, and especially designed monitors have also been developed.

For example, the TEKELEC TE 92 Data Transmission Tester is specially designed for those who are performing measurement experiments on X.25 networks and developing implementations of the X.25 protocols. For instance (*Network News,*

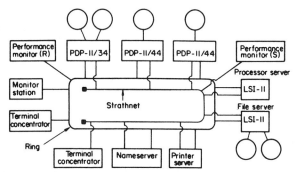

Fig. 10.3. Cambridge Ring and Strathnet systems   SOURCE: Article by Shepherd and Corcoran in *Microprocessors and Microsystems* (Jan/Feb 1982) 6 (1) p. 21

1980), it is being used by the British Joint Network Team, that is sponsored by the Science and Engineering Research Council (SERC).

Black and Brousse (1980) outline in moderate detail the functions and facilities that this sort of device provides. For example, it can record full details of packets passing through it, store data and programs on an attached floppy disk, and carry out measurements in conjunction with network traffic simulations. Tests using such monitors thus seem likely to improve greatly the quality of the empirical data obtainable from measurements and experiments.

Shepherd and Corcoran (1982) describe an experimental LAN, Strathnet, developed at the University of Strathclyde, that is a combined Cambridge Ring and Ethernet-type bus network, and has monitors that measure the performance of both these components of the network; Figure 10.3 shows its configuration. It will be seen that most of the devices are connected to both the ring and the bus, but that one monitor is attached to the ring only and the other monitor is attached to the bus only. These monitors gather statistics that are used to evaluate the relative performances of the ring and the bus. The experiments to be performed on Strathnet are intended also to throw light on the best ways of designing gateways between rings and Ethernets.

THEORETICAL STUDIES OF NETWORKS

In order to obtain a full understanding of the performance of computer networks, it is not only necessary to examine them empiricially, with regular monitoring and experimental measurements and tests, but it is also essential to carry out a wide range of theoretical studies, using mathematical models. Ideally, a unified set of theoretical and empirical methods should be developed, that would allow both general and specific network and protocol design and performance problems to be tackled effectively, and that would lead to the formulation of new network designs, new protocol architectures, and new protocols at all levels. An essential part of this structure would be the cross-validation between these methods.

Considerable progress has been made in this direction during the past decade, and some of it will be reviewed in the following three sections. In the remainder of this section, some of the general principles are outlined, based partly on my own earlier discussion of this subject (Mayne, 1981, especially Section 1).

Measurements and monitoring can provide valuable insights into the performance of networks, together with their attached devices and the user services that they support. The results of network experiments and tests, using measurements, can provide a firm basis for the adequate empirical checking of the predictions made by theoretical models.

Theoretical models first need to be formulated, on the basis of "reasonably realistic" but nevertheless not too complicated asumptions, and then developed to obtain descriptions of network behaviour and predictions of network performance. The formulation of appropriate sets of assumptions, that are not over-simplified, on the one hand, and not too difficult for model development, on the other, is a fine art!

The development of worthwhile results from the network models, arising from the sets of assumptions, requires the application of a wide range of mathematical techniques, including: *analytical techniques*, that use the methods of mathematical analysis to derive explicit formulae that can be used in practical calculations; *probabilistic techniques*, that are in some ways similar to analytical techniques, but use probability theory and are needed because networks have random elements in their behaviour; *numerical techniques*, that calculate numerical estimates and predictions of network behaviour and performance; and *simulation*, that in effect follows through and computes the course of simplified representations of some of the events in a network in order to obtain rough estimates and predictions of its behaviour and performance.

The first three of these techniques, which taken together I call *analytical studies*, make it possible to achieve, with high accuracy, the numerical calculations required for the simpler theoretical models. However, they cannot be applied to models that are too complicated, where analytical answers are too difficult to derive explicitly, and exact numerical calculations, even with the aid of fast computers, are usually too time-consuming.

Simulation can be applied to much more complicated models, but it is much less accurate. Nevertheless it is an essential technique for obtaining reasonably accurate, or at least not wildly inaccurate, initial estimates of the results of calculations for all but the simplest models.

Cross-validation compares the estimates of network behaviour and performance, obtained by various methods, and attempts to find ways of bringing them closer together, by means of further investigations. On the one hand, it uses analytical results, where they are available, to cross-check the accuracy of the simulation methods used. Once the simulation method has been validated thus, it can be used in turn to check the accuracy of analytical approximations used for the more complicated models. On the other hand, cross-validation compares analytical results and simulation results with those of experiments and observations, to test the validity and predictive power of the models that are used. *Cross-validation is especially* strong where close agreement is achieved between analytical, simulation and empirical results for the same situation.

The next section reviews some of the network models, that have actually been used in theoretical studies of computer networks, and have obtained useful analytical and simulation results to estimate and predict various aspects of network behaviour and performance. The two sections after that briefly review the approaches of analytical studies and simulation.

NETWORK MODELS

Mathematical models have been used to investigate many aspects of the performance and operation of all types of computer network, and to throw light on the many problems to which these networks are subject. The published literature on models is already extensive, and there are many unpublished models as well. This section starts with a short general discussion of models and modelling, and then surveys briefly a representative selection of the models that have already been formulated, concentrating especially on models of LANs, but also considering models of broadcast networks, WANs, and specific problems faced by networks.

The purposes for which models and other theoretical studies are used include the following:

1. Mathematical formulation of possible alternative performance criteria, especially combined criteria, that are based on several simple criteria, and the use of optimal trade-offs between different factors affecting performance;

2. Prediction of the behaviour and performance of networks, for different combinations of relevant qualitative and quantitative factors;

3. Investigation of the delays to which data packets are subject, during their journeys across networks, and of the queues where they are likely to be delayed, in nodes and other devices;

4. Investigation of procedures for controlling the flow of packets into and across a network and for preventing congestion inside it;

5. Investigation of reliability problems, including the evaluation of network reliability and the assessment of the effects on network performance of different bit error rates during data transmission;

6. Optimisation of the choice of the numerical values of parameters to be used in network protocols;

7. Optimisation of the policy options for formulating protocols.

As the variety and number of network models at first sight seems bewildering, it would be useful to devise a *classification* of the models, together with a notation to represent different kinds of models. I summarise below the results of a first attempt that I have already made at such a classification, which is as yet only partly developed and has not been published. It takes into account the following five aspects: network type and configuration, nature of the network traffic, other characteristics, protocol(s) used—if specified, and nature of the work done or proposed for the models.

The *model notation* or *model code*, which is *not* described in detail here, consists of the codes for each of the above five aspects, separated by semi-colons. Each aspect has several *components*, each with its own code, so that the code for an aspect consists of the component codes, separated by commas.

Network types include LANs, WANs, and concatenated (multiple linked) networks, together with gateways and other network interconnections. A network configuration is classified according to whether or not the configuration is a linear, ring-like, tree-like, etc. set of links, how many links there are, and whether or not the links are multiple.

Network traffic is specified by a code that has one component for each node that handles traffic; each of these components has *subcomponents* for each node number or name, input specification, and output specification, these sub-components including specifications of traffic types and priorities.

The miscellaneous characteristics at present included are those relating to transmission errors and noise, but other characteristics will doubtless be added later on.

The *protocols code* lists the protocol(s) if any assumed by the model, together with any specific aspects of protocols that are considered.

The *work code* gives a list of aspects covered by current and/or proposed work on the models. The aspect codes included hitherto are: AN for analytical results, expressible by mathematical formulae, AP for specific mathematical or numerical approximations, NUM for numerical calculations based on the mathematical formulation of the model, SIM for the results of simulations based on the mathematical and probabilistic specification of the model, EMP for relevant empirical results such as measurements and observations, and CV for cross-validation studies.

General discussions of network models, together with extensive lists of references to further work on models, have been provided by Kleinrock (1976), Schwartz (1977), Gerla et al (1977). Tobagi et al (1978), and Mayne (1981).

Tropper's (1981) book about LAN technologies gives an extensive discussion of models proposed for ring and bus networks; it also has a bibliography. It aims to synthesise the considerable amount of work done on developing link access protocols for LANs of both types, and to provide a systematic discussion of the protocols and their associated performance models.

Didic and Wolfinger (1982) describe a modelling system that has been applied to model local networks specified in terms of the ISO Reference Model of Open Systems Interconnection. It can be applied to help find optimal network designs and investigate trade-offs between various network configurations.

Bux (1980) provides a comparative evaluation of the performance of ring and bus networks and subnetworks, measuring performance in terms of delay-throughput characteristics. Token-controlled and slotted rings, as well as random-access and ordered access buses, are investigated, using analytical models that describe the various topologies and access mechanisms in considerable detail. There is a comprehensive discussion of how the performance of these different kinds of networks is affected by such system parameters as transmission rate, packet sizes, cable length, and control overhead.

Blair and Shepherd (1982) apply simulation techniques to compare the performance of two leading examples of ring and bus network, the Cambridge Ring and the Ethernet. They evaluate performance mainly in terms of average delay and the variation of delay about its average, and they discuss briefly some of the other factors involved in a complete cost benefit analysis of LANs.

Duce (1981) reports on a conference about a variety of theoretical studies of Cambridge Rings and other LANs; both mathematical models and simulations were presented. Specific simulation studies of rings have also been made by Blair (1982) and Lunn and Bennett (1981). Blair investigates the tuning of system parameters of a Cambridge Ring and indicates how to improve its performance significantly. Lunn and Bennett compare the effects of varying three different parameters on the performance of a Cambridge Ring; these parameters are the ring loading, the number of nodes using the ring, and the message creation rates at each node.

Tanenbaum (1981, Section 7.1) summarises the results of some mathematical models of various bus network protocols, including especially persistent and non-persistent CSMA (Carrier Sense Multiple Access), CSMA-CD the variant of CSMA used by Ethernet, collision-free protocols, and limited-contention protocols. Tobagi and Hunt (1979) give an extensive mathematical performance analysis of CSMA-CD, and Metcalfe and Boggs (1956) present a simple model of Ethernet.

Spaniol (1979) presents a new concept for LAN protocols, including the use of automatic reservations for the retransmission of packets that collide during their first attempts at transmission. His mathematical model shows that nearly optimal throughput can be obtained as a result, even when priority scheduling policies are introduced.

Hamacher and Shedler (1982), Tobagi and Ra (1980), and Watson (1980), for example, have presented other models of bus network performance.

Many mathematical models of broadcast networks have been formulated and developed. As explained in Chapter 9, where some of the protocols of these networks were discussed, the basic ideas arose out of the study of the ALOHA protocol and its variants, the first of which were originally used in the Hawaiian packet radio network (Abramson, 1970 and 1973). These protocols and models for them are surveyed by Tanenbaum (1981, Chapter 6), Tobagi (1980b), Davies et al (1979, Chapter 5), Inose and Saito (1978) and Schwartz (1977, Chapter 13), and also discussed by Metzner (1976) and Tobagi (1980b), for example. From the ALOHA protocols and their mathematical models were evolved many of the bus network protocols and models, already mentioned, other protocols and models for packet radio networks, and protocols and models for satellite networks.

Packet radio models in general are discussed by Tanenbaum (1981, Section 6.2), Tobagi (1980b) and Inose and Saito (1978). More specific packet radio models have been developed by Kleinrock and Tobagi (1975), Tobagi (1980a) and Lam (1981).

Satellite models in general are discussed by Tanenbaum (1981, Section 6.1), Binder (1981), Huynh and Kuo (1981), Inose and Saito (1978), and Gerla et al (1977). More specific satellite models have been developed by Roberts (1972), who first introduced a reservation protocol, Kleinrock and Gerla (1974), and Kleinrock and Lam (1975).

Several theoretical studies have been made of the performance of protocols in

WANs. McGlynn (1978, Chapter 5) includes a comparsion of the performance of data-link protocols. Bux et al (1982) compare the performance of different operational modes of the standard WAN data-link procedure HDLC, which is used in X.25 Level 2. Gelenbe et al (1978) also evaluate the performance of HDLC. Edge and Hinchley (1978) survey end-to-end retransmission techniques, and Edge (1979) compares the performances of the hop-by-hop and endpoint approaches to network interconnection.

Finally, some brief mention is made here of models for the network problems that are discussed in Chapter 17.

The application of queueing theory to network models and to problems of network delay and buffer storage in network nodes and devices are described in great detail by the books by Kleinrock (1976) and Schwarz (1977). Pawlikowski (1980) presents a specific model of this sort.

Inose and Saito (1978) discuss queueing and delay models and other mathematical models relevant to problems of routing, flow control, capacity and flow assignment, network design, and error control. Many flow control models are included in the conference proceedings edited by Grangé and Gien (1979), and further flow control models have been presented by Labetoulle and Pujolle (1981), Pujolle (1978) and Chou and Gerla (1976), for example. Mark (1980) analyses the allocation of channel capacity in multiple access networks.

Kümmerle and Rudin (1978) use mathematical methods to discuss the cost-performance boundaries between packet switching and circuit switching, and the circumstances under which packet switching is better than circuit switching.

Mayne (1981) surveys the work on theoretical studies and models of computer networks, carried out by the INDRA Group in the Department of Computer Science at University College London, to complement their progamme of measurements and experiments and aid their work on protocol development and implementation. This work has been wide-ranging, covering both analytical and simulation studies, investigating a LAN (the Cambridge Ring) as well as X.25 networks and other WANs, and doing work on flow control strategies.

ANALYTICAL STUDIES

As mentioned earlier in this chapter, analytical studies include the use of analytical techniques, probabilistic techniques, and numerical techniques. As the phenomena occurring in computer networks can be represented well by a combination of random and deterministic elements, most network models in practice use *both* analytical and probabilistic techniques.

Perhaps the most important single example of the use of these combined analytical and probabilistic techniques is *queueing theory*, which has provided the basis for many network models. This application of queuing theory is well surveyed by Kleinrock (1976) and Schwartz (1977). These techniques provide formulae which can provide explicit performance evaluations for the simplest network models.

But, in practice, more realistic models are usually needed, that are too complicated to be mathematically tractable using direct methods. Hence the development of numerical approximation techniques has become valuable, and some of them have been discussed by Mayne (1981, Section 8). Perhaps the most important of these approximation methods, and the one most widely applied to computer network models, is the technique of *queueing network models*, which has been surveyed in two special periodical issues, *ACM Computing Surveys*, Vol. **10**, No. 3 (September 1980), and *Computer*, Vol. **13**, No. 4 (April 1980).

SIMULATION STUDIES

Even the use of approximation methods, to strengthen analytical techniques, can handle only a limited range of network models, and the more complicated and realistic models are still too difficult to yield to the analytical approach. Because of this, simulation studies have become vitally important for carrying out preliminary calculations and predictions of network performance.

The uses and methods of simulation are discussed by Mayne (1981, Section 7). Full expositions of simulation methods are given in various books on the subject, including that by Fishman (1978). The implementation of simulations by computers requires the use of simulation programs, using either high level programming languages or specially developed *simulation languages*.

Simulation and its application to a wide range of problems are discussed regularly in a series of Annual Simulation Symposia, sponsored by the IEEE Computer Society. One of the latest of these was the *15th Annual Simulation Symposium* (IEEE Computer Society, 1982).

Several theoretical studies of networks, using simulations, have already been mentioned. This includes the recent studies of local network models by Blair (1982), Blair and Shepherd (1982), Lunn and Bennett (1981), Didic and Wolfinger (1982), and Watson (1980). Price (1976) summarises the earlier work on simulation studies of networks, carried out at the National Physical Laboratory.

Comparative assessments of analytical and simulation studies and of their advantages and disadvantages have been made by Mayne (1981, Section 9) and Kleinrock (1970). Good judgment is needed, both in the choice of specific analytical, probabilistic, numerical and simulation techniques, and in deciding which models should be handled analytically and which should be simulated. The right combination of both approaches can lead to important further advances in the understanding and prediction of network behaviour and performance, similar to those already made in the best of the network models surveyed in this chapter.

REFERENCES

M. D. Abrams et al (Oct 1977) "The NBS Network Measurement System," *IEEE Transactions on Communications*, **COM-25** (10).

N. Abramson (1970) "The ALOHA system—Another alternative for computer communications," *Proceedings Fall Joint Computer Conference*, 281–285.

N. Abramson (1973) "The ALOHA System," pages 501–518 of Ed. N. Abramson and F. F. Kuo *Computer-Communication Networks*, Prentice-Hall, Englewood Cliffs, NJ.

ACM Computing Surveys, Vol. **10,** No. 3 (Sep 1980) Special issue on queueing network models and computer performance modelling.

P. Belanger, C. Hankins and N. Jain (1980) "Performance measurements of a local microcomputer network," *Local Area Network Workshop*, 197–206.

C. J. Bennett and A. J. Hinchley (Sep/Oct 1978) "Measurements of the Transmission Control Protocol," *Computer Networks*, **2**(4/5) 396–408.

R. Binder (1981) "Packet protocols for broadcast satellites," Chapter 5 of Kuo (1981).

P. Black and L. Brousse (Jun 1980) "Monitoring and simulation of X.25 packet switching networks," *Communications International*, **7**(6) 39–40, 42.

G. S. Blair (Feb 1982) "A performance study of the Cambridge Ring," *Computer Networks*, **6**(1) 13–26.

G. S. Blair and D. Shepherd (May 1982) "A performance comparison of Ethernet and the Cambridge Digital Communication Ring," *Computer Networks*, **6**(2) 105–113.

W. Bux (1980) "Local-area subnetworks: A performance comparison," *Local Area Networks Workshop*, 171–196.

W. Bux, K. Kümmerle and H. L. Truong (Feb 1982) "Data link-control performance: Results comparing HDLC operational modes," *Computer Networks*, **6**(1) 37–51.

R. J. Carpenter, T. E. Malcolm and M. L. Strawbridge (1980) "Operational experience with the NBS local area networks," *Local Area Networks Workshop*, 51–66.

W. Chou and M. Gerla (1976) "A unified flow and congestion control model for packet networks," *Proceedings Third ICC*, 475–482.

W. W. Chu, M. Gerla, W. E. Naylor, S. W. Treadwell, D. Mills, P. Spilling and F. A. Aagesen (Nov 1979) "Experimental results on the Packet Satellite Network," *Proceedings NTC, IEEE*, 45.4.1–45.4.12.

N. B. Cohen, J. A. Field and S. N. Kalra (1978) "Measurement of X.25 service," *Proceedings COMPCON*, 330–337.

Computer, Vol. **13,** No. 4 (Apr 1980) Special issue on analytical queueing models and their applications to computer performance models.

D. W. Davies and D. L. A. Barber (1973) *Communication Networks for Computers*, Wiley, Chichester and New York.

D. W. Davies, D. L. A. Barber, W. L. Price and C. M. Solomonides (1979) *Computer Networks and Their Protocols*, Wiley, Chichester and New York.

M. Didic and B. Wolfinger (May 1982) "Simulation of a local computer network architecture applying a unified modeling system," *Computer Networks*, **6**(2) 79–91.

D. A. Duce (Apr 1981) *Report of the Cambridge Ring Modelling and Simultaion Special Interest Group* held on 19 March 1981, Computing Division, Rutherford & Appleton Laboratories.

S. W. Edge (1979) "Comparison of the hop-by-hop and endpoint approaches to network interconnection," pp. 359–373 of Grangé and Gien (1979).

S. W. Edge and A. J. Hinchley (Oct 1978) "A survey of end-to-end retransmission techniques," *Computer Communication Review*, **8**(4) 1–18.

G. S. Fishman (1978) *Principles of Discrete Event Simulation*, Wiley-Interscience, New York.

E. Gelenbe, J. Labetoulle and G. Pujolle (Sep/Oct 1978) "Performance evaluation of the HDLC protocol," *Computer Networks*, **2**(4/5) 409–415.

M. Gerla, L. Nelson and L. R. Kleinrock (1977) "Packet satellite multiple access: Models and measurements," *National Telecommunications Conference Record*, 12:2.1–12:2.8.

Ed. J.-L. Grangé and M. Gien (1979) *Flow Control in Computer Networks*, North-Holland, Amsterdam.

J. L. Grangé and P. Mussard (Feb 1978) "Performance measurement of line control protocols in the CIGALE network," *Proceedings Computer Network protocols Symposium, Liège*, Belgium.

D. S. Grubb and I. W. Cotton (Nov 1977) "Criteria for evaluation of data communications services," *Computer Networks*, **1**(6) 325–340.

V. C. Hamacher and G. S. Shedler (May 1982) "Access response on a collison-free local bus network," *Computer Networks*, **6**(2) 93–103.

D. Huynh and F. F. Kuo (1981) "Mixed-media packet networks," Chapter 6 of Kuo (1981).

IEEE Computer Society (Mar 1982) *15th Annual Simulation Symposium*, and earlier annual symposia in this series.

H. Inose and T. Saito (Nov 1978) "Theoretical aspects in the analysis and synthesis of packet communication networks," *Proceedings of the IEEE*, **66**(11) 1409–1422.

I. M. Jacobs, R. Binder and E. V. Hoversten (Nov 1978) "General purpose satellite networks," *Proceedings of the IEEE*, **66**(11) 1448–1467.

R. E. Kahn, S. A. Gronemeyer, J. Burchfiel and C. Kunzelman (Nov 1978) "Advances in packet radio technology," *P·oceedings of the IEEE*, **66**(11) 1488–1496.

L. R. Kleinrock (1970) "Analytical and simulation methods in computer network design," *Proceedings SJCC*, 569–579.

L. R. Kleinrock (1974) *Communication Nets*, Dover, New York.

L. R. Kleinrock (1976) *Queueing Systems*, Vol. 2, *Computer Applications*, Wiley, New York and Chichester.

L. R. Kleinrock (Nov 1978) "Principles and lessons in packet communications," *Proceedings of the IEEE*, **66**(11) 1320–1329.

L. R. Kleinrock (Sep 1980) "Analysis and design issues addressed at ICCC '78," *Computer Networks*, **4**(4) 175–185.

L. R. Kleinrock and M. Gerla (1978) "On the measured performance of packet satellite access schemes," *Proceedings of the 4th ICCC*, 535–541.

L. R. Kleinrock and S. S. Lam (Apr 1975) "Packet switching in a multiaccess broadcast channel: Performance evaluation," *IEEE Transactions on Communications*, **COM-23**(4) 410–423.

L. R. Kleinrock and W. Naylor (1974) "On the measured behavior of the ARPA network," *Proceedings AFIPS NCC*, **43**, 767–780.

L. R. Kleinrock, W. E. Naylor and H. Opderbeck (Jan 1976) "A study of line overhead in the ARPANET," *Communications of the ACM*, **19**(1) 3–12.

L. R. Kleinrock and F. A. Tobagi (1975) "Random access techniques for data transmission over packet-switched radio channels," *Proceedings NCC*, 187–201.

K. Kümmerle and H. Rudin (Feb 1981) "Packet and circuit switching: Cost/performance boundaries," *Computer Networks*, **2**(1) 3–17.

Ed. F. F. Kuo (1981) *Protocols & Techniques for Data Communications Networks*, Prentice-Hall, Englewood Cliffs, NJ, (with bibliographies).

J. Labetoulle and G. Pujolle (Apr 1981) "A study of flows through virtual circuits computer networks," *Computer Networks*, **5**(2) 119–126.

S. S. Lam (1981) "Design considerations for large mobile packet radio networks," *Local Networks*, 215–231.

Local Area Networks Workshop (1980) Proceedings of the IFIP Working Group 6.4 Local Computer Networks Working Party 80/13 Conference, August 27–29 1980, Zurich, Switzerland.

K. Lunn and K. H. Bennett (Jul 1981) "Message transport on the Cambridge Ring," *Software Practice & Experience*, **11**(7) 711–716.

D. R. McGlynn (1978) *Distributed Processing and Data Communications*, Wiley, New York and Chichester.

J. W. Mark (1980) "Capacity allocation in multiple access networks, *Local Area Networks Workshop*, 151–170.

A. J. Mayne (Jul 1981) "INDRA theoretical and simulation work—A review of progress from 1979-1981," *INDRA Technical Report*, TR-70, University College London.

R. M. Metcalfe and D. R. Boggs (Jul 1976) "Ethernet: Distributed packet switching for local computer networks," *Communications of the ACM*, **19**(7) 395–404.

J. Metzner (Apr 1976) "On improving utilization in ALOHA networks," *IEEE Transactions on Communications*, **COM-24**(4) 447–448.

Network News (May 1980) "TEKELEC TE 92," 6.

K. Pawlikowski (Jan 1980) "Message time waiting in a packet switching system," *Journal of the ACM*, **27**(1) 30–41.

W. L. Price (Dec 1976) "Data network simulation: Experiments at the National Physical Laboratory 1968-1976," *Computer Networks*, **1**(3) 199–210.

G. Pujolle (1978) "Analysis of flow-controls in switched data network by a unified model," *Proceedings 4th ICCC*, 123–128.

L. G. Roberts (1972) "Dynamic allocation of satellite capacity through packet reservation," *Proceedings NCC*, 711–716.

D. Shepherd and P. Corcoran (Jan/Feb 1982) "A gateway development system," *Microprocessors and Microsystems*, **6**(1) 21–24.

J. F. Shoch (Apr 1980) *An annotated bibliography on local computer networks*, Xerox PARC Technical Report.

J. F. Shoch (Sep 1980) "A brief note on performance of an Ethernet system under high loading," *Computer Networks*, **4**(4) 187–188.

J. F. Shoch and J. A. Hupp (Spring 1980) "Performance of an Ethernet local network—A preliminary report," Compcon, 318–322; see also earlier version in *Update Local Area Networks*, 113–125.

M. Schwarz (1977) *Computer-Communication Network Design and Analysis*, Prentice-Hall, Englewood Cliffs, NJ, USA.

O. Spaniol (Nov 1979) "Modelling of local computer networks," *Computer Networks*, **3**(5) 315–326.

A. V. Stokes, D. L. Bates and P. T. Kirstein (1976) "Monitoring and access control of the London node of ARPANET," *Proceedings AFIPS NCC*, **45,** 597–603.

A. S. Tanenbaum (1981) *Computer Networks*, Prentice-Hall, Englewood Cliffs, NJ, (with extensive bibliographies).

F. A. Tobagi (1980a) (Feb 1980) "Analysis of a two hop centralized packet radio network," *IEEE Transactions on Communications*, **COM-28,** 196–216.

F. A. Tobagi (1980b) (Apr 1980) "Multiaccess protocols in packet communication systems," *IEEE Transactions on Communications*, **COM-28**(4) 468–488 (with bibliography).

F. A. Tobagi and V. B. Hunt (1979) "Performance analysis of carrier sense multiple access with collision detection," *Update Local Area Networks*, 217–245.

F. A. Tobagi and R. Ra (1980) "Efficient round-robin and priority schemes for unidirectional broadcasting schemes," *Local Area Networks Workshop*, 131–149.

C. Tropper (1981) *Local Computer Network Technologies*, Academic Press, New York and London.

Update Local Area Networks (May 1979) Proceedings of the Local Area Communications Network Symposium, Boston.

W. B. Watson (Jul 1980) "Performance in contention bus local network interconnection," *Computer Communication Review*, **10**(3) 19–25.

K. Wilkinson (1977) "A network control contre for the European Informatics Network," *ONLINE 1977*, 271–275.

PART THREE

NETWORK APPLICATIONS

Chapter 11

Office Systems
and Business Systems

Computing and information technology are now being applied more vigorously to business offices than to any other area. Following the already extensive and still expanding uses of computing and electronic data processing for such routine commercial operations as accounting, payroll and stock recording, the more direct applications to office work are now being explored vigorously. Originally, they were more or less confined to the use of word processing to speed up clerical and typing work, but far-reaching and dramatic visions of "office automation" and "the office of the future" are being presented to business men more and more.

This chapter tries to show what parts of these visions have already been acheived and what parts are still only experimental and largely potentialities. It shows the decisive parts being played by local area networks in various attempts to implement integrated office information systems, and indicates some possible uses of wide area networks and linked local area networks too, although these are at present used less often. As in Chapter 2, on local area network systems, so here, the claims made by various manufacturers and suppliers should be considered carefully, in relation to the specific requirements of the user organisation that is considering buying their products. Much harm can result from the wrong choices and from the wrong strategy for introducing new technology, just as great benefits can follow from the right policies of office automation.

This chapter starts by considering the requirements for automated and integrated office systems and business systems, together with the planning and implementation of these systems. It then reviews the applications of the available technologies, first presenting the general context and then describing some of them individually, including word processing and text processing, electronic mail and message services, and telefacsimile. After that, it discusses local office systems, based on local area networks, and linked office systems, serving organisations with several premises, using wide area networks by themselves or in conjunction with local area networks. Then the applications of networking to banking and financial transactions are described. Finally, the principles of integrated office information systems and the progress towards the implementation of integrated networks for companies and other organisations are both reviewed briefly.

This chapter is concerned largely with descriptions of the technologies, products and systems that are already available, although to some extent it also discusses their human aspects, problems and possible futures, which are considered further in Chapters 16, 17 and 18, respectively. Recent developments are presented in Chapter 22.

Books on office automation and the use of computer networking and other information technologies in the office include: the introductory book by Price (1979), the tutorial by Thurber (1980), and the discussion by Uhlig et al (1979), which gives a good idea of the general background. There are also four useful volumes of short papers, specially oriented to readers in businesses and companies, that have been published in Gower's *The Office of the Future* series: *Planning for the Office of the Future* (Simpson, 1981), *Planning for Electronic Mail* (Simpson, 1981a), *Planning for Word Processing* (Simpson, 1982b), and *Planning for Telecommunications* (Simpson, 1982c).

There are several films on office automation, including *Office Automation— Planning for Success*, issued by BIS Applied Systems Ltd (undated), and also *Tomorrow's Office* (Rostron, 1981a) and *Office Automation* (Rostron, 1981b).

Collections of relevant articles for the general reader have appeared, for example, in the *Financial Times Surveys* on Computers (18 Jan 1982) and on The Electronic Office (13 Apr 1982), *The Times Guide to Information Technology* (14 Jan 1982), the *Management Today Special Survey* (Apr 1982) on The Automated Office, and the second issue of *IT's Business* (23 Apr 1982) on Office Automation.

Collections of more technical papers on the subject matter of this chapter have appeared in the special issues of *Computer, Vol.* **14,** No. 5 (May 1981), on office information systems; *Computer Networks,* Vol. **5,** No. 6 (Dec 1981), on office automation; and *IEEE Transactions on Communications,* Vol. **COM-30,** No. 1 (Jan 1982), on communications in the automated office. These collections have useful introductions by Maryanski (1981), Uhlig (1981) and Limb (1982), respectively.

Sessions B1, B2, B4, B5, B6 and C9 of the very recent *ICCC 82* (1982) Conference presented many papers about office systems, while Session B9 had three papers on financial applications of computer networking.

The Association for Computing Machinery started publication of its quarterly, *Transactions on Office Information Systems* (*TOOIS*) in 1983. It is concerned with all aspects of office information systems, including: communication systems, distributed processing, data management, office organisation, and user interfaces. It publishes significant original work on the analysis, design, specification and implementation of office information systems, together with reports on experience of these systems.

The books by Corby et al (1982) and Hoare (1980, Part 3, "Key Communications Applications") each have several chapters on applications of networking to office systems and other aspects of business.

Articles giving a general perspective include those by: Davies (1982), on local networks in relation to office automation, Longley (1982), on the integrated information processing systems of the future, Panko (1981), on some of the basic issues of office automation, and Chapter 11 of Mayne (1986), on business and financial applications of videotex.

In the UK, the association OFIX (Office of the Future Information Exchange) was formed early in 1982, as a user-oriented body, welcoming participation by independent consultants but free from any dependence on suppliers. It is aimed at small to medium-sized organisations approaching office automation or going through its early stages. It aims to build up information on a variety of office automation systems, and to include details of user experience, reasons for selection of a given system, and what benefits can be expected. It will develop a user viewpoint on standards and requirements, and publicise this viewpoint in due course. It holds regular meetings in London, publishes *OFIX Newsletter,* and has several working parties, for example, an active working party on electronic mail and electronic filing whose work is indicated in Chapter 22.

PLANNING FOR INTEGRATED OFFICE SYSTEMS AND BUSINESS SYSTEMS

Office automation has been defined as "people using technology to manage and communicate information more effectively" (Wang, 1981a, page 1). Similarly, Uhlig et al (1979, page 20) have defined an *automated office* as "an office in which interactive computer tools are put in the hands of individual knowledge workers, at their desks, in the areas in which they are physically working." The first stage in planning for office automation is an adequate analysis of what activities, processes and procedures are already taking place in the office and of the relationships and interactions between them.

Uhlig et al (1979) sum up the results of general studies of this sort. The most important activity of office workers is communications, and other activties include: gathering, filing, organising, retrieving, modifying, and generating information. Major processes include: planning, resource allocation (sometimes known as programming and budgeting), coordination, monitoring execution of plans, policy formulation, decision making, and directing. Some of these functions are carried out by clerical and secretarial staff; others, at a higher level, are performed by managers and executives.

Bunce (1982) also advocates the use of a functional analysis for planning office information systems. He subdivides integrated information functions into commercial operations functions and office functions. Commercial operations functions are divided into standard functions, such as payroll and invoicing and accounting, that are common to all companies, and functions that are specific to different industrial and service sectors. Office functions are divided into functions like communications, processing, information storage and retrieval, that support general office work, and plant-oriented functions, such as alarm and security systems, monitoring, and control. In order to integrate information processing, the organisation needs a common communications network, that handles voice, data, text and pictures, and a common computing and data processing system.

Rostron (1982) considers that the right way to start office automation is to: establish functional requirements, identify applications, and select appropriate technological solutions. Executives should prepare a strategy and then be prepared to experiment; a properly managed pilot trial is an excellent way of evaluating the opportunities and technical issues. A key question to be settled is whether the chosen option suits the company's style.

Butler (1981) discusses some of the specific problem areas, which companies and other organisations must understand in order to move towards office automation, and advocates a gradual approach to its introduction. Terminals and adequate switching facilities must be installed, together with whatever other equipment is appropriate; the products of the available suppliers must be assessed carefully, preferably using evidence of their previous experience and track record. Economic justifications are needed for any new products and systems introduced. Relevant human aspects should be taken into full account. Management structures may need to be revised; for example, every company needs an *information manager,* coordinating *all three* of the functions of data processing management, telecommunications management, and office management itself. The hardest *technical* problem is to develop appropriate network operating methods to support the multi-function work stations that will eventually be introduced. A coherent overall network structure is needed to integrate all aspects of the office and business system into an integrated whole, and it is by no means clear as yet which, if any, of the LAN systems now on the market can achieve this objective.

Butler (1982) repeats some of these points and also considers some other aspects of office automation. Business aims for office automation include: employee productivity, management productivity, adequate levels of service, and avoiding excessive unemployment. Technological needs include: centralised *and* local computing power and data storage, multiple-function equipment, cheap data storage, good linking and switching between work stations, good networking and good file maintenance. In the UK at least, most potential users still do not fully perceive the need for office automation, and it does not yet seem to have had much impact on business operations. Butler draws the following three major conclusions to be learnt from existing experience of office automation: do not run but walk; do not bother with a detailed long-term plan; the way ahead is through gradual, limited exploitation of information technology, rather than through a grand strategic design.

Agresta (1981) considers that, for a typical large company with many divisions and locations, a phased approach to office automation makes most sense, as it will minimise the shock to the organisation and provide a chance to justify costs at each step. He suggests a ten-year scenario with four stages of development:

1. Word processing, including typing and editing, electronic filing and information retrieval;
2. Communicating word processing, with electronic mail and network access to computers and copiers;

3. Introduction of administrative work stations, providing administrative support systems, and handling internal mail, messages and files;

4. Introduction of management work stations.

In their book on the planning of information management systems, Pritchard and Cole (1982) provide users with advice on the preparation of an office automation strategy, with special reference to the management of personal, departmental, corporate and external information. They take account of views gathered from the UK, USA and Japan.

Blagg (1981) shows how a suitable office system, with staff adequately trained to use it, can lead to great increases in the productivity of an office. He gives a scenario of a typical day in the working of an automated office.

Jones (1982a) discusses an approach to office computing in terms of three aspects, each of which he discusses in turn: departmental processing, inter-departmental communications, and internal department communications.

Collins (1982) examines the need for an office communications system and discusses how to plan it; he gives some indications of the possible cost savings.

In their book on planning electronic message systems, Wilson and Pritchard (1982a) emphasise the need for a strategic approach in developing electronic mail and other office automation facilities. They also outline the character and benefits of office automation, a theme that they develop more fully in their other book (Wilson and Pritchard, 1982b). There, they examine what benefits are being obtained from contemporary information technology, and they describe how to justify the installation of its products and systems.

Not only can office automation offer a range of cost savings; it also provides improved efficiency via value-added applications: increased accessibility to information, allowing the provision of more current and up-to-date information; increased accessibility to people, via message systems and networking; increased control over personal activities, because work can be done from various locations including the home; increased individual contributions, because staff will be able to devote more time to their primary tasks (Price, 1979).

Knight (1982, pages 88–89) lists six key questions that should be asked by any potential user, before he can be confident that an automated office system will serve his organisation reliably over a long period. By obtaining satisfactory answers to these questions, his company is much more likely to gain major and lasting benefits and avoid the liability of unwise choices.

Uhlig et al (1979, Chapter III.2) present a strategy for the implementation of office automation systems, that will help their impact to be beneficial. They describe the steps to be taken by the strategy and the implementation principles, and they indicate the elements of user support that implementation needs, in order to be successful.

Burdett (1981) and Naughton (1981) both examine the justification for companies to move towards greater use of electronic methods and information technology in the office, with special reference to costs.

Other papers on office systems strategy and management include those by: Peters (1982) on an organisations telecommunications potential, Clark (1982) on value added systems, Hawk and Zitzmann (1982) on information management, and Bailey et al (1981) on internal accounting controls.

Cane (1982a) discusses the state of the market for office automation systems and products, and points out that, at present, it is largely only a potential market. Most potential business customers do not see the need to change from their traditional office systems. There are various reasons for this, including high costs and lack of confidence in the ability of suppliers to provide equipment fitting the specific requirements of the organisation. Cane believes that human factors are probably the major hurdle, and that many of the visions of office automation that are presented seem far too fantastic to those who are expected to apply them. Thus progress to office automation will be slow and undramatic, driven by necessity rather than technology.

In my own opinion, this may be true for most companies, which are probably inherently conservative, but there seems to be no reason why a *new* organisation, run by people who are fully aware of the potentials of information technology and office automation, should not deliberately design and implement an *evolving* fully integrated information system from the outset, even if it starts on a relatively small scale.

West (1981) lists some warnings against being over-enthusiastic about the "office of the future," and considers the impact of the new technology on people. He suggests that many of the expected benefits of office automation may not be reaped, in many cases, because the way that things are done in existing offices is upset. It is all too easy merely to mechanise, in the mistaken belief that "automation" has been achieved.

Tsichritzis and Lochovsky (1980) point out that several challenges must be met before office automation can be applied effectively to remedy the information handling problems of an office. Technological and automated solutions to the different aspects of these problems need to be integrated. Models and techniques need to be formulated to represent and analyse the information to flow in the office. Interfaces need to be developed that are easy to use and integrate many different functions. The impact of the proposed office automation needs to be examined, so that solutions and systems can be produced that are acceptable to the office users. These problems need to be tackled with the aid of human factors, software engineering and hardware engineering techniques.

Several technical papers have been written, that present conceptual and mathematical models of office systems. Nutt and Ricci (1981) describe Quinault, an automated system for constructing and analysing office models, whose interactive graphics facilities help managers to understand the structures of their offices and predict the performance of their office information systems.

Svobodova (1981) describes a model of an office automation system, oriented towards its implementation on a computer network; the entities in this model include: work stations, "forms" that define the interface with human workers, and "tasks" that embody the control of how to use the work stations to perform specific functions.

Konsysnski et al (1982) develop a communications model, applicable to office processes, to aid the specification of the requirements for office communications. Chang and Chang (1982) introduce a conceptual framework for office information system design, from the data base viewpoint, that includes an office procedural model.

Arthurs and Stuck (1982) develop a mathematical model for the throughput of jobs and obtain results about the average throughput rate and the average delays that are likely to be experienced; they use a model of an office that handles a mixture of jobs, with each job consisting of one or more steps.

OFFICE AUTOMATION TECHNOLOGIES

Wang Laboratories has developed a strategy that it claims will achieve the successful implementation of office automation in organisations of all sizes (Wang Laboratories, 1981a). This strategy is based on the development and application of six technologies: data processing, word processing, image processing, audio processing, networking, and human factors. The first four of these technologies respectively handle information in the form of numbers, written words, pictures, and spoken words; networking shares information, and human factors is concerned with information for people.

Willams (1982a) indicates some of the technologies used in automated offices and concludes that all sizes of computers will have a role in the "office of the future"; their uses will include provision of personal files and diaries, message storage, control of information flow through the office, and extensive data processing for payrolls and accounts. The right mixture of computers and the correct integration of their functions are both important.

The report by Butler Cox and Partners (1982) examines individual equipment, its costs, and its characteristics, and summarises the experience of over a dozen organisations.

Other reviews and lists of available information technologies and equipment for the automated office are given, for example, by: Agresta (1981), Burns (1980), Buxton (1982), Charlish (1982a), King Taylor (1982), Kjellin (1981), Manley (1981), Mayne (1986, Chapters 6 and 7), Simons (1981a), Wharton (1981) and Williamson (1981). Slonim et al (1981) describe NDX-100, a prototype of an electronic filing machine that integrates several functions of the "office of the future."

McFetrich (1982) points out that office work is concerned with the collection, input, processing, storge, retrieval and communication of information. Therefore managers need to understand and be prepared for the ways in which information technology is modernising and combining these procedures.

WORD PROCESSING AND TEXT PROCESSING

Word processors as pieces of equipment are reviewed in Chapter 7 of this book, by Williams (1982b), and by Broughton (1982), who also discusses sales and service of word processors.

On the other hand, the present section is concerned with various aspects of the *usage and uses* of word processing, including its relation to other office systems.

The book, *Planning for Word Processing,* edited by Simpson (1982b) contains some very useful papers on its practical aspects; reference is made to several of these papers individually later in this section.

The book by Simons (1982b) describes the main characteristics of word processing, and discussed its advantages over conventional typewriting. It considers communication, maintenance, security and costs.

The book by Doswell (1982) covers security aspects of word processing and its associated communications, together with the use of word processors as stand-alone equipment and as part of an automated office. It discusses how far word processors are enhanced typewriters and how far they should be viewed as computers in their own right.

The book by Barton (1981) is a useful practical guide to business uses of word processors.

Periodicals on word processing include *Word & Information Processing* (formerly called *Word Processing Now*) and *Which Wordprocessor.*

Brief general reviews of word processing are given by Corby et al (1982, Chapter 11) and King Taylor (1982), for example. Evans (1981) reviews the history and current status of word processing. Townsend (1981) discusses the technology and history of word processing, and gives four basic rules for planning a successful word processing installation.

Blagg (1981, pages 109–111) considers the requirements and facilities of word processing. Wharton (1982) examines the state of the art of word processing, including communicating word processing and Teletex. Cottle (1981) discusses the application of word processing and related technologies to the management of a company. Word processing, in relation to office systems and office automation is also considered by Holland (1982), Jones (1982b), Pinner (1982) and Sloman (1982).

Wiltshire (1982a) shows how larger companies benefit from centralised systems for office dictation; several pieces of electronic equipment, including PABXs as well as word processors, are available for this purpose. Wiltshire (1982b) describes the benefits brought to the head office of Cadbury, the confectionery firm, by shared-logic word processing used in conjunction with a modern direct-link dictation system from the Dictaphone Company; significant improvements were achieved in the typing service and in the time taken for correspondence. Wiltshire (1982a) reports similar benefits from the use of a Phillips automatic dictation system by the Automobile Association.

Teletex is a sophisticated form of communicating word processing, which is described in the next section, as it is also a form of electronic mail.

Text editing is an important part, not only of word processing, but also of text processing in general, electronic mail, interactive programming, and other forms of online computing. Uhlig et al (1979, Chapter 1.4) discuss at some length several text editing tools for generating, organising, analysing, and transforming information. Sharma and Gruchacz (1982) present the Display Text Editor TED. It is worth noting that sophisticated editors can be provided by good computer operating systems as well as by good word processing systems; for example, this chapter was prepared using a version of the "ded" editor in conjunction with the UNIX operating system.

Allied to text editing facilities are *advanced text management* facilities. For example, computerised dictionaries can provide hyphenation, check spelling (as long as care is taken with variants between British and American English!), and even assist with foreign language translation (Blagg, 1981; pages 114–115). McIlroy (1982) relates the development of the UNIX spelling checker, SPELL, and explains how it works.

Macdonald et al (1982) describe the Writer's Workbench programs, which analyse English prose, and suggest some improvements to them. Cherry (1982) describes a system of programs that help writers to evaluate documents and produce better written, more readable prose. Users without programming experience can quickly learn to use the QBE/OBE language to compose, edit, format and distribute texts, such as letters and reports, and also graphs and diagrams (Zloof, 1981).

Steele (1982) shows how word processing can be viewed as part of a *text processing* technology, as defined for example by a study document of the Computing Services Association. This technology includes: word processing systems with sophisticated editing facilities, a data network and switching system to route letters to their recipients, electronic mail boxes, optical scanners to convert outside documents to machine readable form, keypads and screens for data retrieval, high-quality high-speed printers, and powerful computer software. The UK Department of Industry has sponsored a wide ranging study, to determine its problems and potential benefits.

Kirstein and Treadwell (1982) consider how to integrate document processing with the relevant public telecommunications and networking services.

ELECTRONIC MAIL AND MESSAGE SERVICES

Electronic mail can be defined very generally as any form of electronic communication which is an alternative to at least one of the ordinary postal services. Viewed in this way, it could comprise such services as Telex and Teletex, telefacsimile and digital document storage, together with intercommunicating word processors and message systems having online access to central computers.

More usually, it is defined fairly narrowly, as electronic systems which are designed to handle short messages and those which directly challenge letter post. Its chief features are that the messages for a given recipient are stored safely in a computer system until he is ready to receive them, they are available in electronic form, and they are communicated fast.

The book *Planning for Electronic Mail,* edited by Simpson (1981a), contains a useful collection of papers, oriented especially to the business user. The first of these, by Thompson (1981) reviews the features that would be desirable in a comprehensive electronic mail system, and describes how a company should set about studying its needs for electronic mail and whether it needs it. Rosenberg (1981) considers especially how the telephone system can be used for carrying electronic messages. The papers by Perkins (1981), Mills (1981) and Jones (1981) describe various examples of electronic mail systems on the market.

The Electronic Message System (EMS), marketed by Datapoint (UK) Ltd., can generate a message from a word processor, possibly including information accessed from computer files. The message can then be sent very easily, at whatever level of priority is chosen by its originator; the four priorities used are: immediate, for crisis level messages; urgent, for messages that need to be sent before most other messages; regular, for most messages; and overnight, for long documents and less important messages (Jenner, 1981).

The book by Wilson and Pritchard (1982) emphasises the need for a strategic approach to the development of an electronic mail system and other office automation facilities inside a business, and it gives some of the advice on the design of such a system.

Cane's (1982b) article gives a useful introduction to electronic mail, indicating its nature, giving some arguments for and against its use, and listing some of the considerable number of products and services now on the market.

Uhlig et al (1979, Chapter 1.3) and Crocker (1980a) both present some of the basic concepts of electronic mail and message systems and give examples of their alternative designs.

Perhaps the most usual approach is for the users of a message system to access that system's service computer from their terminals via a network, and have their messages stored in mailbox files on the computer's magnetic disks. Thus a user sends a message to a recipient's mailbox, stored by that computer, and, when he logs in, can retrieve from his own mailbox there whatever messages have arrived for him.

In a *distributed* mail service, at least some of the users have mail delivered to their own computers, as opposed to the remote service storage of the typical mail system.

Distinction should be made too between in-house electronic mail systems, where all the users are attached to the same LAN, remote mail systems, where the users are attached to different nodes of a WAN, and combined systems, using linked LAN's. A typical example of the latter would be where a company has several premises, geographically separated, each of which has its own local mail system, but can also exchange messages electronically with users on another site.

Kirstein (1980) analyses the requirement for message services and briefly surveys the types of facilities now provided for this purpose by WANs, both for public services and for private services. He considers, as illustrative examples, the traditional public Telex service, the proposed new public Telex service (discussed in the next paragraph but one), the Arpanet message systems and services, and Prestel. He suggests services that could become available within the next few years.

Crocker (1980b) and Higginson and Kirstein (1981) both consider the interconnection of mail services using different networks. Here, some degree of compatibility is needed between the networks, and this is achieved by adopting suitable combinations of mutually agreed protocols, including mail protocols. Kerr (1982) discusses the interconnection of public electronic mail systems. Fergus (1982) describes the GILT project, for the interconnection of computer-based message systems via public data networks.

A very important example of an electronic mail service, now being implemented gradually for wide area message exchange, both nationally and internationally, is Teletex, that already has its own set of protocols, agreed by CCITT and mentioned in Chapter 9.

Teletex combines the best features of word processing, Telex and telecommunications. It is concerned with automation of clerical functions, text processing, and electronic processing of documents, including their distribution to stations other than their point of origin. It allows the equipment of different suppliers to be connected to it.

It is now being introduced as an electronic mail system of this kind, in parts of Western Europe and North America. It will be possible to interface and link the Teletex network with the existing Telex network, but Teletex will be much faster, having a data transmission rate of at least 2400 bits/sec, at least on international routes.

Teletex terminals will automatically establish calls, transfer information, and then clear calls, without operator intervention. They will also receive automatically, and be able to store several incoming documents, for later reading and printing on-site and/or for forwarding them to their next destination. Special Teletex terminals, also usable as word processors, have been developed by Philips and Siemens, and Philips has produced a teletex adaptor for its word processors. The Philips terminal has a network controller that will connect it to the PSTN or to X.21 circuit-switched networks or to X.25 packet-switched networks.

Teletex will transmit pages in A4 format, with both upper and lower case letters, accented letters, underlining, and a wide range of characters; in particular, it will allow free use of the character sets of most European languages.

The book by Price (1982) explains the opportunities and the limitations of teletex, and examines how this text communication service can fit into an organisation and interface with local office systems. For useful short introductions to Teletex, see for example *Data Processing* (1981), Corby et al (1982, Chapter 13), Hoare (1980, in Part 3), and Tombs (1981, 1982). Ithell (1982) describes the design and facilities of a new, more powerful, Teletex work station.

Ruggeberg (1982) and Gustawson (1982) report on the development of the Teletex services in West Germany and Sweden, respectively. Kirstein (1980), de Smith(1982)and Reid (1982) discuss developments in electronic message services in general.

Garcia-Lina-Aceves and Kuo (1982) outline an architectural model for large message systems, based on distributed computing. Shicker (1982) proposes a two-stage approach to the problem of naming and addressing an electronic mail system. Tsichritzis et al (1982) outline a prototype system that integrates the facilities of message systems and data base management systems, and manages structured messages according to their contents.

Hattori et al (1982) discuss the problems and technical aspects of designing a flexible real-time voice storage system, with a distributed structure that can be expanded at will. They propose an efficient new method of accessing these distributed voice files in real time, so that continued storing and forwarding of voice messages can be guaranteed. They point out that voice storage systems, allowing telephone communication at any time, will play an important role in the office of the future.

Wagreich (1982) believes that the introduction of electronic message systems in the office will make it much more easy to employ physically disabled individuals, especially those with handicaps to hearing, speech, and sight, as well as those with limited mobility, by reducing many of their barriers to communication. She describes a pilot project with deaf people, that clearly points to the usefulness of computer-based telecommunications in their work situations as well as their personal lives.

TELEFACSIMILE

Telefacsimile, usually just called *facsimile* or *fax,* is the transmission of information about a document along a telephone line or other communications channel, in such a way that the received signals are reconstructed into a form of remote photocopying, as it is the *page image* that is transmitted. Therefore, facsimile can be used to send copies of documents which have diagrams and pictures, and it faithfully reproduces letter headings and signatures in business correspondence.

As a means of transmitting text only, at least in a European language, facsimile is inefficient, as it makes no attempt to use character codes for the letters in the text, but instead sends their much more bit-costly graphical representations. Nevertheless, this particular application of fax turns out to be cost-effective remarkably often. It comes into its own especially when sending texts of languages like Chinese and Japanese, where there is no standard coding of the ideograms that are used.

Until very recently, facsimile has been used mainly for specialist functions, usually either within a company or for sending information to just one other organisation. It is especially useful for sending copies of texts to printers and for sending complete printed page images from one branch of a newspaper to another. Other specialised fax operations are used to transmit information about the weather, and for mobile and military applications.

The now much wider business facsimile market caters for operational fax and convenience fax (Gerrard, 1981). In both cases, they provide electronic mail capability, wherever the PSTN operates, and they need no special document preparation.

Operational fax, covering about 90% of the facsimile market, serves a specific application, such as regular financial information or sales reporting.

Convenience fax machines, usually of the low cost manual variety, are installed on the basis of being "used when required."

At present, there are four grades of public facsimile service and of corresponding facsimile machines. Group 1 machines take between four and six minutes to

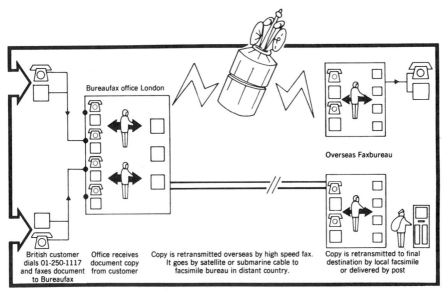

Bureaufax office London

Overseas Faxbureau

| British customer dials 01-250-1117 and faxes document to Bureaufax | Office receives document copy from customer | Copy is retransmitted overseas by high speed fax. It goes by satellite or submarine cable to facsimile bureau in distant country. | Copy is retransmitted to final destination by local facsimile or delivered by post |

Fig. 11.1. BUREAUFAX transmits documents across the world SOURCE: Ed. A. Simpson, *Planning for the Office of the Future,* Gower Publishing Company, Aldershot, Hampshire, England, p. 38 Fig. 4

send a page of A4. Group 2 machines take about three minutes, and, like Group I machines, use analogue transmission. Group 3 machines use digital transmission, and are thus much faster, taking less than a minute a page, sometimes less than half a minute. Group 4 machines allow pages to be sent much faster still. Already, Satellite Business Systems, in the USA, can send 70 pages of fax a minute, thus one page in less than a second!

In 1980, the British Post Office set up Intelpost, the first public international facsimile link, between several cities in the UK and North America; it can send copy across the Atlantic via satellite at about two seconds per A4 page. British Telecom has set up a rival international fascimile service, Bureaufax; see Figure 11.1.

The book by Welch and Wilson (1982b) provides a guide to the practical evaluation of facsimile systems. It describes the features of these systems according to functional criteria, ease of use, and suppliers. It also presents a weighted ranking method of evaluation. Brief introductory descriptions of fax are also given by Corby et al (1982, Chapter 10), Crisp (1982), and Gerrard. British Telecom (1981) refers briefly to fax services. Beckman (1982) and Gerrard (1981) both briefly consider the business market for fax.

LOCAL OFFICE SYSTEMS

"The selling of systems for cabling together all the electronic equipment found in a modern office—personal computers, data terminals, word processors, copiers, printers, telex machines, telephones—will be a billion-pound business some time during this decade. So say analysts of the increasingly look-alike communications and computing industries. In response, the number of suppliers of these systems, known as Local Area Networks (LANs), are multiplying at a breathtaking pace.... Although equally applicable in factories, hospitals and universities, LANs are generally considered to be the foundation upon which the all-electronic office of the future will be built." Having thus summed up the context in which new possibilities for local office systems are emerging, Raggett (1982) briefly considers some of the reasons for using LANs in offices, and reviews bus networks, ring networks, and PABX-based star networks as the main contenders in the field.

The desire to link together different and at first sight incompatible varieties of office equipment is partly motivated by a need to improve efficiency. It is not usually viable to provide one machine of each type to every worker, although it *may* soon become economically feasible to provide each member of office staff with an "intelligent" work station, with local computing power, just because the microprocessors, on which it is based, have now become so cheap. But the prices of other kinds of equipment, including printers and magnetic file stores, are not falling nearly so fast, and thus need to be shared between different users in the same office.

One big advantage of a LAN is that it is able to do just that. As Flint (1982) points out, a LAN, providing a high speed shared channel, is a suitable way of linking individual work stations with shared servers. It can attach to the same bus, string round the same ring, or link to the same PABX, both the individual terminals and work stations, and just a few of the file servers, print servers and not-quite-so-small computers. Furthermore, most LANs are able to support the effective intercommunications of these devices, even though they may be supplied by several different manufacturers. In addition, many LANs offer gateway facilities that enable them to link with other computers, other stations, even other LANs, at a distance, by setting up communications with them over intervening WANs. Thus businesses with several geographically separated premises can often usefully use linked local area networks.

Figure 11.2 shows a typical automated office system and the various facilities to which it gives access, including data processing, text processing, and voice telephony, are linked through a "switch"; this "switch" may be a PABX, if the office uses a star network, or it may be a bus or ring linking the different devices of the system. Figure 11.3 illustrates an office system, using Ethernet technology, and shows the attached devices together with the gateways that link the system to outside networks.

Coen (1982) considers that LANs are important, not so much because of their high data transmission rates, but even more because their high speeds and low error rates can be applied to design information processing systems to meet the needs of specific types of user and user organisation. They allow use-friendly interfaces with the office staff, very rapid response times, very quick access to information centrally stored in office data bases, and almost immediate change of a work station's function when this is required by its user. Another important advantage of LANs is that their high speed channels can transmit *all* kinds of information required in an office: data, text, diagrams, graphics, pictures, and (digitised) voice.

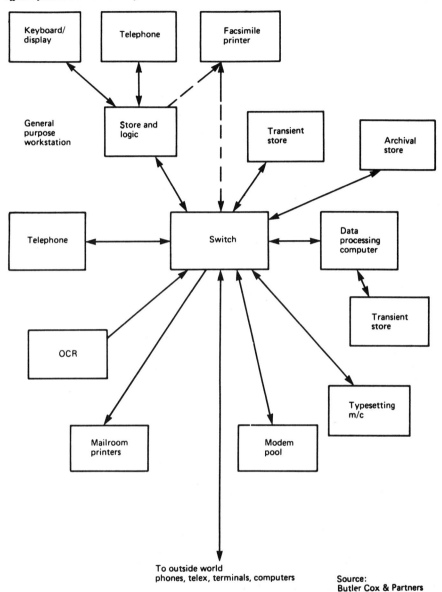

Fig. 11.2. Linkage of multi-function work station to different facilities through a switch SOURCE: Ed. A. Simpson, *Planning for the Office of the Future*, Gower Publishing Company, Aldershot, Hampshire, England, p. 8 Fig 8

Gee's (1982) book on LANs examines their latest techniques, and discusses them, in relation to present and future user needs, as a new means of short-distance, high-speed communications between computers, terminals, and electronic office equipment.

Many of the larger commercially available LAN systems were described in Chapter 2, and some of the smaller ones were described by Chapter 3. In the

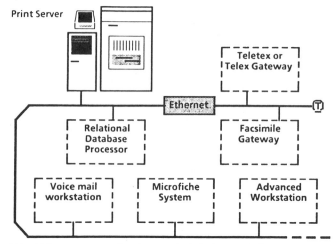

Fig. 11.3. Office Ethernet system showing attached devices and Gateways to outside networks
SOURCE: Paper by Fishburn in *Local Networks* 82, p. 137

present section, references are made to some of the literature that further de-scribes their capabilities as office systems, and their actual use by organisations. Unfortunately, published case studies of these uses still seem to be rare, and, even when they *do* appear, they tend to be very brief.

Perhaps the best known of these systems are XIBUS and its successor MAS-TERNET. Not only are the office applications of these systems well described in their suppliers' own brochures (Master Systems, 1982, 1983a, and 1983b; Xionics, 1982), but their use by organisations has also been fairly well publicised. A Xionics System was installed in the Cabinet Office early in 1982, and it has been used successfully ever since (Brooks, 1981; King Taylor, 1982; Norman, 1982).

Williams (1982c) not only refers to the choice of XIBUS systems by the Cabinet Office and by several large British companies; she also describes the use of such a system by BP Oil at Hemel Hempstead, Herts, England. BP's system, which has 18 work stations, is used by managers at several levels and by secretaries, to handle and store files, send electronic mail and messages, provide work processing and personal computing facilities, and maintain special logs and calendars. While re-maining open-minded about which LAN system on the market will eventually meet its requirements best, BP has already found that its XIBUS system offers significant improvements over less advanced techniques for quick access to shared informa-tion.

Other office LAN systems, whose business applications are well described in their brochures, include: IBIS (Integrated Business Information System) (Plessey Communications System Ltd., 1982), Integrated Electronic Office (Datapoint (U.D.) Ltd., 1982), and the Wang OIS (Office Information System) family (Wang, 1981b).

Cane (1981) describes the Information Management Processor (I.M.P.) system, developed by Office Technology Ltd (OTL), and considers that it offers an ad-vanced set of facilities, and is in some ways ahead of its competitors; for example,

Fig. 11.4. OTL I.M.P. Office System Controller   SOURCE: Office Technology Ltd. Brochure Fig 1

it has included voice processing in its system, and it can act like an "intelligent dictating machine," by turning voice messages into digital signals, which can then be handled like text. Figure 11.4 shows an I.M.P. Office System Controller.

Cane (1982c) describes the activities of GEC's new company GEC Information Systems (GECIS), which brings together the GEC Group's activities in PABXs, telephones, telecommunications, terminals and computers. Although it has tended to be sceptical about those LANs that are not based on PABXs, it is prepared to supply the Magnaloop ring LANs, developed by A.B. Dick in the USA, primarily to link communicating text and graphics processing terminals.

Knippel (1981) describes Nixdorf's Inhouse Network, using Ethernet technology, whose local terminals are able to transfer, access and update information. Facilities include: a data base processor, a message service, fail-safe operating systems, a gateway to communication services, and voice-plus data systems, such as voice electronic mail, speech filing, and local voice conferencing.

Quint et al (1981) discusses the LAN at Laboratoire IMAG in France, which is intended to support experimental distributed applications and systems, and also to provide office services to its users. They describe the approach used for designing and implementing the basic service needed for both types of application.

Scheurer (1981) discusses the two local networks used by INRIA's KAYAK project, at Rocquencourt near Paris. One of the objectives of KAYAK is to build an experimental integrated office system, where the problem of local data communication is fundamental. The approach used has been to develop LANs which would: be cheap enough to be used with small devices based on microprocessors, have low to medium bandwidth, have decentralised control of the network (for improved reliability), have 20 to 200 stations, be wide enough to distribute information round a building.

The first of these networks, TARO, has low bandwidth and only a few stations. It is a token control ring, using twisted pair cable, and has a data rate of 50 Kbits/sec. Computers linked to it include two Apple IIs and an 8080-based microcomputer.

The second network, DANUBE, has a bus configuration with CSMA-CD, as for Ethernet, 1 Km of standard coaxial cable, up to 235 stations, and a data rate of 1 Mbits/sec. An end-to-end transport protocol was developed implemented for use with it.

Recent developments in the PABX approach to office LANs are discussed for example by Pitt (1982), Yoshida et al (1982), and also by Divakaruni et al (1982), who indicate some new directions in enhanced voice networking.

A few mathematical models for aspects of the behaviour of office LANs have been formulated. For example, Nutt and Bayer (1982) describe a simulation study of a class of Ethernet-like bus networks, whose traffic loads are like those that might be found in an office LAN integrating data and voice communication. Niznik (1982) carries out a cost-benefit analysis for integrated facsimile/data/voice LANs.

LINKED OFFICE SYSTEMS

For many years, WANs have been used to link the different branches of certain large business organisations that have many separate premises and customer outlets. The best known examples are the use of networks by the banks and by the airlines. The technology of these private networks is described by Davies and Barber (1973, Chapter 4), who also outline these particular examples of their use.

The applications of networking to banks are discussed fully in the next section. Sheppard and Dickson (1982) discuss their view of bank networks as interconnected open systems.

In 1949, a group of airlines established SITA (Societé Internationale de Télécommunications Aeronautique) as an organisation that would provide them with a cheaper way of exchanging messages. SITA was needed to make it easier to book and sell airline tickets, to exchange operational airline information, and to help locate strayed baggage. Davies and Barber, 1973, (pages 295–300) relate the history of that organisation since then up to the early 1970s.

Originally, SITA set up a worldwide low-speed message-switched network, handling teleprinter traffic. In the 1960s, airline seat reservation systems began to be implemented; Davies and Barber (1973, Section 4.5) describe some early examples. As a result, SITA gradually introduced a high level network, which was completed in 1970, and used Univac 418 II mainfames at Brussels, Frankfurt, Madrid, New York and Rome, and Philips DS714 Mark II mainframes at Amsterdam, London and Paris. The high level network was designed to improve the service for conventional message traffic, provide a service for handling short data messages, and reduce the cost per message. Parallel with the development of this main network, the existing networks were progressively modernised.

Marshall (1981) shows how a worldwide information service, such as the General Electric Mark III service, interrelates with business activities. One technique that Mark III uses is "clustering of the systems," putting up to eight large computers together in a group, in such a way that any one of them can gain access to the files of any other. At that time, General Electric had 21 locations throughout the world, strategically placed on four continents and serving as distribution points to about 600 cities. Both local and long-distance circuits are used for the connections.

Marshall outlines four business applications of Mark III. American Express has been able to monitor the financial affairs of its affiliated companies round the world, and feels as a result that it budgets and expenses are controlled to a degree never before achieved. PSI Energy has developed some sophisticated software packages for oil well exploration firms, and it is able to distribute these packages to its customers via Mark III; it has also been able to send its economic analyses to interested parties all round the world. The European/American Bank has put up a currency data base on a system providing up-to-date figures of worldwide currency values. To remedy difficulties with its export-import paper work, Peugeot installed two data bases, one at its point of manufacture in France, another at its market in the USA, and linked these data bases together.

Cane (1982d) gives some examples of how telecommunications technology can help businesses wishing to use WANs. He refers to the cost savings that can be achieved by the intelligent use of multiplexers and concentrators, and he briefly discusses statistical multiplexing and packet switching, as two powerful techniques for switching data links to match users' needs.

Dalal (1981) expresses the opinion, similar to my own, that LANs are a foundation for the "office of the future," but should also be viewed as components of an internetwork communication system, in other words, as parts of a *linked local area network* (*LLAN*). Naffah's (1981) concept of Integrated Office System, which also adopts this approach, is discussed in the final section of this chapter. Despite this, discussions of the LLAN concept in the computer network literature seem to be rather infrequent.

Figure 11.5 shows a typical example of a configuration, showing two LANs, with their attached devices, the WAN link between these LANs, and another LAN-WAN link.

Kerr and Rhynas (1982) and Crocker (1980b) both discuss the interconnection of different electronic mail networks.

BANKING AND FINANCIAL APPLICATIONS OF NETWORKING

Computer networks are already being used extensively for banking and also for financial operations such as money dealings, stock market transactions, and investment systems. Videotex is being used both for the retrieval of financial information and economic data, and for a variety of financial transactions (Mayne, 1986, Chapter 11). Electronic funds transfer and electronic shopping are now being developed as new sets of facilities, both for businesses and for their customers, including the general public.

The banks began to use computing equipment in the late 1950s, and started

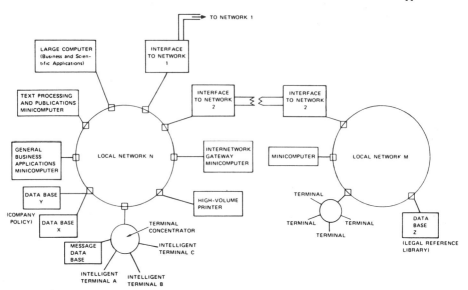

Fig. 11.5. Typical interconnection of terminals, local and remote, processors, and local and remote systems   SOURCE: R. P. Uhlig, D. J. Farber and J. H. Bair, *The Office of the Future*, North-Holland, Amsterdam, Oxford and New York, p. 58

setting up system for data transmission and wide area networking during the 1960s. Davies and Barber (1973, Section 4.4) relate the history of some of these earlier developments, using as an illustrative example the evolution of the use of these facilities by Lloyd's Bank, including the establishment of the Lloyd's Bank teleprocessing network. McGlynn (1978) briefly reviews the use of online processing and distributed processing by the banks.

In the UK, Bankers' Automated Clearing Services (BACS) was set up, together with other special services that the British banks have introduced to aid the transfer of funds between bank accounts (*New Scientist* 1982).

During the 1970s, SWIFT (Society for Worldwide Interbank Financial Telecommunications) set up its network for international financial communications, which is now owned and used by 950 banks in 27 countries and exchanges several hundred thousand messages a day (Evans, 1982; Gourlay, 1982). It can be accessed either by SWIFT-approved devices (SIDs) or by independently supported interfaces. It also imposes strict authentication and security requirements. Chemical Bank and Midland Bank have been collaborating on a project that allows SWIFT to be used for payments in sterling; before that, SWIFT had been used only for payments in currencies other than a bank's domestic currency.

As some banks are not yet on the SWIFT network and still use Telex, computers have been introduced to provide sophisticated message handling systems, to match SWIFT's advanced techniques. For example, Arbat's Intelex system provides store-and-forward switches for use with various Telex, telegraph and local interactive terminals (Evans, 1982).

As computing and communications technologies have converged, so have the data processing and transmission and networking techniques used by the banks

(Gourlay, 1982). For a long time, the banks used WANs, based on mainframe, and then minicomputers were used for in-house banking systems, and real-time techniques were used in message systems. Recently, the banks have implemented some of the most advanced examples of office automation and integrated telecommunication systems.

Cane (1982e) reports several examples of the current use of computing systems by banks; most of these systems are mainframes, but small computers are being used to provide some extra facilities. Hyodo et al (1982) describe a worldwide integrated communications system for the Japanese Sanwa Bank, and Sheppard and Dickson (1982) present a view of banks as interconnected open systems.

Datapoint's integrated international banking package, DataBank, marketed in the UK by Ventek Computers, is designed to meet the business requirements of international banks (Ventek Computers, 1982a). It handles a comprehensive range of enquiries, relating to individual customers, accounts, facilities and deals, providing rapid answers to these questions, through its interactive capabilities. It allows banks considerable flexibility in setting up their computing system. A companion product is DataMap, a powerful and versatile financial planning and modelling system (Ventek Computers, 1982b).

Computer networks have been used for money dealing systems, for example by Citibank (Kennett, 1982; Zynar, 1982), and by Reuters (Driver et al. 1982). They have also been used for stock exchange transactions; for example, the TOPIC private viewdata system at the London Stock Exchange, based on a minicomputer and having hundreds of terminals, provides up-to-the second business information to stockbrokers and their clients throughout the UK (Mayne, 1986).

Renier (1982) describes the Quotrader Investment Center system, which uses the Apple II personal computer as an "intelligent" terminal, and receives raw market data from telephone lines, cable TV, or directly from a communications satellite. It provides its users with continuous market quotations, up-to-the-minute bar charts, automatically generated buy and sell orders, and dynamic accounting. Currently set up to handle the commodities market only, it plans soon to extend its facilities to stock traders.

Ideas for the application of computer networks to *electronic fund transfer* (*EFT*) were first discussed in the 1970s; they are described in some detail by Martin (1977) and more briefly by McGlynn (1978). The types of EFT, representing successive steps towards an EFT society, include:

1. Transfer of money between banks (considered earlier in this chapter);
2. Transfers between the computers of other organisations and the computer of banks, for example for automatic payment of salaries to company employees;
3. Usage of terminals by members of the public to obtain banking services, for example the use of cash-dispensing machines in banks and on the streets;
4. Point-of-sale terminals in shops;
5. Electronic banking facilities and electronic shopping facilities, available in the home.

The first three of these categories of EFT have already been implemented, and the fourth of them has already been widely introduced by many stores and supermarkets. Active steps are now being taken to achieve the fifth stage of EFT.

The Verbraucher Bank in Hamburg has pioneered home banking services, whereby its customers use the German videotex service Bildschirmtext to access the bank's main computer files (Richter, 1981; Cane, 1982e, 1982f). Customers can find out the state of their accounts, make simple payments, and so on. Very strict security precautions are of course taken, and the system is well protected by layers of passwords and access protocols.

The French banks and the French PTT are the driving forces between trials of new electronic shopping systems that are about to start in Caen, France (Charlish, 1982b). Shoppers there will use small customer's terminals in the shops and their own "smart" cards, similar in size to a credit card, instead of paying by cheque, and there will also be retailer's terminals in the shops.

Mayne (1986, Chapter 10) considers some of the personal financial services that videotex provides for citizens, together with its potentialities for electronic shopping. O'Leary (1982a) points out that customers can dial direct to a mail order firm's computer or make airline and holiday reservations, using Prestel's Gateway facility, and remarks that this facility could also lead to the introduction of home banking facilities.

Some recent developments in EFT are described by O'Leary (1982b) and *New Scientist* (1982), and some future possibilities for home banking and electronic funds transfer are discussed by Marsh (1982) and Sutherland (1982) and also in Chapter 18. Hoare (1982) discussed EFT and "cashless living," among other topics.

INTEGRATED NETWORKS FOR COMPANIES AND OTHER ORGANISATIONS

Office automation and computer networking services for business companies and other organisations are unlikely to be really effective unless they are well integrated, unless there different subsystems are brought together according to a unified plan.

The rapid advance of information technology has led to the development of many systems and devices that will become useful components of such integrated systems, but the actual implementation of these systems will need considerable resources and great skill.

Bunce (1982) has given a useful presentation of some of the requirements of integrated office information systems. He believes, probably rightly, that the time has come to begin to formulate the integrated information systems of the future and bring them to reality. Thus development should always be based on functional requirements, and the objectives should be to minimise the total system cost and allow its individual work stations and terminals to have many functions. The family of products, produced for integrated systems, must be open-ended, so that new functional modules can be added to an organisation's installation as new requirements and new technologies merge. Integrated information systems can only come through coordination of the fields of computing, telecommunications and office equipment.

Longley (1982) traces the evolution of data processing techniques up to the advent of distributed data processing. He considers that the current trend is to combine this with word processing and communications, and he identifies some of the new technology required to integrate these many facilities into a unified information processing system. Figure 11.6 shows the sort of integrated system that could be achieved with a bus network, linked by gateways to WANs and by a PABX to the PSTN.

Benjamin (1982) outlines ICL's approach to integrated information management, which is based on the open network philosophy of its Information Processing Architecture (IPA), which is closely aligned with the requirements of the ISO Open System Interconnection model. Users of ICL's systems will be able to build on the foundation of open system networking, choosing work stations and computer systems that are suited to their local needs and controlled by their local managers. In the future, central office functions will be carried out in a more decentralised way, but using the same corporate strategies and standards.

Benstead (1982) presents ITT's approach to the problem of integrating office communications by means of a relatively simple technology and method, allowing PABX equipment, now on the market, to be used as a basis for the next stage for improvement of all three areas of information transfer: voice, text and data. Woolnough (1982) describes the progress that ITT Business System has already made towards integrated office networks. He looks at the way in which they bring telephone systems, facsimile, viewdata, teleprinters, word processors, data terminals and small computers together to form an overall system.

Naffah (1981) conceives an Integrated Office System as a set of distributed work stations, connected by LANs on the same site and using gateways and WANs to link stations of different sites; thus the Integrated Office System is a linked local area network (LLAN). He assumes that the work stations are able to generate, interpret and exchange mixed documents, including voice, images and data, on the same network. He presents the new reference model for the architecture of integrated office systems, that has been adopted by the KAYAK pilot project for Integrated Office Systems and Office Automation, which he is currently leading. It is based on the OSI Reference Model, together with the set of protocols that rule the interworking between the system's different entities. The applications protocols, in the top layer, correspond to the new services to be offered in office systems, including: message services, teleconferencing, information storage and retrieval, and document processing. This new reference model may be viewed as a first step towards defining a universal model, which may be adequate for a wide variety of services, although much experimentation will be needed before a final solution can be reached.

Other recent papers on integrated systems include those by: Anderson et al (1982) on a new communications protocol for integrated digital voice and data, Kirstein and Treadwell (1982) on the integration of public network services relevant

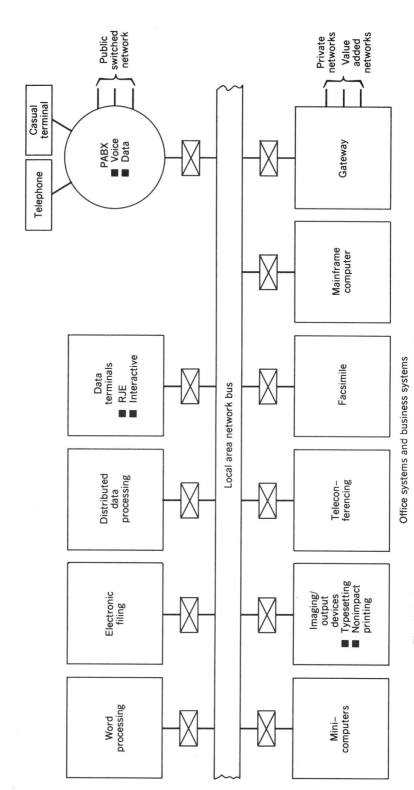

Fig. 11.6. Integrated information processing systems   SOURCE: Ed. A. Simpson, *Planning for Telecommunications*, Gower Publishing Company, Aldershot, Hampshire, England, p. 27 Fig 3

Office systems and business systems

to document processing, Drake (1982) on an integrated business system based on electronic mail, and Yoshida et al (1982) on an integrated system based on a modular integrated EPABX.

Cane (1982a) looks at the approaches to integrated office automation actually being adopted by system suppliers. Most of them provide a multi-function work station as the basic unit, specifying the station as a computer terminal with screen and keyboard, which can be used for word processing, data processing, drawing diagrams, and sending messages. The most advanced work stations incorporate a telephone handset, so as to annotate written text with voice messages, as well as handle ordinary telephone messages. Ways also have to be found for storing vast amounts of text, usually on large magnetic disks, and retrieving this stored information quickly. Printers and facsimile equipment are also needed, together with a LAN adequate to link all the devices together, in order to transfer information quickly and securely between them.

Cane sums up some of the fierce arguments between different suppliers about how to implement this sort of system. For example, the computer manufacturers prefer to base it on special computers, while the telecommunications companies prefer to base it on PABXs. There are also arguments as to whether to send data, picture and voice information together, over the same network, or over separate networks.

As a supplier of integrated office systems, Master Systems (1983) has an open-minded, pragmatic approach to the design of its products, and considers all possible approaches to their architecture. It sees the following consensus emerging about how information systems architecture should look. Its key components would include: multifunction work stations, shared resources, gateways, and a network for interconnecting all the system's devices.

The Plessey IBIS (Integrated Business Information System) is based on a digital PABX called the Plessey PDX, together with Plessey work stations to give users access to the system, and gateways to link it to outside networks (Plessey Communication Systems Ltd., 1982).

The Datapoint Integrated Electronic Office, using the ARC local coaxial network and the ISX Information Switching Exchange, a third-generation digital PABX, is an operational system, already on the market, that links telephones, computers, data terminals, word processing work stations, and electronic mail into one multifunctional system (Datapoint (U.K.) Ltd., 1982). Because of its functional integration, an organisation can start building this system from any direction. The choice of two networking technologies, a local bus network with coaxial cable, and a digital PABX, provides full flexibility.

REFERENCES

J. Agresta (1981) "Office of the Future," pages 93–108 of Burke and Lehman (1981).

G. M. Anderson, J. F. Day and L. A. Spindel (Sep 1982). "A communications protocol for integrated voice and data," *ICCC 82*, 367–372.

E. Arthurs and B. W. Stuck (Jan 1982) "Bounding mean throughput rate and mean delay in office systems," *IEEE Transactions on Communications*, **COM-30**(1) 12–18.

A. D. Bailey, JR, J. Gerlach, R. P. McAfee and A. B. Whinston (May 1981) "Internal accounting controls in the office of the future," *Computer*, **14**(4) 59–70.

J. T. Barton (1981) *Word Processing*, Institute of Management Services, London.

E. C. Beckman (1982) "Facsimile in business," *Planning for Telecommunications*, 90–95.

A. Benjamin (1982) "Managing the centralised office," *Planning for Word Processing*, 12–17.

P. J. Benstead (1982) "The use of an existing PABX as the basis of an integrated office communications system," *Local Networks 82*, 97–708.

BIS Applied Systems Ltd (undated) *Office Automation—Planning for Success*, Film.

R. Blagg (1981) "Planning-scale computer systems for the automated office," *Planning for the Office of the Future*, 105–114.

British Telecom (1981) "The role of British Telecom," *Planning for the Office of the Future*, 28–38.

R. Brooks (11 Oct 1981) "ITT taps into British office of the future," *Sunday Times*, 72.

R. Broughton (1982) "The word processing approach," *Planning for Word Processing*, 24–31.

J. Bunce (Jun 1982) "Integrated information systems—Their time has come," *Communication Systems & Management*, **1**(3) 14–17.

M. Burdett (1981) "Towards the electronic office," *Planning for Electronic Mail*, 28–35.

Ed. T. J. M. Burke and M. Lehman (1981) *Communication Technologies and Information Flow*, Pergamon Press, Oxford England, and Elmsford, NY.

J. C. Burns (1981) "The automated office," pages 220–231 of Ed. T. Forester, *The Microelectronics Revolution*, Blackwell, Oxford.

D. Butler (1981) "Planning for the Office of the Future," *Planning for the Office of the Future*, 3–14.

D. Butler (15 Feb 1982) "Office automation and information technology," Keynote Address to Inaugural Meeting of OFIX.

Butler Cox and Partners (1982) *The Market for Office Technology*, Report.

J. Buxton (13 Apr 1982) "Olivetti's three routes to office automation—Office products, business systems and telecommunications," *Financial Times Survey, The Electronic Office*, XVI.

A. Cane (13 Oct 1981) "UK fledgling spreads wings in office market," *Financial Times*.

A. Cane (1982a) (25 Jun 1982) "The electronic office: Who needs it?," *Financial Times*, 19.

A. Cane (1982b) (13 Apr 1982) "Wide choice of electronic mail systems," *Financial Times Survey, The Electronic Office*, XIX.

A. Cane (1982c) (123 (13 Apr 1982) "GEC unveils strategy on marketing needs—The newly formed GEC Information Systems aims to meet needs of individual customers," *Financial Times Survey, The Electronic Office*, XIX.

A. Cane (1982d) (18 Jan 1982) "Rapid communication within office or factory—Local data networks are the minicomputer's latest offspring," *Financial Times Survey, Computers*, XV.

A. Cane (1982e) "Towards the cashless society—with electronic funds transfer banking takes another big step," *Financial Times Survey, Computers*, XVI—XVII.

A. Cane (1982f) "Secret of the best system—Software is the heart of the electronic office," *Financial Times Survey, The Electronic Office*, V.

J.-M. Chang and S.-K. Chang (1982) "Database alerting techniques for office activities management," *IEEE Transactions on Communications*, **COM-30**(1) 74–81.

G. Charlish (1982a) (18 Jan 1982) "So many developments in the data handling field," *Financial Times Survey, Computers*, XIV.

G. Charlish (1982b) (17 Aug 1982) "Philips first off the mark with the 'smart' card", *Financial Times*, 8.

L. Cherry (Jan 1982) "Writing tools," *IEEE Transactions on Communications*, **COM-30**(1) 100–105.

C. Clark (Sep 1982) "Adding value to value added services," *ICCC 82*, 277–281.

P. Coen (Apr 1982) "The ins and outs of computing," *Management Today Special Survey, The Automated Office*, 13–16.

H. Collins (1982) "Planning your communication system," *Planning for Telecommunications*, 3–10.

Computer, Vol. **14**, No. 5 (May 1981) Special issue on office information systems.

Computer Networks, Vol. **5**, No. 6 (Dec 1981) Special issue on office automation.

M. Corby, E. J. Donohue and M. Hamer (1982) *Telecomm Users' Handbook*. Telecommunications Press, London.

W. Cottle (1981) "Word processing—What and how," *Planning for the Office of the Future*, 50–56.

J. Crisp (13 Apr 1982) "Always the office wallflower—Facsimile transmission, a specialist function," *Financial Times Survey. The Electronic Office*, IX.

D. H. Crocker (1980a) (Oct 1980) "Alternatives in electronic mail networks," *Data Communications*, **9**(10) 95–103.

D. H. Crocker (1980b) (Nov 1980) "Electronic mail, part two: Network integration," *Data Communications*, **9**(11) 109–115.

Y. K. Dalal (1981) "The information outlet: A new tool for office organization," *Local Networks 81*, 11–19.

Data Processing (Jun 1981) "And tomorrow—All the world gets Telex," 29.

Datapoint (U.K.) Ltd. (1982) *The Integrated Electronic Office*, Brochure.

C. A. Davies (1982) "Office automation—The local net in perspective," *Local Networks 82*, 1–13.

D. W. Davies and D. L. A. Barber (1973) *Communication Networks for Computers*, Wiley, Chichester and New York.

M. de Smith (1981) "Developments in electronic message systems," *Business Telecoms—The New Regime*, Online Publications, Northwood Hills, Middlesex, England.

R. S. Divakaruni, G. E. Saltus and B. R. Savage (Sep 1982) "New directions in enhanced voice networking," *ICCC 92*, 362–366.

R. Doswell (1982) *Word Processor Security*, NCC Publications, Manchester, England.

P. Drake (Sep 1982) "An electronic mail based integrated business system," *ICCC 82*.

M. Driver (Sep 1982) "Reuters' money dealing system," *ICCC 82*.

M. Evans (1982) "Message transmission for business in the 1980s," *Planning for Telecommunications*, 42–47.

E. Fergus (Sep 1982) "The GILT Project—Connecting computer-based message systems via public data networks," *ICCC 82*, 407–411.

Financial Times Survey, Computers (18 Jan 1982).

Financial Times Survey, The Electronic Office (23 Apr 1982).

D. Flint (1982) "The local area network as the backbone of new business systems," *Local Networks 82*, 15–32.

J. J. Garcia-Lina-Aceves and F. F. Kuo (Jan 1982) "A hierarchical architecture for computer-based message systems," *IEEE Transactions on Communications*, **COM-30**(1) 37–45.

K. C. E. Gee (1982) *Local Area Networks*, NCC Publications, Manchester, England.

N. H. Gehani (Jan 1982) "The potential of forms in office automation," *IEEE Transactions on Communications*, **COM-30**(1) 120–125.

A. St. F. X. Gerrard (1981) "Focus on Fax," *Planning for Electronic Mail*, 95–103.

C. Gourlay (Jun 1982) "Banking on communications," *Communication Systems & Management*, **1**(3) 20–22.

C. E. Gustawson (Sep 1982) "The teletex service in Sweden," *ICCC 82*, 327–332.

S. Hattori, S. Morita, Y. Fujii and M. W. Kim (Jan 1982) "A design model for a real-time voice storage system," *IEEE Transactions on Communications*, **COM-30**(1) 53–57.

R. C. Hawk and F. R. Zitzmann (Sep 1982) "Information management & the automated office," *ICCC 82*, 357–361.

P. L. Higginson and P. T. Kirstein (1981) "Network interconnection with provision for electronic mail services," *Local Networks 81*, 107–121.

W. C. Hoare (1980) *Electronic Communications Systems*, Petrocelli, New York and Princeton, NJ.

C. Holland (1982) "Word Processing—The micro approach," *Planning for Word Processing*, 103–111.

T. Hyodo, Y. Kudo and M. Seto (Sep 1982) "A worldwide integrated service communication system for the Sanwa Bank," *ICCC 82*, 473–478.

ICCC 82 (Sep 1982) 6th International Conference on Computer Communication, London.

IEEE Transactions on Communications, Vol **COM-30**, No. 1, Part 1 (Jan 1982) Special issue on communications in the automated office.

A. H. Ithell (Sep 1982) "A powerful teletex workstation: Design and facilities," *ICCC 82*, 412–417.

IT's Business, No. 2 (23 Apr 1982) Special issue on office automation.

P. Jenner (Summer 1981) "Electronic mail—ITs time has come," *Datapoint News*, 4–5.

A. Jones (1982a) "Office communications: A management approach," *Planning for Telecommunications*, 31–41.

A. Jones (1982b) "WP—A systems approach," *Planning for Word Processing*, 40–46.

S. Jones (1981) "The electronic scrapbook," *Planning for Electronic Mail*, 68–76.

D. Kennett (9 Jul 1981) "Foreign exchange goes online," *Computer Weekly*.

I. Kerr and D. J. Rhynas (Sep 1982) "The interconnection of public electronic mail systems," *ICCC 82*, 907–912.

L. King Taylor (14 Jan 1982) "Taking the slog out of office routine," *The Times, Guide to Information Technology*, X-XI.

P. T. Kirstein (1978) "Choice of data communication media for transmission of facsimile information," *Computer Networks*, **2**(2) 179–190.

P. T. Kirstein (1980) "New text and message services," pages 521–535 of Ed. S. H. Lavington, *Information Processing 80*, N. Holland, Amsterdam, Oxford, England, and New York.

P. T. Kirstein and S. W. Treadwell (Sep 1982) "Document processing & the integration of relevant public services," *ICCC 82*, 301–306.

H. Kjellin (1981) "Progress in voice communication technologies," *Data Processing International 1981*, 171–174.

D. Knight (1982) "Selecting communications systems for the office of the future," *Planning for Telecommunications*, 80–89.

P. Knippel (1981) "Specification of a commercially viable distributed in-house network," *Local Networks 81*, 123–141.

B. R. Konsynski, L. C. Bracket and W. E. Bracker, Jr. (Jan 1981) "A model for specification of office communications," *IEEE Transactions on Communications*, **COM-30**(1) 27–36.

J. O. Limb (Jan 1982) "Communications in the automated office: Guest Editor's prologue," *IEEE Transactions on Communications*, **COM-30**(1) 1–5.

D. Longley (1982) "The integrated information processing systems of the future," *Planning for Telecommunications*, 11–30.

N. H. Macdonald, L. T. Frase, P. S. Gingrich and S. A. Keenan (Jan 1982) "The Writer's Workbench: Computer aids for text analysis," *IEEE Transactions on Communications*, **COM-30**(1) 105–110.

D. McFetrich (Apr 1982) "Insight on the new technology," *Management Today Special, The Automated Office*, 5–10.

D. R. McGlynn (1978) *Distributed Processing and Data Communications*, Wiley, New York and Chichester, Chapter 8, "Data Communications Applications."

M. D. McIlroy (Jan 1982) "Development of a spelling list," *IEEE Transactions on Communications*, **COM-30**(1) 91–99.

Management Today Special Survey, The Automated Office, (Apr 1982).

B. Manley (1981) "The evolving electronic office market," *Data Processing International 1981*, 123–126.

P. Marsh (29 Apr 1982) "Will Britain buy electronic shopping?" *New Scientist*, **94** (1303) 278–281.

R. W. Marshall (1981) "Worldwide information services," Chapter 7 of Burke and Lehman (1981).

J. Martin (2nd Ed., 1977) *Future Developments in Telecommunications*, Prentice-Hall, Englewood Cliffs, NJ, Chapter 14, "High Velocity Money."

F. Maryanski (May 1981) "Guest Editor's introduction: Office information systems," *Computer*, **14**(5) 11–12.

Master Systems (1982) *XIBUS—The Fully Integrated Electronic Office System*, Master Systems (Data Products) Ltd., Brochure.

Master Systems (1983a) *OFFICEMASTER—The Complete Office from Master Systems*, Master Systems (Data Products) Ltd., Brochure.

Master Systems (1983b) *MASTERNET—The Invisible Network for Master Systems*, Master Systems (Data Products) Ltd., Brochure.

A. J. Mayne (1986) *The Videotex Revolution*, second ed., Wiley, Chichester and New York.

C. Mills (1981) "Electronic message systems," *Planning for Electronic Mail*, 60–67.

N. Naffah (Dec 1981) "Communication protocols for integrated office systems," *Computer Networks*, **5**(6), 445–454.

M. Naughton (1981) "Planning for the office of the future," *Planning for Electronic Mail*, 36–41.

New Scientist (29 Apr 1982) "Banks and stores switch on to electronics—but separately," **94**(1303), 280–281.

C. A. Niznik (Jan 1982) "Cost-benefit analysis for local integrated facsimile/data/voice packet communication networks," *IEEE Transactions on Communications*, **COM-30**(1) 19–27.

A. Norman (2 Sep 1982) "The Comat/Xionics office automation pilot scheme for the Cabinet Office," Presentation to OFIX Meeting.

G. J. Nutt and D. L. Bayer (Jan 1982) "Performance of CSMA/CD networks under combined voice and data loads," *IEEE Transactions on Communications*, **COM-30**(1) 6–11.

G. J. Nutt and P. A. Ricci (May 1981) "Quinault—An Office Modeling System," *Computer*, **14**(5) 41–57.

P. O'Leary (1982a) (14 Jan 1982) "Push-button shopping arrives," *The Times, Guide to Information Technology*, XII.

R. R. Panko (Dec 1981) "Facing basic issues in office automation," *Computer Networks*, **5**(6) 391–399.

F. J. Perkins (1981) "The electronic mailbox," *Planning for Electronic Mail*, 53–59.

W. H. Peters (Sep 1982) "How to determine your organisation's telecommunication potential," *ICCC 82*, 270–276.

A. Pinner (1982) "WP—The total office information systems," *Planning for Word Processing*, 68–74.

D. A. Pitt (Sep 1982) "Alternatives in the use of circuit switching for local area data networks," *ICCC 82*, 351–356.

Plessey Communication Systems Ltd. (Jun 1982) *Plessey IBIS—Integrated Business Information System*, Brochure.

S. G. Price (1979) *Introducing the Electronic Office*, NCC Publications, Manchester, England.

S. G. Price (1982) *Preparing for Teletex*, NCC Publications, Manchester, England.

J. A. T. Pritchard and I. Cole (1982) *Planning Office Automation—Information Management Systems*, NCC Publications, Manchester, England.

V. Quint, H. Pichy, X. Rousett de Pino, S. Sasynn, G. Sergeant and I. Vatton (1981) "Basic services for a local network," *Local Networks 81*, 277–288.

R. Raggett (13 Apr 1982) "Linking systems: Heading for a $1bn business—A big future is seen for

LANs (local area networks) which connect all the equipment needed," *Financial Times Survey, The Electronic Office,* IX.

A.L. Reid (1981) "BT initiatives in electronic message services," *Business Telecoms—The New Regime,* Online Publications, Northwood Hills, Middlesex.

G. J. Renier (Apr 1982) "The electronic investment system: Making money with your computer," *The Futurist,* **16**(2) 18–21.

A. Richter (1981) "Homebanking via Bildschirmtext in the FTR FRG," *Viewdata 81,* 273–279.

A. M. Rosenberg (1981) "The great convergence: The telephone network and message systems," *Planning for Electronic Mail,* 16–27.

S. Rostron (1981a) *Tomorrow's Office,* Management Film.

S. Rostron (1981b) *Office Automation,* Management Film.

S. Rostron (Apr 1982) "How to start becoming automated," *Management Today Special Survey, The Automated Office,* 43–46.

H. Ruggeberg (Sep 1982) "The development of the teletex service in FRG," *ICCC 82,* 338–343.

M. Scaman (1982) "Word processing and the electronic office," *Planning for Word Processing,* 47–53.

B. Scheurer (Sep 1981) "Local network in the Kayak project," *INRIA Report* REL 2.549.

P. Schicker (Dec 1981) "The computer based mail environment—An overview," *Computer Networks,* **5**(6) 435–443.

P. Schicker (Jan 1982) "Naming and addressing in a computer-based mail environment," *IEEE Transactions on Communications,* **COM-30**(1) 46–52.

D. K. Sharma and A. M. Gruchacz (Jan 1982) "The display text editor TED: A case study in the design and implementation of display-oriented interactive human interfaces," *IEEE Transactions on Communications,* **COM-30**(1) 111–119.

D. A. Sheppard and H. C. Dickson (Sep 1982) "A view of banks as interconnected open systems," *ICCC 82,* 479–484.

G. L. Simons (1981a) "Office technology developments," *Planning for the Office of the Future,* 15–27.

G. L. Simons (1981b) *Introducing Word Processing,* NCC Publications, Manchester, England.

Ed. A. Simpson (1981) *Planning for the Office of the Future,* Gower Publishing Company, Aldershot.

Ed. A. Simpson (1981a) *Planning for Electronic Mail,* Gower Publishing Company, Aldershot.

Ed. A. Simpson (1982b) *Planning for Word Processing,* Gower Publishing Company, Aldershot.

Ed. A. Simpson (1982c) *Planning for Telecommunications,* Gower Publishing Company, Aldershot.

J. Slonim, L. J. MacRae, W. E. Mennie and N. Diamond (May 1981) "NDX-100: An electronic filing machine for the office of the future," *Computer,* **14**(5) 24–36.

J. Steele (1982) "Text processing—An integrated approach," *Planning for Word Processing,* 18–23.

R. A. Sutherland (Apr 1982) "Home banking: Electronic money invades the living room," *The Futurist,* **16**(2) 13–17.

L. Svobodova (1981) "Operating system support for distributed office systems," *Local Networks 81,* 329–343.

A. R. Thompson (1981) "Planning for electronic mail," *Planning for Electronic Mail,* 3–15.

K. J. Thurber (Dec 1980) *Tutorial: Office Automation Systems,* IEEE Computer Society, Silver Springs, MD.

The Times, Guide to Information Technology (14 Jan 1982).

D. Tombs (1981) "Teletex—The next major step in office automation," *Planning for the Office of the Future,* 69–75.

D. Tombs (14 Jun 1982) "Teletex—A new concept in electronic mail," Presentation to OFIX Meeting.

K. Townsend (1981) "Planning for word processing," *Planning for the Office of the Future,* 51–68.

D. Tsichritzis, F. A. Rabitti, S. Gibbs, O. Neierstrasz and J. Hogg (Jan 1982) "A system for managing structured messages," *IEEE Transactions on Communications*, **COM-30**(1) 66–73.

F. H. Tsichritzis and F. H. Lochovsky (Sep 1980) "Office information systems: Challenge for the 80's," *Proceedings of the IEEE*, **68**(9) 1054–1059.

R. P. Uhlig (Dec 1981) "Editorial," *Computer Networks*, **5**(6) 389–390.

R. P. Uhlig, D. J. Farber and J. H. Bair (1979) *The Office of the Future—Communication and Computers*, North-Holland, Amsterdam, Oxford, England, and New York.

Ventek Computers (1982a) *DataBank—The International Banking Package*, Brochure.

Ventek Computers (1982b) *DataMap—The Comprehensive Modelling and Planning System*, Brochure.

B. J. Wagreich (Jan 1982) "Electronic mail for the hearing impaired and its potential for other disabilities," *IEEE Transactions on Communications*, **COM-30**(1) 58–65.

Wang (1981a) (Dec 1981) *Office Automation and the Six Technologies*, Wang Laboratories, Inc. Brochure.

Wang (1981b) (Dec 1981) *OIS—Wang Office Information Systems*, Wang Laboratories, Inc. Brochure.

S. W. Watkins (Sep 1982) "National Bureau of Standards' standardization activities for computer based message systems," *ICCC 82*, 289–294.

J. M. West (1981) "Some questions about the new office technology," pages 109–115 of Burke and Lehman (1981).

W. J. Welch and P. A. Wilson (1982a) *Electronic Mail Systems—A Practical Guide*, NCC Publications, Manchester, England.

W. J. Welch and P. A. Wilson (1982b) *Facsimile Equipment—A Practical Evaluation Guide*, NCC Publications, Manchester, England.

K. Wharton (1981) "Electronic office product developments," *Data Processing International 1981*, 133–136.

K. Wharton (1982) "Word processing," *Planning for Word Processing*, 3–11.

E. Williams (1982a) (13 Apr 1982) "When the right mix is important—All sizes of computer will have a role to play in the office of the future," *Financial Times Survey, The Electronic Office*, 11.

E. Williams (1982b) (13 Apr 1982) "Word processors break down the barriers," *Financial Times Survey, The Electronic Office*, 11.

E. Williams (1982c) (13 Apr 1982) "Local area networks deal with Xionics—BP plays the guinea pig," *Financial Times Survey, The Electronic Office*, XVIII.

J. Williamson (Apr 1981) "Telematics and the electronic office," *Communications Engineering International*, **3**(2) 25–37.

P. A. Wilson and J. A. T. Pritchard (1982a) *Planning Office Automation—Electronic Message Systems*, NCC Publications, Manchester.

P. A. Wilson and J. A. T. Pritchard (1982b) *Office Technology Benefits*, NCC Publications, Manchester.

M. Wiltshire (1982a) (13 Apr 1982) "Larger companies benefit from centralised systems—Computerised controls assist documentation workflow," *Financial Times Survey, The Electronic Office*, X.

M. Wiltshire (1982b) (13 Apr 1982) "Looking beyond cost-saving—The benefits that word processing brought to Cadbury," *Financial Times Survey, The Electronic Office*, XI.

R. Woolnough (Mar 1982) "Information transfer for tomorrow's office," *Communications International*, **9**(3), 50, 52, 55.

Xionics (Mar 1982) *XIONICS*, Xionics Ltd., Brochure.

S. Yoshida, T. Nakayama and Y. Hashida (Sep 1982) "A modular integrated EPABX for the office of the future," *ICCC 82*, 345–350.

M. M. Zloof (May 1981) "QBE/OBE—A language for office and business automation," *Computer*, **14**(5) 13–22.

Zynar (Oct 1981) "CITIBANK," **1**(1) 4.

Chapter 12

Distributed Information Systems

To an increasing extent, the information that people need is scattered in a wide variety of different formats, in many different places. More and more of this information is being stored in computer data bases, but these data bases are placed in many different computers. The problems that most people face, when confronted with this rapidly expanding mass of information, are: to know what information they want, to know where to look for it, to know how to recover it, and to know how to integrate it with the information that they already have.

It is not enough for many computer systems, all storing information on a variety of subjects, to be available to these people. To help them find and handle effectively the information that is *relevant* to their needs, but residing in scattered locations, distributed information systems need to be set up, where the different computer data bases are linked by computer networks, in a well integrated way.

These distributed information systems range from those catering for the requirements of single site, that are handled by a local area network, and systems using both local and distant information resources, for which a linked area network is required.

This chapter starts by outlining some of the general principles of information retrieval and data bases. If then discusses distributed data base systems, where an organisation's data base is divided into different parts, held in different locations, with copies of some of the parts being stored at several places. After that, it describes some aspects of local information systems, whose different parts are distributed round a local area network. The next part of the chapter is concerned with distributed systems, where much of the information required must be reached remotely, including the videotex systems and the "conventional" online data base and information retrieval services, and also including the application of gateways and internetworking to access "third party data bases." Another section of the chapter considers pictorial data bases, that store non-textual information and data. Finally, some approaches to the achievement of integrated distributed information systems are outlined, as most of the distributed information systems now in existence are *not* fully integrated. Recent developments are presented in Chapter 22.

DATA BASES AND INFORMATION RETRIEVAL

The information problems that both organisations and individuals face are partly human, partly conceptual, and partly technical.

Firstly, they need to know what information they want, and for what purposes they should use it. An organisation requires various collections of information, related to the different functions that it has to perform; for example, a business company needs to know about the products that it makes and sells, the people who work for it, the customers that it serves and the financial transactions in which it is involved. An individual's information needs range from the important aspects of everyday life and news of current events to particular topics that interest him or form the basis of his hobbies.

In most cases, an enquirer uses some fairly simple classification to provide a framework for his most usual questions; for example, this may be based on the organisation chart and company structure of a business, or on an individual's view of his major needs and activities. An enquiry is thus generally framed in terms of keywords of key phrases, each *keyword* or *key phrase* representing a category in the classification or a specific example of a named member of that category.

But questions also arise which it is not easy, perhaps not possible, to frame in terms of a given classification that is in regular use. The enquiry cannot than be formulated explicity, but instead must "home in" to the required information by judicious use of successive keywords of key phrases, combined with feedback from the user as to whether or not he is getting near the object of his search.

Classification is thus partly a means of codifying known human needs and interests, and partly an approach to conceptual organisation, the arrangement of different ideas and concepts in due relationship to each other. Traditionally, librarians and other designers of standard classifications have usually adopted a hierarchical classification; this worked reasonably well when the things classified, whether knowledge or whether specific subjects organisations were fairly static, and adopted more or less mutually agreed patterns. However, in the present era of dynamic change and "information explosion," this approach is becoming practicable for a more and more limited set of enquiries, and needs to be supplemented by an approach to classification that is evolutionary, much more flexible, and much more adaptable to individual requirements.

To some extent, the computer-based data base and information retrieval systems, already in being and still being developed, take account of this new approach as well as the old one, but it still needs to be properly formulated and much more research needs to be carried out on it. As a first step in this direction, Mayne (1968, 1973, 1974) has proposed the use of non-hierarchical network-like classification. This has the advantage that it can handle enquiries from different directions, and more according to enquirers' ideas of how things should be classified, rather than according to some preconceived arrangement of subject matter. This new sort of classification is especially convenient to use and it should not be too difficult to implement in computer data bases.

Traditionally, the answer of the question of where to look for relevant information has been that it is found in stores of literature, ranging from public libraries and government records to company files and individual collections of books and documents. Recently, more and more of this information has been stored in computers, in explicitly specified collections of information known as *data bases*. These data bases range from loosely structured sets of information about these documents and in many respects rather like a computerised library catalogue, to very well structured and carefully specified groups of records about the different facets of an organisation's operations.

This has led to two broad approaches to searching for information that is relevant from collections of documents and from computer data bases: *information retrieval*, that is concerned mainly with the appropriate choice of keys, to be used in searches, and with other methods of enquiry, and the *data base approach*, where the information is much more systematically organised, very often in records with fixed formats having fixed numbers of fields each of fixed size, and where types of enquiries can usually be clearly defined, with specific sets of rules for answering them.

As Martin (1981, page 307) points out, data bases should also be distinguised from computer files. A *file* is usually a set of records designed for one application or a group of closely related applications; it is often designed by a programmer or user for his own needs. A *data base* is a collection of interrelated data, that are independent of specific applications and can be used for many applications, past, present and future.

There are at least four approaches to handling data bases: the *relational approach*, the *hierarchical approach*, the *network approach*, and the *inverted file approach*. *Data dictionary systems* provide ways of recording and retrieving information about the analysis, design and operational use of data bases. *Data base management systems* (*DBMS*) are software packages, operated in conjunction with application programs, that generate, operate and maintain computer data bases. These aspects of data bases cannot be considered further here, for lack of space, but they are discussed by text books on data bases.

An important preliminary, before applying either the information retrieval or the data base approach, is to know which data bases are likely to hold the relevant information.

The *recovery of information*, its transfer from the data base where it resides to the user's own store of information, is not always an easy matter. In the case of information retrieval from libraries, it is by no means unknown for a relevant document to be identified quite easily, only to find that a physical copy of it is very hard to obtain, as only very few, if any, libraries actually stock it. Ultimately, this problem will be made easier, when computer data bases begin to store the contents as well as the abstracts and bibliographical information, of documents in their records; computer networking will then be used to transfer the copy from the data base to the user.

For organisations whose records are on computer data bases, the recovery problem is usually fairly straightforward, being a matter of local networking, if the data are stored on site, and of wide area networking otherwise.

Having recovered relevant information, users sometimes only have temporary use for it, as for one-off enquiries, but very often they need to incorporate it in their own information stores and *integrate it with the information that they have.* This is made very much easier with modern information technology, as an "intelligent" terminal or work station, interfaced to a computer network can use that network to find, access and recover the relevant information, and then use its own data processing capabilities to transform it, if necessary, and merge it with its local information store.

Another aspect of integration is that the *same* piece of information is often relevant to several *different* user files. Ideally, copies of it should then be stored in each file, or otherwise made readily available to each file. If the records are on paper, this is difficult, as it is expensive to make all the required copies and their physical storage is bulky; on the other hand, if the multiple copies are not made, there are serious risks of misfiling the documents that have to perform one role after another. For computer systems, it is very much easier to make copies, and information stores tend to be more compact; where separate copies are not made, the information in the documents can be displayed on the work station's screen as if separate copies are in the different files, by using the files' pointers to the required documents, making temporary copies of the documents thus identified, and sending them to the station.

It is possible to go further than this. For example, Mayne (1979, 1981, 1982a) has outlined a specification for a very flexible system that allows users to build up their own data bases in formats of their own choice, incorporating both information collected by themselves and information available in other data bases. Mayne (1980) outlines how user-friendly free-format data bases of this sort could be used by voluntary organisations and community information services.

Many books have been written on data bases and computer data base systems, so that only a selection of them can be mentioned here. Robinson (1981) introduces their general principles, while Date (1982) discusses these principles in greater depth. Martin (1981, Chapter 12) provides a preliminary discussion of data base management, and Mayne* (1982b) gives a technical view of DBMS. Lomax (1978) introduces the data dictionary approach and gives details of eight data dictionary software package systems. The book edited by Chu and Chen (1979) contains 44 key papers on data base systems, covering various aspects.

Several books present computer data bases from the user's point of view. NCC's (1980) case study helps prospective users, by describing how a particular user sets about designing a successful application. Davis (1980) analyses user experiences with data base techniques, and indicates objectively what can reasonably be ex-

---

This Alan Mayne is *not* the same person as the author of this book!

pected from their application. Lomax (1979) reports the approaches and views that many users adopted when setting up their data bases and it should help inexperienced users who wish to know where to begin. Elbra (1982) describes some of the ways in which small organisations can use data bases, pointing out both the benefits and the difficulties of their implementation. Douglas (1980) covers the control aspects of handling data bases, including: administration, access, verification, back-up, recovery and audit procedures.

Scheuermann (1978) provides a framework for the design of large data base systems and discusses methods for evaluating their performance.

Many articles about new developments in computer data base systems and techniques are included in recent issues of *ACM Transactions on Data Base Systems* and *IEEE Transactions on Software Engineering*, and also in the proceedings of the *ACM SIGMOD* and *Very Large Data Bases* conferences.

Spennewyn (1982) summarises a forthcoming state of the art report on "second generation" data bases (Gradwell, 1982).

DISTRIBUTED DATA BASE SYSTEMS

One of the most important applications of computer networking is to data bases that are distributed among different network hosts, in different geographical locations. For example, many business companies and other organisations have premises at different places and may wish to have data bases at each of these premises.

These data bases may mostly be accessed locally, but occasions arise when they are accessed externally. In general data are stored at places where they are often used, so that they are retrieved faster and more cheaply than with a centralised system.

With distributed data bases, copies of parts of the data can be duplicated and stored in separate sites, both for convenience of access, and for improved reliability. If each item of data has at least two copies in different places, the data base system is protected against total failure when one computer breaks down.

Distributed data bases can also be required, when a collection of data becomes too large for one computer, even for large main-frame. To allow incremental growth, a group of several interconnected smaller systems is better than one very large one. The data base system can be upgraded and developed by adding new computers to it. Multiple computer systems can also handle more transactions per unit time, and this is liable to be required if many users are interrogating a data base or set of data bases at the same time.

1. Programs in a peripheral computer refer to files obtained from a distant DBMS;
2. Programs using a local DBMS refer to files in a different DBMS, accessed via a WAN;
3. A local DBMS has some of its data stored remotely;

4. Programs in a peripheral computer access data in a data base network, linking DBMS at different sites.

Rothnie et al (1981) surveys work on both special-purpose and general-purpose distributed DBMS, and gives references to further literature about them. Special-purpose distributed DBMS are usually designed to handle the specific needs of a single organisation. The general-purpose distributed DBMS, now being developed, like "conventional" non-distibuted DBMS, are envisaged as systems for solving a wide range of data management problems. Rothnie et al examine some significant research and development projects in this area.

Rothnie et al (1978) provide a tutorial about distributed data base management. Maryanski surveys developments in distributed DBMS. Obana et al (1982) consider the integration of distributed heterogeneous data base systems.

Tanenbaum (1981, Section 10.1) considers some of the specific problems that result from distributing a computer data base where to put the different parts of the data, how to process enquiries, how to prevent the many simultaneous transactions from interfering with each other, and how to maintain the integrity and effective operation of the data base in spite of possible computer system crashes. He discusses these problems with respect to distributed relational data bases especially.

Uhlig et al (1979, Chapter 11.7) explore some issues, relating to the use of distributed data bases, in the following areas:

1. Management—how does distribution help or threaten the data's users and suppliers?
2. Cost—how can the most economical arrangement of the data be judged?
3. Reliability—how does distribution affect the integrity of the data base?
4. What effect does distribution have on security?

The UK Department of Industry has commissioned a study to evaluate distributed data base technology (PACTEL, 1980). Winscom Clarke (1982) considers the influence of network bandwidth on the design of distributed data base systems. Brown (1982) discusses progress towards the implementation of distributed data base systems. Gifford (1981) presents the experience of the design and implementation of Violet, Xerox PARC's experimental decentralised information system.

Collections of papers on distributed data bases are included in the book edited by Chu and Chen (1979), in the conference proceedings edited by Delobel and Litwin (1980), and in the annual *Berkeley Workshop on Distributed Data Management and Computer Networks*.

LOCAL INFORMATION SYSTEMS

In their simplest form, local information systems can be based on magnetic disk stores attached to computers, either single-user small computers or time-shared computers connected to terminals.

More generally, they can be implemented by using networks, with the interrogating user terminals and work stations being on the same LAN as the file server or file store.

Both these types of system have already been discussed in other chapters of this book. This section therefore gives some examples of devices that can be used to enhance such systems.

Barnett and Beckwith (1981) describe the design and use of the Community File Station, an intelligent terminal system in use at Imperial College, London, which has a large central computer facility. This Station allows text preparation, editing, local file management, and rapid text display to be performed locally, without interacting with the central computer. Each user is able to maintain his own permanent files or data base on the local terminal system. The Community File Station is cheap, user friendly and really interactive, with very fast response.

Slonim et al (1981) describe NDX-100, an electonic filing system for the office of the future, that is based on distributed micrpbocessors. While its present model stores and retrieves documents in terms of their textual content, future versions will similarly handle them on the basis of their numerical, graphical or other information.

Back-end data base systems and *back-end storage networks* provide shared storage, which will become essential to the success of many of the large distributed, multiple-host data base systems that are now being developed. They are surveyed in the special issue of *Computer*, Vol. **13,** No. 2 (Feb 1980), and in the article by Maryanski (1980).

Ker (1981) describes the use of photographic techniques, especially the use of microfilm, to enable data, that are not easily input to computers or wordprocessing systems, to be handled efficiently and compactly. While such documents are filmed, information about their location can be keyed into a computer. The Kodak Intelligent Micro-image Terminal (IMT) is a microfilm filing system with built-in microprocessor; its VDU can be interfaced to a computer; to pass on the location of up to 40 microfilmed documents in a brief burst of online communication. The computer then proceeds with other work while the microprocessor in the terminal activates the display of the right images. This is a process of Computer Assisted Retrieval (CAR). Figure 12.1 gives a schematic diagram of this approach to image processing, and Figure 12.2 shows how it could be applied in an automated office.

Computer Output Microform (*COM*) allows data and information, output from computers, to be transferred automatically to microfilm or microfiche, as for example in the Eurocom Fiche Management System (Eurocom, undated).

VIDEOTEX INFORMATION SYSTEMS

Videotex may be defined as the whole class of electronic systems that use a modified television set or visual display terminal to present computer-based information in a user-accessible visual form.

The two major types of videotex are: *teletext*, where information stored in a

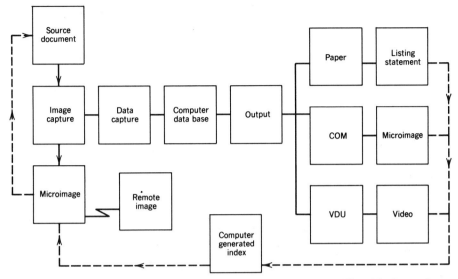

Fig. 12.1. Image processing SOURCE: Ed. A. Simpson, *Planning for the Office of the Future,* Gower Publishing Company, Aldershot, Hampshire, England, p. 83 Fig 6

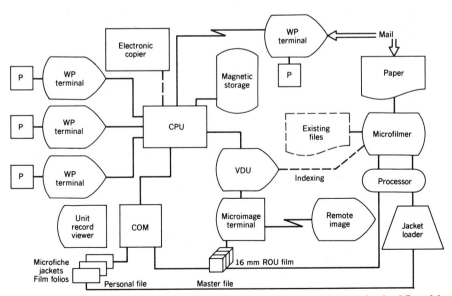

Fig. 12.2. The automated modern office SOURCE: Ed. A. Simpson, *Planning for the Office of the Future,* Gower Publishing Company, Aldershot, Hampshire, England, p. 83 Fig 7

computer is broadcast, usually in conjunction with television signals, to the user's TV set or terminal, and the more sophisticated *viewdata*, where there is a two-way connection, usually via telephone or cable, between the user's TV set and the (usually remote but sometimes local) computer storing information. Whereas teletext is usually one-way, not allowing any feed-back from the user, viewdata allows a user to interact with and respond to the information that he receives.

Both forms of videotex, but especially viewdata, are considered in detail in my book *The Videotex Revolution* (Mayne, 1986), which discusses in turn the videotex systems, technologies and applications, together with the impact of videotex. Chapter 12 of that book, "Data Bases and Information Services," is especially relevant to the theme of the present chapter.

Although videotex was originally designed as a service for retrieving a wide variety of information, stored in computer data bases, it is important to realise that this is by no means its only application; the transaction services, for which it provides a basis, are becoming increasingly important.

ONLINE DATA BASES AND INFORMATION SERVICES

For many years, in what has been a WAN operation, users with computer terminals, linked to computer networks, have been able to recover information stored in large computer data bases. There are already several hundreds of these data bases, on a variety of subjects, including science, technology, medicine, business, economics, the environment, law, current affairs, and education, whose contents have been accessible by means of information retrieval techniques, more sophisticated than those used in most videotex systems of these online data bases, and the Department of Industry's (1981) guide *Technical Services for Industry* describes in moderate detail some of the data base services available in the UK. The book by Hall and Brown (1983) includes a directory of online bibliographic data bases. Deunette (1982) has compiled a list of UK online search services. Moore (1981) reviews recent British research about provision of online information services in public libraries.

These online computer data bases have been developed most extensively in the USA, one of the largest collections being operated by Lockheed DIALOG, but their use has now become widespread in Europe also. British Library's BLAISE system provides access to several major data bases in the UK.

Aslib's Online Information Centre offers advice and services to users who wish to make effective use of online information services in the UK, and covers all publicly available online services, including viewdata and teletext services, as well as services providing bibliographic references services supplying data (Online Information Centre, updated, 1980 and 1984). The UK Online Users Group also caters for users of online information services.

Euronet DIANE, operated over the packet-switched network Euronet, is the first online information service catering for computer data bases in Western Europe as a whole; over 300 of the main data bases in Europe are available on this system.

It was created in order to classify, organise, and make accessible the answers to users' questions and enquiries, at the lowest possible cost. Using a simple terminal, costing little more than a good electric typewriter, at the end of a telephone line, users can carry out searches from information stored on the data bases in a few minutes.

The book edited by Gilchrist (1981) describes the use of small computers and terminals for library systems and information systems.

Martyn (1982) identifies some of the problems to be faced in handling duplicate references arising from online searches of several databases at one, and indicates some approaches to their solution.

GATEWAYS AND THIRD PARTY DATA BASES

In 1980, the Deutsche Bundespost's pilot Bildschirmtext viewdata service pioneered the provision of easy access to ordinary computer data bases by modified TV set viewdata receivers (Green, 1980). This access was made possible by the use of "Gateway" facilities and software, and data bases accessed thus were referred to as *third party data bases (TPDs)*.

Early in 1982, after much prior publicity, the British public viewdata service Prestel announced its service, known as "Prestel Gateway," whereby Prestel users could access third party data bases and outside computer services. Its introduction set a new standard in the capabilities of Prestel.

The facilities that Prestel Gateway can provide include:

1. Real-time interactive use, including a user's ability to handle complete transactions for services within a few seconds;
2. Services providing information specific to individual customers;
3. Data capture, making it easy to collect complex data;
4. Handling of rapidly changing data;
5. Access to "encyclopedic" data bases.

Full details are given in the Prestel brochures *The Possibilities are Infinite* and *Welcome to Gateway* (British Telecom, 1981a and 1981b). Further information is provided by Horne (1982), who predicts that, with the aid of Gateway, Prestel will add more sophisticated and specialist services to its range, while online information services will become oriented to take more account of untrained end users as well as the more expert users that they have at present.

Typical applications, which can benefit from the use of Prestel Gateway and similar gateway facilities provided by the private viewdata systems, include: banking, investment markets, company searches, business services, organisational communications, mail order, and travel reservations. Users of Prestel Gateway and other viewdata gateway services include: financial institutions, manufacturers, farmers, travel agents and operators, computer bureaux, and educational institutions.

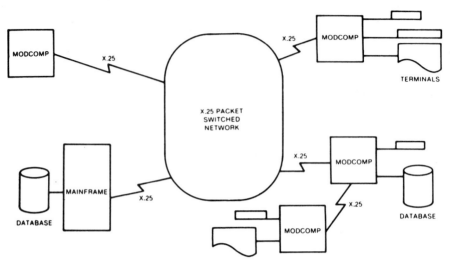

Fig. 12.3. Modcomp third party data base network example   SOURCE: Modcomp Software *Product Bulletin 807*

In the UK, Prestel's third party data base facility uses the packet-switched PSS service as its means of communications with outside computers (Gilbert, 1981, 1982), and some private viewdata systems use it also (See Figure 12.3). This ensures that the costs of data transmission are kept low and that the traffic capacity is high. Private viewdata systems use their gateway facilities to allow companies to use the public viewdata system and other outside data bases, while maintaining full control over their own data bases. By bringing together public and private viewdata systems and other data base systems, gateways allow users to benefit from the advantages of all these systems.

PICTORIAL DATA BASES

The use of computing systems to store pictorial information, especially that collected by satellites and other spacecraft, has expanded rapidly during recent years. The *Computer*, Vol. **14**, No. 11 (Nov 1981), special issue on pictorial information systems, surveys the current state of the art of this new technology. The Editorial by Chang (1981) defines this area and summarises the issue.

A *pictorial image system* is a special type of information system, that supports the manipulation, storage, retrieval and analysis of pictorial data. In the past, pictorial information systems have usually been designed for specific applications. Recent advances in data base technology, computer graphics, and pictorial data structures have led to the development of systems with a more general range.

A *pictorial data base* is a collection of publicly available pictorial data that are encoded there in various formats. A *pictorial data base system* (*PDBS*) provides an integrated collection of pictorial data that are easily reached by a large number of users.

Because of many new potential applications, such as office information systems and computer-aided engineering, pictorial information systems look like becoming an important extension of current information systems, and significant progress has already been made in their design. However, much careful research and development is still needed on the problems of their *standardisation*, including the specification of picture data formats, models of pictorial data bases, data structures, definition languages, and picture manipulation languages.

Change and Kunii (1981) examine recent trends in the design of PDBS, that support pictorial data, encoded in various formats, including vector and raster formats, and provide facilities for automatic conversion of the pictorial data. They also discuss relational and hierarchical approaches to the design of pictorial data bases. They give examples of specific PDBS, mostly for geographical data of various kinds, but also for computer-aided design.

Change and Fu (1981) survey existing query languages for PDBS, and describe in detail a picture-query-by-example approach. For effective man-machine interaction, a flexible user interface is often needed, to make it easier to incorporate a PDBS within a pictorial information system for general problem solving, together with the processing and understanding of images.

Check et al (1981) describe how to manipulate data structures in pictorial information systems. Danielson and Levialdi (1981) discuss the computer architecture of pictorial information systems; the principle of image parallelism is found to be the key to its cost effectiveness.

Zabriot and Nagy (1981) review the pictorial information processing of Landsat geographical data, which have very rich pictorial data structures and whose analysis raises difficult problems. *New Scientist* (2 Sep 1982) reports on the current status of the use of Earth-resources satellites and their attached computer systems, to collect and distribute data about crop conditions, geological deposits, etc.

Szczygiel (1982) briefly discusses image analysis in general, and sees profound implications in the application of image data processing techniques to office systems, libraries, publishing, advertising, and graphic arts. Image processing techniques can improve management information systems, provide mass verification of signatures for banking operations, and give "intelligent vision" to industrial robots. They can also be applied to satellite reconnaissance of the Earth's surface, as already mentioned, to obtain enhanced video images of distant planets, as in the NASA Voyager missions, and medical uses such as computer-assisted body-scanning and tomography.

INTEGRATED DISTRIBUTED INFORMATION SYSTEMS

Integrated distributed information systems can be achieved, for example, as parts of integrated office systems, or by means of integrated distributed data base management systems. The first of these alternatives is discussed at the end of Chapter 11, and the second is considered earlier in the present chapter.

Some other possible approaches will now be mentioned. One of these could well emerge from my own studies of user-friendly free-format data bases (Mayne, 1979,

1980, 1981, 1982a) and of nonhierachical "network" classifications (Mayne, 1968, 1973, 1974). Systems, combining these principles, are envisaged in the first instance for community information services, but could be applied to bibliograhic and library services, research and development establishments, and business offices, indeed to almost any area of application of information systems.

Nelson (1982) presents his vision of "Hyperworld," as a vast new realm of published documents, both text and graphics, that would be available instantly to its users, and provide all of them with a "grand library" in which they could store their own ideas. His Project Xanadu (Nelson, 1981) is building an advanced public-access storage and publishing system to provide a dynamic example of a preliminary attempt to implement this approach.

Lederberg (1978) states his personal views on the possible emergence of a new form of communication, which he calls the *EUGRAM*, which is based on the convergence of economical digital communications with computer-aided file management and protocols for the easier interconnection of users separated in both time and space. One key element of this proposed technology is the combination of electronic mail with the computer management of textual data. Another is that users would be able to share, in ways that would otherwise not be widely available, in the development, refinement and application of complex knowledge-based computer systems for handling a particular field of science, technology, or human activity.

REFERENCES

R. Barnett and R. C. Beckwith (Oct 1981) "The Community File Station," *Software—Practice and Experience*, **11**(10) 1001–1008.

British Telecom (1981a) *The Possibilities are Infinite—Prestel Gateway*, Prestel Brochure P520 5/81.

A. P. G. Brown (1982) "Progress towards distributed database systems," *ICCC 92*, 831–837.

N. S. Chang and K. S. Fu (Nov 1981) "Picture query languages for pictorial data-base systems," *Computer*, **14**(11) 23–33.

S. K. Chang (Nov 1981) "Pictorial information systems: Guest Editor's introduction," *Computer*, **14**(11) 10–11.

S. K. Chang and T. L. Kunii (Nov 1981) "Pictorial data-base systems," *Computer*, **14**(11) 13–21.

M. Check, A. F. Cardenas and A. Klinger (Nov 1981) "Manipulating data structures in pictorial information systems," *Computer*, **14**(11) 43–50.

W. W. Chu and P. P. Chen (Oct 1979) *Tutorial: Centralized and Distributed Data Base Systems*, IEEE Computer Society, Silver Springs, MD, USA.

Computer, **13**(2) (Feb 1980) Special issue on back-end storage networks.

Computer, **14**(11) (Nov 1981) Special issue on pictorial information systems.

P. E. Danielson and S. Levialdi (Nov. 1981) "Computer architecture for pictorial intormation systems," *Computer*, **11**(4) 53–67.

C. J. Date (3rd Ed., 1982) *An Introduction to Database Systems*, Addison-Wesley, Reading MA, and London.

B. Davis (1980) *Database in Perspective*, NCC Publications, Manchester, England.

Ed. C. Delobel and W. Litwin (1980) *Distributed Data Bases*, N. Holland, Amsterdam, Oxford, England, and New York.

Department of Industry (1981) *Technical Services for Industry*, Directory.

J. B. Deunette (Compiled by) (2nd. Ed., Oct 1982) *UK Online Search Services*, Aslib, London.

I. J. Douglas (1980) *Security and Audit of Database Systems*, NCC Publications, Manchester.

R. A. Elbra (1982) *Database for the Small Computer User*, NCC Publications, Manchester, England.

Eurocom (undated) *Fiche Management Systems*, Leaflet.

R. J. Firth (1982) *Viewdata Systems—A Practical Evaluation Guide*, NCC Publications, Manchester, England.

D. K. Gifford (Dec 1981) "Violet, an experimental decentralized system," *Computer Networks*, **5**(6) 423–433.

D. Gilbert (1981) "Videotex gateways, Linking Prestel to data processing systems," *Viewdata 81*, 619–636.

D. Gilbert (1982) "A new communication medium—Prestel Gateway," pages 116–118 of Ed. A. Simpson (1982) *Planning for Electronic Mail*, Gower Publishing Company, Aldershot, Hampshire, England.

Ed. A. Gilchrist (1981) *Minis, Micros and Terminals for Library and Information Systems*, Heyden, London.

Ed. D. Gradwell (1982) *Database—The Second Generation*, Pergamon Infotech State of the Art Report.

R. Green (10 Oct 1980) "Germans sell UK software back to Britian," *Computer Talk*, **3**.

J. L. Hall and M. J. Brown (3rd Ed., 1983) *Online Bibliographic Databases, A Directory and Sourcebook*, Aslib, London.

C. Horne (May 1982) "Gateway—An enhancement of Prestel," *Aslib Proceedings*, **34**(5) 266–270.

N. Ker (1981) "Planning for the microfilm system," pages 76–83 of Ed. A. Simpson (1981) *Planning for the Office of the Future*, Gower Publishing Company, Aldershot, Hampshire, England.

J. Lederberg (Nov 1978) "Digital communications and the conduct of science: The new literacy," *Proceedings of the IEEE*, **66**(11) 1320–1329.

J. D. Lomax (1978) *Data Dictionary Systems*, NCC Publications, Manchester, England.

J. D. Lomax (1979) *Evaluating the Database Approach*, NCC Publications, Manchester, England.

J. Martin (1981) *Design and Strategy for Distributed Data Processing*, Prentice-Hall, Englewood Cliffs, NJ, Part 4, "Design of Distributed Data."

J. Martyn (Aug 1982) "Unification of the results of online searches of several databases," *Aslib Proceedings*, **34**(8) 358–363.

F. J. Maryanski (Feb 1978) "A survey of developments in distributed data base management systems," *Computer*, **11**(2) 28–38.

F. J. Maryanski (Mar 1980) "Backend data base systems," *ACM Computing Surveys*, **12**(1) 3–25.

A. Mayne (Mayne, 1982b) (1982) *Database Management Systems—A Technical Review*, NCC Publications, Manchester, England.

A. J. Mayne (1978) "Some modern approaches to the classification of knowledge," *Classification Society Bulletin*, **1**(4) 12–17.

A. J. Mayne (Apr 1973) "Towards a new scheme for the classification of knowledge," *Informatics 1*, 43–54.

A. J. Mayne (May 1974) "Progress report on a new scheme for the classification of knowledge," *International Classification*, **1**(1) 27–32.

A. J. Mayne (Apr 1979) "A new system for handling data bses," *Journal of Informatics*, **3**(1) 33–36.

A. J. Mayne (Apr 1980) "Data base developments and user requirements—Development and design of data bases for human needs," Abstract of paper presented at the British Computer Society, *Communications 80 User Forum*, Brimingham, England.

A. J. Mayne (Jul 1981) "Experience with small user-oriented data base systems," *Papers Presented at the Third Research Colloquium of the British Computer Society Information Retrieval Specialist Group*.

A. J. Mayne (Mayne, 1982a) (Oct 1982) "Some preliminary results on the implementation of free-format data bases on personal computers," Papers presented at 25 Years of Computing Conference, University of Leeds.

A. J. Mayne (Mayne, 1986) *The Videotex Revolution*, second ed., Wiley, Chichester and New York, Chapter 12, "Data Bases and Information Services,"

W. N. Moore (1981) "On-line information in public libraries: A review of recent British research," *British Library R & D Report* **5648**.

NCC (1980) *Database Application Design—A Case Study*, NCC Publications, Manchester, England.

T. Nelson (1981) "Why not have it all?" *Videotex 81*, 309–315.

T. Nelson (Mar 1982) "A new home for the mind," *Datamation*, **28**(3) 168–180.

New Scientist (2 Sep 1982) "French mapping satellites knock spots off," **95**(1321) 624–625.

S. Obana, Y. Urano and K. Suzuki (1982) "The integration of distributed heterogeneous database systems based on entity-relationship model," *ICCC 82*, 763–768.

Online Information Centre (undated) *Online Information Centre*, Leaflet.

Online Information Centre (Nov 1980) *Selecting a Terminal for Online Information Retrieval*.

Online Information Centre (1984) *The Online Information Centre—Publications and Services*, Leaflet.

PACTEL (1980) *Distributed Database Technology*, NCC Publications, Manchester, England.

H. Robinson (1982) *Database Analysis and Design—An Undergraduate Text*, Chartwell-Bratt, Bromley, Kent, England.

J. B. Rothnie, Jr., P. A. Bernstein and D. W. Shipman (Oct 1978) *Tutorial: Distributed Data Base Management*, IEEE Computer Society, Silver Springs, MD.

J. B. Rothnie, Jr., N. Goodman and T. Marill (1981) "Data-base management in distributed networks," Chapter 10 of Ed. F. F. Kuo (1981) *Protocols & Techniques for Data Communication Networks*, Prentice-Hall, Englewood Cliffs, NJ.

P. Scheuermann (Feb 1978) "On the design and evaluation of large data bases," *Computer*, **11**(2) 46–55.

D. Spennewyn (2 Sep 1982) "The wind of change in dbms," *Computing*, 18–19.

M. Szczygiel (2 Sep 1982) "Business is booming in image analysis," *Computer Weekly*, 13.

A. S. Tanenbaum (1981) *Computer Networks*, Prentice-Hall, Englewood Cliffs, NJ.

D. A. Winscom Clarke (1982) "The influence of network bandwidth on the design of distributed database systems," *ICCC 82*, 753–756.

A. L. Zabriot and G. Nagy (Nov 1981) "Pictorial information processing of Landsat data for geographic analysis," *Computer*, **14**(11) 43–50.

Chapter 13

Distributed Computing Systems

Distributed computing systems may be defined as systems where computations and data processing operations are carried out over several linked but separate computers or computing devices. The allied terms *distributed processing* and *distributed data processing* have been defined in many senses (Martin, 1981, pages 87 to 88; Uhlig et al, 1979, pages 175–176.

This chapter discusses various aspects of distributed computing systems. Recent developments are presented in Chapter 22.

DISTRIBUTED DATA PROCESSING AND DISTRIBUTED COMPUTING

Uhlig et al (1979, Chapter 11.6) present a model for distributed processing, that can be used as a framework for discussing it; they apply it to develop the concepts of this field and to discuss various examples of distributed computing systems, displaying a range of future directions and possibilities. According to them, such a model should be general enough to represent a significant number of the distributed computer architectures now in use. It should allow the formulation of distributed systems that might be appropriate in the future and perhaps enable insight to be obtained about future directions. It should lead to predictions of possible future paths in architecture and applications. In their own model, all flow of information between devices, device handlers, file handlers and applications programs uses the distributed system's program-to-program communications (PPC) mechanism; the implementation and structure of PPCs is one of the current areas of research in distributed processing.

Martin's (1981) book *Design and Strategy for Distributed Data Processing* discuss distributed processing in considerable detail, especially the different forms of distributed processing and the strategies that can be used. Chapter 6 of that book gives some examples of the great variety of forms that it can take and configurations of computing devices that it can use. Connections between computers, processors and devices include: computer buses and machine room channels that are very fast, LANs, WANs, both leased and public telephone lines, and manual transport of magnetic stores such as tapes and disks. Ways of distributing the processing include *vertical distribution*, where there is a hierarchy of processors, at different levels, and *horizontal distribution*, where the processors are of equal or comparable rank. More general types of distributed system use both these approaches. Many distributed computing systems also allocate specific *processing functions* to processors or other particular types of device at each given level.

The amounts and degrees of distribution in a computing system cover a wide spectrum, ranging from loosely connected WANs, where computers communicate with each other relatively rarely, to tightly coupled *data flow machines*, whose different processors interact instruction by instruction.

Tanenbaum (1981, Section 10.2) outlines several different models for distributing the computation, with different degrees of coupling from loose to tight, and including both static and dynamic partitioning of tasks between devices.

In the *hierarchical model*, different functions are carried out by devices at different levels. For example, in a typical distributed computing system for a factory, a mainframe at the top level would coordinate all computing, minicomputers at the level below would analyse and store data, and microcomputers would control equipment and collect data on the shop floor; here, each processor handles a different level of detail, corresponding to the needs of the different people who need information.

In the *CPU cache model*, parts of the computation are done on a central computer, say, and parts done on local minicomputers. Decisions as to which parts to run on which machine depend on the suitabilities of the machines, their relative costs, the bandwidths of the lines between them, and the current workload.

In the *user-server model*, no central computer is used; instead, the users' personal computers and/or work stations, together with special devices such as file servers, data base servers and print servers, are all attached to the same LAN, which may also have at least one gateway to outside networks.

In the *pool processor model*, computing and data processing are carried out by a group of processors, constituting the *pool*, and all these processors, together with the fixed function servers, gateway(s) and user terminals are attached to a LAN.

In the *data flow model*, the basic distributed computing system is no longer a computer network but a computer of a special design, called a *data flow machine*, containing several suitably interconnected processors. The different steps of a calculation or data processing function are here distributed between the processors, according to an arrangement that is specified by the program being run.

One of the original intentions of WANs was to allow host computers to share resources (Cole, 1982, Section 10.1). For example, special devices, such as microfilm plotters and fast array processors, may be too expensive to have at each computer centre, yet users at any of these centres may wish to use any of the facilities provided by these devices. A WAN between the computing centres allows these users to access the resources that require, at an overall cost that is lower.

The IEEE Computer Society has published several tutorials on distributed computing systems. The tutorial by Liebowitz and Carson (1981) gives an introductory survey of distributed processing, defining three major areas: points-of-use systems, resource-sharing networks, and multiple-processor systems; it discusses several case histories, providing insights into design issues, cost-effectiveness and management problems. The tutorial by Thurber (1980) uses a top-down approach, from the overall concepts down to implemented hardware structures; it illustrates the problems and potentialities, and informs about the pitfalls and the progress already made. The other tutorials are those by Palmer and Mariani (1979) on methods of designing distributed computing systems, Larson (1979) on the application of decentralised control theory to distributed systems, and Kuhn and Padua (1981) on the wide variety of parallel processing computers now available.

The IEEE Computer Society has also published the proceedings of the important international conferences on distributed computing systems, DCS 79 (1979) and DCS 81 (1981), which include many useful papers on computer networks, as well as papers on distributed computing as such, and the proceedings of an international conference on parallel processing (IEEE Computer Society, 1981).

The National Computing Centre has published three books on distributed computing systems. NCC (1978) examines trends in distributed systems, with special reference to the impact of different computer technologies of them and on computer communications. Down and Taylor (1976) report on developments in distributed computing systems, and give general information on experience of these systems. Green (1978) describes techniques and aids, that may be useful to people thinking of using minicomputers in a distributed system.

The Prime Computer (1980) brochure describes the distributed computing system, using intercontinental WANs to interconnect Prime computers, that is operated by this company.

TIME SHARING

One of the simplest forms of distributed computing is *time sharing*, where any number of terminals, up to a few hundred, share the access to the processing power of a central computer. The principles involved are outlined, for example, by Cole (1982, Chapters 4 and 5).

Most time-shared computers, that are used from interactive but "unintelligent" terminals, operate character-by-character, via full duplex connections to the terminals. If the number of terminals is not too large, the terminals may be linked directly to the computer in a star network. More generally, a snowflake network is used, with the computer linked to multiplexers, each of which serves a cluster of terminals, although some terminals may be connected directly to the computer. As the terminals have to share access to the computer, some scheme must be used for assigning this access, for example a *round robin scheme* where each terminal in a cluster or each multiplexer is allotted access in turn.

Figure 13.1 shows the configuration of the APL Time-Sharing Network, devel-

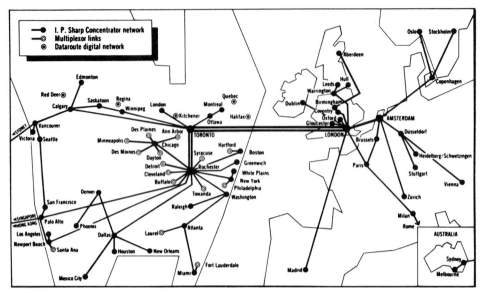

Fig. 13.1. APL time-sharing network   SOURCE: Ed. A. Simpson, *Planning for Electronic Mail*, Gower Publishing Company, Aldershot, Hampshire, England, p. 59

oped by I. P. Sharp Associates Ltd. It is a WAN with international and inter-continental coverage.

Simple message-based systems are available, that can handle the communication between more intelligent terminals and a central computer. Time-shared systems using *multipoint* (*multidrop*) lines connect as many terminals as possible to one line, thus reducing transmission costs. Each line can carry only one message at a time, either from a terminal to a computer or from the computer to a terminal. To avoid interference between communications intended for different terminals, the message transmissions from the terminals must be controlled by a *polling discipline*, where the computer polls each terminal to ask if it has a message and, if it has, assigns a slot for that message. The computer can send a message to any terminal as soon as the line is free.

Multipoint terminals are not very useful in interactive general purpose time-shared computers, where users often need responses to single characters. But they can be very useful where fairly large chunks of information are entered at once, for example in transaction processing systems for entering invoices and in airline ticket booking systems.

The DPTX Product Bulletin (Prime Computer, 1981a) describes various ways in which Prime's DPTX software allows users of Prime terminals to link with main-frames. The DPTX/DSC software allows a Prime system to share a multidrop communication line with IBM 3271 controllers.

Terminal protocols make it easier to connect different models of terminals to the same computer network; they are described by Day (1981), for example, and more briefly towards the end of Chapter 9.

REMOTE JOB ENTRY

Although terminals are most often used for interactive computing and data processing, they can also be used for *remote job entry* (*RJE*), where they activate the running of batch-processed jobs in distant computers. When such a job is finished, a notification of this can be sent to the terminal, and the output can be posted or otherwise recovered from the computer centre.

An *RJE station* is a small group of peripherals, such as a console, a card reader, and a line printer, that allows users both to enter batch jobs and to receive their usually fairly extensive output, locally, usually at some distance from the central computer. Although the peripherals are mainly character-based, the characters entered are organised into files, which are transferred in blocks to the remote computer, with the RJEs using a synchronous medium in the same way as multipoint lines (Cole, 1982, page 74). Although the earlier RJE stations are going out of fashion, the concept of RJE has been extended into a form of true distributed computing, by using small computer as the RJE controller (Cole, 1982, page 75).

Prime's RJE products allows multi-user Prime systems to emulate IBM, CDC, Univac, Honeywell and ICL RJE terminals over synchronous terminals (Prime Computer, 1981b). They are designed to communicate with many remote sites at once. Any terminal, connected to a Prime system, can submit jobs for transmission to remote processors, eliminating the need for local RJE stations or dedicated terminals. Prime mainframes can run together RJE emulators, program development and production work.

RJE protocols have been devised, that allow network users to operate a variety of computer batch systems with one implementation of RJE software; they are described by Day (1981), for example, and are also considered briefly towards the end of Chapter 9.

LOCAL AREA NETWORK OPERATING SYSTEMS

In order that network users may avoid having to handle each computer on a network differently and having to learn its systems and languages separately, there is a need for network-wide operating systems, which have the job of managing the data and the communication in a uniform, computer-independent way (Tanenbaum, 1981, page 476).

For LANs, the approach of replacing the operating systems of the connected computers by one homogeneous *distributed operating system* is beginning to be adopted. Systems of this sort are described briefly by Tanenbaum (1981, Section 10.3.2). Much research is still being done on how to design them; most researchers use one of two models.

In the *process model*, each resource, such as a file, disk, or peripheral, is managed by some process, and the operating system only manages the communication between the processes. Traditional operating system functions, such as file handling, processor scheduling, and terminal control, are managed by specific server processors that can be called by programs.

In the *object model*, the computing system's "world" has various objects, each of which has a type, a representation, and a set of operations that can be performed on it. In order to carry out any operation on an object, for example read a file, a user process must obtain the necessary permission. The basic task of the operating system here is to manage these permissions and allow operations to be performed.

The Apollo Domain system has evolved as a direct result of improvements in technology; it combines the good parts of time-shared systems and dedicated mini-computers, but claims to have overcome their disadvantages (Apollo Computer, 1981). It uses a high speed interactive wideband LAN, and provides a dedicated processor for each user, who thus has a high level of interactive parallel perfor-mance. Its LAN enables a community of users to coordinate their computing in a comprehensive way.

Schutt and Welch (1981) and Spratt (1981) describe the distributed computing facilities provided by the Cambridge Ring system at the University of Kent, which is essentially an example of the user-server type of system. Such a network of communicating, dynamically variable, servers has the potential of combining the advantages of a central time-shared mainframe with those of stand-alone personal computers. Schutt and Welch list some of these advantages:

1. Access to a wide range of standard services;
2. Ability to upgrade hardware and software according to user demand and technical innovations;
3. Physical security of data and software;
4. Ability to share data and software, at the user's discretion;
5. Faster responses.

Rubinstein et al (1981) describe the operation of the Cambridge Ring system at University College London, which handles several time-shared systems, based on the UNIX operating system, and supporting over a hundred research users and student users. They discuss the principles behind the protocols used, together with the performance characteristics of the whole system.

Whitehouse (1981) considers, in a rather abstract way, how distributed systems, based on LANs, can support application programs, by means of the characteristics of these LANs.

Svobodova (1981) describes how a LAN operating system can support a distrib-uted office system, in terms of a model of an office information system.

Tanenbaum and Mullender (1981) describe Amoeba, a distributed operating sys-tem, designed to run on many processors, which includes a protection system. It uses six levels of protocol: on top, an Application Layer, where users' programs are run; below that, a System Call Layer, providing library routines and a user interface to the operating system; below that, and still part of the operating system, a Transport Layer and a Monitor Layer; these four layers sit on top of the Data Link Layer and the Physical Layer, which are not part of Amoeba, but belong to whatever LAN it uses.

Sincoskie and Farber (1981) describe the SODS/OS operating system, used at the University of Delaware, USA.

Donnelley (1981) considers distributed computing systems, built from modules operating in separate domains, and discusses the problems of manaaging these domains at the levels of process-to-process communication.

WIDE AREA NETWORK OPERATING SYSTEMS

The operating system of a time-shared computer is a computer resource-management system (Cole, 1982, page 169). In order to provide users with a reasonable-service, it allocates resources such as central processing time, memory, and access to peripheral devices. The user perceives the quality of the service in terms of how easily he accesses its resources and how well it responds to his commands.

WANs· with large multiprogrammed host computers and large amounts of existing software tend to use *network operating systems*, which are implemented as a collection of user programs running on the various hosts, while each host continues to run its old (non-network) operating system (Tanenbaum, 1981, page 476). Tanenbaum (1981, Section 10.3.1) discusses network operating systems briefly, considering as an illustrative example the National Software Works (NSW) system, that runs on the Arpanet.

McGlynn (1978) describes the three layers of software that must be considered in WAN data communications systems: host operating system, communications-based access software, and application programs.

Thurber (1979) introduces a collection of papers on the subject of distributed processing communication architecture, including interconnection switches and digital paths. It starts by considering system configurations and then discusses packet switching, circuit switching and bus structure.

All Prime computer systems use the multi-function PRIMOS operating system, which supports many functions, including a wide range of communications facilities (Prime Computer, 1981c). These include the RJE products and DPTX, mentioned earlier in this chapter, and the PRIMENET networking software.

FILE TRANSFER

File transfer between computers in distributed computing systems is best handled by file transfer protocols. These are discussed, for example, by Day (1981), and are also considered briefly by Cole (1982, pages 164–165) and towards the end of Chapter 9.

MEDIA CONVERSION

Media conversion is the process of changing the representation of a specific piece of data of information one one medium into a corresponding representation on another medium. In its simplest form, the two media are of the same general type, but belong to two different variants of that type. In its more general form, often more difficult to handle, the media themselves are of different types.

Media conversion as such is not a primary function of computer networks, but this topic is mentioned here, because it is often found that the best way of performing a conversion between two specific media involves the use of some form of networking. Some examples are now considered briefly.

A good example of simple media conversion, for which there is probably a considerable demand, is the conversion of files between different magnetic media, for example between two different floppy disks formats or between two magnetic tape formats. This can quite often be done by direct use of a computer system, running online both the original storage medium and the medium on which the new files are to be placed. However, quite often unexpected difficulties arise, which make this direct approach difficult, if not impossible; this can arise from certain types of incompatibilities between the specific ways in which the data on the two storage media are formatted.

When such cases arise, a simple application of networking should usually make it possible to achieve the conversion successfully. The approach to be used is to place medium 1 online on computer 1 and medium 2 online on computer 2, and at the same time to activate a data link between computer 1 and computer 2. Such a data link could either belong to a LAN, to which both computers are connected, or it could be a WAN-type line between both computers. In the latter case, the connecting link can be purely local, but each of the communicating computers would contain inside it a suitable interface such as a communications card.

The reason why this approach would work is that a communications link between two computers transfers a stream of bits or a stream of bytes. A program in computer 1 would convert the data representation on medium 1 into an explicit transformation of that representation, residing in the memory of computer 1, which would be the representation of the data to be transferred between the two computers. This representation would not change while being transferred, so that it would have the same pattern of bits and bytes when it ultimately reaches the memory of computer 2. Therefore, another piece of software, this time situated in computer 2, could convert it into the representation appropriate for storage on medium 2.

This explanation can be made clearer by an analogy. Text in medium 1 is in German, and a version of the text in French is required in medium 2. Neither computer 1 nor computer 2 can perform the translation direct, but both computers have interpreters who know English. Thus the interpreter in computer 1 translates the German text on medium 1 into an intermediate text, in English, which is posted, via the communication link, to computer 2. The interpreter in computer 2, who also knows English, can translate the intermediate text into French, and place that translated version in medium 2.

For some types of conversion between different types of media, as opposed to different variants of the same type of medium, the same principle will work. This is possible when converting from one digital data medium to another, as it is then *always* possible to use as intermediary some well defined pattern of bits and bytes, that can be sent reliably along a communication channel. In other words, in terms of the analogy, interpreters are always available, who can translate from a given digital data language into English, and there are other interpreters who can translate from English into the required new digital data language.

The situation is less simple when at least one of the media involved is analogue, for example voice or non-digital pictorial information. Even though it is usually possible to translate from analogue form into digital form and vice versa, the translation processes, *unlike* the translations between two digital "languages," can no longer be done with arbitrarily high reliability. Thus the media conversion cannot now be done without inaccuracies. To make matters worse, the translation between an analogue "language" and a digital "language" may no longer be straightforward, as it now requires a more or less complicated pattern recognition process.

This is true, for example, of computer recognition of spoken language, where the state of the art is advancing slowly, compared with most parts of information technology. It is also true, though to a lesser extent, of optical character recognition of text, which can be done reliably for printed text, fairly reliably for typed text, but which is much more uncertain for handwritten text, unless the handwriting is remarkably good! Another snag, of course, is that even when these recognition technologies *do* work adequately, their use in media conversion is much more expensive, at least when all but the most elementary, and usually much less useful, forms are being carried out.

REMOTE RUNNING OF COMPUTER PROGRAMS

Terminal access protocols are used to allow a user at an asynchronous terminal to access a remote host computer *across a network, as if* he were directly connected to the host and using a time-shared service directly linked to that host (Cole, 1982, page 165). For most such terminals, it is necessary to connect them directly or via a telephone to a special intermediary processor, that can act as an interface between the terminal and the WAN. A processor of this sort is called a *packet assembler and disassembler (PAD)* on X.25 networks, and a *terminal interface processor (TIP)* on the Arpanet.

Terminal access protocols, including the Arpanet Telnet protocol, are described by Day (1981) and Cole (1982, pages 165–167), and are also mentioned towards the end of Chapter 9.

TELESOFTWARE

In its original form, *telesoftware* was defined as a facility for distributing and storing computer programs through a teletext and/or viewdata system. More generally, it can be defined as the transmission of programs from one computer to another by broadcast radio or broadcast television or via telephone lines or computer network, together with the recording of these programs on the receiving computer's storage media.

In a typical example of a telesoftware system, the receiving computer, usually a personal computer, automatically retrieves a program, required by one of its users, from another computer, usually a mainframe. It checks that the program data have been transmitted correctly, and then stores the program on one of its cassette or disk stores, where it can be used when required. Reliable transmission can be ensured, partly by including error checks at the receiving end, which are almost certainly activated if a transmission error occurs, and partly by retransmitting any block of data found to be erroneous when it is received. This is in accordance with the standard practice of low level data transmission protocols.

Mayne (1986, Chapter 13) outlines the earlier history of telesoftware, "including its" emergence as a facility provided by the British public videotex services Prestel, Ceefax and Oracle. Reference is given there to the considerable earlier work that was done in this field.

The Council for Educational Technology (1982) provides a comprehensive brief review of the current situation of telesoftware provision and development in the UK. Broadcast telesoftware uses the BBC's Ceefax and IBA's Oracle teletext services. Telesoftware, sent via the PSTN, can be based on any viewdata system, public or private, or on locally established links between the transmitting and receiving computers; in practice, Prestel at present provides by far the most important service of this sort.

Telesoftware procedures have been especially well developed for the Research Machines 380Z and the Apple II personal computers, but they are rapidly becoming available for other makes of personal computers, including the Pet, Tandy and BBC Microcomputer.

With support from the Department of Industry, the Council for Educational Technology (CET) set up the CET Telesoftware Project as a trial scheme for the distribution and reception of computer programs via Prestel. Prestel also collects programs from other sources, including the BBC and the magazine *Practical Computing*.

The BBC Computer Literacy Project, launched in January 1982, provides appropriate facilities for telesoftware, as optional extras for use with the BBC microcomputer system.

All Prestel users, who have a suitable telesoftware package, together with the right sort of personal computer, can obtain and run these programs. The CET Information Sheet on telesoftware, mentioned above, provides the necessary details, with indications of costs and further information sources.

The educational uses of software are considered briefly in the section on educational applications of networking in the next chapter.

INTEGRATED DISTRIBUTED COMPUTING SYSTEMS

The objective of a distributed processing strategy should be to establish an integrated framework, within which distributed processing can grow rapidly involving its users as much as possible, leading to highly productive development of applications, and avoiding the pitfalls of distributed computing (Martin, 1981, Chapter

10). Because of these pitfalls, some of the early distributed computing systems and computer networks were disasters; to avoid this happening and gain the benefits of these systems, informed planning is needed.

Martin (1981, Chapter 10) goes on to discuss how this can be approached and carried out. For each of the following aspects of systems management, a choice has to be made between centralised and decentralised management: setting standards, selecting architectures, choosing hardware and software, usage decisions, the design of data, and the development of applications. The appropriate combination of these choices varies from one organisation to another, according to their management styles and structures.

The design of distributed data processing cannot be done at one particular time by one group of people; it evolves over many years in an organisation or company (Martin, 1981, page 161).

Thus the need is *not* for one comprehensive, grandiose plan, but for a framework that allows step-by-step growth, with none of the steps being too large. The separate steps should fit into a unified pattern, with whatever degrees of compatibility and interconnection are best suited to the organisation. Although the implementations are likely to take years, the strategic plan should be created at the outset, but modified from time to time as new experience is gained and new facilities become available. The management patterns, computer and network architectures, and controls need to be set before too much ad hoc implementation has been done.

Uhlig et al. (1979, Chapter II.8) briefly describe two separate but complementary systems, that indicate the types of distributed computing systems and software that will appear in the future. The Distributed Computing System (DCS), developed by one of these authors under the sponsorship of the USA National Science Foundation, was one of the first functional distributed computing systems to be developed. Its goals are: system reliability, modular growth, modernisation by stages, dynamic restructuring and use of resources. The hardware system used in a collection of devices, mostly minicomputers, linked by a ring. The Modular Office System (MOS), is intended to bring together, in one design, current LSI computer technology, the best current set of personal computer based services and services interconnecting personal computers, and a "clean" man-computer interface that is easy to use. This system is designed for executives, designers, and others not expert in computing, rather than for programmers.

REFERENCES

Apollo Computer (1981) *Apollo Domain Architecture*, Apollo Computers Inc., Brochure.

R. Cole (1982) *Computer Communication*, Macmillan, Basingstoke, Hampshire.

Council for Educational Technology (Mar 1982) "Telesoftware," *CET Information Sheet No. 3*.

J. D. Day (1981) "Terminal, file transfer, and remote job protocols," Chapter 3 of Ed. F. F. Kuo (1981) *Protocols and Techniques for Data Communication Networks*, Prentice-Hall, Englewood Cliffs, NJ.

DCS 79 (Oct 1979) *First International Conference on Distributed Computing Systems*, Huntsville, AL, USA, IEEE Computer Society, Silver Springs, MD.

DCS 81 (Apr 1981) *Second International Conference on Distributed Computing Systems*, Versailles, France, IEEE Computer Society, Silver Springs, MD.

J. E. Donnelley (1981) "Managing domains in a network operating system," *Local Networks 81*, 345–361.

P. J. Down and F. E. Taylor (1976) *Why Distributed Computing?*, NCC Publications, Manchester, England.

R. G. Green (1978) *Using Minicomputers in Distributed Systems*, NCC Publications, Manchester, England.

IEEE Computer Society (Aug 1981) *International Conference on Parallel Processing*, IEEE Computer Society, Silver Springs, MD.

R. H. Kuhn and D. A. Padua (Aug 1981) *Tutorial: Parallel Processing*, IEEE Computer Society, Silver Springs, MD.

R. E. Larson (Oct. 1979) *Tutorial: Distributed Control*, IEEE Computer Society, Silver Springs, MD.

B. H. Liebowitz and J. H. Carson (3rd Ed., Apr 1981) *Tutorial: Distributed Processing*, IEEE Computer Society, Silver Springs, MD.

D. R. McGlynn (1978) *Distributed Processing and Data Communications*, Wiley, New York and Chichester, Chapter 3, "Data Communications Software."

J. Martin (1981) *Design and Strategy for Distributed Data Processing*, Prentice-Hall, Englewood Cliffs, NJ.

A. J. Mayne (1986) *The Videotex Revolution*, second ed., Wiley, Chichester and New York.

NCC (1978) *Trends in Distributed Systems*, NCC Peblications, Manchester, England.

D. Palmer and M. Mariani (Oct 1979) *Tutorial: Distributed System Design*, IEEE Computer Society, Silver Springs, MD, USA.

Prime Computer (1980) *Distributed Processing*, Prime Computer Inc., Brochure.

Prime Computer (1981a) *Distributed Processing Terminal Executive (DPTX)*, Prime Computer Inc., Product Bulletin.

Prime Computer (1981b) *RJE*, Prime Computer, Inc., Product Bulletin.

Prime Computer (1981c) *PRIMOS Operating System*, Prime Computer Inc., Product Bulletin.

M. J. Rubinstein, C. J. Kennington and G. T. Knight (1981) "Terminal support on the Cambridge Ring," *Local Networks 81*, 475–490.

T. Schutt and P. H. Welch (1981) "Applying micro-computers in a local area network," *Local Networks 81*, 491–501.

W. D. Sincoskie and D. J. Faber (1981) "The Series/1 distributed operating system," *Local Networks 81*, 319–328.

E. B. Spratt (1981) "Developments of the Cambridge Ring at the University of Kent," *Local Networks 81*, 503–518.

L. Svobodova (1981) "Operating system support for distributed office systems," *Local Networks 81*, 329–343.

A. S. Tanenbaum (1981) *Computer Networks*, Prentice-Hall, Englewood Cliffs, NJ.

A. S. Tanenbaum and S. J. Mullender (1981) "Amoeba—A capability based distributed operating system," *Local Networks 81*, 363–377.

K. J. Thurber (Oct 1979) *Tutorial: Distributed Processing Computer Architecture*, IEEE Computer Society, Silver Springs, MD.

K. J. Thurber (May 1980) *Tutorial: A Pragmatic View of Distributed Processing Systems*, IEEE Computer Society, Silver Springs, MD.

R. P. Uhlig, D. J. Farber and J. H. Bair (1979) *The Office of the Future*, North-Holland, Amsterdam, Oxford, England, and New York.

P. Whitehouse (1981) "Design of application programs for distributed systems," *Local Networks 81*, 85–95.

Chapter 14

Other Applications of Networks

This chapter presents some of the applications of computer networks that are not covered by Chapters 11 to 13. It considers in turn applications to: public services and utilities, electronic publishing, computer conferencing and teleconferencing, education and training, community information services, home information systems, medicine and health care, and industry. Its final section considers some miscellaneous applications. Recent developments are presented in Chapter 22.

PUBLIC SERVICES AND UTILITIES

Actual and potential applications of networking by national and local government services include administration, information, law enforcement, protection against crime and other hazards, and social security. Networking is also used by public utility services such as gas and electricity.

Though some of these applications are important, there seems to be very little published literature about them. Licklider and Vezza (1978) consider them briefly and describe a few examples.

The USA Social Security Administration (SSA) distributes many billions of dollars a year to over 20 million people, and interacts with millions of clients a year through its many offices. In 1976, the SSA began planning the modernisation of its massive data processing activities, by expanding its already extensive use of computers and installing a major communications subsystem. The SSA carries out much consultation and updating of central and regional data bases from its local offices.

The USA National Crime Information Centre is operated by the FBI, and uses a network to communicate with state and local police units. It has had difficulties in obtaining full networking facilities, because its requirements for them tend to conflict with Congressional concern for the right of privacy of information.

There are several potential applications of computer networking to the transmission of alarms and emergency messages from people's homes to local organisations that can act on them effectively. For example, warnings of intruders, fire, gas leakage, and water leakage can be sent, "electronic babysitting" can be carried out, and the well-being of old and sick people can be monitored. The actual use of such services does not seem to be widespread as yet.

Carne (1981) gives some examples of miscellaneous ways in which communications systems can be used in the home. He shows a load control and energy management system, with communications between the electric power utility with the homes that it serves, via radio, CATV, telephone or power line. These connections are controlled by commands from the utility and/or the householder, and they can address individually such major power loads as water heaters, space heaters, and air-conditioning; the householder can also address individual lights and appliances.

Carne also shows the design of a remote control and monitor telephone system, which adds a microprocessor and other devices to a conventional telephone. This allows equipment to be monitored and controlled remotely, emergency services to be called automatically when required, and selected information to be displayed to the householder as he desires.

The London Borough of Hackney is one example of a British local authority that is embarking on a fundamental change in the way in which it provides community services, by decentralising a wide range of these services and their staff to about thirty neighbourhood offices. The provision of local computing and networking facilities is crucial to the success of this decentralisation policy. Data, text and voice facilities are provided, together with electronic mail and viewdata systems; the network links local personal computers and intelligent terminals to central minicomputers and mainframes.

ELECTRONIC PUBLISHING

Electronic publishing is a group of various ways of applying computing, information technology and electronics to the dissemination of information that would previously have been distributed by conventional methods of printing or reproducing paper documents. It includes: videotex news services, described by Mayne (1986); the automatic generation of viewdata frames from information already stored in a computer system; word processing, described in Chapters 7 and 11; and the use of computer typesetters, also mentioned in Chapter 7.

Haslam (1981) considers some of the attitudes of existing print publishers, in the UK and Western Europe and North America, to electronic publishing. He reports that some of them have invested heavily in new information technologies, while others of comparable importance have spent nothing on them. He gives examples of reasons for publishers' decisions on electronic publishing technologies, and he provides a checklist for publishers who still have to decide whether or not to use them.

Langton Information Systems Ltd. is a leading electronic publishing company in the UK, and it has pioneered several new techniques in this field (Langton Information Systems, 1982). It issues *Langton Electronic Publishing News* quarterly. It offers a total service for electronic publishing applications, well adapted to the needs of individual customers.

Its COMPUSET package provides fully automatic production of complete publications from text or data files on word processors, minicomputers or mainframes. Xerox has officially adopted COMPUSET as the standard composition system for its internationally successful laser printer.

Langston also provides photocomposition, laser printing, microfiche publishing, and distribution services. It has a comprehensive system for integrating graphics with text, for the production of both hard copy and microfiche publications. It can help clients convert their existing records into computer data bases ready for electronic publishing; in fact, the same computer files can be used as the bases for printed documents or microforms or videotex displays.

The product literature of Word-Set Systems Ltd. (1982) describes its "Complete Electronic Office" services, in data formatting and extraction, data processing, word processing, and phototypesetting. Its electronic publishing service, the Word-Set Publishers Manuscript Managers Service, can handle all the stages of the production of a document by its author, editor, publisher and printer. This service is based on its Word-Set range of word processors and work stations, which can act also as microcomputers, with full data processing and information retrieval capabilities, phototypesetter terminals, and remote terminals. Authors, editors and publishers can use them to key in, modify, and correct text, until it is in a form ready for typesetting. Between 160,000 and 15 million characters of text can be stored, according to the system configuration, and text can be exchanged by delivering or posting floppy disks or by transmitting it between work stations over the PSTN. A bureau service is operated for authors who cannot affort their own equipment.

The collection of papers edited by Hills (1981) provides one of the first statements of viewpoints on the future of the printed word, in what may well become a continuing debate of increasing importance in this area of new information and communication technologies. Specialists in publishing, librarianship, information science, computing and education present detailed surveys of their fields, together with statements on the futures of the printed word and such other readable media as video displays, computer print-outs, microfiche and microfilm.

COMPUTER CONFERENCING AND TELECONFERENCING

Teleconferencing is an extended communication between at least two individuals, using facilities that range from telephone and radio to high speed telefacsimile, integrated graphics projection, and computer-aided information transfer and retrieval (Future Systems Inc., 1980; Raitt, 1982, page 66).

Computer conferencing is an extension of teleconferencing, where messages and comments on papers and other documents can be entered, recorded, distributed to selected participants, stored, retrieved, and commented on. In some respects, Teletex and other electronic mail and communicating word processing systems, that allow the storage, retrieval and manipulation of texts by several remote users, are similar.

However, computer conferencing systems carry sophisticated message systems one stage further. Their basic principle of operation is to have all messages for a "computer conference" on a given subject placed in a given set of files, which is then shared between those participating in the conference.

Martin (1981, Chapter 11), Uhlig et al (1979, Chapters I.7 and I.10), Clark (1981), Licklider and Vezza (1978, page 1332), and British Telecom (1980, pages 12–14) give brief introductions of teleconferencing and computer conferencing in relatively non-technical language. Fuller descriptions are given in the reports *Teleconferencing* (Future Systems, Inc., 1980) and *Teleconferencing Systems* (Hough and Panko, 1977), and in the books by Johansen et al (1979), Hiltz and Turoff (1978), and Kerr and Hiltz (1982).

Pioneering work on computer conferencing has been done since 1975 by the Computerized Conference & Communications Center at New Jersey Institute of Technology, which has developed the Electronic Information Exchange System (EIES). Turoff and Hiltz (1978) review the earlier stages of the development and implementation of EIES. Recent work there, investigating the use of EIES as a laboratory tool for conducting information experiments, is described by Hiltz et al (1982). Hiltz (1982) has investigated the impact of computer conferencing on the use of other methods of communication.

Other examples of computer conferencing systems are reviewed briefly by Hiltz and Turoff (1978, Chapter 2); they include the EMISARI system of the Office of Emergency Preparedness in the USA, and the FORUM and PLANET systems of the Institute for the Future in California. The PLANET system is now available commercially from the InfoMedia Corporation, and allows geographically separated people to engage in group planning and information retrieval, either by agreeing in advance to a particular "meeting" time or by running the PLANET program at times of their own choice to review each other's comments (InfoMedia Corp., 1979a). InfoMedia also markets the NOTEPAD system, which allows members of an organisation to manage and control a project with several activities; it can be accessed by local telephone calls, from many locations in the USA and around the world (InfoMedia Corp., 1979b).

In Europe, the COM computer conferencing system has been in regular use at the Stockholm University Computing Centre since 1979. Palme (1981) describes experience of its use, and gives information about how much KOM, its Swedish language version, is used, what it is used for, which people use it, users' opinions of the system, and its costs compared with those of other communications media. The English language version of COM is available at several sites in the UK.

Pieper (1982) briefly describes a field trail of the KOMEX computer conferencing in Germany, and finds that they indicate a lack of the originally intended computer assistance for group problem-solving and decision-making processes.

Vialaron and Girard (1981) present the "audiographic teleconference" as implemented recently in France; they describe the service that it provides and the equipment that it uses, and then indicate possible future developments. Wilkens (1981) specifies some systems for audiovisual man-machine dialogue for a very large number of subscribers.

The social impact of computer conferencing, and its effects on other modes of communications, are discussed in Chapter 16.

NETWORKS FOR EDUCATION AND TRAINING

The Council for Educational Technology (CET) is concerned with the applications of various new technologies to education, and it has been especially active in promoting the use of information technology. Its recent work is summarised in its report *Education and Information Technology* (Council for Educational Technology, 1982a).

As far as its implications for education are concerned, information technology has three main elements:

1. Information handling, the storage and retrieval of information;
2. Communications technology, the transmission of information;
3. Information transformation, the manipulation of information, putting it into forms that can be used for specific purposes.

The power of information technology results from the combination of these three aspects. Areas of application include: libraries, computers, and the use of radio, television, and other audiovisual media.

CET advises education and training institutions on the advantages and disadvantages of introducing new technologies. It undertakes trials, both to explore what these technologies have to offer, and to assess its potential ability to meet specific needs. It follows new developments actively, in order to uphold the interests of educational users. It tries to integrate new technology into existing teaching methods, and it seeks opportunities for new ways of learning.

It is interested in exploring the educational applications of all aspects of videotex, but it has so far concentrated on working with Prestel. It has about 200 pages on Prestel about education and training offered by colleges, polytechnics and other places of education. Under its "umbrella," it offers a comprehensive service to education and training institutions and helps them to publish information on Prestel pages (Council for Educational Technology, 1982b). It also uses Prestel to explore its potential as a teaching and learning resource. Its Curriculum Index links together pages of information useful in education.

Thompson (1981) reports on the CET educational trial of Prestel, which provided a range of educational establishments with Prestel terminals and monitored their use. This trial provided a practical opportunity for educational users to experience information technology. Mayne (1986) gives further information on this trial and on other uses of videotex in education.

The CET's Telesoftware Project and other educational uses of telesoftware are outlined in the section on telesoftware in Chapter 13, and references to further relevant work are given there. CET supports educational users of telesoftware and computers, not only with advice and guidance on equipment and appropriate software, but also with information and training literature on the use of these systems.

CET also has links with the Microelectronics Education Programme (MEP), and the Scottish Microelectronic Development Programme (SMDP), and has assisted in setting up the UK's twelve Regional Information Centres.

In the field of teleconferencing, CET has run an experiment in Cambridgshire, coordinated by the Ely Resources and Technology Centre, designed to link six small and remote primary schools and encourage communication between children which might otherwise not occur. CET has carried out additional teleconferencing trials and it has already learned from its own experience that teleconferencing has clear advantages when meetings are carefully structured and their participants already know each other.

The Open University has set up a private viewdata system, Optel, in order to reach its many part-time tutors at their homes and overcome the limitations of access to terminals that would have been imposed if they had been placed at study centres (Bacsich, 1981). An earlier version of Optel had a fully evaluated user trial, whose outcome was positive enough to allow the Optel project to continue.

More recently, in order to enhance its communications with students learning at a distance, the Open University has set up its Radiotext project, which has involved the design of a system for transmitting computer-coded text and graphics over an unmodified VHF radio broadcast network (Smith and Zorkoczy, 1982). Besides providing a rapid communications medium for course management, it can be used to deliver audio-visual pacakges and computer software for appropriate courses. In this system, the transmitter sends data from a data preparation terminal, via a tape recorder, and the receiver has a Radiotext interface with an audiocassette recorder, a low-cost printer, and a TV set.

The New Jersey Institute of Technology (1982) was planning a new kind of seminar, to be introduced early in 1983, where students can participate, on their own schedules, in their homes or work places, in educational courses taught by instructors and experts from all parts of the USA. The students have more personal involvement in these courses than in an any other non-credit continuing education programme. They are conducted via students' terminals or personal computers, connected to the USA-side EIES computer conferencing system, already described in the previous section. Students take part in online sessions, ask and answer questions, and communicate as often as they wish with their instructors and other participants, at any hour of the day, any day of the week. They are able to do this through EIES' message system, which places the participants' communications into the electronic mailboxes of their recipients.

The Video Response System in Japan provides remote users with various service courses, by presenting audio-visual information, such as colour photographs, sound and films, through 4 MHz bandwidth transmission lines (Magara et al, 1982).

The system has a wide range of applications, including information retrieval, entertainment and computer-aided instruction. The system already provides some educational training courses for internal use by the Nippon Telegraph and Telephone Public Corporation (NTT).

The Anik B communications satellite has been used to carry several tele-education experiments (Marchand, 1981). The Ontario Educational Communications Authority has been interested in using it to bring to the North of Canada the educational facilities at present available in the South. In the Atlantic region and maritime provinces of Canada, there have been several experiments involving universities.

Schools using microcomputers can extend the use of computing to a wide range of subjects, beyond computer studies and data processing themselves (Dixon, 1982). For example, computers can be used to automate fundamental scientific experiments and log data for a variety of education projects. With computer-aided learning as well, the use of computing can become an integral part of the whole learning process. With simple local networking, large numbers of children can be given access to computers through suitably linked VDUs.

Some schools have already installed their LANs or are beginning to plan them. For example, Dudley College of Technology uses a Nestar Cluster One (*Educational Computing*, Sep 1982). As well as providing a powerful training facility, this network has provided students, staff and administrators with early experience of computing techniques that will be important during the 1980s. The installation was completed in February 1982 and student courses started in March, on business and management studies and word processing as well as computing itself. The College's administrators are also using it for word processing and handling student records. A work station in the College library runs OverView, a Prestel-compatible viewdata system; it can link to Prestel, and even capture Prestel frames and manipulate them locally. The Dudley LAN's link to Nestar's in-house network at Uxbridge is part of a growing WAN, indeed of a linked LAN system.

COMMUNITY INFORMATION SERVICES

Applications of networking to community information services are mentioned only briefly here, as they are considered more fully, in relation to their human and social impacts, in Chapter 16. Their possible future, as a major force for social transformation, is discussed at the end of Chapter 18 and in the Epilogue.

Hitherto, the most important computer-based community information services have been developed through Prestel in the UK and The Source, CompuServe and other similar services in the USA. They are described by Mayne (1980).

Mayne (1980) outlines how user-friendly free-format computer data base systems, which are considered very briefly in Chapter 12, could be used by voluntary organisations and community information services.

HOME INFORMATION SYSTEMS

Most of the home information systems available at the moment are either videotex systems, which can provide people with access to a wide variety of information and stored in public data bases, or information services, such as The Source and CompuServe, that link to personal computers in people's homes. These are described in detail by Mayne (1986).

Mayne (1986) describes the principles, procedures and some of the applications of "home videotex systems," based on personal computers, and gives some examples of these systems. For example, many if not most types of personal computers can now be fitted with suitable adaptors that make them viewdata terminals as well. Personal computers can also be programmed to carry small private viewdata systems.

In principle, some of the cheaper personal computer networks and micronets, described in Chapter 3, could be used to link personal computers in different homes in the same street or neighbourhood; the PSTN is already being used for communications between different owners of personal computers. The chief obstacle to the widespread use of personal computers, so linked, is that the costs of personal computer systems with communications facilities are still too high for more than a small minority of people.

Carne (1981) reviews some of the possibilities for home information systems, including videotex, and describes the design of a programmable entertainment/ information centre for use in the home. For example, it can be used for automatic reception of specific TV channels at specific times for viewing or recording, for a simple household electronic message service, for access to teletext, and for generating graphics displays and playing computer games.

Gaffner (1981) indicates through diagrams several aspects of home information system, including the role of videotex and allied technologies in their applications. He points out the common elements of the new electronic media: software (e.g., TV programmes, computer programs, education, transaction services, electronic mail), distribution vehicles (e.g., telephone lines, cable TV, broadcasting, data storage media), and terminals (e.g., TV sets, adapted TV sets, personal computers, point-of-sale terminals, electronic directory devices, handheld devices).

MEDICAL APPLICATIONS OF NETWORKS

Although there have been extensive applications of computing to medicine, there has as yet been relatively little use of computer networking techniques there, apart from their application to on-line information retrieval from large computerised medical data bases such as Medlars.

As Licklider and Vezza (1978, page 1334) point out, the potentialities for medical computer networking are there; for example, it could make medical records available wherever they are needed, even for patients having accidents of medical emergencies far away from their regular doctors and local hospitals. The use of networking for remote medical diagnosis is also possible (McGlynn, Chapter 8).

One problem here is that medical records impose strong requirements for privacy, data security and data management, and these requirements must be met by the computer networks as well as by the computer data bases that handle the records.

Another problem is that most medical records have been handwritten, incomplete and in incompatible formats; in addition, many patients move from one doctor to another, making good record-keeping even harder. This situation is beginning to be changed by recent advances in computerisation of medical records. For example, data from clinical tests can be recorded directly, computers can prompt data entry on the basis of check lists, patients can enter their own case histories, paramedics can contribute to the records, and personal computer systems can help local general practitioners set up and maintain their medical records.

Although little seems to have been published about medical computer networking, it does now have some interesting applications.

For example, Fairhurst (1982) describes the use of the Geisco Mark III WAN to handle the international communications for Europ Assistance Group's international medical rescue system. Founded in France in 1963, this Group provides medical and technical assistance on a worldwide basis for the nationals of twelve countries. More than seven million people subscribe to the service each year, and it handles about 30,000 cases a year. Each of its National Companies maintains a 24-hour operations centre, to deal with its own subscribers. A central principle of its operation is that, when people are taken ill or injured abroad, the whole of their treatment, together with decisions about their transport, must be monitored by physicians. The system's programs belong to two main groups: programs giving details of services which can be applied to any particular medical case, and programs to help the coordination of the Group's administration.

Computer information systems, including videotex, could provide greatly improved aids for the disabled; indeed there is widespread and increasing interest in the application of computing to their problems and to the improvements of their facilities for communicating with other people and with the outside world. The first basic principle is that computing systems can in principle display information in a variety of sensory modes, not only visually but also audibly and even by touch and perhaps also smell. The second basic principle is that disabled people could have a wider choice of input devices, not only ordinary or modified keyboards and keypads but also cruder tactile inputters and devices activated by speech and other sounds and patterns of light. The third principle is that, through computer software, these unusual forms of information input and output can be transformed fairly easily to and from forms that are normally used. The fourth principle is that the usual computer communications facilities can then be applied. These possibilities have as yet only begun to be implemented, but they should be realised before many years have passed.

INDUSTRIAL APPLICATIONS OF NETWORKS

Computer networks have been used in manufacturing and on the factory floor, for regular company communications; see, for example, McGlynn (1978, Chapter 8). However, their more interesting and demanding applications are to online industrial control systems.

IEE Conference Publications, No. **208** (1982) is the proceedings of the 4th International Conference on Trends in On-Line Computer-Control Systems. It contains papers on: control systems and their design, control system management, trends in equipment configurations, software, and applications. Several of these papers are now outlined.

Halley and Davie (1982) describe a fault-tolerant communications ring for online distributed control systems. It provides reliable communications between up to 255 work stations, each containing a microprocessor-based digital controller. The system can cope with the failures of individual controllers, and the ring itself has built-in redundancy. Various tests carried out on this prototype system show that the objectives of its design have been met substantially, and that a production version of it could be made. It can be used for security systems and alarm systems as well as industrial control.

Sheppard (1982) shows how advances in microprocessor technology and the stricter requirements of industrial users have had a marked effect on instrumentation and control, whose present and long-term trends are for "Distributed Control and Data Acquisition Systems." For example, the Kent P4000 Distributed System, is a product resulting from extensive research into the characteristics needed for a distributed control system. Sheppard presents the design of the system as a whole, the capabilities of its functional units, and the advanced communications systems that link these distributed units, which can be geographically separated.

Hirst (1982) describes the use of videotex as a control tool. A vital aspect of successful control is getting right information to the right people at the right time. As control systems become more complex, sophisticated and distributed, the number of right people rises, the range of right information becomes more extensive, the speed of communication becomes more crucial, and the design of control systems becomes harder. He shows how videotex offers a range of economical solutions to these problems, without the risk of flooding the wrong people with the wrong information, and how its potentials go beyond information and offer the right people opportunities to control industrial processes in new, more convenient ways. Figure 14.1 is a schematic diagram of a typical example of a distributed industrial control system with viewdata access.

MISCELLANEOUS APPLICATIONS OF NETWORKS

Distributed communications and control systems have been used fairly widely in transport, by land, air and sea. Although their detailed consideration is beyond the scope of this book, a few examples are mentioned. Area control of groups of many

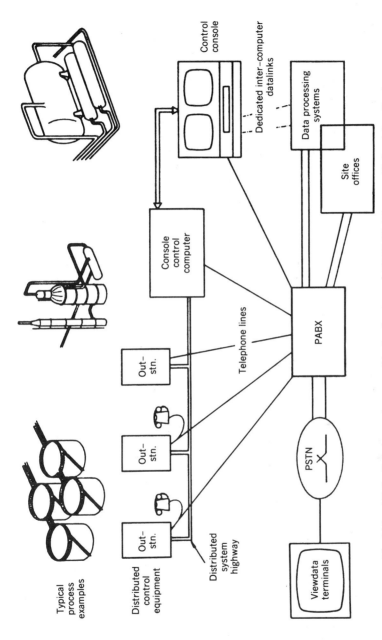

Fig. 14.1. AS distributed control system with viewdata access SOURCE: Diagram of industrial application of viewdata in article by Hirst in *IEE Conference Publications*, **208**, pp. 71–79

traffic signals, at the centres of large cities, is well-known, as is the use of computers to aid air traffic control.

Some examples of computer control of urban traffic systems are described in the conference proceedings edited by Levine et al (1979). The use of distributed control, with local traffic detection and control functions being carried out by microprocessor-based devices on site, and larger, more centrally placed, computers coordinating their activities, is advocated by several of the papers, and some preliminary work in this direction is outlined.

Ballam (1982) relates the story of British Telecom's highly successful ACP80 (air cargo processing in the 80s) operation. It started as the result of London Airport's introduction in 1971 of Laces, its system to handle cargo documentation and administration. This system was widely praised by air freight concerns and overseas airport authorities. Laces' successor, ACP80, is accepted by many as a world leader. It is the only cargo processing facility to enable private companies to link their own systems into a public service; it is the only facility to handle both imports and exports; and it is the first system with the potential to handle both air and sea freight.

Humphrey and Fielden (1982) describe a distributed information system for use in British lighthouses and other navigational aids. As a step towards a largely integrated system of unmanned navigational aids, supported at high efficiency by a small team of experienced maintenance personnel, Trinity House started introducing DARIC (Distributed Automated Remote Indicating and Control System) as an advanced system of communication and control of selected stations, currently being run as a pilot trial, in preparation for the specification of a fully operational system later on. It uses mainly 1200 baud PSTN links, but it supplements these by radio links where necessary.

Silverstein (1982) reviews the problem of national and international disasters, due to bad weather, earthquakes, fires, major transport accidents, etc., and concludes that the public services for coping with them are still relatively primitive. He points out that the greatest need here is for a complex worldwide communications system, able to override the destruction of local communication systems in many of these disasters, and fulfil the needs for real-time communications, global intelligence, and access to computer data bases. The communication subsystems needed would include: systems for local hazard assessment and preparedness; global, national and regional warning systems; mobilisation and early rescue systems. Such a disaster communications system faces several difficulties, which have to be considered when designing it.

Licklider and Vezza (1978, page 1335) mention applications of networks to defence, and especially to military command and control and military communication. They attribute the origin of both interactive computing and computer networking to the SAGE system (Semi-Automatic Ground Environment for air defence), and view many of the American military systems, to command forces and control weapons, as being essentially computer-communications networks.

The Arpanet, although operated by American and British universities as well as by defence computer experts, has been sponsored by the Defense Advanced Projects Research Agency (DARPA) in the USA, and much of the technology that it has developed has been applied to the design of military networks such as Autodin II. Military networks of course have very severe security and reliability problems, and must be able to operate when many of their individual components and sub-systems have been put out of action, and when the enemy makes attempts to jam their communications.

Other applications of networking to military systems include systems for the handling and distribution of intelligence information, and military logistics and inventory systems.

REFERENCES

P. Bacsich (1981) "The Open University viewdata system," *Viewdata 81*, 647–657.

A. Ballam (8 Jul 1982) "Successful BT product may ruin companies it serves," *Computer Weekly*, 16.

British Telecom (1980) *Telecom Research Laboratories*, British Telecom, Brochure.

Ed. T. J. M. Burke and M. Lehman (1981) *Communication Technologies and Information Flow*, Pergamon Press, Oxford, England, and Elmsford, NY.

Ed. G. Cantraine and J. Destine (1981) *New Systems and Services in Telecommunications*, North-Holland, Amsterdam, Oxford, England, and New York.

E. B. Carne (1981) "Future household communications-information systems," Chapter 6 of Burke and Lehman (1981).

Centre for Educational Technology (1982a) "Education and information technology," *CET Information Sheet* No. 2.

Centre for Educational Technology (1982b) *The CET Prestel Educational Umbrella Service*, Report.

L. G. S. Clark (1981) "Teleconferencing for all," pages 104–108 of Ed. A. Simpson (1980) *Planning for Electronic Mail*, Gower Publishing Company, Aldershot, Hampshire, England.

M. Dixon (18 Jan 1982) "Making the classroom a livelier place," *Financial Times Survey, Computing*, XX.

Educational Computing (Sep 1982) "The net benefits," **3**(7) 18.

R. J. Fairhurst (1982) "Computer communications for an international rescue system," *ICCC 82*, 697–701.

Future Systems Inc. (1980) "Teleconferencing: A new communications service for the 1980s," *Future Systems Inc.*, Report No. 108.

H. B. Gaffner (1981) "Home information systems—The place of videotex," *Videotex 81*, 295–302, and *Viewdata 81*, 549–556.

A. P. B. Halley and H. Davie (1982) "A fault tolerant communications ring for on-line distributed control systems," *IEE Conference Publications*, **208**, 30–33.

G. Haslam (1981) "The publisher's dilemma: How much, how soon?," *Viewdata 81*, 192–201.

Ed. P. Hills (1981) *The Future of the Printed Word*, Open University Educational Enterprises, Milton Keynes, England.

S. R. Hiltz (1982) "The impact of a computer conferencing system upon use of other communication modes," *ICCC 82*, 577–582.

S. R. Hiltz and M. Turoff (1978) *The Network Nation—Human Communication via Computer*, Addison-Wesley, Reading, MA, and London.

S. H. Hiltz, M. Turoff, K. Johnson and C. Aronovitch (Apr 1982) "Using a computerized conferencing system as a laboratory tool," *ACM SIGSOC Bulletin*, **13**(4) 5–9.

D. R. Hirst (1982) "Viewdata as a control tool," *IEE Conference Publications*, **208**, 10–13.

R. W. Hough and R. R. Panko (Apr 1977) *Teleconferencing Systems: A State-of-the-Art Survey and Preliminary Analysis*, National Science Foundation Report.

E. D. Humphrey and C. J. Fielden (1982) "A distributed automation system for use in UK lighthouses and other navigation aids," *IEE Conference Publications*, **208**, 71–79.

IEE Conference Publications, **208** (1982) *Trends in On-Line Computer Control Systems*.

Infomedia Corp. (1979a) *The PLANET System—A User's Guide*.

Infomedia Corp. (1979b) *The Infomedia Notepad System—A User's Guide*.

R. Johansen, J. Vallee and K. Spangler (1979) *Electronic Meetings: Technical Alternatives and Social Choices,* Addison-Wesley, Reading MA, and London.

E. B. Kerr and S. R. Hiltz (1982) *Computer-Mediated Communications Systems: Status and Evaluation*, Academic Press, New York and London.

Langton Information Systems (1982) *Langton Electronic Publishing Systems*, Langton Information Systems Ltd., Brochure.

Ed. W. S. Levine, E. Lieberman and J. J. Fearnsides (1979) *Research Directions in Computer Control of Urban Traffic Systems*, American Society of Civil Engineers, New York.

J. C. R. Licklider and A. Vezza (Nov 1978) "Applications of information networks," *Proceedings of the IEEE*, **66**(11) 1330–1346.

D. R. McGlynn (1978) *Distributed Processing and Data Communications*, Wiley, New York and Chichester.

M. Magara, M. Takei and J. Tamura (1982) "Use of the Video Response System in Education," *ICCC 82*, 595–600.

J. R. Marchand (1981) "Applying new communication technologies in Canada: A case study," Chapter 10 of Burke and Lehman (1981).

J. Martin (1981) *The Telematic Society*, Prentice-Hall, Englewood Cliffs, NJ.

A. J. Mayne (1980) "Data base developments and user requirements—Development and design of data bases for human needs," Abstract of paper presented at the British Computer Society *Communications 80 User Forum*, Birmingham, England.

A. J. Mayne (1986) *The Videotex Revolution*, second ed., Wiley, Chichester and New York.

New Jersey Institute of Technology (1982) *Continuing Education Participatory Seminars via Computer Communications*, Division of Continuing Education Leaflet.

J. Palme (Dec 1981) "Experience with the Use of the COM computerized conferencing system," *FOA Rapport*, C 101 66E-M6(H9), Stockholm, Sweden.

M. Pieper (1982) "Computer conferencing and human interaction," *ICCC 82*, 653–657.

D. I. Raitt (Jan 1982) "Recent developments in telecommunications and their current impact on information services," *Aslib Proceedings*, **34**(1) 54–76.

P. F. Sheppard (1982) "International and geographical distributed control of industrial processes," *IEE Conference Publications*, **208**, 22–25.

M. E. Silverstein (1982) "The role of computer communications in disasterology as we approach the year 2000," *ICCC 82*, 702–705.

P. Smith and P. I. Zorkoczy (1982) "Radiotext," *ICCC 82*, 612–617.

V. Thompson (1981) "Educational trial of Prestel," *Viewdata 81*, 303–311.

M. Turoff and S. R. Hiltz (1978) "Development and field testing of an electronic information exchange system: Final report on the EIES Development Project," *Computerized Conferencing and Communications Center, New Jersey Institute of Technology, Research Report*, No. 9.

R. P. Uhlig, D. J. Farber and J. H. Bair (1979) *The Office of the Future*, North-Holland, Amsterdam, Oxford, England, and New York.

M. Vialaron and T. Girard (1981) "The audiographic teleconference: A method of communication of groups," (In French), *New Systems and Services in Telecommunications*, 289–297.

H. Wilkens (1981) "Systems for audio-visual man-machine dialogue for a very large number of subscribers," *New Systems and Services in Telecommunications*, 341–345.

Word-Set Systems Ltd. (1982) *Word-Set*, Product Literature.

PART FOUR

WIDER ASPECTS
OF NETWORKS

Chapter 15

Network Costs and Economics

This chapter discusses briefly the costs, financial savings, and other economic aspects of running and using computer networks, both local area networks and wide area networks. It shows that economic decisions, about whether or not it is financially justified to instal and use a network, or become connected to existing network services, are fairly complicated, and need to be based on a careful analysis of both costs and benefits. One difficulty here is that there seems to be a shortage of published reports of case histories of computer network use, giving full specifications and numerical details of the specific costs and benefits in actual practical situations.

This chapter starts by considering the operating costs and also the ongoing financial benefits of local area networks and wide area networks. The costs and revenues of network services, especially public network services, are then analysed. After that, some illustrative examples of network tariffs are given, quoting figures of some of the British Telecom tariffs, and pricing strategies are discussed. Finally, some remarks are made about the demand and market for network systems and services. The economic impact of networking is considered in the next chapter. Some further, more recent, figures of network costs are given in Chapter 24.

OPERATING COSTS OF LOCAL AREA NETWORKS

For isolated LANs, the chief capital costs are the costs of the local communications infrastructure, which may be a ring, bus or PABX, for example, and the costs of the work stations and special devices attached to the network. Typically, the equivalent cost per active work station ranges from somewhat below £500 for a personal computer network, like the Acorn Econet, that has small personal computers, such as the Acorn Atom and the BBC Microcomputer as stations, to well over £5,000 for an elaborate office LAN system, such as MASTERNET. In between come intermediate-sized LANs, such as the Nestar Cluster/One Model A, which is at the top of the personal computer—micronet range, and typically uses Apple II and/or Apple /// as stations, at an equivalent cost of about £2,000 to £3,000 each. Costs for the smaller office LANs proper are similar.

These figures should be construed only as order of magnitude guides, as much depends on the specific details of implementation. Costs per station tend to decrease considerably when the number of station rises from just a few to a few dozen; the quoted estimates are more accurate for the latter case. Costs of interconnection increase when the average lengths of connections and the reliability of the connections rises.

The estimates of costs given above also assume somewhere near a bare minimum of attached special devices, such as printers and file stores; total network costs can rise considerably or even a great deal if specially expensive devices of this sort are used, due to the additional facilities or higher qualities of services that are required. The costs of attached devices, such as printers, can vary between £50 and £100,000, according to their capabilities, and there are even greater ranges in costs of data storage devices and media (Hayes, 1981). Costs of storage are falling much faster than those of printers, and costs of processing units and computing devices are falling faster still.

The capital costs of the network devices and equipment, mentioned so far, is only one part of the costs. There are also running costs, such as power consumption and maintenance, together with software costs, both for provision and again for maintenance, and perhaps interest charges and loan charges, if the equipment is leased and not bought outright, or if it is bought on borrowed money.

If the LAN is also part of a linked LAN system, or otherwise connected to at least one WAN, there are further charges of all these kinds, due to the necessity of providing modems and/or other physical gateway devices and the software to operate these as well as the LAN connections. On top of this are the WAN service charges, of the sorts listed later in this chapter.

For many organisations, these costs, all taken together, may seem high, even allowing for the actual and potential benefits, but there are often possibilities for substantial savings for organisations of most sizes, with the possible exception of some of the very small organisations.

In very many if not most cases, an organisation considering the acquisition of a LAN is a business, wishing to automate its office. For small businesses and many medium-sized ones, operating from one site, the main requirement is for a stand-alone LAN, possibly also having limited access to the PSTN or some other WAN. For medium-large and large companies, with several premises or many, the demand for a linked LAN is likely to emerge, again providing local office automation services, but this time at least largely in a distributed mode.

Burdett (1982) and Naughton (1982) have examined some of the justifications for business companies to move towards electronic methods and the use of information technology in the office. Burdett points out that many of the substantial costs of running an office are unlikely to be reduced much by applying information technology. He quotes the rough breakdowns of office costs as: face-to-face communication (25%), analysis and decision (21%), telephone (20%), preparation of letters and reports (15%), moving paper (12%), typing (4%) and copying (3%). Although information technology could substantially decrease some of these costs, its overall impact on the total costs of the organisation is much less dramatic. The gains that could be achieved, even though seeming relatively marginal, could still be very worthwhile.

Naughton points out that the relative amounts of the costs of human services and the running of equipment are shifting very considerably, with a change over a period of about five years that *is* dramatic. Salaries of all categories of staff, from the clerical and secretarial to the professional and managerial, are rising inexorably, while the actual costs of most kinds of equipment are falling sharply, though much more rapidly for some kinds than for others. For example, in the mid-1970s, the annual cost of a secretary, including overheads, was about four or five times less than the capital cost of a typical word processing work station; now it is over three or four times as much! When managers also start to use suitably designed work stations on a fairly large scale, much of their precious time will be saved, again with substantial savings of costs.

In very many cases, there may be a net economic balance in favour of installing a network system or accessing an existing service, but no very clear general rules can be given as to the appropriate decisions to be made by businesses and other organisations of specific sizes and types. Much will depend on various specific circumstances, including the degree to which existing staff can actually use or be trained to use the equipment effectively.

Thus *organisations would be well advised not to rush in and acquire a LAN, without due thought and expert advice*, even if the initial cost analyses give indications clearly in favour of this action. Again, it depends very much on the specific organisation whether it should jump straight to an advanced system or take a slower evolution towards it, step by step; most experts tend to advocate the latter course in most cases.

OPERATING COSTS OF WIDE AREA NETWORKS

For an organisation using only WANs, and not having a LAN, the capital costs of the system are the costs of the terminals and other communicating devices, and the costs of modems, multiplexers, concentrators and similar equipment. In the simplest case, each device just has a modem or acoustic coupler, linked directly to the PSTN. Besides the power consumption and maintenance of this equipment, there are other running costs that are usually much more substantial, namely the telecommunications charges levied by the PTT or other carrier, and the online computing or other service charges made by the organisation(s) being accessed on the other side of the WAN. The most usual operating telecommunications costs are described by Corby et al (1982), Chapter 14 of which discusses budgeting for telecommunications, while Chapter 15 considers costing.

Mayne (1986, Chapter 14) analyses the costs of using videotex services. These vary considerably, teletext being much cheaper but providing much less, while the cost patterns are quite different, for example, for home users of teletext, home users of viewdata, business users of public viewdata services, organisations using stand-alone private viewdata systems, and organisations using private viewdata systems that are also able to access remote computers and other viewdata services.

For organisations using LANs to connect with WAN services, these charges will mostly be of a similar nature, although they are liable to be considerably higher, especially when the LANs use expensive gateway facilities, and also when they access more costly equipment and services at the other end. Panko (1981) and Kirstein (1978) analyse and consider the costs of electronic mail systems and facsimile systems, respectively.

For organisations using linked LANs, interconnected over the PSTN or other WANs, the costs are again mostly similar, except that the cost of end-user services may no longer be levied, as facilities in the same company or business group may be accessed. Again, costs may be somewhat less than otherwise, if judicious use is made of leased lines of packet-switched services.

COSTS AND REVENUES OF NETWORK SERVICES

For network services operated by PTTs and other public carriers, the costs incurred include: capital costs of telecommunications lines, nodes, exchanges and other equipment used, costs of buildings to house some of that equipment, ongoing costs of keeping that equipment maintained and in good working order, salaries of staff, and, in many cases, costs of research and development. The chief revenues are: income from tariffs charged for services, income from leased lines, and income from modems and other equipment hired by network users.

Network services not operated by public carriers, and also some of the special services provided by public carriers, are usually *value-added services*, providing services, such as time-shared computing, online information retrieval, and videotex, that make use of the public network services providing basic data communication facilities. Thus their costs are similar to those incurred by network users in general. Income will be mainly from tariffs charged to customers for services provided. Additional cash flows are involved if the service commissions subcontractors to carry out parts of the service, such as provision of data bases and information retrieval facilities.

For example, Mayne (1986, Chapter 14) analyses costs and revenues of videotex systems and services. Here, the cash flow pattern is unusually complicated, as money is exchanged between four groups of people: the system's operators, the system's information providers, the system's users, and also the PTTs and other telecommunications, television and computing organisations.

Gitman and Frank (1978) present the results of an economic analysis of alternative network strategies, based on typical requirements for voice and data communications. They consider the economics of integrating voice and data communications in a common communications system, together with the cost-effectiveness of alternative voice digitisation rates and strategies. They compare three switching technologies: circuit switching, packet switching, and hybrid (circuit-packet) switching.

The intention is to identify and quantify network technologies that show low long-term operating costs. This information, together with information about transition problems and their associated costs, is needed in order to find the most cost-effective evolutionary path for future communications systems. Gitman and Franks' study provides a framework and a target technology for detailed analysis of network evolution, planning and costs.

On the basis of total network cost, lines and switching, they find packet switching to be the cheapest and circuit switching to be the most expensive of the three switching technologies. This ranking is virtually unchanged under a variety of assumptions about traffic, costs and parameters; it is independent of whether voice and data are carried in separate networks or in the same integrated network.

They find that the cost of two separate packet-switching networks, one for voice and one for data, is lower than the cost of an integrated voice and data system under any of the three switching technologies, for the wholed range of voice-digitisation rate considered.

Figures 15.1 and 15.2 give two examples of Gitman and Frank's cost comparisons of switching technologies with voice digitisation.

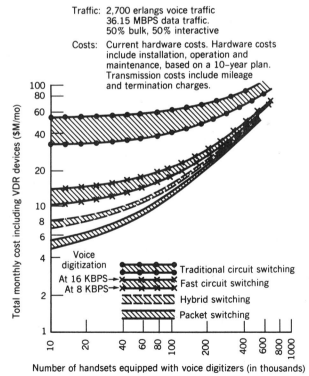

Fig. 15.1. Comparison of switching technologies with voice digitization between 8 kbps and 16 kbps; total monthly costs include backbone network, estimated cost of voice digitization device in handsets   SOURCE: Copyright © 1978 IEEE *Proceedings of the IEEE* (Nov 1978), **66** (11) p. 1567 Fig. 13

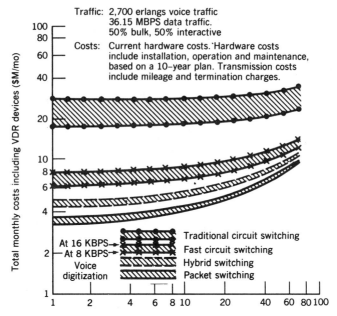

Fig. 15.2. Comparison of switching technologies under voice digitization   SOURCE: Copyright ©
1978 IEEE *Proceedings of the IEEE* (Nov 1978), **66** (11) p. 1567 Fig. 14

Bella and Corsi (1982) present some results obtained, using tools developed for
general network optimisation problems, to evaluate the cost-effectiveness of various
alternatives in the access part of the network, between the user's site and the neighbouring data switching exchange. They give numerical examples, showing the impact of various mixtures of services on the possible network structures, and they
compare them from a technical-economic point of view.

They find that there is a significant advantage of using, in the access network,
intelligent network concentrators rather than pure time division multiplexers. These
advantages can be even greater if the concentrators can support a relatively high
number of terminals, typically 256, and also integrate local switching capability.

TARIFFS AND PRICING STRATEGIES

Corby et al (1982, Chapter 20) gives British Telecom's 1981–82 price schedule and
tariffs for its public switched telephone network, its Datel services, and its packet-
switched network services. The tariffs for the latter are now outlined.

The charges for using PSS are made up of three parts, covering access to the
service, usage of the service, and special facilities provided by the service (British
Telecom National Network, 1984). VAT (currently 15%) is charged on the total
bill.

For packet terminals, access charges consist of a connection charge and a quarterly rental, and one of the British Telecom Dataline services is used. The Dataline rental includes charges for modem, line between terminal and exchange, and a dedicated port at the exchange. These charges are independent of the distance between the terminal and the exchange, and no telephone charges are incurred. For Dataline 2400, Dataline 4800, Dataline 9600, and Dataline 48K, the respective connection charges are £450, (*new* connections not available), £800, and charge dependent on distance to PSS node, and the respective quarterly rentals are £437.50, £700 (for existing connections), £825, and £2000. The minimum period of service is one year for the first three and three years for Dataline 48K.

For character terminals using Dataline, the basis is the same. For Dataline 300 and Dataline 1200, the respective connection charges are £200 and £350, and the quarterly rental is £275.

For character terminals using dial-up, the only PSS access charges £25 are for the NUI (Network User Identity) connection, and £6.25 quarterly connection per PAD. There are also charges for whichever of Datel 200 or Datel 600 is used, and these charges are shown on the user's *telephone* bill.

PSS usage charges are divided into a call duration charge, payable on Datacalls and Converted Minicalls only, and a charge for data carried, charged for all calls. The call duration charge is 23p per hour for terminals using Dataline, 88p per hour for Datel 200 terminals, and £1.23 per hour for Datel 600 terminals. In each case, the chargeable unit of time is 2 seconds. The charge for data carried is 25p per Kilosegment (1000 segments), and the chargeable unit is one segment of 64 8-bit bytes. These charges are reduced for duration per quarter over 1000 hours and volume per quarter over 1500 Ksegments. There are cheap rates for usage after 6 pm and before 8 am, Monday to Friday, and all day Saturday, Sunday, Christmas Day, and New Years Day.

There are also charges for any special PSS facilities used; note that none of these facilities is essential for effective use of PSS, although some users will find them useful. These charges are divided into single payments for change of facility and, for some of the facilities only, quarterly rentals. For example the single payment and quarterly rental, respectively, are: £20 and £5 for a Closed User Group (CUG), £20 and £5 for each logical channel (other than the first) and £20 and £5 for call redirection. For transfer charge acceptance, Minicall acceptance, and Direct Calling, the single payments are £4 each, and there is no rental. For connection of Datalines to alternative exchanges, other than the one normally used, a quarterly rental of £625 is payable, in addition to the standard charges. A customer may have more than one Dataline to his PSS exchange (Multiline facility), in which case there are standard charges for each line.

British Telecom brought the PSS-IPSS link into service on 21 December 1981, to provide PSS users with access to and from packet-switched services in countries served by IPSS. British Telecom International (1985) gives details of the services available and tariffs charged.

PSS-IPSS services are now available between the UK and USA, Canada, Japan, and several European countries, including West Germany, Sweden and Switzerland. Incoming services are also available to the UK from Australia, Hong Kong, Irish Republic and Israel. British Telecom is still extending this service to other countries, and connection to Euronet is planned very soon. Current news about the PSS-IPSS network is available to all PSS users via PSS' Hostess computer, whose Network User Address (NUA) is 234 21920101013.

Access charges are the same as for PSS, as entry to IPSS is via PSS, and no separate equipment is needed to reach IPSS. Duration charges are £1.32 per hour for Europe and £6.00 per hour for North America and the rest of the world. Volume charges per Ksegment are £1.20 for Europe and £3.50 for North America, and £4.00 for the rest of the world.

Mayne (1986, Chapter 14) gives details of the tariffs for the Prestel public viewdata service, that applied early in 1982.

In describing their Micronet 800 service, launched in 1983, which links personal computer users to each other and to Prestel, British Telecom et al (1982a and 1982b) point out that the *only* tariff charged by the service, during off-peak hours, is a flat rate subscription of £52 a year. In addition, connection the service via the PSTN is charge of the telephone bill at the usual telephone rates. Users of the system also have to buy a low-cost adaptor for a simple connection between their microcomputer and telephone. Advertising "page" rates range from £50 per year up to the £400 per month charged for advertising space on the "Welcome" page accessed every time a user logs in.

Kelly (1978) provides information about the UK tariffs for Euronet and IPSS (for North America) that were valid in 1978. He describes the charging principles adopted in Euronet, and mentions the work of CCITT Study Group III on the preparation of Recommendations, relating to the principles to be adopted for international charging and accounting for public network services.

Mathison (1978) discusses the general principles of international tariffs, including: basis for charges, reverse charging, packet size conversion, volume discounts, volume-sensitive line pricing, and the possibility of uniform international charges.

Muller (1982) argues for a change to a cost-based tariff policy, instead of the "second best" pricing policy, currently advocated in the literature, or the "value of service" principle now used by many PTTs. He advocates that this principle be combined with greater freedom for network users, together with the possibility of competition between networks, in the face of the emerging integrated digital network services.

Ratz and Field (1980) use mathematical models of tariffs, to compare different communications services, and investigate the conditions under which each service is the most economical.

Gale and Koenker (1982) suggest a theoretical basis for pricing an interactive time-shared computer service, and provide some empirical evidence on congestion in systems, using the UNIX operating system, that leads to specific proposals for UNIX pricing. Congestion is an inherent problem of shared resources like interactive computer systems; every user contributes to the general deterioration of response time as loads on the computer system increase. Prices can be used to encourage the efficient use of shared resources, by equating the prices of the computer services with the value of the marginal congestion delay imposed on others.

DEMAND AND MARKET FOR NETWORK SYSTEMS AND SERVICES

Flint (1981) considers the nature of the demand and market for LAN products and services in Europe. For any given user organisation's LAN, a variety of devices and services are needed, perhaps not all provided by the same vendor.

There are four reasons, associated with the inherent nature of a LAN, why an organisation might decide to install one:

1. To support resource sharing;
2. To provide networking between incompatible devices;
3. As a local connection source;
4. As a network architecture.

Flint then balances the arguments, that he has put forward in favour of using LANs, with some arguments against. He quotes an example where a linked LAN solution would *not* be cheaper than a WAN solution using multiplexers.

He then presents the results of market forecasts of the LAN networks, for the period 1980–1990, both for large sites and for medium-sized sites, and subdivided between different types of LAN. He also presents forecasts of prices of LANs and revenue from LANs, during this period. These forecasts show that the total revenue from LAN sales is likely to be only a small proportion of the total revenue from the computer industry as a whole, during the 1980s.

He points out that this does *not* imply that LANs are unimportant; on the contrary, they are likely to become very important. This is because the next decade will see a vast increase in the number of computer-based devices used in offices, factories and laboratories. Inside any organisation using more than a very few of these devices, a LAN will often be essential to ensure the required cooperation between these devices.

Kelly (1978) refers to past attempts to forecast the demand for both national and international data traffic; he points out that most of them have failed to take into account the common carriers' plans for new data services and tariffs. Demand is highly conditioned by tariffs; once tariffs are announced, it is not long before the resulting demand is indicated. Judging by the British experience, there is a small but significant demand for packet-switched data network services. To meet this, care is needed in designing networks; in particular, packet-switched exchanges should be designed so that they can be expanded rapidly to support most terminals and offer extra facilities.

Although a public packet-switched data network service is intended primarily for data, it can be used for any suitable digitally encoded transmission. Time will tell whether services other than data, such as teletex, electronic mail, and viewdata, will provide more traffic for these networks than traditional data traffic.

Oren and Smith (1982) provide a mathematical framework for modelling demand and finding optimal tariffs in markets that have positive demand externalities and can sustain volume discounts. This theory applies in particular to computer networks, where the benefit derived by a subscriber increases as more subscribers join the network service. They give an example of a nonlinear price strategy, that will make a network affordable to more users, with a lower "critical mass" of subscribers needed to start it.

REFERENCES

L. Bella and N. Corsi (1982) "Evaluation of the impact of different services on the access to a packet switched network," *ICC 82*, 669–674.

British Telecom International (1985) *IPSS - Meeting the Business Challenges of Today and Tomorrow for the Internationally Active Business*, Brochure.

British Telecom National Networks (1984) *Packet SwitchStream*, Folder of Leaflets.

British Telecom/Prestel, EMAP Computers & Business Publications Ltd./Telemap Ltd., ECC Publications Ltd., and Prism Micro-products (1982a) *How You Can Connect to a Nationwide Network of Computer Users*, Brochure.

British Telecom/Prestel, EMAP Computers & Business Publications Ltd./Telemap Ltd., ECC Publications Ltd., and Prism Micro-products (1982b) *Micronet 800 Brings Your Computer to Life!*, Leaflet.

M. Burdett (1982) "Towards the electronic office," pages 28–35 of Ed. A. Simpson (1982) *Planning for Electronic Mail*, Gower Publishing Company, Aldershot, Hampshire, England.

M. Corby, E. J. Donohue and M. Hamer (1982) *Telecomms Users' Handbook*, Telecommunications press, London.

D. Flint (1981) "The European market for local area networks," *Local Networks 81*, 573–590.

W. A. Gale and R. W. Koenker (1982) "Pricing interactive computer services: A rationale and some proposals for UNIX implementation," *ICCC 82*, 675–680.

I. Gitman and H. Frank (Nov 1978) "Economic analysis of integrated voice and data networks: A case study," *Proceedings of the IEEE*, **66**(11) 1549–1570.

R. J. Hayes (1981) "The new generation of graphics in the information business," pages 55–70 of Ed. T. J. M. Burke and M. Lehman (1981) *Communications Technologies and Information Flow*, Pergamon Press, Oxford, England, and Elmsford, NY.

P. T. F. Kelly (Nov 1978) "Public packet switched data networks, international plans and standards," *Proceedings of the IEEE*, **66**(11) 1539–1549.

P. T. Kirstein (May 1978) "Choice of data communication media for transmission of facsimile information," *Proceedings of the IEEE*, **2**(2) 179–190.

J. Martin (1981) *Design and Strategy for Distributed Data Processing*, Prentice-Hall, Englewood Cliffs, NJ, Chapter 14, "Cost and Benefit Analysis."

S. L. Mathison (Nov 1978) "Commercial, legal, and international aspects of packet communications," *Proceedings of the IEEE*, **66**(11) 1527–1539.

A. J. Mayne (1986) *The Videotex Revolution*, second ed., Wiley, Chichester and New York.

J. Muller (1982) "Cost-based tariffs, integrated network use and network competition in the telecommunication sector," *ICCC 82*, 681–684.

M. Naughton (1982) "Planning for the office of the future," pages 36–41 of Ed. A. Simpson (1982) *Planning for Electronic Mail*, Gower Publishing Company, Aldershot, Hampshire, England.

S. S. Oren and S. A. Smith (1982) "Nonlinear pricing and network externalities in telecommunications," *ICCC 82*, 685–690.

R. R. Panko (Feb 1981) "The cost of EMS," *Computer Networks*, **5**(1) 35–46.

H. C. Ratz and J. A. Field (Sep 1980) "Economic comparisons of data communication services," *Computer Networks*, **4**(4) 143–155.

Chapter 16

The Impact of Networks

The impact of networks and networking should be viewed firstly as part of the total economic, social, political and human impacts of computing and information technology as a whole, because they deal with communication and distributed information, they have several more specific impacts as well.

The overall effects of computing and information technology on human life and human society have been considered in some detail in *The Computer Age* (Dertouzos and Moses, 1979), *Communication Technologies and Information Technologies* (Burke and Lehman, 1981), *The Future with Microelectronics* (Curnow and Barron, 1979), *Gutenberg 2* (Godfrey and Parkhill, 1979), *The Microchip* (Burns, 1981), *The Microelectronics Revolution* (Forester, 1980), and *Microelectronics and Society* (Friedrichs and Schaff, 1982), for example. More specifically, the Nora-Minc Report (Nora and Minc, 1979) considers the development of the resulting information society in relation to the situation in France, but it has implications for developments in other countries too.

These books do not discuss the impact of networks, as distinct from the general impact of information technology, in very great detail, although this chapter considers some of the specific references that some of them make. Much more reference to networking is made in the recent books *The Telematic Society* (Martin, 1981a), which presents many of its aspects, *The Network Nation* (Hiltz and Turoff, 1978), which considers it in relation to computer conferencing and other forms of human communication, *The Videotex Revolution* (Mayne, 1986), which describes the part that it plays in videotex, and *The Office of the Future* (Uhlig et al., 1979), which discusses it in connection with office automation.

McCrum and Ryan (1981) discuss the wide range of impacts of new forms of data communications services, from a Canadian perspective.

This chapter begins by considering the human interfaces with networks, including human factors and man-machine interfaces. It then discusses in turn different aspects of the impact of networks: their impact on public awareness, their social impact, security in networks, telecommunications regulations and networks, their legal aspects including especially privacy, and their political impact. Recent developments are presented in Chapter 24.

HUMAN INTERFACES WITH NETWORKS

The two chief aspect of human interfaces with computer systems and networks are the physical interfaces between the devices and their users, and the psychological interfaces, the extent to which terminals and work stations present barriers to their users or encourage their effective operation. This section considers both these aspects in turn, and ends by discussing human interfaces with electronic message systems. There has been a recent upsurge of interest in human factors in computer networks; the fairly recent ICCC 82 Conference had no less than three sessions on this topic, and several of its papers are cited here.

Davies (1982a) discusses the user interface and human factors, as one of four important trends, that will dominate the emerging generation of office information system. He considers the needs for work station displays, that are improved in several respects, movable screens, and separate adjustable keyboards, as examples of better adaptations of equipment for human users, and he calls for systems that are more user-friendly and approachable, for example having carefully designed menu facilities.

Coulouris (1981) describes some experiments in the design of user interfaces for office work stations, that have been carried out at Queen Mary College, London. These experiments use a design methodology, based on constructing an "activity model," that describes the information processing activities to be performed and the information structures on which they operate. Activity models are outlined for a word processor and for an office filing system. The experimental work station at Queen Mary College is designed to manage office information processing and associated tasks, and uses an "animated desktop," based on a new colour display system.

Atkinson and Lipson (1980) describe several ways in which computer peripherals can in effect add extra "senses" and "motor controls" to people, and especially to the disabled, who will be able to communicate more effectively with computer systems and computer networks as a result. For example, special keyboards and other control devices allow handicapped people, with limited muscular control, to use the full power of the computer, and thus participate in a wide range of human activities. Speech synthesis and speech recognition devices should both greatly aid people with learning disabilities. Myers (1982) describes how personal computers aid the handicapped, and *Byte* (Sep 1982) has a special issue on this subject.

Jarrett (1982, pages 135–139) discusses the question of possible health hazards from VDUs, used in the office and elsewhere. Visual fatigue and eyestrain is the most important health risk, caused by glare, reflections, and lack of contrast. There is some evidence that VDUs can worsen, if not actually cause, certain eye disorders. Screens *can* flicker at a rate that brings on fits in epileptics, although this can usually be avoided by proper adjustment of VDU controls. There is probably negligible risk from X rays produced by VDUs, although this is not yet known for sure. Most VDUs, having their screen above a keyboard, can cause their operators to adopt bad postures, causing headaches (also a result of eyestrain) and aching muscles in head and shoulders; the best remedy here is well-designed seats, desks of the right height, and regular breaks for the operators. Psychological stress can also result from slow computer response times (in some systems), lack of user-friendliness, general information load, poor environmental conditions, etc.

Not only do computer systems and computer networks need to have interfaces, between their terminals or work stations and their users, that are well adapted physically. These interfaces also need to have the right psychological qualities, so that they are not intimidating and over-complicated, but convenient and comfortable to operate. In other words, they need to be *user-friendly*, and this is largely a matter of presentation and software design.

The book by Abbott (1982) aims to help computer systems designers produce input and output specifically for users rather than purely for the benefit of the computer.

Huckle (1982) points out that heterogeneous computer networks often, if not usually, present very complex interfaces to their users. She believes that, typically, they act as a deterrent to potential users, who lack confidence in their ability to communicate effectively with machines, and to people who do not have time to learn the complicated and often demanding network procedures. While she was at Hatfield Polytechnic, she and her colleagues there designed a system that allows users to view networks in a uniform way, providing a communication medium, that can be tailored to their needs, and a network-wide filing system. Some of the distributed software for this system has already been implemented, and the principles of the system have been shown to be feasible. It provides the potential for greater efficiency and faster response time than for a centralised system.

Huckle has found that one major difficulty, with users of time-shared systems, is that different systems have different log-in and operating procedures; the presence of these different environments is a major cause of user errors. The users thus need to view the network as *one* entity, with a consistent user interface. They should not be required to log in to the network more than once during a session, and they should be able to access a succession of different computers during that session, in such a way that the system carries out automatically all necessary log-ins to the individual computers. The network facilities should be uniformly available to the users, no matter what computer is being addressed. Users and user programs should be able to reach and manipulate files, without any need to specify where they are stored.

The networks under consideration consist of several host computer systems, terminals, and a communications sub-network, which can be anything from a LAN to a public data network. Figure 16.1 is a schematic diagram of the configuration used by this sort of system. Here, each *user interface process (UIP)* provides an interface between a group of users and the network, and each *host interface process (HIP)* provides an interface between its host and the network, and modifies the interactions betweeen the UIPs and the host. Figure 16.2 shows which computer languages are used for different parts of the network operations; note that there are three groups of languages, for users, host computers, and the network; inside each group, the languages are divided into languages, giving commands to the computers, and languages, sending responses back to the users.

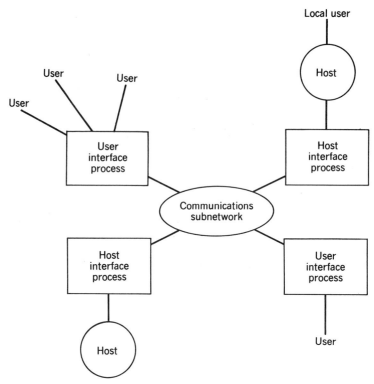

Fig. 16.1. Elements of a network at Hatfield Polytechnic, including HIPs and UIPs SOURCE: © 1982, ICCC, Int'l Council for Computer Communication, Reprinted from *Procs ICCC '82,* North-Holland Publ., Amsterdam. Article by Huckle in *ICCC 82* Conference Proceedings, p. 590 Fig 1

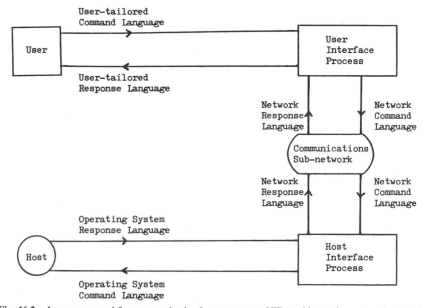

Fig. 16.2. Languages used for communication between users, UIPs and hosts, in a network at Hatfield Polytechnic SOURCE: © 1982, ICCC, Int'l Council for Computer Communication, Reprinted from *Procs ICCC '82,* North-Holland Publ., Amsterdam. Article by Huckle in *ICCC 82* Conference Proceedings, p. 592 Fig 2

Endicott (1982) discusses an experimental project at the IBM System Products Division development laboratory in Rochester, MN, USA, for developing a system interface which makes available to an untrained user all or most of the data processing functions needed by the owner or manager of a small business. The NPS experimental system, which operates on an IBM System/34, uses a specific sequence of menus and prompts, that do not end until a legitimate function has been performed or defined. A complete set of system documentation is available online, which can usually be reached by a "help," response. Manual office procedure concepts and terminology are used wherever possible.

Thimbleby (1982) provides a preliminary set of guidelines for user interfaces, and especially for the design of better text editors and word processing procedures. The user interface should be predictable enough to allow its effective use without requiring the user's undivided attention; few actual systems meet even this minimal requirement. The interface should also provide current feedback, that is kept continually up-to-date; it should be independent of context, and it should respond to each user action immediately.

Schicker (1981) discusses the user interface to a work station that handles text. He shows how the same basic text-moving commands can maintain unstructured as well as structured text data; they can also create, send and receive both personal and administrative messages. They allow information to be moved or copied easily, within one of the contexts, structured and unstructured, or between them.

Kidd (1982) points out that, if interactive computer systems are to communicate easily and efficiently with their users, then their dialogue design must be compatible with the information processing capabilities of the human mind. He illustrates this point by considering how to design "spoken" menus for interactive voice information systems. He suggests that the critical factor in successful user performance is the amount of problem solving needed to select the appropriate choice from a spoken menu list.

Willis (1982) describes some applications of voice input/output systems to telephone services; all these new services would be based on man-computer communication using voice. For example, the system can give "spoken" replies to numbers that are dialled from a telephone; there is no reason why similar systems, also responding to keyboard input and to the human voice, should not be used in the human interface to computer networks.

Barber (1982) raises the important question of how far the present system of protocol levels, based on the ISO Model of Open System Interconnection, provides the best interface between computer networks and their users; he notes that most of the OSI work on layered protocols is concerned mainly with computer systems programmed to behave as interacting automata. He suggests the possibility of further layers above the present ones, to provide some kind of user-friendly interface, although these layers might be hard to define. He also considers the alternative possibility that the human interface of a "User Agent" will have to be outside the OSI protocols structure.

Smith (1982) discusses some of the human factors issues, that need to be addressed before national and international computer-based message systems become widely used in the public domain; he outlines the kinds of service requirements that their users will need. He explores several of the issues and suggests an additional class of service to provide more comprehensive user protection.

Biran and Feldman (1982) describe the human factors, influencing the proper choice of an electronic mail system, with special reference to the user needs of multi-language countries. In a given document, there may be problems of simultaneous use of different languages, alphabet differences, and even whether text is read from left to right or right to left.

THE ECONOMIC IMPACT OF NETWORKING

Between them, advances in telecommunications, computing and information services seem likely to have at least four very important general economic effects;

1. There will be a move to an "information economy," where over half of all "production" will be in the information and services sector.

2. To an increasing extent, people will be able to carry out a variety of economic transactions from their homes, and more and more of those employed in offices and businesses will be able to work in their own neighbourhoods or even at home.

3. As a result, demands for transport will begin to decline, slowly at first, then rapidly, and this will in turn have other economic effects, in general leading to less wasteful use of energy and other resources.

4. There will be a very big effect on patterns of employment; how far this is good and how far it is bad depends very much on what economic, social, and political policies are devised to meet this challenge.

McCrum and Ryan (1981) comment briefly on the concept of an "information economy," whose introduction is being made easier by new forms of data communication. The "information sector," which will dominate it, includes all resources used in producing, processing and distributing information goods and services; new data communication services are essential for the information economy, as they make it much easier to provide these goods and services. Data communication networks serve as a central nervous system for that economy, through which many of its transactions will take place. Thus a nation's "balance of payments" in electronics and communications will become critically important.

Marsh (1982) discusses the social impact of electronic funds transfer (EFT) and electronic shopping. The could greatly reduce the needs to send mountains of paper, in the form of cheques and cash, through the banking system, and they would save the banks a lot of trouble. On the other hand, EFT could lead to a nightmare, by threatening people's privacy and their rights under consumer protection legislation. Some forms of financial fraud would become much more difficult, but possibilities for other forms would open up. With due safeguards, EFT could make life more comfortable and rewarding in many ways. No country is yet anywhere near achieving an EFT network, and careful studies will be needed before any such network is introduced.

In their two papers, Kraemer (1982) and Kraemer and King (1982) examine in detail the hypothesis that there will be a major substitution of telecommunications for journeys to work and other business trips, and that a great deal of energy will be saved as a result. The first paper examines the potential for such substitution, mainly through video and audio teleconferencing and computer conferencing, and finds that a significant amount of energy saving could occur as a result, even though it might be considerably less than some people suppose. Then it reviews recent research on public attitudes towards substitution of telecommunications for travel and on the operational experience with substitution experiments in organisations. The second paper investigates the major factors, that influence the choice between telecommunications and travel by individuals and institutions, and discusses what kinds of public policies could make the substitution easier.

McCrum and Ryan (1981) view unemployment as the major labour-related risk, arising from the introduction of new telecommunication services. As old jobs and roles disappear, new ones will evolve to evaluate, develop, implement, manage, and market new forms of data communications, but the transition period may be difficult. Increased concentration of capital in the service sector, and the higher productivity of that sector, will both reduce its labour requirements; for example, this could lead to a reduction of 16% in the total requirement for the British labour force (Barron and Curnow, 1979). The impact on employment could be reduced, because the spread of new computing and data communications services is being slowed down by the shortage of skilled engineers and technicians and by a backlog of orders for silicon chips. The overall effect will be a loss of many existing jobs, but the creation of many new jobs, together with demands for new sets of labour skills. It remains to be seen how orderly the transition to the new pattern of employment is, and how far it is painful and destructive, how far it is constructive.

Uhlig et al (1979, Chapter III.7) offer some ideas about how to translate the impact of office automation into economic payoffs and benefits. There will be savings from word processing, but these will apply to only a small part of the total business costs. The major impact is likely to be reduction of labour costs of managers and professional staff, as they spend most of their time communicating; new developments in office applications of computer networking should make this process much more cost-effective and less time-consuming.

Gollin (1981) considers the potential of electronic information media, in the context of economic challenges faced by American daily newspapers. Little is really known yet about consumer response to these media. Their rate and extent of market penetration, determined by what consumers and advertisers will be willing to pay, seems likely to be evolutionary rather than revolutionary. They may well gain only slow and restricted acceptance, in the light of social, economic, and psychological constraints.

Turoff and Chinai (1982) describe the Electronic Information Marketplace, that has been implemented as a specialised subsytem on the Electronic Information Exchange System (EIES). This system allows any user of the EIES computer conferencing system to sell and barter information, services and goods to other EIES members. It is designed as a direct user-to-user marketplace, and it completely eliminates the need for a special class of "information providers," of the sort required by many videotex systems and other computer information services. The implications of this electronic marketplace are discussed, in terms of individual and public use, industry structure, costs, cooperative computing, and user expectations and impacts.

THE IMPACT OF NETWORKS ON PUBLIC AWARENESS

Computer networks can increase public awareness by providing the infrastructure for a variety of online computer data bases, computer-based videotex information services, "home encyclopedias," new educational services, and computer conferencing. Their applications to computer information services are described in Chapter 12 and to education and computer conferencing in Chapter 14.

Mayne (1986, Chapter 15) briefly considers the impact of videotex on public awareness, and summarises some recent views on this topic. For example, Burns (1981, pages 160–162) points out that videotex can bring information to the community and also convey the opinions of individuals to central bodies. He gives some of the conditions for improved public awareness as a result of the use of videotex.

Aubrac (1980) considers possible applications of modern technology to improve the use of information in developing countries. They are just beginning to use some of the possibilities, but they have a long way to go before they use information effectively, and it is still uncertain who will control its sources there. Most of the technology is already available, for providing a satisfactory system for the international exchange of information. The full organisation of such a system could provide more equal opportunities for those contributing information, and open up great prospects for international cooperation to benefit the poorest countries, whose information needs are especially urgent.

In combination with videodisks, which are beginning to become accessible to the consumer market and which store thousands of pages of information each, at a reasonable cost, videotex services are opening up prospects for "home encyclopedias," together with access to a wide range of outside information sources. Both videodisk players and videotex services can be linked to home TV sets. Both these technologies have already had extensive impacts on educational technology and learning methods. As a result, people will not only be able to reach more easily the sources of information that will make them more aware; they will also be able to use that information more effectively, and learn better *how* to become more aware.

Nor need people any longer confine their sources of information to well-known information providers, with large audiences. The combination of electronic publishing, local videodisk systems based on home computers, and videotex technology, provides scope for "narrowcasting" of relevant information between widely scattered people with similar mutual interests and hobbies. In this way, an invaluable complement is provided to the *broadcast* information and entertainment services of today.

Licklider and Vezza (1978, page 1336) consider that networking has the potential of changing the news into a multidimensional dynamic model of the world, that each individual can explore in his own way, choosing for himself the time scales, the amount of detail, and the modes of presentation. In principle, networking could open the way to self-directed exploration and investigation by the receiver of the news. In practice, the evolution, from the present newspaper/magazine format to a truly user-determined interaction with a global knowledge base, will probably be long and slow.

Computer conferencing is a new form of computer communication, using the computer, that could eventually become a mass medium, as widely used as the telephone (Hiltz and Turoff, 1978). It constitutes a new alternative method for conducting communication among groups or networks of people or organisations, for meetings, study groups, and teacher-learning exchanges. Its participants type their written comments and contributions into a terminal, attached to a telephone, which then send the material by network to the host computer. Thus they can all send and receive materials at a pace, time and place of their own choice.

In their book, Hiltz and Turoff (1978), as pioneers of computer conferencing, cover its different aspects, including its impact on public awareness and its social impacts, in great detail. They describe some of the existing computer conferencing systems, including EMISARI and PLANET/FORUM, as well as EIES, the system that they have developed. They consider the social and psychological processes used in computer conferencing. They discuss its impacts on education, public use of information, communications with handicapped people, home life, business management, and scientific research, for example.

Hiltz (1982) considers the impact of a computer conferencing system on the use of other communication modes. Three models of the nature of this impact are tested on data from the operational trials of the use of the EIES system by scientific researchers. Use of computer conferencing tends to be treated as an additional communications mode, and if anything to increase, not decrease, the use of other communication modes, although there is some replacement of telephone and mail by computer communication. Most users did not significantly alter their travel to professional meetings or their visits to other researchers.

Bamford (1980) considers computer conferencing within a larger framework, and shows its relationship to other forms of information exchange. He describes the experience of operational trials of small research communities, begun in 1977. These trials allow electronic information exchange to be assessed, and they encourage the existence of a population of experienced users.

At the end of their paper, Van der Loos and Slaa (1982) urge that priority be given to increasing public awareness about the possibilities and problems of information technology, and especially the social consequences, in order to stimulate social discussion about these issues. In this way, better public policies will emerge in this area. Hiltz and Turoff (1978, pages 209–210) make a similar plea, for adequate education about computing and information technology in the schools, so that the younger citizens of the future, at least, can be well informed about them.

THE SOCIAL IMPACT OF NETWORKS

Like other information technologies, computer networking is contributing in several ways to the change of individual and social life. This subject is so large that only a few aspects of it are considered in this section, while other sections, on the regulatory, legal and political aspects, consider related issues, such as the right to communicate, privacy and public policies.

Bell (1979) points to five major areas where significant new trends are developing, that could have important social impact and implications:

1. The merging of telephone and computer systems, telecommunications and teleprocessing, into a single mode of communication.
2. The progressive substitution of electronic media for paper information processing.
3. The expansion of TV services through cable services, videotex, etc.
4. The reorganisation of computer-based storage and retrieval systems to include interactive computer network communication, using terminals based in the library and the home.
5. The expansion of education systems and facilities brought about by information technology.

Hiltz and Turoff (1978, Chapter 13) consider some of the social impacts of computer conferencing. If communication replaces commuting to work to a significant extent, much time and energy would be saved, various patterns of decentralised work would emerge, and there would be effects on productivity, morale, and family relationships, that would need to be carefully considered, as these effects are not necessarily all good. Large, more fluid, social networks seem likely to emerge, and will be viewed perhaps as "extended families," perhaps as "electronic tribes."

Mayne (1986, Chapter 15) considers the social impact of videotex, and outlines various views that have been expressed about it. The most extensive published discussion on the social effects of videotex seems to be the report *New Views* (1979), prepared by the Commission on New Information Technology, in Sweden. Although it refers to the Swedish scene, most of what it says is generally applicable to developed countries. There, the Commission made proposals about the use and conditions of use of these media in Sweden; many of their recommendations may apply to Europe as a whole and to other parts of the world. One of its aims was to stimulate a general debate about the new media, their possibilities and their dangers, their good and bad effects.

Uhlig et al (1979, Chapters III.4 to III.6) discuss at some length the impacts of office automation and information technology on the organisation, groups, and individuals in the working environment. Jarrett (1982) also considers the effects of office automation on the working environment, the work patterns and roles of office staff, both managers and secretaries, and the relationships between these staff.

SECURITY IN NETWORKS

This section starts by briefly considering computer security in general, then discusses computer security in networks, and finally outlines some relevant work on cryptography. It reviews some of the very considerable amount of literature that has been written on computer security in general and security in computer networks in particular.

The National Computing Centre has published quite a number of books on general aspects of computer security. The book by Wood (1982) is an introductory text, for all people involved with the security of computer operations; it covers computer security in relation to the physical environment, personnel, systems design, contingency planning, insurance, and security audit. NACCS (1979) gives management some brief guidelines on the potential threats to security, together with some feasible countermeasures. Squires (1981) covers a range of activities, that could be undertaken at the computer systems design stage, to ensure the security of that system. It includes discussions of planning, systems definition, management, organisation and personnel aspects, together with design methods, documentation, and security control.

Pritchard (1979a) gathers together information about breaches of security that have actually occurred. Pritchard (1979b) examines the various types of computer security that are available, including both hardware systems and software systems for achieving security; he lists types of breaches of security, and discusses human aspects. Pritchard (1979c) provides information and advice on all aspects of security in online systems. Squires (1980a, 1980b) discusses human factors in security, and security measures to be taken with reference to people working in computer departments and installations.

The IEEE Computer Society's (1980, 1981, 1982) annual conference proceedings on security and privacy are also relevant.

Martin (1981b, Chapter 35) introduces those aspects of computer security that are most relevant to computer networks. Security is especially important here, because many people in many places may have access to a particular network. Some of the information, stored in the network, may be of great value to the organisation(s) using the network, so that it must not be lost, stolen, or damaged. Protection is needed, not only from hardware and software failures and from physical disasters, but also from people who are careless or have criminal intentions.

Security thus includes protection of resources from damage and loss, together with protection of data against unauthorised disclosure, modification and destruction.

Network security is a very complicated subject, because of its many aspects, and it can only be considered in outline here. Martin lists 10 essentials for its achievement:

1. Network users must be properly *identifiable.*
2. It must be possible to check that network user's actions are *authorised.*
3. Network users' actions should be *monitored.*
4. Data, software, and hardware must be protected from physical destruction.
5. These resources should be *locked, to prevent unauthorised use.*
6. The data should be *reconstructable.*
7. The data should be *auditable.*

8. The computer systems and computer network should be *protected against tampering.*
9. Transmission over the network should be *failsafe.*
10. Data sent over the network, should be *private, with the more important parts of it being protected by crytography.*

Martin also proposes attacking each security risk in three ways:

1. Minimise the chance that it happens.
2. Minimise the damage that results if it *does* happen.
3. Plan to recover from the damage as well as possible, if it *does* occur.

Martin then discusses a variety of ways of implementing network security, including: layers of protection, privacy locks, authorisation schemes, alarms, identification of users, message authentication, closed user groups, and cryptography.

Kent (1981) also discusses security in computer networks, and starts with a statement of principles. He points out that it has been extremely difficult to develop secure general-purpose computer systems; indeed, no such systems have been achieved as yet. He lists eight principles of secure system design:

1. Economy of mechanism, using the simplest design that achieves the desired effect.
2. Fail-safe defaults, requiring access decisions to be based on permission rather than exclusion.
3. Complete mediation, requiring every access to every object to be checked against an access control data base.
4. Open design, so that the *design* of the protection mechanism is not secret.
5. Separation of privilege, requiring at least two "keys" to unlock the system.
6. Least privilege, requiring that each program and each user should operate with the smallest set of privileges needed to perform a given task.
7. Least common mechanism, minimising the amounts of system common to more than one user and shared between all users.
8. Psychological acceptability, designing the human interface for ease of use, so that all users routinely and automatically apply the system's protection mechanisms.

Kent considers link-oriented, end-to-end, and connection-oriented security measures. Attacks on communication security can be *passive*, in which case the intruders just watch the network message, or *active*, in which case they also tamper with them. Kent discusses various measures against them in some detail, including especially the use of cryptography. He ends with a discussion of authentication and access control in networks, considering as an illustrative example the methods used in the Arpanet.

In his tutorial on network security, Davies (1981) presents the major advances in the applications of cryptography to security since the mid-1970s. He covers the main components, from which a secure data network can be designed, and describes some of the potential weaknesses of such a system. He explores techniques to keep data secure from "line tapping", as well as methods for developing and evaluating the security of networks. The tutorial includes reprints of 22 papers, extensive original work, an annotated bibliography, and a subject index

Cryptography, already mentioned briefly near the end of Chapter 8, has been presented in detail in the semi-popular book by Kahn (1967) and more technically by Konheim (1981) and Baker and Piper (1982). Brief outlines are given, for example, by Davies (1979), Davies et al (1979, Chapter 9), and Tanenbaum (1981, Section 9.1).Davies (1982) reviews some recent advances in cryptography.

TELECOMMUNICATIONS REGULATIONS AND NETWORKS

In almost every country, the provision of long-distance telecommunications transmission and switching, including the data communications services provided for WANs, is provided by a carrier subject to public control and regulations. Usually, the carrier is a single organization, the PTT for that country. In some countries, for example Italy, there are different carriers for different services, such as telegraph, local telephone, intercity telephone, and international telephone.

In North America, there are several carriers, each privately owned but usually having a monopoly on public switched voice traffic in its own area; however, data networks, such as Telenet and Tymnet, have transcontinental coverage. The "Record Carriers" have some degree of monopoply on "record traffic," i.e., message traffic. In the USA, the operation of the carriers is subject to the regulations of the FCC.

In a *value added network* (*VAN*), the network operators rent transmission equipment from the carriers, and then instal their own switching equipment. VANs are subject to public regulations about what they are allowed to do, what traffic they can carry, and what rates they may charge. These regulations take into account who owns the host computers, terminals and switches, who rents the transmission lines, what types of traffic are carried, and what transmission technologies are used (Cerf and Kirstein, 1978, p. 1404).

Mathison (1978, pages 1529–1534) discuss the regulatory framework for networks, including some of its history, with special reference to the situation in the USA. US policy on packet network services is based on the Communications Act of 1934, which provides for FCC regulation of communication services that are "common carrier in nature"; the exact criteria for these services are not defined, although they include all communication services offered to the public for hire.

In 1966 and 1976 respectively, the FCC initiated its rule-making First Computer Inquiry and Second Chapter Inquiry, about policy problems resulting from the growing interdependence of computers and communications. The Second Inquiry proposed a more precise distinction between data processing and communications, together with a proposed rule, but there was an almost universal consensus from interested parties that they were unworkable, would discourage development of new services and technologies, and would be impossible to enforce.

In the UK, the regulatory situation has been made more liberal, as a result of the separation of British Telecom from the Post Office and as a result of the loss of monopoly powers and the privatisation of British Telecom. However, British Telecom still provides the basic infrastructure for data communication services and for transmission of data over WANs in the UK, both over the PSTN and through its Packet Switched Service (PCC). In addition, computer network communications between the UK and other countries now has to pass over the international telephone network or via PSS, with the exception of a few experimental network projects, such as the Arpanet, some of whose traffic only is allowed to cross the Atlantic via Satnet.

Cawkell (1980) discusses some aspects of the regulatory situation, in the USA, UK and Europe, and contrasts the more liberal attitude of the USA, including the FCC's encouragement of innovation, with the more restrictive approach in Europe, although this is now beginning to thaw, at least in the UK.

Irwin and Ela (1981) review past US telecommunications policy and question the assumptions of the current search for a policy for the future. They discuss both static and dynamic regulatory models, together with attempts to formulate a hybrid model; they conclude that a hybrid model is an essentially unworkable combination of the static and dynamic approaches. They believe that institutions and restraints need to be removed altogether, in order to allow the telecommunications industry to develop.

Cerf and Kirstein (1978, pages 1405–1406) briefly discuss some regulatory problems and issues, which are discussed in the relevant section of Chapter 17.

LEGAL ASPECTS OF NETWORKS

Apart from telecommunications regulations, the most important legal aspects of networks are trans-border data flow and privacy.

Transborder data flow has been discussed by Lenk (1982, pages 296–298), McCrum and Ryan (1981, pages 35–36), Mathison (1978, pages 1536–1538), and, very briefly, by Licklider and Vezza (1978, pages 1343–1344).

Although communication over packet-switched networks is technically able to improve international information flow and make it easier, unfortunately this flow is to some extent threatened by "data protection laws" and other regulations that have been passed by several countries. These laws are being advocated for reasons such as "protection of individual privacy," "preservation of national sovereignty," and "protection of growing national industries."

These regulations restrict the free flow of information across national boundaries, and are thus similar to customs regulations, which restrict the free flow of goods between nations. Besides their effects of freedom of expression, they could also have harmful effects on businesses, reducing their productivity, limiting their technology transfer, and making it harder for them to avoid fragmentation into uneconomic units. On the other hand, unrestricted international data flow could have its disadvantages and dangers too, and its possible effects on national cultures, privacy and security need to be considered carefully

The threat of computers and information technology to individual privacy has been discussed very often. References to it in the literature on computer networks and information technology include: Martin (1981b, Chapter 36), Dunn (1982, pages 35–36), Lenk (1982, pages 283–290), McCrum and Ryan (1981, pages 36–37), Licklider and Vezza (1978, page 1343). The IEEE Computer Society (1980, 1981, 1982) has been holding annual conferences on security and privacy.

The book by Simons (1982) discusses privacy in connection with computerisation in industrial, social and service sectors. It considers especially the specific legislation on privacy in various countries, and the recommendations of working parties on privacy in the UK and elsewhere. It includes brief information about systems and programming safeguards.

The issue of privacy has already been made serious by the presence of computer systems that can store very large data bases, and by the establishment of many such data bases by government departments and other public authorities in quite a number of countries, especially in Europe and North America. Computer networking makes the problems even more serious, because it is now much easier to transfer information from one data base to another and even distribute it to many data bases. Thus some form of legislative protection is needed to ensure that given pieces of information about an individual can only enter the data bases of authorities and organisations that are entitled to hold them, and that only authorised people are allowed to access these pieces of information. In most cases, each individual should have a right to know and check at any time, free of charge, what information is held about him/her.

The problems and issues of privacy are also mentioned at the end of Chapter 17.

Uhlig et al (1979, Chapter III.8) recommend that, in future, there should be a legal requirement for all technological innovation and implementation to be accompanied by a "human impact statement," to ensure the preservation of the quality of human working life. Care should be taken that an undue bureaucratic load is not introduced as a result.

THE POLITICAL IMPACT OF NETWORKS

This section considers some of the ways in which computer networking and other information technologies could modify, if not transform, political processes. It then gives examples of public debates on the impact of information technology, and ideas for public information policies.

Hiltz and Turoff (1978, pages 197–201) consider that the most exciting and far-reaching political application of a computer conferencing system could be the possibilities that it opens up for the direct participation and voting of citizens on important national and local issues. They outline several models of participatory democracy, based on this concept. They describe J. W. Huston's Constitutional Convention (Con-Con) project, to establish 21 community centres throughout that state, to allow public participation in the 1978 Hawaii Constitutional Convention, through computer conferencing and videotapes.

Computer conferencing would make it much less expensive to organise political lobbies, thus opening up this approach to many groups of citizens who would otherwise be unable to afford it. In principle at least, a computer conferencing system would make it very easy for individuals with common objectives to find each other and organise as a group.

Computer-linked community councils could be set up, consisting of representatives of neighbourhood, racial, or other groups. Leaders of various community groups would have better opportunities to meet each other. Citizen groups in different areas would be able to pool the technical and professional talent available to them.

Computer conferencing would allow citizen advisory groups to governments to become more effective, by being able to hold a continual "meeting" between their face-to-face sessions. Government officials would be able to participate more selectively, concentrating on those parts of the discussion where their information, advice and encouragement are needed. They would be able to retrieve the citizens' advice, or poll the members of these groups, when a decision is about to be made.

Legislators and other elected officials could use computer conferencing in many ways. They could keep in better touch with advisers in their constituencies and elsewhere. Political negotiations could be made much less time-consuming, and traditional political decision making processes could become more efficient. In the long run, some legislative sessions, particularly special sessions or emergency sessions called on a specific issue or problems, could be held through computer conferences.

Computer networks could be used to poll opinions, and register consumer choices; at a later stage, "electronic" voting would become possible, although its effects might be mixed (Lenk, 1982). Such votes could strengthen horizontal communication structures, and it would not necessarily help social sub-groups to express their opinions. "Instant referenda" could well benefit existing power structures more than citizens, as those in power would pose the relevant questions and the conditions of feedback.

On the other hand, with computing and communication facilities become muchmore widespread than before, independent groups of citizens could also initiate *their* referenda and political campaigns, and publicise their results. In view of this factor, Lenk's view, that information technology is unlikely to change existing power structures and institutions, that have prevented the achievement of alternative forms of democracy so far, seems to be too pessimistic.

Lenk also has some rather gloomy views on the extent to which information technology would make bureaucracy more powerful. According to him, it has immediately caused the growing significance of formal elements in society, and been the vehicle of their introduction. In this sense, bureaucratisation is more than the existence of large hierarchical, highly regulated, organisations. It also means that an increasing part of social relations consists of human interaction via bureaucracies. As bureaucracies assume more functions of social service and control, they become a major factor of social integration. This dependence of society on large bureaucracies for some of the most important things also makes society more vulnerable, and information technology aggravates this vulnerability. It is especially dangerous to leave to computers or other machines alone vital decisions affecting the survival or quality of life of human beings.

On the other hand, computer networks could open the way to a less bureaucratic society by encouraging decentralisation of decision making and administration into local groups. New-style villages, whose coherence could be increased by the presence of local area networks, could well emerge as an important pattern of life, and they would be connected into wider federal political structures with the aid of linked local area networks.

Burns, (1981, pages 160–162) and Mayne (1986, Chapter 15) briefly mention some aspects of the political impact of videotex and other information technologies. Especially notable here are the general discussions by the Swedish Commission on New Information Technology (*New Views*, 1979; Ohlin, 1981), which has both formulated recommendations for government information policies and encouraged their public debate.

Van der Loo and Slaa (1982) look at the impact of information technology in the Netherlands. They analyse the public debate on information technology there, and they appraise government policies on socioeconomics, microelectronics and information technology. They conclude that the government must play a more active part in making citizens more aware of the issues.

McCrum and Ryan (1981) see the need for national policies for the coordinated development of new communications networks. The evolving complex and comprehensive networks of data highways need national direction and standards for their orderly development, just as public road systems do.

According to them, there needs to be a detailed understanding of services and total system concepts, about the network structures and their economical application. National objectives need to be stated about the industrial exploitation of new communications services, so that national industries obtain important benefits. They believe that the time for national action and exercise of sovereignty is now. Dunn (1982) considers some of the policy issues, arising in connection with the creation of new information, and then discusses specific policy problems arising from communications and information storage and retrieval systems and their use. He considers that a broader, more integrated, view of this field could help the development of future national information policies, and he makes some suggestions for further studies in this area.

REFERENCES

J. Abbott (1982) *Man-Machine Interface Design*, NCC Publications, Manchester, England.

R. C. Atkinson and J. I. Lipson (Sep 1980) "Instructional technologies of the future," Paper delivered at the *APA 8'th Annual Convention*, Montreal, Canada.

R. Aubrac (Jan–Feb 1980) "Tele-knowledge," *Development Forum*, 7.

Lord Avebury (1978) *The Impact of Computers in Society Seen from the Western Viewpoint*, Digico Publications, Letchworth, Herts, England.

H. Baker and F. Piper (1982) *Cipher Systems—The Protection of Communications*, Northwood Books, London.

H.E. Bamford (Sep 1980) "Computer conferencing—The exchange of experience," *Telecommunications Policy*, **4**(3) 215–220.

D. L. A. Barber (Sep 1982) "Human factors in open system interconnection," *ICC 82*, 823–830.

I. Barron and R. C. Curnow (1981) *The Future with Microelectronics*, Frances Pinter, London, and Nichols Publishing, New York.

D. Bell (1979) "The social framework of the information society," *The Computer Age*, 163–211.

D. Biran and F. Feldman (Sep 1982) "Human factors in designing an electronic mail system for a multilanguage country," *ICC82*, 658–663.

T. J. M. Burke and M. Lehman (1981) *Communication Technologies and Information Flow*, Pergamon Press, Oxford England and Elmsford, NY.

A. Burns (1981) *The Microchip—Appropriate or Inappropriate Technology?*, Ellis Horwood, Chichester.

Byte, Vol. **7**, No. 9 (Sep 1982) Computers and the Disabled, Special Issue.

A. E. Cawkell (1980) "Forces controlling the paperless revolution," *The Microelectronics Revolution*, 244–274.

V. G. Cerf and P. T. Kirstein (Nov. 1978) "Issues in packet-network interconnection," *Proceedings of the IEEE*, **66**(11) 1386–1408.

G. F. Coulouris (1981) "Experiments in user interface design for office workstations," *Local Networks 81*, 519–530.

C. A. Davies (1982a) "New systems and services for tomorrow's office," *Local Networks 82*, 1–13.

D. W. Davies (1979) 'Cryptography and crypto-systems," *Interlinking of Computer Networks*, 201–237.

D. W. Davies (Aug 1981) *Tutorial: The Security of Data in Networks*, IEEE Computer Society, Silver Springs, MD.

D. W. Davies (1982b) (17 May 1982) "New developments in cryptography," Lecture to British Computer Society Data Security Specialist Group.

D. W. Davies, D. L. A. Barber, W. L. Price and C. M. Solomonides (1979) *Computer Networks and Their Protocols*, Wiley, Chichester and New York.

Ed. M. L. Dertouzos and J. Moses (1979) *The Computer Age: A Twenty-Year View*, The MIT Press, Cambridge, MA and London.

D. A.Dunn (Mar 1982) "Developing information policy," *Telecommunications Policy*, **6**(1) 21–38.

L. J. Endicott (Sep 1982) "A carefully structured system interface," ICCC 82, 647—652.

Ed. T. Forrester (1980) *The Microelectronics Revolution*, Blackwell, Oxford, England.

Ed. G. Friedrichs and Adam Schaff (1982) *Microelectronics and Society For Better or For Worse*, Pergamon Press, Oxford, England, and Elmsford, NY.

Ed. D. Godfrey and D. Parkhill (1979) *Gutenberg 2: The New Electronics and Social Change*, Press Porcepic, Toronto, Canada.

A. E. Gollin (Sep 1981) "Consumers and advertisers in the electronic market place—Implications for newspapers and other media," *Telecommunications Policy*, **5**(3) 171–180.

S. R. Hiltz (Sep 1982) "Impact of a computerized conferencing system upon use of other communication modes," *ICCC 82*, 577—582.

S. R. Hiltz and M. Turoff (1978) *The Network Nation—Human Communication via Computer*, Addison-Wesley, Reading, MA and London.

B. A. Huckle (Sep 1982) "A proposal for improving access to heterogenous computer networks," *ICCC 82*, 589–594.

IEEE Computer Society (Apr 1980) *Proceedings, 1980 Symposium on Security and Privacy*, Silver Springs, MD.

IEEE Computer Society (Apr 1981) *Proceedings, 1981 Symposium on Security and Privacy*, Silver Springs, MD.

IEEE Computer Society (Oct 1982) *Proceedings, 1982 Symposium on Security and Privacy*, Silver Springs, MD.

M. R. Irwin and J. D. Ela (Mar 1981) "US telecommunications regulation—Will technology decide?," *Telecommunications Policy*, **5**(1) 24–32.

D. Jarrett (1982) *The Electronic Officer—A Management Guide to the Office of the Future*, Gower Publishing Company, Aldershot, Hampshire, with Philips Business Systems.

D. Kahn (1967) *The Codebreakers*, The Macmillan Company, New York.

S. T. Kent (1981) "Security in computer networks," Chapter 9 of Ed. F. F. Kuo (1981) *Protocols & Techniques for Data Communications Networks*, Prentice-Hall, Englewood Cliffs, NJ.

A. L. Kidd (Sep 1982) "Problems in man-machine dialogue design," *ICCC 82*, 531—536.

A. G. Konheim (1981) *Cryptography*, Wiley, New York and Chichester.

K. L. Kraemer (Mar 1982) "Telecommunications/transportation substitution and energy conservation—Part 1," *Telecommunications Policy*, **6**(1) 39–59.

K. L. Kraemer and J.L. King (Jun 1982) "Telecommunications/transportation substitution and energy conservation—Part 2," *Telecommunications Policy*, **6**(2) 87–99.

K. Lenk (1982) "Information technology and society," Chapter 9 of Friedrichs and Schaff (1982).

J. C. R. Licklider and A. Vezza (Nov 1978) "Applications of information networks," *Proceedings of the IEEE*, **66**(11) 1330–1346.

W. A. McCrum and M. G. Ryan (Mar 1981) "Risks and benefits of new communications services," *Telecommunications Policy*, **5**(1) 33–39.

P. Marsh (29 Apr 1982) "Will Britain buy electronics shopping?," *New Scientist*, **94**(1303) 278–281.

J. Martin (1981a) *The Telematic Society*, Prentice-Hall, England Cliffs, NJ.

J. Martin (1981b) *Design and Strategy for Distributed Data Processing*, Prentice-Hall, Englewood Cliffs, NJ.

S. L. Mathison (Nov 1978) "Commercial, legal and international aspects of packet communications," *Proceedings of the IEEE*, **66**(11) 1527–1539.

A. J. Mayne (1986) *The Videotex Revolution*, second ed., Wiley, Chichester and New York.

W. Myers (Feb 1982) "Personal computers and the disabled," *IEEE Micro*, **2**(1) 26–40.

NACCS (1979) *Computing Practice—Security Aspects*, NCC Publications, Manchester, England.

New Views (1979) "Computers and new media—Anxiety and hopes." Report by the Commission on New Information Technology, Sweden.

S. Nora and A.Minc (1978) *L'Informatisation de la Société* (*The Information Society*, In French), Documentation Francaise, Paris.

T. Ohlin (1981) "Videotex and Teletext in Sweden—A nation decides," *Viewdata 81*, 215–230.

J. A. T. Pritchard (1979a) *Computer Security—Facts and Figures*, NCC Publications, Manchester, England.

J. A. T. Pritchard (1979b) *Security in Communications Systems*, NCC Publications, Manchester, England.

J. A. T. Pritchard (1979c) *Security in Online Systems*, NCC Publications, Manchester, England.

J. A. T. Pritchard (1980) *Data Encryption*, NCC Publications, Manchester, England.

P. Schicker (1981) "A workstation user interface with a minimal command set," *Local Networks 81*, 531–542.

G. L. Simons (1982) *Privacy in the Computer Age*, NCC Publications, Manchester, England.

H.T. Smith (Sep 1982) "Human factors issues in network communications systems," *ICCC 82*, 644–668.

T. Squires (1980a) *Computer Security—The Personnel Aspect*, NCC Publications, Manchester, England.

T. Squires (1980b) *People and Security—An Introduction*, NCC Publications, Manchester, England.

T. Squires (1981) *Security in Systems Design*, NCC Publications, Manchester, England.

A. S. Tanenbaum (1981) *Computer Networks*, Prentice-Hall, Englewood Cliffs, NJ.

H. Thimbleby (Sep 1982) "Basic user engineering principles for display editors," *ICCC 82*, 537–542.

M. Turoff and S. Chinai (Jul 1982) "An electronic information market place," Computer Conferencing and Communications Center, New Jersey Institute of Technology, Research Report.

R. P. Uhlig, D. J. Farber and J.H. Bair (1979) *The Office of the Future*, North Holland, Amsterdam Oxford, England, and New York.

H. van der Loo and P. Slaa (Jun 1982) "Information technology—Public debate in the Netherlands," *Telecommunications Policy*, **6**(2) 100–110.

A. R. Willis (Sep 1982) "Voice I/O System design," *ICCC 82*, 583–588.

M. B. Wood (1982) *Introducing Computer Security*, NCC Publications, Manchester, England.

Chapter 17

Network Problems and Issues

This chapter discusses briefly some of the most important of the network problems and issues. Inevitably, most of its discussion gives only an outline of the many different areas that are relevant, and often this is because the literature on network problems and issues is so extensive that even a full summary of it could fill several volumes.

This chapter considers in turn: network design, congestion and flow control, routing, addressing, transmission errors, deadlocks, network protocol problems and issues, network operating problems and issues including standardisation, regulatory problems and issues, economic problems and issues, and finally human and social problems and issues. Network problems and issues are discussed further in Chapter 24.

Quite a number of the relevant papers on network problems and issues, that are cited individually in this chapter, are contained in the conference proceedings edited by Pujolle (1981) in the book edited by Kuo (1981), and in the special issue of *Proceedings of the IEEE* on packet communication networks (Vol. **66**, No.11, Nov 1978). Also specially relevant are the book by Schwartz (1977), and the papers by Cerf (1981), Cerf and Kirstein (1978), who include a list or unresolved research questions, and Kleinrock (1978, 1980). Mayne (1986, Chapter 17) briefly reviews some of the problems arising in videotex, one particular area of computer networking.

NETWORK DESIGN

One of the most extensive discussions of network design is given in the book by Schwartz (1977), that discusses mostly packet-switched and message-switched networks, although it gives some consideration to circuit-switched data networks.

Global network design covers at least the following four aspects:

1. *Topological design* Given the geographical location of messages and the traffic expected over the network, where should the network nodes be located and how should they be connected? What type of configuration—tree, ring, mesh, ... should the network take?

2. *Line capacity allocation* What data rates should be used in the different links of the network?

3. *Routing procedures* What routing procedure or algorithm be used? Should control of routing be localised or centralised? How often and in what ways should routing information and routing control be updated? What parameters have a significant effect on routing?

4. *Flow control procedures* What are the best ways of ensuring smooth traffic flow throughout the network? How are bottlenecks and deadlocks prevented? How can particular uses, data sources and nodes be prevented from monopolising and "tying up" the network?

Flow control and routing procedures are considered in the next two sections of this chapter.

Performance critera, that are used in network design, include the following:

1. Response times and delays can be required to be less than a given amount for most of the time, e.g. less than one second for 95% of the time, or their overall averages, or averages on given links, can be minimised.

2. Maximum network cost can be specified, or response time minimised for a given cost, or cost minimised for a given response time.

3. Maximum reliability or at least a specified reliability.

In addition to the global network design problems and criteria summarised above, there are also questions of local design, what should be done at specific nodes and local groupings of nodes. For linked local area networks, there are not only the problems of designing the individual LANs and designing the WAN that interconnects them, but further stages of design may be needed, considering all these aspects in relation to each other, and mutually adjusting their parameters in the most advantageous way.

Much of the detailed design of networks may require mathematical methods, taking into account the numerical values of the characteristics of the network components, the distances between them, traffic characteristics, and link data rates and channel capacities. Schwartz's (1977) book discusses the principles of many of these methods.

For other general discussions of network design, see, for example, Davies et al (1979, Chapter 10), who discuss network optimisation, Davies and Barber (1973, Chapter 14), who review general design principles. Tanenbaum (1981, Chapter 2), who introduces the mathematics of network topology design, and Martin (1981, Chapter 10), who considers strategies for distributed data processing.

Akavia and Kleinrock (1979) consider the design of a distributed communication system, with many terminals wishing to communicate with each other. They discuss several related questions, such as: how to access the communications resources effectively, what trade-offs are basic to the design, how far the design should be hierarchical, how a large network should be decomposed into smaller parts. Using mathematical models, they consider two technologies, line and broadcast, and both star networks and distributed networks.

Branscomb (1981, Section 10) points out that, for LANs as well as WANs, the options involved in specifying a network are so numerous that simulation and modelling tools are becoming essential for network designers. It is *not* a trivial matter to find the optimal configuration of a network, and calculate its throughput, performance and cost, given assumptions about bandwidth, traffic, computer power, and tariffs. IBM has built two very useful network design tools, to aid this process. SNAP/SHOT is a discrete simulation model, that allows users to "test drive" their new computer-communications system, while it is still in a planning stage. NET-PAK helps users to configure the most economical set of telecommunications facilities and services, that meet specific performance requirements. Over 1000 IBM customers have used these facilities so far.

Shoch et al (1982) have highlighted several important considerations that affect the design of an Ethernet LAN. They have traced the evolution of the system from Experimental Ethernet, a research prototype, to Ethernet Specification, a multi-company standard, by discussing stategies and trade-offs between alternative implementations. Ethernet is intended chiefly for use in office automation, distributed data processing, terminal access, and other situations requiring economical connection to a LAN carrying bursts of traffic at high peak data rates. Experience with Experimental Ethernet, which has been used to build distributed systems supporting electronic mail, distributed filing, etc., has confirmed many of the original design goals and decisions. Metcalfe and Boggs (1976) include a brief discussion of the Experimental Ethernet design problems.

Zachmann (1981) shows how CSMA bus networks, of which Ethernet is an example, have important properties, not found in older network arthitectures, that extend the horizons available for designers of network application systems and operating systems. New, quite different approaches are needed to system design, in order to take advantage of these opportunities. Zachmann discusses some of the design opportunities now available. In a rather abstract paper, Whitehouse (1981) considers how to match LAN characteristics to the characteristics of application systems.

McQuillan and Walden (1977) examine in detail the design decisions made in constructing the Arpanet; they provide considerable insight into the problems encountered by this network in its early days, and how they were solved.

Huynh et al (1976) and Huynh and Kuo (1981) present some of the important design isses for *mixed-media* packet-switched networks, combining terrestrial WANs with satellite networks. Satellite networks offer considerable scope for cheap, high bandwidth data communications, but they suffer from large inherent delays not present in ground links. Thus a mixture of both these communication media seems to offer the best of both worlds. Both these papers discuss trade-offs, that should offer guidelines for the design and best usage of mixed-media networks.

Tanenbaum (1981, Section 6.2) and Lam (1981) discuss routing and other design considerations for packet radio networks. Packet radio is similar to satellite broadcasting, but the problem of the long propagation delays in the satellite network is replaced by the problem of where to place the repeater stations that enable messages to be conveyed beyond the range of single short wave radio transmitters.

CONGESTION AND FLOW CONTROL

A packet-switched network has two major resources that are limited, that must be shared between its users, and that therefore need efficient management; these resources are the buffer space within the network nodes and the bandwidth of the communication lines between the nodes. This management problem is discussed, for example, by Cole (1982, Section 10.1), who points out that this model of a network, as the interconnection of store-and-forward nodes by fixed bandwidth channels, leads to the following basic characteristics.

There is a *delay* to each packet, between its entry into the network at its source, and its departure from the network at its destination. This delay is due mainly to queueing of packets at the nodes, although a small part of it is due to transmission time. Delay increases rapidly as the traffic intensity in the network rises.

Throughput is the rate at which a source can transmit packets into the network along a particular link. Its maximum value depends on the bandwidths of the network's communication channels and on the processing speed of its nodes. As traffic increases, throughput first rises to a peak, and then falls again, as conditions become congested.

Thus *congestion* is a result of traffic that is heavy enough to fill at least the most critical links in the network, with the result that delays to traffic increase, throughput becomes limited, and queues buildup. These characteristics of heavy traffic are not confined to packet-switched networks, and occur in message-switched and circuit-switched networks as well; indeed, they occur in road networks as well as computer networks.

Because it is not possible to have perfectly secure transmission, some packets are lost, and others are duplicated through attempts to prevent loss due to time-outs.

The network nodes have only *finite storage*. A node that fills all its buffers cannot accept any more traffic, until some of its packets have been forwarded and accepted by the next node. If two full nodes try to send to each other, there is an example of the phenomenon of *deadlock*, which is discussed later in this chapter.

In order to solve congestion, deadlock and other problems, resulting from heavy traffic in networks, various methods of *flow control* have been devised; its aims are to: maintain efficient network operation, guarantee fair sharing of limited resources, and protect the network from the effects of congestion (Gerla, 1981). These goals are achieved by properly regulating and, if necessary, blocking the flow of packets into the network and also inside it. Different flow control procedures may be applied at different levels of network protocol.

Flow control may need some exchange of information between nodes, to choose the control strategy, and perhaps some exchange of commands, to implement that strategy; these exchanges occur as overheads to channel and processor loads. Flow control may also require bandwidth, buffers and other resources to be reserved to individual users or classes of users. This trade-off between gain of efficiency, due to controls, and loss of efficiency, due to limited sharing and overheads, must be considered carefully when designing flow control strategies.

Levels of flow control include: node-to-node (hop-by-hop) control, network acess (entry-to-network) control, entry-to-exit (end-to-end) control, virtual-circuit control, and process-to-process control.

One of the best-known techniques of flow control is to require packets to be sent in sequence order and acknowledged on receipt; this system is described by Cole (1982, Section 6.6), for example. Here, the transmitter is given a *window size*, that is the maximum number of unacknowledged packets that it is allowed to send. A packet may be *retransmitted*, either if its *acknowledgment* is not received within a *time-out* period, or if a *negative acknowledgment* is received, sent when the receiver has noted the arrival of a damaged packet or a packet out of order.

Flow control is also discussed by Davies et al. (1979, Chapter 4), Schwartz (Chapter 11), Tanenbaum (1981, Section 5.3), and Inose and Saito (1978). Special collections of papers on flow control include the proceedings of the Versailles conference on flow control (Grangé and Gien, 1979), and the April 1981 issue of *IEEE Transactions on Communications* (Rubin, 1981). Gerla and Kleinrock (1980) provide a comparative survey of different methods of flow control; they describe the need for flow control, examine the functions required, and describe in detail various mechanisms of flow control.

Pujolle (1978) develops a mathematical model of a packet-switched network, with special reference to flow control, and shows how necessary it is. Labetoulle and Pujolle (1981) attempt to evaluate the flow control performance of an X.25 network; they develop several models, and evaluate the response time and stability of such a network. Chammas (1982) discusses responses times over packet-switched networks, with special reference to X.25 networks. Jacobsen and Thisted (1980) discuss X.25's flow control principles, and recommend a modification, whose effect would be to prevent possible network congestion due to the frequent retransmission of duplicate packets.

Ahuja (1979) describes the flow control mechanisms and procedures, used by Release 4.2 of SNA (IBM's System Network Architecture) to prevent network congestion. Herrman (1976) describes several flow control procedures, including those used by the Arapanet in its early days. Jacobs et al (1978, p. 1459) outline the flow control and congestion control methods used in packet satellite networks. Raubold (1979) describes flow control in the GMD network, and gives a clear view of the practical problems met in achieving acceptable flow control.

The conference proceedings edited by Pujolle (1981) contains six recent papers on flow control and allied topics. Arthurs and Stuck (1981) mention two fundamental ways of improving the traffic-handling capabilities of digital systems; increasing the speeds of their subsystems, and attempting to have as many tasks executed in parallel as possible; they consider how to maximise the mean throughput of completed work through the system, using the latter approach, and they apply it to link level flow control over LANs and satellite networks. Geissler et al (1981) use simulation methods to study the problem of guaranteeing throughputs in an X.25 network. Kermani (1981) analyses the performance of a feedback scheme for controlling congestion. Takashi et al (1981) use queueing theory and simulation to analyse approximately a composite congestion control scheme. Using analytical models and simulation methods, Omidyar and Sohraby (1981) present results on average delays of voice and data packets in an integrated voice and data network, for two different local flow control schemes. Majus and Hohe (1981) discuss deadline-oriented critera, with respect to the objective of minimising "bad" cases.

ROUTING

Like flow control, routing procedures aim to control the traffic within a network, so that data are transferred efficiently. *Routing* procedures aim to provide the best sets of paths between sources and destinations, given the traffic requirements and the network configuration. The definition of "best path" here may depend on the types of traffic carried (interactive, batch, data, voice, etc.) and outside constraints (e.g. security, legal, policy, political) that are not necessarily related to network performance. Paths of minimum delay are often sought, to obtain at least first approximations to good routes. Two approaches may be adopted: *system optimisation*, which minimises total average delay, and *user optimisation*, which minimises individual source-to-destination delays until an equilibrium is reached.

Although simpler routing procedures assume a static network, routing procedures in practice need to be *dynamic* and *adaptive*, i.e. they must be able to adjust their routes to time-varying network conditions. They attempt to optimise the network's use of resources, as long as the offered traffic can be accommodated by the network. When this traffic becomes too large, it must be regulated by flow control until it becomes less congested.

Many classifications of adaptive routing policies have been proposed. For example, in *isolated policies*, each node performs its routing computation independently, using local information. In *distributed policies*, nodes exchange information and cooperate to perform the routing computation in parallel. In *centralised policies*, a network routing centre computes minimum delay routes, using information about the whole network, and distributes routing tables or routing commands to all nodes. These policies may also be combined.

Useful general discussions of routing are given by Davies et al (1979, Chapter 3). Davies and Barber (1973, Chapter 12), Gerla (1981), Inose and Saito (1978), Schwartz (1977, Chapter 11). Schwartz and Stern (1980), and Tanenbaum (1981, Section 5.2).

Doss and Smetanka (1982) point out that, in large networks, it may become undesirable to maintain network topology information for routing, either in a central data base in one node, or distributed between all nodes. They consider an intermediate solution, using *locally centralised nodes*, containing network topology information about the nodes in their area.

Bharath-Kumar and Jaffe (1982) study algorithms for the effective routing of messages from a source to multiple-destination nodes in a store-and-forward network. They aim to minimise the "network cost", which is the sum of weights of links on the routing path, and compare this measure with "destination cost," which is the sum of the shortest path distances to all destinations.

Ossola (1981) summarises experience and theoretical results in network routing, and proposes a set of principles for routing in packet-switched networks. Purely distributed and adaptive routing is found to be both advantageous and feasible, even in large networks. The same principles, that are used for packet-switched networks, can be used for other types of networks, as long as various adaptations are done for the choice of cost functions and for very large networks. Ossola conjectures that a routing algorithm can be designed, where nodes need only know their neighbours, and where a given destination may appear in many nodes.

McQuillan (1977) surveys routing algorithms used for packet-switched networks over the period 1974–1977. McQuillan et al (1980) and Rosen (1980) discuss the Arpanet's new routing algorithm. Ahuja (1979) describes in detail the routing concepts of Release 4.2 of SNA (IBM's System Network Architecture), that allows multiple routes between network users. Kahn et al (1978, Sections IV and V) and Lam (1981) discuss routing in packet radio networks.

ADDRESSING

Shoch et al (1982, p. 20) discuss problems of addressing packets in local area networks, with special reference to Ethernet, where each packet has a source address and a destination address. A LAN design can use either *network-specific (network-relative)* station addresses, that must be unique on *their* network, but may be the same as other addresses held by other stations on other networks, and *unique (universal, absolute)* station addresses, that are unique over *all* networks to which the station is or can be connected.

To allow internetwork communication, the address of a station, if network-specific, must usually be combined with a unique network number, to produce an unambiguous address at the next higher level of protocol. Systems, using universal station addresses, may also use unique network numbers, to aid routing.

The Experimental Ethernet used network-specific addressing, with eight-bit fields for each of the source and destination addresses, enough to accommodate the maximum number of stations in that network.

However, for LANs with many stations, and for internetworks with many LANs, a universial address is much more convenient, especially for higher-level routing and addressing procedures. For this reason, the Ethernet Specification uses 48-bit universal station addresses.

Both Experimental Ethernet and Ethernet Specification support *broadcast* addressing, where packets may be sent to all active stations. Ethernet Specification also supports *multicast* addressing, where packets may be aimed at more than one specific destination. For example, multicast addresses may be represented by *log-*

ical addresses, where a permanently assigned address denotes one or more physical addresses. Multicast addressing is especially useful for such applications as access and update of distributed data bases, teleconferencing, and the distributed algorithms for managing LANs and the internetwork connecting them. Serious consideration should be given to aspects of design that reduce the load imposed on the system for filtering unwanted multicast packets.

These forms of addressing are also discussed by McQuillan (1978), in his paper on enhanced message-addressing capabilities for computer networks. He shows that these concepts and methods make it easier to implement many ways of using networks. For each of the methods discussed, McQuillan emphasises efficiency and reliability, and recommends implementation approaches. He shows how performance can be improved significantly, if these addressing methods are implemented with efficient delivery mechanisms. He finds that virtual circuit systems are better than datagrams, when logical addressing is used, while datagrams are preferable for broadcast, group, and multi-destination addressing.

Cerf and Kirstein (1978, pages 1399–1400) consider names, addresses and routes in relation to each other. They quote Shoch as saying that a *name* states what an object is, an *address* specifies where it is, and a *route* tells how to reach it. The "obvious" model, where host computers transform names into addresses and networks transform addresses into routes, if necessary, is over-simplified. Cerf and Kirstein raise some of the major issues, arising in connection with the joint use of names, addresses and routes, and they offer some partial solutions.

Jacobs et al (1978, pages 1459–1460) consider addressing in relation to satellite networks, whose broadcasting facility makes them especially attractive for applications, such as speech conferencing, that need addresses.

TRANSMISSION ERRORS

All network transmission media are subjected to "noise" and interference of various sorts, although some, such as telephone lines and certain radio channels, are much more liable than others, such as LAN buses and cables and optical fibres. As a result, the bits and bytes, in packets and other sets of data sent over networks, are subject to *transmission errors*, and these errors are likely to occur in *bursts*, rather than independently. In "bad" lines, an appreciable proportion of bytes can be received incorrectly or even lost, whereas, in the more reliable media, there is only one error on average for many millions of bytes sent. The nature of transmission errors and how to deal with them discussed by Cole (1982, Sections 6.1 to 6.5) and Tanenbaum (1981, Section 3.5).

Computer networks thus need to take special steps in order to achieve reliable data transfer. Each receiving node has to know if there are any errors in the data sent to it, and the node or the network then needs to take the appropriate corrective actions. In order to obtain more reliable transmission, there must be some sacrifice of the efficiency of that transmission.

The three methods of error control, used in computer communications, are: echo checking, forward error correction and automatic repeat request.

Echo checking sends each piece of data back to the sender for checking. It is typically used on full duplex connections between asynchronous terminals and computers in time-shared computer systems. When a user types a character on the terminal's keyboard, it is sent to the computer and then returned, so that it appears on the terminal's display or printer. If the character is wrong, the user types it in again. This technique is not very suitable for general network applications, because it wastes channel capacity, and because most communications need to be automatic.

Forward error correction (FEC) involves adding extra bits to the data, so that the receiver can not only detect the occurrence of an error, very nearly every time that it occurs, but also find which bit(s) have changed and correct them. The *Hamming coding technique* provides a simple FEC, but, like other FECs, it has low efficiency, due to the large proportion of redundant bits that need to be sent. However, it has some advantages. It is the only error system that can be used with simplex connections. It can also be useful in satellite communications, and in situations where the noise characteristics of a channel are known.

In *automatic repeat request (ARQ)*, the receiver checks the received bit pattern against a check precalculated by the sender, and added to the sequence of bits or bytes that is transmitted. If the checks do not agree, an error is assumed to have occurred, the whole message, on which the checks were carried out, is thrown away, and the receiver asks the sender to transmit the message again. If the checks are well designed, the probability of an error being present, when both checks agree, is negligible although not quite zero. ARQ techniques are used most widely in synchronous computer communications, where channels are relatively free from errors, and the data are usually sent in blocks or packets, to each of which the checks are applied, with one or two *cyclic redundancy check (CRC)* bytes being placed at the end of each block or packet.

The error detection and correction codes, needed to handle FEC and ARQ methods, are discussed by Cole and Tanenbaum, and also by Davies and Barber (1973, Section 6.4). The end of Chapter 8 briefly considers error correction and detection codes in general, and gives references to literature that provides further details about them.

Davies et al (1982) consider compensation for transmission line errors, by applying FEC, either by protocol at the data link level or directly at the data transmission level. They look at FEC methods and some recent data link protocols, in terms of throughput efficiency. Finally, they present a new selective repeat protocol, which has the advantages of both these types of FEC.

Conrads and Kermani (1982) discuss the problem of error checking for voice packets, and show that it is not feasible not to check voice packets for errors, in an environment where voice and data coexist. Through mathematical models, they show that there is no significant advantage in providing special, less restrictive, checking for voice packets, and they provide some guidelines for the design of a data network that can be used to transmit voice as well.

Duma and Zbăganu (1981) present two mathematical models for the occurrence of errors in digital communication channels; these two models include many earlier error models as special cases, but do not seem to be unduly difficult to compute.

They state that further investigations are needed, to establish the validity of these models and estimate their parameters in real communications channels.

RELIABILITY

Network failures can happen both in nodes and in links. Careful design and duplication of equipment can largely remove failure in nodes, if the cost is considered to be justified. Failure of individual links, at least in WANs, where they are exposed to external hazards, is harder to avoid.

Bus LANs are believed to be more reliable than rings, although the reliability of rings can be improved, for example, by using more than one station per attached device, by using double rings, and by adopting a "braided ring" topology, so that alternative paths are available between given pairs of stations.

WANs are more resistant to breakdowns of links and nodes, because it is easier for them to use alternative routes, to bypass sections that are temporarily out of order. However, the actual equipment in LANs is often inherently more reliable than that in WANs.

Literature describing LAN reliability seems to be scarce, and this chapter thus includes no references to papers specifically concerned with this topic; however, it is sometimes mentioned in passing in papers dealing with more general aspects of LANs.

Davies and Barber (1973, Section 12.4) and Davies et al (1979, Section 10.3) briefly discuss the reliability of WANs, and outline some mathematical methods for its calculations, in terms of the network configuration and the failure probabilities of individual components.

Lohwasser (1982) shows how the Deutsche Bundespost meets network users' demands for extremely high availability and reliability of their data connections by good network management, based on organisation, network operation, maintenance of staff. Data communications are managed centrally by the Telecommunication Engineering Centre in Darmstadt. The staff of the telecommunication offices maintain and operate the data transmission and data switching equipment.

Nakamura et al (1978) describe the DDX-2 circuit-switched system, which the Japanese PTT has developed for a new data network, and include a section on the reliability of this sytem.

Nilsson et al (1980) describe the framework of a packet radio communicator system and network architecture in a hostile and noisy environment, with a high density of users, i.e. under conditions where high reliability is much harder to achieve.

DEADLOCKS

Deadlock has been a continual threat in computer networks, especially in terminal-oriented systems. It can occur in many ways, for example when the nodes at both ends of a link both have full buffers, so that neither end of the link can communicate with the other. Deadlock is less liable to occur when traffic conditions are not congested, and where adequate flow control procedures are applied.

Nevertheless, the Arpanet has experienced serious deadlock and "lockup" conditions on several occasions, as a result of which it has had to change its operating procedures and protocols from time to time (Davies and Barber, 1973, pages 399–404; Kleinrock, 1978, pages 1324–1325; Tanenbaum, 1981, Section 5.3.6). Experience has shown that it is fairly easy to avoid the recurrence of specific types of deadlock, *once they have been discovered*; the hardest part of the problem is to find them!

Isloor and Marsland (1980) give a general review of the deadlock problem, with special reference to their occurrence in distributed data bases. They discuss the basic approaches to deadlock handling: detection techniques, prevention mechanisms, avoidance schemes and methods. They consider various mathematical models for detecting and analysing deadlocks, together with a combined approach to deadlock handling, and they report on some current implementations of systems for dealing with deadlocks.

Lai (1982) provides a comprehensive compendium of potential protocol "traps," that can lead to deadlocks, which have been compiled from the literature on computer networks. He describes ten different kinds of deadlock and four different kinds of message "ping-ponging", that can occur in computer networks. He concludes that, once the conditions for deadlock have been identified, it is relatively easy to solve them. The difficulty is to isolate them to prevent them at the design stage. Even with available automatic verification systems, it is still necessary to rely on human intuition and experience to deal with them.

Gelernter (1981) discusses a technique used to prevent "store-and-forward deadlock" on the Stony Brook microprocessor network, which is a sort of "network computer," with a ringlike configuration. Its users log in to the network as a whole, their jobs move from node to node, and the network is controlled by a distributed operating system, running on many nodes at once.

NETWORK PROTOCOL PROBLEMS AND ISSUES

Besides the problem of deadlock, considered in the previous section, network protocol problems include those arising in connection with: protocol architectures and layers, protocols for interconnected networks, specific protocols, the encryption of protocols, the formal specification, verification, validation and checking of protocols, and the assessment of protocol implementations. This section briefly considers each of these aspects in turn.

For WANs, it is generally agreed that the use of the ISO Reference Model for Open Systems Interconnection is usually appropriate. Kalin and Le Moli (1978) discuss the protocol architecture of LANS, and conclude that the use of this model seems to be sensible for LANs also.

Shoch et al (1981) examine the problems caused by mutual *encapsulation* of network protocols, where the protocol for one level is treated as data by a lower level of protocol. Although the concept has often been extended to internetwork protocols, the situation has occurred where different internetwork protocols have arisen. Several solutions have been proposed, including an even higher level of protocol; Shoch et al propose a simpler solution, for a specific example.

Cerf and Kirstein (1978, Section VI) discuss some problems of interconnection between packet-switched networks. All the proposed methods of interconnection aim to provide the physical means for a host computer on one network to be accessed by all hosts and users on all the interconnected networks. In order to achieve this objective, data, produced by a source in one network, must be delivered to its destination(s) in another network, and correctly interpreted on arrival there. Thus interprocess communication must be provided across network boundaries.

No such communication can occur without some agreed conventions. The communicating processes must share some transmission medium, and they must use common data conventions or use agreed translation methods, in order to exchange and interpret their data successfully. Sometimes, the required commonality can be obtained by translating one protocol into another at a gateway between networks; in other cases, the communicating parties can use the same protocols.

Issues that must be resolved, before a coherent network strategy can be defined, include: level of interconnection, naming, addressing, routing, flow control, congestion control, accounting, access control, and interest services.

As the behaviour of a network depends on its transmission medium and type, as well as on the specific implementation and control techniques that it uses, the interconnection of networks requires a simple and accurate classification of these networks, together with the development of mathematical tools which help to predict the performance of various interconnection topologies (Tobagi et al, 1978, page 1445). The coordination, control and collection of simultaneous measurements in several interconnected networks is of the greatest importance here, and experiments have been carried out to evaluate internetwork protocols and end-to-end user performance in a multi-network environment. Jacobs et al (1978, page 1460) refer briefly to the special network interconnection problems that arise in a configuration of neighbouring networks that includes a packet satellite network.

In the USA and the UK, research on wide area internetworking has predominantly considered the Arpanet or the value-added X.25 networks operated by the PTTs. Researchers at University College London have been building an interconnection facility, linking both these major internet systems, for use in these investigations. The services to be supported by this facility include interactive terminal traffic, file transfer, and electronic mail. Braden and Cole (1982) briefly describe these internets and the protocols, services and hardware used for UCL's interconnection facility. They end with a discussion, summarising the general interconnection problems that they have met.

Kirstein and Wilbur (1980) discuss the applications being developed on the Cambridge Ring at UCL, that include access between terminals and file stores, attached to the Ring, and resources on outside networks, and protocol conversion services, so that terminal users on one network can use another, and so that file and message services can be received from one network and transferred in another form to another network.

Higginson and Moulton (1982) describe the implementation of the UK Network Independent File Transfer protocol (NIFTP) over three different types of network: X.25, datagram (Arpanet), and local ring. They discuss the problems encountered, the performance achieved, and the impact of network characteristics on file transfer activities.

Price (1982) reviews work on data encryption techniques for assuring the integrity of data carried by computer networks, and defending it against passive and active intrusion. Standardisation of encryption algorithms and safe modes of operation is proceeding fast, and standards are also being prepared for incorporating encryption enhancements to lower level protocols. However, little has yet been done to encrypt higher level protocols.

Bochmann and Sunshine (1980) and Sunshine (1979, 1981) give general expositions of some of the methods for formal specification, verification and checking of protocols, with some reference to the requirements of LANs in the latter paper. Danthine (1980) considers the use of *Petri nets* for this purpose, and Symons (1977a, 1977b and 1978) considers the similar use of a more general technique, *numerical Petri nets*. Rubin and West (1982) propose an improved technique for the validation of protocols. Rudin (1982) gives some practical examples of automatic protocol validation.

In order to give users confidence in the protocol products that they need to buy, implementations of protocols need to be tested by a trusted independent assessment centre, which can ensure that they conform to agreed standards. The National Physical Laboratory (NPL) has developed suitable testing techniques for use by such centres. Rayner (1982) describes the theoretical basis that has been established for this work. Implementation assessment is being investigated by an international collaborative study, which will hopefully lead to the establishment of international assessment centres using internationally accepted testing procedures.

NETWORK OPERATING PROBLEMS AND ISSUES

Spratt (1982) discusses problems of management and control of the Cambridge Ring LAN at the University of Kent, which has been fully operational since the end of 1979. Cole (1982) considers the organisational problems, met in on-site computer communication, and discusses some of the opportunities provided by local networking. Gibson (1981) discusses ITT's networking problem as a multinational, trying to link its LANs. Branscomb (1981, Section 8) discusses several approaches to setting up and operating LAN communications within an organisation; for example, should the management of its facilities be carried out by a single computer, or should it be distributed between all the "intelligent" devices on the network?

Martin (1981) discusses operating problems and issues for WANs in Part 3 of his book, on strategy for distributed data processing; Chapters 10 to 13 are especially relevant.

Cerf and Kirstein (1978) raise the question of what network services are needed on an internetwork level. Obviously, interactive computing and bulk data transport services must be supported, but should facilities to support voice, teleconferencing and telemetry by provided as well?

Douglas (1981, page 7) points out that the installation of a computer-communications system within an organisation is fraught with difficulties; it is rather like carrying out a heart transplant. This is a socio-technical area where further research is needed, and implementers of networks will continue to have problems here for some years.

One of the most important considerations and problems in network operation is the adoption of standards appropriate for that network. Work on LAN standardisation has been carried out by the IEEE Standards Project 802 in the USA and by ECMA (European Computer Manufacturers Association) and other bodies in Europe.

The IEEE standards work has been described by Graube (1982), Myers (1982) and Sze (1982), for example. Bearing in mind the needs of the market and the different types of LAN already on offer, the IEE 802 Committee has proposed standards for two types of LAN access: contention access and token passing, and for three kinds of LAN: CSMA bus, token bus, and token ring.

Brenner (1982) reports on the progress towards LAN standardisation in ECMA; he briefly surveys the set of ECMA LAN standards, ratified by ECMA in June 1982, and comments on their significance as a step towards Open Systems Interconnection. In particular, the ECMA CSMA/CD standards are based on the Ethernet Specification and its progression by IEEE Project 802.

Heard (1982) discusses LAN standardisation activities in Europe, including the work by ECMA, CCITT, and CEC (Commission of the European Communities). He also describes the work of the FOCUS LAN project team in the UK.

REGULATORY PROBLEMS AND ISSUES

In almost all countries, transmission and switching services for long distance communication are provided by a regulated carrier, which is the national PTT in most countries outside North America, and which is one of the many public carriers in the USA and Canada. The operators of Value Added Networks (VANs) rent transmission equipment from the carriers but add their own switching equipment; they are themselves subject to regulations about what they may do, what traffic they may carry and what tariffs they may charge.

Cerf and Kirstein (1978, Section IX) discuss regulatory issues in relation to several types of network configuration and interconnection; Figures 17.1 to 17.4 originally appeared in their paper and are used to illustrate some of their comments about regulatory issues. In these figures, the letter H stands for host computer, T stands for terminal, S stands for switch, DN stands for data network. Figure 17.1

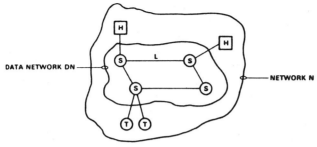

Fig. 17.1. Schematic of one network SOURCE: Copyright © 1978 IEEE *Proceedings of the IEEE* (Nov 1978), **66** (11) p. 1405, Fig. 15

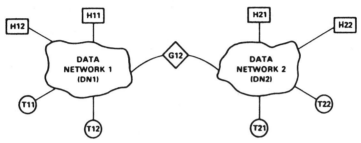

Fig. 17.2. Schematic of two connected networks SOURCE: Copyright © 1978 IEEE *Proceedings of the IEEE* (Nov 1978) p. 1405, Fig 16

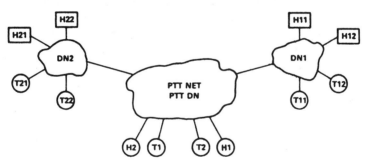

Fig. 17.3. Schematic of PTT model SOURCE: Copyright © 1978 IEEE *Proceedings of the IEEE* (Nov 1978) p. 1405, Fig 17

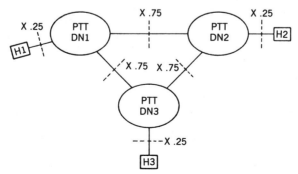

Fig. 17.4. Multiple PTT network interconnection SOURCE: Copyright © 1978 IEEE *Proceedings of the IEEE* (Nov 1978), **66** (11) p. 1405 Fig 18

shows a single network; if it is a LAN, for example, it can be treated as a single "host" when connected to outside networks. In Figure 17.2, the connection of DN2 to DN1 immediately changes DN2 to a VAN; in Europe, such networks, if private, may not connect directly to each other, but only through a PTT network, as shown in Figure 17.3. In the USA, the regulations are rather less strict. Figure 17.4 shows how different PTT data networks interconnect; note that the interfaces between them use the X.75 protocol, while their interfaces with host computers or LANs use X.25.

Mathison (1978) reviews the policy issues, relating to the structure and regulation of national data networks, and relating to the interconnection of national networks into an international packet-switched network system. He concludes that all public packet-switched network services will continue to be regulated, that competitive packet-switched networks will coexist in the USA and Canada, but that only one public packet-switched network will be allowed to exist in most other countries. He predicts that packet networks will worsen the problem of distinguishing between non-regulated data processing services and regulated data communications services, that public packet networks, using CCITT standards, will rapidly be interconnected internationally, and that there will eventually be a unified international packet-switched network system, similar to today's international PSTN and Telex systems.

Douglas (1981, Section 3) briefly discusses how commercial and political considerations are likely to restrict access to data. Douglas (1981, Section 8) considers that some degrees of government regulation of data communications must continue, as unrestricted competition between computer networks seems to be unworkable. Geller (1981) discusses bottlenecks to communication that are imposed by regulations, even in the USA, which is relatively liberal in this respect, and advocates that competition should be allowed to play a more important role, in an environment with fewer regulations.

Tyler (1982) reports that, in many parts of the world, the established "European model" of industry structure for telecommunications, which is basically monopolistic, is now being challenged. The rapid evolution of competitive telecommunications services in the USA has encouraged consideration of a more competitive approach elsewhere. Tyler reviews the issues involved in deregulation, defines broad policy alternatives, considers their advantages and disadvantages, and discusses some lessons from recent experience. While not taking sides on this issue, Hughes (1982) states some of the advantages of the monopoly supply of the main data transmission and switching network, and discusses some of the problems that may arise if deregulation is carried out.

ECONOMIC PROBLEMS AND ISSUES

This section is only brief, as most of the economic problems and issues are discussed in Chapters 15 and 16 and to some extent also in Chapter 18. For example, Chapter 15 discusses the study by Gitman and Frank (1978), that aims to identify and quantify network technologies that show low long-term operating costs.

Benstead (1982) points out an important economic problem that is faced by directors and managers of organisations considering the installation of LANs, computers, and other electronic office equipment. Many of these people are concerned by the very rapid rate of change of information technology and what seems like a flood of new products; these trends bring several dangers. Some companies may face too many upheavals, due to too frequent investment in new products. There are serious risks of obsolescence, and there is not yet any way to ensure the protection of capital investment in equipment, as user needs change.

Jarrett (1982, pages 119–122) briefly discusses some of the economic problems of office automation.

HUMAN AND SOCIAL PROBLEMS AND ISSUES

Like the previous section, this section is brief because most of the human and social problems and issues, arising from the impact of networking, are discussed in other chapters, especially Chaptesr 16 and 18.

Smith (1982) discusses some of the human factors that need to be considered, before national and international computer-based message systems become widespread in the public domain. Users need to be protected in several ways, especially from unwanted and unsolicited communications. While the present tendency is to increase the provision of communication resources, to bring facilities to more and more people, the emphasis may well switch, in the not too distant future, to the control and limitation of these resources.

Jarrett (1982) discusses some of the human factors arising from the introduction of office automation; for example, he considers the health hazards of VDUs, which can be minimised if due precautions are taken (page 135 to 139), and he considers the effect of information technology on the design and content of office jobs (pages 138–144).

Licklider and Vezza (1978, page 1344) state that some computer network applications will tend to alter significantly the nature of office work and the skills required at work. This will give rise to issues of education and retraining, appropriate pay for increased responsibility, and possible displacement of labour by automation. Another important issue is the impact of networking on productivity.

Davies (1982) considers several aspects of the man-machine interface in offices, and suggests several ways in which it could be improved. He also discusses the need to improve the productivity of professional and managerial staff, if the introduction of new technology is to become fully effective.

Hiltz and Turoff (1978) and Uhlig et al (1979, page 105) discuss some potential human problems of computer conferencing.

Lenk (1982) considers several problems arising from the social impact of information technology, including computer networks. Administrations may become less human and more bureaucratic, and their decision making may become more centralised. Trans-border data flow is becoming an important issue. Invasions of privacy, especially by bureaucratic authorities, could give rise to concern. In general, information technology makes society more vulnerable. Although Lenk's views may well be too pessimistic, the problems that he considers certainly give no reason for complacency, and they should be carefully investigated.

Douglas (1981, Sections 4 to 6) briefly discusses three examples of the social effects of computer networks, on automation, the availability of raw materials, and political control.

REFERENCES

V. Ahuja (1979) "Routing and flow control in systems network architecture," *IBM Systems Journal*, **18,** 298–314.

G. Akavia and L. R. Kleinrock (Sep 1979) "Performance tradeoffs and hierarchical designs of distributed packet-switching communication networks," Report UCLA-Eng-7952, Computer Science Department, University of California, Los Angeles.

E. Arthurs and B. W. Stuck (Sep 1981) "Multiple resource systems maximum mean throughput analysis," pages 201–211 of Pujolle (1981).

P. J. Benstead (1982) "The use of an existing PABX as the basis of an integrated office communications system," *Local Networks 82*, 97–108.

K. Bharath-Kumar and J. M. Jaffe (Sep 1982) "Routing to multiple destinations in computer networks," *ICCC 82*, 949–954.

G. V. Bochmann and C. A. Sunshine (Apr 1980) "Formal methods in communication protocol design," *IEEE Transactions on Communications*, **COM-28**(4) 624–631.

R. T. Braden and R. H. Cole (Sep 1982) "Some problems in the interconnection of computer networks," *ICCC 82*, 969–974.

L. M. Branscomb (Feb 1981) "Computer communications in the eighties—Time to put it all together," *Computer Networks*, **5**(1) 3–8.

W. Bux (Sep 1981) "Analysis of a local-area bus system with controlled access," pages 11–22 of Pujolle (1981).

V. G. Cerf (1981) "Packet communication technology," Chapter 1 of Kuo (1981).

V. G. Cerf and P. T. Kirstein (Nov 1978) "Issues in packet-network interconnection," *Proceedings of the IEEE*, **66**(11) 1386–1408.

J. Chammas (Sep 1982) "Response times over packet-switched networks—Some performance issues," *ICCC 82*, 993–998.

M. Cole (1981) "Organisational problems and opportunities," *Local Networks 81*, 21–29.

R. H. Cole (1982) *Computer Communications*, Macmillan, London and Basingstoke, England.

D. Conrads and P. Kermani (Sep 1982) "Some issues of transmission of packetized voice through store-and-forward data communication networks," *ICCC 82*, 725–729.

A. A. S. Danthine (Apr 1980) "Protocol representation with finite-state models," *IEEE Transactions on Communications*, **COM-28,** 632–643.

C. A. Davies (1982) "New systems and services for tomorrow's office," *Local Networks 82*, 1–13.

D. W. Davies and D. L. A. Barber (1973) *Communication Networks for Computers*, Wiley, Chichester and New York.

D. W. Davies, D. L. A. Barber, W. L. Price and C. M. Solomonides (1979) *Computer Networks and Their Protocols*, Wiley, Chichester and New York.

M. C. Davies, I. W. Barley and P. E. Smith (Sep 1982) "The effect of line errors on the maximum throughput of packet type computer communication and a solution to the problem," *ICCC 82*, 943–948.

A. S. Douglas (Feb 1981) "Computers and communications in the 1980's: Benefits and problems," *Computer Networks*, **5**(1) 9–14.

C. L. Doss II and T. D. Smetanka (Sep 1982) "The use of distributed topology databases for network routing," *ICCC 82*, 962–967.

I. Duma and G. Zbaganu (Sep 1981) "Markov renewal processes in modelling binary communication channels," pages 261–268 of Pujolle (1981).

D. Gelernter (Sep 1981) "Prevention of store-and-forward deadlock on a microprocessor network," pages 305–314 of Pujolle (1981).

H. Geller (Feb 1981) "Progress and problems in the 1980's," *Computer Networks*, **5**(1) 15–18.

M. Gerla (1981) "Routing and Flow Control," Chapter 4 of Kuo (1981).

M. Gerla and L. R. Kleinrock (Apr 1980) "Flow control: A comparative survey," *IEEE Transactions on Communications*, **COM-28**(4), 553–574.

P. J. Gibson (1981) "Local networks and the Multinationals," *Local Networks 81*, 31–45.

A. Giessler, A. Jagemann and E. Maser (Sep 1981) "Simulation of an X.25 network providing throughput guarantees," pages 279–290 of Pujolle (1981).

I. Gitman and H. Frank (Nov 1978) "Economic analysis of integrated voice and data networks: A case study," *Proceedings of the IEEE*, **66**(11) 1549–1570.

Ed. J.-L. Grangé and M. Gien (Feb 1979) *Flow Control in Computer Networks*, N. Holland, Amsterdam, Oxford and New York.

K. S. Heard (1982) "LAN standardization activities in Europe," *Local Networks 82*, 121–129.

J. Herrman (1976) "Flow control in the ARPA network," *Computer Networks*, **1**(1) 65–76.

P. L. Higginson and R. Moulton (Sep 1982) "Experiences with use of the UK Network Independent File Transfer Protocol on several networks," *ICCC 82*, 913–918.

S. R. Hiltz and M. Turoff (1978) *The Network Nation—Human Communication via Computer*, Addison-Wesley, Reading, MA and London.

P. A. B. Hughes (Sep 1982) "Monopoly—Do the advantages outweigh the disadvantages?," *ICCC 82*, 564–569.

D. Huynh and F. F. Kuo (1981) "Mixed-media packet networks," Chapter 6 of Kuo (1981).

D. Huynh, H. Kobayashi and F. F. Kuo (1976) "Design issues for mixed media packet switching networks," *Proceedings NCC 1976*, 541–549.

H. Inose and T. Saito (Nov 1978) "Theoretical aspects in the analysis and synthesis of packet communication networks," *Proceedings of the IEEE*, **66**(11) 1409–1422.

S. S. Isloor and T. A. Marsland (Sep 1980) "The deadlock problem: An overview," *Computer*, **13**(9) 58–78.

I. M. Jacobs, R. Binder and E. V. Hoversten (Nov 1978) "General purpose satellite networks," *Proceedings of the IEEE*, **66**(11) 1448–1467.

T. Jacobsen and P. Thisted (Jan/Apr 1980) "CCITT Recommendation X.25 as part of the ISO Reference Model of Open Systems Interconnection," *Computer Communications Review*, **120**(1/2) 48–55.

D. Jarrett (1982) *The Electronic Office—A Management Guide to the Office of the Future*, Gower Publishing Company, Aldershot, Hampshire, England, with Philips Business Systems.

R. E. Kahn, S. A. Gronemeyer, J. Burchfiel and C. Kunzelman (Nov 1978) "Advances in packet radic technology," *Proceedings of the IEEE*, **66**(11) 1468–1496.

T. Kalin and G. Le Moli (Sep 1982) "Standardisation issues and protocol architecutre for LANs ir view of OSI Reference Model," *ICCC 82*, 111–114.

P. Kermani (Sep 1981) "Analysis of a feedback scheme for congestion control in computer networks," pages 331–343 of Pujolle (1981).

P. T. Kirstein and S. R. Wilbur (Aug 1980) "University College London activities with the Cambridge Ring," *Local Area Network Workshop*, 115–130.

L. R. Kleinrock (Nov 1978) "Principles and lessons and packet communications," *Proceedings of the IEEE*, **66**(11) 1320–1329.

L. R. Kleinrock (Sep 1980) "Analysis and design issues addressed at ICCC '78," *Computer Networks*, **4**(4) 175–185.

Ed. F. F. Kuo (1981) *Protocols & Techniques for Data Communications Networks*, Prentice-Hall, Englewood Cliffs, NJ (with bibliographies).

W. S. Lai (Jun 1982) "Protocol traps in computer networks—A catalog," *IEEE Transactions on Communications*, **COM-30**(6) 1434–1449; an earlier version of this paper was published in *Local Networks 81*, 289–301.

J. Labetoulle and G. Pujolle (1981) "A study of flows through virtual circuits computer networks," *Computer Networks*, **5**, 116–126.

S. S. Lam (1981) "Design considerations for large mobile packet radio networks," *Local Networks 81*, 215–231.

K. Lenk (1982) "Information technology and society," Chapter 9 of Ed. G. Friedrichs and A. Schaff (1982) *Microelectronics and Society*, Pergamon Press, Oxford, England, and Elmsford, NY.

J. C. R. Licklider and A. Vezza (Nov 1978) "Applications of information networks," *Proceedings of the IEEE*, **66**(11) 1330–1346.

Local Area Networks Workshop (1980) Proceedings of the IFIP Working Group 6.4 Local Computer Networks Working Party 80/13 Conference, August 27–29 1980, Zurich, Switzerland.

F. N. Lohwasser (Sep 1982) "Network management for performance and reliability in integrated text and data network of the Deutsche Bundespost," *ICCC 82*, 748–752.

J. M. McQuillan (1977) "Routing algorithms for computer networks—A survey," *Proceedings of the National Telecommunications Conference*, 2.

J. M. McQuillan (Nov 1978) "Enhanced message addressing capabilities for computer networks," *Proceedings of the IEEE*, **66**(11) 1517–1527.

J. M. McQuillan and D. C. Walden (1977) "The ARPA network design decisions," *Computer Networks*, **1**243–289.

J. M. McQuillan et al (May 1980) "The new routing algorithm for the Arpanet," *IEEE Transactions on Communications*, **COM-28** (5) 711–719.

J. Majus and L. Hohe (Sep 1981) "Scheduling in packet switching systems with delay—Advantages and constraints," pages 399–408 of Pujolle (1981).

J. Martin (1981) *Design and Strategy for Distributed Data Processing*, Prentice-Hall, Englewood Cliffs, NJ, especially Part 5, "Software and Network Strategy."

S. L. Mathison (Nov 1978) "Commercial, legal, and international aspects of packet communications," *Proceedings of the IEEE*, **66**(11) 1527–1539.

A. J. Mayne (1986) *The Videotex Revolution*, second ed., Wiley, Chichester and New York.

R. M. Metcalfe and D. R. Boggs (Jul 1976) "Ethernet: Distributed packet switching for local computer networks," *Communications of the ACM*, **19**(7) 395–404.

W. Myers (Aug 1982) "Towards a local network standard," *IEEE Micro*, **2**(3) 28–45.

R. Nakamura, S. Tomita and S. Yoshida (1978) "DDX-2 field trial experience," *ICCC 78*, 17–22.

A. Nilsson, W. Chou and C. J. Graff (1980) "A packet radio communication system architecture in a mixed traffic and dynamic environment," *Proceedings Computer Networking Symposium*, 51–66.

C. G. Omidyar and K. A. Sohraby (Sep 1981) "Local control for integrated voice/data networks," pages 355–365 of Pujolle (1981).

M. Ossola (Sep 1981) "Routing principles for the eighties: Are experience and theory sufficient to settle for distributed and adaptive routing?" pages 35–44 of Pujolle (1981).

W. L. Price (Sep 1982) "Encryption implementation in a layered network architecture," *ICCC 82*, 883–887.

G. Pujolle (1978) "Analysis of flow-controls in switched data network by a unified model," *ICCC 78*, 123–128.

Ed. G. Pujolle (Sep 1981) *Performance of Data Communications Systems and Their Applications* (Proceedings of the Paris Conference, 14–16 Sep 1981), N. Holland, Amsterdam, Oxford, England, and New York.

E. Raubold (1979) "Flow control on the GMD-Network," *Interconnection of Computer Networks*, 431–468.

D. Rayner (Sep 1978) "Protocol impelemetation assessment," *ICCC 82*, 931–936.

E. C. Rosen (Feb 1980) "The updating protocol of ARPANET's new routing algorithm," *Computer Networks*, **4**(1) 11–19.

J. Rubin and C. H. West (May 1982) "An improved protocol validation technique," *Computer Networks*, **6**(2) 65–73.

Ed. H. Rudin (Apr 1981) Special issue on congestion control in computer networks, *IEEE Transactions on Communications*, Vol. **COM-29**, No. 4.

H. Rudin (Sep 1982) "Automated protocol validation: Some practical examples," *ICCC 82*, 919–924.

M. Schwartz (1977) *Computer-Communication Network Design and Analysis*, Prentice-Hall, Englewood Cliffs, NJ.

M. Schwartz and T. E. Stern (Apr 1980) "Routing techniques used in computer communication networks," *IEEE Transactions on Communications*, **COM-28**(4) 539–552.

J. F. Shoch, D. Cohen and E. A. Taft (1981) "Mutual encapsulation of internetwork protocols," *Computer Networks*, **5**(4) 287–300.

J. F. Shoch, Y. K. Dalal, D. D. Redell and R. C. Crane (Aug 1982) "Evolution of the Ethernet local computer network," *Computer*, **15**(8) 10–26.

H. T. Smith (Sep 1982) "Human factor issues in network communication systems," *ICCC 82*, 664–668.

E. B. Spratt (Sep 1982) "Local area networks: Management and quasi-political issues," *ICCC 82*, 143–148.

C. A. Sunshine (Sep 1979) "Formal techniques for protocol specification and verification," *Computer*, **12**(9) 20–27.

C. A. Sunshine (1981) "Protocols for local networks," *Local Networks 81*, 245–261.

F. J. W. Symons (1977a) (Mar 1977) "The description and definition of queueing systems, using numerical Petri nets," *University of Essex Telecommunication Systems Group Report*, **143**.

F. J. W. Symons (1977b) (May 1977) "The application of numerical Petri nets to the analysis of communication protocols and signalling systems," *University of Essex Telecommunication Systems Group Report*, **144**.

F. J. W. Symons (May 1978) "Modelling and analysis of communication protocols using numerical Petri nets," *University of Essex Telecommunication Systems Group Report*, **152** (Ph.D. Thesis).

D. T. W. Sze (1982) "IEEE LAN Project 802—A current status," *Local Networks 82*, 109–120.

Y. Takahashi, N. Shigeta and T. Hasegawa (Sep 1981) "An approximation analysis for congestion control scheme in distributed processing systems," pages 345–354 of Pujolle (1981).

A. S. Tanenbaum (1981) *Computer Networks*, Prentice-Hall, Englewood Cliffs, NJ.

F. A. Tobagi, M. Gerla, R. W. Peebles and E. G. Manning (Nov 1978) "Modeling and measurement techniques in packet communication networks," *Proceedings of the IEEE*, **66**(11) 1423–1447.

M. Tyler (Sep 1978) "Regulation and monopoly in public telecommunications: Theory and international experience," *ICCC 82*, 559–563.

R. P. Uhlig, D. J. Farber and J. H. Bair (1979) *The Office of the Future*, North-Holland, Amsterdam, Oxford, England, and New York.

P. Whitehouse (1981) "Design of application programs for distributed systems," *Local Networks 81*, 85–95.

W. F. Zachmann (1981) "Operating and applications system design opportunities for Carrier Sense Multiple Access bus local area networks," *Local Networks 81*, 379–389.

Chapter 18

Future Prospects of Networks

By combining the technologies of telecommunications and computing, computer networks are playing a vital and leading part in the development of information technology, which is rapidly transforming office work and business operations in particular, and the pattern of human life in general.

After considering briefly the experience of networking so far, and indicating some of the lessons to be learnt from it, this chapter describes some of the future prospects for computer networks and for information technology, taking into account significant developments that are either already in progress or seem likely to occur soon. On the technical side, it reviews prospects for computer network technologies and some of the allied technologies, for interconnection of local network systems, for network services, and for "intelligent" computer networks. On the human side, which is at least as important, it discusses some of the future economic, social and human impacts and potentialities of computer networks, and it ends by presenting some possibilities for social networks. Recent developments and views are presented in Chapter 24.

The Epilogue outlines the work and plans of the 'Peace Network,' a new initiative that is attempting the gradual conscious development of a new computer network for the benefit of mankind.

Martin (1981) describes computer network and other information technologies, their applications, and their possible future impact on human life. Jarrett's (1982) book on the electronic office includes discussions of the present and future effects of office automation, including networking, on the business and work environments.

Hiltz and Turoff (1978) and several recent articles in `The Futurist` explore various aspects of the human impacts of computer networking and information technology in general. For example, the North American Telephone Association recently collected and published the views of a wide range of people on the future of telecommunications (*The Futurist*, Apr 1982). The World Future Society (1982) has published a collection of papers, *Communications and the Future*, prepared mainly by presenters of papers at its conference on this topic in Washington in July 1982.

Mayne (1986, Chapter 16) surveys the present experience of videotex, one of the most important areas of application of computer networks, and discusses many of its possible future developments, together with some wider economic and social implications.

LESSONS TO BE LEARNT FROM PAST EXPERIENCE OF NETWORKING

This section considers in turn some experience of local area networks, office applications of networking, and wide area networks. It concludes by summarising some of the lessons learnt from the operation of wide area networks.

Rubinstein et al (1981), Spratt (1981), and Sweetman (1981) include reviews of their experience of Cambridge Ring installations at University College London, the University of Kent at Canterbury, and Logica, respectively.

Shoch et al (1982) give a very thorough description of Ethernet, and report on experience of its development from Experimental Ethernet, several years ago, to the Ethernet Specification, introduced fairly recently.

Pliner and Hunter (1981) review the properties of Sytek's LocalNet, a broadband LAN, and compare them with actual user requirements. They conclude that a broadband LAN, incorporating an open network philosophy, provides a wide range of benefits for users. They consider that LocalNet tends to enhance these benefits, and has been used successfully in a wide range of applications, including office automation, manufacturing data collection, and process control.

After discussing the range of applications of LANs and giving some examples of LAN configurations, Bass (1982) concludes that LANs can be used either to meet conventional communications requirements or as a basis for unconventional distributed network architecture.

In his discussion of LANs for new business systems, Fling (1982) concludes that LANs can provide a very convenient and cost-effective basis for future office systems. They have only recently become commercially available and he considers that they are still technically immature. Although they present opportunities for designers of new systems, care is still needed if users are to avoid the problems of over-sold systems that are not yet able to meet their requirements fully.

Naffah (1981) presents the results of INRIA's Kayak project in France, that is now investigating the prototype of a distributed office system, corresponding to the next generation of systems, and is integrating a set of compatible services offered via new work stations and server devices that are connected by a LAN.

Tapscott (1982) reports an experiment, carried out by Bell-Northern Research in Canada, to test the hypothesis that automated offce systems improve the productivity of office workers. A pilot system was developed, that had subsystems for: electronic message service, text processing, information retrieval, administrative functions, and analytical tools. It was found that the pilot system apparently improved the users' communications, use of time, attitudes towards office system techology, and quality of working life. In later tests, Bell-Northern will improve its ability to collect valid evidence, and obtain more evidence, of higher quality. These tests are expected to provide the information needed for useful product design, effective marketing, and successful implementation of the new technology. Tapscott believes that they should provide better designed office systems, using LANs, that are used, accepted and enjoyed by more office workers.

Taylor (1982) describes his experience of becoming a Telex user, during the initial period, 1982–1985, during which Telex services will be provided by several public data networks and be introduced into most of Western Europe.

Barnes and Graves (1982) review the operational and maintenance experience, gained in running British Telecom's PSS service; they include a report on experience of its pre-operational phase, starting with a public trial in September 1980 and continuing until PSS became fully operational on 20 August 1981.

The French public data network, TRANSPAC, opened in 1978, now has over 6000 X.25 subscribers and probably over 10,000 users. It has gained significant experience in managing, operating and maintaining its service, providing a considerable variety of data processing applications. Huet and Trottin (1982) survey the organisational and technical problems that it encountered, and describe some of the relevant solutions and methods that were chosen.

Runkel (1982) reviews the first year of experience with DATEX-P, the Deutsche Bundespost's public packet-switched data network. They describe this experience from the operators' and users' viewpoints, and report the results of some measurements of thoughput and delay, taken during field trials.

Kleinrock (1978) sums up some of the lessons learnt during the first ten years' experience of communication over packet-switched wide area networks. It was evident that users of these networks cannot insulate themselves completely from the underlying technology. Indeed, the service appears to them quite different from leased line services, and they may have certain decisios and options "thrust upon them" due to the nature of the service offered. Users should be aware of the consequences of certain decisions and network parameter settings, if they wish to avoid serious degradation of service.

Kleinrock shows how experience of the Arpanet and other packet-switched WANs led to important lessons being learnt about how to avoid network deadlocks and degradation of network service, and about distributed control, broadcast channels and hierarchical design; he outlines these lessons themselves.

He also states several principles, that can be viewed as lessons of special importance. The performance of WANs improves significantly as systems become larger. It pays to use "intelligent" network nodes, and the cost of providing that computing capability is falling far faster than the cost of telecommunications. Constraints on network design and operation are often necessary, but quite often also lead to risks of deadlock and degradation of service. The price to pay for organisation a collection of distributed resources into a cooperating group includes "collisions," control overheads, and idle capacity. Flow control is a critically important function in packet-switched networks, but much more needs to be known about it.

It can be dangerous to use old protocols in new network environments. It can be even more dangerous to leave network design to those inexperienced in it. The true sharing of data processing facilities in networks has still not been fully realised.

FUTURE PROSPECTS FOR NETWORK TECHNOLOGIES

Healey (1982) discusses future strategies for local area networks. He considers that at present the importance of LANs has been overestimated, but that investment in research and development on LANs and in pilot projects for new types of LANs is essential now, as LANs will be important subsystems in tomorrow's information systems. He thinks that, today, with a few exceptions, it is not economical to instal LANs, but that any large organisations, who are not prepared to instal some LANs now, on a trial basis, will be in danger of falling behind within a few years, when LANs do become economic.

Considering advances in information technology, he predicts that, in less than ten year's time, cheap desktop computers will have the power and storage capacity of today's mainframes. When digital telephone systems are introduced, data transmission rates over WANs will be increased by about ten times. Users will ask for more local control of resources, and distributed computing and storage will become easier. Such applications as text storage and retrieval and electronic mail will need much higher storage capacity than before, so that new mass stores, such as video-disks, will need to be developed further. The increased use of personal computers as work stations will make networking more attractive; its applications to the integration of voice and text, video and fax, communications and electronic mail, will make it essential. A growing number of vendors are supplying "intelligent" work stations, but, for local networking to "take off" fully, its media, such as coaxial cable, twisted pairs and optical fibres, need to become cheap, and connection of devices to networks needs to become easier.

Myers (1982a, pages 42–43) points out that the advent of LANs is bringing about quite extensive improvements in network technology. For example, the costs of station interfaces could drop from thousands to hundreds of dollars, when these interfaces become VLSI chips. LAN data transmission rates are already millions of bits per second. Bus networks are beginning to handle hundreds of stations, spread over distances of several kms. This growth in LAN capabilities is leading to more extensive use of distributed computing, resource sharing, and common data bases. Individual users will have access to more computing power, more peripherals and more information; as a result, they will be able to communicate more widely and work better. LANs will provide a new generation of network applications, some of which will perhaps be unsuspected.

Myers (1982b) reviews some trends in office automation technology. He envisages the possibility that the "office of the future" will have: a telephone-like terminal for speech input–output, an optical scanner, and a keyboard; a colour TV display with a resolution of one to four million points; a quality colour printer; local processing power between one and ten million instructions per second; optical fibre communications at 100–200 Mbits/sec. He foresees multi-function work stations handling word processing, data processing, and scientific and engineering calculations. However, he points out that none of these developments is inevitable, and that new applications and functions will be unduly accepted by users only if they can show improved productivity; those applications showing the best gains will be adopted first.

Yamazaki et al (1982) propose a design for a Broadcast Architecture Network (BANET) for distributed office systems. This would be a bus LAN, using a layered network architecture. It would provide special facilities for forming and dissolving "Communication Groups" among its users.

British Telecom's (1980) brochure about the British Telecom Research Laboratories at Martlesham Heath gives illustrative examples of the wide variety of research and development being carried out there at that time, not only on new telephone systems but also on new data communications and computer networking technologies as well as allied technologies. Projects have been started in the field of wideband transmission, which may have far-reaching effects for customer services that cannot yet be perceived clearly. Communication systems will become more and more interactive, with more facilities for feedback from users, and subscribers may soon be able to watch films and TV programmes of their choice at times that they choose.

Carne (1981) considers that future progress in telecommunications will depend largely on continuing advances in three major areas: the attainment of higher levels of integration (i.e. more active components per unit area) in digital circuits, the operation of communications satellite circuits at higher frequencies, and the development of a complete range of optical communications products.

Fibre optics is one of the new technologies that is making rapid progress and will contribute to the introduction of communications services with very high bandwidth. For example, Conway (1982) envisages that, in offices, wideband LANs will make possible television conferences for businessmen, who will be provided with two-way video channels as well as extra channels for fast data transmission, facsimile and other services. Petritsch (1982) shows how to introduce optical technology into a local ring, to increase its reliability; he considers an example of such a ring, with 27 customer locations, that can access each other, together with 20,000 special circuits, soon to be increased to 50,000. Schäffner et al (1982) consider the use of optical fibres for integrated broadband communications, which could well become the most economical way of implementing public telecommunications networks in the future.

Van Trees et al (1977) point out that satellite communication technologies, now being developed and expected to be implemented in the 1980s, can influence the economic viability of various satellite network applications and system concepts. According to Jacobs et al (1978, page 1466), the developments most likely to have significant impact include: the use of higher transmission frequencies, multibeam satellites, satellite on-board processing, and intersatellite links.

Leakey (1982) looks at computer communications from a rather original and unusual point of view. He sees their present trend as an evolution to increasing complexity of user requirements, systems, and technology, and wonders how far existing design and specification procedures will be able to cope with this situation. He suggests a radical change of approach, to match technologies of the future more adequately to user needs, and to make systems less susceptible to the effects of errors. Important future needs will include: incorporation of devices with high levels of integration, large increases in channel capacity together with dynamic allocation of channel capacity, ability to adapt rapidly to different mixtures of data, text, speech and vision, and ability to adapt to a limited number of system specification and implementation errors without having to redesign the system.

More specifically, he advocates the development of a new combination of circuit switching and packet switching, that he calls *code division multiplexing* (*CDM*), where sequences of pseudorandom numbers would act as message carriers, and where pattern recognition, rather than channel timing or headers, would be the chief technique for separating different messages. This would be a move away from present systems of precise information transmission towards systems catering for errors in an integrated way, with the necessary redundancy forming part of the message structure; Leakey believes that communication and pattern recognition systems inside animals and humans already operate according to these principles, which are thus "the natural way."

He states the following advantages of the proposed new approach:

1. Channels would no longer have to be defined precisely, and thus become more flexible.

2. Systems could be made more adaptable by building in self-optimization.

3. Each message would pervade a whole channel, so that messages would overlap in the time and frequency domains, and thus become less sensitive to the effects of noise.

Yasaki (1982) describes the Japanese ten-year research and development programme, that is intended to yield a "fifth generation" computer system, showing a considerable degree of "artificial intelligence." As it is envisaged that computers of this sort should have telecommunication links, genuinely intelligent computer networks may well become possible when these computers have been developed.

Herbert (1982) describes the design of a large distributed computing system at Cambridge University, that uses its Cambridge Ring network. This project aims to provide the sort of facilities, that are offered by time-shared systems using mainframes, but using distributed components. The key to its approach is that users are better served by personal computers than by sharing the limited resources of one central computer; but, instead of allocating one personal computer to each user, it has a central pool of small computers, allocated to users on demand for the duration of their sessions only; users still access the system through terminals. Users can also share the use of more sophisticated and expensive facilities, on a time-shared basis. This sort of hybrid approach, combining the principles of time sharing and distributed personal computing, could well become important in many of the office LANs and other LANs of the future.

Morgan (1979) considers that the convergence of personal computing, data processing and office automation is likely to play an important part in many business systems of the future, leading to substantial improvements in productivity and business methods. In his view, personal computers and other intelligent work stations will provide interfaces to users, and be able to access data processing and office automation services. Wide bandwidth links, using optical fibres for example, will be needed, in order to provide users with the full potential benefits of this approach. At present, the two chief obstacles to its implementation are that existing user interfaces to most personal computer, data processing and office automation systems are inadequate and not very user-friendly, and that much work still needs to be done on interfacing many different types of devices together in an intelligent way.

Morgan suggests that user organisations should take the following steps to prepare for the "interconnected future" that he envisages:

1. Whenever old office equipment is scrapped, consider replacing it by computer-based communicating equipment; this need not cost much more and should be very worthwhile in the long run.

2. If possible, user organisations should introduce pilot office automation projects, to find out the ways in which they are best suited to the larger-scale office automation that they may introduce later.

3. Make a long-range plan for the distribution and interconnection of information resources within the organisation, comprising both its structured data bases and its unstructured managers' and secretaries' files.

4. Educate all staff into present facilities and future possibilities for the applications of office automation and information technology.

Watanabe (1980) considers a strategy for the study of visual communications in the 1980s. He reports the findings of market research that was carried out to find out the major visual communications needs in leading Japanese business organisations. The system found to have greatest potential were: videoconferencing, interactive information retrieval, facsimile, document processing, and an office automation system combining all four of these functions. In the light of these findings, Watanabe describes a study programme for the 1980s and indicates which visual communications technologies should be developed.

Kornbluh (1982) looks briefly at some of the time-saving and energy-saving innovations that could transform the office world. These include: personal desktop terminals and work stations, "intelligent" word processors and telephones and communicating copiers, electronic mail, teleconferencing and computer conferencing, "electronic blackboards," computerised training devices, micrographic storage, and new devices for voice input/output and speech compression. Especially important will be the portable office, based on the "electronic briefcase," radio paging, and mobile telecommunications links. These new devices and techniques will make it possible to reduce interruptions and time-wasting "shadow functions," due to defects in present less advanced systems; they will automate several steps in the communication process, now carried out manually, and they will reduce the number of transformations needed between different communication media.

One part of this "office revolution" will be greatly improved facilities for test processing and preparation; a few examples of this are mentioned. Margerison (1982) describes some ways in which enhanced word processing facilities can be integrated with electronic mail and other forms of office automation. The book edited by Hills (1981) contains detailed surveys of various fields, such as publishing and librarianship, and presents well-informed and perceptive statements on the future of the printed word and other readable forms of text. Friedman (1981) discusses the extent to which paper will continue to have a role in the information systems of the future, with special reference to CAMIS (Computer Assisted Makeup and Imaging Systems) printing-on-demand, and Harman (1981) discusses recent developments of micrographics in relation to computing. Videodisks will play a progressively important part as very compact, relatively cheap, stores of pictorial, text, and digital information, as well as sound and voice.

FUTURE PROSPECTS FOR INTERCONNECTION OF LOCAL NETWORK SYSTEMS

Thurber (1982) considers various apsects of future LAN systems, including their connection of WANs and their linking with each other via WANs. LANs are already connected to X.25 networks, satellite networks, packet radio networks, networks using fibre optics, and back-end storage networks, providing massive amounts of online storage, and many more of these connections are likely in the future.

According to Thurber, LANs will be grouped hierarchically, within regions comprising cities and countries, through the use of public and private data networks and the use of radio and microwave technologies. Eventually, they will be linked across nations and continents. LAN technology is bringing about a reassessment of network architecture concepts, and is leading designers into the view of a "network" as a hierarchically organised group of cooperating LANs. The development and implementation of such linked local area networks are just beginning.

Healey (1982) points out that the linking of LANs to remote networks via gateways is becoming essential, as more and more users plan for a mixture of networks and services. Both manufacturers and PTTs will develop gateways, which will act as buffers and protocol converters to allow user-transparent interfaces. Some people in user organisations will need to become aware of the technical problems of coping with the conflicting claims of vendors and providing their own network services. Without some technical awareness, user organisations are likely to inflict severe problems on their real users, the work station operators who need transparency above all else, so that they can be free from worries about the operation of the network infrastructures on which they rely.

Tombs (1982) considers why the electronic office is still not much more than a theoretical concept, in spite of all the publicity that it has received and the optimistic predictions that have been made about it. He examines why this is so, and suggests that the "missing link" is a simple economical way of connecting word processing and text processing systems at different sites. He predicts that the international Teletex standard, recommended by CCITT, will provide the answer, as Teletex services, able to link distant word processors over LANs, will come into operation in Europe during the next few years, and will eventually appear worldwide.

Fergus (1982) describes GILT, a collaborative research project, where several European institutions are collaborating on the development of techniques and protocols to interconnect computer-based message systems via public data networks. GILT is developing protocols for message systems according to the principles of Open Systems Interconnection, and it is making full use of the existing X.25 and Teletex protocols.

Murray (1982) describes how British Telecom has already started to modernise its telephone network, by conversion to digital operations, using a range of digital transmission systems, based on the internationally agreed hierarchy of data transmission rates, 2, 8, 34, and 140 Mbits/sec, for operation over copper cables, optical fibres, and microwave radio links. British Telecom intends to accelerate its conversion rate, in order to achieve more quickly a high quality telephone service, offering enhanced facilities, as well as creating an Integrated Services Digital Network (ISDN), to meet more complex future requirements for mixed voice, text, data and image traffic. Hughes (1982) outlines a strategy for the evolution of British Telecom's network from a circuit-switched network to an ISDN providing variable-bit-rate channels. Arita et al (1982) propose a future digital network configuration evolving towards an ISDN.

Several projects are experimenting with the interconnection of local area networks by means of a satellite network. Kirstein et al (1982) describe the UNIVERSE project, where several British universities are collaborating with British Telecom, Logica and GEC, to investigate the use of concatenated Cambridge Rings, linked via small satellite Earth stations to the DTS satellite. The project plans to use UNIVERSE heavily for document and message traffic, multimedia conferencing, cross-network loading of computer programs, acquisition of network measurement data, and coordination of experiments, distributed computing, network performance, and encryption and authentication of messages. There will be demonstrations of voice, Teletex, videotex, and graphic messages.

Celandroni et al (1982) describe the current status and future plans of the STELLA experiment for satellite interconnection of LANs. STELLA was the first European wideband data transmission experiment to become operational. It is collaborating with the UNIVERSE project. Huitema and Radureau (1982) report on the NADIR project, which is studying the interconnection of DANUBE coaxial cable bus LANs through satellite links.

FUTURE PROSPECTS FOR NETWORK SERVICES

British Telecom has extensive programmes already in progress for the progressive improvement of its telephone and data network services; these have been described in several places (e.g., British Telecom, 1982; Jarrett, 1982, pages 85–93; Jefferson, 1982; McMorrin, 1982; Oliver, 1982; Smith, 1982)

British Telecom's installation of digital transmission systems and System X exchanges in the UK is the first step towards the development of an Integrated Services Digital Network (ISDN), which will eventually operate, not only throughout the UK, but also internationally. The ISDN will be able to provide end-to-end digital communications and support a wide variety of network services, including voice, text, data, graphics, images, and pictures.

British Telecom introduced IDA (Integrated Digital Access) as a pilot service in 1984; this will evolve into a rapidly developing full ISDN service during subsequent years. Proposed initial ISDN services in the UK include: circuit-switched data (2.4, 4.8, 8, 9.6, 48, and 64 kbits/sec), fax (64 kbits/sec), Teletex, viewdata (8 and 64 kbits/sec), private digital circuits, access to packet-switched services, slow-scan TV, and digital telephone services.

Each ISDN customer will be allocated an 80 kbits/sec channel, multiplexed in both directions on a single line pair in the existing local distribution network. This channel is subdivided into a main channel of 64 kbits/sec, for voice or data, an extra 8 kbits/sec channel for data, and an 8 kbits/sec signalling channel. The capabilities of the network can evolve in future to include packet and wideband switching. International standards will be adopted as they become available, so that the new services may be applied worldwide.

British Telecom already markets a separate Packet Switched Service (PSS), also known as Switchstream 1, carrying data at rates up to 48 kbits/sec, and offering customers significant improvements in service, including error checking and data protection, together with connections to similar data networks overseas, via its International Packet Switched Service (IPPS).

As a first stage, British Telecom will introduce an extensive dedicated private circuit digital network, able to carry its KiloStream services, at rates ranging from 2.4 kbits/sec to 48 kbits/sec, and its broadband MegaStream services, ranging from Mbits/sec upwards, and able to access its SwitchStream and SatStream services; all these services together constitute its range of digital services, the X-Stream services.

British Telecom is also modernising its long-established Telex service, which has over 90,000 users, by introducing computer-controlled Telex exchanges with store-and-forward, multiple delivery, and broadcast facilities, together with provisions for the interconnection of devices operating at different speeds with different codes.

British Telecom is already using Intelsat communications satellites over the Atlantic and Indian Oceans to obtain direct access to over 80 countries. From 1984, it will also be able to reach European telephone by Eutelsat. As the ECS satellite will be digital, British Telecom's first digital international switching centre will open in London in 1984, thus complementing the conversion of the land transmission and switching network to digital operation, and bringing nearer the implementation of the international ISDN.

Kelly (1982) reports on the interconnection of national packet-switched data networks in Europe, together with the resulting impact on new network services.

Four of these data networks are already operational, and 17 of them are expected to be running by the end of 1984. The Conference of European Postal and Telecommunications Administrations (CEPT) has agreed on plans for the international interconnection of these networks with each other, with Euronet (which was established late in 1979 to allow EEC users to gain access to scientific, technical and socio-economic data bases), and with overseas data networks.

Harris (1982) describes the trial of a fibre optic transmission system, installed in the rural communities of Elie and St. Eustache in Manitoba, Canada, to bring a variety of integrated telecommunications services to 150 subscribers. Each subscriber receives individual line telephone service, the Telidon viewdata system, nine TV channels, and six stereo radio channels.

Ramani and Miller (1982) propose the use of an inexpensive communications satellite in low orbit (100 to 5000 kms above the earth's surface), to provide an international telecommunications service, adapted especially to the needs of developing countries, where no data networks exist at present. The satellite would operate in a relatively narrow bandwidth (64 to 256 kbits/sec), and have a computer on board, which would poll the ground stations, and which would collect and store messages that it would distribute around the world.

Mayne (1986, Chapter 16) considers the present experience and future prospects of videotex, including public and private videotex services and videotex information services. British Telecom et al (1982a, 1982b) outline the Micronet 800 service, which was started in 1983, as a nationwide network of British personal computer users, who will be linked to Prestel data bases and telesoftware services.

Durkin (1982) examines the full potential of viewdata, especially in the context of business information systems. For example, it could alert busy executives to frames of data showing information on which they should take action, and it could provide an "electronic memo" service. Word processing operators could key letters, memos, reminders, reports, and minutes into a combined word processing-viewdata system, which could store most if not all the information now kept in bulky filing cabinets.

Rosner (1982) describes a project, now in progress, to establish a unified network and a homogeneous set of protocols, so that people working in British universities can access computing resources wherever they are. He describes the background to this project, explains the choice of protocols, reports on the methods used to implement them, and shows some of the benefits already achieved. *Computer Weekly* (23 Sep 1982) reports that plans for this network are now nearly complete, and that British Telecom is now discussing tariffs for this service. The network will use X.25 protocols, either over private lines, or through PSS. Universities will have gateways built into their mainframes or provided on separate small computers.

Muehldorf et al (1981) describe Worldcom, a worldwide automatic communication system, which is intended to monitor sensors at many sites round the Earth. This experimental system has been designed for the benefit of mankind, and the non-technical obstacles to its operation have already been overcome through special agreements.

It has been implemented and tested at ten sites in eight countries: Australia, Austria, Belgium, Canada, West Germany, Japan, UK, and USA. Ultimately, it can serve 500 sites, using the PSTN and robust 300 bits/sec data transmission channels. It continually monitors the integrity of its sensors, and it can detect any tampering with its own data and hardware. It can also monitor mobile facilities, as these carry satellite communications terminals.

With this system, it would become possible to construct data bases of global scope, which could be accessed quickly and reliably, at low cost, from any part of the world. Its potential applications include: monitoring United Nations safeguards and safety sensors, disseminating world weather information, providing worldwide medical information services, giving agricultural support to developing countries, and international banking.

"INTELLIGENT" COMPUTER NETWORKS

An "intelligent" computer network provides its users with versatile work stations, for example personal computers, that can be used to access a wide variety of facilities, available on the network or on other networks to which it is linked, and, above all, user-friendly, so that they can be operated with little or no previous training. This concept is best explained through an illustrative example.

Begbie et al (1982) describe iNet, the "Intelligent Network," that has been set up by Bell-Northern Research and the Computer Communications Group of TransCanada Telephone System, to provide a new set of value-added network services. It offers a wide set of user functions, including directories, access to information, filing, and message services. It builds on existing data network services, and it is an infrastructure for an information marketplace, including a videotex centre. After its completion and testing, it was offered to subscribers of the TransCanada Telephone System, and accessed from terminals located in their offices. Before this happened, a version of this service, with a limited set of facilities, was given user trials with 250 Telidon terminals and 150 alphanumeric terminals.

Whereas many if not most computer systems·put up barriers to online information usage, for people who have not had special training, iNET helps its users to gather, apply and communicate the information that they handle. It has three types of directories to help users find the information that they need: personal directories, organisation directories, and gateway directories, respectively provide guides to information about personal services, information relevant to the user's organisation, and external information, including that provided by national and regional information services. Other facilities provide assistance to users, when they want it, and help them remember the commands for accessing and using the system; they enable users to communicate with other users and send messages; they provide users with personal workspaces, where they can manipulate their own information and combine it with information retrieved from elsewhere; they include aids to administration.

FUTURE ECONOMIC IMPACTS AND POTENTIALITIES OF NETWORKS

As already mentioned in Chapter 16, computer networking and other forms of information technology seem likely to have at least four very important economic impacts: a move to an "information economy," a progressive extension of financial transaction services based on telecommunications, a substantial reduction in the demand for transport with accompanying savings of energy, and large effects on patterns of employment and work.

In Chapter 16 of *The Videotex Revolution* (Mayne, 1986), I discuss these impacts in general terms and also discuss the sharp challenge that they present to the present conventional approaches to economics, both capitalist and collectivist. Instead of repeating these arguments here, this section considers further some of the possible developments in electronic financial transactions.

Telecommunications facilities and information technology have already made possible a wide range of financial information services, available for example from both public and private videotex services, together with potentially extensive facilities for home banking, electronic funds transfer, and electronic shopping, already partially provided by some videotex services. Videodisk technology also seems likely to make important contributions to home information services though, at least not yet, to transaction services. Sutherland (1982) describes in moderate detail some of the financial information and home banking services that are actually or potentially available.

He also discusses the question of how far a public demand is likely to be generated from them. As for many other services based on new technologies, their initial marketing and development is largely a "chicken and egg" situation. While the services and the facilities that they use are still expensive, the demand stays low; while the market is still small, it is not possible to produce equipment on the scale that allows it to be cheap. In the case of services based on computer networks, this vicious circle is usually gradually removed with the aid of the rapid drop in prices of many though not all of the components of devices attached to networks and some of the equipment inside the networks.

Sutherland considers that the achievement of the "critical mass" for the electronic financial transactions market will depend largely on compatibility between various components of home information systems, which would be helped greatly by the adoption of suitable network standards. Those services most likely to use the PSTN are already beginning to provide electronic alternatives to several "ordinary" transaction services. They will be provided, and to some extent are already being provided by organisations such as banks, retailers, and both public and private communications companies. However, these organisations will not market them vigorously until much more consumer demand is evident. At best, market penetration seems likely to be fairly slow, with not more than about ten per cent of households likely to adopt these services by 1990.

To be accepted, these services must make it economically attractive for customers to retrieve relevant information from home, shop and buy from home, solve home management problems, and handle automatically such transactions as banking, personal investments, transport and hotel reservations, ticket bookings and purchases. In other words, these services must be able to deal with much if not most of the enormous amount of details which have to be attended to in contemporary living, as well as enrich and improve people's quality of life. Technically, all this is feasible, but much depends on what initiatives are taken by the organisations that can provide these services.

FUTURE SOCIAL AND HUMAN IMPACTS AND POTENTIALITIES OF NETWORKS

Several of the possible future, as well as present, social and human impacts of computer networks and information technology are considered in Chapter 16, so that they are not discussed again here. This section indicates some possible developments for new man-machine interfaces, and home information-communication systems. It then considers the human aspects of office automation, and finally makes some remarks on the impact on society in general.

The Telematic Society (Martin, 1981) discusses the following impacts of computer networks and information technology, among others: the changed patterns of urban life (Chapter 17), the shortened working week (Chapter 19), freedom and privacy and information (Chapters 21 and 22), and people's reactions to these new developments (Chapter 23). Martin advocates building the greatest diversity of information channels today, to maximise the chance of freedom tomorrow. Society should eventually formulate its laws and safeguards, so that computers can police the actions of other computers.

User interfaces with computer systems and computer networks need to be made much more accessible and user-friendly. Although some important progress has already been made in this direction, which is described in Chapter 16, many further improvements are needed.

The low resolution displays that are prevalent today are adequate for only some, but by no means all, of the complicated tasks for which they are needed. When high resolution displays become more widely available, they will be used in office systems and work stations to display clear images of whole A4 pages and simulate the handling of many pieces of paper at the same time; in the latter case, they will use existing techniques for dividing the screen up into several display windows.

Several attempts have already been made to introduce new types of keyboard, to make it easier for users to input information into computer systems. For example, the Microwriter, described in Chapter 7, uses a greatly simplified keyboard, that some users claim to find more convenient to use. Montgomery (1982) advocates radical changes; both by rearranging the keys, and by replacing key strokes by wiping movements across the keyboard. He has developed a prototype keyboard that uses these principles. One very simple improvement, that could be made to many, if not most, keyboards for terminals and computer systems, is to include facilities for adjusting the intensity of pressure that activates the key depressions;

in my own experience, keyboards are usually rather "sticky" and need fairly heavy pressure to register their key strokes.

Chapter 16 gives several examples of ways in which computer input/output devices can help disabled and handicapped people communicate more effectively with computer systems and with other people. Myers (1982c) surveys the contemporary state of the art of this application, and makes some future projections. In particular, he shows how personal computers could be used to improve the quality of life for the handicapped, and indeed recover a wealth of human resources that would otherwise be lost. He predicts that systems, catering for the blind, deaf, movement-handicapped, and voiceless, could reach a large proportion of people, handicapped in these ways, during the 1980s.

Carne (1981) presents his ideas for a comprehensive household communications-information system, illustrated in Figure 18.1. It would use a combination of new technologies, and be based on a home computer, supporting the functions of information and entertainment, command and control, and administration. He outlines the functions that the system would perform, in these different categories. His ideas illustrate the potential of advanced technologies to provide extra communications and information services that could be attractive to consumers and manufacturers. However, he points out that a total system of this sort will not necessarily emerge; much depends on the influence of existing interests and the importance of existing facilities.

Neill (1982) shows how computerised information, videotex, and other information technologies may shape libraries in the future. He emphasises that libraries may also be viewed as storehouses of traditional information, so that they will continue to provide books for their readers, in an environment not unlike that of today, in addition to providing terminals to computer data bases and information services. He sees four fundamental principles underlying the changes now taking place or being considered in libraries: the "right to know," the need for libraries to package information into the media most convenient for their users, the need for librarians to be involved in social changes and in the life of their own neighbourhoods, and the provision of information and knowledge needed by people.

Nelson (1982) presents a vision of a "hyperworld," a vast new realm of published text and graphics, all available instantly, a grand library in which anyone could place anything that he wishes to publish. He envisages that as a result people will be brought together by computer, rather than driven apart by television. As explorable graphics and simulations are added to the "hyperworld," the computer screen would become more and more a kind of shared social environment. He sees the need for these worlds, and they could soon become a new product that would pay. Their software is being developed. However, there is at present a shortage of the creative visionary artists, writers, publishers and investors, able to see the possibilities and translate these ideas into reality.

The June 1982 issue of *The Futurist* contains several papers about the office of the future. The paper by Kornbluh (1982) is summarised in the section on the future of network technology, earlier in this chapter. Mandin et al (1982) show that the office of the future could at best be a place of unparalleled creativity, providing

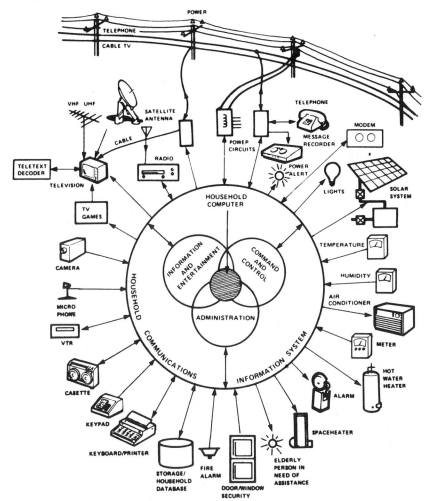

Fig. 18.1 A total household communications-information system   SOURCE: Article by Carne in Burke and Lehman, *Communication Technologies and Information Flow* p. 83 Fig 6.4, Pergamon Press

plenty of opportunities for its workers, or, at worst, a prison with a regimented work environment. They argue that its working atmosphere will be determined by management, not by new technology. Renfro (1982) views the prospect of office work in the home with mixed feelings; he discusses several psychological problems that could result, for example the invasion of the privacy of the home by a boss calling to check up on progress, and the lack of contact between employers and their workers. Applegath (1982) puts the case for working at an office in the home; regular office routine can stifle productivity and creativity, and work at home can save time, money, and mental energy. Probably there is no one clear cut answer as to whether people should work at home or not, when practicable; some people and families seem to be well-suited to it, while it would have bad effects on others.

What *does* seem possible is for most office staff to be able to work in offices much nearer to their homes, rather than commute regularly to city centres, as a result of new improvements in computer communications.

Business Systems and Equipment (July 1982) quotes a selection of views on the office of the future, including its human as well as technical aspects.

Computer networks will eventually have wide impacts on social life, especially through videotex and other home information systems. I state some of my own views on the future social and human impacts of videotex, in relation also to allied technologies, in *The Videotex Revolution* (Mayne, 1986, Chapter 18).

Computer conferencing is discussed in Chapter 14, and described in detail by Hiltz and Turoff (1978); recent developments are reported by Turoff and Hiltz (1982). One of its social consequences could be the emergence of "electronic tribes," a sort of "extended family." Perhaps the most important qualitative impacts of this new communication medium are the increased connectivity to ideas and people, that it brings about, and the liberating attitudes that it creates.

In their extensive discussion of the human and social impacts of computer conferencing, another very important form of computer networking, Hiltz and Turoff (1978, pages 489-490) express their belief that computer-based communications can be used to make human lives richer and freer, by enabling people to reach and use vast stores of information, and by providing them with opportunities for work and social intercourse on a more flexible, convenient and cheap basis than before. Although this is the vision behind their concept of a "Network Nation," they warn that policies and safeguards should be introduced, to choose and guide the implementation of alternative forms of these services and alternative systems for guaranteeing their security from interference or abuse. Otherwise, these networks could become the basis for a totalitarian network of control, much more comprehensive and efficient than hitherto.

Garrett and Wright (1980, pages 492 to 493) consider that computer networks could help to bring about a very fast and efficient decision making system, that could be used by a decentralised democratic society, and would be far more desirable than the top-heavy bureaucracies of modern parliamentary democracies. Networks could enable decisions to be made much more quickly, with much better responses to events, and at least in principle allowing all people in a group, instead of a delegate, to be consulted. This could lead to a form of participatory democracy, where many more people could become politicians if they choose. However, care should be taken to avoid any computer network or collection of information being controlled by any one group; this could be prevented by use of data bases distributed round the network. Central computers, if any, would merely route messages and transmissions to their appropriate destinations.

SOCIAL NETWORKS

During recent years, not only have computer networks been developed; there has also been a parallel evolution of "social networks," an increasing coming together of different groups and associations working on a wide variety of humanitarian projects.

This phenomenon has been especially marked in the USA, where it has come to be known as the "Aquarian Conspiracy" (Ferguson, 1980), and it has also been very evident in the UK. Social networks, that have arisen in the fields of culture, education, ecology and the environment, healing, medicine, business, and politics, are beginning to come together into a leaderless but potentially powerful broader network, working to bring about radical change in individual countries and in the world. This wider network, the "Aquarian Conspiracy," has already enlisted the minds, hearts and resources of people in all walks of life, covering a wide range of viewpoints, and several of mankind's most advanced thinkers are contributing to it. In the United Kingdom, movements such as Turning Point and communities such as Findhorn provide foci for members of this network.

A few years ago, several leading members of the network began to become aware of the potential of computer networks for helping their exchange of ideas and mutual cooperation on a variety of projects. In April 1979, the World Symposium for Humanity was held simultaneously in London, Toronto and Los Angeles. Unfortunately, its attempt to link its three conferences by satellite communications was unsuccessful, but it *did* gather some information from those attending, that was placed in a computer data base. Although it was a "failure," due to financial and other difficulties, it *did* bring together a remarkable and varied collection of people with mutual interests, and much cross-fertilisation of ideas took place and many new human links were forged. To this extent, the "Aquarian" network increased its size and coverage at that point in time.

Several new "social networks" emerged out of the Symposium. One of these, Nucleus, a small group of people based mainly in London, set up in May 1981 a project on "Cooperation for New Age Computers," in which I took part, just as I had attended the end of the Symposium itself. Another of them, Centre Link, proposed the use of Apple II computers to help bring together many groups and associations with similar interests. Although hampered by lack of financial resources, these projects usefully brought together representatives from quite a number of social networks, several of which have been actively considering the use of computer data bases and even computer networks. The Peace Network, one of the proposed projects arising out of these discussions, is described in the Epilogue. Since then, several other important social networks have developed and are continuing to emerge.

At the Onearth Gathering at Findhorn, Scotland, in October 1982, several of the "social networkers" present expressed keen interest in the possibility of using networks of small computers to aid their work; they clearly appreciated the potential of computing and information technology in general, when used in the right ways.

REFERENCES

J. Applegath (Jun 1982) "What's good about the home office," *The Futurist*, **16**(3)46.

T. Arita, S. Yoshida and K. Imai (Sep 1982) "Future facilities in digital network," *ICCC 82*, 19–24.

A. C. Barnes and J. Graves (Sep 1982) "Operational & maintenance experience of PSS," *ICCC 82*, 237–240.

C. C. Bass (1982) "Market development and user experience," *Local Networks 81*, 33–41.

R. Begbie, I. M. Cunningham and H. Williamson (Sep 1982) "INET: The intelligent network," *ICCC 82*, 285–300.

British Telecom (1980) *Telecom Research Laboratories*, Brochure.

British Telecom (1982) *Telecommunications for the 1980's*, Brochure with leaflets.

British Telecom/Prestel, Emap computers & Business Publications Ltd./Telemap Ltd., ECC Publications Ltd., and Prism Microproducts (1982a) *How You Can Connect to a Nationwide Network of Computer users*, Brochure.

British Telecom/Prestel, Emap Computers & Business Publications Lts./Telemap Ltd., ECC Publications Ltd., and Prism Microcomputers (1982b) *Micronet 800 Brings Your Computer to Life!*, Leaflet.

Business Systems and Equipment (Jul 1982) "The office of the future," 14–16.

E. B. Carne (1981) "Future household communications-information systems," pages 71–86 of Ed. T. J. M. Burke and M. Lehman (1981) *Communication Technologies and Information Flow*, Pergamon Press, Oxford, England, and Elmsford, NY.

N. Celandroni, E. Ferro, L. Lenzini, B. M. Segal and K. S. Olofsson (Sep 1982) "STELLA—Satellite interconnection of local area networks: Present state and future trends," *ICCC 82*, 425–430.

Computer Weekly (23 Sep 1982) "Plans for university net nearly ready," 6.

A. Conway (Summer 1982) "The significance of fibre optics," *dp International*, 9–11.

T. Durkin (1982) "Viewdata's role, present and future," pages 101–107 of Simpson (1982).

E. Fergus (Sep 1982) "The GILT project—Connecting computer-based message systems via public data networks," *ICCC 82*, 407–411.

M. Ferguson (1980) *The Aquarian Conspiracy—Personal and Social Transformation into the 1980s*, J. P. Tarcher, Inc., Los Angeles.

D. Flint (1982) "The local area network as the backbone of new business systems," *Local Networks 82*, 15–32.

H. B. Freedman (Oct 1981) "Paper's role in the electronic world," *The Futurist*, **15**(5) 11–16.

The Futurist (Apr 1982) "Telefutures: Prospects for telecommunications," **16**(2) 57–62.

J. Garrett and G. Wright (1980) "Micro is beautiful," pages 488–406 of Ed. T. Forester (1980) *The Microelectronics Revolution*, Blackwell, Oxford, England.

G. H. Harmon (Oct 1981) "Micrographics—Return of the 25-cent book?," *The Futurist*, **15**(5) 61–62.

K. B. Harris (Sep 1982) "Computer communications for rural subscribers, using a fibre optic transmission system," *ICCC 82*, 507–512.

M. Healey (1982) "Local area networks: Strategies for the future and alternatives for the user," *Local Networks 82*, 143–148.

A. J. Herbert (1 Oct 1982) "Distributed computing systems: Computing services of the future?," Paper presented at 25 Years of Computing Conference, University of Leeds, England.

Ed. P. Hills (1981) *The Future of the Printed Word*, Open University Educational Enterprises, Milton Keynes, England.

S. R. Hiltz and M. Turoff (1978) *The Network Nation—Human Communication via Computer*, Prentice-Hall, Englewood Cliffs, NJ.

M. Huet and J. J. Trottin (Sep 1982) "Field technical experience in the use of a packet switching public network," *ICCC 82*, 241–246.

C. J. Hughes (Sep 1982) "The long term future of circuit & non-circuit switching in multiservice networks," *ICCC 82*, 13–18.

C. Huitema and J. Radureau (Sep 1982) "Interconnecting local area networks through satellite links," *ICCC 82*, 431–435.

I. M. Jacobs, R. Binder and E. V. Hoversten (Nov 1978) "General purpose satellite networks," *Proceedings of the IEEE*, **66**(11) 1448–1467.

D. Jarrett (1982) *The Electronic Office—Management Guide to the Office of the Future*, Gower Publishing Company, Aldershot, Hampshire, England, and Philips Business Systems.

Sir G. Jefferson (Jun 1982) "Trends in telecommunications," *Electronics and Power*, **28**(6) 438–442.

P. T. F. Kelly (Sep 1982) "Interconnection of national packet switched data networks in Europe and their impact on new services," *ICCC 82*, 85–90.

P. T. Kirstein, J. Burren, R. Daniels, J. W. R. Griffiths, D. King and R. M. Needham (Sep 1982) "The UNIVERSE project," *ICCC 82*, 442–447.

L. R. Kleinrock (Nov 1978) "Principles and lessons in packet communication," *Proceedings of the IEEE*, **66**(11) 1320–1329.

M. Kornbluh (Jun 1982) "The electronic office—How it will change the way you work," *The Futurist*, **16**(3) 37–42.

D. M. Leakey (Sep 1982) "Possible trends in computer communications," *ICCC 82*, 8–11.

G. McMorrin (1982) "British Telecom's network for the future," pages 126–133 of Simpson (1982).

D. Mankin, T. K. Bikson and B. Gutek (Jun 1982) "The office of the future-Prison or paradise?," *The Futurist*, **16**(3) 33–36.

T. A. Margerison (1982) "Focus on word processing," pages 32–39 of Ed. A. Simpson (1982) *Planning for Word Processing*, Gower Publishing Company, Aldershot, Hampshire, England.

J. Martin (1981) *The Telematic Society*, Prentice-Hall, Englewood Cliffs, NJ.

A. J. Mayne (1986) *The Videotex Revolution*, second ed., Wiley, Chichester and New York.

E. B. Montgomery (Mar 1982) "Bringing manual input into the 20th century: New keyboard concepts," *Computer*, **15**(3) 11–18.

H. L. Morgan (May 1979) "The interconnected future: Data processing, office automation, personal computing," *Update Local Area Networks*, 291–299.

E. I. Muehldorf, F. J. Prokoski and R. Eier (Sep 1981) "A global data communications system," pages 367–377 of Ed. G. Pujolle (1981) *Performance of Data Communications Systems and Their Applications*, N. Holland, Amsterdam, Oxford, England, and New York.

W. J. Murray (Sep 1982) "The emerging digital transmission network," *ICCC 82*, 712–717.

R. A. Myers (Myers, 1982b) (Sep 1982) "Trends in office automation technology," *IEEE Communications Magazine*, **20**(5) 10–14.

W. Myers (Myers, 1982a) (Aug 1982) "Towards a local network standard," *IEEE Micro*, **2**(3) 28–45.

W. Myers (1982c) (Feb 1982) "Personal computers aid the handicapped," *IEEE Micro*, **2**(1) 26–40.

N. Naffah (1981) "Distributed office systems in practice," *Local Networks 81*, 627–641.

S. D. Neill (Oct 1981) "Libraries in 2010: The information brokers," *The Futurist*, **15**(5) 47–51.

T. Nelson (Mar 1982) "A new home for the mind," *Datamation*, **28**(3) 168–180.

G. P. Oliver (1982) "The Integrated Services Digital Network," *IEEE Conference Publication*, **209**, 8–13.

G. A. Petritsch (Sep 1982) "Introducing lightwave technology to customers' premises," *ICCC 82*, 502–506.

M. S. Pliner and J. S. Hunter (1982) "Operational experience with open broadband local area networks," *Local Networks 82*, 71–86.

S. Ramani and R. Miller (Sep 1982) "A new type of communication satellite needed for computer based messaging," *ICCC 82*, 322–326.

W. L. Renfro (Jun 1982) "Second thoughts on moving the office home," *The Futurist*, **16**(3) 43–45, 47–48.

G. J. Renier (Apr 1982) "The electronic investment system: Making money with your computer," *The Futurist*, **16**(2) 18–21.

R. A. Rosner (Sep 1982) "Towards OSI among UK universities," *ICCC 82*, 607–611.

M. J. Rubinstein, C. J. Kennington and G. J. Knight (1981) "Terminal support on the Cambridge Ring," *Local Networks 81*, 475–490.

D. Runkel (Sep 1982) "Experience with & performance measurements of the packet switching network in FRG," *ICCC 82*, 253–257.

H. Schäffner, H. J. Matt and K. Fussgänger (Sep 1982) "Optical networks for integrated broadband communication," *ICCC 82*, 518–583.

J. F. Shoch, Y. K. Dalal, D. D. Redell and R. C. Crane (Aug 1982) "Evolution of the Ethernet local computer network," *Computer*, **15**(8) 10–26.

Ed. A. Simpson (1982) *Planning for Telecommunications*, Gower Publishing Company, Aldershot, Hampshire, England.

M. Smith (1982) "A new network for digital data services," *IEE Conference Publication*, **209**, 177–187.

E. B. Spratt (1981) "Developments of the Cambridge Ring at the University of Kent," *Local Networks 81*, 503–518.

R. A. Sutherland (Apr 1982) "Home banking: Electronic money invades the living room," *The Futurist*, **16**(2) 13–17.

D. Sweetman (1981) "A distributed system built with a Cambridge Ring," *Local Networks 81*, 451–464.

D. Tapscott (Mar 1982) "Investigating the electronic office," *Datamation*, **28**(3) 130–138.

G. Taylor (Sep 1982) "Dateline 1985—A user's experience with Teletex," *ICCC 82*, 418–423.

K. J. Thurber (1982) "Open networks for mixed supplier terminal and minicomputer support," *Local Networks 82*, 61–70.

D. Tombs (Summer 1982) "The key to the electronic office," *dp International*, 29–30.

M. Turoff and S. R. Hiltz (1982) "Exploring the future of human communication via computer," *Technology & Society*.

H. L. Van Trees, E. V. Hoversten and T. P. McGarty (Dec 1977) "Communications satellite technology," *IEEE Spectrum*, **14**(12) 42–51.

T. Watanabe (Dec 1980) "Visual communication technology—Priorities for the 1980s," *Telecommunications Policy*, **4**(4).

H. Yamazaki. I. Yoshida and K. Hasegawa (Sep 1982) "A proposal for Broadcast Architecture Network (BANET)," *ICCC 82*, 115–120.

E. K. Yasaki (Jan 1982) "Tokyo looks to the 90's," *Datamation*, **28**(1) 110–115.

PART FIVE

RECENT DEVELOPMENTS

Chapter 19

Recent Developments in Network Systems and Services

This chapter describes some of the recent developments in commercially available systems for local area networks, personal computer networks and micronets, and wide area networks. Since the first edition of this book, new systems have come on the market for all these types of network, but they have been especially numerous for personal computer networks, micronets, and systems based on digital private automatic branch exchanges (PABXs). This chapter ends by reviewing some recent and prospective developments in computer network services.

References are given not only to literature about these new network systems and services, but also to some recent literature on systems and services already mentioned in the first edition.

LOCAL AREA NETWORKS

Several important books have recently been written about local area networks, including the following eight books.

Local Area Networks (Cheong and Hirschheim, 1983) aims to describe and classify LANs and their development. It provides a fairly detailed independent assessment of two of the major approaches to LANs, the Cambridge Ring and the Ethernet, and describes over 20 major LAN systems now on the market. Besides providing a broad overview of interest to actual and prospective network users, it contains a considerable amount of technical detail, especially in its Appendices. It is also oriented to the needs of user organisations, as it includes chapters on the capabilities and desirable features of LANs, the evaluation of LANs, future developments affecting LANs, and the organisational aspects of LANs with special reference to the human aspects of the implementation of LANs. It should do much to reduce the widespread confusion about what LANs aim to do and what can actually be achieved with the local network products currently available.

The *Data Ring Main* (Flint, 1983) describes what LANs are and what they can do. It discusses why they are needed, and how they can be used effectively to link together different pieces of computing and communications equipment in an office building or factory. It considers the classification of network systems, and includes a comprehensive description of existing network systems and technologies. It includes a presentation of local network architectures, standards, and protocols. Turning to aspects of special interest to network users, it considers the potentialities and role of LANs in a changing business environment, and gives guidance on how an organisation can establish its requirements for a LAN and make a suitable choice; it includes a list of questions which can be put to a potential supplier of a network.

Digital Equipment Corporation's book *Introduction to Local Area Networks* (DEC, 1982a) gives a very useful explanation of the general principles and some of the technical details of local area networking. After giving a brief history of the evolution of LANs, it has chapters on network topology and control, channel control and allocation and access, circuit switching and packet switching, transmission media, communication standards and network architecture, LAN components, private bench exchanges, broadband LANs and baseband LANs. It makes relatively little mention of specific LAN systems and products, apart from its descriptions of the Ethernet LAN system (developed and marketed jointly by Xerox, DEC, and Intel), other DEC products, and Digital Network Architecture (DNA).

Local Networks (Franta and Chlamtac, 1983) is aimed mainly at on-site network technologists and engineers, and is concerned with technical rather than management aspects. It covers local network structures and organisation, protocols, modelling, and measurement.

Local Networks—An Introduction (Stallings, 1984) is a useful user-oriented introduction. *Local Network Technology* (Stallings, 1983) is a companion to this textbook, covering the same topics and containing reprints of many key references.

The *Local Network Handbook* (Davis, 1982) is a collection of 37 articles from the journal *Data Communications*. It has sections on technology, software, equipment, implementation, applications, and selections of LANs.

Another book with the title *Local Area Networks* (Gee, 1982) describes the various types of LANs and indicates their chief application areas. It describes available network technologies and network sharing techniques, the PABX approach, research systems, and recent developments. It then discusses the LAN standards situation, the choice of a LAN, and future possibilities.

The same author's later book *Introduction to Local Area Computer Networks* (Gee, 1983) presents the characteristics, topologies, and data transmission technologies of LANs. It describes examples of LAN systems and applications, and discusses software and hardware requirements and performance characteristics.

The book edited by Ravasio et al (1982) is the published proceedings of the Symposium on Local Computer Networks, held in Florence in April 1982; it contains a useful collection of papers about research on LANs.

Computer Networks (1983) reports on another fairly recent event, the 7th Conference on Local Computer Networks, held in Minneapolis in October 1982. It had sessions on: implementation strategies, modelling and performance, system concepts, user considerations, and protocol concepts.

The November 1983 issue of *IEEE Journal on Selected Areas in Communications*, Vol. **SAC-1**, No. 5, is a special issue on local area networks (Kuemmerle et al, 1983).

Useful articles, reviewing the different kinds of LANs and the available LAN systems, include those by Gee (1984), Hart (1984), Jennings (1983a), Bradshaw (1983) and Ditlea (1982); *Communications Management* (1984a) provides a buyer's guide to a typical selection of LANs now on the market in the UK.

Mills (1984) classifies LANs into local computer access networks, local computer networks, and integrated networks.

In *local computer access networks*, most of the computing resources reside in relatively few locations, and the requirement is just to provide terminal users with access. For most applications, data rates up to 9.6 kbits/sec are adequate, a terminal interface can cost less than $250, perhaps much less, and a terminal can cost around $600. Local computer access networks with 400 to 500 nodes are quite common, and networks of this type can have thousands of nodes. All LAN vendors consider this aspect of networking, although cost and effectiveness vary considerably between different techniques.

Local computer networks support high-speed, high-volume applications, such as large file transfers, distributed processing, and load sharing between closely located devices communicating over a shared medium. Data rates for attached devices may range from a few tens of kbits/sec, for word processors and personal computers, to tens of Mbits/sec for communications between mainframes. Networks of this sort should provide an error-control protocol. They are limited to about 256 nodes, and usually have less than 16 nodes. Each such network uses a shared distribution medium, has half-duplex transmission, and adopts a special (non-X.25) form of packet switching. Costs tend to be high. Well-known examples include Ethernet, Hyperchannel, and Cluster One.

Integrated networks go beyond local computer networks, by handling voice and/ or image data, as well as ordinary data. However, few applications need simultaneous real-time voice and text input/output. The two approaches currently offered to integrated networking are broadband (CATV-based) and PABX-based, but neither of them is cost-effective for terminal-to-computer applications. Broadband systems on the market include LocalNet, Net/One (broadband version), and Wangnet. Vendors of PABX-based systems include InteCom, Northern telecom, and Rolm.

Davidson (1981) introduces yet another classification of LANs into: *processing nets*, whose components provide an environment for executing user-oriented computing and information processing tasks; *communication nets*, whose components are used to interface pieces of equipment to the net's communication mechanisms, so that user devices can exchange information with each other; *standardised nets*, such as Ethernet, which provide network services for a wide range of vendor devices that can be attached. He argues that, of these three types, communication nets are most likely to meet the varied needs for communication in the "office of the future."

Chapter 3 of the book by Needham and Herbert (1982) describes the original Cambridge Ring, at Cambridge University, with special reference to its packet protocol (also considered in its Appendix) and its performance. Most of the book is about the use of the Cambridge Ring as a distributed computing system.

IBM has been working on a new type of LAN using token passing control in a star-ring configuration. This type of token ring is described by Terrell (1983), Strole and Andrews (1983), Dixon et al (1983), Reagan (1983), and Voysey (1984a). It is claimed that this approach will make it easier to integrate the required functions into future office systems and terminal-based systems; in particular, that it will be able to cope better with a wide variety of attached devices and cater for traffic between LANs at different sites.

The IBM token ring has a data rate of at least 4 Mbits/sec, and it is fault tolerant, with automatic bypassing of nodes that fail. Rings of this sort are believed to be easily accessible, very reliable, and easily extensible in both function and physical size. Different IBM rings, including those of all three types, with different operating speeds, can be linked by a "ring backbone" (Reagan, 1983).

IBM has announced its intention to implement an SNA-compatible token ring LAN on its cabling system. It has also announced its intention for a broadband token bus LAN for industrial applications, implemented on CATV cable.

NEC Information Systems has developed the C&C-Net Loop 6770, a fiber optic ring LAN, using token passing access, and designed chiefly for high-speed data transfer between computers (Campbell, 1983). It has a data rate of 32 Mbits/sec and is easy to modify, expand, and maintain.

Master Systems (Data Products) Ltd. has developed a small low-cost star network, Officemaster, linking up to eight multi-function work stations, and easy to integrate with this company's MASTERNET LAN, previously known as the Xionics XINET (Master Systems, 1983a).

Ebiharo et al (1983) present the concept and structure of GAMMA-NET, a full-scale high-performance LAN, linked by a dual optical fibre ring bus, with data rate 32 Mbits/sec, and they give some of its experimental results. The design goals of this LAN are efficient resource sharing and improved reliability, serviceability, and availability.

Stevens (983) describes ICL's new MACROLAN high-performance LAN, which was designed to meet the needs of those users who require a LAN to have a performance level more like that of a dedicated link. Its network topology is typically a network of linked stars, and it uses fibre-optics transmission at a data rate of 50 Mbits/sec.

Boulton and Lee (1983) and Voysey (1984b) describe the University of Toronto's Hubnet, an experimental LAN using optical fibres, which has a data rate up to 50 Mbits/sec and a "dual rooted tree" configuration which is not unlike a multiple star. It is said to produce better performance than other types of LAN for heavy or sudden traffic loads.

Lindsay (1982) proposes a LAN design that is potentially more powerful than other approaches. It has a "coincident star" configuration, which could be very reliable, simple to build, and able to support such new services as video conferencing.

Hill (1982) describes the "Dragnet" topology, which is in some ways like that of Ethernet, but differs in other respects. He discusses the strengths and weaknesses of the Dragnet approach and states that Dragnet and Ethernet are compatible and could be combined into a hybrid network.

Sikora and Franke (1983) describe American Bell's new LAN using a centralised-bus architecture, which is said to combine many of the advantages of distributed and centralised approaches to LAN organisation, and to fit in well with voice-oriented PABXs, thus allowing close integration of voice and data nets. Its modular approach allows it to interface to many types of devices, to link easily with other LANs, and to communicate with WANs via gateways.

ICL's Microlan uses a simple coaxial cable, of length up to 300 metres, to join up to 16 ICL DRS 20 work stations (ICL, 1983a). It has a data rate up to 1 Mbits/sec, and its work stations can perform either different aspects of the same job or totally different office jobs.

ICL's *OSLAN (Open Systems Local Area Network)* provides a main data highway to carry voice, data and text along an office building (ICL, 1983b). It is suitable for office applications that are too large to be handled by Microlan. It can link up to 100 work stations, and it has length up to 1500 metres, and data rate up to 10 Mbits/sec. As shown in Figure 19.1, it can handle a wide range of business services, and it can use a DNX-2000 PABX to access WANs and remote LANs at other sites of a company.

Reagan (1983) describes the AT&T LAN, whose "Databit" nodes have unconstrained topologies and can be linked over long distances. It has modular construction, and is accessed by asynchronous terminals.

The Lanier System 5000 is an office LAN, using a coaxial cable with data rate 1.25 Mbits/sec (*Computer Weekly*, 1983a). It provides support for word processing, electronic mail and filing, personal computing, and management decision support, together with instant access to information through colour graphics displays. The system carries out four functions: network management, data base service, background computing, and communications; as many as 4000 stations can be attached to it if multiple System 5000 processors are used.

Comm Ponents is a modular data communications system, developed by the British company, Network Products (*Computer Weekly*, 1984). It offers a set of hardware and software modules, allowing users to create a versatile network, which can be expanded and adapted to future requirements, by adding and changing modules. Modules, contained in a chassis, can communicate at up to 48 Mbits/sec, and an interchange bus between chassis has data rate up to 80 Mbits/sec.

Several new broadband LANs have been developed. Hackett (1983) describes the present state of the art of the Interactive Systems/3M Videodata system, which has a bandwidth of 449 MHz, and can handle over 2000 attached devices. It can support many services together, and be applied to videoconferencing, surveillance, energy management, and factory automation, besides the usual LAN functions.

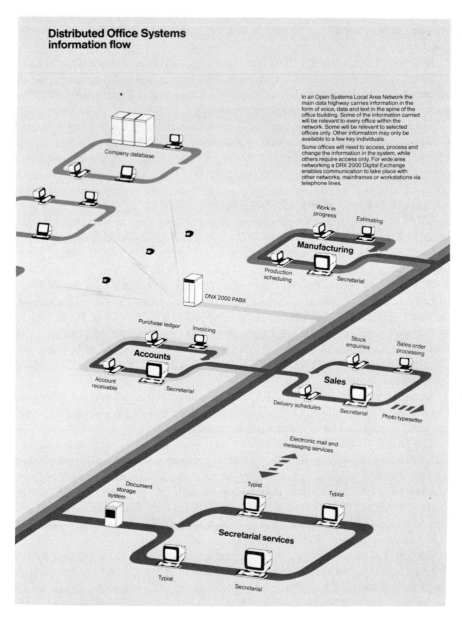

Distributed Office Systems information flow

In an Open Systems Local Area Network the main data highway carries information in the form of voice, data and text in the spine of the office building. Some of the information carried will be relevant to every office within the network. Some will be relevant to selected offices only. Other information may only be available to a few key individuals.

Some offices will need to access, process and change the information in the system, while others require access only. For wide area networking a DRX 2000 Digital Exchange enables communication to take place with other networks, mainframes or workstations via telephone lines.

Fig. 19.1. Distributed office systems information flow   SOURCE: *ICL Distributed Office Systems Wordprocessing,* ICL Brochure, p. 11

The Philips SOPHO-LAN uses a single CATV cable, with bandwidth 440 MHz, to carry audio, image, and video information, as well as text and data; the data can be carried on high-speed, medium-speed, or low-speed data channels (Philips Business Communications, 1983a). It allows any compatible equipment on the network, which can include devices made by many manufacturers, to communicate directly with any other without using an expensive "switch." It has modular construction and multi-mode operation, and is claimed to be user-friendly, flexible, reliable, and easy to integrate into wide area networking and global communications, especially through the SOPHO-NET WAN described later in this chapter.

Ferranti Broadband uses a coaxial cable of bandwidth up to 440 MHz to link one or more host computers to a wide variety of remote terminals (Ferranti, 1983). It is said to be convenient to use, easy to expand, and economical to operate.

Computer Automation's *SyFAnet*™ (*System For Access network*) is a broadband-bus network, which uses the *CSMA/CA (Carrier Sense Multiple Access/Collision Avoidance)* access method to increase throughput. Colvin (1983) describes SyFAnet and the CSMA/CA protocol in some detail. SyFAnet can link microprocessor-based, multifunction work stations, using the CP/M-86 operating system. It can have X.25 and SNA connections to mainframes and WANs round the world. It is fully integrated, flexible, and capable of expansion. Its powerful processors, one for applications and another for sharing resources, make it more reliable.

There has been increasing interest in the implementation of LANs based on private automatic branch exchanges (PABXs), and several new products have been developed here.

Roberts (1983) reviews the status of integrated voice/data PABX-based systems and outlines the characteristics of systems of this sort, already available on the American market or to be launched there soon. The companies supplying these systems or about to supply them include: ROLM, GTE, NEC, Harris/DTX, Ericsson, American Bell, Mitel, Plessey, and Siemens.

Camrass (1983) discusses current developments in PABX-based systems, and shows how PABX suppliers are now actively exploiting new technologies, in order to add value to their traditional switching products. As a result, network users are faced with a wide, sometimes rather confusing, choice of alternative systems. According to Camrass, changing market conditions are stimulating new product development here, especially for the larger systems. PABX systems have evolved from the first generation stand-alone PABXs to the second generation digital network PABX systems; and third generation integrated switching networks are now beginning to emerge.

The CASE Beeline system uses a compact PABX, which can give all the existing and future computers, terminals, word processors, and telex machines of an office site the potential ability to contact each other, whatever the types and models of these devices (CASE, 1983a). Beeline offers direct connections to up to 1024 local devices at speeds up to 9600 bits/sec, as well as to WANs.

The IAL Flexinet Local Area Distribution System (LADDS) allows a user organisation to interconnect and integrate new and existing office data processing equipment into its local and outside computing services, using its existing telephone wires without interruption of normal speech operation (IAL Data Communications, 1983a). Thus, the installation of Flexinet is easy and causes no disruption. Flexinet equipment consists of access units in offices, which link users' terminals to the office telephone lines, and a data PABX, to which each terminal's data stream is connected after separation from the telephone system. Other IAL products may be introduced, to satisfy the specific needs of an individual organisation. Applications of Flexinet include office-to-office data communications, shared computing and word processing facilities, and office links to outside computers; a user needs only one terminal to perform all of these applications.

The IAL Datex-90 system provides independent full duplex data links, by allowing speech plus data to be transmitted rapidly over existing telephone networks (IAL Data Communications, 1983b). Its subscriber unit can be installed quickly, next to any data terminal and telephone. An exchange unit at the user's PABX separates data and voice channels.

ICL's DNX-2000 PABX, starting as a telephone exchange, can be extended to handle integrated voice and data, becoming part of a full-scale office system (ICL, 1983d, page 32). Such a system might include PABXs, LANs such as ICL's OS-LAN, mainframe computers, terminals, electronic mail stations, word processors, and electronic printers. It is very compact, can handle economically at least 250 extensions, and eventually up to 10,000 extensions.

Micom Systems Inc. has recently developed the INSTANET™ LAN (Micom Systems and Micom-Borer, 1983; Holder, 1983). It is designed as a star network round a Micom Micro 600 data PABX, which can provide port selection and switching for up to 1500 input/output lines with data rates up to 9600 bits/sec. Figure 19.2 shows a typical configuration, with a variety of local device connections, together with PSTN and WAN access to remote terminals, WANs, and other INSTANET LANs.

Bain (1983) discusses the co-located system approach to LANs, which he considers able to meet the criteria applied by most organisations when choosing a LAN system. It uses a central PABX for switching and for carrying voice traffic. It directs non-voice traffic, through a LAN technology switch in the PABX, to separate LANs, cluster controllers, and gateways to other networks. Each user of the system can access both voice and data through existing telephone wiring.

Additional references to Cambridge Rings and allied LANs: Coen (1983), Enrico et al (1983), Hutchison (1983), Locke-Wheaton (1983), Logica VTS (1983), Lees (1983), Racal-Milgo (1983), Roworth and Cole (1983).

Additional references to other ring LANs: Hawker Siddeley (1983), Master Systems (1983b).

Additional references to Ethernet: Enrico et al (1983), Hutchison (1983), Kellond (1983), Wolfberg (1982).

Additional references to the Datapoint ARC bus network: (Datapoint, 1982; 1983a to 1983c).

Additional references to the Sytek LocalNet™ broadband network: Network Technology and Sytek (1983).

Additional reference to CASE Grapevine network: CASE (1983b).

Additional references to LANs using PABXs: CASE (1983b), Fratta et al (1981), Gandalf (1982), Hara (1983), Kingsmill (1983), Plessey Communications Systems (1983).

PERSONAL COMPUTER NETWORKS AND MICRONETS

A considerable number of new personal computer network systems have come on the market during the last year or two. Some of them are described briefly in this section, and most of them are bus networks.

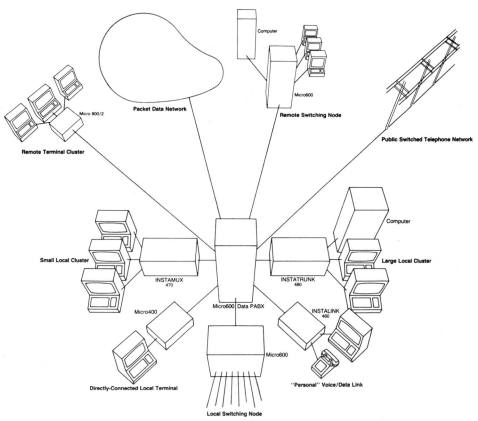

Fig. 19.2. INSTANET™ ... MICOM's Instant Local Network SOURCE: Courtesy of Micom Systems, Inc. and Micom-Borer Ltd. (INSTANET Brochure, inside back cover)

CLEARWAY is a low-cost ring network, developed by the British company Real Time Developments (1982). It can connect with almost any personal computer, printer, or modem that has an RS-232 interface. It can use ordinary home TV cable and is very simple to install. It can link up to 99 nodes, each attached to an RS-232 device, and can handle up to about 25 devices without noticeable loss of speed. Its ring speed is 56 kbits/sec and its device interface speed is up to 9600 bits/sec. This means that it can perform data transfers to and from floppy disks, but not to and from hard disks for which a more expensive networking system is needed.

V-NET is a low-cost, very easy to install, modular system for connecting up to 32 microcomputers into a simple LAN (Midlectron, 1983; *Communications Management*, 1984b). It uses the RS-232-C interface, and allows data to be transmitted between micros at rates up to 9.6 kbits/sec. Normally, its stations should be within 75 metres of each other, but the range can be extended up to 1000 metres, using special cables and interfaces. Communication over WANs can be added by attaching a modem to any station. V-NET interfaces with Ethernets and Cambridge Rings are being developed. Midlectron claims that V-NET has the lowest price for any fully functional LAN now on the market.

TORCHNET is a combined hardware/software package for inexpensive linking of between two and 254 TORCH personal computers in a simple, easily expandable way (Torch Computers, 1983). It allows TORCH computers, running sophisticated business programs, to communicate with each other and share information. It also offers the capability of running NET-MAIL, a complete electronic mail system, which can be run locally and access external electronic mail, for example, Telecom Gold, initiate telex transfers, and communicate with IBM, ICL, and other TORCH systems.

Vector Graphic has developed the low cost SABER-NET micronet, using the LINC™ (Local Interactive Network Communications) operating system. This network can connect different Vector 4 microcomputers without the need for special file servers, print servers, and communication servers (Vector Graphic, 1982; *The Vector Graphic Journal*, 1983; Reichert, 1983). It uses an ingenious combination of ring and bus technologies with a token passing system, and achieves a data rate of 750 kbits/sec over ordinary telephone cable. Ordinary CP/M software applications, including word processing and data base, can be run on LINC, together with electronic mail, using Vector Graphic MaiLINC software. Vector Graphics is about to upgrade its system in several respects, for example, by introducing its Vector VSX work stations, with 16-bit as well as 8-bit microprocessors, and by improving its operating systems. It maintains full compatibility between successive generations of its products.

The Altos TeamNet II allows up to 32 Altos 586/986 16-bit Teamcomputers with up to 288 terminals to be linked together (Altos Computer Systems, 1983). The system can also be connected to an Ethernet, and to outside WANs for remote data transmission. Because of the wide range of software packages available on Altos computers, it can be used to support all kinds of data processing, file handling, and word processing normally required by a business.

Compucorp's OmegaNet® provides an efficient, cost effective way of sharing information between Compucorp Information Processors (Systrex, 1983). it can have up to 32 stations, connected by coaxial cable with a data rate up to 500 kbits/sec, and using CSMA/CA. It is flexible and easily expandable, and it can use hard disks for shared file storage and a variety of shared printers, to support data process and word processing applications.

TECNET™ is a powerful LAN developed for Hytec's range of microcomputers and terminals (Hytec Microsystems, 1983). It uses low-cost coaxial cable, with a data rate up to 750 kbits/sec, to connect up to 255 devices, at distances up to 1 km (farther, if repeaters are used). It conforms to the ECMA 72 CSMA/CD LAN standard, and can link to micros, minis, ICL, Burroughs and Honeywell mainframes, and other networks, via the PSTN.

The Plessey ISLAND LAN is a low-cost, easily installable and flexible system for connecting Plessey Business Computers (Plessey Office Systems, 1983). It uses a token polling bus with twisted pair cable and has a data rate up to 800 kbits/sec. It provides cost effective shared file storage and printing and can be linked to other networks via a PABX.

Since launching Cluster/One, Nestar Inc. has developed three other personal computer networks, all marketed in the UK by Nestar Systems Ltd. (formerly Zynar Ltd). ELF is a smaller version of Cluster/One, using a similar technology, and it links up to ten computers, compared with up to 64 for Cluster/One (Zynar, 1983a, 1983b). Both Elf and Cluster/One have data rates up to 240 kbits/sec, with a maximum cable length of 1000 feet.

PLAN 2000 uses ARCNET^{TM} Technology, to link up to 255 IBM Personal Computers (Zynar, 1983e). PLAN 400 is similar but can link any combination of up to 255 Apple and IBM personal computers (Zynar, 1983d, 1983e). Both PLAN networks have data rates up to 2.5 Mbits/sec with a maximum cable length of 4 miles (Zynar, 1983a).

IBM has its own networking systems for linking IBM Personal Computers: PC Network and, on a smaller scale, PC Cluster.

The Symbiotic Computer Systems SyMBnet uses recent fibre-optic technology to provide an effective long-range LAN linking Apple personal computers (Symbiotic Computer Systems, 1983). It is versatile and adaptable and can access shared SyMBfile hard disk stores, which can have SyMBstore magnetic tape back-up.

Quorum Computers' Q-LAN links up to 64 processor units with a total cable length of up to 600 metres (Quorum Computers, 1983). Each user has a dual processor, one half of which runs CP/M software in the usual way, and the other half provides network communication and additional memory. Q-Lan also uses shared hard disk storage, and its data rate is up to 625 kbits/sec.

Markoff (1982) briefly describes a proposal for an alternative low-cost computer network.

The Irish company Transtec recently announced its Transnet LAN with shared-hard-disk storage, which should be able to link up to 250 work stations in a typical office application (Kennett, 1984). It has a data rate up to 500 kbits/sec, soon to be increased to 1 Mbits/sec in a new version. It already has an IBM Personal Computer interface; and interfaces to Apple, DEC, and some other personal computers are expected in due course.

The book *Micros and Modems* (1983) gives a broad overview of telecommunications with personal computers. It includes chapters on hardware and software aspects, network concepts, interactions between people and computers, and the future of telecommunications with computers.

Data Communications for Microcomputers (Nichols et al, 1982) is a book which provides some technical information about linking of personal computers via the PSTN and discusses data transfers, RS-232-C and other Physical Layer protocols, modems, and practical applications and experiments.

The book *Microcomputer Data Communication Systems* (Derfler, 1982a) provides a guide to the operations of modems, terminals, communications software, and connection to other computer systems via the PSTN, for the Apple II, TRS-80 and other personal computers. Derfler (1982b) is a similar book for TRS-80 personal computers.

The British weekly *Personal Computer News* (1984a) recently issued a special feature on modems and communications. It includes tables of modems and accompanying software available for various personal computers, including modems that can be used for connection to the British viewdata service Prestel. At the time of writing, *Personal Computer News* (1984b) had just started to issue further features on micros, modems, and communications.

Held (1983) points out that personal computers are becoming better and cheaper; at the same time their network concepts are becoming clearer and more explicit. In most cases, the best choice of communications for a personal computer still tends to be determined by the applications that its users require. Table 5 of this article usefully relates application needs to networking strategies.

Custance (1983) gives a brief introduction to networking with micros, including access to public services like viewdata, for example, Prestel and Micronet 800, and electronic mail, for example, Telecom Gold. Her article includes a table listing a selection of personal computer network and other LAN suppliers.

Micronet 800 has recently been set up as a service, operating as part of the British viewdata system Prestel, that enables users of certain personal computers, including the BBC Micro, Sinclair Spectrum, TRS-80, and Apple II, to load and use microcomputer software stored in the Micronet 800 data base and access other Prestel information (Micronet, 1983).

According to a recent extensive survey, microcomputer vendors' support for communications varies from the bare minimum, an RS-232-C port, all the way to an X.25 interface (Jordan, 1983). Jordan provides a very extensive table, showing, for models sold by many vendors, the nature of the micro and its communications lines, the maximum transmission speed of these lines, protocols supported, associated LAN (if any), gateway (if any), electronic mail (if any), and basic purchase price.

Campt (1984) gives further information about available products, linking micros to mainframes, with details of prices, micro data formats supported, and compatible sources of mainframe data. He feels that there is still much room for improvement in "intelligent" links between micros and mainframes.

So many communications software packages have now been developed for different models of personal computer that no attempt is made to summarise them here. Useful introductions are given in some of the books just cited and in the article by Rolander (1982), for example.

Of special interest is Software Connections' Data Core local network data base management system that is described by Gee (1983). Its data base and information sharing facilities are said to be so powerful that they will open up a vast market for software for personal computer networks, and enable these networks to handle many applications previously reserved for minicomputer systems.

Additional reference to Nestar Cluster/One: Zynar 1982).

Additional references to Corvus Systems Constellation and Omninet: Keen Computers (1983a to 1983c), Warshaw (1983). Note that, although originally developed for the Apple personal computers, these networks can now be linked to many microcomputers, including: IBM, DEC VT180, DEC Rainbow 100, Xerox 820 and 820II, Commodore 2000, 3000, 4000 and 8000 Series, TRS-80 Models II, III, and 12, and the Corvus Concept Personal Workstation.

Additional reference to HiNet: Digital Microsystems (1983).

Additional reference to U-NET: U-Microcomputers (1983).

WIDE AREA NETWORKS

Public wide area networks based on conventional technologies are described in Chapter 4; see also the general review by Slana and Lehman (1981). The book by Yakubaitis (1983) includes brief descriptions of the packet-switched networks Euronet (Europe), PSS (UK), TRANSPAC (France), ECN (Latvian SSR), and DATAPAC (Canada). Kamae (1982) describes a public fax network.

The December 1983 issue of *IEEE Journal on Selected Areas in Communications*, Vol. **SAC-1**, No. 6, is a special issue on packet-switched voice and data communications (Vlack and Decina, 1983).

Kuwabara (1983) describes public circuit-switched and packet-switched networks in Japan, and examines the possibilities of linking them with other networks, both inside and outside Japan. Murakami (1983) outlines work on domestic satellite communications in Japan, whose first commercial satellite network, using two satellites, was set up in 1983. Ejiri (1981) and Nakajima (1983) describe the advanced facsimile communication network and visual communications system now being developed in Japan.

Wide area networking systems, being developed by the major manufacturers, especially DEC, IBM, and ICL, are making gradual but steady progress. In all cases, they provide WAN interfaces for their terminals, computers, and LANs, and these interfaces are available for packet-switched networks, using X.25, as well as for networking services based on the PSTN.

Although DEC, IBM, and ICL have their own networking architectures, called DNA, SNA, and IPA, respectively, these architectures are all closely related to the international standard networking architecture, OSI, and are gradually converging towards it. Both DNA and IPA can already interwork with SNA to a considerable extent. These architectures and the associated standards are considered more fully in Chapter 21.

The DEC approach to networking is outlined in various publications of DEC (1982a to 1982c, 1983a to 1983c); its latest version, Phase IV, is also described by Thurk and Twaits (1983). DEC computers can work together in a dynamic network, that can change as its users' needs change. The network system can be an office LAN, or it can operate over a WAN, or it can be a linked local area network, a system of LANs linked by one or more WANs. This capability is supported by Digital's network software DECnet.

More specifically, DECnet is the family of Digital's software products, protocols, interfaces, and other supporting services, which allows DEC computer systems to be linked into distributed processing networks. Networks using DECnet make individual systems more powerful, productive and efficient, by joining them together and enabling them to communicate effectively with each other.

DECnet is now in its fourth phase, which has greatly simplified the configurations of its local networking, now that it supports Ethernet with its bus structure. The maximum number of nodes in a network supported by DECnet has been increased from 255 to 1023.

Youett (1983) discusses IBM's current reappraisal of its network products. The newest variant of SNA, Version 4.2, was released in June 1979. However, IBM users are not bound to use SNA for packet-switched networking, based on X.25; there are three other options available to them. For the future, IBM may decide to concentrate on a digital broadband network technology using time division multiplexing; this would at least have a lower software overhead and make full use of the potential of fibre optics.

ICL Technical Journal, Vol. **3**, No. 3 (May 1983), is a special issue on communication (ICL, 1983d), which is devoted mostly to the presentation of the IPA networking architecture and the associated networking system.

Philips Communication Network Structure is an extension and refinement of the OSI layered network architecture, and it comprises two types of network: SOPHO-LAN and SOPHO-NET. SOPHO-LAN is described earlier in this chapter. SOPHO-NET is Philips' packet-switched business communications network (Philips Business Communications, 1983b; Philips Business Systems, 1984).

It can link a variety of devices and also several SOPHO-LANs to X.25 data networks, SNA networks, PABX-based private telephone networks, and the public switched telephone network (PSTN). It is not restricted by different protocols from different manufacturers and networks, as its network undertakes all necessary protocol conversions. It thus protects investment in existing data equipment and services.

According to Philips, its multi-microprocessor architecture makes SOPHO-NET very reliable and flexible, with a very good performance. It anticipates the latest advances in communications technology, including LAN technology, fibre optics, and satellites. It provides the means to build a fully integrated office communications network, independent of the models and types of equipment attached to it, and it significantly reduces data transmission costs.

Rauzino (1983) gives a guide to data communications software for use with equipment linked to LANs. This software is usually available from the software vendors of this equipment, but there are dozens of other suppliers for the communications software available on the most popular computers. This article gives a very extensive table of the teleprocessing monitors, terminal managers, and terminal support packages now on the market. It is a condensed version of a survey of data communications software, published by Data Decisions Software Information Service, Cherry Hill, NJ.

Casey (1984) describes the private WANs developed by DEC and Texas Instruments for connecting all the divisions within their organisations around the world. DEC's network has nearly 16,000 users, accessing 1,700 DEC minicomputers and an unspecified number of personal computers and other intelligent terminals. The Texas Instruments network links about 13,000 interactive terminals.

British Telecom (1984) presents an up-to-date description of its *ISDN (Integrated Services Digital Network)*, based on System X; the earlier work on both of these systems is described in Chapter 4, 6, and 18. ISDN now uses *IDA (Integrated Digital Access)*, a new digital transmission between System X exchanges and users' equipment. Single line IDA links an exchange to a user's data terminal and telephone via an NTE (Network Terminating Equipment). Multiline IDA links an exchange to local telephones and data terminals via a digital PABX. ISDN also has gateways to the PSTN, KiloStream, and Packet SwitchStream networks.

Mercury Communications, the new British telecommunications service which has been set up in competition to British Telecom, is developing an IDN (Integrated Digital Network), carrying all services, including voice, data, and image in digital form. This network will use several transmission technologies including radio, optical fibre, cable, and wire. Links are being developed between London, the Midlands, the Bristol area, and the North of England, but not to Wales or Scotland yet. Some of the technical aspects of the Mercury network are described by Cott (1983), Mead (1983), and Willett (1983).

Telecom Canada is now developing an integrated national satellite network, Stratoroute 2000, which will offer transmission paths for a variety of applications and become operational late in 1984 (Hubert and Gaumond, 1984). It will at first support voice communications and synchronous data transmission at speeds up to 56 kbits/sec; it will be possible to select several data rates between 2.4 and 56 kbits/sec. The ground trunk lines to the earth stations will support multiplexed transmissions at 1.544 Mbits/sec. The total data rate of the satellite channels will start at 30 Mbits/sec, then, after a year, be increased to 45 Mbits/sec; later on, 90 Mbits/sec bursts will be overlayed.

NETWORK SERVICES

The book *Evaluating Data Transmission Services* (Bleazard, 1983) provides guidelines to help users to evaluate currently available data transmission services in the UK, together with new services expected to start by early 1985, in terms of the facilities that they offer. He identifies possible applications and opportunities for improved cost/benefit. The book is likely to interest people choosing, managing, or using data communications services. It has a bibliography and includes a survey of users' experience of PSS.

Spencer (1983) describes the current and future developments in the data networks, services, and products provided by British Telecom. He discusses British Telecom's overall medium-term and long-term plans, reviewing them in the context of market changes and organisational changes within British Telecom. He considers the development of data services and networks in the light of users' increasing need to plan strategically the development and growth of their company networks.

Services discussed include improvement to Telex, Packet SwitchStream, KiloStream, MegaStream, Telecom Gold (also described in British Telecom's (1983) brochure), and Telecom Silver. According to Spencer, Videoconferencing looks like being the most publicised service of 1984. He concludes that, in practice, British Telecom now has a combination of services that meets all user needs; it is committed to a responsible provision of what users want, and it plans to continue vigorous development of its services.

Letford (1983) describes British Telecom's advanced voice and data services for international communication, including IPSS and SatStream (also described by Shorrock (1983)). The following digital services are offered or planned:

1. For data, high-speed data links, computer data base transfer, wide area networking;

2. For image, high-speed fax, electronic mail for decentralised distribution, remote printing of newspapers;

3. For voice, digitised voice, store-and-forward voice, links via digital PABXs;

4. Teleconferencing (frame video at 64 kbits/sec) and Videoconferencing (at 2 Mbits/sec) (see also *Computer Weekly* (1983b)).

Mildenhall (1983) discusses the role of British Telecom's ISDN, mainly from a user's viewpoint; he highlights the general features and user benefits of the ISDN. He compares these long-term objectives with the shorter-term users of the early version of ISDN, especially British Telecom's IDA "Pilot" Service, which is also described in British Telecom's (1984) brochure.

Mercury Communications is the new telecommunications system, recently set up in the UK in competition with British Telecom. Its Technical Director describes its integrated approach to its new services, catering for voice, data, and image, all in digital form. Further overviews of its services, together with assessments of its prospects, are given by Condon (1983), Frampton (1983), and Walton (1984).

Mercury intends to compete directly with British Telecom's international telecommunications service (*Computer News*, 1984a). It has agreed to set up Transatlantic satellite links, in collaboration with several American companies, and it also plans links to West European countries.

Kuwabara (1983) describes how the Japanese plan to expand their circuit-switched and packet-switched network services. He suggests possible future trends for applications in both services, including applications using facsimile. Murakami (1983) reports a commercial communications satellite service started in Japan in August 1983. Ejiri (1981) and Nakajima (1983) describe existing and proposed facsimile network services in Japan.

Value added networks are essentially computer networks that provide services other than communication and conveying messages. Hugill (1983) discusses what VANs are, what they offer, and who provides them. He points out that the official definition of *Value Added Network Services* (VANS) is linked to the published standard for OSI (Open Systems Interconnection) and the essential clause of the VANS General Licence. VANS provide applications of the OSI standard, which is discussed further in Chapters 9 and 21. Hugill gives some examples of VANS, provided by a whole range of companies and organisations; these services include: network management, protocol conversion, videotex, and electronic publishing.

Reid (1983) presents the work of British Telecom Spectrum, of which he is Chief Executive. Spectrum is the division of British Telecom with responsibility for value added services, including: Telecom Gold (electronic mail), Telecom Tan (computer-assisted telephone answering), Telecom Red (alarm control stations), and Telecom Silver (credit card authorisation). Reid describes Spectrum's activities and plans, product approach, and management philosophy.

Tamworth (1983) briefly presents the existing facilities and proposed future enhancements of Teletex, the first fully compatible international service, other than fax, for users in all parts of the world wishing to exchange text. It will be possible to use both circuit-switched networks, with X.21 and X.71 protocols, and packet-switched networks, with X.25 and X.75 protocols, to carry Teletex. Jagger (1984) also describes the Teletex service, and considers that it will eventually take over from Telex, fax, and business mail. Kamae (1982) describes a public fax service in Japan, where fax is especially important because of the complexity of the written language!

Berman (1984) reports that the market for British Telecom's new "cabletext" services has expanded considerably. It has just launched a Cable Interactive Services Division, which will supply cable TV operators with text information channels that can be received only on teletex sets. It is also offering telesoftware, video games, home banking, and electronic shopping services.

Hubert and Gaumond (1983) describe Stratoroute 2000, the satellite network service to be started by Telecom Canada late in 1984. It will at first be offered across Canada, and then have some overseas extensions. It will offer a variety of services including: voice transmission, terminal-to-terminal, computer-to-computer, communicating word processing, fax, freeze-frame video, and other digital image applications.

Several computer networks have been set up to help researchers. In the UK, an extensive computer network has been set up to link computer centres and services at British universities (Rosner, 1983). It has major centres at London, Manchester, the Rutherford Appleton Laboratory, and the Daresbury Laboratory, together with about 60 smaller centres. It is very heterogeneous, and links mainframes, minis, micros, and LANs. It provides a framework for remote job entry, terminal access, file transfer, data bases, electronic mail, shared facilities, major applications in new areas, and other services.

The *Alvey Network (Alvey Communication Environment)* is being set up in the UK as a high-performance network, using megabit links to join LANs at various sites participating in the Alvey Programme for Advanced Information Technology (Black, 1984). The aim was to have an electronic mail service for Alvey participants operating fully by May 1984, and to have the full service running by the end of 1984. Attempts will be made to provide interworking between all kinds of equipment. Progress in developing and implementing this service is reported from time to time in *Alvey News*, the newsletter issued on behalf of the Alvey Programme.

CSNET is being developed cooperatively within the American computer science community, to provide them with file transfer, access to remote data bases, electronic mail, and other services (Gait, 1982). It has taken over some of the functions previously carried out by The Arpanet in this area.

Labadi and Sebestyén (1983) describe various aspects of the IIASA TPA/70 X.25 Gateway-Network, which has been set up by *IIASA (International Institute of Applied Systems Analysis)*, to promote the online exchange of scientific information between national and international institutions and organisations.

Additional references: *Computer News* (1984b), Jennings, (1983b, 1983c), Kehoe (1982), Part 5 of Rosner (1982), Thurman (1982), Whitehouse (1983).

REFERENCES

Altos Computer Systems (1983) *Team Computing—The New Concept for Business Automation*, Altos Computer Systems Ltd., Brochure.

P. Bain (1983) "The LAN in a PABX dominated environment," *LocalNet 83 (Europe)*, 209–221.

C. Berman (12 Jan 1984) "BT's market for 'cabletext' set to grow," *Computing*, 8.

G. Black (5 Jan 1984) "Alvey aims at comms network," *Computer Weekly*, 3.

G. B. Bleazard (1983) *Evaluating Data Transmission Services*, NCC Publications, Manchester, England.

P. I. B. Boulton and E. S. Lea (Jul 1983) "Bus, ring, star and tree local area networks," *Computer Communications Review*, **13**(3) 19–24.

D. Bradshaw (Nov 1983) "Networks: Ready for shakeout?," *Software*, 22–26.

British Telecom (1983) *Telecom Gold—Electronic Mail from British Telecom*, Telecom Gold, London, Brochure.

British Telecom (Jan 1984) *IDA—Integrated Data Access*, British Telecom, London, Brochure PH3489 (1/84).

A. D. Campbell (1983) "Fiber optic data communications C&C Loop 6770," *LocalNet 83 (New York)*, 307–318.

D. W. Campt (Mar 1984) "Missing: The universal micro-to-mainframe link," *Data Communications*, **13**(3) 125–130.

R. J. Camrass (1983) "Current developments in computerised PABX systems," *Business Telecom 83*, 243–250.

CASE (1983a) *Beeline from Case-Breaking the Communication Barrier*, CASE plc, Watford, Herts., England, Brochure.

CASE (1983b) *CASE Grapevine—Local Area Networking Made Simple*, CASE plc, Watford, Herts., England, Brochure A997.

D. Casey (12 Jan 1984) "DEC and Texas set net trends for users," *Computing, Communications Supplement*, 10–11.

V. E. Cheong and R. A. Hirschheim (1983) *Local Area Networks—Issues, Products, and Developments*, Wiley-Interscience, Chichester and New York.

P. J. Coen (1983) "Local area networks and distributed office systems," *Business Telecom 83*, 219–230.

A. Colvin (Oct 1983) "CSMA with collision avoidance," *Computer Communications*, **6**(5) 227–235.

Communications Management (1984a) (Feb 1984) "A buyer's guide to local area networks," 40–41.

Communications Management (1984b) (Feb 1984) "Star network from Midlectron," 52.

Computer Networks (Aug 1983) "Local computer networks," Vol. **7**(4) 273–275.

Computer News (1984a) (2 Feb 1984) "Mercury is on the rise," 2.

Computer News (1984b) (12 Jan 1984) "BT plans expansion in packet switching," 3.

Computer Weekly (1983a) (17 Nov 1983) "Office network handles up to 4,000 stations," 4.

Computer Weekly (1983b) (13 Oct 1983) "BT revives the prospect of meetings by TV," 20.

Computer Weekly (5 Jan 1984) " 'Major change' in concept of comms network," 26.

R. Condon (Apr 1983) "Sir Michael and Mercury: The view from the top floor," *Communications Management*, 21–24.

P. J. Cott (1983) "Business demand for digital telecoms: An integrated system approach," *Business Telecom 83*, 197–201.

K. Custance (Nov 1983) "All the right connections," *Practical Computing*, **6**(11) 111–113.

Datapoint (1982) *Networking—The Datapoint Networking Perspective*, Datapoint Corporation, San Antonio, TX, Brochure.

Datapoint (1983a) *The Datapoint ARC Local Area Network—Factsheet*, Datapoint Corporation, San Antonio, TX, Document No. 61528.

Datapoint (1983b) *The Datapoint ARC Local Area Network—Milestones*, Datapoint Corporation, San Antonio, TX, Document No. 61590.

Datapoint (1983c) *The Datapoint ARC Local Area Network—Gateways from the ARC Network*, Datapoint Corporation, San Antonio, TX, Document No. 61560.

J. M. Davidson (Apr 1981) "Local network technologies for the office," Ungermann-Bass, Inc., Santa Clara, CA, *Net/One™ Technical Papers Series*, 2.

Ed. G. R. Davis (1982) *The Local Network Handbook*, McGraw Hill, New York.

DEC (1982) *Introduction to Local Area Networks*, Digital Equipment Corporation, Maynard, MA, Book, Order No. EB-22714-18.

DEC (1982b) *Networking—Distributed Processing—Application Stories by Digital*, Digital Equipment Corporation, Maynard, MA, Brochure.

DEC (1982c) *Distributed Processing and Networks—A Technical Overview of Digital Networking Products and Capabilities*, Digital Equipment Corporation, Maynard, MA, Brochure, Order No. EA-22505-18.

DEC (1983a) *DECnet-11S Phase III*, Digital Equipment Corporation, Maynard, MA, Data Sheet, Order No. ED-23014-20.

DEC (1983b) *Networks—DECnet Phase IV*, Digital Equipment Corporation, Maynard, MA., Brochure, Order No. ED-24622-42.

DEC (1983c) *Networks System and Options Catalog*, Digital Equipment Corporation, Maynard, MA, Order No. EB-24467-18.

F. J. Derfler, Jr. (1982a) *Microcomputer Data Communication Systems*, Prentice-Hall, Englewood Cliffs, NJ.

F. J. Derfler, Jr. (1982b) *TRS-80 Data Communication Systems*, Prentice-Hall, Englewood Cliffs, NJ.

Digital Microsystems (1983) *HiNet—Travel the Network*, Digital Microsystems Ltd., Brochure.

S. Ditlea (Nov 1982) "Joining the network," *Inc. Magazine*.

R. C. Dixon, N. C. Strole and J. O. Markov (Jan 1983) "A token-ring network for local data communications," *IBM Systems Journal*, **22**(1/2) 47–62.

Y. Ebihara et al (Dec 1983) "GAMMA-NET: A local computer network coupled by a high speed optical fiber ring bus—System structure and concept," *Computer Networks*, **7**(6) 375–388.

M. Ejiri (Jul 1983) "Advanced facsimile communication network," *Japan Telecommunications Review*, **25**(3) 176–183.

G. Enrico, F. Malpeli and E. Valdevit (1983) "An Ethernet based communications network: Technology and services," *LocalNet 83 (Europe)*, 481–489.

Ferranti (1983) *Ferranti BROADBAND Cable Networks*, Ferranti Computer Systems Ltd., Brochure A004 Issue 3.

D. C. Flint (1983) *The Data Ring Main: An Introduction to Local Area Networks*, Wiley Heyden, Chichester and New York.

R. Frampton (Apr 1983) "Mercury: Can it prove to be a worthy challenger to the might of Telecom?," *Communications Management*, 18–19.

W. R. Franta and I. Chlamtac (1983) *Local Networks*, Gower Publishing Company, Aldershot, Hampshire, England.

L. Fratta, F. Borgonovo and F. A. Tobagi (1981) "The Express-Net: A local communication network integrating voice and data," 77–88 of Ed. G. Pujolle (1981) *Performance of Data Communication Systems and Their Applications*, North-Holland, Amsterdam, Oxford, England, and New York.

J. Gait (Jul 1982) "A coordination and information center for a research-oriented computer communications network," *Information Services & Use*, **2**(1) 41–51.

Gandalf (Oct 1982) *PACXNET*, Gandalf Technologies, Inc., Manotick, Ont., Canada, Brochure.

B. J. Gee (1983) "Database design on a personal computer network," *LocalNet 83 (New York)*, 207–212.

K. C. E. Gee (1982) *Local Area Networks*, NCC Publications, Manchester, England and Wiley, Chichester and New York.

K. C. E. Gee (1983) *Introduction to Local Area Computer Networks*, Macmillan, London and Basingstoke.

K. C. E. Gee (16 Feb 1984) "Station shall talk unto station," *Computer News*, 12–13.

B. K. Hackett (1983) "Recent developments with the Videodata broadband network," *LocalNet 83 (New York)*, 261–271.

E. Hara (Oct 1983) "A fiber-optic broadband LAN/OCS using a PBX," *IEEE Communications Magazine*, **21**(7) 22–27.

M. Hart (Feb 1984) "Should you wish upon a star or take a bus?," *Communications Management*, 36, 39.

Hawker Siddeley (Aug 1983) *MULTILINK— Technical Guide*, Hawker Siddeley Dynamics Engineering Ltd., Welwyn Garden City, England, Document TML 0256 Issue 1.

G. Held (May 1983) "Strategies and concepts for linking today's personal computers," *Data Communications*, **12**(5), 211–219.

D. D. Hill (Jul/Oct 1982) "Dragnet—A local network with protection," *Computer Communications Review*, **12**(3/4) 92–98.

K. Holder (17 Nov 1983) "Micom launches easy-to-use local net," *Computer Weekly*, 4.

P. M. Hubert and J. Gaumond (Jan 1984) "Canada combines voice, data and images on national satellite network," *Data Communications*, **13**(1) 177–184.

D. Hugill (1983) "What are VANS? What do they offer and who provides them?," *Business Telecom 83*, 299–305.

D. Hutchison (Dec 1983) "Ethernet and the Cambridge Ring," *Computer Bulletin*, **II/38**, 17–20.

Hytec Microsystems (1983) *TECNET Local Area Network*, Hytec Microsystems Ltd., Oxford, England.

IAL Data Communications (1983a) *IAL Flexinet Local Area Distribution System (LADDS)*, IAL Data Communications, Basingstoke, Hampshire, England, Leaflet.

IAL Data Communications 81983b) *Datex-90 Speech plus Data—Offers a Cost Effective Data Transmission Network*, IAL Data Communications, Basingstoke, Hampshire, England, Leaflet.

ICL (1983a) *ICL Distributed Office Systems—DRS20 Series*, International Computers Ltd., London, Brochure P1449.

ICL (1983b) *ICL Distributed Office Systems—Wordprocessing*, International Computers Ltd., London, Brochure.

ICL (1983c) *ICL Information Systems*, International Computers Ltd., London, Brochure P1565.

ICL (1983d) (May 1983) *ICL Technical Journal*, Vol. **3**, No. 3, Issue on Communications.

H. Jagger (Jan 1984) "Teletex—Electronic mail's great leap forward," *Communications Management*, 32–34.

F. Jennings (1983a) (17 Nov 1983) "Hobnobbing with the LANs," *Computer Weekly*, 20–21.

F. Jennings (1983b) (20 Oct 1983) "How to lease a line to a user—Leased telephone lines," *Computer Weekly*, 18.

F. Jennings (1983c) (3 Nov 1983) "How to understand the public data service," *Computer Weekly*, 16.

P. Jordan (Dec 1983) "How much support for communications do microcomputer vendors offer?," *Data Communications*, **12**(12) 197–208, with supplement (Jan 1984), *Data Communications*, **13**(1) 196–197.

T. Kamae (Mar 1982) "Public facsimile communication network," *IEEE Communications Magazine*, **20**(2) 47–51.

Keen Computers (1983a) *Corvus Networks—A Short Guide*, Keen Computers, London, Leaflet.

Keen Computers (1983b) *Power plus Economy—Corvus Constellation Network*, Keen Computers, London, Brochure.

Keen Computers (1983c) *A Network You Can Afford—with Benefits You Can't Afford to Miss—Corvus Omninet*, Keen Computers, London, Brochure.

L. Kehoe (19 Feb 1982) "How we get West Coast news cheaper," *Financial Times*, 16.

G. Kellond (1983) "Ethernet—Its past, present and future," *LocalNet 83 (Europe)*, 277-282.

D. Kennett (23 Feb 1984) "Transnet opens to large users," *Computer Weekly*, 9.

A. Kingsmill (1983) "A PABX based integrated business information system," *LocalNet 83 (Europe)*, 195-207.

Ed. K. Kuemmerle, B. W. Stuck and F. A. Tobagi (Nov 1983) *IEEE Journal on Selected Areas in Communications*, Vol. **SAC-1,** No. 5, special issue on local area networks.

M. Kuwabara (Apr 1983) "Trends in Japanese DDX applications," *Computer Communications*, **6**(2) 73-77, reprinted from *Japan Telecommunications Review*, **24**(3) 199-208 (Jul 1982).

A. Labadi, I. Sebestyén (Apr 1983) "The IIASA TPA/70—X.25 Gateway-Network Promotes International Flow of Scientific Information," *Computer Networks*, **7**(2) 113-121.

W. Lees (1983) "The UNIVERSE network at Logica," *LocalNet 83 (Europe)*, 311-326.

A. Letford (1983) "Advanced voice and data services for international communications," *Business Telecom 83*, 177-185.

D. C. Lindsay (Jul/Oct 1982) "Local area networks: Bus and ring vs. coincident star," *Computer Communications Review*, **12**(3/4) 83-91.

J. Locke-Wheaton (Jul 1983) "Choosing a network for in-house development," *DEC User*, 33-35.

Logica VTS (1983) *Polynet*, Logica VTS Ltd., London, Brochure.

J. Markoff (28 Jun 1982) "Group proposes an alternative, low-cost computer network," *InfoWorld*, 28.

Master Systems (1983a) *OFFICEMASTER—The Complete Office from Master Systems*, Master Systems (Data Products) Ltd., Camberley, Surrey, England, Brochure.

Master Systems (1983b) *MASTERNET—The Invisible Network for Master Systems*, Master Systems (Data Products) Ltd., Camberley, Surrey, England, Brochure.

P. C. Mead (1983) "A wideband intercity network using optical fibers," *Business Telecom 83*, 203-211.

Micom Systems and Micom-Borer (1983) *Local Network Costs Getting Out of Hand?*, Micom Systems, Inc., Chatsworth, CA, and Micom-Borer Ltd., Reading, Berkshire, England, Brochure.

Micronet 800 (1983) *Micronet 800—It Brings Your Micro to Life!*, Micronet 800, EMAP Business & Computer Publications Ltd., London, Brochure.

Midlectron (1983) *Your Link with the Future*, Midlectron Ltd., Belper, Derbyshire, England, Leaflet.

R. Mildenhall (1983) "Developing the ISDN," *Business Telecom 83*, 187-196.

K. L. Mills (Mar 1984) "Testing OSI protocols: NBS advances the state of the art," *Data Communications*, **13**(3) 277-296.

T. Murakami (Jan 1983) "Domestic satellite communications in NTT," *Japan Telecommunications Review*, **25**(1) 7-16.

H. Nakajima (Jul 1983) "Recent trends in the development of facsimile and visual communication system in NTT," *Japan Telecommunications Review*, **25**(3) 156-165.

R. M. Needham and A. J. Herbert (1982) *The Cambridge Distributed Computing System*, Addison-Wesley, London and Reading, MA.

Network Technology and Sytek (1983) *LocalNet™ Broadband Network Technology—Linking Today with Tomorrow*, Network Technology, Ltd., Reading, Berkshire, England, and Sytek, Inc., Sunnyvale, CA.

E. A. Nichols, J. C. Nichols, and K. P. Musson (1982) *Data Communications for Microcomputers—with Practical Applications*, McGraw Hill, New York.

J. M. Nilles (1983) *Micros and Modems: Telecommunicating with Personal Computers*, Reston Publishing Company, Reston, VA.

Personal Computer News (1984a) (28 Jan 1984) "Modems and communications," No. 46 (*PCN Micropaedia*, Vol. **16,** Part 1).

Personal Computer News (1984b) (31 Mar 1984 on) "COMMUNICATE: PCN's guide to micros, communications and modems," No. 55 and subsequent issues (PCN Micropaedia, Vol. **20**).

Philips Business Communications (1983a) *SOPHO-LAN—Synergetic Open Philips Local Area Network*, Philips' Telecommunicatie Industrie BV, Hilversum, Netherlands, Brochure TDS 3047-09-83/E.

Philips Business Communications (1983b) *SOPHO-NET—Synergistic Open Philips Network*, Philips' Telecommunicatie Industrie BV, Hilversum, Netherlands, Brochure TDS 3495-09-83E.

Philips Business Systems (1984) *SOPHO-NET—A Unique Advanced Wide Area Network Providing Protocol Compatibility and Significant Reductions in Data Transmission Costs*, Philips Business Systems, Colchester, Essex, England, Brochure.

Plessey Communications Systems (May 1983) *Plessey IDX Integrated Digital Exchange*, Plessey Communication Systems Ltd., Nottingham, England, Publication No. 8031.

Plessey Office Systems (Dec 1983) *The Plessey Business Computer for a New Generation of Business Users*, Plessey Office Systems Ltd., Nottingham, England, Publication No. 9723 12/83 5M.

Quorum Computers (1983) *Q-LAN*, Quorum Computers Ltd., Southampton, England, Brochure.

Racal-Milgo (1983) *PLANET Private Local Area NETwork*, Rascal-Milgo Ltd., Hook, Hampshire, England, Brochure.

V. Rauzino (Nov 1983) "A guide to data communications software," *Data Communications*, **12**(11) 211–219.

Ed. P. Ravasio, G. Hopkins and N. Naffah (1982) *Local Computer Networks*, North-Holland, Amsterdam, Oxford, England, and New York. (Proceedings of the IFIP TC.6 International Symposium on Local Computer Networks, Florence, Italy, April 1982).

P. Reagan (Dec 1983) "AT&T, IBM aiming for local net war of '84," *Data Communications*, **12**(12) 163–175.

Real Time Developments (Aug 1982) *Clearway—The Low Cost Networking System*, Real Time Developments Ltd., Farnborough, Hampshire, England, Brochure.

A. Reichert (1983) "Beyond the bus and the ring," *LocalNet 83 (New York)*, 213–226.

A. A. L. Reid (1983) "Value Added Network Services," *Business Telecom 83*, 307—314.

P. Roberts (1983) "Where have all the integrated PBXs gone?," *Local Networks 83 (New York)*, 1–18.

T. A. Rolander (27 Jan 1982) "Microcomputer software meshes with local nets," *Electronics*.

R. Rosner (16 Nov 1983) "OSI among British Universities," Lecture to British Computer Society, Data Communications Specialist Group.

R. D. Rosner (1982) *Packet Switching*, Lifetime Learning Publications, Belmont, CA.

D. Roworth and M. Cole (1983) "Fibre optic developments for the Cambridge Ring," *LocalNet (Europe)*, 519–535.

D. Shorrock (Nov 1983) "Satellites take off," *DEC User*, 61, 63, 66.

J. J. Sikora and D. C. Franke (1983) "A LAN based on a centralized-bus architecture," *LocalNet 83 (New York)*, 147–157.

G. Spencer (1983) "Inland data services from British Telecom," *Business Telecom 83*, 169–176.

W. Stallings (1983) *Tutorial: Local Network Technology*, IEEE Computer Society Press, Silver Spring, MD.

W. Stallings (1984) *Local Networks—An Introduction*, Macmillan Publishing Company, New York, and Collier Macmillan, London.

N. C. Strole and D. W. Andrews (1983) "Design and architecture of a token-ring local area network," *LocalNet 83 (New York)*, 171–187.

Symbiotic Computer Systems (1983) *Product Information*, Symbiotic Computer Systems Inc., Fairfield, CT, and Symbiotic Computer Systems Ltd., Croydon, Surrey, England, Literature Pack.

Systrex (1983) *Compucorp's OmegaNet*, Systrex Ltd., London, Brochure.

M. E. Tamworth (1983) "Teletex: A true international standard," *Business Telecom 83*, 315—323.

P. Terrell, Jr. (1983) "A local area network," *LocalNet 83 (New York)*, 251–259.

M. Thurk and L. Twaits (Sep 1983) "Inside DEC's newest networking phase," *Data Communications*, **12**(9) 215-223.

W. H. Thurman (Mar 1982) "Telecommunications down under," *IEEE Communications Magazine*, **20**(2) 31–44.

Torch Computers (1983) *TORCHNET Local Area Networking*, Torch Computers Ltd., Shelford, Cambridge, England, Leaflet.

U-Microcomputers (1983) *U-NET Professional Standard Micronetwork System*, U-Microcomuters Ltd., Warrington, Cheshire, England, Literature Pack.

Vector Graphic (1982) *LINC™—The Company Network*, Vector Graphic Inc., Thousand Oaks, CA, Brochure P/N 8001-0059.

The Vector Graphic Journal (1 Jul 1983) "LINC Local Area Network," Vol. **II**, No. 2, 6, 7, 9, 15.

Ed. D. Vlack and M. Decina (Dec 1983) *IEEE Journal on Selected Areas in Communications*, Vol. **SAC-1**, No. 6, special issue on packet-switched voice and data communications.

H. Voysey (1984a) (Feb 1984) "Lord of the rings—IBM and its token offering for LANs," *Communications Management*, 22-23.

H. Voysey (1984b) (12 Jan 1984) "Making effective use of the speed of fibre optics," *Computing, Communications Supplement*, 20-21.

P. Walton (12 Jan 1984) "Double act or deadly rivalry for carriers?," *Computing, Communications Supplement*, 14-15.

M. Warshaw (1983) "Network hierarchies and PC networks," *LocalNet 83 (New York)*, 495-498.

P. Whitehouse (Jul/Aug 1983) "A machine to ring the changes," *Computer Management*, 23-26.

R. J. Willett (1983) "The Design and Implementation of Mercury's London Network," *Business Telecom 83*, 213-217.

Ed. N. E. Wolfberg (1982) *The Ethernet Handbook*, Shotwell and Associates, San Francisco, CA.

E. A. Yakubaitis 91983) *Computer Network Architecture*, Allerton Press, New York (English translation of 1980 Russian Edition).

C. Youett (6 Oct 1983) "The new route to net profits," *Computing*, IBM Supplement, 25.

Zynar (1982) *Zynar Cluster/One Local Computer Network—General Information Manual*, Zynar Ltd., Uxbridge, Middlesex, England, Document GX001-M001-01.

Zynar (1983a) *ZYNAR NETWORKS: Comparison*, Zynar Ltd., Uxbridge, Middlesex, England, Leaflet.

Zynar (1983b) *ELF—Link Your Apple at Low Cost*, Zynar Ltd., Uxbridge, Middlesex, England, Leaflet.

Zynar (1983c) *PLAN 2000—Zynar has Plans for Your IBM PC's*, Zynar Ltd., Uxbridge, Middlesex, England, Brochure.

Zynar (1983d) *Turn Personal Computers into a Network of Shared Resources*, Zynar Ltd., Uxbridge, Middlesex, England, Brochure.

Zynar (1983e) *Here's the PLAN . . . the PLAN 4000 Personal Computer Network*, Zynar Ltd., Uxbridge, Middlesex, England, Brochure.

(Zynar Ltd. has now been renamed "Nestar Systems Ltd.")

Chapter 20

Recent Developments in Network Technologies

This chapter starts by discussing some recent ideas on network structures and network interconnection, giving some examples of structures used in new network systems, and describing some recent work on network interconnection and network gateways. It then lists some of the equipment recently developed for use inside networks and for attachment to networks. After that it describes some further developments in transmission technologies, especially in the use of fibre optics and satellites in networks. Finally, it reviews some of the equipment, methods, and models used in network monitoring, control, and performance analysis.

This chapter provides a more comprehensive description of network equipment than was given in Part 2 of this book.

NETWORK STRUCTURES AND NETWORK INTERCONNECTION

Hill (1982) proposes a "Dragnet" topology, which is like that of Ethernet in some respects but differs in others. Instead of using one long two-way cable, it has many short one-way cables linked to concentrators, so that each station in the network has a transmit cable to a concentrator and a receive cable from that concentrator. Concentrators in turn have transmit and receive cables, linked to other concentrators. Eventually, all the links converge on a central node or hub, where all packet collisions are detected.

The Dragnet topology is thus a *dual rooted tree*, consisting of a tree of transmit links, connected via the hub to a tree of receive links. This sort of structure was originally proposed by Closs and Lee (1980), whose paper is mentioned in Chapter 6. It has also been used in the Hubnet LAN at the University of Toronto, and it is advocated and described by Boulton and Lee (1982) after their examination of some relative merits of the star, ring, bus, and tree topologies for LANs.

Lindsay (1982) proposes a coincident star LAN topology, which he considers to be potentially more powerful than existing LAN structures.

Reagan (1983) outlines AT&T's new network architecture, using multiple "Databit" nodes. Each Databit node is a cluster of linked star networks, and there are also long distance links between stars in different Databit nodes.

In their discussion of fibre optic ring networks, Warrior and Husain (1983) include a useful classification of fibre optic network topologies and of fibre optic ring topologies; these are illustrated in Figures 20.1 and 20.2, reproduced from their paper.

Strole and Andrews (1983) summarise the fundamental aspects of the star ring architecture of the IBM token ring, which has been designed to meet the needs of very small LANs, with only a few terminals, up to those of very large LANs, with thousands of terminals. The design emphasises fault detection and isolation facilities, together with mechanisms for network expansion and growth. Rings of this sort can be linked with each other in various ways, for example by bridges, via a "backbone" ring, or via bridge/modems connecting to a broadband medium. The typical packet format is a header (15 bytes), followed by data (variable number of bytes), and ending with a trailer (6 bytes). The IBM token ring system is also described by Dixon et al (1983), Reagan (1983), and Terrell (1983).

Grandi et al (1983) describe the fibre optic ring, used by the HERMES Project of the Commission of European Communities' Joint Research Centre informatics programme, which aims at studying advanced concepts in networking. Its network

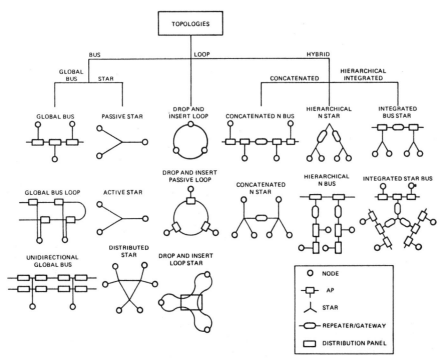

Fig. 20.1. Taxonomy of fibre optic topologies   SOURCE: Paper by Warrior and Husain in *LocalNet 83 (New York)*, Online Publications Inc., p. 327

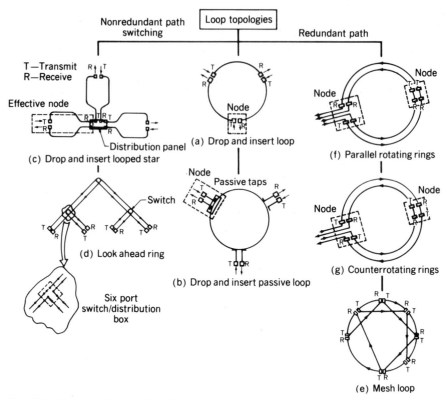

Fig. 20.2. Loop topologies SOURCE: Paper by Warrior and Husain in *LocalNet 83 (New York)*, Online Publications Inc., p. 328.

is intended to act as a test-bed, perhaps also as a catalyst, for the description and operation of distributed data bases, parallel processing, and data conferencing applications.

Takeyama et al (1983) describe a new fibre optic ring LAN, FACOM 2880, which has two types of rings based on the same design architecture. The minor ring, FACOM 2881, is designed to accommodate up to 240 terminals, using a 4.096 Mbits/sec cable. The major ring, FACOM 2883, can connect up to 4096 terminals, using a 22.768 Mbits/sec data highway. A typical configuration has a major processor, special processors, several minor rings, and at least one gateway, all connected to a major ring.

Ebihara et al (1983) present the concept and structure of GAMMA-NET, a full-scale high-performance optical fibre ring bus LAN.

Reichert (1983) describes the new topology, combining ring and bus concepts, of the Vector Graphic SABER-Net, using the LINC operating system.

Sikora and Frank (1983) present American Bell's new LAN architecture, using a centralised bus, which is said to combine many of the advantages of distributed and centralised LAN systems. It offers a modular approach for interfacing to many types of devices, linking multiple LANs and providing gateways to other networks.

Hubley and McDonald (1983) describe American Bell's Net 1000 "intelligent network," whose major elements are port interfaces, storage, communications processing, and information movement.

Ennis (1983a) discusses the design considerations of the architecture of "Metronet," a broadband network, developed jointly by Sytek and General Instrument, to support various urban data applications. It uses multiple 128 kbits/sec CSMA/CD channels to support up to 100,000 videotex terminals per hub.

Broomall and Heath (1983) give a broad tutorial survey of the various topologies available for use in parallel/distributed computer systems. They classify circuit-switched networks by connection capability, topology, and basis of development.

Leiden (1983) introduces the concept of "logical local area," in connection with nonstandard LAN solutions to the problem of networking a large industrial site and perhaps also several remote locations. A *logical local area* is defined as a configuration, at least 80% of whose traffic is "internal," that is, between nodes in that area. A logical local area differs from a local area, as usually defined, in that it need not be physically contiguous, so that its nodes could constitute more than one physical cluster.

Brayer (1983) describes the structure of an experimental radio network with 25 mobile stations and without fixed topology.

The book *Local Area Network Gateways* (Gee, 1983) includes chapters on the reasons for interconnecting networks, gateway functions, gateway location, gateway limitations, user interfaces, and current research on gateways; it gives references to relevant further reading.

The September 1983 issue of *Computer*, Vol. **16**, No. 9, is a special Issue on Network Interconnection (*Computer*, 1983a); three of its papers are now summarised. Shneiderwind (1983) discusses three approaches to network interconnection: network access, network services, and protocol functions; he considers how they are related and in what respects they overlap. Benhamou and Estrin (1983) show how the use of high-performance gateways and bridges will allow the development of "hybrid networks," in their view the only real way to achieve an integrated network system able to support the products of many vendors. Hinden et al (1983) describe how the DARPA Internet uses gateways to form a packet-switched network system of several underlying networks; the Internet successfully links between 400 and 500 host computers in the USA and Europe.

Three recent papers present British Telecom's work on network interconnection. Best and Fineman (1983) give a historical perspective, see LAN-WAN gateways as critical to British Telecom's aim of stimulating a market for advanced communications inside and between businesses, and discuss British Telecom's development of a gateway, with special reference to the protocols likely to be included. Marshall and Spieglhalter (1983) describe SESNET, which acts as a test bed for British Telecom's internetworking activities; it links several LANs and various types of equipment. Childs (1983) describes the range of LAN-WAN-LAN communications facilities, to be provided by means of British Telecom's new ISDN, and gives details of the practical realisations achieved. Especially important is the adoption of a standard internetworking protocol, covering ISO Levels 1 to 3, which will allow LANs of different types and manufacturers to exchange useful information.

Grant et al (1983) describe their approach to building a gateway between X.25 WANs (e.g., PSS) and LANs (e.g., Cambridge Ring and Ethernet). They explain the purpose of such a gateway, outline the hardware on which it is based, give details of its software implementation, and show how the gateway will be used after its installation at the University of Strathclyde, Glasgow, Scotland.

Sherman (1983) describes a working internetworking architecture, for interconnecting different LANs. Potter and St. Amand (1983) advocate a modular approach to the connection of minicomputers to LANs.

In three brochures, Amdahl Communications System Division shows examples of the network configurations that it uses to link different network systems (Amdahl, 1983a to 1983c). They give examples of configurations for private and public X.25 data networks, terminal services networks, and WANs with one, two, and many nodes.

Micom Systems (1983a) discusses its INSTANET™ LAN based on the Micro600 data PABX, and its communications with outside WANs. Figure 20.3 shows a typical configuration for INSTANET Remote Communication Gateways. A special version of the Micro600/X.25 Concentrator PAD is used as gateway to an X.25 network, an INSTATRUNK 480 is used to link to a remote computer and its remote terminals, and other facilities are used to connect to isolated terminals and the PSTN.

Figure 20.4 shows a typical configuration of WANs, linked by the Plessey 8600 family of telex and data switches, Telex/Packet Gateway, and Teletex Conversion Facility (Plessey Controls, 1983a). Figure 20.5 shows in more detail the configuration of a packet-switched network and a Telex network, linked by a Plessey 8687 Telex/Packet Gateway (Plessey Controls, 1983b).

Datapoint (1983) shows how its ARCNET LANs are linked to other networks. ARCGATE™ products are used to link an ARCNET with an IBM mainframe, by means of IBM3270 emulation, and ARCLINK connects different ARCNETs over long distances.

Ennis (1983b) describes the interconnection strategies and issues for an installation covering broadband cable systems. He illustrates the use of broadband as a "backbone" distributed system, by examining the LocalNet/Ethernet Gateway, now being developed jointly by Sytek and Bridge Communications.

Rutkowski and Markus (1982) introduce the ISDN (Integrated Services Digital Network) concept, as a continually evolving multi-faceted approach, and state some of the important issues associated with its development.

Ellis (1983) introduces the concept of *ISLN* (*Integrated Services Local Network*), to describe an integrated voice/text/data/image network within a site, thus complementing the concept of ISDN, which performs the same functions between sites. ISLN differs from ISDN mainly in requiring a higher data rate. It is not proposed as a solution to the problem of linking major computer nodes, but it is intended to cover the communications needs of a user and his equipment at a work station. In the first phase of introducing ISLN, Ellis proposes a data rate of 64 kbits/sec able to handle voice, data, and still images. In the second phase, he proposes a data rate of 2 Mbits/sec able to handle full moving video. He views an ISLN connected

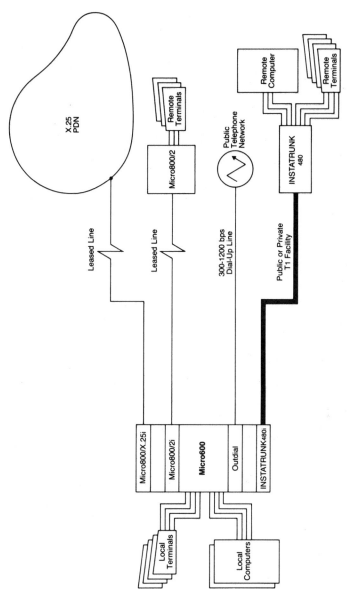

Fig. 20.3. INSTANET remote communications gateways   SOURCE: Courtesy of Micom Systems, Inc. and Micom-Borer Ltd. (INSTANET™ Brochure, last page)

THE PLESSEY 8600 RANGE

The new 8600 range of telex and data switches brings together the proven technology of the successful 4660 range and new developments which Plessey has produced to fulfil requirements for "value-added" services and interworking with new data networks.

The essence of the 8600 is its special ability to grow to very large exchange sizes, and to incorporate as integral units new interworking facilities.

This has been made possible with the fulfilment of important evolutionary developments in designs for multi-computer systems. The result is one family of compatible hardware and software products for telex and data switching. The range of the 8600 family extends from small limited facility telex/data concentrators to full subscriber/trunk gateways of 32768 ports. Any size may be enhanced, with the addition of specialised units for interworking telex with other message and data services on public switched data and telephone networks.

The 8600 design is based on modular processor unit principles and the features which are unique to its architecture are:

★ A flexible software architecture which allows a variety of management and switching functions to be assembled into an integrated, single unit package when the requirement is for modest size and functions.

★ An inter-unit bus system which allows exchange management functions to be centralised while traffic switching and processing functions are dispersed among several load sharing units when the requirement is for large exchanges.

★ Flexible hardware and software structures which maximises the benefits of standard computer and logic modules without restricting capability for a wide size range and versatility in application.

★ "Value-added" services units which are available as integral parts of 8600 exchanges or as free-standing products.

The diagram below illustrates the situations to which 8600 products may be applied.

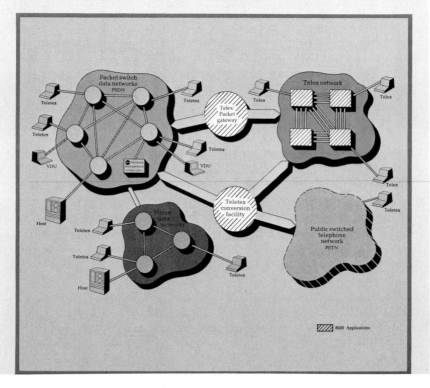

Fig. 20.4. Typical configuration of WANs linked by Plessey 8600 telex and data switches   SOURCE: The copyright for the illustration featured is vested in Plessey UK plc. Plessey Controls Ltd. *8600 Series* Brochure, diagram on inside front page

382

INTRODUCTION

The Telex/Packet Gateway (TPG) is part of the 8600 range of Plessey telex, data and packet switching/communication systems, which is specifically designed to meet the growing demand for data switching and interworking between data networks and services.

The TPG is an interface between telex and packet switched networks providing a service which enables intercommunication between subscribers on the telex network and any terminal (or host computer) on the packet switched network. The subscribers of the telex network may be directly and individually connected to the TPG or connected via trunk circuits.

The provision of a Telex/Packet network interworking facility paves the way for Telex users to access mailboxes and databases hosted on packet networks.

Where the packet network can be accessed from the public telephone network, the modern executive on the move, carrying a portable data terminal with acoustic coupler, will be able to call any telex terminal in the world from an ordinary telephone.

The TPG incorporates Plessey's well proven and established techniques in telex and packet switching and complies with the relevant CCITT recommendations.

This brochure describes the free-standing version of the TPG facility. It is also available in an alternative form for integration into 8600 range designs for main exchanges, and in this case reference should be made to our 8667 leaflet.

A companion brochure gives reference details of the full range of 8600 products.

FACILITIES

★ Up to 512 telex subscriber/trunk circuits operating at 50 bits/sec. with CCITT Type A, B, C and D signalling.

★ Two (or more) synchronous data links (X75) operating at speeds from 2400 to 64,000 bits/sec.

★ Up to 350 simultaneous calls.

★ Packet assembly and disassembly (PAD) in accordance with CCITT X3, X28 and X29 recommendations.

★ Speed and code conversion.

★ Comprehensive call statistics.

★ Automatic fault detection and error reporting.

★ Extensive range of system supervisory, reconfiguration and maintenance commands.

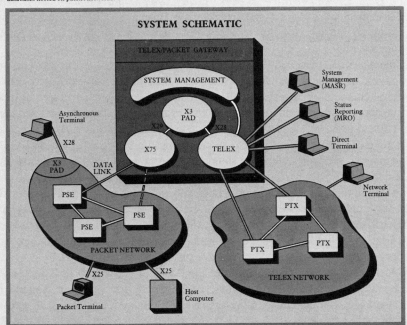

SYSTEM SCHEMATIC

Software

The TPG software can be divided into six functional areas – the telex signalling protocol, the packet assembly/disassembly (PAD) functions, the terminal – PAD protocols, the packet switching protocols, the PAD – packet terminal/host computer protocols, and system management functions.

Telex Signalling Protocols

Calls from the telex network are established using a two-stage selection process. The first stage establishes a connection between the calling terminal and the TPG whilst the second stage establishes the end to end connection between the telex terminal and the called terminal or host computer. The first stage is established using the telex signalling protocols appropriate to the application.

For calls to the telex network, standard call set up procedures are used to establish the connection from the TPG to the called terminal.

PAD

In order to provide a real-time communication between the telex and packet switched data networks (PSDN), the TPG must convert the character

Fig. 20.5. Typical configuration of Plessey Linked Telex/Packet Gateway   SOURCE: The copyright for the illustration featured is vested in Plessey UK plc. Plessey Controls Ltd. *8687 Telex/Packet Gateway* Brochure, diagram on inside front page

to an ISDN as logically a PABX, and he considers that standardisation will be as important for ISLN as it is for ISDN.

Additional references describing network structures in general: Chapters 3 and 8 of Black (1983), Chapter 1 of Chou (1983), Chapter 9 of Pooch et al (1982).

EQUIPMENT INSIDE NETWORKS

This section indicates the range of equipment currently available for use inside networks. It considers in turn: modems, multiplexers, concentrators, other network nodes, PABXs and other network exchanges. For each type of equipment, it lists a wide selection of the models available from various manufacturers and vendors.

The *Data Communications Buyers' Guide 1984* (*Data Comunications*, Dec 1983) contains lists of vendors and products, available in the USA, for various types of network equipment, including equipment for data concentration, data transmission, and switching.

Computer Management (1982) lists message switching equipment, modems and multiplexors available in the UK two years ago. Scheren-Guivel (1983) gives tables of general characteristics, physical characteristics, functional characteristics, tests and diagnostics of synchronous modems now available. *Communications Management* (1983a) provides a buyers' guide to modems currently on the British market.

Jennings (1983a) includes a table summarising modems for use on the PSTN, and Jennings (1983b) describes the standards currently available for modems.

Crandall (1983) discusses the basic theory of the operation of the Z19 RF modem, which interfaces serial data communications equipment to broadband coaxial cable communications systems, and gives examples of its applications to data and voice local/metropolitan area networks. Ratner (1983) gives a tutorial on broadband modems. Ziener and Ryan (1983) examine methods for implementing modems suitable for applications with high data rates, over 100 Mbits/sec.

Modems now on the market include: the AJ 4048 High Speed Modem, 4800 bits/sec full duplex (Anderson Jacobson, 1982); CASE 460/343 Data Modem, for time sharing at 120 chars/sec, 1200 bits/sec full duplex (CASE, 1983a); several series of Codex modems (Codex, 1983); Dynatech-Nolton Data Modems and Radio Modems (Dynatech-Nolton, 1983); Ericsson's new range of Series 7 modems, with speeds up to 19200 bits/sec (Ericsson, 1983a); the IAL range of modems (IAL Data Communicatons, 1983); the IBM 3863, 3864, and 3865 Modems, with speeds up to 9600 bits/sec (IBM, 1983a); the Interlekt IDC30 Series Modems and Portman Multi-Speed Modems for attachment to microcomputers and terminals; the Micom-Borer Micro4000 Series Data Modems, with speeds up to 9600 bits/sec (Micom-Borer, 1982); the Modular Technology V21, V22, V23, and V26 Modems and 3005 Acoustic Coupler; the very inexpensive Prism VTX 500 Modem for the Sinclair Spectrum personal computer (Prism, 1983); and the Userlink range of modems (Userlink Systems, 1984).

There is a wide variety of multiplexers, concentrators, X.25 PADs (Packet Assembler/Disassemblers), and other network nodes now on the market. Sudan and

Brohm (1983) give a guide to the choice of statistical multiplexers, and *Communications Management* (1984) gives a guide to multiplexers now available in the UK.

Statistical multiplexers can handle variable-length data block transmission and dynamic bandwidth assignment, with the aid of buffer storage to accommodate temporary peak loading on individual channels or groups of channels. They allow much better use to be made of shared data channels than would otherwise be possible.

Amdahl Communications Systems Division has several ranges of network equipment of modular design, including its 2000 Series Time Division Multiplexer (TDM) Systems, 3000 Series Switched Network Systems, and 4000 Series X.25 Systems, together with modems and test equipment. Its Series 4000 Network concentrator can perform many functions, including protocol translation, data routing, statistical multiplexing, providing error-free communications links and access to WANs (Amdahl, 1983b). Its 4075E Communications Processor is a high-performance front end or remote concentrator for networks using IBM's SNA (Amdahl, 1983e).

Anderson Jacobson's BABYNET AJ788 Multipoint Multiplexer allows many terminals to use a few computer ports, and also lets single terminals switch between several different computer systems (Anderson Jacobson, 1983).

DEC has a range of Ethernet Hardware Products for use with Ethernet LANs (DEC, 1983a), together with a range of WAN products, for use with DNA and SNA (DEC, 1983b). DEC's KMS11-BD Intelligent Multiplexer is designed to produce efficient, high-speed X.25 communications between a DEC PDP-11 or VAX computer and up to eight serial synchronous lines (DEC, 1982).

CASE has developed Series DCX, a complete range of statistical networking multiplexers, which can be formed into an integrated data exchange system to provide a flexible cost-effective data communications network (CASE, 1983b). Its DCX 815 Intelligent Multiplexer can handle up to eight asynchronous data channels over a single modem link (CASE, 1983b). Also in this range of multiplexers, and progressively more sophisticated, are the DCX 817 and DCX 825 Intelligent Multiplexers, the DCX 725 Dynamic Bandwidth Allocation (DBA) Multiplexer, the DCX 849 Intelligent Networking Multiplexer, and the DCX 850 data Exchange, handling up to 255 nodes (CASE, 1983b). For a further discussion of CASE Data Exchanges see Richards (1983).

The CASE DCX 816 PAD is a very efficient protocol converter, allowing up to eight asynchronous devices to share a single X.25 data link (CASE, 1983c). Its XGATE Gateway acts as a "PAD," allowing up to 125 DCX users access to PSS or other X.25 networks, and its BLUEGATE Gateway brings IBM compatibility to up to 32 asynchronous terminals, letting them emulate terminals on an IBM 3271/3274 cluster controller (CASE, 1983d).

Codex markets the 6000 Series of Intelligent Network Processors (Codex, 1983).

The TELEBOX II provides a simple system for connecting the widest range of computers, ranging from micros and word processors to mainframes, to the Telex network (Data & Control Equipment, 1983).

Dynatech's DynaPac X.25 range includes a MultiPad X.25 PAD, a MultiPlex X.25 PAD, and a MultiSwitch X.25 network switching device; Dynatech Communications (1983) describes this equipment and some of its applications, as well as giving some useful background information about X.25 networks. The Dynatech (1984) catalogue is a comprehensive list of the range of Dynatech network equipment marketed in the UK.

The Ferranti Telex Manager uses advanced message preparation and storage techniques, and automatically routes messages between terminals and the Telex network (Ferranti, 1981). The Ferranti Teletex Adaptor provides a simple interface to the Teletex service for computer-based products with a V.24 interface; it can be used in synchronous or asynchronous operation at speeds for 50 to 9600 bits/sec (Ferranti, 1983a).

The IAL FLEXIMUX B10 statistical multiplexer handles up to 32 asynchronous or synchronous channels and has automatic diagnostics (IAL Data Communications, 1983). The IAL 6PA 124 Speech-plus Multiplexer provides simultaneous combination of speech or high-speed data with low-speed telegraph channels.

Infotron's ANI™ (Advanced Network Integration) is a concept guiding Infotron's family of LAN systems, network concentrators, and statistical and wideband multiplexers; it is based on the idea that a user's network should evolve, not become obsolete (Infotron, 1983a). It provides for local area networking, LAN-WAN interconnection and interaction, and centralised network control (Infotron, 1983b).

Micom Systems (1983a, 1983b) describes the equipment used in the INSTA-NET™ LAN, including the Micro800/2i Data Concentrator Module, the INSTA-LINK™ Voice/Data Multiplexor, the INSTAMUX™ 470 Local Multiplexer, allowing terminals to operate up to 19.2 kbits/sec, and the INSTATRUNK™ 480 T1 Local Multiplexer, with total data rate of up to 1.544 Mbits/sec.

Micom wide area networking equipment includes: the Micro500 Error Controllers (Micom Systems, 1982), the Micro750 Intelligent TDM (Micom Systems, 1983c), the Micro800/X.25 Concentrator PAD (Micom Systems, 1983d), the Micro860/2 Data Concentrators (Micom Systems, 1983e), the Micro860 Concentrator Switch (Micom Systems, 1983f), and the Micro600 and Micro650 Port Selectors (Micom Systems, 1983g).

The Micro800/X.25 is easy to install and operate. It can be configured to fit existing equipment, so that no changes are needed in the use of terminals that access X.25 networks through it; terminal operators do not even have to learn to set up X.25 calls. The Micro600 and Micro650 are intelligent data PABXs, designed to manage the interconnections of many terminals and computer ports, especially for minicomputers; they handle asynchronous and synchronous data terminals, respectively.

Norsk Data's ND-100CC communications controller is a stand-alone device, that can link almost any mainframe, mini or micro (*The Times*, 1984). It is a powerful 16-bit minicomputer in its own right, and allows up to 25 micros, terminals and/or printers simultaneous access to between one and four computers.

The brochure *Plessey Controls in Data Communication* (Plessey Controls, 1983c) gives an overview of the Plessey wide area networking equipment. Specific items of equipment include; the TP 3010 Network Interface Processor (Plessey

Controls, 1982a), the TP 4000 Communications Processor for Packet Switching (Plessey Controls, 1982b), and the MX System 16002, offering a full range of multiplexer facilities, and designed to accommodate all types of data transmission, while incorporating a 16 kbits/sec modem (Plessey Controls, 1983d, 1983e).

The new Plessey 8600 range of Telex and Data Switches allows data exchanges to grow to very large sizes, and uses a very flexible modular design (Plessey Controls, 1983a). It includes the Plessey 8687 Telex/Packet Gateway (Plessey Controls, 1983b). Brown (1983) describes the Plessey Telex Network Adapter, which also enables Telex users to communicate with the users of packet-switched networks.

The RENEX TRANSLATOR protocol converting controller allows almost any asynchronous personal computer, terminal, or printer to communicate with a host computer, as if it were an IBM or 327X or 328X (Renex, 1983). According to version, it can handle between 5 and 33 ports, one of which is a synchronous link, while the others are asynchronous.

The Symicron MIGROGATE™ range of equipment is a modular multiprocessor system, adapted to communications and designed for use with small networks (Symicron, undated). Up to 64 ports may share one gateway link through its muldy'lexer. It is not restricted to any particular vendor's hardware, software, or networking approach.

Sytek has developed the LocalNet 20/™ Series and LocalNet 50/™ Series of equipment for use with its LocalNet broadband LAN (Sytek, 1983a).

Ungermann-Bass (undated) briefly describes the two versions of its NetOne™ LAN Communications System, together with the equipment that they use. Baseband Net/One has an Ethernet-compatible configuration, consisting of coaxial cable, transceivers, and network interface units; it uses CSMA/CD. Broadband Net/One has a CATV-compatible configuration, consisting of a CATV coaxial cable plant, head-end frequency remodulator, and network interface units equipped with radio frequency modems. Ungermann-Bass (various dates) describes some of the specific components used in Net/One.

Hutchison and Grant (1983) describe the design and implementation of a terminal concentrator for Strathnet, a combined Ethernet and Cambridge Ring LAN at the university of Strathclyde, Glasgow, Scotland.

The development of PABXs and network exchanges has been proceeding especially fast during recent years. The report *Integrated Voice/Data PBXs* (Architecture Technology, 1983) explains and illustrates the basic operation of integrated voice/data PABXs, showing what they can do and how they do it. It describes and evaluates the systems now on the American market or likely to appear soon.

The May 1983 issue of *IEEE Communications Magazine*, Vol. **21**, No. 3, is an issue on digital switching, including PABX technology (McDonald, 1983).

The June 1983 issue of *Communications Management* contains a special supplement on PABXs, including a full listing of PABXs available in the UK (*Communications Management*, 1983a). PABXs now on the market are also discussed by Kenyon (1984b) and Whitehead (1983a). Miles (1983) gives a state-of-the-art review of computer-controlled PABXs. Tremewan (1984) compares and contrasts PABXs with "ordinary" LANs, and gives some advice about the choice of a PABX.

Cohen (1983) describes M/A-Com Linkabit's IDX-300 Digital Exchange and its development. Ztel's Private Network Exchange (PNX) is designed to integrate voice and data by combining the voice features of a sophisticated PABX with a token ring LAN (Kay, 1983). Hasui et al (1983) propose an integrated PABX allowing switching of handwritten messages.

Camrass (1983) gives a management guide to the selection of a PABX and includes an evaluation of different PABX technologies.

Gandalf uses PABX and digital exchange technology in its PACXNET LAN and PACX Data Communications Management System (Gandalf, 1982a, 1982b); see also Chapter 6.

ICL uses its DNX-200 Distributed Network Exchange as a gateway between its OSLAN local networking system and wide area networks.

The Plessey IDX (IBIS Digital Exchange) is a third-generation digital exchange, where voice, text, and data traffic are controlled and switched in an integrated way (Plessey Office Systems, 1983a). It is designed to be the heart of the Plessey IBIS (Integrated Business Information System) LAN, described briefly in Chapters 6 and 11. Communications Management (1983a, pages 34–36) looks at how Plessey's IDX might develop as data and voice communications in the office become better integrated.

Magnusson and Jinbo (1983) review the GTD-5 EAX Series, a family of stored program, distributed process control, switching systems.

Rolm has recently launched the CBX11, a powerful new end-to-end digital communications system, with 4400 Mbits/sec data rate, distributed architecture, fiber optic links, and advanced digital telephones (Segerdahl, 1984a). It has been designed for both voice and data communications with tremendous information handling capabilities. It can be expanded in a modular way to support between 16 and over 10,000 users of both voice and data. There are over 13,000 existing Rolm CBXs, installed throughout the world; all of them can be upgraded fairly cheaply to the full capabilities of the CBX11, which is also believed to be widely compatible with many if not most computers and computer networking systems.

EQUIPMENT LINKED TO NETWORKS

This section updates Chapter 7 by giving some examples of terminals, displays, word processors, multi-purpose work stations, and voice equipment that have recently become available and can be attached to networks. However, it makes no attempt to survey the large number of new computers, especially personal computers and portable computers, which have recently appeared on the market usually with communications options available. It ends by considering recent advances in optical information storage devices.

The *Workstation Server News* is a monthly newsletter, written for all those interested in equipment attached to LANs; it specifically focuses on work stations and servers. It describes new items of equipment, specially emphasising how they work in operational environments.

The *Data Communications Buyers' Guide 1984* (*Data Communications*, Dec

1983) contains lists of vendors and products, available in the USA, for terminals, storage devices, and media, as well as support equipment.

In its feature on terminals, *Computer Weekly* (1983a) shows that terminals have evolved dramatically during the last 20 years and may have further radical changes during the next five years; it also warns of the rapid obsolescence of the older types of work stations. The 29 March 1984 issue of *Computer Weekly's Management Review Supplement* is a special issue on printers and terminals, containing much useful information on recent developments (*Computer Weekly, Management Review*, 1984).

Stewart (1983) points out that vendors now recognise the benefits to user efficiency and productivity that can result by applying ergonomics to the design of terminals. Holder (1983) describes a new terminal, developed by Aregon, that is already accessible to a wider range of users as it no longer requires the use of a keyboard and can also be operated by a light pen or graphics tablet.

Beishon (1983) provides a table giving the characteristics of several dozen terminals compatible with DEC's VT100 series of terminals. DEC has recently introduced a new range of terminals, the VT200 family, that integrates human engineering with full VT100 performance (DEC, 1983d).

Besides its usual terminals and work stations, ICL has introduced the 9500 range of retail terminals for use in shops and stores, and the 9600 range of terminals for data collection in factories and warehouses and also for recording workers' hours of attendance.

Aihara et al (1983) describe the multiple-bit-rate digital synchronous terminal system, with bit rates 8×2^n kbits/sec and 384×2^n bits/sec, for various integral values of n, which is being developed in Japan. An experimental prototype system has been designed, and field trials have been started.

Tulley (1983) gives details of those Teletex terminals that are nearest to appearing on the market and describes their nature. A typical Teletex terminal has a local part consisting of keyboard, printer display, local control and local memory, and a communication part consisting of receiving memory, sending memory, communication control, and a link to the Teletex network; its two parts communicate with each other via their respective memories. He distinguishes four types of Teletex terminals: Teletex adaptors, communicating typewriters, purpose-built terminals, and word processors and microcomputers, only a few models of which can yet be connected to the Teletex service. Kenyon (1984) discusses currently available teletex terminals and classifies them into: stand-alone terminals, Teletex adaptors, and Teletex cluster controllers.

The Userlink Integrated Terminal and Userlink Briefcase Terminal can be used with all networks and most internal systems (Userlink Systems, 1984). Their applications include: time-sharing computing, online data entry, electronic mail, viewdata, and online information retrieval from remote computer data bases.

Goodyear (1984) reviews some of the trends in portable terminals, including hand-held, "briefcase," and special purpose portable terminals; well over 50 models are now available in the UK. As almost all of them transmit and receive information in a serial asynchronous mode, which may not be directly compatible with the host computers to which they are to be linked, their users need to know at an early stage what extra hardware and software are needed to provide a suitable interface. Communications between portable terminals and hosts are usually by direct link, telephone line, radio, infra-red, or a combination of these methods. Goodyear includes a check list of 15 questions to ask before acquiring portable terminals.

British Telecom's Merlin M100 VDU Terminal contains a modem and has facilities for automatic dialing, connection, and log-on to a computer system via the PSTN (British Telecom, 1983). It can also store frequently dialed telephone numbers. Besides acting as a computer terminal, it can link to other services, including packet-switched networks (e.g., PSS and IPSS), electronic mail (e.g., Telecom Gold), and viewdata (e.g., Prestel).

The Braid Telex Manager allows an IBM Personal Computer to be used as a telex terminal (Braid Systems, 1983).

IBM has a wide range of "high function" displays, including: the 3278 range of monochrome displays, the 3279 range of the colour displays, and the 8775 stand-alone display, which can be used as a terminal for SNA networks (IBM, 1983b). These displays have good graphics as well as text facilities and are specially designed to be comfortable and convenient for their operators. The 3270 range of controllers allows these IBM display terminals to be clustered for access to computer networks.

Griffiths (1983) provides a basic introduction to facsimile transmission, shows how it compares with other communication techniques, outlines the fax standards in use, and indicates some likely future developments of fax including its integration with data processing systems. Griffiths (1984) briefly describes the Group I, Group II, and Group III types of fax machines, and lists the wide range of optional facilities now available for them. He gives a check list of questions that users can ask their suppliers. He mentions the available fax standards and outlines the work of the British Facsimile Industry Consultative Committee (BFICC).

Gee (1984) and Weinstein (1984) report on recent developments in "smart cards," which are portable plastic cards, with built-in memory and "intelligence," that can be used for financial transactions. Their two main European manufacturers, Bull and Philips, have joined forces; IBM and the Japanese are also interested. Mills (1984) describes memory card technology, systems, and applications, and reviews their potential as portable personal computers.

ICL's DRS word processing system has been designed to function, not only as a sophisticated word processor in its own right, but also as part of an integrated office system, providing a complete range of secretarial support services (ICL, 1983b). Its word processors are easily linked to ICL's LANs and, through them, to WAN facilities.

Henson (1983) identifies the market forces driving the evolution of word processors from stand-alone systems to components of multi-function information processing networks. He discusses some of the factors relevant to the connection of word processors to various types of network.

Several leading manufacturers and vendors have designed multi-purpose work stations, specially adapted for well integrated use with their LANs.

CAP's Mobile Office can be used at temporary work locations, including construction sites and on oil platforms and ships (CAP, 1982). It uses a CAP Multi-Function Workstation, which can carry out the following functions: computer terminal, office computer, word processor, Teletex unit, telex editor and terminal, facsimile terminal, satellite terminal, viewdata terminal, viewdata information provider terminal, and TV receiver.

The ICL DRS 20 Series of work stations is an evolutionary distributed office system, designed to meet the real needs of the business world (ICL, 1983a, 1983c). Each work station can function as a "dumb" terminal, a personal computer in its own right, or as a computer working with the rest of a computer network. The ICL PERQ is a very sophisticated computer and work station, with high resolution black and white graphics, specially adapted to the needs of scientists, engineers, and designers (ICL, 1983a; Hopwood and Witty, 1982; Loveluck, 1982).

The MASTERNET Multi-function Workstation, similar to the Xionics work station described in Chapter 7, offers users without technical expertise a wide range of facilities some of which are local while others access outside networks and services (Master Systems, 1983). This system guides its users with helpful messages and presents them with menus to help them choose the information that they require.

The Plessey IBIS Integrated Workstation provides a full range of integrated electronic office and communications applications together with full personal computing facilities (Plessey Office Systems, 1983a). It has full networking facilities, as part of the Plessey IBIS Integrated Business Information System.

The Prime Producer 100™ Office Workstation is integrated with the Prime Office Automation System (OAS), which has document transfer, electronic mail, and filing facilities, and performs a wide range of integrated office tasks (Prime, 1983). It can access information on any Prime 50 Series computer, and it has good word processing software.

Xerox in the USA and Rank Xerox in the UK have a range of work stations, differing in capabilities and facilities, to match the chief needs of different users (Rank Xerox, 1983). For example, the Xerox 860 word processor has comprehensive text processing facilities, and the Xerox 8010 work station is designed specifically for the professional information worker. These work stations can be used with the Xerox 8000 Network Systems, including Ethernet, to carry out a wide variety of office functions and also access external communications and computing services.

STC's Executel work station is specially designed to cater for the communications requirements of senior managers and executives (STC, 1983). It has a multi-facility telephone and a keyboard and display screen with many functions and capabilities. It can be used as a telex, electronic mail, or viewdata terminal.

Recently developed digital voice equipment includes: the Ferranti Computer Systems Voice Manager (Ferranti, 1983b), the Plessey Integrated Voice Messaging System (Plessey Office Systems, 1983b), and Wang's Automated Voice Communications System DVX (Wang, 1981). The possibilities for voice message systems and other aspects of voice communications are discussed in the December 1983 issue of *IEEE Communications Magazine*, Vol. **21,** No. 9, an issue on speech communications (Sekey, 1983).

Videodisk technology is continuing to progress, although most of its potentialities for integration with computing systems and computer networks have yet to be realised. Mayne (1982) surveys the state of the art of this new technology and its possible convergence with computing.

Segerdahl (1984b) and Rothchild (1983) survey the work now being done on the development of optical memory media. They describe how optical disks work, who makes them, and how much data they can hold.

The MNEMOS SYSTEM 6000 can store more than 6000 A4 pages of text or graphics information, together with about one MB of digital information for indexing purposes and users' application software (Mnemos, 1982). Its work station can be connected to local or remote computer systems for exchanging digital data.

Videodisk systems now on the market include Philips Professional LaserVision (Philips Electronics, 1983) and Philips Megadoc (Philips, 1983; Nevinson, 1983). Megadoc accepts input in digital form with equal ease from document readers, word processors, and other types of communicating devices. Its indexing and information retrieval procedures are controlled by an integrated package of software modules.

A document system, soon to be completed for the Library of Congress, will use 100 Thomson-CSF optical disks in a data "juke box" able to store about 100 GB of data at a data storage cost of about $150 per GB (a *GB—gigabyte—*is a unit of a billion bytes) (Charlish, 1984a). The new DOC Wheel Mass Storage System, now being developed by Docdata of Venlo, Netherlands, can store about 6 GB per cassette at an estimated cost of $20 per cassette (Charlish, 1984b).

Bearing in mind that one GB of storage is equivalent to about 400,000 A4 pages of text, and that optical storage costs, as opposed to optical storage device costs, are already hundreds of times cheaper than those of corresponding magnetic media, optical memories are thus beginning to become competitive. However, they have a long way to go as most optical disk systems are not yet designed to interact with computer systems.

Those few that do interact with them, such as the Optimem 1 GB disk announced by Shugart (Moody, 1984), the 7600 4 GB disk announced by Storage Technology (*Computing*, 1984; Holder, 1984), and the 1.31 GB disk announced by Hitachi (*Wireless World*, 1984), have computer read-write facilities and interfaces, but memories that cannot be erased; this lack of erasability does not matter too much, considering the very large and inexpensive memories used. No truly erasable read–write optical memory seems to have developed yet beyond the fairly early experimental stage.

TRANSMISSION TECHNOLOGIES

This section updates Chapter 8 by reporting on recent development in transmission technologies. Although considering other aspects of data transmission, it concentrates on fibre optic and satellite communications, where these new developments have been most rapid. It ends by referring to some recent literature on data compression and on transmission errors.

Data Channels is a fortnightly newsletter on data transmission and on some other aspects of networking.

Sklar (1983) gives a tutorial, though fairly mathematical, overview of digital communications with 74 references to the relevant literature. The first part of his review discusses the steps in signal processing, formatting and source coding, digital modulation formats, demodulation, and trade-offs between different digital transmission parameters. The second part presents channel coding, multiplexing and multiple access, frequency spreading, encryption, synchronisation, and communications link analysis together with some conclusions. Although this paper surveys digital communications in general, it specially emphasises communication over satellite links.

Part 1 of the book *Packet Switching* (Rosner, 1982) introduces the concepts of packet switching, giving both qualitative and quantitative comparisons between circuit switching, message switching and packet switching; it also considers the traffic characteristics of voice and data messages. Part 6 of the book deals briefly with the future of packet switching, especially its use in ISDNs; it describes some approaches combining switching and packet switching in integrated voice-data networks.

Haselton (1983) and Amstutz (1983) present the basic concepts of *burst switching*, a new approach to switching especially designed for use in integrated voice-data networks. *Burst-switched networks* have many, highly dispersed, small link switches, each handling about 16 lines or trunks, and usually also have at least one high-capacity hub switch. The connections between these switches are called links, and many links may pass through a single hub. Ports, that is, lines or trunks, access the network via the link switches. This sort of network corresponds to a central PABX of up to 65,000 lines and trunks.

In *burst switching*, data and voice characters are both switched in the same way, through the same circuits. However, data bursts and voice bursts are treated differently, to allow for the fact that voice characters need to be transmitted rapidly, otherwise they become useless, while data characters may be delayed but must not be lost.

A *burst* is a continuous piece of voice or a data message or a system command. A channel is allocated for a burst for the duration of its transmission, but becomes available for another burst, after the end of the transmission. A burst consists of a four-byte header, followed by variable length information, and ending with a distinctive end-of-message byte.

The header contains routing information, control information, and an error-checking byte. The control information specifies whether the burst carries digital voice, image, text, data, or control information. The header effectively reserves the contiguous network channels that are needed to convey the burst from its source to its destination for the duration of its tranmission. In the event of contention between bursts, voice bursts are given priority, but delayed voice bursts, unlike delayed data bursts, are discarded.

From this description, it is evident that burst switching is intermediate between circuit switching and packet switching. A total message is divided into bursts, but these bursts may often be longer, perhaps much longer than packets; in the case of voice, a burst corresponds to an element of speech where the sound-level is appreciable—speech typically has sound bursts, separated by short silent intervals. As in circuit switching, the whole of a burst is sent along the network route that is allocated to it; this contrasts with packet switching, where the route taken by a packet is not necessarily given in advance but may be determined, link by link, as the packet passes through the network. However, circuits are reserved for much shorter periods than with circuit switching. The store and forward facility for non-voice bursts is similar to that of packet switching and message switching.

Burst switching has the following advantages:

1. Shorter loop lengths allowing the use of higher bandwidths and less wiring;
2. Integrated networking allowing more flexibility as the mixture of traffic changes;
3. Dispersed control allowing support of higher calling rates;
4. Detection of silent intervals in speech so that voice bandwidth is used nearly three times as effectively as with circuit switching;
5. Very low overheads so that transmission channel utilisation can exceed 99% when burst time lengths exceed .1 sec.

Burst switching also has the following disadvantages:

1. Delays to messages tend to be greater than with circuit switching, although they are comparable to those with voice packet switching;
2. Network complexity is increased, in the sense that automatic test and system diagnostic routines are essential, together with facilities for initiating testing remotely.

Morse and Kopec (1983) discuss the evaluation of the performance of a distributed burst-switched communication system.

Gerla (1983) defines a *transport technique* as a method used to establish a channel over a communications link, with the aid of multiplexing. He considers circuit switching and packet switching and their variants, in relation to the following transport and multiplexing schemes: *space division* (dividing a trunk into different physical channels), *frequency division* (assigning different frequency bands to different channels), *time division* (assigning different time slots to different channels), *statistical time division* (assigning different time slots to channels only when these channels have data to send), and *block division* (devoting a whole trunk to a given pair of users only for the time needed to send a packet message between them).

From the user's viewpoint, he suggests that it may be better to distinguish between services rather than between the many different combinations of switching and transport schemes. He compares the following three services:

1. A *circuit service* provides protocol transparency between speed-matched source-destination pairs, but it gives no protection against errors and failures;

2. A *packet service* provides speed conversion and recovery from errors and failures, and perhaps also provides code conversion and protocol conversion, but it cannot guarantee a low delay or adequate bandwidth, nor can it support arbitrary protocols;

3. An *integrated services network* combines circuit-switched and packet-switched services, and it is usually based on a hybrid transport and switching implementation.

Charlish (1984c) describes the Versa-Track flat cabling system developed by the US-based company Thomas and Betts. It allows power, telephone and data cables to be taken under office carpets to office work stations, at low cost and without disruption. It could thus be especially helpful to orgnisations rearranging their office space to cope with an influx of word processors, personal computers, work stations, and other equipment.

Charlish (1982) describes how the British Central Electricity Generating Board moves messages through its electricity grid, making use of the power that is generated.

Willett (1983) discusses the transmission technologies used by the Mercury telecommunications network, now being developed in the UK, including: wire, cable, radio, and fibre optics.

IEEE Transactions on Selected Areas in Communications, Vol. **SAC-1,** No. 3 (April 1983) is a special Issue on fibre optic systems (Personick, 1983). It includes papers on: fibre optical systems in general, trunk transmission systems, field trials, broadband distribution systems, undersea cable systems, fibre optic LANs, subsystems and components, and special applications.

Communications International, Vol. **10,** No. 4 (Apr 1983) has a *Focus Supplement: Fibre Optics*, that includes articles on fiber optic systems in Canada and the cost-benefits of fibre optic systems.

The report *Optical Fiber Communications* (Future Systems, 1982) reviews current developments and future systems. *Optical Fiber Communications* (Keiser, 1983) is a recent book on fiber optic communications systems.

An article in *Computer Weekly* (1983b) reviews modern fibre optics technology and considers that it is probably the best way of meeting the rapidly expanding demand for voice and data communications. Systems, soon to be installed as part of British Telecom's ISDN, will transmit data at 500 Mbits/sec or even faster. The article predicts that fibre optics will first be applied to trunk telecommunications traffic, which needs links of very high capacity, then to LANs, especially in factories, and then to undersea cables.

British Telecom has already awarded Plessey a contract to lay a 565 Mbits/sec fibre optic communications system between Nottingham and Sheffield, in England; this is believed to be the first commercial system of its kind in the world.

Fibre/Laser News is a fortnightly newsletter on optical fibre and laser technologies, including their applications to communications and information technology.

Baack et al (1983) describe several experimental digital and analog broadband optical transmission systems, and conclude that there are disadvantages in using analog broadband optical transmission techniques. The second section of their paper gives a comprehensive list of the data rates achieved in a variety of operational and experimental systems. They report successful field trials on systems with data rates up to 400 Mbits/sec, and successful laboratory tests on systems with data rates up to 2000 Mbits/sec. Their paper has many references to other relevant literature.

Bell (1984) reviews the current status of fibre optic telecommunications systems, and includes tables indicating the characteristics of the systems, installed or being built in the USA, Canada, the UK, Western Europe, Japan, and Saudi Arabia. Some of the fibre optic trunks will be hundreds of miles long. Their data rates are to be 400 Mibts/sec in Japan, 280 Mbits/sec in the UK-Belgium trunk, and up to 140 Mbits/sec elsewhere.

Martin-Royle and Bennett (1983) survey optical fibre transmission systems in British Telecom's network, which already has fully operational systems at data rates of 8, 34, and 140 Mbits/sec. About a half of its trunks will use optical fibres by 1990.

Garner (1984) reports that optical fibre technology is becoming an essential part of Japan's Information Network System (INS) and describes some of this technology. The current focus of interest is the 2800 km optical trunk line between Fukuoka and Sapporo, at different ends of Japan. Towards the end of the 1980s optical fibre cable TV systems and LANs will become widespread in Japan.

Kennedy (1983) discusses the prospects for the use of fibre optics in LANs. Hitherto, local data communications systems have generally limited the use of fibre optics to point-to-point multiplexed data links. Recently, costs of optical fibres have dropped enough, and fibre optics technology has improved enough, to allow highly reliable fibre optic systems to be useful in LANs at a reasonable cost. Kennedy examines the economics of fibre optic systems in comparison with baseband and broadband cable systems and gives some numerical cost figures.

Warrior and Husain (1983) examine the reliability of fibre optic rings from a system viewpoint. They evaluate simplex, duplex, and counter-rotating ring structures to find out how much ring reliability can be improved.

Campbell (1983), De Grandi et al (1983), Ebihara et al (1983), and Takeyama et al (1983) describe fibre optic rings that have already been built; Roworth and Cole (1983) discuss the use of optical fibre links in the Cambridge Ring. Laviola (1983) describes Citibank's extensive fibre optic metropolitan network, linking major buildings in midtown and downtown Manhattan, and also using a digital microwave link to duplicate its longest optical fibre link.

The British company, Focom, recently introduced its DART distributed high-speed fibre optic data communications network, which was designed in modular form to meet the needs of a wide range of users (*Computer Weekly*, 1983c). It can be expanded from a basic unit of 16 data ports up to integrated networks with thousands of terminals. It uses fibre optic rings, each with up to 480 data ports. These rings can be interconnected locally, and also for multi-site organisations via long distance links over British Telecom's MegaStream and KiloStream networks. As a result, DART can support full local networking together with national and international networking.

Dowling (1983) describes the installation of a fibre optic 80-terminal network at Lansing Bagnall's 16-acre site in Basingstoke, England. Dowling (1983) and Harwood (1983) point out several advantages of using optical fibres here, not only lower cost, but also easy installation, flexible routing, freedom from electrial interference and lightning strikes, increased safety, and improved protection against unauthorised data access.

Hara (1983) presents a design for a fibre optic broadband LAN using a PABX in an office environment. The channels allocated for transmitter and for receiver are 55.25 MHz for closed circuit TV and 64 kbits/sec each for telephone, data, signal, and two special-purpose channels.

Katz (1983) describes some semiconductor optoelectronic devices for optical communications in free space.

Walker (1983) reports on some recent developments in radio communications, together with its likely future. He mainly considers the following four aspects: digital microwave systems, single sideband systems, cellular mobile systems, and digital electronic message services.

Meteor burst communications uses the ionised trails, left by meteors passing through the Earth's atmosphere, to reflect or reradiate VHF radio signals. Later in 1984, the US Air Force will install the first operational data communications network, using this principle (Fitzgerald, 1984). It will run under minicomputer control with full duplex transmission. Because the meteor trails do not last long, this sytem cannot handle voice communications, but it can support data traffic at rates from 2000 to 4800 bits/sec on a 25 kHz bandwidth. The system is able to work because about 50,000 meteors of the right kind enter the atmosphere each second.

The 1983 Satellite Directory (Phillips, 1983) gives useful information about satellite communications in general. *Satellite News* is a weekly newsletter on satellite communications.

The book *Satellites Today* (Baylin and Toner, 1983) discusses the history, technology, concerns, and future of satellite communications. It is intended for intelligent laymen as well as telecommunications professionals.

New periodicals on satellite communications include the quarterly *International Journal of Satellite Communications*, the monthly *Cable & Satellite Europe*, and the newsletter *Cable & Satellite News*.

IEEE Transactions on Selected Areas in Communications, Vol. **SAC-1**, No. 1 (Jan 1983) is a special issue on digital satellite communications (Feher et al, 1983). *Computer Networks*, Vol. **7**, No. 6 (Dec 1983) reports on the International Symposium on Satellite and Computer Communications, held at Versailles, France, in April 1983. *Computer*, Vol. **16**, No. 4 (Apr 1983) is an issue on communications satellite software.

Communications International, Vol. **10**, No. 11 (Nov 1983) has a *Focus Supplement: Satellite Communications*, which has articles on satellite systems and technology, the potential applications of the Inmarsat satellite system to the guidance of aircraft as well as ships, satellites for business communications, and the uses of satellites in Canada.

Bell (1984) reviews the current status of satellite communications in the USA. Comsat is using an uplink band of 14 to 14.5 GHz and a downlink band of 11.7 to 12.2 GHz for a variety of services, including the distribution of NBC broadcasts. A 1983 FCC ruling allows spacing of communications satellites in geostationary orbits every two degrees instead of the previous spacing of four degrees, but requires stricter technical standards as a result. Also in 1983, the FCC approved an uplink band of 17.3 to 17.8 GHz and a downlink band of 12.2 to 12.7 GHz for domestic direct broadcast services.

Shorrock (1983) describes the current state of satellite communications in the UK, and believes that satellites can provide substantial savings over the costs of conventional networks. He gives some details of SatStream, the British Telecom's satellite communications to be launched in 1984, and of INMARSAT, the International Marine Satellite Organisation.

Hubert and Gaumond (1984) describe the Stratoroute 2000 Network, to be opened by Telecom Canada late in 1984. It will use time division multiple access and spot beam technology, and operate in the 14/12 GHz band on the ANIK C satellite.

Murakami (1983) describes the Nippon Telegraph & Telephone Public Corporation's research and development on satellite communications, which began in the 1960s and is now being applied to technologies for high capacity satellite systems. NTT's commercial service, using two satellites, started in August 1983.

Raghbati (1981) reviews data compression techniques, and gives references to further literature. He points out that reducing redundancy in data representation leads to decreased data storage requirements and reduces data communications costs; care should of course be taken that the reliability of data transmission is not made unacceptably low as a result.

Johannes (1983) describes the specification of performance and down time of a digital system. He refers to international standards work on measures of this sort (CCITT, 1980 and 1982), and notes that CCITT uses the term "error ratio" to define error rate averaged over an interval.

CCITT (1980) uses a performance parameter the percentage of time intervals having more than a given error rate. CCITT requires an international 64 kbits/sec digital connection to have at least 90% of one-minute intervals with error rate $\leqslant .000001$, averaged over that minute, and at least 92% of one-second intervals to be error-free. For reasons noted by Newcombe and Pasupathy (1982), the one-minute interval criterion is appropriate to voice transmission, and the one-second interval criterion is suitable for data transmission.

An additional specification, based on seconds with error rate .001 at most, averaged over that second, has more recently been advanced, together with proposals suggesting a .1 second interval, probably in view of increasing data rates (Johannes, 1983).

This more general performance parameter has also been used in a proposed definition of failure for a digital system, so that outage and availability can be determined without ambiguity; here, a one-second interval and an error rate .001 at most have been used. CCITT (1982) has tentatively defined complete failure as beginning when ten consecutive seconds each have error rate .001 or worse, and ending when ten consecutive seconds each have error rate better than .001. The beginning and end of the complete failure period are both taken back to the first seconds of the consecutive ten seconds defining them.

Sastry (1984) also discusses CCITT's approach to performance specification (CCITT, 1980). He suggests a new parameter, *percentage error-free blocks*, as an additional performance measure, to be specified for different block lengths.

Newcombe and Pasupathy (1982) discuss error monitoring for digital communications, and Podell (1982) formulates the probability of reliable information completion, within a tolerable delay, as a measure of effectiveness for digital communication paths.

Additional references to data transmission in general: Chapters 5 and 7 of Black (1983), Chapters 5 to 8 of Chou (1983), Part II of Pooch et al (1982).

Additional reference to transmission via the PSTN: Baynton (1984), Jennings (1983c).

Additional references to fibre optic transmission and communications: Personick (1981), Howes and Morgan (1980), Sandbank (1980), Miller and Chynoweth (1979).

Additional references to satellite communications: Feher (1983), Jain (1983), Menzies (1983), Nirenberg (1983), Parker (1983), *Financial Times* (1982), Macclesfield (1982), Bhargava et al (1981), Online Publications (1980).

NETWORK CONTROL AND PERFORMANCE

This section updates Chapter 10 by reporting on recent developments in network measurement, monitoring, control, performance analysis, modelling and simulation. It also includes extensive information about commercially available equipment for network monitoring, management, and control.

Amer et al (1983) describe the work of the network measurement centre at the National Bureau of Standards, Washington, DC, and the techniques used there for measuring NBS' own CSMA/CD bus LAN, NBSNET. These methods can be applied to the measurement of other LANs. Table 2 in this paper summarises ten types of measurement reports. Toense (1983) gives further details of the measurement of NBSNET. Traffic generators send packets of given length distributions at known rates along an isolated network segment; these packets are recorded and time-stamped for analysis. Toense concludes, from analysis of the empirical laboratory data, that the behavior of NBSNET is fair, stable and predictable, under the operating conditions that were observed.

Seitz et al (1983) describe performance measurements of the Arpanet, the transatlantic research network, that have been oriented to the needs of its users. These experiments have been based largely on the proposed measurements standard (proposed Federal Standard 1043), and have shown the feasibility of using it to measure the performance of a modern data communications network. The tools and techniques, developed by the Arpanet project, made it easier to prepare a later version of the standard, American National Standard X3.102.

The measurement results show some significant difference between the performance of the subnetwork and the (much lower) performance of some of the services usually delivered to some of Arpanet's end users. Delays at the user interfaces were often two to four times as much as the corresponding subnetwork delays, and the observed throughputs were proportionally lower.

Most of these extra delays seem to have been introduced by communications support software in the host computers, rather than by user programs. The measurements confirmed that transmission errors are extremely rare on the Arpanet, but that loss of data, in transit between users' application programs, is relatively common. Such failures seem to be caused by hardware and software "crashes" and subnetwork delays, in addition to the lateness of Arpanet hosts in accepting transferred messages. The loss of users' data was by far the most serious defect observed in the network during these measurements; that one phenomenon was more important than all other factors influencing the quality of the Arpanet's service to its users.

Wilbur (1983) reports on the work, carried out at University College London, on the measurement and monitoring of the UNIVERSE network, that uses satellite communications to link Cambridge Rings at various sites. One aim of this work is to collect information about traffic patterns and the results of performance measurements; another is to use monitoring to find the reliability of the network's components.

Bernstein et al (1983) discuss the requirements for a network control centre for broadband LANs. It should provide a wide range of functions, including: configuration control, security and access control, administrative recording, and performance monitoring. It should be designed for easy expansion, as the number of attached devices and the number of device types increase. The Sytek LocalNet network control centre is described as an example, that achieves many of these objectives.

Swanson (1983) discusses three types of data communications test equipment, useful for network monitoring: protocol testers (data line monitors), voice frequency analysers, and non-protocol-oriented test sets. Veith (1983) states that any moden diagnostics system should include a data analyser, which has a monitor and which can simulate other equipment on its network.

Dadzie (1983) and Marchbanks (1984) describe the functions of a network control system. It should identify, immediately after they occur, any faults affecting network operation, and ideally it should attempt to predict network problems before they occur, in order for remedial action to be taken before users are affected. To do this, the network should be set, so that a warning can be given and corrections made, whenever a threshold is exceeded; a data base of performance statistics should be maintained and analysed.

In advanced network control systems, monitoring is performed automatically by systems based on microprocessors or minicomputers. A network control system needs to test the network, and maintain control over various data collection activities. It should provide a single point of contact for network users, who should be able to view the network as a single resource, not as a mass of complexities. It should have facilities for configuration control, including the variation of lines, modems and terminals; in this way, the network can be modified more easily in order to meet its performance objectives better.

Network measurement and monitoring equipment on the market include: the Atlantic Research INTERVIEW Data Analyzers, Protocol Analyzer and Protocol Test Equipment (Atlantic Research, 1983a to 1983c); the Dynatech DYNA-TEST™ 1600 Protocol Monitor/Simulator (Dynatech Data Systems, 1983); IAL Network Management (IAL Data Communications, 1983); the Sytek LocalNet 50/120™ Statistical Monitor, for collecting performance statistics on a selected LocalNet channel for a specific time interval (Sytek, 1983b); the TEKELEC TE 820 PCM Frame Simulator & Analyzer (Tekelec, 1981); and the Tektronix Communications Analyzers and Testers (Tektronix, 1980a to 1980c).

The TEKELEC CHAMELEON is a versatile, comprehensive, flexible, and easy-to-use Data Communications Simulator/Analyzer (Tekelec, 1983). Its monitoring facilities allow the display of line activities at high speed. The CHAMELEON uses a wide range of simulation software packages, that are easily adapted to most network environments. A series of menus enable its users to select the functions they wish to apply in a straightforward way. It is specially designed to analyse the performance of X.25 and IBM protocols.

The Micom Micro800/X.25 collects operational data on X.25 network usage, performance statistics, call duration times, and other data about calls (Micom Systems, 1982d).

Quite a number of network management and control systems are now available.

The DynaPac Network Control Center controls X.25 networks (Dynatech Communications, 1983). The Dynanet-200 network management system monitors, tests, and controls data communications networks from a central work station with a colour graphics display (Dynatech, 1984).

EDNET, the Ericsson Data NETwork management system, is a modular system for automatic monitoring and centralised control of data transmission networks (Ericsson, 1983b).

The Gandalf PACX network exchange provides central management control of local and remote networking facilities, including the provision of complete statistical data and system security facilities (Gandalf, 1982b).

The British data communications company IAL has just launched its Medius network management system, with colour monitor displays of network faults, which aims to provide network users with a range of resource management functions for all aspects of networking (*Computer News*, 1984).

The Infotron ANM-800 Advanced Network Manager forms the nucleus of Infotron's Advanced Network Integration (Infotron, a to c). It provides a comprehensive network planning and control system and reports real time status information, statistics, and events on a colour graphics display.

The Micom Micro600 is not only a stand-alone data PABX; it can be used for

LAN management, when linked with Micom's INSTANET products (Micom Systems, 1983f). The Micom 860 Concentrator Switch performs centralised management of a WAN; it can configure remote channels, gather network operating statistics, and allow remote modems to operate unattended (Micom Systems, 1983g).

The Plessey TP5000 control centre is based on a powerful minicomputer (Plessey Controls, 1982c). It performs all network data management functions, including: acting as command centre, collecting data for traffic and statistical and accounting analyses, holding the data base used to manage network equipment, and providing consoles to help the network control supervisors isolate faults and take remedial action.

The Sytek LocalNet 50/100™ Network Control Center provides automatic services for access control, performance monitoring, and secure communications of the Sytek LocalNet™ broadband LAN (Sytek, 1983c).

The Racal-Milgo Communications Management Systems provide complete and powerful network management systems for handling up to 10,000 addressable devices; they include a range of systems for all sizes of networks (Racal-Milgo, 1983a and 1983b). They provide diagnostic information and automatic alarm collection, via independent management channels, separate from the network's primary data channels. Sophisticated high resolution colour graphics displays can be provided, to help system operators to understand the network's structure and behaviour.

SMART (Systems Monitoring And Reporting by Tesdata) provides the information needed to analyse and manage network performance (Tesdata Systems, a to c). Through sophisticated high resolution colour graphics, it can translate detailed technical data into graphs, bar charts, pie charts, and other displays that are easy to understand. It can be used for configuration management, prediction of response times and throughputs, and network planning, based on calculations using mathematical models. It can evaluate hardware requirements and software options, and it is easily tailored to individual user requirements.

IBM has several recent software products that are useful for network management (IBM, 1983c).

Version 2 of the Series/1 Realtime Programming System Communications Manager is an upgrade of Version 1; as such, it significantly strengthens the Series/1 communications capabilities in addressing front end processing, performing distributed applications, and providing full networking functions. Maximum flexibility and control are emphasised, and full compatibility with X.25 is intended. The Remote Manager similarly allows management of non-SNA networks from a host-computer using SNA.

The Communications Manager supports a wide range of IBM devices, including the IBM 3270 family, IBM office automation equipment, and the IBM Personal Computer. LANs can be established with the Communications Manager, using the Series/1 Local Communications Controller. Up to 16 Series/1 systems may be connected in a ring configuration. Larger LANs may be built up, using interconnected rings of this sort.

Version 3 of Network Problem Determination Application (NPDA) is designed to increase network operators' ability to detect and resolve problem situations. Its *alert management* feature monitors alert messages and automatically notifies the network manager of error situations or threshold conditions. The alerts can be displayed dynamically at selected operator stations.

NPDA collects and interprets information about detected errors and events, and maintains statistical data originated by those hardware and software components that provide such information. It also recommends possible actions that users can take to locate and relieve network problems. NPDA Version 3 offers enhanced support of several kinds in addition to previously announced NPDA functions.

Version 2 Release 2 of Teleprocessing Network Simulator (TPNS) is designed to test and evaluate online application programs, control programs, and networks, before actual network installation. It simulates terminal and subarea network traffic for the purpose of driving telecommunications systems. Its users can reduce the amount of test time for these systems and at the same time test them more effectively.

The analysis and mathematical modeling of network performance are presented in the books *Performance Models of Distributed Systems* (Gelenbe, 1983) and *Performance Analysis of Data Systems and Their Applications* (Pujolle, 1981). The book *Principles of Computer Communication Network Design* (Seidler, 1983) presents mathematical models for computer network design, access methods, routing, congestion, and optimisation.

The January 1984 issue of *IEEE Journal on Selected Areas in Communications*, Vol. **SAC-2,** No. 1 is a special issue on computer/aided modeling, analysis, and design of communications systems (Shanmugan and Balaban, 1984). Also relevant are some of the most advanced recent research on LANs and in the ACM SIGCOMM (1983) conference proceedings.

Stallings (1984) aims to show which factors are important in determining LAN performance and also summarises recent comparative performance studies.

The performance parameters, usually considered in performance analyses of networks, include throughput and delay characteristics of network links and longer paths through networks, together with mean queue sizes and other characteristics of queues at network nodes.

Grubb and Abrams (1981) consider user-oriented performance parameters. Goel and Amer (1983) develop a much wider class of network performance metrics, using a mathematical formulation in terms of finite state models. Johannes (1983) and Sastry (1984) briefly discuss some performance parameters related to transmission errors.

In their general discussion of LANs, Kümmerle and Reiser (1983) consider their performance. In particular, they compare the delay and throughput characteristics of the CSMA/CD and token-passing access methods, and they discuss some significant differences between ring and bus systems with respect to wiring, media, transmission, and reliability.

Stuck (1983) presents the results of the calculation of maximum mean data rates for LANs using token-passing access via a ring, token-passing access via a bus, and CSMA/CD; he gives formulae for maximum mean throughput rate and for slot time. He provides graphs of maximum mean carried data rate versus actual transmission, for a LAN with 100 stations, for the cases when only one station is active and when all stations are active, and for packet sizes of 500, 1000, and 2000 bits.

Davies and Ghani (1983) discuss the design of a high-speed LAN, using an optical-fibre ring. They compare the performance of token ring, slotted ring, register insertion ring, and CSMA ring protocols. They conclude that the token ring usually performs best, but that the register insertion ring is a useful alternative under certain conditions.

Li et al (1983) study the behaviour of a token bus LAN under different configurations and constraints. They evaluate bounds for the maximum queue and delay, the performance trade-offs of baseband versus broadband networks, and the effects of several connecting stations, cable length, packet sizes, and round-robin transmission methods. They compare the performance of an approach, using linked subnets, with another approach, using a single LAN.

Acampora et al (1983a) examine the performance of media access schemes used by a centralised-bus LAN. Because the centralised bus is short, packet transmissions are scheduled "perfectly," without destructive collisions and without periods when the bus is idle and packets await transmission. The scheduling of packet transmissions is distributed and flexible, allowing for multiple priority classes, round-robin-like scheduling within a priority class, and integrated circuit switching and packet switching. The performance of this access method is compared with that of other popular contention schemes; the results indicate clearly the better performance of the proposed new bus contention scheme. For further details, see Acampora et al (1983b) and Hluchyj et al (1983).

Carpenter (1984) compares the performance of two LAN access methods, the token bus (IEEE Standard 802.4) and LODI (the Local Distributed Data Interface specification, ANSI Standard X3T9.5).

Alton et al (1981) report the results of their study of Euronet.

Brayer (1983) discusses the expected performance of a mobile radio network which does not have a fixed topology.

Recent papers on mathematical modelling of networks include the above mentioned papers by Davies and Ghani (1983), Li et al (1983), Acampora et al (1983a and 1983b), Hluchyj et al (1983), and Stuck (1983), together with the following papers: Bux and Schlatter (1983), on the performance analysis of buffer insertion rings; Sykas et al (1983), on a new family of multiple-access protocols for resolving contention in LANs; Chlamtac and Eisenger (1983), on the performance of CSMA/CD in an Ethernet with mixed voice and data traffic; Majithia and Li (1983), on the performance of a terminal that integrates voice and data services; Tham and Hume (1983), on the analysis of a network system carrying voice traffic and data traffic of both low and high priorities; Hsieh et al (1983), on performance analysis of an end-to-end flow control mechanism; Borgonovo and Fratta (1983), Gold et al (1983), Liu et al (1983), Malcolm et al (1983), Riordon et al (1983), and Szpankowski (1983), on access methods for radio networks; Guilbur et al (1983) on satellite multiple access; Gopal and Kermani (1983), on the performance of stop-and-wait protocols over satellite links; and Podell (1982) on the evaluation of the probability of reliable completion of information transfer within a tolerable delay time.

Stallings (1984) provides some useful examples of the results of simple performance modelling.

He shows that propagation delay D and data rate R set an upper bound on performance that is independent of the medium-access control protocol. If L is the mean packet length in bits, then a, the ratio of packet propagation time to packet transmission time, is given by the formula

$$a = RD/L$$

The parameter a typically has values between .01 and 1, assuming a signal propagation velocity of 200,000 km/sec. He shows that the maximum network utilisation is

$$U = \text{Throughput}/R$$
$$= (1/(\text{propagation time} + \text{transmission time}))/R$$
$$= 1/(1 + a)$$

Using simple models of token-passing and CSMA/CD access methods, he then shows that, as the number of active stations becomes very large, the maximum achievable throughput tends to

$1/\max (a, 1)$ for token bus LANs,

and to

$1/(1 + 3.44\, a)$ for CSMA/CD bus LANs.

Stallings finally compares results from analytical and simulation models for CSMA/CD bus, token bus, token ring, slotted ring, and register insertion ring LANs; agreement between corresponding models was generally good. He refers especially to the studies of Stuck (1983) and Liu et al (1982), mentioned above. Between them, these studies give the following results:

The performance of CSMA/CD depends strongly on the parameter a, and is best for low a; it offers the least delay under a light load, but is most sensitive to work load when this is heavy. The token ring is least sensitive to work load. For really heavy loads, leading to congested conditions, the register insertion ring performs best. The slotted ring usually gives the poorest performance.

Other recent simulation studies include: the above mentioned work by Chalamtac and Eisenger (1983); an investigation of collision-control algorithms in CSMA/CD LANs (Moura and Field, 1981); a study of satellite multiple access, including a comparison with corresponding calculated analytical results (Guilbur et al, 1983); and a discussion of the results of some simulations of the application of the IEEE Standard 802.3 and 802.4 medium access protocols to factory floor LANs (Sweeton, 1983).

Ramshaw and Amer (1983) describe the simulation of artifical network traffic over a LAN, using pseudorandom number generators.

REFERENCES

The 1983 Satellite Directory (1983) Phillips Publishing, Bethesda, MD.

A. S. Acampora, M. G. Hluchyj and C. D. Tsao (1983) "Performance of a centralized-bus local area network," *LocalNet 83 (New York)*, 159–169.

A. S. Acampora, M. G. Hluchyj and C. D. Tsao (Jun 1983) "A centralized-bus architecture for local area networks," *Proceedings of the International Conference on Communications*, 932–938.

ACM SIGCOMM (1983) *Communication Architectures and Protocols*, Proceedings of ACM Sigcomm Symposium, Austin, TX, 8–9 March 1983, also published as *Computer Communications Review*, Vol. **13**, No. 2.

K. I. Aihara, K. Kikuchi and H. Yamaguchi (Aug 1983) "Multiple-bit-rate synchronous terminals towards ISDN," *IEEE Communications Magazine*, **21**(5) 45–50.

B. Alton, A. Patel, M. Purser and J. Sheehan (1981) "The performance of a packet switched network—A study of Euronet," pages 379–389 of *Pujolle* (1981).

Amdahl (1983a) *The Invisible Link for Cost-Effective Access to Private and Public X.25 Networks*, Amdahl Communications Systems Division, Marina del Rey, CA, Brochure M1122 5-82.

Amdahl (1983b) *The Invisible Link for Uniting Dispersed, X.25-Compatible Systems*, Amdahl Communications Systems Division, Marina del Rey, CA, Brochure M283.2.

Amdahl (1983c) *The Invisible Link for Integrating a Variety of Systems into One Network*, Amdahl Communications Systems Division, Marina del Rey, CA, Brochure M783.2.

Amdahl (1983d) *Series 4400 Network Concentrator—Overview*, Amdahl Communications Systems Division, Marina del Rey, CA, Report GI-0006B.

Amdahl (1983e) *4705E Communications Processor*, Amdahl Communications Systems Division, Marina del Rey, CA, Brochure M1143 10/83.

P. D. Amer, R. Rosenthal and R. Toense (Apr 1983) "Measuring a local network's performance," *Data Communications*, **12**(4) 173–182.

S. R. Amstutz (Nov 1983) "Burst switching: An introduction," *IEEE Communications Magazine*, **21**(8) 36–42.

Anderson Jacobson (1982) *AJ 4048 High Speed Modem*, Anderson Jacobson, Inc., San Jose, CA, Brochure.

Anderson Jacobson (1983) *BABYNET AJ788*—The Switching Multipoint Multiplexer, Anderson Jacobson, Inc., San Jose, CA, Leaflet.

Architecture Technology (1983) *Integrated Voice/Data PBXs*, Architecture Technology Corporation, Minneapolis, MN.

Atlantic Research (1983a) *INTERVIEW™ Series 29A/30A/40A Data Analyzers*, Atlantic Research Corporation, Springfield, VA, Leaflet tp-276-9-83.

Atlantic Research (1983b) *INTERVIEW™ 3600 Protocol Analyzer*, Atlantic Research Corporation, Springfield, VA, Leaflet tp-290-03-83.

Atlantic Research (1983c) *INTERVIEW™ Data Communications Protocol Test Equipment*, Atlantic Research Corporation, Springfield, VA, Leaflet tp-327A-09-83.

C. Baack, G. Elze, G. Grosskopf and G. Wolf (Feb 1983) "Digital and analog optical broad-band transmission," *Proceedings of the IEEE*, **71**(2) 198–208.

F. Baylin and A. Toner (1983) *Satellites Today—Microwaves to Movies*, Satellites Today, Boulder, CO.

K. Baynton (Mar 1984) "Bits, bytes and blocks—Conquering the data transmission jungle," *Communications Management*, 38–44.

M. Beishon (Apr. 1983) "Imitation is the sincerest form of flattery," *Dec User*, 19–26.

T. E. Bell (Jan 1984) "Technology '84: Communications," *IEEE Spectrum*, **21**(1) 53–57.

E. Benhamou and J. Estrin (Sep 1983) "Multilevel internetworking gateways: Architecture and applications," *Computer*, **16**(9) 27–34.

M. Bernstein, C. Sunshine and D. Kaufman (1983) "A network control center for broadband local area networks," *LocalNet 83 (New York)*, 425–434.

J. Best and L. Fineman (1983) "LAN gateways to wide area networks," *LocalNet 83 (Europe)*, 124–135.

V. K. Bhargava, D. Haccounb, R. Matyas and P. P. Nuspl (1981) *Digital Communications by Satellite—Modulation, Access and Coding*, Wiley-Interscience, Chichester and New York.

U. D. Black (1983) *Data Communications, Networks and Distributed Processing*, Reston Publishing Company, Reston, VA.

F. Borgonovo and L. Fratta (Jan 1983) "A collision resolution algorithm for random-access channels with echo," *Computer Communications Review*, **13**(1) 31–39.

P. I. P. Boulton and E. S. Lee (Jul 1983) "Bus, ring, star and tree local area networks," *Computer Communications Review*, **13**(3) 19–24.

Braid Systems (1983) *A New Era in Telex. . . . The Braid Telex Manager*, Braid Systems Ltd., London, Brochure.

K. Brayer (Nov 1983) "An adaptive computer communications network designed with decentralized control," *IEEE Communications Magazine*, **21**(8) 30–35.

British Telecom (1983) *Merlin M110 Communicating VDU Terminal*, British Telecom Business Systems, London, Brochure MER 55 (9/83).

G. Broomall and J. R. Heath (Jun 1983) "Classification categories and historical development of circuit switching topologies," *ACM Computing Surveys*, **15**(2) 95–133.

R. S. Brown (Apr 1983) "Telex-packet switching interworking in the UK," *British Telecommunications Engineering*, **2**(1) 27–31.

W. Bux and M. Schlatter (Jan 1983) "An approximate method for the performance analysis of buffer insertion rings," *IEEE Transactions on Communications*, **COM-31**(1) 50–55.

Cable & Satellite Europe (ongoing) Cable & Satellite Europe, London, Monthly Magazine.

Cable & Satellite News (ongoing) Cable & Satellite Europe, London, Newsletter.

A. D. Campbell (1983) "Fiber optic data communications C&C Loop 6770," *LocalNet 83 (New York)*, 307–318.

R. Camrass (1983) *Buying a PABX—How to Make a Sensible Choice*, Oyez Scientific & Technical Services, London.

CAP (1982) *Sea View—The World's First Mobile Office*, CAP Group, London, Brochure BCD/CPR/1082.

R. Carpenter (Feb 1984) "A comparison of two 'guaranteed' local network access methods," *Data Communications*, **13**(2) 143–152.

CASE (1983a) *CASE 460/34 Data Modem*, CASE plc, Watford, Herts., England, Leaflet.

CASE (1983b) *CASE Series DCX Multiplexers*, CASE plc, Watford, Herts., England, Brochure.

CASE (1983c) *CASE DCX 816 X25 Packet Assembler/Disassembler*, CASE plc, Watford, Herts., England, Leaflet.

CASE (1983d) *Series DCX Gateways*, CASE plc, Watford, Herts., England, Leaflet.

CCITT (1980) "Error performance in an integrated digital connection forming part of an integrated digital services network." CCITT Recommendation G.821 in *VIIth Plenary Assembly Yellow Book*, Vol. III, Facsicle III.2, Geneva.

CCITT (Jul 1982) *Report of Meeting of Working Party XVIII/3 (Network Performance Objectives)*, Com. XVIII–No. RS-E.

Gl Charlish (27 Sep. 1982) "CEGB moves messages with power through the grid," *Financial Times*, 27.

G. Charlish (1984a) (17 Feb 1984) "Optical disks for data 'juke box'," *Financial Times*, 14.

G. Charlish (1984b) (7 Mar 1984) "Carousels of data for mass storage," *Financial Times*, 14.

G. Charlish (1984c) (6 Feb. 1984) "Flat cables for the long run," *Financial Times*, 10.

V. E. Cheong and R. A. Hirschheim (1983) *Local Area Networks—Issues, Products, and Developments*, Wiley-Interscience, Chichester and New York.

G. Childs (1983) "LAN/WAN networking," *LocalNet 83 (Europe)*, 137–147.

I. Chlamtac and M. Eisenger (Oct. 1983) "Voice/data integration in Ethernet—Backoff and priority considerations," *Computer Communications*, **6**(5) 236–244.

Ed. W. Chou (1983) *Computer Communications, Vol. 1, Principles*, Prentice-Hall, Englewood Cliffs, NJ.

F. Closs and R. P. Lee (Aug. 1980) "A multistar broadcast network for local-area communication," *Local Area Network Workshop*, 67–88.

Codex (1983) *Codex Integrated Communications*, Codex Ltd., Thronton Heath, Surrey, England, Leaflet.

K. Cohen (Aug 1983) "Major vendor designs switch for own use," *Data Communications*, **12**(8) 107–109.

Communications International (Apr 1983) Vol. **10**, No. 4, Focus Supplement: Fibre Optics.

Communications International (Nov 1983) Vol. **10**, No. 11, Focus Supplement: Satellite Communications.

Communications Management (1983a) (Aug 1983) "Buyer's guide to the modem market," 26–27.

Communications Management (1983b) (Jun 1983) "PABXs: Let competition commence," 26–38.

Communications Management (Mar 1984) "Multiplexers—Cutting the cake," 58–59.

Computer (1983a) (Sep 1983) Vol. **16**, No. 9, issue on network interconnection.

Computer (1983b) (Apr 1983) Vol. **16**, No. 4, issue on communications satellite software.

Computer Management (Feb 1982) "Lines of Communications," 19–31.

Computer Networks (Dec 1983) "Conference Report—Satellite and Computer Communications," Vol. **7**, No. 6, 413–418.

Computer News (22 Mar 1984) "New Medius promises network users a cheap and simple system," 15.

Computer Weekly (1983a) (13 Oct 1983) Feature on Terminals, 27–33.

Computer Weekly (1983b) (10 Nov 1983) "Long distance calls cost is set to tumble," 34.

Computer Weekly (1983c) (1 Nov 1983) "Datacomms network makes debut at the Compec show," 51.

Computer Weekly (5 Jan 1984) "'Major change' in concept of comms network," 26.

Computer Weekly, Management Review (29 Mar 1984) special issue on printers and terminals.

K. C. Crandall (1983) "Application of the Z19 RF modem to broadband local networks," *LocalNet 83 (New York)*, 273–280.

D. Dadzie (1983) "Network management techniques," *dp International 1983*, 153–156.

Data & Control Equipment (1983) *The New TELEBOX II*, Data & Control Equipment Ltd., Aylesbury, Bucks., England, Leaflet.

Data Channels (ongoing) Phillips Publishing, Bethesda, MD, Fortnightly Newsletter.

Data Communications (Dec d1983) *Data Communications Buyers' Guide 1984*, McGraw-Hill, New York.

Datapoint (1983) *Gateways from the ARC Local Area Network*, Datapoint Corporation, San Antonio, TX, Document No. 61560.

P. Davies and F. A. Ghani (Aug 1983) "Access protocols for an optical-fibre ring network," *Computer Communications*, **6**(4) 185–191.

G. De Grandi, R. Brisset et al (1983) "HERMES: A research project to implement advanced service on a fibre optic ring," *LocalNet 83 (New York)*, 295–305.

DEC (1982) *KMS11-BD Intelligent Multiplexer for X.25 Applications*, Digital Equipment Corporation, Maynard, MA, Brochure YK-AA01A-05.

DEC (1983a) *Networks—Ethernet Hardware Products*, Digital Equipment Corporation, Maynard, MA, Brochure ED-25443-42.

DEC (1983b) *Networks System and Options Catalog*, Digital Equipment Corporation, Maynard, MA, Brochure EB-24467-18.

DEC (1983d) *Advancing the Standard—Digital Introduces the VT200 Family*, Digital Equipment Corporation, Maynard, MA, Brochure, Order No. ED-25812-56.

S. Dowling (10 Nov 1983) "Eliminate sleepless nights," *Computer Weekly*, 35.

Dynatech Communications (1983) *DynaPac X.25 Communications Processors*, Dynatech Communications, European Marketing Headquarters Fresnes, France, Brochure and Catalog.

Dynatech Communications (Apr 1984) *Data Communications Equipment (3rd. Ed.)*, Dynatech Communications Ltd., Chesthunt, Herts., England, Brochure and Catalog.

Dynatech Data Systems (1983) Dyna-Test™ 1600, Dynatech Data Systems, Springfield, VA, Leaflet.

Y. Ebihara et al (Dec 1983) "GAMMA-NET: A local computer network coupled by a high speed optical fiber ring bus—System concept and structure," *Computer Networks*, 7(6) 375—388.

C. W. H. Ellis (1983) "The PABX as a LAN after liberalization," *Business Telecom 83*, 251–255.

G. Ennis (1983a) "Design considerations for broadband metropolitan networks," *LocalNet 83 (New York)*, 333–345.

G. Ennis (1983b) "Some interconnection strategies for broadband networks," *LocalNet 83 (Europe)*, 165–177.

Ericsson (1983a) *Making the Right Connections*, Ericsson Information Systems AB, Tyreso, Sweden, Brochure 2/LZT 102 382 RA.

Ericsson (1983b) *EDNET Network Management System*, Ericsson Information Systems AB, Tyreso, Sweden, Leaflet.

K. Feher (1983) *Digital Communications Satellite/Earth Station Engineering*, Prentice-Hall, Englewood Cliffs, NJ.

Ed. K. Feher, L. J. Greenstein, D. Lombard and L. Pollack (Jan 1983) *IEEE Journal on Selected Areas in Communications*, Vol. **SAC-1,** No. 1, special issue on digital satellite communications.

Ferranti (1981) *Ferranti Telex Manager*, Ferranti Computer Systems, Manchester, England, Leaflet B00164.

Ferranti (1983a) *Ferranti Teletex Adaptor*, Ferranti Computer Systems, Manchester, England, Leaflet A200.

Ferranti (1983b) *Voice Manager VM600—A Breakthrough in Telephone Communications*, Ferranti Computer Systems, Manchester, England, Brochure B00197/2.

Fiber/Laser News (ongoing) Phillips Publishing, USA, Fortnightly Newsletter.

Financial Times (7 Jun 1982) Survey on Satellite Communications.

P. Fitzgerald (9 Feb 1984) "How message meteors harness the heavens," *Computer News*, 12.

Future Systems (1982) *Optical Fiber Communications—Current Systems and Future Developments*, Future Systems Inc., Gaithersburg, MD, Report No. 116.

Gandalf (1982a) *PACXNET*, Gandalf Technologies, Inc., Manotick, Ont., Canada, Brochure and Folder of Leaflets about PACXNET Component Products.

Gandalf (1982b) *PACX—The Proven Data Communications Management System*, Gandalf Technologies, Inc., Manotick, Ont., Canada, Brochure.

R. Garner (9 Mar 1984) "Light links for Japan's future," *Financial Times*, 12.

J. Gee (16 Feb 1984) "Smart card war hots up," *Computer Weekly*, 19.

K. C. E. Gee (1983) *Local Area Network Gateways*, NCC Publications, Manchester, England.

E. Gelenbe (1983) *Performance Models of Distributed Systems*, Addison-Wesley, London and Reading, MA.

M. Gerla (May 1983) "Understanding switching and transport schemes," *Data Communications*, **12**(5) 155–165.

A. K. Goel and P. D. Amer (Summer 1983) "Performance matrices for bus and token ring local area networks," *Journal of Telecommunication Networks*, **2**(2) 187–209.

Y. I. Gold and W. R. Franta (Apr 1983) "An efficient colllision-free protocol for prioritized access-control of cable or radio channels," *Computer Networks*, **7**(2) 83–98.

K. H. Goodyear (1984) "Data entry: Portable terminals," *dp International 1984*, 275–279.

I. Gopal and P. Kermani (Jun 1983) "Performance of stop-and-wait protocols over high delay links," *Computer Communications*, **6**(3) 115–119.

A. Grant, D. Hutchison and D. Shepherd (1983) "Implementation of a local area network—X25 gateway," *LocalNet 83 (Europe)*, 149–163.

R. Griffiths (1983) "An introduction to facsimile transmission," *dp International 1983*, 165–168.

R. Griffiths (1984) "Facsimile transmission and reception," *dp International 1984*, 279–282.

D. S. Grubb and M. D. Abrams (1981) "User-oriented data communication performance parameters," 145–154 of Pujolle (1981).

R. Guilbur and J. M. Pellaumeil (Dec 1983) "An analytical study of packet satellite multiple access," *Computer Networks*, **7**(6) 389–393.

H. D. Haback (Feb 1983) "Putting Micros to work in the office," *Data Communications*, **12**(2) 127–135.

E. Hara (Oct 1983) "A fiber-optic broadband LAN/OCS using a PBX," *IEEE Communications Magazine*, **21**(7) 22–27.

P. Harwood (Feb 1983) "Fibre optics for short-haul communications links," *Computer Communications*, **6**(1) 32–35.

E. F. Haselton (Sep 1983) "A PCM frame switching concept leading to burst switching network architecture," *IEEE Communications Magazine*, **21**(6) 13–16.

K. Hasui, S. Hatori, M. Kato and T. Katsuyama (1983) "Handwritten message switching via an integrated EPBX," *LocalNet 83 (New York)*, 19–29.

D. Henson (1983) "Wordprocessors in communications networks," *dp International 1983*, 159–164.

D. D. Hill (Jul/Oct 1982) "Dragnet—A local network with protection," *Computer Communications Review*, **12**(3/4) 92–98.

R. Hinden, J. Haverty and A. Sheltzer (Sep 1983) "The DARPA Internet: Interconnecting heterogeneous computer networks with gateways, *Computer*, **16**(9) 38–48.

M. G. Hluchyj, C. D. Tsao and R. R. Boorstyn (Dec 1983) "Performance analysis of a preemptive priority queue with applications to packet communication systems," *Bell System Telephone Journal*, **62**(10–Part 2) 3225–3245.

K. Holder (24 Nov 1983) "Centre improves communications," *Computer Weekly*, 2.

K. Holder (22 Mar 1984) "Storage launches optical system," *Computer Weekly*, 8.

F. R. A. Hopwood and R. W. Witty (Sep 1982) "PERQ and advanced master graphics workstations," *IEEE Computer Graphics and Applications*, **2**(7) 9–15.

Ed. M. J. Howes and D. V. Morgan (1980) *Optical Fibre Communications—Devices, Circuits and Systems*, Wiley-Interscience, Chichester and New York.

W. N. Hsieh and B. Kraimeche (Spring 1983) "Performance analysis of an end-to-end flow control mechanism in a packet-switched network," *Journal of Telecommunication Networks*, **2**(1) 103–116.

P. M. Hubert and J. Gaumond (Jan 1984) "Canada combines voice, data, and images on national satellite network," *Data Communications*, **13**(1) 177–184.

J. S. Hubley and J. F. McDonald (Jun 1983) "What's behind American Bell's long awaited Net 1000?," *Data Communications*, **12**(61) 195–203.

D. Hutchison and A. Grant (Dec 1983) "Terminal concentrator for an Ethernet-style local network," *Computer Communications*, **6**(6) 291–296.

IAL Data Communications (1983) *Data Products Short Form Catalogue 1983*, IAL Data Communications, Basingstoke, Hampshire, England, Catalogue.

IBM (1983) *The IBM 3863, 3864 and 3865 Modems*, IBM United Kingdom Ltd., Portsmouth, England, UK Form 24-8002.

IBM (1983b) *Talking Points on High Function Display Products*, IBM United Kingdom Ltd., Portsmouth, England, UK Form No. 24-8046-1.

IBM (1983c) *IBM Europe Programming Announcements*, Received via IBM United Kingdom Ltd., Portsmouth, England.

ICL (1982) *DNX-2000 Distributed Network Exchange*, International Computers Ltd., London, Leaflet.

ICL (1983a) *ICL Information Systems—An Introduction to Information Technology*, International Computers Ltd., London, Brochure.

ICL (1983) *ICL Distributed Office Systems—Wordprocessing*, International Computers Ltd., London, Brochure.

ICL (1983c) *ICL Distributed Office Systems—DRS 20 Series*, International Computers Ltd., London, Brochure.

Infotron (a) (undated) *Introducing Advanced Network Integration From Infotron*, Infotron Systems Corporation, Cherry Hill, NJ, Brochure.

Infotron (b) (undated) *ANI Advanced Network Integration*, Infotron Systems Corporation, Cherry Hill, NJ, Leaflet 583.

Infotron (c) (undated) *ANM-800 Advanced Network Manager*, Infotron Systems Corporation, Cherry Hill, NJ, Leaflet 983.

International Journal of Satellite Communications (ongoing) Wiley-Interscience, Chichester and New York.

P. C. Jain (Summer 1983) "Onboard processing in future satellite communication systems," *Journal of Telecommunication Networks*, **2**(2) 139–151.

F. Jennings (1983a) (27 Oct 1983) "Data communication is just a telephone call away," *Computer Weekly*, 18.

F. Jennings (1983b) (24 Nov 1983) "What the user needs to know about modems," *Computer Weekly*, 22.

F. Jennings (1983c) (20 Oct 1983) "How to lease a line to a user—Leased telephone lines," *Computer Weekly*, 18.

V. I. Johannes (Apr 1983) "Performance parameters for digital communication," *Proceedings of the IEEE*, **71**(4) 539.

J. Katz (Sep 1983) "Semiconductor optoelectronic devices for free-space optical communications," *IEEE Communications Magazine*, **21**(6) 20–27.

P. M. Kay (1983) "A new distributed PABX for voice/data integration," *LocalNet 83 (New York)*, 19–29.

G. Keiser (1983) *Optical Fiber Communications*, McGraw Hill, New York.

J. Kennedy (1983) "Fibre optics in local area networks," *LocalNet 83 (Europe)*, 327–341.

A. Kenyon (1984a) (19 Jan 1984) "Life grows hectic for the exchange makers," *Computer Weekly*, *Management Review*, 14–15.

M. Kenyon (1984b) (Jan 1984) "The text for 1984—The year of the Teletex terminal," *Communications Management*, 36–37.

K. Kümmerle and M. Reiser (Winter 1982) "Local-area communication networks–An overview," *Journal of Telecommunication Networks*, **1**(4) 349–370.

M. A. Laviola (1983) "Citibank's fiber optic metropolitan network," *LocalNet 83 (New York)*, 347–355.

P. J. Leach et al (Nov 1983) "The architecture of an integrated local area network," *IEEE Journal on Selected Areas in Communications*, **SAC-1**(5) 842–857.

S. H. Leiden (1983) "The geographically distributed local area network: A case study," *LocalNet 83 (New York)*, 79–89.

L. Li, R. Cherukuri and R. Bergman (1983) "Performance characteristics of token bus networks," *LocalNet 83 (Europe)*, 261–275.

D. C. Lindsay (Jul/Oct 1982) "Local area networks: Bus and ring vs. coincident star," *Computer Communications Review*, **12**(3/4) 83–91.

M. T. Liu, W. Hilal and B. H. Groomes (1982) "Performance evaluation of channel access protocols for local computer networks," *Proceedings COMPCON Fall '82*, 417–426.

J. M. Loveluck (Nov 1982) "The PERQ workstation and the distributed computing environment," *ICL Technical Journal*, **3**(2) 155–174.

P. Macclesfield (Nov 1982) "Patrolling the data highways of tomorrow," *Computer Management*, 19–22.

Ed. J. McDonald (May 1983) *IEEE Communications Magazine*, **21**(6) Issue on Digital Switching.

S. Magnusson and W. S. Jinbo (Sep 1983) "GTD-5 EAX hardware overview," *IEEE Communications Magazine*, **21**(6) 6–12.

M. Majithia and S. G. Li (Aug 1983) Buffer analysis of an integrated voice and data terminal," *Computer Communications*, **6**(4) 171–177.

M. A. Malcolm, L. D. Rogers and J. C. Spracklen (Feb 1983) "An acknowledging contention algorithm suitable for local radio networks," *Computer Networks*, **7**(1) 1–8.

P. Manchester (Sep 1983) "Has anyone a manageable solution?," *Computer Management*, 34–36.

I. Marchbanks (Mar 1984) "Controlling the data network—No longer an optional 'extra'," *Communications Management*, 54.

J. Marshall and B. Spiegelhalter (1983) "Experiences with Net/One at British Telecom," *LocalNet 83 (Europe)*, 67–79.

R. D. Martin-Royle and G. H. Bennett (Jan 1983) "Optical-fibre transmission systems in the British Telecom network: An overview," *British Telecommunications Engineering*, **1**(4) 190–199.

Master Systems (1983) *MASTERNET*, Master Systems (Data Products) Ltd., Camberley, Surrey, England, Brochure.

Ed. A. J. Mayne (Oct 1982) *Computers & Video Convergence—State of the Art Report*, Office of the Future Ltd., Richmond, Surrey, England, Report.

M. Medina (1983) "Interactive session service implementation over a local area network," *LocalNet 83 (Europe)*, 437–445.

P. Menzies (May 1983) "Extraterrestrial merger: Satellite carriers, computer vendors join forces," *Data Communications*, **12**(5) 179–188.

Micom-Borer (1981) *Micro4000 Series Data Modems*, Micom-Borer Ltd., Reading, Berkshire, England, Leaflets.

Micom Systems (1982) *Dumb Terminal Transmission Errors Souring Your Outlook?*, Micom Systems, Inc., Chatsworth, CA, Brochure.

Micom Systems (1983a) *Local Network Costs Getting Out of Hand?*, Micom Systems, Inc., Chatsworth, CA, Brochure.

Micom Systems (1983b) Instanet™ Leaflets, Micom Systems, Inc., Chatsworth, CA.

Micom Systems (1983c) *Tempted by the Low Cost of 56K DDS or a Wideband Data Link? Looking for the Best Way to Cut It up? Introducing the Micro750—The Intelligent TDM*, Micom Systems, Inc., Chatsworth, CA, Brochure.

Micom Systems (1983d) *Want to Squeeze More out of Packet Switching? You Can with Micom's Concentrator PAD ... Anywhere in the World!*, Micom Systems, Inc., Chatsworth, CA, Brochure.

Micom Systems (1983e) *Still Squeezing Data through the Old-Fashioned Way? Concentrate. It's Cheaper ... and Better!*, Micom Systems, Inc., Chatsworth, CA, Brochure.

Micom Systems (1983f) *Why a Data PABX? Introducing the Micro600 and the Micro650,* Micom Systems, Inc., Chatsworth, CA, Brochure.

Micom Systems (1983g) *Are Your Data Concentrators Multiplying? Like to Switch Terminals between Different Computers? Integrate Your Network with a Concentrator Switch,* Micom Systems, Inc., Chatsworth, CA, Brochure.

R. Miles (1983) "The computer-controlled PABX," *dp International 1983,* 169–174.

Ed. S. E. Miller and A. G. Chynoweth (1979) *Optical Fiber Telecommunications,* Academic Press, New York and London.

M. Mills (Jan 1984) "Memory cards: A new concept in personal computing," *Byte,* **9**(1) 154–168.

Mnemos (1982) *MNEMOS,* Mnemos Inc., Lawrenceville, NJ, and Mnemos Europe Ltd., Teddington, Middlesex, England, Leaflet.

G. Moody (Jan 1984) "Mass storage," *Practical Computing,* **7**(1) 80–81.

J. D. Morse and S. J. Kopec, Jr (Mar 1983) "Performance evaluation of a distributed burst-switched communications system," *Proceedings Phoenix Conference on Computing in Communications,* 41–46.

A. Moura and J. Field (Feb 1981) "Collision-control algorithms in carrier-sense multiple-access (collision-detection) networks," *Computer Communications,* **4**(1) 10–18.

T. Murakami (Jan 1983) "Domestic satellite communications in NTT," *Japan Telecommunications Review,* **25**(1) 7–16.

T. Nevinson (Autumn/Winter 1983) "A new concept in office automation," *dp International,* 17–18.

E. A. Newcombe and S. Pasupathy (Aug 1982) "Error rate monitoring for data communications," *Proceedings of the IEEE,* **70**(8) 805–828.

L. Nirenberg (Jun 1983) "How much should a satellite earth station cost?," *Data Communications,* **12**(6) 99–114.

Online Publications (1980) *Satellite Communications,* Online Publications Ltd., Northwood Hills, Middlesex, England.

E. B. Parker (Jan 1983) "Satellite micro earth stations—A small investment with big returns," *Data Communications,* **12**(1) 97–104.

S. D. Personick (1981) *Optical Fibre Transmission Systems,* Plenum Press, New York.

Ed. S. D. Personick (Apr 1983) *IEEE Journal on Selected Areas in Communications,* Vol. **SAC-1,** No. 3, special issue on fiber optic systems.

Philips (1983) *Megadoc System Description,* Philips, Eindhoven, Netherlands, Document 8798. 732.03211.

Philips Electronics (1983) *Philips Professional Laser Vision,* Philips Electronics Brochure, Croydon, Surrey, England, Brochure.

Phillips Publications (1983) *The 1983 Satellite Directory,* Phillips Publications, Bethesda, MD.

Plessey Communication Systems (May 1983) *Plessey IDX Integrated Digital Exchange,* Plessey Communication Systems Ltd., Nottingham, England, Publication No. 8031.

Plessey Controls (1982a) *TP 3010 Network Interface Processor,* Plessey Controls Ltd., Poole, Dorset, England, Publication No. 7927/1.

Plessey Controls (1982b) *TP 4000 Communications Processor for Packet Switching,* Plessey Controls Ltd., Poole, Dorset, England, Publication No. 79631/1.

Plessey Controls (1982c) *Corporate Data Networking,* Plessey Controls Ltd., Poole, Dorset, England, Publication No. 7999.

Plessey Controls (1983a) *8600 Series,* Plessey Controls Ltd., Poole, Dorset, England, Publication No. 8068.

Plessey Controls (1983b) *8687 Telex/Packet Gateway,* Plessey Controls Ltd., Poole, Dorset, England, Publication No. 8069.

Plessey Controls (1983c) *Plessey Controls in Data Communication,* Plessey Controls Ltd., Poole, Dorset, England, Publication No. 8019.

Plessey Controls (1983d) *MX System 16002—Multipurpose Data Transmission,* Plessey Controls Ltd., Poole, Dorset, England, Publication No. 7995/1.

Plessey Controls (1983e) *MX System 16002—Statistical Multiplexer,* Plessey Controls Ltd., Poole, Dorset, England, Publication No. 7995/b.

Plessey Office Systems (1983a) *Plessey IBIS Integrated Business Information System—Integrated Workstation,* Plessey Office Systems Ltd., Nottingham, England, Publication No. 8052/1.

Plessey Office Systems (1983b) *Plessey Voice Messaging for Telephone Messages that Always Get Through,* Plessey Office Systems Ltd., Publication No. 8065.

R. L. Podell (Winter 1982) "A measure of effectiveness for telecommunications," *Journal of Telecommunication Networks,* **1**(4) 371–384.

U. W. Pooch, W. H. Greene and G. G. Moss (1982) *Telecommunications and Networking,* Little, Brown and Company, Boston, MA and Toronto, Canada.

D. Potter and J. St. Amand (Jun 1983) "Connecting minis to local nets with discrete terminals," *Data Communications,* **12**(6) 161–164.

Prime (1983) *Prime Producer 100™ Office Workstation,* Prime Computer, Inc., Natick, MA, Leaflet PB 1478.

Prism (1983) *PRISM VTX 5000—The Unique Modem for the Sinclair Spectrum,* Prism Micro Products Ltd., London, Leaflet.

Ed. G. Pujolle (1981) *Performance Analysis of Data Communication Systems and Their Applications,* North Holland, Amsterdam, Oxford, England and New York.

Racal-Milgo Ltd. (1983a) *Communications Management Systems CMS Series,* Racal-Milgo Ltd., Hook, Hampshire, England, Publication No. 4085-1.

Racal-Milgo Ltd. (1983b) *Communications Management Systems CMS Series 2,* Racal-Milgo Ltd., Hook, Hampshire, England, Publication No. 4325-1.

H. K. Raghbati (Apr 1981) "An overview of data compression techniques," *Computer,* **14**(4) 71–75.

L. Ramshaw and P. O. Amer (Aug 1983) "Generating artificial traffic over a local area network using random number generators," *Computer Networks,* **7**(4) 233–251.

Rank Xerox (1983) *Xerox 8000 Network System,* Rank Xerox Ltd., London, Brochure RX919 CO782.

D. V. Ratner (Jun 1983) "How broadband modems operate on token-passing nets," *Data Communications,* **12**(6) 225–227.

Ed. P. Ravasio, G. Hopkins and N. Naffah (1982) *Local Computer Networks,* North-Holland, Amsterdam, Oxford, England and New York. (Proceedings of the IFIP TC.6 International Symposium on Local Computer Networks, Florence, Italy, April 1982).

P. Reagan (Dec 1983) "AT&T, IBM gunning for local net war of '84," *Data Communications,* **12**(12) 181–190.

A. Reichert (1983) "Beyond the bus and the ring," *LocalNet 83 (New York),* 213–226.

Renex (1983) *The TRANSLATOR,* Renex Corporation, Springfield, VA, Brochure.

T. G. Richards (1983) "Towards an Integrated Communications Exchange," CASE plc, Watford, Herts., England, Application Note.

J. S. Riordon et al (Aug 1983) "Access strategies in packet mobile radio data networks," *Computer Networks,* **7**(4) 211–221.

R. D. Rosner (1983) *Packet Switching,* Lifetime Learning Publications, Belmont, CA.

E. Rothchild (Mar 1983) "Optical memory media," *Byte,* **8**(3) 86–106.

D. Roworth and M. Cole (1983) "Fibre optic developments for the Cambridge Ring," *LocalNet 83 (Europe),* 519–535.

A. M. Rutkowski and M. J. Markus (Jul/Oct 1982) "The Integrated Services Digital Network: Developments and regulatory issues," *Computer Communications Review,* **12**(3/4) 68–82.

J. Saint-Remi (Jan 1984) "The many sounds of voice digitization," *Data Communications,* **13**(1) 169–170.

Ed. C. P. Sandbank (1980) *Optical Fibre Communication Systems,* Wiley-Interscience, Chichester and New York.

A. R. K. Sastry (Jan 1984) "Performance objectives for ISDN's," *IEEE Communications Magazine,* **22**(1) 49–55.

J. H. Scheren-Guivel (Dec 1983) "What's available in today's sync modem marketplace," *Data Communications,* **12**(12) 141–182.

A. Segerdahl (1984a) (2 Feb 1984) "Dialling the Future—Today," *Computing,* 24.

A. Segerdahl (1984b) (1 Mar 1984) "Looking to a future for the optical disk," *Computing,* 26–27.

J. Seidler (1983) *Principles of Computer Communication Network Design,* Ellis Horwood, Chichester, and Halsted-Wiley, New York.

N. B. Seitz (Mar 1984) "User-oriented data communication performance standards," *Communications International,* **11**(3) 21–30.

N. B. Seitz, D.R. Wortendyke and K. P. Spies (Aug 1983) 'User-oriented performance measurement on the ARPANET," *IEEE Communications Magazine,* **21**(5) 28–44.

Ed. A. Sekey (Dec 1983) *IEEE Communications Magazine,* Vol. **21**, No. 9, issue on speech communications.

Ed. K. S. Shanmugan and P. Balaban (Jan 1984) *IEEE Journal on Selected Areas in Communications,* Vol. **SAC-2**, No. 1, special issue on computer-aided modelling, analysis, and design of communications systems.

R. H. Sherman and M. G. Gable (Jun 1983) "Considerations in interconnecting diverse local nets," *Data Communications,* **12**(6) 145–154.

N. Shneiderwind (Sep 1983) "Interconnecting local networks to long-distance networks," *Computer,* **16**(9) 15–24.

D. Shorrock (Nov 1983) "Satellites take off," *Dec User,* 61–66.

J. J. Sikora and D. C. Franke (1983) "A LAN based on a centralized-bus architecture," *LocalNet 83 (New York),* 147–157.

B. Sklar (Aug 1983 and Oct 1983) "A structural overview of digital communications: A tutorial review," *IEEE Communications Magazine,* **21**(5) 4–17 and **21**(7) 6–21.

W. Stallings (Feb 1984) "Local network performance," *IEEE Communications Magazine,* **22**(2) 27–36.

STC (1983) *Executel,* STC Business Systems, Brighton, England, Brochure 177-1E.

T. Stewart (May 1983) "Terminal design: A European perspective," *Data Communications,* **12**(5) 195–203.

N. C. Strole and D. W. Andrews (1983) "Design and architecture of a token-ring local area network," *LocalNet 83 (New York),* 171–187.

B. W. Stuck (May 1983) "Calculating the maximum data rate in local area networks," *Computer,* **16**(5) 72–76.

L. Sudan and E. G. Brohm (May 1983) "What to look for when choosing a stat mux," *Data Communications,* **12**(5) 125–130.

R. H. Swanson (Nov 1983) "Beyond vendor support: Putting network analysis into users' hands," *Data Communications,* **12**(11) 169–176.

D. C. Sweeton (1983) "Simulation results for factory floor networks," *LocalNet 83 (New York),* 411–423.

E. D. Sykas, D. W. Karvelas and E. N. Protonotarios (Aug 1983) "Combined URN and TDMA scheme for multiple-access protocols," *Computer Communications,* **6**(4) 199–207.

Symicron (undated) *Sub-Networking,* Symicron Ltd., London, Brochure.

Sytek (1983a) *LocalNet 20/™ Series and 50/™ Series Equipment,* Sytek, Inc., Mountain View, CA, Various Leaflets.

Sytek (1983b) *LocalNet 50/120™ Statistical Monitor,* Sytek, Inc. Mountain View, CA, Leaflet 5120-0383.

Sytek (1983c) *LocalNet 50/100™ Network Control Center,* Sytek, Inc., Mountain View, CA, Leaflet 0000-1001.

W. Szpankowski (Feb 1983) "Packet switching in multiple radio channes: Analysis and stability of a random access system," *Computer Networks,* **7**(1) 17–26.

A. Takeyama, N. Sata and S. Hinoshita (1983) "Major and minor ring architecture using fibre optics," *LocalNet 83 (New York),* 281–294.

Tekelec (1981) *PCM Frame Simulator & Analyzer TE 820,* Tekelec, Inc., Santa Monica, CA, Brochure.

Tekelec (1983) *Tekelec Presents the Chameleon: An Advanced Data Communications Analyzer and Simulator,* Tekelec, Inc., Santa Monica, CA, Brochure.

Tektronix (1980a) *TEK 830 Series Data Communications Analyzers,* Catalog No. 1, Tektronix, Inc., Beaverton, OR, Brochure 35X-4581.

Tektronix (1980b) *Tektronix Data Communications Testers 834,* Tektronix, Inc., Beaverton, OR, Brochure AX-4344.

Tektronix (1980c) *Tektronix Data Communications Tester 834,* Tektronix,Inc. Beaverton, OR, Leaflet x-4378-1.

P. Terrell, Jr. (1983) "A local area network," *LocalNet 83 (Europe),* 251–259.

Tesdata Systems (a) (undated) *SMART by Tesdata—New Technology to Meet New Demand in Network Management,* Tesdata Systems Corporation, McLean, VA, Brochure.

Tesdata Systems (b) (undated) *SMART by Tesdata,* Tesdata Systems Corporation, McLean, VA, Leaflet.

Tesdata Systems (c) (undated) *The SMART Way,* Tesdata Systems Corporation, McLean, VA, Leaflet.

Y. K. Than and J. N. P. Hume (Feb 1983) "Analysis of voice and low-priority data traffic by means of brisk periods and slack periods," *Computer Communications,* **6**(1) 14–22.

The Times (17 Jan 1984) "Computer briefing," 17.

R. E. Toense (Summer 1983) "Performance analysis of NBSNET," *Journal of Telecommunication Networks,* **2**(2) 177–186.

P.Tremewan (2 Feb 1984) "Changing a pabx to suit your needs," *Computing,* 36.

C. Tulley (1983) "Teletex: A status report on terminal choice," *Business Telecom 83,* 323–344.

Ungermann-Bass (undated) *Net/One™ Local Area Network Communications System,* Ungermann Bass, Inc., Santa Clara, CA, Leaflet.

Ungermann-Bass (various dates) *Net/One Equipment,* Ungermann Bass, Inc., Santa Clara, CA, Various Leaflets.

Userlink Systems (1984) *The Userlink Systems for User Friendly Access* and other Leaflets, Userlink Systems Ltd., Stockport, Cheshire, England.

P. Veith (June 1983) "Diagnostic systems for data networks," *Communications International,* **10**(6) 69–70.

A. Walker (Aug 1983) "Some recent advances in radio communications," *IEEE Communications Magazine,* **21**(5) 51–54.

Wang (1981) *DVX—An Automated Voice Communications System from Wang,* Wang Laboratories, Inc., Lowell, MA, Brochure 10-81-30M.

J. Warrior and A. Husain (1983) "Reliability in fiber optic ring networks," *LocalNet 83 (New York),* 319–331.

S. B. Weinstein (Feb 1984) "Smart credit cards: The answer to cashless shopping," *IEEE Spectrum,* **21**(2) 43–49.

P. Whitehouse (Jul/Aug 1983) "A machine to ring the changes," *Computer Management,* 23–26.

S. Wilbur (1983) "Initial experience with Universe at University College London," *LocalNet 83 (Europe),* 297–309.

R. U. Willett (1983) "The design and implementation of Mercury's London network," *Business Telecom 83,* 213–217.

Wireless World (Feb 1984) "Optical memory," 61.

The Workstation Server News (ongoing) Architecture Technology Corporation, Minneapolis, MN, Monthly Newsletter.

F. Yuan, V. Jeybalen and M. G. Gable (1983) "MACS: A mini-packet switched multi-network bridge," *LocalNet 83 (New York)*, 401–410.

R. E. Ziener and C. R. Ryan (Oct 1983) "Minimum-shift-keyed modem implementations for high data rates," *IEEE Communications Magazine*, **21**(7) 28–37.

Chapter 21

Recent Developments in Network Architectures, Standards and Protocols

National and international work on the formulation of new standards for local and wide area networks and for their protocols has been developing rapidly and expanding during recent years. Effort has been concentrated on the creation and implementation of an "open systems environment," that will allow network systems, standards, and protocols to evolve continually as new requirements emerge and technology advances. As a result, the *ISO Reference Model for Open Systems Interconnection (OSI)* has become the dominant approach to network architecture, as well as the basis for most of the work on network standards and for the classification or different layers of network protocols. It has opened the way to meeting the increasingly urgent requirement for mutual compatibility of different network systems and different devices attached to networks.

In December 1983, the *Proceedings of the IEEE* published a very important special issue on open systems interconnection (Folts and des Jardins, 1983), covering all these topics. Several of its important findings are summarised in this chapter.

NETWORK ARCHITECTURES

In his overview of OSI, Folts (1983) starts by relating its history. To meet the problem of achieving an "open system environment," ISO Technical Committee 97 established a new subcommittee, SC 16, on OSI, whose task was to develop the ISO Reference Model for OSI, which would provide an architecture to serve as a worldwide basis for all future development of standards for distributed information systems throughout the world. It first met in March 1978, and its first two years involved considerable technical and political controversy; after this, agreement gradually emerged. In May 1983, ISO International Standard 7498 and CCITT Recommendation X.200, specifying the basic architecture of OSI, were approved; their texts were slightly different, but ISO and CCITT ratified mutually compatible standards in 1984.

There is support for these new standards in the USA, UK, France, and other countries. CCITT's new work for ISDNs also incorporates the principles of OSI, and is developing standards for a worldwide switched digital telecommunications system, supporting services for voice, data, electronic mail, fax, video, and so forth. Newer requirements will be fed back to OSI to ensure its continuing evolution.

Although OSI's architectural principles, including the definition of its seven layers, have now been firmly established, Folts points out that OSI itself will never be completed as it will continually evolve; its principles should now be applied to new requirements and new applications, to the improvement of existing implementations, and to the preparation of new designs to meet the next generation of user needs.

Interim protocols and standards can be used in those application areas where work on OSI is still developing. As OSI advances, the modular design of its layered architecture makes it easier to incorporate and integrate new protocols and new technologies, without disrupting those elements that are already in place. OSI has thus emerged as an essential foundation for advancing technology and for establishing distributed information systems all around the world.

Day and Zimmermann (1983) describe the current state of the art of the ISO Reference Model. They present its essential concepts and elements, define the functions of each of its seven layers, and discuss briefly some of the outstanding architectural issues, which constitute areas for further development and study by SC16 and associated committees.

Their formulation of the functions of the seven layers is as follows:

1. *Physical Layer*, providing the mechanical, electrical, functional, and procedural standards needed to access the physical communications medium;

2. *Data Link Layer*, providing functional and procedural ways of transferring data between network entities and detecting and possibly correcting any error occurring in the physical layer;

3. *Network Layer*, providing independence from data transfer technology and from relaying and routing considerations, and having the following sublayers:

    a. *Subnetwork Access Sublayer*, concerned with directly using the available data link service to provide an abstract subnetwork,

    b. *Subnetwork Enhancement Sublayer*, concerned with enhancing a particular subnetwork to allow data transfer across it to meet the required quality of service,

    c. *Internetting Sublayer*, carrying out concatenation and routing between neighboring subnetworks, together with global addressing and congestion control;

4. *Transport Layer*, providing transparent transfer of data between end systems, as well as error recovery and flow control, so that the upper layers need have no concern about providing reliable and cost-effective data transfer;

5. *Session Layer*, aiming chiefly to provide mechanisms for organising and structuring the interactions between application processes;

6. *Presentation Layer*, aiming chiefly to make application processes independent of differences in data presentation;

7. *Application Layer*, primarily concerned with the semantics of applications; those aspects of an application process, that are concerned with communication between processes, are within the OSI environment.

Day and Zimmermann conclude that the ISO Reference Model has made a major contribution to the recent more rapid and effective development of international network standards, and that it has been very useful in helping to coordinate different groups, working on different standards and aspects of standards.

Jenkins and Knightson (1984) give a brief introduction to the concepts and structure of the ISO Reference Model for OSI.

Linington (1983) discusses the modelling techniques used in standardising OSI. He presents various extensions to the basic concepts of service and protocol, together with the conventions that they use. For example, a *service primitive* is an abstract element of the interaction between a service user and a service provider, that is independent of implementation. There are four major types of service primitive, corresponding to important stages in a dialogue or exchange between users: *request*, *indication*, *response*, and *confirm*. Linington also discusses the relations to the real world of the models of services and protocols that he develops.

Chapin (1983) presents the concepts of connection-mode and connectionless data transmission that have already been applied successfully by international and national standards bodies to develop OSI service and protocol standards. *Connection-mode* data transmission involves the establishment and maintenance of a connection, which represents a dynamically negotiated agreement about the transfer of a series of related units. *Connectionless-mode* data transmission allows comparable entities to communicate independent unrelated data units between each other, without establishing a connection, but relying only on the prior knowledge that these entities have about each other.

Langsford (1982) provides a tutorial discussion of OSI assuming no special knowledge. He analyses the requirement for OSI in terms of users' needs to transfer data objects between information processing systems, the range of protocols relevant to users, and the available carrier networks. He emphasises the need to distinguish between *interconnection*, the mechanism of providing a channel for data transfer, and *intercommunication*, the transfer of information. He points out that current standards activities have tended to interpret OSI fairly narrowly, as an architecture for interconnection, and that a wider view of OSI can be applied, which considers OSI as a method allowing the exchange of information between information processing systems.

Harper (1984) discusses what users can expect from OSI, now that the OSI

Reference Model has become a full International Standard, IS 7498. He points out that OSI is definitely not intended to be a standard general purpose architecture, either for communications or for a wider range of functions; it just represents a division of functions into manageable pieces, to allow the developments of international standards based on it.

One reason why manufacturers try to show that their proprietary network architectures are aligned to OSI is that their actual implementations can be made consistent with emerging OSI standards much more easily if their architectures are similar to the OSI architecture.

Harper predicts that a wide range of functions can be expected for open systems by the early 1990s, making it possible to build useful computer networks with equipment from different vendors, a problem that is often considered very difficult today. He thinks that it will always be easier to use established proprietary architectures, which will fit in with new technology more rapidly.

Larson and Chestnut (1983) advocate the division of the Data link Layer of OSI into Hardware-Dependent and Hardware-Independent Sublayers, in order to cut costs and support more networks.

Dennis (1983) and Knightson (1982) discuss the Transport Layer. Schindler et al (1982a) propose a specification of the Presentation Layer.

Potter (1983) describes NET/PLUS, an architecture designed for truly compatible communications in LANs between products of different vendors attached to them. This architecture is based on the ISO model and on existing standards where they are available.

ISONET™ has been developed by the British Company, LDR Systems Ltd., as a package of well-structured communications software, written in a high level programming language, which can be implemented on a wide variety of computers (LDR Systems, 1984). It provides its users with facilities to communicate and process data and handle text, through a readily available tool that is easy to use. It uses the principles of layering, established in the ISO Reference Model, and applies international standards to implement the services and protocols at each of these layers.

Despite its wide acceptance, the ISO Reference Model may not be as universal as some of its advocates would like to think. Much, if not most, of the current communication between linked personal computers, or even between personal computers and minicomputers or mainframes, is governed by protocols that are relatively simple, compared with the ISO protocols for packet-switched networks. It is arguable that most users and programmers of personal computers, being fairly unsophisticated, should continue to use protocols that are simple but meet most of their requirements; although it has many advantages, the ISO approach does have the drawback that its protocols are complicated to formulate and thus not very easy to implement.

Riley (1983) reports John Burren, Head of Information Systems at the Rutherford Appleton Laboratory, UK, as having some reservations about how far the ISO Model can be applied to exchange information between systems. He felt that it did not cater for voice communication, nor did it allow sufficiently for recent changes in data transmission technologies, nor did it cater well enough for the high speeds of information transfer made possible by these technologies.

Computer Networks (1983) reports on the ACM SIGCOMM '83 Symposium, which included sessions on the current status of network architectures and on network architectures and algorithms; the full proceedings of this conference are published in *Computer Communications Review*, Vol. **13,** No. 2 (ACM SIGCOMM, 1983a).

The February 1984 issue of *Computer Networks*, Vol. **8,** No. 1, is a special issue on programming languages and open systems interconnection.

Several network architectures, other than OSI, are now being widely used especially SNA, DNA, IPA, and Philips Communication Network Structures, which have been developed by leading computer manufacturers, and DCNA, which has been developed by NTT (Nippon Telegraph & Telephone Public Corporation) in Japan. They are now gradually being adapted so that they will eventually converge towards OSI and become more or less compatible with it.

Systems Network Architecture (*SNA*), introduced in 1974, is the communciations architecture used by IBM; it is described fully by Cypser (1978), in IBM document SC30-3112, and briefly in a fairly recent brochure (IBM, 1981). It allows the separate functions, built into its terminal products, network products, and communications software, to be brought together into a unified system. As a result, it provides terminal users with better facilities for receiving, processing and transmitting information; it relieves network designers and managers of much of their burden. Because it is a basis for the development of IBM's future as well as current network products, it provides users with a stable infrastructure which they can adopt over long periods of time.

SNA has the following seven layers, which are like those of the ISO model (des Jardins, 1983):

1. *Physical control*, connecting adjacent nodes physically and electrically;
2. *Data link control*, transmitting data reliably along links;
3. *Path control*, routing data in packets between source and destination and controlling data traffic in a network;
4. *Transmission control*, pacing data exchange to match data processing rates at source and destination, also enciphering user data for security if necessary;
5. *Data flow control*, synchronising flow between source and destination, correlating exchanges, grouping related data into units;
6. *Presentation services*, formatting data for different modes of presentation, coordinating resource sharing;
7. *Transaction services*, providing various application services.

Gray and Mitchell (1979) describe the major enhancements to SNA that have enabled it to evolve from an architecture, supporting tree networks based on a single computer system, to an architecture supporting multiple-system networks with alternative paths and parallel links.

Jones (1983) reports on the success of SNA, due to its highly structured and modular arrangement, and indicates some likely candidates for enhancement of its facilities.

Rutledge (1982) considers the simularities of OSI and SNA, although they originated in different ways and started with different objectives. He concludes that they could become generally compatible and that implementations of both could be mapped together if there is enough motivation to do this.

Digital Network Architecture (*DNA*) is designed to help users of DEC's computer systems and terminals create integrated networking systems; it is described briefly in DEC's book on LANs (DEC, 1982a) and in a special brochure (DEC, 1982b). It is both flexible and easy to use, and it can help user organisations to increase productivity, improve efficiency, reduce data processing costs, and manage open-ended growth.

DNA has the following eight layers, which are in many respects comparable to those of the ISO model (DEC, 1982a, 1982b; des Jardins, 1983):

1. *Physical Link*, managing physical network channels;
2. *Data Link*, providing communication along links;
   (Layers 1 and 2 jointly handle Ethernet LAN low level protocols, communication with X.25 networks, and DDCMP (Digital Data Communications Message Protocol multi-point and point-to-point communications.)
3. *Routing*, providing adaptive routing for data packets between source and destination;
4. *End-to-end communications*, providing a transport service;
5. *Session control*, providing system integration and performing naming functions;
   (Layers 4 and 5 jointly perform task-to-task communication functions.)
6. *Network application*, performing commonly used application functions;
7. *Network management*, including provision of modules for network maintenance;
8. *User*, providing application services for users.
   (Layers 6 and 8 jointly cover such functions as virtual terminal, remote command file submission, downline system loading, remote resource access, and file transfer.)

DNA can connect LANs and WANs, and also link the LANs at different sites of an organisation. It can provide links between DEC systems and those of other manufacturers; for example, it can connect DNA networks with SNA networks (Eakin, 1983; Morency and Flakes, 1984; DEC, 1982b).

Information Processing Architecture (*IPA*) is the networking architecture for ICL's Networked Product Line. Besides being designed to ensure compatibility across ICL's wide range of products and to provide a clearly defined path for growth in their use, it is structured to meet international standards, based on OSI, so that it is an imporant practical step towards open systems (ICL, 1983a, p. 8). It also allows ICL to provide SNA capabilities on many of its products.

IPA is described in some detail in several papers in the May 1983 issue on communications of *ICL Technical Journal* (ICL, 1983b). For example, Brenner (1983) gives a general overview of IPA, Lloyd (1983) describes IPA's data interchange and networking facilities, Turner (1983) discusses the IPA telecommunications function, which realises Layers 1 to 4 of OSI, and Goss (983) presents the concepts of IPA community management, which is a set of tools, facilities, and methodologies, to cater for management functions in IPA networks.

Philips Communication Network Structure has been formulated as an extension and refinement of OSI and has been designed to operate on the Philips SOPHO-LAN and Philips SOPHO-NET WAN, as well as on both these systems working together (Philips Business Communications, 1983). It has the following seven domains:

1. *Physical Domain*, corresponding to OSI Physical Layer;
2. *Link Domain*, corresponding to OSI Data Link Layer;
3. *LAN Domain*, corresponding to OSI Subnetwork Access Sublayer and intended for communication over LANs;
4. *Packet Domain*, corresponding to OSI Subnetwork Access Sublayer and OSI Subnetwork Enhancement Sublayer together and intended for X.25 communications over WANs;
5. *Transfer Domain*, corresponding to OSI Internetting Sublayer;
6. *Communication Domain*, corresponding to OSI Transport Layer;
7. *Information Domain*, corresponding to OSI Session Layer, OSI Presentation Layer, and OSI Application Layer together.

Morino and Mishimura (1981) outline the logical structure and protocols for *Data Communication Network Architecture (DCNA)*, which is also discussed by Imai et al (1982). Joint research and development on DCNA was started in April 1977 by NTT and four Japanese computer/communications manufacturers: Fujitsu, Hitachi, Nippon Electric, and Oki Electric Industry. Its third version was completed in July 1980. Its protocols are applicable to various data communications networks in heterogeneous environments, and they include several high level protocols. Its applications are being investigated by various users in Japan. DCNA's designers have made vigorous efforts to have its features reflected in international standards; NTT participates positively in CCITT and ISO activities and promotes DCNA concepts in their discussions.

DCNA has the following levels and sublevels:

1. *Physical Level*, corresponding to OSI Physical Layer;
2. *Data Link Control Level*, corresponding to OSI Data Link Layer;
3. *Transport Level*, performing the functions of OSI Network Layer and OSI Transport Layer and having the following sublevels:

   a. *Routing Control Sublevel*, performing routing functions,
   b. *Transport Unit Control Sublevel*, setting up and clearing logical com-

munication paths between source and destination nodes connected by one or more links, controlling flow to prevent congestion, and confirming delivery (acknowledging) to prevent loss;

4. *Function Control Level*, corresponding to the three top layers of OSI and having the following sublevels:
   a. *Data Unit Control Sublevel*, setting up and clearing logical communication paths between an applications program and data transfer over the paths, corresponding to the OSI Session Layer,
   b. *Fundamental Attribute Processing Sublevel*, performing transformations of data attributes common to various kinds of higher level common functions (e.g., code conversion), corresponding to the OSI Presentation Layer,
   c. *System Function Sublevel*, performing functions specific to each kind of higher level common function but not specific to each application,
   d. *Application Function Sublevel*, performing functions specific to each kind of higher level common function and also specific to each application;
   (Sublayers 4c and 4d jointly correspond to the OSI Application Layer.)

5. *Information Processing Level*, processing specific applications (e.g., scientific and engineering calculations) and thus above the seven OSI layers.

Imai et al (1982) show how DCNA has been extended to acquire multi-media capabilities and become able to handle combinations of data, video, and voice. The requirements for media handling included the ability to deal with the following situations:

1. Media from a given terminal differing from media to that terminal;
2. Different media at source and destination;
3. Different media transferred on the same line between source and destination on a time-shared basis;
4. Separate line for each medium between a given source and a given destination;
5. The media used for transfer differ from the media used for input, output, and storage.

The US Department of Defense has developed its own *Internet Architecture Model*, together with an associated set of protocols; its principles are outlined by Cerf and Cain (1983). Major factors, which influenced the development of this architectural model, include DoD's experimental and operational experience with many interconnected networks, assessments and evaluations of military requirements, and specific concerns about network security, survivability, and operation under crisis conditions.

The book *Computer Network Architectures* (Meijer and Peters, 1982) is intended as a comprehensive introduction to network architectures, and provides a good source of information for practicing engineers; it contains many references to the relevant literature. It gives detailed treatments of OSI and of the network architectures developed by IBM, DEC, Univac, and Burroughs, and it briefly describes those developed by Siemens, Honeywell, and ICL. It considers some of the problems of interconnecting different network architectures, especially over public data networks.

The book *Proprietary Network Architectures* (Gee, 1981) discusses network architectures in general, and gives details of OSI, SNA, DNA, and Hewlett Packard's Distributed Systems Network. It ends with discussions of user requirements and the evaluation of network architectures.

The book *Computer Network Architecture* (Yakubaitis, 1983) covers network architecture, including the upper layers of the ISO model, in considerable detail. Black (1983) discusses network architecture in Chapter 8 of his book *Data Communications, Networks and Distributed Processing*.

Konongi and Das (1983) give a brief introduction to network architecture, and discuss protocols and interfaces between interconnected systems.

Ennis and Filice (1983) present the architecture used with the Sytek LocalNet™ LAN. Leach et al (1983) describe the architecture used with the Apollo DOMAIN LAN.

Mimice and Marsden (1982) point out that current developments in network architectures and protocol standards are not suitable for small microcomputers with limited storage and processing capability. They propose a distributed systems architecture for these computers; it is based on datagrams, maintains compatibility with OSI wherever possible, and supports internetworking.

NETWORK STANDARDS

Des Jardins (1983) gives a detailed review of the current status of international (OSI) and US computer networking computer standards.

He reports that, as a result of the work of ISO, CCITT, ECMA, and national standards bodies, the status of the OSI standards was as follows at the time when he wrote his paper:

Layer 1 (Physical Layer)

The EIA electrical interface standards RS-232, RS-422, and RS-423 have been widely adopted. The IEEE-802 Layer 1 LAN standards are in their final stages, with Baseband CSMA/CD and Token Bus being completed in 1983, Broadband CSMA/CD and Token Ring in 1984; all major manufacturers have indicated that they will implement IEEE-802. ECMA plans to publish a Digital PBX to Host Computer standard in 1984. CCITT Recommendations for ISDN interfaces and universal miniconnector standards should be adopted in 1984.

Layer 2 (Data Link Layer)

HDLC has been an international standard for several years, and the HDLC Consolidated Classes of Procedure progressed to an ISO Draft Proposal in 1983. IEEE-

802 Logical Link Control was adopted as a LAN standard in 1983. These two standards will provide the basis for all data link control across LANs and WANs.

Layer 3 (Network Layer)

Standardisation work in 1983 concentrated on defining the internal structure of this layer and the types of service available from it. Progress has been made in defining the layer's address structure and in developing a connectionless-mode internetwork protocol. It is expected that both these areas, together with LAN-WAN interfaces, will be standardised in 1984.

Layer 4 Transport Layer

World agreement has been reached on the Transport Protocol, which advanced to ISO DIS (Draft International Standard) status in September 1983. CCITT is expected to adopt Transport Protocol at its Plenary Session in 1984.

Layer 5 (Session Layer)

Session Layer Service and Protocol Standard will probably become a DIS early in 1984 and is expected to be adopted by CCITT at its Plenary Session in 1984.

Layer 6 (Presentation Layer)

ISO anticipates publishing a Draft Proposal for the Presentation Protocol by early 1984.

Layer 7 (Application Layer)

Developing standards are expected in 1984 for: ISO file transfer, CCITT videotex and Teletex, CCITT electronic message handling.

Thus, by the end of 1984, international, OSI-based, standards should be available for:

1. Worldwide digital networking through LANs, public and private WANs, and the early versions of the evolving new ISDNs;
2. End-to-end universal Transport and Session control;
3. Several important application protocols, together with a canonical transfer syntax, defined in the Presentation Layer for each application context.

These standards will form the basic worldwide capabilities of OSI, which should become widely available and then routine in the late 1980s.

Chapin (1983) has written the first two of a series of reports on computer communications standards, motivated by the belief that better, more timely, more relevant standards, closer to the state of the art, will result if the people interested in these standards are more widely informed. He points out that, although it has become increasingly urgent to develop high quality standards for networking services, protocols and interfaces, the process of developing these standards is not widely understood and often seems confusing. Chapin's first report surveys recent work on OSI, transport protocols, LAN standards, and internetworking; it lists the US and international standards bodies involved. His second report surveys recent work on OSI, X.25, Network Layer, Transport Layer, Session Layer, and LAN standards.

Owen (1983) discusses the importance of the international exchange of information about data communications, both within and between the developed and developing countries. Communication and exchange of ideas is essential between individuals and groups from a variety of backgrounds, who are involved in developing new systems. Owen indicates the part played by IFIP Technical Committee 6: Data Communications, and the ways in which it achieves its aims. Topics in which it is interested include protocols, local networks and messaging, covered by its Working Groups 6.1, 6.4, and 6.5, respectively.

The US Government has set up the *Federal Telecommunicatons Standards Program (FTSP)*, administered by the National Communications System (NCS), and the *Federal Information Processing Standards Program (FIPSP)*, conducted by the NBS. FTSP has been active in developing and promoting Federal versions of X.25 (FED-STD-1041), user-oriented digital communications performance parameters (FED-STD-1033 and FED-STD-1043), data link control (FED-STD-1003A), and Physical Layer encryption (FED-STD-1026). NCS has been a major participation in developing ISDN standards, scheduled for initial adoption in 1984.

NBS has been very active in developing draft *FIPS (Federal Information Processing Standards)* in the Transport Layer and higher Layers. FIPS for LANs, Transport Protocols, Session Protocols, Internetwork Protocols, Message Systems, and File Transfer Protocols were published in 1983 or due to appear in 1984; all of them are coordinated with the corresponding IEEE, ISO, and CCITT standards now being developed.

In one massive volume, Folts (1983) gives all 123 interface protocol standards that had been set by ISO, CCITT, ECMA, EIA, and the US Government, at the time when it was compiled.

Nelson (1983) gives a detailed progress report on the LAN standards emerging from the work of IEEE Project 802, Local Area Network Communication Standards. Standards are being proposed for the baseband and broadband LANs, and, for each of these types, for several access methods:

1. Standard 802.3, Baseband CSMA/CD, at 10 Mbits/sec, was approved by the IEEE Standards Board in June 1983. A standard for Broadband CSMA/CD is still in fairly early stages of discussion; variants for 5 Mbits/sec and 10 Mbits/sec per sub-channel are envisaged.

2. Standard 802.4, Baseband Token Ring, has been accepted, with formal confirmation expected very soon; it specifies admissible data rates of 1, 5, 10, and 20 Mbits/sec. Standard 802.4, Broadband Token Bus, is now being developed, with admissible data rates of 1, 5, and 10 Mbits/sec per sub-channel.

3. Standard 802.5, Baseband Token Ring, is now being drafted and may be approved in mid-1984; it has admissible data rates of 1 to 4 Mbits/sec, if twisted pairs are used and higher than that if coaxial cables or optical fibers are used.

4. All LANs using IEEE standards, will work under the IEEE Logical Link Control Standard 802 and Higher Layer Interface, Standards 802.1.

Rance (1983) relates the history and describes the status, at that time, of the IEEE Project 802. He discusses some of the remaining issues in each of the three access methods considered: CSMA/CD, token bus, token ring. Fromm (1983) presents the crucial part played by ECMA, as well as IEEE, in the development of LAN standards. This IEEE and ECMA work has been reviewed briefly in Appendices F and G, respectively, of the recent book *Local Area Networks* (Cheong and Hirschheim, 1983).

The proposed IEEE standard is also reviewed by Burr (1983), and by Dahod (1983), who argue that it is unrealistic to expect only one LAN standard to emerge, because LAN technology is innovative and users' objectives are varied. This view is borne out by the current situation, namely that there is a triple IEEE LAN Standard, jointly supporting standards for Ethernet, token bus, and token ring LANs.

Norton (1983) describes the work of the *Focus Committee on Information Technology*, set up by the Department of Industry in the UK, with special reference to the FOCUS initiatives in the area of LAN standards (Meadowcroft, 1982; O'Connor, 1981). The FOCUS Report on LANs (Meadowcroft, 1982) classifies LANs broadly into four groups, in order of increasing cost and complexity: micronets, data nets, integrated networks, and "video nets," which can carry video and voice as well as text and data. It includes projection of the future development of these groups, and foresees especially rapid growth for data nets.

In August 1982, the Department of Industry also set up the *Information Technology Standards Unit (ITSU)*, directed by Keith Bartlett. In these ways, the Department of Industry has acted decisively to provide the essential public advice, support, and research needed to allow British industry and business to take full advantage of the new opportunities provided by information technology. OSI (1983) is the published proceedings of a conference, organised in conjunction with ITSU and held in London in December 1982.

ITSU has assembled a collection of "Intercept Recommendations," in an attempt to speed up the normal process of standardisation. ITSU assesses when a given DIS is likely to be adopted with only minor changes that can be accommodated later with minimal difficulty. Norton (1983) gives a list of four draft LAN standards for Media Access Techniques and three for OSI Data Link Layer, that seem likely to be made Intercept Recommendations. Foremski (1984) considers that it latest recommendations, now being issued, will effectively let British manufacturers and system builders start to implement the OSI standards before their full ratification.

Kennett (1984a) reports that the UK's biggest telecommunications user, the British government, is leading the demand for network and telecommunications standards in the UK.

Twelve top European computer companies, including GEC, ICL, Philips, Plessey, and Siemens, have agreed to implement all levels of OSI standards in their products from 1985 on (Riley, 1984; Ring, 1984).

Members of the British Computer Society are actively involved in developing standards in most areas of computing. Some of their work is outlined in a recent article (*British Computer Society*, 1984).

There have been several general reviews of recent standards work, for example by Williams (1983), Kennett (1983), Chapter 12 of Black (1983) and *Which Computer?* (1984). Charlish (1984) comments on the discrepancies between the standards of official bodies, unofficial groupings, and manufacturers that are becoming increasingly frustrating and irritating to users of equipment from different vendors.

Saal (1983) discusses standardisations of LANs and personal computer networks. He points out that only a few microcomputer vendors have yet recognised the advantage of adopting standards and avoided the pitfalls of going it alone.

De Haas (1982) discusses the current status of CCITT's intensive efforts on standards for integrated services digital networks (ISDNs). Because of the substantial technical and economic consequences of the decisions to be taken, much of this standardisation is being based on existing, though advanced technology, and is being worked out *a priori,* before even pilot systems have been tested. The paper by Collie et al (1983) is also relevant.

Jennings (1983) outlines current modem standards and indicates the purposes of the CCITT V standards and X standards, as well as the standards ISO 2110, ISO 2593, ISO 4902, and EIA RS-232-C.

Panko (1981) reviews the standards that had been recommended for electronic message systems at the time of his article.

Tamworth (1983) describes the CCITT Recommendations for Teletex standards: F.200, Teletex Service; S.60, Terminal Equipment; S.61, Character Repertoire/ Codes; S.62, Control Procedures; S.70, Transport Service; S.90, Teletext/Telex Conversion Facility. Also relevant are the international circuit-switched data network standards X.21 and X.71, and the international packet-switched data network standards X.25 and X.75. Now that CCITT has defined its standards, Teletex will be the first international service, after fax, which is able to provide compatibility between users, in all parts of the world, wishing to exchange text. Kennett (1984) reports that a new standard for combining Teletex and facsimile transmission is expected to be accepted soon by CCITT.

Smith (1984a) reviews the international standards on Coded Character Set for Information Processing Interchange, namely: ISO 646, the 7-bit standard, ISO 4873 (1973), the 8-bit set (1979), and the more comprehensive ISO 6937, now being developed. ISO 6937 Part 1, General Introduction, and Part 2, Latin Alphabetic and Non-Alphabetic Graphic Characters, have been approved and are now being published; Part 3, Control Functions for Page-Image Format, has been released as a DIS and will be published later. Smith (1984b) discusses work done on setting standards for non-Latin alphabets, and lists some of the ISO character sets.

Blyth (1983) examines the current status of ISO's proposals for OSI standards on text interchange. Without such standards, incompatibilities in media, communications protocols, and document structure often make it difficult, if not impossible, to interchange text between different word processors. Work on text interchange standards has begun only recently, and it still has some way to go before working drafts will reach stability and agreement. Once this has been achieved, interactions between the text services and the file service can be investigated.

The Data Interchange Format (DIF™) is a popular de facto "standard" in the US, although it has not yet been adopted by any of the standards bodies. It was developed by Robert M. Frankston, President of Software Arts, Inc., as a method of communicating data between VisiCalc and other software, and it can be viewed as a first attempt for exchanging numerical tables and simple text data between personal computers. Its principles and applications are described fully in the book by Beil (1983), which includes the DIF Technical Specification as Appendix A and gives extensive references to the literature on DIF.

Harper (1984) considers that standards for new areas will emerge as users see the demand for them. ISO and other standards bodies are now working on the management of systems, communications, and resources, a very important but very complicated area, which is at present linked closely with implementation.

Mullen (1983) argues that the networks of the future will be based not on common hardware but on common applications. He cites AT&T Information Systems' Net/1000 network, which is just starting, as a good potential model for an industry-wide applications network. He points out that the industry-specific standards for common applications networks are beginning to emerge. As examples, he lists the ISO and ANSI standards on banking, together with three standards for videotex.

Selvaggi (1983) provides background information for the US Department of Defense (DoD) *Data Protocol Standardization Program* and outlines current DoD planning for future work in this area. Cerf and Lyons also comment on this programme, identifying deficiencies in existing standards for military applications; they outline a strategy for military standardisation; adopt commercial standards where they apply, and supplement these with special military standards when necessary.

Berman (1984) reports that British Telecom, in collaboration with major manufacturers has developed a new *digital private network signalling system (dpnss)* standard, which allows the new facilities on PABXs from different vendors to be linked in a private network. Dpnss developed out of the earlier *Digital Access Signalling System (Dass)*; Dass 1 and Dass 2 are signaling systems for British Telecom's PSTN. Plessey, GEC Reliance, GTE Ferranti, Mitel and STC are all collaborating in implementing dpnss, but there has not yet been any consortium of companies, producing any similar standard in any country other than the UK. It has been said that dpnss is the voice equivalent of X.25.

US government and industry standards organisations have defined a set of user-oriented performance parameters that may be applied to any data communications service (Seitz, 1984). Twenty-one of these parameters are defined in the American National Standard X3.102-1983 (ANSI, 1983). Seitz et al (1983) describe the predecessor of this standard, proposed Federal Standard 1043, which has four major sections: data extraction, data files, performance assessment, and statistical design and analysis. As a result of their own user-oriented performance measurements, they suggested some improvements, that have been incorporated in the new standard, ANS X3.102.

The proposed standard ANS X335/135 defines the comparison of network measurement methods. Both this standard and ANS X3.102 are expected to be useful in comparing performance between alternative network services, products, and suppliers (Seitz, 1984).

CCITT Study Group VII has been attempting to define Quality of Service parameters and values for public data networks (Seitz, 1984). Draft CCITT Recommendation X.140 specifies user-oriented network-independent Quality of Service parameters like those defined in ANS X3.102.

Schindler (1982) attempts to clear up confusions about communications and networking terminology. He considers such terms as "Teletex," "videotex," and "network integration," and indicates their relative positions within the ISO Reference Model for OSI. He discusses in detail the terminology and concepts of transmission, switching, internetworking, network integration, LANs and ISDNs. He also considers keywords relating to applications such as office automation and text processing.

NETWORK PROTOCOLS

The special issue of the *Proceedings of the IEEE* on OSI includes papers discussing work on the development of OSI protocols in all seven OSI Layers. McClelland (1983) reports on new developments in services and protocols of the Physical Layer. Conard (1983) reviews services and protocols of the Data Link Layer. Ware (1983) describes the work of CCITT and ISO on the Network Layer. Callon (1983a) discusses an Internetwork Protocol. Knightson (1983) reports on Transport Layer standardisation. Emmons and Chandler (1983) consider Session Layer services and protocols. Hollis (1983) discusses the current status of standards work on the Presentation Layer.

Bartoli (1983) presents the work of ISO, CCITT and ANSI on the Applications Layer, together with some of its concepts. The papers by Lowe (1983), Lewan and Long (1983), Langsford et al (1983), and Cunningham (1983), describe the OSI Virtual Terminal Service, the OSI File Service, the OSI Management and Job Transfer Services, and Message-Handling Systems and Protocols, respectively.

The book by Pužman and Pořízék (1981) contains an extensive discussion of communications protocols. Protocols are also discussed in Chapters 2 to 4 of Computer Communications (1983) and in Chapters 6 and 8 of the book by Black (1983).

The book by Needham and Herbert (1982) includes a description of the protocols used in the Cambridge Ring LAN.

Murphy (1982) describes the ARCnet token-passing network protocol and shows how it increases LAN throughput.

Computer Networks (1983) reports on the ACM SIGCOMM '83 Symposium on Communication Architectures and Protocols, held at Austin, Texas, in March 1983; its full proceedings are published by ACM SIGCOMM (1983a). Its keynote session was on the theme "Putting Protocols to Work," and there were also sessions on: protocol implementation experience, protocol verification methods, specification and testing and performance analysis of protocols, local network access protocols, gateways and protocol compatibility issues, queueing models of protocols, and other topics.

Other conferences with papers on protocols and architectures have included the Seventh and Eighth Data Communications Symposia, at Mexico City and at North Falmouth, Massachusetts; their proceedings have been published by ACM SIGCOMM (1981, 1983b).

Colvin (1983a and 1983b) claims that the SyFAnet LAN combines the best features of baseband and broadband technologies without the pitfalls of either, by using CSMA/CA (Carrier Sense Multiple Access with Collision Avoidance) in its low level protocols. CSMA/CA requires a node to "listen," that is, sense the carrier, twice, before sending a packet. Potential collisions are detected during an initial "carrier burst," before data transmission.

In their presentation of Toronto University's Hubnet LAN, which has a dual rooted tree topology, Boulton and Lee (1983) describe in detail the hub protocol and access control protocol that it uses. These protocols have several advantages, including the avoidance of collisions between contending packets, the absence of limits to packet size, a good performance in heavy traffic.

Dahod and Grobicki (1983) Present the new Unilink distributed LAN access method, which attempts to combine the benefits of CSMA/CD and token passing. This approach defines a "message slot" as a period, during which a packet (of fixed or variable length), may be transmitted; each message slot is implicitly numbered. A given device in the LAN can send a packet only during a message slot whose number is allocated to it. An automatic numbering process sometimes assigns a message number to one device only, sometimes to several devices. In the former case, dedicated assignment, only the assigned device may transmit a packet during the slot with that number. In the latter case, contention assignment, several devices may attempt to transmit, with any "collisions" being handled in much the same way as the CSMA/CD.

Sykas et al (1983) propose a new family of hybrid multiple access protocols, designed to reduce contention between packets in LANs with low access time and high channel utilisation; they combine features of existing deterministic and random multiple access schemes. They use dynamic frames, whose length depends on the number of stations busy at the time. Each frame is divided into a status slot, a sequence of reserved TDMA slots, one for each active station, and a sequence of unreserved slots, in which the URN protocol or some other random access protocol operates. Sykas et al show that this scheme provides stability under any circumstances, and allows the achievement of good throughput and delay characteristics. Under normal traffic conditions, access time is low; under heavy traffic conditions, channel utilisation remains high, and delays are "not too long" and thus still acceptable.

Stokesberry (1983) describes NBS' work on the use of the ISO/NBS Class 4 Transport Protocol on LANs, interworking with the IEEE 802 LAN protocols.

Ellis et al (1983) describe the choice of protocols used with the Nestar PLAN 4000 network. They also discuss some of their experience in implementing them on the network, stressing the problems met and how they were solved.

Yeomans (1983) reviews the progress of work on LAN standards for multi-media office documents combining data, text, graphics, image, and voice information. Practical constraints on their implementation include economics, human factors, and regulatory issues. He suggests that further high level protocol standards for LANs will not be needed in the short term, to meet these needs, but that there will be a continuing need for some standardisation above the Transport and Session Layers to provide gateway standards to interconnect LANs and WANs.

Gold and Franta (1983) discuss an efficient collision-free protocol, providing distributed access control for cable networks or radio networks operating under various priority disciplines.

Pearson (1983) shows how to apply the OSI model, to design protocols that can provide effective communications services to microcomputers. One of these protocols, the *Microcom Networking Protocol* (*MNP*), is now marketed by Microcom, Inc. in the USA (Microcom, 1983), and by British Telecom Merlin in the UK under the name of *T-Link* (British Telecom, 1984). It uses the OSI Physical, Data Link, Session, and Application Layers.

It could well enable all models of personal computers and micros to share and exchange their information freely, and it seems likely to become a de facto standard. Its other advantages include: reliable data transfer, flexibility, flow control, data transparency, low cost, compact software, and implementation independence.

Morino and Nishimura (1981) describe some of the protocols used by DCNA. There are DCNA "common protocols" for the Data Link Control and Transport Levels and for the Data Unit Control and Fundamental Attribute Processing Sublevels. DCNA applications protocols include virtual terminal, file transfer/access, job transfer, data base access, and network management protocols; they are also discussed by Toda (1980). Imai et al (1982) give some details of the DCNA multi-media communication protocols, for multi-media indirect control, character image mixed text control, and graphic control.

In a recent series of articles, Jennings (1984a to 1984d) considers various aspects of WAN line protocols, operating in the Data Link Layer. Besides presenting some of the general principles, he considers some specific protocols including: IBM Binary Synchronous Communications (BSC) (Jennings, 1984a), HDLC and SDLC (Jennings, 1984b and 1984d), and the IBM 2780 contention protocol for use with the IBM 2780 RJE terminal (Jennings, 1984c), and the "glass teletype" protocol (Jennings, 1984e).

In his book *Packet Switching,* Rosner (1982) discusses several aspects of protocols. Part 2 of his book deals with X.25 and other operational protocols in a packet-switched network. Part 4 describes resource-sharing multi-access techniques for packet radio networks and satellite networks.

Brodd (1983) shows that the WAN level 2 protocols HDLC, ADCCP, and SDLC correspond closely, even though the first two were produced by two different standards bodies, ISO and ANSI, while SDLC was developed by IBM as a commercial subset of both of them.

Schindler et al (1982b) argue that X.21 is one of the most important candidates for a *Universal Digital Service Access* (*UDSA*) interface using OSI. As a basis for discussion of X.21's suitability for this purpose, they explain its context and underlying philosophy, and they present a formal specification for it. They then discuss the architectural issues related to X.21, the UDSA interface, and the ISDN interface.

Poussard (1983) describes the CCITT protocol X.22, which designates a multiplexed link-to-user interface, and which is valuable in both circuit-switched and packet-switched networks despite being relatively little known. It is now being actively implemented in Australian, West German, and Swedish networks.

CAPX25 is communications software, implementing X.25 for Data Terminal Equipment, for use in private networks, national networks, and international networks (CAP, 1983a and 1983b). It operates on the Intel range of MULTIBUS®-based data communications processor boards. It provides an interface procedure library, supporting small applications on a single board configuration and large applications on a multiboard configuration.

Callon (1983) briefly introduces the current OSI approaches to internetworking, discusses the need for a connection-oriented internetwork protocol, and proposes a design for it. This proposed new protocol includes connection setup, data transfer, and connection termination phases.

Von Studnitz (1983) reports on the actual status and short-term expectations of the agreements about Transport Layer protocols between ISO, CCITT, and ECMA. Mapstone (1983) gives a detailed specification of the ECMA-72 Class 4 Transport Protocol.

Schindler et al (1983) discuss the ISO and ECMA draft proposals for a Teletex-based Session Protocol, and suggest possible developments that could lead to an international standard there.

Listanti and Villani (1983) discuss some basic requirements for integrating voice and data traffic; they propose a communications protocol for voice transmission with X.25 networks. They use voice "packets" imbedded in data packets, a virtual circuit routing technique, and flow control at Levels 3 and 4; packet retransmission after error detection is limited to the packet header.

Kohler (1982) examines the use of OSI protocols in the communications systems used by public administration in West Germany. Common data communications protocols have been proposed by a working group of the Federal Republic's public administration. Protocols for Layers 4 through 6 have been approved by the Co-ordination Committee for Data Processing.

Xionics and the Mond Division of ICI have jointly developed ISOLINK, a set of communications software modules, as an advanced implementation of OSI. ISOLINK has four stages of development and allows nontechnical users of the XINET and MASTERNET LAN systems to use computer systems, networks, network services, applications, and data bases, without any knowledge of networking protocols, procedures, or conventions.

The XOREN File Transfer Packages have been developed to implement file transfer to and from DEC computers (Xoren 1983a, 1983b). XOREN IPL-11 is an easy-to-use set of programs, which allows data and program files to be transferred economically over asynchronous links between two DEC computers, either on the same site, via a direct line, or in different sites, via a telephone line. VAX-11, PDP-11, LSI-11, and DEC Professional 300 computers can be linked in this way. XOREN IPL-11/POS is a software package which allows a Professional 300 to be linked to another computer, over a direct line or a telephone line.

Lees (1983) describes some of the protocols used by the UNIVERSE network, which has linked various Cambridge Ring LANs in the UK via satellite and via high-speed land lines.

Einert and Glas (1983) present the gateway concept, based on the ISO Reference Model as a solution for "opening" previously incompatible manufacturers' networks. This solution implies the mapping of network architectures and protocols, and in particular it must translate high level, end-to-end protocols.

Bracker (1983) discusses the capabilities of today's protocol conversion products and interfaces, and specifies whether they convert by means of hardware or software or both. He includes a table that sums up the characteristics of dozens of these products that are on the market. Wiley (1983) shows that the newest protocol converters can easily be integrated to improve networking functions in a surprising variety of ways.

Haverty and Gurwicz (1983) point out that selecting a protocol for a particular task and choosing a method of implementing that protocol both need close attention to a specific environment. They outline some general rules for solving these problems, and they illustrate their remarks by discussing a case study of protocol implementation.

Dickson and de Chazal (1983) discuss the status of CCITT formal description techniques, especially the revised Specification and Description Language (SDL), which is a candidate language for protocol specification in CCITT Recommendations. They explain the relationships between the key concepts in SDL and OSI. They give an illustrative example of the benefits of applying SDL to protocol specification.

Vissers et al (1983) recall that, early in the development of OSI, it was recognized that formal description techniques would be needed to achieve its goals. They give a brief history and report on the status of the ISO/TC97/SC16/WG1 ad hoc group on Formal Description Techniques and its three subgroups. They survey the techniques developed by each of these subgroups, up to the end of 1982.

Computer Networks (1984, pages 57-65) reports the Conference on Protocol Specification, Testing and Verification, held at Zurich, Switzerland from 31 May to 2 June 1982, under the auspices of IFIP WG 6.1; full proceedings have been published (Rudin and West, 1983). The conference had sessions on: protocol theory and analysis, specification and formal models, theory and applications of Petri nets, protocol validation and verification, protocol performance, protocol design and implementation, integrated systems, and protocol testing.

In December 1982, the *IEEE Transactions on Communications* published a special section on protocol specification, testing, and verification (Sunshine, 1982). Its four papers discuss the use of three mathematical tools for these purposes: finite state machines, Petri nets, and extended state transition models.

Vuong and Gowan (1983) "prove" the X.75 Level 3 protocol as an example of protocol validation by the method of resynthesis and decomposition.

The report, edited by Rayner (1982), discusses a system for testing protocol implementation. Davidson (1982) discusses the feasibility of setting up a centre for testing protocols. Linn and Nightingale (1983) and Mills (1984) describe how the national Bureau of Standards (NBS) tests implementations of OSI protocols.

REFERENCES

ACM SIGCOMM (1981) *Proceedings Seventh Data Communications Symposium,* Mexico City, 27–29 Oct 1981, also published as *Computer Communications Review,* Vol. **11,** No. 4.

ACM SIGCOMM (1983a) *Communication Architectures and Protocols,* Proceedings of ACM SIGCOMM '83 Symposium, Austin, TX, also published as *Computer Communications Review,* Vol. **13,** No. 2.

ACM SIGCOMM (1983b) *Eighth Data Communications Symposium,* North Falmouth, MA, 3–6 Oct 1983, also published as *Computer Communications Review,* Vol **13,** No. 4.

ANSI (1983) American National Standard X3.102-1983, "Data communication user-oriented performance parameters," Computer and Business Equipment Manufacturers' Association, Washington, DC.

P. D. Bartoli (Dec 1983) "The Application Layer of the Reference Model of Open Systems Interconnection," *Proceedings of the IEEE,* **71**(12) 1404–1407.

D. H. Beil (1983) *The DIF™ File,* Reston Publishing Company, Reston, VA.

C. Berman (9 Feb 1984) "UK takes the lead in open PABX standard," *Computing,* 16.

U. D. Black (1983) *Data Communications, Networks and Distributed Processing,* Reston Publishing Company, Reston, VA.

D. Blyth (Oct 1983) "Standardization of text transfer in open systems," *Computer Communications,* **6**(5) 253–257.

P. I. P. Boulton and E. S. Lee (Jul 1983) "Bus, ring, star and tree local area networks," *Computer Communications Review,* **13**(3) 19–24.

W. E. Bracker, Jr. (Aug 1983) "Surveying the protocol conversion vendors' offerings," *Data Communications,* **12**(8) 89–101.

J. B. Brenner (May 1983) "IPA networking architecture," *ICL Technical Journal,* **3**(3) 234–239.

British Computer Society (22 Mar 1984) "Standards: The Society helps to develop and promote them," *Computing,* 16.

British Telecom (1984) *T-Link,* British Telecom Merlin, Felixstowe, Suffolk, England, Leaflet.

W. D. Brodd (Aug 1983) "HDLC, ADCCP, and SDLC: What's the Difference?," *Data Communications,* **12**(8) 115–122.

W. E. Burr (Aug 1983) "An overview of the Proposed American Standard for Local Distributed Data Interchange," *Communications of the ACM,* **26**(8) 554–561.

R. Callon (1983a) (Dec 1983) "Internetwork protocol," *Proceedings of the IEEE,* **71**(12) 1388–1393.

R. Callon (1983b) (Jul 1983) "Proposal for a connection-oriented internetwork protocol," *Computer Communications Review,* **13**(3) 10–18.

CAP (1983a) *CAPX25 Packet Switching Network Interface,* CAP Group, London, Brochure BCD/SP/MAY83.

CAP (1983b) *CAPX25—High Performance Low Cost Communications on an Intel MULTIBUS® Board,* CAP Group, London, Leaflet.

V. G. Cerf and E. Cain (Oct 1983) "The DoD Internet Architecture Model,"*Computer Networks*, **7**(5) 307–318.

V. G. Cerf and R. E. Lyons (Oct 1983) "Military requirements for packet-switched networks and their implications for protocol standardization," *Computer Networks*, **7**(5) 293–306.

A. L. Chapin (1983a) (Dec 1983) "Connections and connectionless data transmission," *Proceedings of the IEEE*, **71**(12) 1365–1371.

A. L. Chapin (1983b) "Computer Communications Standards," *Computer Communications Review*, **13**(1) 40–46 (Jan 1983) and **13**(3) 36–42 (1 Jul 1983).

G. Charlish (9 Mar 1984) "'Bizarre' standards confusion," *Financial Times*, 10.

V. E. Cheong and R. A. Hirschheim (1983) *Local Area Networks—Issues, Products, and Developments*, Wiley-Interscience, Chichester and New York.

Ed. W. Chou (1983) *Computer Communications, Vol. 1, Principles*, Prentice-Hall, Englewood Cliffs, NJ.

B. E. Collie, L. B. Kayser and A. M. Rybczynski (1983) "Looking at the ISDN interfaces: Issues and answers," *Data Communications*, **12**(6) 125–136.

A. Colvin (1983a) (Oct 1983) "CSMA with collision avoidance," *Computer Communications*, **6**(5) 227–235.

A. Colvin (1983b) "CSMA with collision avoidance—A new technique for cost reduction," *LocalNet 83 (Europe)*, 223–238.

Computer Networks (Oct 1983) "SIGCOMM '83 Symposium—Communication Architectures and Protocols," Vol. **7**, No. 5, 351–359.

Computer Networks (Feb 1984) Vol. **8**, No. 1, special issue: programming languages and open systems interconnection.

J. W. Conard (Dec 1983) "Services and protocols of the Data Link Layer," *Proceedings of the IEEE*, **71**(12) 1378–1383.

I. Cunningham, (Dec 1983) "Message-handling systems and protocols," *Proceedings of the IEEE*, **71**(12) 1425–1430.

R. J. Cypser (1978) *Communications Architecture for Distributed Systems*, Addison-Wesley, London and Reading, MA.

A. M. Dahod (Mar 1983) "Local network standards: No utopia," *Data Communications*, **12**(3) 173–180.

A. M. Dahod and C. J. Grobicki (Nov 1983) "Multiple access method embraces popular local net schemes," *Data Communications*, **12**(11) 237–245.

I. C. Davidson (Aug 198') "A report on the feasibility of a National Protocol Testing Centre," NCC, Manchester, England, Report.

J. D. Day and H. Zimmerman (Dec 1983) "The OSI Reference Model," *Proceedings of the IEEE*, **71**(12) 1334–1340.

T. de Haas (1982) "International Standardization and the ISDN," *Journal of Telecommunication Networks*, **1**(4) 333–340.

DEC (1982a) *Introduction to Local Area Networks*, Digital Equipment Corporation, Maynard, MA, Order No. EB-22714-18.

DEC (1982b) *Networks—Digital Network Architecture for the 1980s*, Digital Equipment Corporation, Maynard, MA, Brochure, Order No. EA-23404-18.

G. Dennis (Jun 1983) "Transport Services Layers in OSI," *Communications International*, **10**(6) 67–70.

R. des Jardins (Dec 1983) "Afterword: Evolving Towards OSI," *Proceedings of the IEEE*, **71**(12) 1446–1448.

G. J. Dickson and P. E. de Chazal (Dec 1983) "Status of CCITT description techniques and application to protocol specification," *Proceedings of the IEEE*, **71**(12) 1346–1355.

D. Eakin (Feb 1983) "Gaining access to IBM's SNA,"*DEC User*, 26–32.

D. Einert and G. Glas (Spring 1983) "The SNATCH Gateway: Translation of higher level protocols," *Journal of Telecommunication Networks*, **2**(1) 83–102.

G. M. Ellis, S. Dillon, S. Stritter and J. Whitnell (Nov 1983) "Experiences with a layered approach to local area network design,"*IEEE Journal on Selected Areas in Communications*, **SAC-1**(5) 852–868.

W. F. Emmons and A. S. Chandler (Dec 1983) "OSI Session Layer: Services and protocols," *Proceedings of the IEEE*, **71**(12) 1397–1400.

G. Ennis and P. Filice (Nov 1983) "Overview of a broad-band local area network protocol architecture," *IEEE Journal on Selected Areas in Communications*, **SAC-1**(5) 832–841.

H. C. Folts (Dec 1983) "Scanning the issue," *Proceedings of the IEEE*, **71**(12) 1331–1333.

Ed. H. C. Folts (1982) *McGraw Hill's Compilation of Data Communications Standards Edition II*, McGraw Hill, New York.

Ed. H. C. Folts and R. des Jardins (Dec 1983) *Proceedings of the IEEE*, Vol. **71**, No. 12, special issue on open systems interconnection (OSI)—new standard architecture and protocols for distributed information systems.

T. Foremski (8 Mar 1984) "OSI standards to get boost," *Computing*, 3.

I. Fromm (1983) "ECMA's role in the standardization of local area networks," *LocalNet 83 (Europe)*, 415–423.

K. C. E. Gee (1981) *Proprietary Network Architectures*, NCC Publications, Manchester, England.

Y. I. Gold and W. R. Franta (Apr 1984) "An efficient collision-free protocol for prioritized access-control of cable or radio channels," *Computer Networks*, **7**(2) 83–98.

S. T. F. Goss (May 1983) "IPA community management," *ICL Technical Journal*, **3**(3) 278–288.

J. B. Gray and T. B. McNeill (1979) "SNA multiple-system networking," *IBM Systems Journal*, **18**(2) 263–297.

J. Harper (15 Mar 1984) "The Model answer to the standard problems," *Computing*, 38–39.

J. Haverty and R. Gurwitz (Mar 1983) "Protocols and their implementation: A matter of choice," *Data Communications*, **12**(3) 153–166.

L. L. Hollis (Dec 1983) "OSI Presentation Layer activities," *Proceedings of the IEEE*, **71**(12) 1401–1403.

IBM (undated) *Systems Network Architecture Format and Protocol Reference Manual: Architecture Logic*, International Business Machines, Document SC30-3112.

IBM (1981) *IBM 3705-80 Communications Controllers . . . . . . The Benefits of SNA for Intermediate Systems*, IBM World Trade Brochure, GK10-6330-0 (05/81).

ICL (1983a) *ICL Information Systems—An Introduction to Information Technology*, International Computers Limited, London, Brochure P1565.

ICL (1983b) (May 1983) *ICL Technical Journal*, Vol. **3**, No. 3, issue on communications.

Y. Imai, O. Takahashi and S. Fujinami (Oct 1982) "Network architecture expansion for INS-DCNA multi-media communications protocols," *Japan Telecommunications Review*, **14**(4) 345–351.

P. A. Jenkins and K. G. Knightson (Jul 1984) "Open Systems Interconnection—An introductory guide," *British Telecommunications Engineering*, **3**(2) 86–91.

F. Jennings (24 Nov 1983) "What the user needs to know about modems—Modem standards," *Computer Weekly*, 22.

F. Jennings (1984a) (26 Jan 1984) "Protocols you will need before and after LANs," *Computer Weekly*, 20.

F. Jennings (1984b) (2 Feb 1984) "All you need to know about synch and asynch operation," *Computer Weekly*, 38.

F. Jennings (1984c) (9 Feb 1984) "Contention protocol that has become a standard," *Computer Weekly*, 20–21.

F. Jennings (1984d) (16 Feb 1984) "All about protocols," *Computer Weekly*, 16.

F. Jennings (1984e) (1 Mar 1984) "Configuring out your links," *Computer Weekly*, 25.

R. Jones (6 Oct 1983) "Going strong ten years on," *Computing, IBM Supplement*, 14.

D. Kennett (24 Nov. 1983) "Standards work nears fruition," *Computer Weekly*, 4.

D. Kennett (1984a) (26 Jan 1984) "Government sets standards rolling," *Computer Weekly*, 9.

D. Kennett, (1984b) (9 Feb 1984) "Mixing fax and teletex draws near," *Computer Weekly*, 11.

K. G. Knightson (Jul/Oct 1982) "The Transport Layer," *Computer Communications Review*, **12**(3/4) 14–23.

K. G. Knightson (Dec 1983) "The Transport Layer standardisation," *Proceedings of the IEEE*, **71**(12) 1394–1396.

W. Köhler (Dec 1983) "Common data communications protocols in the FRG," *Computer Communications*, **6**(6) 283–290.

V. K. Konongi and C. R. Das (Oct 1983) "An introduction to network architecture," *IEEE Communications Magazine*, **21**(7) 44–50.

A. Langsford (Fall 1982) "Open Systems Interconnection—An architecture for interconnection or for distributed processing?," *Journal of Telecommunication Networks*, **1**(3) 253–263.

A. Langsford, K. Naemura and R. Speth (Dec 1983) "OSI management and job transfer services," *Proceedings of the IEEE*, **71**(12) 1420–1424.

K. N. Larson and W. R. Chestnut (Mar 1983) "Adding another layer to the ISO net architecture reduces costs," *Data Communications*, **12**(3) 215–222.

LDR Systems (1984) *ISONET—General Description*, LDR Systems Ltd., Aldershot, Hampshire, England, Document P1005-GD02 (1.84).

P. J. Leach et al (Nov 1983) "The architecture of an integrated local network," *IEEE Journal on Selected Areas in Communications*, **SAC-1**(5) 842–857.

W. Lees (1983) "The UNIVERSE network at Logica," *LocalNet 83 (Europe)*, 311–326.

D. Lewan and H. G. Long (Dec 1983) "The OSI File Services," *Proceedings of the IEEE*, **71**(12) 1414–1419.

P. F. Linington (Dec 1983) "Fundamentals of the layer service definitions and protocol specifications," *Proceedings of the IEEE*, **71**(12) 1341–1345.

R. J. Linn and J. S. Nightingale (Dec 1983) "Testing of OSI protocols of the National Bureau of Standards," *Proceedings of the IEEE*, **71**(12) 1431–1434.

M. Listanti and F. Villani (Feb 1983) "An X.25-compatible protocol for packet voice communications," *Computer Communications*, **6**(1) 23–31.

R. V. S. Lloyd (May 1983) "IPA data interchange and networking facilities," *ICL Technical Journal*, **3**(3) 250–264.

H. Lowe (Dec 1983) "OSI Virtual Terminal Service," *Proceedings of the IEEE*, **71**(12) 1408–1413.

F. M. McClelland (Dec 1983) "Services and protocols of the Physical Layer," *Proceedings of the IEEE*, **71**(12) 1372–1377.

A. S. Mapstone (May 1983) "Specification in CSP Language of the ECMA-72 Class 4 Transport Protocol," *ICL Technical Journal*, **3**(3) 297–312.

G. Meadowcroft (Aug 1982) "Local area networks," Report to the FOCUS Committee, UK.

A. Meijer and P. Peters (1982) *Computer Network Architectures*, Pitman, London, and Computer Science Press, Rockville, MD.

Microcom (1983) *The Microcom Networking Protocol (MNP)—An Introduction*, Microcom, Inc., Norwood, MA, Leaflet.

K. L. Mills (Mar 1984) "Testing OSI protocols: NBS advances the state of the art," *Data Communications*, **13**(3) 277–296.

O. Mimice and B. Marsden (Jun 1982) "A datagram-based network architecture for microcomputers," *Computer Communications*, **5**(3) 128–139.

J. P. Morency and R. Flakes (Jan 1984) "Gateways: A vital link to SNA network environment," *Data Communications*, **13**(1) 159–166.

H. Morino and T. Nishimura (Jan 1981) "DCNA—A standard network architecture for the 1980s," *Japan Telecommunicatons Review*, **23**(1) 78–88.

J. Mullen (Nov 1983) "In pursuit of industry-specific standards," *Data Communications*, **12**(11) 187–201.

J. A. Murphy (8 Sep 1982) "Token passing protocol boosts throughput in local networks," *Electronics*.

R. M. Needham and A. J. Herbert (1982) *The Cambridge Distributed Computing System*, Addison-Wesley, London and Reading, MA.

J. Nelson (Sep 1983) "802: A progress report," *Datamation*, **29**(9) 136–152.

J. Norton (1983) "The DoI FOCUS Committee—A status report on activities and results," *LocalNet 83 (Europe)*, 425–436.

R. M. O'Connor (Dec 1981) "Information technology standards, strategy and priorities," Report to the FOCUS Committee, UK.

OSI (1983) *Open Systems Interconnection—Technical Strategies for the 1980s*, Oyez Scientific and Technical Services, London.

K. Owen (Jun 1983) "Data communications: IFIP's international 'network' of experts," *Computer Communications*, **6**(3) 141–146.

R. R. Panko (Sep 1981) "Standards for electronic message systems," *Telecommunications Policy*, **5**(3) 181–197.

G. Pearson (Mar 1983) "Anatomy of a microcomputer protocol," *Data Communications*, **12**(3) 231–239.

Philips Business Communications (1983) *SOPHO-NET—Synergistic Open Philips Network*, Philips' Telecommunicatie Industrie BV, Hiversum, Netherlands, Brochure TD 3495-09-83E.

D. Potter (1983) "NET/PLUS: A local network architecture for multi-vendor capability," *LocalNet 83 (New York)*, 227–237.

T. J. Poussard, (Sep 1983) "The X.22 interface: An economic standard for multiplexing," *Data Communications*, **12**(9) 193–196.

J. Pužman and R. Pořížek (1981) *Communication Control in Computer Networks*, Wiley, Chichester and New York.

J. Rance (1983) "IEEE Project 802—A status review," *LocalNet 83 (Europe)*, 399–413.

Ed. D. Rayner (Aug 1982) "A system for testing protocol implementation," National Physical Laboratory, Teddington, Middlesex, England, Report DITC 9/82.

J. Riley (22 Mar 1984) "Europe forces standardisation," *Computer Weekly*, 1.

T. Ring (22 Mar 1984) "Esprit asked to back standards," *Computing*, 3.

R. D. Rosner (1982) *Packet Switching*, Lifetime Learning Publications, Belmont, CA.

Ed. H. Rudin and C. West (1983) *Protocol Specification, Testing and Verification III*, North Holland, Amsterdam, Oxford, England, and New York.

H. Saal (May 1983) "Local area networks—An update on microcomputers in the office," *Byte*, **8**(5) 60–79.

S. Schindler (Jun 1982) "Keywords in communication technology," *Computer Communications*, **5**(3) 140–147.

S. Schindler, C. Bormann, U. Flasche and H. Wilke (1982a) (Apr 1982) "Open Systems Interconnection—The Presentation Service," *Computer Communications*, **5**(2) 79–95.

S. Schindler, U Flasche, U. Oranen and H. Widlewski (1983) "Open Systems Interconnection: The Teletex-based Session Protocol," *Computer Communications*, **6**(2) 78–89 (Apr 1983) and **6**(3) 126–140 (Jun 1983).

S. Schindler, T. Luckenbach and M. Steinacker (1982b) (Dec 1982) "X.21 as a universal digital service access interface, *Computer Communications*, **5**(6) 298–307.

N. B. Seitz (Mar 1984) "User-oriented data communications performance standards," *Communications International*, **11**(3) 21–30.

N. B. Seitz, D. R. Wortendyke and K. P. Spies (Aug 1983) "User-oriented performance measurements on the ARPANET," *IEEE Communications Magazine*, **21**(5) 28–44.

P. S. Selvaggi (Oct 1983) "The Department of Defense Data Protocol Standardisation Program," *Computer Networks*, **7**(5) 319–328 (Oct 1983).

J. M. Smith (1984a) (23 Feb 1984) "A standard to satisfy 41 languages," *Computer Weekly*, 24–25.

J. M. Smith (1984b) (1 Mar 1984) "Setting standards for some sophisticated characters," *Computer Weekly*, 32.

D. Stokesbury (1983) "Use of ISO Class 4 Transport on local area networks," *LocalNet 83 (New York)*, 371–383.

Ed. C. A. Sunshine (Dec 1982) *IEEE Transactions on Communications*, Vol. **COM-30**, No. 12, 2485–2512, special section on protocol specification, testing and verification.

E. D. Sykas, D. E. Karvelos and E. N. Protonotarios (Aug 1983) "Combined urn and TDMA scheme for multiple access protocols," *Computer Communications*, **6**(4) 199–207.

M. E. Tamworth (1983) "Teletex: A true international standard," *Business Telecom 83*, 315–323.

I. Toda (Apr 1980) "DCNA higher level protocols," *IEEE Transactions on Communications*, **COM-28**(4) 575–584.

K. J. Turner (May 1983) "The IPA telecommunications function," *ICL Technical Journal*, **3**(3) 265–277.

C. A. Vissers, R. L. Tenny and G. V. Bochmann (Dec 1983) "Formal description techniques," *Proceedings of the IEEE*, **71**(12) 1356–1364.

P. von Studnitz (Feb 1983) "Transport protocols: Their performance and status in international standardization," *Computer Networks*, **7**(1) 27–35.

S. T. Vuong and D. D. Gowan (Summer 1983) "Protocol validation via resynthesized decomposition: The X.75 protocol as an example," *Journal of Telecommunication Networks*, **2**(2) 153–178.

C. Ware (Dec 1983) "The OSI Network Layer: Standards to cope with the real world," *Proceedings of the IEEE*, **71**(12) 1384–1387.

Which Computer? (Feb 1984) 61–64, special feature: standards.

J. M. Wiley (Jul 1983) "New networking horizons with protocol converters," *Data Communications*, **12**(7) 127–133.

D. Williams (1983) "The road to open systems," *dp International 1983*, 143–146.

Xoren (1983a) (Sep 1983) *XOREN IPL-11 File Transfer Package for the Digital PDP-11, LSI-11 and VAX-11—User Guide*, Xoren Computing Ltd., London, Brochure.

Xoren (1983b) (Jul 1983) *XOREN IPL-11/POS File Transfer Package for the Digital Professional—User Guide*, Xoren Computing Ltd., London, Brochure.

E. A. Yakubaitis (1983) *Computer Network Architecture*, Allerton Press, New York (English Translation of 1980 Russian Edition).

J. Yeomans (1983) "Do local networks require further high level protocols to be useful?," *LocalNet 83 (Europe)*, 469–479.

Chapter 22

Recent Developments
in Network Applications

This chapter starts by describing three of the networked office systems now on the market, and discussing recent developments are current issues in office automation and other applications of computer networks to business. It continues by outlining recent developments in media conversion, electronic mail and message services, banking and financial applications of networking, distributed information systems, and distributed computing systems. It ends by giving some recent examples of miscellaneous applications, in electronic publishing, teleconferencing, education, health care, industry, and defence.

Over 60 case studies, giving illustrative examples of a variety of network applications, are outlined in Chapter 23.

OFFICE AUTOMATION AND BUSINESS APPLICATIONS

Digital Equipment Corporation's approach to office automation aims to apply computer-based systems to improve the effectiveness of people working in an office environment (Hewitt, 1983; DEC, 1983a). it recognises that people are the most important resource in any office, and that it is essential to begin to learn how automation affects the office worker. It recommends that the best way to do this to start implementing office automation by introducing a pilot system first; this is what DEC did when installing its own electronic mail system. DEC's approach caters for word processing, electronic mail, communications, and integrated publishing. DEC (1983b and 1983c) provide diagrams of its VAX-based Office Architecture and Office Product Set.

DEC's approach handles word processing, electronic mail, communications, and integrated publishing. DEC (1983b and 1983c) provide diagrams of its VAX-based Office Architecture and Office Product Set.

ICL's Distributed Office Systems provide a new framework for office integration and are designed to meet the needs of actual offices (ICL, 1983a to 1983d). ICL's approach is evolutionary and identifies four distinct but interrelated types of office services: personal computing, local computing using a LAN, distributed access using a LAN or WAN, and distributed processing, combining different applications and using both local and remote environments. ICL's "families" of office systems are based on these four categories, and include: the DRS 20 family of purpose work stations, the DRS 20 range of distributed access terminals, the DRS 8800 word processing systems, and Bulletin, ICL's private videotex system. Figure 22.1

How a networked system can improve productivity

The ability to communicate is as important for computers as it is for people. Communication allows information and brain power to be shared, so that a group can accomplish far more than can the individual members working separately. Computer networking operates in the same way, with the same balance of individual and shared resources.

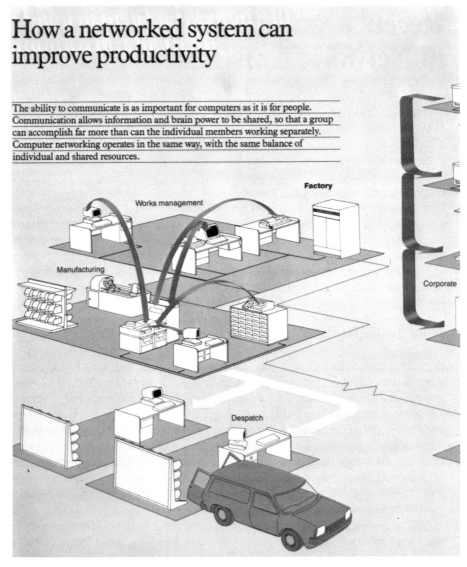

Fig. 22.1. How a networked system can improve productivity   SOURCE: *ICL Information Systems,* ICL Brochure, pp. 6 and 7

shows how an ICL networked system can improve productivity, both in the office and in the factory of an industrial company.

Which Computer? (1984) discusses Plessey's radical approach to office automation, using the Plessey IBIS Integrated Business Information System, and compares it with more conventional office automation systems. Plessey is attempting to integrate data, text, and electronic mail with its communications expertise, and uses interconnection, via its Integrated Data Exchange (IDX), as the key to its

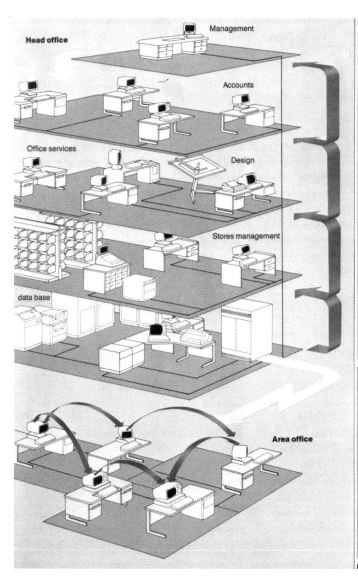

The products in the ICL networked range are designed to communicate easily with one another and with other manufacturers' products, including IBM mainframes.

In a networked system, processing power is placed where it is needed and used, thus saving delays in transmission and the costs of landlines or other links from remote sites. At the same time, each networked device can share the information held in the databases, can access the central files, and can call on supplementary computing power or programmes from the mainframe, or other local processors, when necessary.

Each networked system thus consists of a number of linked units whose total power and performance is far greater than the sum of the various parts. Since they are communicating electronically, there are none of the delays normally associated with post or staff absence. Since all the networked devices can share the same information base, productivity is increased.

With the installation of microwave and optical-fibre networks across the country, and the adoption of international standards for open systems networks, it will be possible to "plug in" to existing networks for immediate communication with a wide variety of networked systems throughout the world.

Types of networked systems

A network can be *local*, looking after the communication requirements of a single site which might include accounting, sales ledgers, sales order processing, word processing and perhaps stock and production control.

Or the network can embrace a *wide area*, linking remote terminals or local networks to an area office or HQ, across PTT communication services.

Both local and wide area networks are developing towards the *open system* which can interconnect any terminal, peripheral or system from ICL or any other manufacturer providing they conform to recognised communication standards.

office automation system. Its word processing facilities are very sophisticated and include access to other systems and transfer of documents between them. Other applications supported include financial spreadsheets, graphics, file handling, and electronic mail. Security is well maintained.

Other leading companies selling integrated office systems include Burroughs, Honeywell, Philips, and Xerox.

The book *A Manager's Guide to Local Area Networks* (Derfler and Skilling, 1983) clearly presents LANs and their applications to busy managers and executives. It is quick and easy to read, discusses LAN and PABX technologies, how to plan office automation, how to buy a network, and how to manage data bases. There is good coverage of the search for standards via OSI, and IBM's SNA is described. The book includes a helpful glossary. It presents three examples of network options and how they work: the Rolm CBX voice-data-switching network, the Amdax Cablenet broadband system, and Ethernet.

The recent book *Office Automation* (Doswell, 1983) describes applications of computer technology to information processing in the office and business environments. It gives understandable introductions to computers, systems analysis, and human factors. It provides a conceptual framework which will equip its readers for likely technological changes. It examines in detail the present state of the art of information processing in offices and in businesses. It integrates these developments into a wider framework of social changes, so that it is not only of interest to those concerned with improving office productivity.

Other presentations of the current state of the art and recent developments in office automation are given, for example, in: two fairly recent conference proceedings (Naffah, 1980 and 1982); the special section on office automation in the April 1983 issue of *Proceedings of the IEEE* (Bridge, 1983); the articles on the electronic office in the May 1983 issue of Byte (Clark, 1983); the office automation feature in the July 1983 issue of *Dec User* (1983a); The issue on office automation of *Computer Weekly's Management Review* supplement (*Computer Weekly, Management Review*, 19 January 1984); the book *Human Factors in Office Automation* (Galitz, 1980).

The newly launched newsletter *Electronic Office* covers significant developments in office automation in the USA, Canada, UK, Europe, Japan, and other parts of the world. *Which Office?* is a monthly magazine reporting on office automation developments in the UK. Also very useful are *The International Office Automation Guide* and *The International Word Processing Report. The International Communications Report* provides relevant information about computer networking, network services, and telecommunications to busy executives who need to use communications technologies.

Tucker (1984) reviews the January 1984 report on office automation by the British company Eosys, and assesses the attitudes of the managers surveyed to various issues. They perceived the major problems in tackling office automation as being: ensuring compatibility of systems (65% of them), adapting available products to their own needs (55%), high equipment costs (39%), allocating organisational responsibility for office automation (30%), finding sufficiently expert and experienced staff (22%) (the shortage of communications engineers is especially acute in the UK), "go it alone" users in their own organisation (12%), and lack of interest among potential users (8%). Interest in advanced office equipment was concentrated on microcomputer, word processor, management work stations, and executive terminals; there was a good deal less but still considerable interest in microfilm/microfiche, electronic mail, message switching, and videotex, less still in fax, and not much yet in optical character reading.

Lacey (1984) reviews some of the major ideas and trends in office automation during 1983, including developments in word processing and text processing, and new products launched by IBM, ICL, DEC, Plessey and British Telecom Merlin. He expresses the hope that further extensions of office automation will not take away social contact between different people in an office, as they could all too easily do if all the technological potentialities are followed through fully.

Cluff (1984) presents the challenges that office automation presents to business management. Far too many offices have introduced word processors and microcomputers in an unstructured, piecemeal way. Such an approach will not only be too expensive for the 1980s, it will also be highly dangerous. Many companies will no longer remain competitive if they do not introduce office automation, but their situation will become worse still if they mismanage its implementation. Success will depend on a new conceptual framework, concentrating on the patterns of relationships in the office, between people and people, people and machines, machines and machines. For a typical company, Cluff sees the data processing manager as probably the best person to guide it to success through office automation in the increasingly competitive 1980s, but only if he is forward-looking and aware of ongoing developments.

The book *New Office Technology—Human and Organisational Aspects* (Otway and Peltu, 1983) provides a flexible strategic plan for carrying through office automation and office technology projects. It shows how to design office systems so that human and organisation aims are combined with technical and economic objectives. It examines and discusses a variety of relevant problems and issues, summarizes them and gives practical recommendations for their solution.

Taylor (1983) discusses how the revolution in office technology affected one particular company and shows how its application influenced organisational structures and patterns of human interactions there. Human aspects of office automation are also considered by Coffey (1982). Bernhard (1982) discusses the "quandary" of office automation.

In Chaper 3 of his book on LANs, Flint (1983) discusses the changing business environment in relation to information technology, including the role of support systems, the nature of office work, tools for office workers, interpersonal communications, and work stations. In Chapter 4 of his book, he considers the role of the network in the organisation and states the four chief reasons for computer networks as: providing communications between organisations, supporting communications between people, accessing shared data, and sharing expensive resources.

In Chapter 9 of their book on LANs, Cheong and Hirschheim (1983) indicate some organisational implications of LANs and in Chapter 10 discuss at some length the organisational, as opposed to the technical, implementations of LANs, using a *socio-technical systems approach.*

Teger (1983) examines some of the market factors central to the evolution of office automation, and considers some possible trends for their future evolution. Office workers spend a substantial proportion of their time in interpersonal communications, especially by telephone, at meetings, and via documents. Because of the benefits of automating a whole business communications cycle, office automation is seen to be especially useful when it logically integrates multiple applications and modes of communication.

King and Maryanski (1983) view information management as a key element of office automation. By having computers keep track of the details of their increasingly heavy load of information, people in organisations can concentrate on higher level duties like planning and decision making. This paper discusses in turn the evolution of computer-based documents, the management and distribution of office data, and future management information systems.

Lochovsky (1983) considers that emerging information technology provides great scope for improving office productivity, by introducing specific support tools to aid office staff, and that the greatest productivity gains will be achieved by supporting office workers better, rather than trying to displace them. Bechhofer (1983) also discusses how to improve productivity in the office; he believes that the conversion to automated tools in an office must take account of many aspects, especially human factors. Goodyear (1984) sees portable terminals as a specific aid to office productivity, by eliminating some of the bottlenecks in existing data entry systems; they are likely to reduce significantly the amount of paper records, and the time devoted to data collection and transmission.

Walker (1983) shows how LANs can help the more effective use of business microcomputers. Whereas present office computing systems often use dedicated micros for specialised applications, businesses increasingly need to bring their applications together into one system. LANs can help here, and different LANs in an organisation can be linked together through gateways. For small business systems, micronets, or personal computer networks are sufficient, and full-scale LANs are not needed.

Davis et al (1983) point out that a computerised diary facility is a typical function that a computer communication system can make available. They examine such a diary facility in terms of the relevant social factors, the system needed to introduce it, and the system details needed for support.

Foley (1983) considers that Open Systems Interconnection (OSI) will play a major part in supporting business data communications, for example, finance, commerce, and electronic mail. He examines the business application standards, especially protocols and formats, dealing with information movement, and analyses selected business data standards for their relevance to OSI.

Morgan (1984) discusses the implications of OSI for the operation of organisations and businesses and especially for their data processing managers and professional staff. Standards bodies have now made sufficient progress towards implementing OSI that users need to ask themselves how they are preparing themselves, their staffs, and their companies for its application. OSI will usually imply a new approach to systems design, and all data processing staff will need to keep up to date with the latest OSI concepts, techniques, and standards.

MEDIA CONVERSION

Several products have recently come on the market for transferring data between floppy disks and other magnetic storage media with different formats.

Ott and Ruoff (1983) explain how the Trans/Media 500 media translation system, from Applied Data Communications Inc., solves the problem of incompatible disk formats, by using a Z80A microprocessor and Basic translation routines to resolve the format differences. A typical Trans/Media 500 configuration includes various $5\frac{1}{4}''$ and $8''$ floppy disk drives, a streaming-tape drive, and a terminal. Although the system is designed for conversion between floppy disks, it can also handle up to four 800 or 1600 bits/inch tape drives and up to two 10 MB hard disks as input/output media. The Trans/Media 500 is already being used by a media conversion service that handles over 440 different floppy disk formats, including those for Apple, DEC, IBM, TRS80, and many other personal computers as well as many models of word processors (Serious Software, 1983).

However, media conversion facilities for the smaller personal computers, used in the home, are still rather limited.

Another device that can convert data between a wide range of floppy disk formats for word processors and personal computers is the Shaffstall MediaCom 5000 Floppy Disk Converter, which can also be interfaced to phototypesetter editing systems and output data to a variety of phototypesetters and front end systems (Shaffstall, 1983a, 1983b; FormScan, 1983a). The MediaCom 5000 can receive information, sent by telecommunications, from a remote word processor or optical character reader, and it can act as a host for both asynchronous and bisynchronous communications and other widely used protocols.

The InterMedia Multi Disk Reader and Protocol Converter can read and convert disk formats used by many word processors and personal computers, and be linked to the most popular phototypesetting systems (InterMedia, 1983).

The FormScan Codem series of protocol translators, based on the Data General MBC3 communications microprocessor, can be used as the central node of a low cost star network, providing communication between different types of word processors, and integrating word processing with data processing and phototypesetting (FormScan, 1983b).

It is also possible to input data from typed and printed documents directly into computing systems, using optical character readers. For example, the Lexisystems Workless Station can automatically read documents into a word processor; it can accept most of the popular typefaces, and handle up to eight on each machine (Lexisystems, 1983). The Kurzweil 4000 Intelligent Scanning System is an exceptionally versatile reader, which combines "artificial intelligence" techniques with optical scanning capability (Kurzweil, 1983). Because it can learn the characteristics of different typefaces, it can handle printed documents with a wide variety of fonts and type sizes.

ELECTRONIC MAIL AND MESSAGE SERVICES

OFIX (Office of the Future Information Exchange), a British independent user-oriented body already described at the beginning of Chapter 11, in January 1984 issued the Interim Report of its Working Party on Electronic Mail and Filing (Crawford et al, 1984). The Working Party aimed to review the experience of users of electronic mail, in order to:

1. Identity OFIX members' needs for electronic mail and the benefits which they could gain from it;
2. Establish guidelines, difficulties, and product selection criteria;
3. Report back to OFIX.

Its definition of electronic mail was as follows: "*Electronic Mail (EM)* is an electronic carrier or transmission service using which an enfranchised user can, at any time, compose and send human-comprehensible text which will be retained in the system until it is cleared by the designated receiver (or receivers) or is purged. All users are capable, equally, of being senders and receivers."

This definition was chosen to give the widest possible definition of EM, compatible with some of its basic concepts. An essential part of EM is the ability of its system to hold a communication, either in a central mailbox or in a distributed node, until the person to whom it is addressed deals with it. Thus direct communication between a sender's machine and a receiver's machine are excluded, so that Telex and telefacsimile, for example, are not classified as EM.

Having decided its definition and scope, as given above, the Working Party "brainstormed" the main issues: concept of EM, users' likely need and motivations, and key questions. It then questioned and visited users and gained its own experience of the use of electronic mail bureau and mailboxes. Twenty one user organisations, including public bodies and commercial and industrial companies, were contacted, and three composite case studies were presented: traveling salesmen using a viewdata type system, using a bureau mailbox, and a big paper user.

The Working Party also prepared some notes on international communications, the transfer of mail electronically across national boundaries; these notes considered especially aspects that must be catered for in an "open" national or international communications environment

Finally it analysed its data and drew its conclusions. It considered the potential benefits of EM to be: speed of distribution, wider awareness, better feedback, staff savings, paper savings, overhead costs savings, and increased effectiveness of traveling staff. It saw good payoffs for EM in the areas of: traveling staff, international communications, communications with remote offices, and solution of paper problems. It would like to see further investigation of the following issues: shared (corporate) electronic filing, review of software products including their categorisation, the possibility of a consumer group to influence suppliers, and the updating of information about user experiences. It identified 18 common pitfalls and guidelines for avoiding them, 15 likely needs of users, and 14 criteria for product selection. It provides a list of EM products and suppliers.

Wilson (1984) summarises some of the findings of a recent study of electronic mailbox systems in the UK, jointly soponsored by the Electronics and Aeronautics Requirements Board and the National Computing Centre (NCC, 1984). One of its findings was that mailbox systems will dramatically improve productivity and effectiveness; thus organisations should implement them as quickly as possible.

The study surveyed 34 mailbox products now on the British market, with over 100,000 users around the world, but it excluded mailbox products not sold in the UK (and perhaps mainly used in the USA) and mailbox systems developed by organisations for their internal use. The study identified 13 types of applications for structured mailbox systems, including: communication with branches, education and training, project teams and working parties, transaction processing, and communications between suppliers and their customers. The study recommended further research on mailbox structuring to be started immediately.

Telecom Gold is an electronic mail service, marketed by British Telecom as part of a worldwide communications network (British Telecom, 1982 and 1983)). It uses the Dialcom system, developed in the USA by ITT Dialcom. It uses powerful central computers to obtain many of the benefits of office automation, without the need to acquire expensive equipment or recruit specialist staff. Each of its users has a private workspace in one of its central computers, for receiving and transmitting messages, memos, letters and other information; he can also set up and manage a complete record-keeping system from his desk. Messages can be edited by Dialcom's Text Editor, then sent instantly, and on request distributed simultaneously to several destinations at no extra cost. Shared information files can be set up, which can be reached and processed only by a specific group of users. Almost any terminal can be linked to the service.

Ferris (1983) describes several electronic mail services, including Telecom Gold, Dialcom (to which it is linked), and British Leyland's service bureau of Comet. Ferris argues that the prevalence of personal computers is likely to increase the appeal of electronic mail still further.

DEC started its own pilot electronic mail service in 1978 (DEC, 1983a; Hewitt, 1983). It started with 40 users and rapidly grew to 750 users, its maximum capacity. It ran for 18 months, and was then replaced by a production system, which has been running successfully ever since its start in 1979; a major part of its success is due to the lessons learnt from the pilot project. The system now has 15 user nodes and 15,000 users round the world. The typical user accesses the system several times a day, sending, receiving, and filing messages and memos. As a result, DEC has reduced its telephone costs appreciably, and its telex costs and paper usage dramatically.

Usenet is a worldwide network of Unix users, providing an electronic mail service, and circulating an electronic newspaper among its members (Beishon, 1983).

It is layered on the UUCP (Unix-to-Unix-copy programs), that first appeared in Version 6 of Unix in 1975. It sends mail to people as if they are all on one machine. It broadcasts news in its huge electronic journal, which circulates intermittently round the network. It has gateways to other networks, including the Arpanet.

Panko (1981) surveys standards for electronic message systems.

Additional references to electronic mail and message systems: Uhlig (1981), Cohen and Postel (1983), Palme (1983), Piquer (1983), Vallee (1983).

BANKING AND FINANCIAL APPLICATIONS

Financial Technology Bulletin is a monthly newsletter, providing banks and other financial institutions, insurance companies, stockbrokers, retailers, and company financial staff with important and up-to-date information about the applications of information technology to financial services. Topics covered include: financial uses and users of information technology; banking networks; computerised cash management and real-time dealing systems; "smart cards" and other payment systems; information-based services; satellite, cable and other communications systems; hardware and software products on the market; developments, trials, and installations; security and protection against fraud and theft; and relevant laws and regulations.

The book *Multinational Computer Nets* (Veith, 1983) reviews the major international banks' progress with multinational computer networks. The leading US, German, and Japanese banks are shown to use international telecommunications more than British banks use it. The book reviews technologies and procedures in banking communications, and it includes an extensive bibliography.

Weinstein (1982) briefly surveys some of the important financial networks now being used. He describes the banking networks SWIFT (Society for Worldwide Interbank Funds Transfer), CHIPS (Clearing House Interbank Payment System, operated by the New York Clearing House Association), BankWire (linking 300 US commercial banks), FedWire and FRCS 80 (operated by the Federal Reserve System), the AIM (Automatic Teller Machines) networks, and various home terminal networks linked to banks. SIAC (Securities Industry Automation Corporation) operates a securities trading network for the New York and American Stock Exchanges in New York. Credit authentication networks include those operated by American Express and VISA. Looking to the future, Weinstein suggests that financial institutions will adopt whatever mixture of proprietary industry networking and public networking facilities meets their immediate and short-term needs.

Porter (1983) states that the availability and flow of information to those who must use it as a key to continuing success in banking, now and in the future. The provision of networks, which can achieve this goal economically and efficiently, is a challenge to the financial institutions, the PTTs, and the suppliers of hardware and software. Porter discusses the banks' requirements for communications at and between their head offices and branches.

Youett (1983) describes some of the applications of communications technology in the City of London, including the world's largest private viewdata network at the London Stock Exchange and the Midland Bank's private voice and data communications network, to be designed and supplied by Plessey Communications Systems. The May 1983 issue of *Dec User* includes a computers in banking feature with papers on international banking, dealing with terminals and making fast communication systems secure.

French (1983) describes the City Business System, a piece of equipment specially designed to meet the needs of London's business trading community. It has a terminal with a touch-sensitive screen, enabling its users to access private circuits, exchange lines and switchboards, as well as a range of information stored on computers. There are also facilities for wide area networking with remote terminals, PSS, the telex network, and viewdata systems. This system is an interesting example of the convergence of computer and communications design; and its software structure allows new facilities to be added easily to it. Since the first installation in July 1982, many systems of this sort have been installed in the UK and other countries.

Weinstein (1984) reports on the use of "smart cards" in large-scale trials in France. They represent an emerging means of electronic payment and personal record transfer and updating. For security, a card's memory is divided into user-accessible, conditionally accessible, and user-inaccessible sections. A user has to enter the correct *PIN (personal identification number)* in order to use the card at all.

Recent developments in *EFT (electronic funds transfer)* in the USA and Europe are described in the book *Banking and Electronic Fund Transfers* (Revell, 1983) and are outlined by Repton (1983). Cane (1984) discusses some recent applications of computing to EFT and banking in the USA.

The newsletter *Teleservices Report* covers electronic financial and business services, electronic merchandising, interactive video marketing, at-home shopping and banking, and other financial applications of information technology.

Bechhofer (1983) tells how the traditional newsletter of the Independent Investors Forum, Washington, DC, became an interactive computer-accessed investment advisory service.

DISTRIBUTED INFORMATION SYSTEMS

One of the problems in handling distributed information systems is that information about them has already become very extensive—and widely distributed between a variety of sources! A considerable number of periodicals and conference proceedings already describe and discuss them, including the following: the ongoing series of conference proceedings, *International Online Information Meetings* and *Proceedings of the National Online Meetings*, and the journal *Online Review*, all covering various aspects of distributed information systems; *Monitor* and *UK Online User Group Newsletter*, providing information about recent developments in online information services; the series of books *Electronic Document Delivery*, about document delivery systems to back up online information services; *The Electronic Library*, a journal on computer applications in libraries, and *Library Micromation News*, providing news and views for microcomputer users in libraries.

This section reports on a selection of recent developments in distributed data bases, online information services, and library automation. It does not consider recent developments in videotex, although they are very relevant, as these are covered thoroughly in the forthcoming second edition of my book *The Videotex Revolution*, (Mayne, 1986).

DataBase/Electronic Publishing is an extensive report on the data base publishing industry and forecasts its future growth; it covers major developments in new data bases and data base distributors, videotex, teletext, and online access to data bases using personal computers and low cost terminals.

The book *Database Management Systems for the 80s* (Atre, 1983) takes a pragmatic approach to data bases and *data base management systems (DBMS)*, which he considers in detail. He describes some of the available DBMS products, data base management, data administration and manipulation, query and report generation, and data communications.

The manual *Controls for Advanced Online/Database Systems* (Kuong, 1983) gives practical and straightforward descriptions of online data base systems controls and should help data processing, audit and security specialists to review existing controls and specify improved controls in advanced data base systems.

The report *Network Database Systems* (Lehot and Kaisler, 1982) is designed to help users decide on their requirements for DBMS in a network environment and evaluate the relative capabilities of the different DBMS on the market. It surveys many of the available systems and gives selection criteria, together with a glossary and references.

The book *Database & Data Communications Systems* (Walsh, 1983) provides data processing managers and management information system managers with a very detailed examination of information storage in computer systems. It attempts to guide them towards the successful installation, operation, and support of a data base system with communications facilities, and it is especially concerned with making systems work for their users.

The book *Distributed Data Sharing Systems* (Van der Riet and Litwin, 1982) is fairly technical, and includes discussions of models and architecture of distributed data bases, distributed knowledge systems, query processing, resource allocation, security and privacy, and integrity of data base information.

The Fall 1983 issue of *Journal of Telecommunication Networks*, Vol. **2**, No. 3, is a special issue on distributed database technology (Wood, 1983).

EUSIDIC Database Guide 1983 (1983) lists over 1,800 data bases in various parts of the world, available in machine-readable form. Readers can obtain rapid access to its information, by organisation, data base, or subject. They can find out quickly who has put up which data base, which data bases a given organisation has produced, or which data bases can be reached publicly through a given operator. For each of 49 subject categories, there is a comprehensive alphabetical listing of relevant data bases and organisations.

The Nov 1982 issue of *Information Services & Use*, Vol. **2,** Nos. 3–5, is a special issue on transborder data flows: access to the international on-line data-base market. It devotes special attention to the role of transnational corporations in this area of computer-based information transfer and to the significance of this area to the developing countries.

Auld (1983) discusses briefly the future of data base information services; relevant developments include: personal computing, word processing, videotex, videodisks, communications software, electronic mail, and teleconferencing. He draws the following conclusions:

1. Data base providers will adopt various spacing strategies;
2. Downloading of information and programs into personal computers is here to stay;
3. Changes in information technology will accelerate;
4. Most professionals will become "computerate";
5. Handling of computer-based data will become as frequent as reading printed publications;
6. To prosper, data base publishers will have to offer many more products;
7. Traditional printed publications will increase in number, having a role complementary to online publications, and both will take on new shapes as a result.

Esculier (1984) mentions some ISO standards relevant to distributed data base systems. Gallagher (1984) discusses several aspects of the proposed American National Standard on DBMS, developed by ANSI Committee X3H2.

Gee (1983) describes the revolutionary new local network DBMS, DataCore, introduced by Software Connections. It expands networking into a whole new applications area, information sharing. It is said to solve the deficiencies of single user data bases, and to meet the security and performance requirements of serious business applications. It has modern relational data base architecture with subschema capabilities, a data dictionary, and field level access.

Kavanagh (1984) reports that Ashton-Tate, a leading American supplier of microcomputer data base systems, has developed a multi-user version of its dBase II package, which runs on Ethernet LANs under Microsoft's MS-DOS operating system. It is preparing versions for other networks and multi-user operating sytems. A private file can be accessed only through a specific combination of terminal and password; a shared file can be read and written by any terminal with the right password.

The British company Userlink Systems has pioneered the development of low-cost microcomputer systems to simplify online access to remote computers, viewdata information systems and electronic mail (Userlink systems, 1984). With its aid, a user can contact a computer data base with one key stroke only, and can set up messages and searches before picking up the telephone. This saves time, telephone costs, and data base charges. Userlink Systems has recently developed the

Userlink Dataferry, a microfilm interface for the Derwent patent information data bases. It is a terminal attachment, that automatically retrieves the microfilm frame numbers from records retrieved in a search, and sends them to user's microfilm reader.

The book *Online Searching: A Primer* (Fenichel and Hogan, 1983) assumes no previous knowledge of online searching of computer data bases, and explains step by step how to get started. It includes chapters on: types of data base, what to expect from their vendors, the role of intermediary help for users, how to choose a terminal, the basic principles of searching techniques, and how to charge for online searching. It briefly reviews searching of data bases containing numerical and other non-bibliographic data. It contains a glossary of online terminology and lists the names and addresses of organisations in the online data base business.

Rush (1982) surveys some fairly recent developments in library automation systems and networks.

Barnholdt and Nybroe (1983) describe Alis, the Automated Library Information System at the Datacentralen af 1959 Service Centre in Copenhagen, which has a data base of over 125,000 bibliographic records. It has a catalogue search system, combined with a circulation control system with bar-code readers. Its users can obtain bibliographic records for retrieved documents, together with information about their current status, for example, whether on shelf, on loan, or reserved. The search system is based on STAIRS/CICS and offers English and Danish dialog. The system can be reached by direct call from Euronet, SCANNET, or the local university network DTH-NET.

Collier (1983) and Venner and Walker (1983) describe a project at the Polytechnic of Central London for exploring the potential of microcomputer networks and office automation for libraries. It has concentrated on a specific application, the development of an online public access catalogue for the largest of the six sites of PCL's library. This site contains about 30,000 volumes on social science, business studies, and communication. The project started with the design and implementation of software and has been followed by a trial and evaluation of the system.

Additional references to distributed data bases: Adiletta (1984), Chapter 10 of Black (1983), Date (1983), *Distributed Database* (1981), Garcia-Molina (1982), Houston (1983), Kehoe (1982).

DISTRIBUTED COMPUTING SYSTEMS

The book *The Cambridge Distributed Computing System* (Needham and Herbert, 1982) describes the University of Cambridge Computer Laboratory's experimental distributed computing system, based on the original Cambridge Ring LAN. It gives a full account of this integrated system, and discusses its main design issues in detail; as such, it is a useful guide for computer experts seeking real solutions to distributed systems problems. In the Cambridge system, users are allowed exclusive access to powerful, centrally located computers and services when they require them; this is an interesting contrast with the alternative approach of providing LAN users with personal computers or multi-purpose work stations.

Other recent books on distributed computing systems include: *Distributed Computing Systems* (Paker et al, 1983), *Multi-Microprocessor Systems* (Paker, 1983), and *Performance Models of Distributed Systems* (Gelenbe, 1983).

Computer Weekly has had special features on distributed computing (*Computer Weekly*, 1982 and 1983).

Which Computer? (1984b) describes NCR's Tower multi-user computing system, using the UNIX operating system. As hardware, the Tower is somewhere between a microcomputer and a minicomputer; it has a 10 MHz Motorola 68000 processor, and a dual bus allowing concurrent activities, which do not interface with each other and do not compete for resources. Its main unit has up to 7 I/O controllers, that can support up to three floppy disk drives, three hard disks, and a streaming tape controller for back-up. Up to 16 terminals, either local or remote, can be connected. A multi-protocol communications controller supports up to four communications links, for example, Tower to Tower links, using the UNET communications system, or links to IBM or IBM-compatible systems, using SNA. Teletype links to terminals and printers can also be made.

The Tower operating system is based on the UNIX operating system, but NCR has added some important extensions to UNIX to make it more acceptable to commercial users. NCR's version has left the full facilities of UNIX, for those who can use them, but added a user interface for the benefit of those who know what applications to do but do not know much about computing. Tower-UNIX utilities include: Office Procedure Analysts, Application Developer, text processing, "camera ready" document production, electronic mail, print spooling, file transfer to other systems in a network, and a comprehensive system log. Further applications, supported by Tower, include: Multiplan, an electronic spreadsheet for financial modelling; Ingres, a relational DBMS, previously available on DEC/VAX computers; and colour graphics software, for two- and three-dimensional image creation and viewing, shading and patterning, and "real-time" image manipulation.

Commercially available extensions to UNIX, which allow it to be used for networking, include NETIX (NETwork UNIX) and XENIX. NETIX was developed by the Bell Telephone Manufacturing Company (Bell Information Systems, 1983); further details are given by Wambecq (1983) and Rowe et al (1982). It enables work stations, host computers, and other equipment to work together in a coordinated way, and it gives an integrated view of all services in a network; thus it can be used to build systems for various application areas, such as office systems, newspapers, and factory control.

XENIX was developed by Microsoft Corporation, and is rapidly becoming a standard for 16-bit microcomputers, providing an extensive set of program development tools and a solid base for running applications software. Kavaler and Greenspan (1983) describe its use with ALTOS-NET II software for file handling and remote processor execution on the ALTOS LAN.

Blair et al (1983) describe the development of Mimas, an experimental network operating system at the University of Strathclyde, Glasgow, Scotland, which links and unifies several computers all running UNIX. The design criteria for this system are resource sharing, high availability, and ease of extension. Blair et al argue that the ISO Reference Model is of limited use in designing such a system, and they present the Mimas model as an alternative. It has five layers, as follows:

Physical Layer
LAN, in this case Strathnet

Local Resource Management Layer
UNIX kernel, IPC primitives

Global Resource Management Layer
Process manager, File manager, Device managers

Server Layer
Extended operating system functions, Server support environment

Applications Layer
Mimas shell, User programs

Pogran (1983) and Hoffman et al (1982) describe the Cronus Distributed Operating System, being developed by Bolt, Beranek and Newman. Cronus has been designed to support general-purpose interactive processing as a base for command and control applications. It places special emphasis on: *adaptability* and *reliability*, via redundant equipment; *accommodation*, that is, the ability to integrate new processors and operating systems to provide special-purpose services and devices; *scaleability*, supporting cluster sizes up to several hundred nodes; *accessibility*, making all resources available from all its terminals and work stations; and *buy-in-cost*, a variety of methods for offering a range of cost and performance.

Additional references to distributed computing systems: Cypser (1978), Chapter 12 of Black (1983), Bruins et al (1983), Coen (1983), Hollingsworth (1983), Howlett et al (1983), Loveluck (1982), Manchester (1984), Nelson (1983), Phillips (1983), Piquer (1983), Willson (1983).

OTHER APPLICATIONS OF NETWORKS

This section gives examples of recent applications of networks to public services, electronic publishing, teleconferencing, education, health care, industry, and defence.

Fortgang and Frisch (1983) describe Contel Information Systems' experience of the installation of LANs in US government facilities, to meet the needs of the 1980s and beyond. They point out that these applications of networks make special demands on system customisation, expansion, and interfacing, as well as on vendor field service and training.

Youett (1983a) shows how British national and local government organisations use data communications to cope with their vast amounts of paper work and information exchange. He describes the networks used by the Cabinet Office, the Office of Population Surveys & Censuses, and Coventry County Council.

The Rank Xerox Graphics System for electronic publishing consists of: a Xerox 150 Graphic Input Station, Electronic Printer Image Construction (EPIC) software, a Graphics-Handling Option, and a Xerox Integrated Composition System (XICS) including a Xerox 9700 Printing System (Rank Xerox, 1983a). Besides the Xerox 9700 Printing System, the Rank Xerox 8700 Printing System and the Rank Xerox 2700 Distributed Electronic Printer are also available; the latter can be used for printing on a distributed basis (Rank Xerox, 1981, 1983b, and 1983c).

This sort of electronic publishing, sometimes called *on-demand publishing*, makes it possible for either short-run or long-run publications to be produced very quickly at reasonable cost; extra copies of an already set document can be run off very conveniently, at a moment's notice.

DataBase/Electronic Publishing (1983) includes a review and forecast of the electronic publishing industry, and details of its leading organisations.

Ongoing sources of information on electronic publishing include: the journal *Electronic Publishing Review*, the newsletters *Monitor* and *Communication Technology Impact*, and the book series *Electronic Document Delivery*.

Computer Compacts is a new electronic journal, available both in paper format and as an experimental online retrieval system and journal. Its total subject coverage includes: programming, microprocessing and hardware, communications and standards, performance analysis, computer graphics, CAD/CAM, industrial applications, medical applications, information systems, regulations, transborder data flow and allied issues, and impacts of computing and information technology on society. The online version aims to provide news in key computer areas, while the paper version will provide updated access information and serve as a forum related to international electronic publishing.

Wilson (1984) describes a three-year experiment, sponsored by the British Library, to produce electronically a refereed journal of scientific papers, *Linc* (*Loughborough Information Network Community*), on the theme of human factors in computing. Its features include a Noticeboard facility, whereby draft papers can be presented informally for information and comment, and a structured mailbox facility, which will also be of great interest to businesses.

Gurnsey (1983) considers some of the factors which influence the market for electronic publishing, and indicates several factors that seem to indicate likely success, at least in the short term.

British Telecom is one of the pioneers of teleconferencing, and has run its Confravision service for over ten years; it is now planning to extend the service so that it can be run from users' own premises (Cluff, 1983). It is also moving into international teleconferencing, and has given several demonstrations of it. It plans a videoconferencing service for 1984 (Spencer, 1983).

Cluff (1983) discusses some American research findings, which suggests that teleconferencing has in the past been oversold to management; he sees a big gap between many businessmen's initial expectations and what is currently practical here.

Lerch (1983) reviews several computer conferencing systems, including most of those mentioned in Chapter 14. He lists the systems commercially available today;

most of them can be accessed by a personal computer or a terminal, and the software for some of these systems can be licensed for operation on a mainframe.

The book *Teleconferencing and Beyond: Communications in the Office of the Future* (Johansen, 1983) is one of the most comprehensive recent discussions of teleconferencing and allied areas.

Teleconferencing and Electronic Communications (Parker and Olgren, 1982) is the published proceedings of a conference held at Madison, WI, in Spring 1982. *Teleconferencing—New Media for Business Meetings* (Ebon, 1982) is a short book, intended for managers not specialising in telecommunications.

Hunter (1983) reports on some uses of teleconferencing in the developing countries. The University of the West Indies is installing a satellite-based audio teleconferencing system to broaden its medical, agricultural advisory, and educational services throughout the Caribbean islands. Brazil's Federal University of Rio Grande de Sol has designed its own teleconferencing system. A meeting of specialists from many countries and international organisations decided that teleconferencing is an essential tool for the development of the Third World.

The book *New Information Technology in Education* (Hawkridge, 1983) describes technologies and techniques being used by educators in their attempts to teach more effectively. It includes full discussions of many experiments, ideas and projects, involving the application of information technology to all kinds of education. It has a good bibliography.

Bramer (1983) describes the Open University's wide area star network, based on its central computer at Milton Keynes, England, and the participation by some of the British Microelectronics Education Program (MEP) Regional Centres in an experiment using this network. The network can be accessed by teletype-compatible terminals with acoustic couplers or modems, and also by some models of personal computer including the Apple. Its facilities include electronic mail, automatic file transfer, telesoftware, and information retrieval. The MEP experiment is still in its early stages, and will concentrate on the use of electronic mail facilities, although individual centers are experimenting with other options.

Bramer's personal view is that education needs an electronic communications system, not only for messages, but also as a focus for centralised information and software libraries. For several reasons, he considers that the Open University seems the ideal institution to host such a system in the UK.

HealthNet is a fast, secure and effective information and communications system, for transferring the British National Health Service's forms, memos and letters over the PSTN (Britsh Telecom, 1984). It uses microcomputer-based multipurpose terminals, which plug into and share existing telephone sockets. It is designed to improve communications, make more effective use of staff time, manage information more rapidly and at lower cost, and help analyse clinical data, in the National Health Service. It was developed as the result of a detailed and wide ranging study in several major health districts.

Computer Networks (Aug 1983) reports on an IFIP-IMIA Working Conference on Communication Networks in Health Care, held at Ulvsunde Palace, Sweden, from 14 to 18 June 1982. Besides the keynote address on "Meaning and role," there were sessions on principles of communication networks, multi-media communication, data protection, requirements and needs, computer networks within health care, and other topics.

McLean et al (1983) discuss a computer architecture for small-batch manufacturing. They consider that industry will benefit from a system that defines the functions of its parts-manufacturing modules and standardises the interfaces between them. A scheme of this sort is being studied at an NBS facility in Gaithersburg, MD. Some of the standards to be used could evolve from the IEEE 802 LAN Standards.

Youett (1983b) describes three very different approaches to the applications of telecommunications and networking to shipping and freight transport in the UK, at Lloyd's of London, the National Freight Corporation, and British Rail's Railfreight.

Cerf and Lyons (1983) outline the nature of the requirements for military packet-switched data communications, contrasting them with those of commercial, industrial, and private users, served by common carrier public packet-switched networks. They identify deficiencies in the existing standards for military applications, and outline a strategy for standardisation of military networks. Davidson (1983) discusses practical experiences in an early application of the ISO Reference Model to a military LAN. The July 1983 issue of *IEEE Communications Magazine*, Vol. **21,** No. 4, is devoted to military communications (Ricci, 1983).

REFERENCES

W. F. Adilatta (Feb 1984) "Packet network proven best for optimizing a library operation," *Data Communications*, **13**(2) 125–134.

S. Atre (1983) *Detection Management Systems for the 80s*, QED Information Services.

D. Auld (Spring 1983) "The future of database information services," *Information Services & Use*, **3**(1/2) 11–15.

B. Barnholdt and J. Nybrae (Dec 1983) "ALIS—The On-line literature localization and document ordering system of the National Technological Library of Denmark," *Computer Networks*, **7**(6) 407–411.

A. S. Bechhoefer (May 1983) "Electronic publishing: The new newsletter," *Byte*, **8**(5) 124–130.

M. Beishon (Jan 1984) "Unofficial network," *DEC User*, 21–23.

Bell Information Systems (1983) "Description of NETIX, the UNIX based LAN network operating system," Bell Information Systems, Antwerp, Report.

R. Bernhard (Sep 1982) "The quandary of office automation," *IEEE Spectrum*, **19**(9) 34–39.

U. D. Black (1983) *Data Communications, Networks and Distributed Processing*, Reston Publishing Company, Reston, VA.

G. Blair, D. Hutchison and D. Shepherd (1983) "Implementation of a local network operating system," *LocalNet 83 (Europe)*, 387–398.

M. Bramer (Nov 1983) "Towards an electronic communications network for education," *Computer Education*, 45, 25–27.

Ed. R. F. Bridge (Apr 1983) *Proceedings of the IEEE*, Vol. **71**, No. 4, 451–528, special section on office automation.

British Telecom (1982) *Telecom Gold*, British Telecom, Telecom Gold, London, Literature Pack.

British Telecom (1983) *Telecom Gold—Electronic Mail from British Telecom*, British Telecom, Telecom Gold, London, Brochure.

British Telecom (1984) *Merlin HealthNet—Community Health Advanced Communications and Information System*, British Telecom Merlin, Felixstowe, Suffolk, England, Leaflet.

T. Bruins, W. Vree, G. Reijns and C. van Spronsen (1983) "A layered distributed operating system," *LocalNet 83 (Europe)*, 351–371.

A. Cane (30 Mar 1984) "Why Citibank loves computing—Electronics opens up competition in banking," *Financial Times*, 14.

V. G. Cerf and R. E. Lyons (Oct 1983) "Military requirements for packet-switched networks and their implications for protocol standardization," *Computer Networks*, 7(5) 293–306.

V. E. Cheong and R. A. Hirschheim (1983) *Local Area Networks—Issues, Products, and Developments*, Wiley-Interscience, Chichester and New York.

Ed. P. C. Clark (May 1983) *Byte*, Vol. **8**, No. 5, includes articles on the electronic office.

E. G. Cluff (Spring 1983) "Thoughts on teleconferencing," *dp International*, 34–35.

E. G. Cluff (Mar 1984) "Open those office doors," *Which Office System?*, 33–34.

P. J. Coen (1983) "Local area networks and distributed office systems," *Business Telecom 83*, 219–230.

M. Coffey (4 Feb 1982) "Watching the human factor in office automation," *Computing*, 20.

D. Cohen and J. Postel (1983) "Gateways, bridges and tunnels in computer mail," *LocalNet 83 (New York)*, 385–400, and *LocalNet 83 (Europe)*, 109–123.

M. Collier (May 1983) "Microcomputer networking in libraries (I) Background and aims of the project," *VINE*, No. 48, 21, The Library, University of Southampton, England.

Communication Technology Impact (ongoing) Elsevier International Bulletin, Amsterdam, Oxford, England, and New York, Newsletter.

Computer Compacts (ongoing) North-Holland, Amsterdam, and Elsevier Science Publishing Company, New York.

Computer Networks (Aug 1983) "Conference Report—Communication networks in health care," 7(4) 276–281.

Computer Weekly (19 Aug 1982) feature on distributed computing, 14–17.

Computer Weekly (27 Oct 1983) special feature on distributed computing, 20–26.

Computer Weekly, Management Review (19 Jan 1984) issue on office automation.

N. Crawford et al (Jan 1984) *OFIX Working Party Report on Electronic Mail and Filing, Interim Report*, OFIX, Hemel Hempstead, Herts., England.

R. J. Cypser (1978) *Communications Architecture for Distributed Systems*, Addison-Wesley, London and Reading, MA.

C. J. Date (1983) *An Introduction to Database Systems, Vol II*, Chapter 7, "Distributed databases," Addison-Wesley, Reading, MA, and London.

J. A. Davidson (Dec 1983) "OSI layering of a military local network," *Proceedings of the IEEE*, **71**(12) 1435–1441.

R. H. Davis, K. Saunders and T. Shannon (Dec 1983) "A computerized diary facility," *Computer Communications*, **6**(6) 297–307.

DEC (1983a) *Digital's Experience Using Office Systems*, Digital Equipment Co. Ltd., Reading, England, Document OSB-1-3/83.

DEC (1983b) *Digital's Office Architecture*, Digital Equipment Co. Ltd., Reading, England, Leaflet.

DEC (1983c) *VAX Office Product Set*, Digital Equipment Co. Ltd., Reading, England, Leaflet.

Dec User (1983a) (Jul 1983) 20–32, office automation feature.

Dec User (1983b) (May 1983) 29–40, computers in banking feature.

F. Derfler, Jr. and W. Skillings (1983) *A Manager's Guide to Local Area Networks*, Prentice Hall, Englewood Cliffs, NJ.

Distributed Database (1981) Online Publications, Pinner, Middlesex, England.

A. Doswell (1983) *Office Automation*, Wiley, Chichester, and New York.

M. C. J. Ebon (1982) *Teleconferencing—New Media for Business Meetings*, American Management Associates, New York.

Electronic Document Delivery (ongoing) Learned Information, Oxford, England Series of Books.

The Electronic Library (ongoing) *The International Journal for Minicomputer, Microcomputer & Software Applications in Libraries*, Learned Information, Oxford, England, Quarterly Journal.

Electronic Office (ongoing) FinTech, London, Fortnightly Newsletter.

Electronic Publishing Review (ongoing) *The International Journal of the Transfer of Published Information via Videotex and Online Media*, Learned Information, Oxford, England Quarterly Journal.

C. Esculier (Feb 1984) "The SIRIUS-DELTA Architecture: A framework for co-operating database systems," *Computer Networks*, **8**() 43–48.

EUSIDIC Database Guide 1983 (1983) Learned Information, Oxford, England.

C. Fenichel and T. Hogan (1983) *Online Searching: A Primer*, Learned Information, Oxford, England.

D. Ferris (1 Dec 1983) "Mail is partner in an electronic marriage," *Computer Weekly*, 9.

Financial Technology Bulletin (ongoing) Oyex IBC Ltd., Monthly Newsletter.

D. C. Flint (1983) *The Data Ring Main—An Introduction to Local Area Networks*, Wiley Heyden, Chichester and New York.

J. S. Foley (Dec 1983) "Business data usage of OSI," *Proceedings of the IEEE*, **71**(12) 1442–1445.

FormScan (1983a) *The Shortest Path from Copy to Setting—The MediaCom 5000*, FormScan Ltd., Frome, Somerset, England, Brochure.

FormScan (1983b) *Breaking the Language Barrier—The Codem*, FormScan Ltd., Frome, Somerset, England, Brochure.

M. Fortgang and I. T. Frisch (1983) "Local area network installations in government facilities," *LocalNet 83 (New York)*, 137–146.

D. J. French (Oct 1983) "The City Business System," *British Telecommunications Engineering*, **2**(3) 174–178.

W. D. Galitz (1980) *Human Factors in Office Automation*, QED/Life Office Management Association.

L. J. Gallagher (Feb 1984) "Procedure language access to proposed American National Standard database management systems," *Computer Networks*, **8**(1) 31–42.

H. Garcia-Molina (Sep 1982) "Reliability issues for fully replicated data bases," *Computer*, **15**(9) 34–42.

B. J. Gee (1983) "Database design on a personal computer network," *LocalNet 83 (New York)*, 207–212.

E. Gelenbe (1983) *Performance Models of Distributed Systems*, Addison-Wesley, London and Reading, MA.

R.J. Goldfield (May 1983) "Achieving greater white-collar productivity in the office," *Byte* **8**(5) 154–172.

K. H. Goodyear (1984) "Data entry: Portable terminals," *dp Internationl* 1984, 275–279.

W. Günsteide (Mar 1982) "Man and automation in the office," *Information Systems & Use*, **1**(5) 263–270.

J. Gurnsey (Oct 1983) "Electronic publishing: A market perspective," *ASLIB Proceedings*, **35**(10) 389–397.

D. Hawkridge (1983) *New Information Technology in Education*, Croom Helm, London.

J. Hewitt (1983) *Office Automation Today and Tomorrow*, Digital Equipment Co. Ltd., Reading, England, Document OSB-2-4/83, reprinted from *Minicomputer News* (Oct 1982).

M. Hoffman, W. MacGregor, R. Schantz and P. Thomas (Jun 1982) "Cronus—A distributed operating system," Bolt, Beranek and Newman, Cambridge, MA, Report No. 5041.

S. Hollingsworth (Jul 1983) "Is time sharing trying for a comeback?," *Data Communications*, **12**(7) 83–88.

G. B. Houston (Apr 1983) "Tightening up software on a distributed database," *Data Communications*, **12**(4) 133–150.

J. Howlett, D. Parkinson and A. Sylvestrowicz (May 1983) "DAP in action," *ICL Technical Journal*, **3**(3) 330–334.

P. Hunter (6 Oct 1983) "University brings telecomms to the world's hungry belt," *Computer Weekly*, 18.

ICL (1983a) *ICL Distributed Office Systems—A New Era in Office Technology*, International Computers Limited, Brochure P1449.

ICL (1983b) *ICL Distributed Office Systems—DRS 20 Series*, International Computers Limited, Brochure P1468.

ICL (1983c) *ICL Distributed Office Systems—Wordprocessing*, International Computers Limited, Brochure.

ICL (1983d) *ICL Information Systems—An Introduction to Information Technology*, International Computers Limited, Brochure P1565.

Information Services & Use (Nov 1982) Vol.2, Nos. 3–5, special issue: transborder data flows: access to the international on-line data-base market.

InterMedia (1983) *Multi Disk Readers and Protocol Converters*, Inter Media Graphic Systems, Aldershot, Hampshire, England, Brochure.

The International Communications Reporter (ongoing) Keith Wharton Consultants, Richmond, Surrey, England.

The International Office Automation Guide, Keith Wharton Consultants, Richmond, Surrey, England.

International Online Information Meeting (ongoing) Learned Information, Oxford, England, Conference Proceedings Series, six published so far.

The International Word Processing Report (ongoing) Keith Wharton Consultants, Richmond, Surrey, England.

R. Johansen (1983) *Teleconferencing and Beyond: Communications in the Office of the Future*, McGraw Hill, New York and Maidenhead, England.

P. Kavaler and A. Greenspan (Sep 1983) "Extending UNIX to local-area networks," *Mini-Micro Systems*, 197–202.

J. Kavanagh (22 Mar 1984) "Ashton-Tate moves to multi-users," *Computer Weekly*, 13.

L. Kehoe (24 Mar 1982) "Making the best use of stored data," *Financial Times*, 12.

K. J. King and F. J. Maryanski (Apr 1983) "Information management trends in office automation," *Proceedings of the IEEE*, **71**(4) 519–528.

Knowledge Industry (1983) *DataBase/Electronic Publishing: Review & Forecast, 1983*, Knowledge Industry Publications, White Plains, NY.

J. F. Kuong (1983) *Controls for Advanced Online/Database Systems*, Management Advisory Publications.

Kurzweil (1983) *Kurzweil 4000 Intelligent Scanning System*, Cambridge, MA, Brochure.

M. Lacey (1984) "Developments in office automation," *dp International 1984*, 117–122.

P. G. Lehot and S. H. Kaisler (1982) *Network Database Systems*, Architecture Technology, Minneapolis, MN.

I. A. Lerch (May 1983) "The movable conference," *Byte*, **8**(5) 104–120.

Lexisystems (1983) *Work Less, Do More—the Workless Station*, Lexisystems Ltd., Frome, Somerset, England, Brochure.

Library Micromation News (ongoing) Polytechnic of Central London, London, Quarterly Newsletter.

F. H. Lochovsky (Apr 1983) "Improving office productivity: A technology perspective," *Proceedings of the IEEE*, **71**(4) 512–518.

J. M. Loveluck (Nov 1982) "The PERQ workstation and the distributed computing environment," *ICL Technical Journal*, **3**(2) 155–174.

C. McLean, M. Mitchell and E. Barkmeyer (May 1983) "A computer architecture for small-batch manufacturing," *IEEE Spectrum*, **20**(5) 59–64.

P. Manchester (Jan 1984) "Distributed data processing revisited," *Computer Management*, 31–33.

A. J. Mayne (1986) *The Videotex Revolution*, second ed., Wiley, Chichester and New York.

Monitor (ongoing) Learned Information, Oxford, England, Monthly Review.

L. Morgan (1984) "The challenge of OSI," *dp International 1984*, 165–186.

Ed. N. Naffah (1980) *Integrated Office Systems—Burotics*, North-Holland, Amsterdam, Oxford, England, and New York, Proceedings of IFIP-TC-6 International Workshop on Integrated Office Information Systems—Burotics, Versailles, France, 6–9 Nov 1979.

Ed. N. Naffah (1982) *Office Information Systems*, North-Holland, Amsterdam, Oxford, England, and New York, Proceedings, Second International Workshop on Office Information Systems, Couvent Royal de St.-Maximin, France, 13–15 Oct 1981.

NCC (1984) *Introducing the Electronic Mailbox*, NCC Publications, Manchester, England.

R. M. Needham and A. J. Herbert (1982) *The Cambridge Distributed Computing System*, Addison-Wesley, London and Reading, MA.

D. Nelson (1983) "Network protocols for Apollo's DOMAIN System," *LocalNet 83 (Europe)*, 343–349.

G. Neumann (1981) "An operating system for a microcomputer network," 213–227 of Ed. G. Pujolle (1981) *Performance Analysis of Data Communication Systems and Their Applications*, North-Holland, Amsterdam, Oxford, England, and New York.

Online Review (ongoing) *The International Journal of Online Information Systems*, Learned Information, Oxford, England, Bi-monthly Journal.

B. Ott and J. Ruoff (Sep 1983) "Universal diskette reader resolves different formats," Mini-Micro Systems.

Ed. H. Otway and M. Peltu (1983) *New Office Technology—Human and Organisational Aspects*, Frances Pinter, London.

Y. Paker (1983) *Multi-Microprocessor Systems*, Academic Press, New York and London.

Ed. Y. Paker and J. P. Verjus (1983) *Distributed Computing Systems—Synchronization, Control and Communication*, Academic Press, New York and London.

J. Palme (Aug 1983) "On preserving identity and references between documents in distributed computerized message systems," *Computer Networks*, **7**(4) 269–272.

R. R. Panko (Sep 1981) "Standards for electronic message systems," *Telecommunications Policy*, **5**(3) 181–197.

Ed. L. A. Parker and C. H. Olgren (1982) *Teleconferencing and Electronic Communications—Applications, Technologies and Human Factors*, University of Wisconsin—Extension, Madison, WI.

S. Phillips (1983) "Distributed systems and their protocols," *LocalNet 83 (Europe)*, 373–385 and *LocalNet 83 (New York)*, 357–369.

A. R. Piquer (Apr 1983) "On ordering requests to servers in a distributed system," *Computer Networks*, **7**(2) 69–81.

K. T. Pogran (Jul 1983) "Selection of a local area network for the Cronus distributed operating system," *Computer Communications Review*, **13**(3) 25–35.

I. Porter (Dec 1983) "Information availability in banking," *Communications International*, **10**(12) 51–52.

Proceedings of the .... National Online Meeting (ongoing) Learned Information, Oxford, England, Conference Proceedings Series, four published so far.

Rank Xerox (1981) *Xerox 9700 Electronic Printing System*, Rank Xerox Ltd., London, Brochure RX893 CT0381.

Rank Xerox (1983a) *Xerox Graphics System—Electronic Publishing*, Rank Xerox Ltd., London, Brochure RX944 M083.

Rank Xerox (1983b) *Xerox 8700 Electronic Printing System*, Rank Xerox Ltd., London, Brochure RX943 MO383.

Rank Xerox (1983c) *Xerox 2700 Distributed Electronic Printer*, Rank Xerox Ltd., London, Brochure RX942 MO383.

D. O. Redell and J.E. White (Sep 1983) "Interconnecting electronic mail systems," *Computer*, **16**(9) 55–63.

C. S. Repton (Jun 1983) "Electronic funds transfer in the USA and Europe," *Communications International*, **10**(6) 55–58.

J. R. S. Revell (1982) *Banking and Electronic Fund Transfers*, OECD, Paris.

Ed. F. Ricci (Jul 1983) *IEEE Communications Magazine*, Vol. **21**, No. 4, issue on military communications.

L. A. Rowe and K. P. Birman (Mar 1982) "A local network based on UNIX operating system," *IEEE Transactions on Software Engineering*, **SE-8**(2).

J. E. Rush (1982) "Library automation systems and networks," 333–422 of Ed. M. C. Yovits (1982) *Advances in Computers*, Vol **21**, Academic Press, New York and London.

J.P. Schmader (Dec 1983) "Data transmission techniques alter energy management," *Data Communications*, **12**(12) 126–134.

Serious Software (1983) *Media Conversion*, Serious Software, London, Brochure and Leaflets.

Shaffstall (1983a) *MediaCom 5000 Floppy Disk Converter*, Shaffstall (U.K.) Ltd., Windsor, Berkshire, England, Leaflet.

Shaffstall (1983b) *The Shaffstall MediaCom 5000 Phototypesetter Interface*, Shaffstall Corporation, Indianapolis, IN.

L. Southworth (Sep 1983) "Basics of EFT network switching," *Data Communications*, **12**(9) 175–186.

G. Spencer (1983) "Inland data services from British Telecom," *Business Telecom 83*, 169–176.

J. Taylor (Aug 1982) "Office communications: Reshaping our society?," *Computer Communications*, **5**(4) 176–180.

S. L. Teger (Apr 1983) "Factors impacting the evolution of office automation," *Computer Networks*, **7**(4) 503–511.

Teleservices Report (ongoing) Arlen Communications, Bethesda, MD.

O. Tucker (22 Mar 1984) "Micros and wp-top firms' shopping lists," *Computing*, 38–39.

Ed. R. P. Uhlig (1981) *Computer Message Systems*, North-Holland, Amsterdam, Oxford, England, and New York, Proceedings IFIP-TC-6 International Workshop on Computer Message Systems, Ottawa, Canada, 6–8 April 1981.

UK Online User Group Newsletter (ongoing) Abington, Cambridge, England.

Userlink Systems (1984) *The Userlink Systems for User Friendly Access* and other Leaflets, Userlink Systems Ltd., Stockport, Cheshire, England.

J. Vallee (1983) *Computer Message Systems*, McGraw Hill, New York and Maidenhead, England.

Ed. R.P. Van de Riet and W. Litwin (1982) *Distributed Data Sharing Systems*, North-Holland, Amsterdam, Oxford, England, and New York.

R. Veith (1983) *Multinational Computer Nets*, Gower Publishing Company, Aldershot, Hampshire, England.

G. Venner and S. Walker (May 1983) "Microcomputer networking in libraries (II)," *VINE*, No. 48, 22–26, The Library, University of Southampton, England.

G. Walker (Nov/Dec 1983) "Networks make the most of business computers," *Mind your Own Business*, **6**(10) 74–75.

M. E. Walsh (1983) *Database and Data Communications Systems: A Guide for Managers*, Prentice-Hall, Englewood Cliff, NJ.

A. J. M. Wambecq (1983) "NETIX—A distributed operating system based on Unix software and local networking," Bell Information Systems, Antwerp, Report.

S. B. Weinstein (Winter 1982) "A perspective in financial industry networking," *Journal of Telecommunication Networks*, **1**(4) 317–332.

S. B. Weinstein (Feb 1984) "Smart credit cards: The answer to cashless shopping," *IEEE Spectrum*, **21**(2) 43–49.

Which Computer? (1984a) (Mar 1984) "Office automation," 85–88.

Which Computer? (1984b) (Feb 1984) "Tower of power," 67–71.

Which Office System? (ongoing) EMAP Publications, London, Monthly Magazine.

P. Willson (1983) "Progress in TP monitors," *dp International 1983*, 177–180.

P. Wilson (1984a) (1 Mar 1984) "Let's get mailboxes moving," *Computer Weekly*, 26.

P. Wilson (1984b) (2 Feb 1984) "Transmitting scientific knowhow," *Computing,* 29.

Ed. H. M.. Wood (Fall 1983) *Journal of Telecommunication Networks*, Vol. **2**, No. 3, special issue: distributed database technology.

C. Youett (1983a) (Dec 1983) "How comms keeps the information flowing in the corridors of power," *Communications Management*, 44–47.

C. Youett (1983b) (Sep 1983) "Shipping and freight: Trailing in the wake of the telecoms advance," *Communications Management*, 58–61.

C. Youett (Mar 1984) "The City: Where time and comms is king with capital," *Communications Management*, 47–50.

Chapter 23

Case Studies of Networks

This chapter outlines case studies of over 60 operating networks, mostly in the USA and UK. It gives examples of case studies of local area networks, personal computer networks and micronets, wide area networks, and linked local area networks. Finally, it describes some case studies of applications of DECnet (DEC, 1982).

CASE STUDIES OF LOCAL AREA NETWORKS

Morris (1984) discusses Strategic Incorporated's (1983) massive report, *Local Communications Systems*, which analyses and forecasts product opportunities resulting from the impact of LANs and PABXs on local communications systems users. It is based on detailed interviews with 50 of these users in the USA. Each of these large organisations, ranging from giant companies to smaller dispersed businesses with many computer users, was interviewed over a period of one year, in an attempt to clarify what types of LANs were being used, why, and how effectively.

Collinson (1983) describes the computing systems at the University of Kent, Canterbury, England, where there is a network of Cambridge Rings and VAX computers. This local network also has outside communications via PSS and Usenet.

Patton (1983) discusses the experiences with token ring networks of three different types of user: managers and secretaries, development programmers, and system administrators. Most of the users were comparatively unaware of the ring, and many of them began to use and think of the ring network as an extended single system.

Green (1983) discusses the British Cabinet Office's pioneering use of an early model of Xionics' XINET LAN system; see also Youett (1983a). The initial users of the system were the small team of information technology advisors, established to stimulate the use of this new technology in government departments. Typical applications have included: the use of word processing to draft and redraft memos and reports, electronic mail, maintaining appointments diaries and telephone directories, and accessing computer data.

Christy (1983) discusses DEC's experience of the installation and use of Ethernets in support of the design of VLSI chips. In the light of this experience, he recommends that network support staff need to understand a considerable amount about hardware and software as well as communications.

Nall (1983) discusses the selection and management of a networking system spread over the five buildings of the Harbor Branch Foundation in Florida. An Ethernet-type system was chosen, but with a fibre optic cable, connected to a baseband Ethernet cable.

Ross (1983) describes the installation and operation of one of the UK Department of Industry-sponsored Pilot Office Systems, a 27-work station Ethernet of the Greater London council's Scientific Branch. All of the Branch's 140 scientific, technical, and administrative staff have access to the facilities, which include electronic mail, filing, word processing, and document production, and graphics. The four phases of equipment installation and user training schedules were:

1. Introduction of stand-alone word processors;
2. Linking of these word processors, together with file servers and print servers, to form a network;
3. Adding 8010 work stations, to provide more advanced facilities;
4. Extending the network to provide communications with mainframes, incorporate new products, and add facilities in the light of experience gained and needs previously identified.

Pogran (1983) gives the reasons why Ethernet technology was chosen for the LAN that was used for the development of the Cronus Distributed Operating System by Bolt, Beranek and Newman.

Georganas and Mwikalo (1982) discuss the implementation and operation of Platon, a CSMA/CD bus LAN, with data rate 1 Mbit/sec, at the Department of Electrical Engineering, University of Ottawa. Platon interconnects the department's computers, terminals, peripherals, and various instruments, and the university's mainframe. Its chief objectives are to facilitate network evolution and provide resource sharing for network access, file transfers, and other applications. Platon is also used for research on distributed systems, in connection with which a packet voice system and packet radio gateway are now being developed.

Favre (1983) describes Yorkshire Alloy's experience of a Datapoint ARC LAN; this sort of network was originally chosen as the least expensive way of developing the company's online order processing system. Benefits arising from the system included faster software development and dramatically improved information flow. The LAN can expand or adapt to meet any new requirement easily and quickly.

Datapoint (1983) has given several case histories of the use of its ARC LAN. Triple-A Specialty Co., Chicago, has been gathering and using information so effectively that its way of doing business has been revolutionised; thanks to manufacturing resource planning and computerisation, it now has precise control over all phases of its operations. Because its ARC network handles their everyday business administration, the C. F. Martin Company can still take the time to produce quality guitars, that its craftsmen make by hand. Worsley's, the London wholesale paper merchants, uses an ARCNET to streamline the office operation of its sales headquarters; in addition, a "talking terminal" has been developed and attached to the network for the benefit of a key member of staff who is totally blind. The Diakonessenhuis Refaja hospital in Dordrecht, Netherlands, has installed an ARC-NET to automate its medical and administrative operations; as a result, the information flow is being handled much more quickly, leaving staff free to attend to the more urgent needs of their patients.

Frisch (1983) discusses as a case history the LAN specified for the House of Representatives and installed as a standard there. Mazutis and Phillips (1983) describe COMNET, the broadband voice, video, and radio network for the Canadian House of Commons. Youett (1984a) reports on some of the possible uses of networking, now being considered by the British House of Commons and House of Lords.

Ambler (1983) reports that, after making a careful study, the American Stock Exchange decided that a LAN would best serve its increasing information needs.

Rankins (1983) describes AppalNet, a broadband LAN that now meets Appalachian State University's needs for internal data communications and distribution of TV programs. This LAN supports wideband video, voice, and data communications.

Beauchamp (1983) discusses the implementation of Kiewiet, a high-speed decentralised LAN, now being developed to link all the terminals and computers, both on and off campus at Dartmouth College, NH. It makes extensive use of multipurpose gateways to provide several alternative protocols.

Knight (1983) discusses the implementation of a Hyperchannel System at the Data Processing Division of the Royal Bank of Scotland, at Edinburgh. It connects two large computer systems at opposite ends of a building; each system provides back up for the other in event of breakdown. These two systems are at the centre of a WAN linking the bank's terminals at its branches. Plans for future development and expansion of the network include the installation of a Hyperbus.

Gibson (1983) discusses frankly Boeing Computer Services' successes and failures with LANs from six different vendors. Despite software glitches and poor diagnostics, they all work!

Kaufman (1983) describes the comprehensive LAN that TRW has developed for data communications between many different kinds of computers and related support devices. It operates over a very high bandwidth coaxial cable system, using interface devices based on microprocessors. TRW has recently upgraded this network to include security features, using the Data Encryption Standard (DES) for cryptographic data protection.

Keil (1983) explains briefly the specification that General Motors has developed for LANs in the manufacturing environment; broadband coaxial cable is the preferred medium for this standard LAN. General Motors' expanding needs and the emergence of the General Motors LAN specification increases by an order of magnitude the number of devices attached to their broadband systems. There are now nearly a thousand devices, and there could be over 150,000 by 1990, most of which will need to be attached to LANs.

Freeman and Thurber (1982) give five examples to illustrate how LANs can be designed to meet the tough demands of military, factory, and elementary school environments. By describing specific designs, prototypes, customised networks, and standardised commercial products, they show by examples how specific needs are met.

CASE STUDIES OF PERSONAL COMPUTER NETWORKS AND MICRONETS

Pickwell (1983) describes the HiNet micronet used by the headquarters of the Fisons Group in England. This network, using intelligent terminals that can be located almost anywhere in the building, has provided Fisons with a very reliable, versatile, and cost-effective facility for data processing and text processing, needing minimum effort from its increasing number of users. There are 16 terminals, likely to rise to 30 within about a year; all these work stations are linked to a central 27 MB hard disk.

Hubbard (1983) describes the use of a Nestar network of several dozen Apple IIs and Apple ///s at Citibank's dealing rooms in London; this sort of network was chosen because of its high speed, which was required for this particular application.

Ham (1983) discusses the plans that Dolby Laboratories had for integrating incompatible products, improving departmental data transactions, and streamlining office operations. They chose the solution of distributed microcomputers, linked and switched by a Rolm CBX.

As Carnegie Mellon University's plans for personal computing have evolved, its administration has concluded that the abilities of personal computers provide only part of the answer's to the university's information processing needs (Van Houweling, 1983). As a result, the university's effort, to provide each of its members with a personal computer by 1990, depends more critically on LAN software and communications technology than it does on the development of personal computers.

Walsh (1983) describes a semiautomated computer facility based on a Corvus Constellation star network, at Plymouth Polytechnic in England. The network has 33 Apple II personal computers, 2 printers, and a 40 MB central hard disk; it is now used by about 1,500 students for introductory courses in Basic and Pascal, together with other programming languages and software packages.

Hopkins et al (1983) describe the installation and use of a Nestar Cluster/One network at Dudley College of Technology, England.

The Polytechnic of Central London Library Services has been awarded a contract, by the British Library and the Department of Industry, to investigate the potential of microcomputer networking and office automation for libraries (Collier,

1983). A major objective is to develop an online public access catalog (OPAC), one of the most demanding problems of library automation. Venner and Walker (1983) describe the work being done on the OPAC, using a Nestar PLAN 4000 system, with attached Apple II and IBM personal computers and a dedicated file server based on 137 MB hard disk.

CASE STUDIES OF WIDE AREA NETWORKS

Sinclair et al (1983) describe the evolution of the Honeywell Information Systems internal data communications network, and consider that both designers and users of multi-site computer facilities can benefit from the experiences of this upgraded network. This massive LAN took four years to develop, and has over a hundred nodes, including Honeywell DPS 8 mainframes and DPS 6 minicomputers, together with about 3,000 asynchronous and synchronous terminals at data rates of 300 to 9600 bits/sec, and over 170 inter-computer ports at rates up to 56 kbits/sec. The network has over 80,000 connect hours a month, comprising about 200,000 individual sessions, generating a billion characters of user input and five billion characters of user output.

Communications Management (1983) describes the WAN operated by Union Texas Petroleum in Houston, TX and based on the philosophy that multi-vendor computing equipment provides maximum flexibility. This company's computer centre has four large computers from two mainframe suppliers, and supports a network that includes 350 dial-up asynchronous and binary synchronous private line terminals from many suppliers. A Paradyne 850 DCX statistical multiplexer and port selector acts as a central interface between the computers and the terminals, and makes sure that the right machines and devices are connected to each other at the right time.

Youett (1983b) gives three case studies of the use of WANs in retailing in the UK. The furniture and carpet suppliers Waring & Gillow use nine IBM System 34 computers sited at different cities, for the control of its complex accounting operations and elimination of much of its previous paper work; each computer acts as an autonomous unit with up to 16 remote terminals attached, and the computers communicate with each other via IBM's Interactive Communications Facility software package. Amoco is experimenting with "intelligent" electronic debiting and checking devices on petrol pumps at some of its petrol stations, linked to Barclaycard's central computer during off-peak hours. The Debenhams store in Oxford Street at the centre of London uses a Racal Transcom 100 TCL credit verification machine, containing a card reader and built-in modem, and linked to a central computer.

Youett (1983c) gives two examples of the use of wide area networking by the press. The *Financial Times* uses Kalle and Muirhead facsimile systems to transmit page images of its newspaper from its editorial offices in London, to Frankfurt in West Germany, where its European edition is printed. With the aid of a Honeywell H153 modem, data are transmitted overland at 153 kbits/sec; eventually, satellite transmission is envisaged. United Press International (UPI) has recently installed a CASE MSX message switch to handle its international wire news service. For example, journalists in London can send stories via the MSX to the UPI data base in Dallas, TX.

Levin (1983) reports that the Media Data Division of Katz Communications, a media sales representative for the American commercial broadcasting industry, reevaluated its network options in terms of its corporate structure, scrapped most of its old network, but retained its IBM 4341 and chose a statistical multiplexer topology round this. Their new WAN links 23 Katz sales offices, located in 21 US cities.

Higgins (1983) tells how protocol converters opened the way for wider access of City College of San Francisco's terminals to its central computer, thus avoiding the need to obtain much costly equipment.

Ciepelewski et al (1983) discuss the use of a PDP-11 at the Royal Institute of Technology, Stockholm, for wide area networking. A connection to the Swedish X.25 network TELPAK was implemented, to gain experience of network interfacing, create a base for experiments on high level protocols, and provide communications facilities for users.

Weaving (1983) describes the network of minicomputers at the Joint Research Centre of the Commission of the European Communities. A broadcast service has been implemented as a basic facility of the Joint Research Centre's packet-switched network. Weaving presents the interface that the broadcast service gives to applications programs and discusses their current use of it. This service, as implemented, could become a useful and powerful tool to support distributed applications.

Fisher (1984) gives an overview of the integrated communications system for transmitting and exchanging voice, fax, teletype, and computer data required for the design of the Boeing 767 aircraft, which is being designed at various places in Italy and Japan, by teams that need to be coordinated effectively with engineers and designers in the USA.

Youett (1983d) briefly describes Mercedes Benz's WAN for use inside the UK, which is based on IBM 1431 minis at its Brentford headquarters. The terminals at the company's scattered sites are linked via leased lines, and Racal modems operating at 9.6 kbits/sec handle the message traffic. Youett (1984a) describes the WAN, used by the Austin Rover Group of British Leyland, to link its centres in Britain and Europe, using IBM 4300 computers and 9.6 and 14.4 kbits/sec land lines.

Youett (1983e) describes British Leyland's broadband network, originally designed to link its four main production to its London head office. It is probably one of the most advanced communications networks in Europe, and is already saving over $3 million a year in telecommunications charges. This network also handles British Leyland Systems' well-known Comet electronic mail service and its viewdata service. BL Systems has been looking closely at the possibility of implementing LANs, which it sees as a crucial way of improving BL's manufacturing operations.

Youett (1984b) presents the networking strategy of Harris Corporation. In 1980, it installed its own private satellite network, which linked its principal factories in Florida, Texas, and Rhode Island. Using its own PABX, radio, microwave, and fibre optics communications equipment, Harris has expanded this WAN to handle its international communications. It now provides telex, electronic mail, fax, and voice services between 20 sites.

Johnson and Faulkner (1983) relate how RCA's Cylix Communications Network turned from land lines to satellites, in order to serve more users and apply a wider range of protocols, while growing gradually.

CASE STUDIES OF LINKED LOCAL AREA NETWORKS

Citibank has implemented an extensive fibre optic network together with a digital microwave link, joining its five major buildings in Manhattan, and providing access to the Citicorp Satellite Network (Laviola, 1983). This network has comprehensive voice, data, and video transmission facilities, to support Citibank's financial services and operations. Its versatile designs allows a wide choice of voice and data services.

British Petroleum has been evaluating carefully the alternative approaches that it could adopt to office automation (*Dec User,* 1983). In 1980 it started a pilot project at Aberdeen, Scotland, running on three PDP-11 computers. Since then, several PDPs and VAXs have been linked to over 200 terminals in the "Development" office automation project. For the next trial, incorporating three terminals at remote offshore sites, as well as about 40 in offices on the mainland, an Officeman software system was used.

Robinson (1983) describes Shell UK's'uxperience of selecting, planning, installing, and operating a pilot broadband network at two separate sites. He stresses the essentially special approach to LANs of the large organisation with wide area sites, distant from each other but needing to be linked in an integrated telecommunications network. The experience gained by Shell has been satisfactory, and it should be relevant to most organisations considering the use of broadband LANs.

Ratnayake (1983) reviews Overseas Containers Limited's experiences of a Datapoint ARC LAN, which is one significant component of its much broader network system. It has had computer networks and worldwide telex networks since its start in 1969. It has used its own WANs in the UK and Europe since 1984, and a few international data communications links since 1980. One of its key objectives in the 1980s is to exploit the converging technologies of computing, office systems, and telecommunications, by realising the opportunities and avoiding the pitfalls implicit in this convergence.

Bothner-By (1983) describes the composite network for voice, data, and text, at the Oslo Head Office of the *Det norske VERITAS* newspaper. Several communication nodes, PABX systems, and LANs have been interconnected to form this network. A new network of digital service integrated PABXs is emerging at various VERITAS offices. WANs and new public network services, as well as LANs, are being used.

Guerro (1983) describes a linked local area network project, using the technology of Sytek's Local Net™ system. When completed, this project will correct to the same LAN about 400 computers and over 600 terminals, spread over several sites several miles apart, at the Zürich Polytechnic (ETH).

SESNET was established to provide a service for British Telecom's System Software Engineering Centre, and act as a test bed for internetworking activities. Marshall and Spiegelhalter (1983) discuss the factors governing the choice of network and the planning considerations leading up to its installation. They report on the problems met and experience gained during the implementation of SESNET. They describe its constituent LANs and the types of equipment attached to them, together with its gateways to PSS and the PSTN. They also indicate the services offered to its users, including office automation facilities, computer resources, and data networking.

Project UNIVERSE, already described in Chapter 18, is an advanced experiment in the linking of Cambridge Ring LANs at various sites in the UK via the OTS communications satellite, via high-speed terrestrial links, and via the British X.25 networks PSS and SERCNET. The Department of Industry (1983a and 1983b) describes its recent developments, including the exploration of practical applications to internetworking and office automation. Specific facilities that have been demonstrated include: multi-function work stations, multi-media document transfer via satellite, transfer of slow-scan television images, retrieval of stored images, videotex service, and recorded voice service. Kirstein and Wilbur (1983) describe its basic configuration, networks, gateways, common servers, and the programme for its use. Ackroyd (1983), Cunningham (1983), and Gourd (1983) give some further details of the UNIVERSE network technology. Childs and Morrow (1983) describe British Telecom's involvement in Project UNIVERSE. Wilbur (1983) discusses initial experience with UNIVERSE at its University College London site.

The Alvey Programme for development of Advanced Information Technology in the UK is developing the Alvey Network to link its own offices to the 10 new Alvey research centres and also to the European Esprit programme (Goodwin, 1984). A Xionics XINET LAN was installed at its London headquarters, late in 1983, and consists of 26 Xionics work stations and four printers. It is being implemented in stages, starting with basic office automation tasks, and later proceeding with wide area network links.

CASE STUDIES OF APPLICATIONS OF DECnet

A fairly recent brochure of Digital Equipment Corporation (DEC, 1982) presents five case studies applications of DECnet, describing them in some detail and including network configuration diagrams.

Digital's own engineering network includes over a hundred VAXs, many PDP-11s, several DEC SYSTEM-20s, and about 4,000 terminals. Over 200 nodes at more than a dozen sites cover several parts of the USA and overseas locations in Reading, England, Geneva, Switzerland, and Sydney, Australia. This large and varied network demonstrates well the flexibility of DECnet and it adaptability to changing organisational requirements. It supports: software development, sophisticated hardware engineering design (including CAD), new product manufacturing, development of educational services courses, word processing, and electronic publishing.

The wind tunnels at NASA's Ames research centre were crucial for the testing of the Space Shuttle Columbia. They are equipped with DECnet and DEC interactive computer systems, which form part of an advanced 34-node network of VAX 11-780s, a VAX-11/750, and PDP-11s. By means of DECnet, NASA at Ames is obtaining all the benefits of resource sharing in a coherent digital processing network, which allows its users access to special computer graphics and editing services, as well as to large remote computers for number-crunching. Ames originally had a DECnet Phase II network, but upgraded to DECnet Phase III, without having to alter existing applications. Ames' second network, the Share Program, uses four VAX-11/780s, communicating with the same Cyber 7600 computer, to support administrative tasks, CAD/CAM software development, and extensive numerical calculations. Ames' long-term plan is to use DECnet over a satellite to Ames with NASA's Lewis and Langley sites.

Bird & Son, a leading manufacturer of roofing and other building products, is transforming its data processing from the centralised batch-oriented approach, which it used in the 1970s, to a distributed interactive system for the 1980s. It already uses a VAX-11/780, various PDP-11s, and DECnet for a typical distributed processing application. It developed BASIS (Bird And Son Information System) as the foundation for its integrated interactive administrative system, which has largely replaced written documents. BASIS automatically generates invoices, shipping papers, bills of lading, and even instructions for forklift operators; it will eventually include: factory data collection, accounts receivable, payroll, financial planning, sales planning, word processing, electronic mail, and even the provision of portable terminals for all company sales staff.

At the Volkswagen Plant in Wolfsburg, West Germany, more than 70 Digital minicomputers, including a VAX-11/780, various PDP-11s, and DECnet Phase III form a responsive distributed process control network, which is vital for its design, testing, and production operations. This distributed network allows different kinds of process feedback, ranging from those related to ongoing production and needing immediate attention, to post-access analyses useful for planning future process control procedures. DECnet Phase III features used include: route-through capability, file transfer, task-to-task communication, a network command terminal, remote booting, and downline loading. Volkswagen and Digital also jointly developed some additional DECnet facilities to meet special Volkswagen requirements, such as accounting statistics, completely automatic file transfer and transaction transfer in both directions between different computers, and supervision of priority-ordered queues of test-stand requests for connection to process control computers. Despite the network's complexity, its users perceive only one computer system.

At the University of Washington, in Washington State, DECnet has achieved more efficient use of available computer ports, together with a more convenient and economical use of computer systems. It turned to networking, to keep up with the rapidly increasing demands for computing by both staff and students, and to allow full sharing of its computer resources. The network now has VAX-11/780s, connected by DECnet Phase III, and used for instruction; there are plans to link them both to a CDC 179-750 computer, used for both research and teaching. The network has been found specially convenient for software development and maintenance, and also promises to help speed up learning by students.

The Department of Computer Science, at the University of Washington, was recently awarded a very large National Science Foundation grant for computer research, $4.2 million over five years of the Eden Project on local area networks. This Project has developed an experimental network based on Ethernet and is using three VAXs to create its software. Analysis of projected traffic loads and network stability led to the choice of Ethernet. The Eden Project aims to create a largely new combination of existing computer capabilities. It envisages a system much larger than that provided by conventional time sharing, with much more immediate responses. The system differs from existing LANs by integrating its components much more closely into a functional whole, thus constituting a "building-size highly parallel computer." The system will be used for various computing projects, including distributed concurrent computation, programming, image analysis, and office automation.

REFERENCES

B. R. Ackroyd (Jul 1983) "Project UNIVERSE—Local area networks and satellite communications," *British Telecommunications Engineering,* **2**(3) 121–125, reprinted from *Communication & Broadcasting,* **8**(2) 3–8 (Feb 1983).

J. Ambler (1983) "American Stock Exchange trades old network for streamlined setup," *Data Communications,* **12**(12) 255–262.

K. Beauchamp (Dec 1983) "Computer network development at Dartmouth College," *Computer Communications,* **6**(6) 308–312.

H. Bothner-By (1983) "A corporate service integrated digital PABX network," *Business Telecom 83,* 283–297.

G. H. L. Childs and G. Morrow (Jul 1983) "British Telecom and Project UNIVERSE," *British Telecommunications Engineering,* **2**(2) 91–93.

P. Christy (1983) "User experiences with production Ethernet," *LocalNet 83 (New York),* 109–115.

Ciepelewski, T. Jungefeldt and J. Linnell (Jan 1983) "Connecting a minicomputer to an X.25 network— A case study," *Computer Communications Review,* **13**(1) 11–30.

M. Collier (May 1983) "Microcomputer networking in libraries (I) Background and aims of the project," *VINE,* No. 48, 21, The Library, University of Southampton, England.

P. Collinson (Sep 1983) "Ringing the changes at College," *Dec User,* 16–20.

Communications Management (Aug 1983) "A 'traffic cop' keeps the data flowing in downtown Houston," 31.

C. Cunningham (May 1983) "Project Universe—The ultimate in resource sharing," *Communications Management,* 16–22.

Datapoint (1983) *ARC Case Histories,* Datapoint Corporation, San Antonio, TX, Leaflets.

DEC (1982) *Networking—Distributed Computing—Application Stories by Digital,* Digital Equipment Corporation, Maynard, MA, Brochure EA-21796-18.

Dec User (Aug 1983) "Pilot project for system specification," 45–48.

Department of Industry (1983a) *Project UNIVERSE,* UK Department of Industry, Information Technology Division, London, Brochure and associated Leaflets.

Department of Industry (1983b) *Project UNIVERSE,* UK Department of Industry, Information Technology Division, London, Booklet prepared for Telecom 83, Geneva.

D. Favre (1983) "LAN experience at Yorkshire Imperial Alloys," *dp International,* 185–188.

D. E. Fisher (Jan 1984) "Integrated digital communications networking," *IEEE Communications Magazine,* **22**(1) 42–48.

H. A. Freeman and K. J. Thurber (Sprint 1982) "Local networks for the specialized environment," *Journal of Telecommunications Networks,* **1**(1) 59–70.

I. T. Frisch (Spring 1983) "The evolution of local area networks," *Journal of Telecommunication Networks,* **2**(1) 7–23.

N. Georganas and R. Mwikalo (Dec 1982) "Platon: A university local area network," *Computer Communications,* **5**(6) 308–313.

R. W. Gibson (Mar 1983) "Local net user relates trials, tribulations," *Data Communications,* **12**(3) 121–129.

C. Goodwin (9 Feb 1984) "Xionics net will link Alvey centres," *Computing,* 1.

R. Gourd (Aug 1983) "Project Universe demonstrates future networks," *Communications International,* **10**(8) 62–63.

R. Green (22 Sep 1983) "Is this the highest powered LAN of all?," *Computer Weekly, Management Review,* 4.

M. Guerro (1983) "Experience with a wide area broadband network," LocalNet 83 (Europe), 501–508.

M. R. Ham (Jul 1983) "Complex revamp of network steers user to a digital PBX solution," *Data Communications,* **12**(7) 157–160.

M. Higgins (Apr 1983) "College network passes test, despite limited computer resources," *Data Communications,* **12**(4) 125–127.

G. Hopkins, P. Davies and B. Green (1983) "The net benefit of a local microcomputer network in a college of technology," *LocalNet 83 (Europe),* 57–66.

R. Johnson and S. Faulkner (Jul 1983) "Great leap upward serves computers and applications in mid-size firms," *Data Communications,* **12**(7) 93–99.

L. J. Kaufman (1983) "Application of the DES Standard to the TRW Local area network," *LocalNet 83 (New York),* 473–484.

B. R. Keil (1983) "Broadband coax—A media for productivity improvement in the auto industry," *LocalNEet 83 (New York),* 127–136.

P. T. Kirstein and S. R. Wilbur (Summer 1983) "The UNIVERSE Project," *IUCC Bulletin,* **5**(2) 86–90.

A. Knight (Aug 1983) "Local networking at the Royal Bank of Scotland," *Computer Communications,* **6**(4) 192–198.

M. A. Laviola (1983) "Citibank's fiber optic metropolitan network," *LocalNet 83 (New York),* 347–355.

D. P. Levin (Dec 1983) "Building a network around an IBM 4300 mainframe," *Data Communications,* **12**(12) 163–175.

J. Marshall and B. Spiegelhalter (1983) "Experiences with Net/One at British Telecom," *LocalNet 83 (Europe),* 67–79.

J. Mazutis and J. Phillips (1983) "COMNET: A broadband voice, video and radio network for the Canadian House of Commons," *LocalNet 83 (Europe)* 239–249.

J. Morris (23 Feb 1984) "LANs play roles of all things to all men," *Computer Weekly, Management Review,* 16–17.

K. L. Nall (1983) "System selection and management of fiber optic Ethernet," *LocalNet 83 (New York)*, 91–100.

C. Patton (1983) "User experiences with ring networks," *LocalNet 83 (New York)*, 101–107.

P. Pickwell (1983) "A micronet case study in a commercial environment," *LocalNet 83 (Europe)*, 49–55.

K. J. Pogran (Jul 1983) "Selection of a local area network for the Cronus Distributed Operating System," *Computer Communications Review*, **13**(3) 25–35.

R. P. Rankins (1983) "AppalNet—A local network for Appalachian State University," *LocalNet 83 (New York)*, 117–125.

A. Ratnayake (1983) "The Datapoint ARC in a commercial environment," *LocalNet 83 (Europe)*, 105–108.

J. Riley (29 Mar 1984) "Routine work needs a change," *Computer Weekly, Management Review*, 4–5.

A. Robinson (1983) "Experiences with a broadband network in Shell UK," *LocalNet 83 (Europe)*, 80–91.

G. Ross (1983) "Implementing on Ethernet based advanced office systems," *LocalNet 83 (Europe)*, 93–103.

J. T. Sinclair, W. E. Lewis and R. B. Wall (Oct 1983) "Data communications networks evolution has lessons for all," *Data Communications*, **12**(9) 199–209.

Strategic Incorporated (1983) *Local Communications Systems*, Strategic Incorporated, CA.

D. Van Houweling (1983) "Workstations for all at Carnegie Mellon," *LocalNet 83 (New York)*, 513–524.

G. Venner and S. Walker (May 1983) "Microcomputer networking in libraries (II) A public access catalogue system," *VINE*, No. 48, 22–26, The Library, University of Southampton, England.

C. Walsh (1983) "Personal computer network in a teaching environment," *LocalNet 83 (Europe)*, 39–48.

K. Weaving (Aug 1983) "Broadcast service implementation on a packet-switched network," *Computer Communications*, **6**(4) 178–184.

S. Wilbur (1983) "Initial experience with Universe at University College London," *LocalNet 83 (Europe)*, 297–309.

C. Youett (1983a) (Dec 1983) "How comms keeps the information flowing in the corridors of power," *Communications Management*, 44–47.

C. Youett (1983b) (Aug 1983) "Retailing—Technology's proving ground for data/comms convergence," *Communications Management*, 33–35.

C. Youett (1983c) (Sep 1983) "Little and often: How Britain's communicators are learning the ways to communicate," *Communications Management*, 33–35.

C. Youett (1983d) (Apr 1983) "World-wide strategy of Mercedes Benz," *Communications Management*, 66–68.

C. Youett (1983e) (Apr 1983) "How BL's own network saves 2m every year in telephone charges," *Communications Management*, 60–66.

C. Youett (1984a) (Feb 1984) "How comms helps BL keep its European distributors informed," *Communications Management*, 28–32.

C. Youett (1984b) (Feb 1984) "The Harris Corporation strategy," *Communications Management*, 32–34.

Chapter 24

Current Network
Problems and Prospects

Like Part 4, this chapter discusses the wider aspects of computer networks, but takes account of recent developments, most of which have occurred since the first edition of this book was written. It summarises some of the recent literature on network problems, both those that were already known and those that have come to light during the last year or two. It outlines some of the ideas recently expressed about the future of networking and its applications, and considers further the relationships between networking and information technology in general.

This chapter considers in turn: technical network problems and prospects; the choice, design, operation, and management of networks, together with other topics relevant to those who run or install networks; economic aspects; human and social aspects, including such political issues as privacy and freedom of information; network security and some other aspects of computer security; network ownership, planning, and regulation; further impacts and potentialities of computer networks during the next two decades.

TECHNICAL NETWORK PROBLEMS AND PROSPECTS

The first part of this section outlines some recent work on the following technical network problems: congestion, flow control, routing, naming and addressing, transmission errors, reliability, network failure, network interconnection, and other network protocol problems and issues.

The second part briefly reviews some of the prospects for local area networks and integrated services digital networks. It then considers recent developments and prospects for networks based on cable TV, optical transmission technology, radio technology, and satellites.

Bernstein (1982) proposes a terminology for computer communication problems faced in synchronous polled networks.

Chapter 7 of the book by Seidler (1983) discusses network congestion and ways of counteracting it. Stuck (1983a and 1983b) analyses the behaviour of several different LAN access methods under congested traffic conditions.

Moura (1983) shows how flow control can optimise the operation of a packet-switched network. Data regulation ensures proper store-and-forward traffic flow, and allows speed matching and error-free transmission.

Chapters 5 and 6 of the book by Seidler (1983) discuss network routing in considerable detail. Topics discussed there include: shortest paths and how to find them, parameters of routing rules, optimisation of routing rules, adaptive routing rules, random routing rules, and routing rules based on optimal flows. Chapter 10 of the book by Pooch et al (1982) presents some algorithms for routing and flow control. Rosner (1982) considers routing in Part 3 of his book.

Perlman (1983) proposes an algorithm for broadcasting of reliable routing information through a network, and presents its basic principles and design details. After equipment failure, the algorithm enables a network to stabilise without human intervention reasonably soon after any malfunctioning component has been repaired or disconnected.

In a fairly mathematical paper, which presents its results with the aid of graphs, Brayer (1983) discusses a self-configuring routing algorithm for a mobile radio network.

Cole et al (1983) discuss several of the problems faced by the Arpanet and DARPA Catenet in handling electronic mail and file transfers. They conclude that naming, addressing and routing are the major difficulties in a multi-layer multi-network environment of this sort, which caters for a variety of users.

The book by Blahut (1983) introduces the theory and practice of error control codes.

Error control coding and error correction coding for digital communications are discussed in the books by Lin and Costello (1983) and Clark and Cain (1981), respectively Bhargava (1983) presents a forward error correction scheme for digital communications. Newcombe and Pasupathy (1982) describe error rate monitoring for digital communications.

The July 1982 issue of *IEEE Transactions on Computing*, Vol. **C-31,** No. 7, is a special issue on reliable and fault-tolerant computing.

Salwen (1983) considers various factors that influence LAN reliability, including: aspects related to communications, architectural considerations, and network hardware reliability.

Podell (1982) discusses a fairly complicated probabilistic model of reliability in a packet-switched network, and evaluates the probability of reliable information completion, within a tolerable delay, for various situations.

Findlow (1982) points out that network failures can be nightmares, and explains how to use network management systems to avoid them.

Various approaches to network interconnection are discussed in Chapter 19, "Communications Gateways," in the book by Fling (1983), in pages 98 to 102 of the book by Cheong and Hirschheim (1983), and in the papers by Heard (1983) and Higginson and Cole (1983).

Frisch (1983) considers the past, present, and future evolution of LANs from the viewpoint of users. He surveys users' requirements and expectations for LANs, based on the results of several market research studies. He attempts to assess the future impact on LANs of standards, software requirements, and voice and data integration.

Durham (1983) reports on the work being done at Cambridge University to improve the performance of the Cambridge Ring. A speed of 50 MHz is envisaged for the fast version of the Ring, now being developed; as technology advances, this speed could gradually advance to 100 MHz or beyond.

De Grandi et al (1983) describe the HERMES Project at the Joint Research Centre of the Commission of the European Communities, which aims to study advanced concepts in networking; they outline the far reaching goals of the Project.

Hooley (1983) predicts that the development of future generation computer systems will dramatically affect the PABX during the next 10 years. He thinks that the coming fourth generation of digital PABX systems will probably replace the present centralised switching by smaller distributed switching systems, sharing some centrally located facilities such as gateways; they will also use optical fibre transmission. Later generations of PABX systems will begin to use the new fifth generation computer technologies as they emerge.

Computer Management (1984a) notes that data communications are changing as users ask for personal access. Despite the present focussing of attention on LANs, this article considers that the arrival of the digital telephone service as a commercial reality is likely to affect mainframe data communications strategies much more immediately.

Part 6 of the book by Rosner (1982) deals with integrated networks and the future of packet switching; after describing some approaches combining circuit switching and packet switching, it introduces voice-data ISDNs. Kostas (1984) and Andrews (1984) both discuss the possible further development of ISDNs in fairly general terms. Kitahara (1983) describes the Information Network System (INS), now being developed as an integrated network in Japan.

Hughes (1983) presents some of the principles used in the ISDN now being developed by British Telecom. It is designed as a unified network, able to carry out both present and future services; restrictions, that might prejudice improvements to existing services or hinder the introduction of new services, are avoided. ISDN services, using a data rate of 64 kbits/sec, will start coming into operation during 1984. The design of a variable-bit-rate network should not have too many difficulties; the rate of progress to such a network will depend on various technical, economic, and political factors.

At the end of its discussion of the changing tone of telecommunications, *Which Computer?* (1984) considers the possible role of cable TV networks, which will make wide use of switched star technology, which allows two-way communications and various switched services. The proposed new systems, at least in the UK, will still have plenty of room for interactive services, such as viewdata with electronic mail, home banking, and home shopping; there will also be services specially oriented to business users. Eventually, the cable network will carry voice, text, data, and pictures, as well as providing communications between microcomputer users.

Powers and Mahajan (1983) consider the history and characteristics of optical transmission and satellite communications systems, and compare these two technologies in terms of their qualities, cost trade-offs and trends. Optical transmission has large bandwidths, compatibility with other terrestrial systems, and relative immunity from interference. Satellite systems have large bandwidths, extensive coverage, and flexibility, but there is limited room for them in geostationary orbits. Jones (1984) outlines some of the characteristics of fibre optic and satellite systems, in relation to their future prospects.

Martin-Royle and Bennett (1983) survey British Telecom's current and projected use of optical fibre transmission systems in its telecommunications networks. By the end of the 1980s, about 50% of the main network links and much of the junction network will use optical fibres; studies are in hand for the local use of optical fibres. Transatlantic submarine cables, using optical fibres, are expected in the late 1980s.

Garner (1984) reports on the extensive part already being played by optical fibre technology in all parts of Japanese telecommunications, so much so that they could have a clear international lead in the applications of this technology. Fibre optic trunk lines are to play an essential part in INS, enabling it to provide advanced information services at very high data rates throughout Japan. In the late 1980s, there will also be extensive use of fiber optic LANs and CATV systems.

Murakami (1982) describes the present status and future trends of mobile communications service using radio technology. The future services will have more varied functions and use a wider variety of transmitted information than at present.

Chitre (1983) discusses the relationships between different factors, which determine trends in future satellite communications systems. In the future, the diversity of launch options, improvements in earth stations, and demand for new services will influence the trends in satellite technology.

The book *Satellites Today* (Baylin and Toner, 1983) gives a clear and concise but fairly extensive coverage of the history, technology, legal issues, and future of satellite communications.

NETWORK CHOICE, DESIGN, OPERATION, AND MANAGEMENT

This section discusses some of the important problems and issues facing those who have to run or install computer networks. An organisation, which is considering the possibility of installing or using a network, first has to consider whether to do this, and if so, what sort to acquire or access. Once it has decided to obtain a network, it may choose a system already on the market or it may be faced with the problem of designing its network, in which case it almost certainly needs the help of outside experts. Once a network has been installed and is in use, there are various problems concerned with its operation and management. All these aspects are considered in turn.

Flint (1983a, Part V, and 1983b) discusses network choice, especially the choice of LANs, in considerable detail. The first question to consider is whether the user organisation needs an applications system or a communications utility. The choice of an applications system should depend chiefly on how well the system meets the requirements of the applications. The best choice of a network utility depends on the nature of the organisations site(s) and on the devices that need to communicate with each other. In both cases, the user should consider his requirements first, not the network technology; his estimate of future requirements should start from an assessment of existing systems.

Flint lists the following eleven key issues in network requirements:

1. How many sites need to be linked? How similar are their communications requirements?
2. What availability is needed for communications between sites?
3. What types of traffic must be carried between sites?
4. What are the requirements for data communications between each pair of sites?
5. What requirements are there for video communications?
6. What special data requirements are there?
7. How reliable and available do local communications need to be?
8. Do computers and work stations with high transmission rates need to be supported?
9. How many host computers need to be supported, with what interfaces?
10. How many terminals and other simple digital devices need to be supported? What are their interfaces and protocols? How much will they be used? Where are they located?
11. What special facilities, such as gateways and servers and electronic mail, does the network need?

He discusses them in detail in Chapters 24 and 25 of his book (Flint, 1983a). In Chapter 26 of his book, he describes the network procurement process.

Walker (1983) gives two "golden rules" for anyone establishing and running a sensible office network:

1. Choose the network best able to meet the existing and anticipated needs for information and resource sharing in the business;
2. Have a good supply of the knowledge and commitment needed to optimise the many benefits that networking can provide.

Gee (1983) discusses the applications of LANs, together with the considerations and pitfalls that should be borne in mind when choosing a LAN. Hom (1983) and Langford (1983) consider LAN user needs in relation to network choice. Jackson (1983) reviews some of the different LANs on the market, in relation to network choice. Network choice is also discussed in the book by Derfler and Skilling (1983).

The report *Multi-Vendor Data Communications Networks* (QED, 1982), based on experience of networks in the USA, discusses in depth how to integrate different vendors' equipment with maximum flexibility and economy. It shows how to link one LAN to outside WANs and to other LANs, and considers how to find the best configuration for an individual user organisation. Eakin (1983) also considers the question of compatibility between equipment from different manufacturers, and discusses some approaches for upgrading or replacing an organisation's existing system, which may have a varied selection of equipment from several different suppliers.

Appendix 2 of the book by Flint (1983) presents an example of the sort of questionnaire that a user organisation should submit to vendors offering to supply a communications network. Frisch (1983) formulates some questions that users should ask LAN vendors. Whitehouse (1983) warns users not to buy a network "too easily" after hearing vendors' sales talk.

Akhtar (1983), Leiden (1983), and Locke-Wheaton (1983) give case histories of how their organisations actually choose their LANs.

Another question allied to network choice and facing certain user organisations, especially the larger ones, is voice-data integration in networks. Klineman (1983) tells how five executives, from large companies already deeply committed to data communications, considered the major issues of voice-data integration and discussed the arguments for and against different approaches to it. These issues are also discussed by Ditlefsen (1983), Hart (1983), and Wiley (1983a). Houldsworth (1983) discusses the related topic of the convergence between PABX-based systems and other kinds of LANs.

Recent books on network design include *Data Network Design Structures* (Sarch, 1983) and *Principles of Computer Communication Network Design* (Seidler, 1983); Seidler's book has a fairly mathematical presentation. Design considerations are also discussed in Chapter 11 of the book by Black (1983) and Part 3 of the book by Rosner (1982).

Dadzie (1983) points out that network design is concerned with the initial planning and continuing evolution of a network. Its chief concern is to ensure that the network achieves its design objectives, in terms of function, performance, availability, and cost. He indicates various responsibilities of network designers.

Saltzer et al (1983) explore some of the engineering problems involved in designing a ring with no central control. Cooper and Edholm (1983) discuss design issues in broadband LANs.

Metropolitan area networks (*MANs*) are beginning to emerge as a new category of computer network, intermediate in size between LANs and WANs. Typically, they are integrated networks, covering areas larger than one block, and operating over distances up to about 20 miles. Ennis (1983) presents some design considerations for broadband metropolitan networks. Sazegari (1983) suggests that cities design and build their own networks, if they become tired of waiting for vendors to offer a suitable high-speed metropolitan integrated voice and data network; he gives some helpful hints as to how they should do this.

Jennings (1983) lists the following questions to be put when designing a network, especially a WAN, or network usage for an organisation:

1. What type of network is required. Should it be a LAN or a WAN? If it is a WAN, should it use the PSTN, leased lines, or a packet-switched network?
2. What types and speeds of modems are required?
3. For what operations is the PSTN to be used?
4. What communication protocols and line codes are used?
5. Are time division multiplexers to be used?
6. Is a network management system required?
7. What standby arrangements cover line, modem, and other failures?
8. Has the network been designed to minimise costs?
9. Will the network provide the required types of service and response times?
10. Has the network been designed to take advantage of future telecommunications services and facilities?

Wiley (1983b) suggests how to optimise WAN design and obtain compatibility by choosing the most suitable switching technique: circuit switching, packet switching, or a combination of the two. Minoli (1983) proposes a new design approach for store-and-forward networks. Brayer (1983) describes the design of a 25-node mobile radio network, which does not have a fixed topology.

Hughes (1983) discusses several aspects of the design and implementation of the ISDN now being developed in the UK by British Telecom. Bhagri (1984) and Kostas (1984) also present considerations for ISDN design and implementation. Gerla and Pazos-Rangel (1984) present a method for optimal design of ISDNs.

Network operation and management are becoming increasingly hard, because of more sophisticated user requirements and requests. The network manager's job is become much more demanding because of the increasing complexity of networks and network equipment, and because of the many new types of network coming on the market. An article in *Computer Management* (Feb. 1984) gives some advice to network managers trying to find their way through this maze. Richards (1983) explores some "do's and dont's" of network creation and management by means of a "case study," based on the experience of several companies.

Freeman (1983) and Lefavi (1983) both discuss how to minimise network downtime; Freeman indicates how to achieve this by diagnosing problems online, and Lefavi advocates the careful identification of problems during initial planning and daily network operation.

Kenyon (1983) examines some network management functions, which he considers essential for the successful operation of a LAN; he also considers briefly centralised and distributed implementations of network management systems. Marchbanks (1984) argues the case for network management controls.

Dadzie (1983) discusses the management needed to ensure the continuing smooth operation of a teleprocessing network. It covers a wide range of control techniques, which can be subdivided into three functional areas: control, administration, and design.

ECONOMIC ASPECTS

This section starts by giving some additional information on network costs and tariffs, supplementing some of the information in Chapter 15. It then assesses current demands and possible future markets for different types of network systems and services. It ends by commenting further on some of the economic impacts of computer networks.

Some examples of the costs of networks and network equipment are now given. Many of the figures are taken from various parts of the book *The Data Ring Main* (Flint, 1983a), others are taken from different sources. Some of the costs are quoted in US dollars ($) and some in pounds sterling (£); it is impossible to translate accurately between dollar and sterling values, because of recent fluctuations of the exchange rate between about $1.03 and $1.43 per £.

Costs of computer processing units and memories are still falling rapidly by a factor between 6 and 8 every ten years (Flint, 1983a, 21). Costs of other types of equipment are also dropping, though not so fast.

Recent trends in cost per interconnection in the USA are estimated by Flint, 1983a, 337: for minicomputer LANs they are $800 to $8,000 (1982), $400 to $2,500 (1984), $200 to $700 (1986), $60 to $400 (1990); for personal computer networks and micronets, $100 to $600 (1982), $40 to $200 (1984), up to $60 (1986), up to $20 (1990).

From my own observations of typical personal computer network costs in the UK in late 1983, the networking cost per device is usually at least £100 and can be considerably more. For networks of this sort with about 10 personal computers, which also have at least one server and at least one print server, the networking plus servers cost per computer typically ranges from about £500 to £2,000, according to the quality and capabilities of network and servers.

Custance (1984) quotes some estimates of cost per connection made by Ken Baynton, the Managing Director of Micom-Borer Ltd.: about £850 for a bus LAN such as Ethernet, £650 to £1,600 for a ring LAN, and £85 to £550 for WAN connections using his own company's equipment. Walker (1983) estimates rather higher prices of £1,500 to £2,000 per channel attached to a LAN.

Other estimates of WAN access costs are roughly £200 to £450 per multiplexed connection (Flint, 1983a, 242, 1982 figures) and roughly £1,200 to £2,000 per synchronous port connection including terminal cost (Flint, 1983a, 244). Flint (1983a, 305) estimates the costs of a five-site, 200-device LAN-WAN configuration at $360 to $140 per attached device at 1980 prices.

Flint (1983a, 90) estimates the costs of several types of network wiring and wiring connection. Costs per metre range from £0.10 to £2.30 for all types, £0.20 to £1.50 for coaxial cable, and are about £0.50 for optical fibre. Costs per wiring connector range from £3 to £30 for all types, £4.50 to £12 for coaxial cable, and are about £30 for optical fibre. Optical fibre costs are falling rapidly and are now well below those of corresponding systems based on computer wires.

An "acceptable cost" for networking an attached device is usually considered to be somewhere between 10% and 20% of the cost of the device (Flint, 1983a,

40). However, the cost of providing access to networked devices, even to sophisticated networked work stations, is already low compared with the costs of capital equipment per worker in the USA, which are of the order of $25,000 for factory workers and even more for farm workers, although they are still very low for office and professional workers (Flint, 1983a, 20).

Kelley (1983) discusses office LAN requirements from an analysis of office activities, and examines their economic feasibility. He gives some specific examples with numerical data.

Nirenberg (1983) discusses how much a satellite earth station, an essential component of a satellite network, should cost.

Part 5 of the book *Packet Switching* (Rosner, 1982) describes some common carrier network services, and gives examples of their tariffs. Jagger (1984) quotes some examples of tariffs for the Teletex service to be launched in the UK. A recent leaflet from British Telecom (1984) gives the initial tariffs for the IDA Service, using the British ISDN now being developed.

Kitahara (1983) proposes a *bit-based tariff structure*, based on the number of bits sent in a message and independent of distance traveled and time taken. He has advocated this since 1977, and now sees good prospects for its application in the Japanese Information Network System, now being developed, as soon as advances in optical fibre and other technologies make network costs low enough.

Various commercially available reports have from time to time estimated demands for digital communications and computer networks. These include Logica's (1981) report *The Data Communications Market in Western Europe 1981–1987*, and several reports issued by Frost and Sullivan. Lawrence (1984) reviews *The Report on European Telecommunications* (The Yankee Group, 1984) which predicts that this market will change more over the next five years than during the past century.

Langford (1983) states that LANs are coming to fruition now, because of growing data communications needs and reduced costs of moving data within a site. Data processing costs have now fallen to a level where users can easily afford their own terminals, micros, or minis. The resulting proliferation of data processing on a site has created a requirement for LANs, in order to use these data processing resources more effectively. Judging by many interviews with users, the success of a particular LAN is determined largely by its ability to meet the following types of user needs: connectivity, compatibility, network management, cost control, distribution, networking, and integration.

Burgess (1983) quotes Tim Holley, the Managing Director of Racal-Milgo Ltd., as saying that the market for LANs is about to take off into a multimillion pound business, and perhaps reaching over a hundred times its present level by 1987. It has been predicted that by the early 1990s there will be one work station per office worker in the USA.

Computing (1984a) announces the finding of a recent report by the US research firm International Resource Development which says that the growth in the market for LANs is being hindered by too many products and by the resulting confusion among users.

Woolnough (1984) summarises recent reports by Mackintosh International and

Enlon Associates and by Frost and Sullivan on the future growth of the microcomputer market. Forecasters of this market generally agree that data communications will be the next big growth area for microcomputers.

Iliffe (1984) discusses some of the possibilities that will be opened up for interactive business services by the emerging newer types of cable networks. They will provide person-to-person message services, electronic mail order, home shopping, and remote computing facilities. Although the initial risks of investing in cable systems are high, wealthy backers should become available, as the potential returns from their business applications may well be worth thousands of millions.

Powers and Mahajan (1983) consider the market for optical and satellite transmission systems. They present cost comparisons and cost trends. Optical transmission systems tend to have lower starting costs, but their costs are more sensitive to distance and depend on rights of way. Satellite systems have high starting costs, but their costs are relatively independent of distance. Powers and Mahajan conclude that these two technologies are inherently suited to different complementary markets with the major factors determined by the relevant economics of the network providers. Shackman (1983) considers that Western Europe is not a natural market for satellite communications.

Leighfield (1983) believes that recent developments in communications legislation and information technology have opened up new opportunities for organisations to become more effective. In order to maximise such opportunities, they need to take a comprehensive and strategic view of information technology, and adopt a pragmatic approach to realising these opportunities as facilities become available.

In 1982, the International Telecommunications Union set up a Commission, led by Sir Donald Maitland, to investigate why the telecommunications of the developing countries has lagged so far behind the developed world and how that situation could be improved. Johnstone (1984) reports that one of the Commission's preliminary findings is that both Third World governments and manufacturers of sophisticated telecommunications equipment must reassess the commercial potential of the developing countries. In a report on world communications, the consultants Arthur D. Little concluded that the world market for telecommunications could double during the 1980s, with the lead being taken by Asia.

Johnstone points out that telecommunications has become as vital to economic development as finance and energy. Without sophisticated telecommunications, industry cannot flourish, nor can education and emergency services be developed to anything like their full potential.

In her Christmas address in 1983, Her Majesty The Queen said that we want to see still more modern technology being used by the poorer countries, to provide employment and produce primary products and goods that will be bought by the richer nations at competitive prices.

Rivera and Briceño (1982) discuss various viewpoints about the impact of emerging communications and information technologies on unemployment, with special reference to the situation in the developing countries.

Maurer et al (1982) state that, in principle, new methods of telecommunications and information technology require fewer materials and use less energy than traditional methods. However, carelessly designed systems and applications could cause tremendous increases in the use of these resources. To avoid this happening, it is necessary to design a new technological system and take account of human attitudes, so that the modes of communication can be changed appropriately.

The quarterly journal, *Information Economics and Policy*, is concerned mainly with telecommunications economics and policy, and includes discussions on related issues of information economics and media planning. It is intended for researchers, expert consultants, and policy makers in these fields.

HUMAN AND SOCIAL ASPECTS

This section considers the human factors in office automation and other aspects of information technology, their general impact on work and society, and the political issues that arise, including privacy, data protection, and freedom of information.

Hasui et al (1983) give figures of the rates of information transfer to and from a person. The total sensory input rate is of the order of 1000 Mbits/sec, including visual input of order 1 to 100 Mbits/sec, audio input of order 10 to 100 kbits/sec, but effective information input to the brain only about 40 bits/sec. The brain's rate of information transfer to human memory is about 100 bits/sec. The brain sends motor control information to hands, arms, legs, and body at a total rate of order 10 Mbits/sec.

The book *Human Factors in Office Automation* (Galitz, 1980) gives practical guidelines for designing user-friendly office systems. Topics that it covers include: keyboard and screen design for input and output, data collection techniques, causes and remedies of operator error, office environment, and management of change.

The book *Office Automation* (Doswell, 1983) devotes considerable attention to human factors, including discussions of the ways in which office workers actually work and could work, the management of change, the individual job, and wider social aspects.

In Chapter 10 of their book, Cheong and Hirschheim (1983) consider the human aspects of implementing new technology. A branch of sociology called "implementation research" has led to the conclusions that implementation is a process rather than a product and that it is necessary to consider and manage the behavioural aspects of the change process.

The *socio-technical systems approach*, which Cheong and Hirschheim apply to the process of LAN implementation, sees any technological intervention as consisting of a *technical system*, involving various technologies and job tasks, and a *social system*, involving people with their various roles and behaviours. Once the requirements of these two systems have been ascertained, their variables are recombined in such a way that the two systems together are eventually jointly optimised. This approach is said to provide a work environment and task structure where people can achieve personal development and satisfaction.

The book *New Office Technology—Human and Organisational Aspects* (Otway and Peltu, 1983) examines and discusses a variety of human and social questions with summaries and recommendations. For example, how will office automation systems affect the ability of organisations to adapt and survive? What will be their impact on people working in offices? What are the ergonomic requirements of the new systems? How far will information destroy some jobs but create others?

Human factors in office automation are also considered by Coffey (1982), Goldfield (1983), Günsteide (1982), and Taylor (1982); Taylor suggests that information technology in the office will have greater impact on society than most people now expect.

In these days of chronic high unemployment, it is not surprising that there are widespread fears that computing and information technology will take away far more jobs than they produce, nor is it yet at all clear whether there will be a net loss or gain of jobs as a result. In the UK at least, the trade unions by no means always welcome the advance of information technology; for example, in the newspaper industry, they have been fighting a rearguard action against the introduction of new printing technology, and the new Mercury telecommunications network has suffered some delays as a result of industrial action. Some trade unionists are very critical of the British government's policy for information technology.

Remarkably few articles discuss specific examples of the impact of information technology on work and employment; one example is Oppenheim's (1981) discussion of the likely impact of information technology on the work of librarians, information scientists, and data base producers during the next 10 years.

Kavanagh (1982) reports an imaginative £4 million project where the Greater London Council is setting up "technology networks" to make computing expertise and equipment at London's polytechnics and universities available to "ordinary people" including the unemployed. GLEB (1984) reports on the recent progress and current status of these networks.

Custance (1983) examines the arguments for and against working at home. Many companies now realise that the cost of office rents and overheads in the heart of a large city far exceeds the cost of setting up an employee or former employee at home with a personal computer, modem, and printer. Rank Xerox has pioneered a project where it has sent some of its staff and former staff back to work in their homes, using networking to keep them in touch with each other and with their offices (Kransdorff, 1982).

Yet, a recent survey of 200 senior business managers, commissioned by Philips Business Systems, showed over half of them against the idea or thinking it unlikely to happen, while only about 5% would like to work from home or thought it likely to happen (Custance, 1983). The main reason why they opposed working from home was the importance of interactions between people in the office world. With widespread electronic mail, these objections might gradually be overcome, but there is another problem—that of trying to keep work and home life separate.

In his book *The Network Revolution*, Vallee (1982) warns that mankind is in danger of being taken over by information technology. Drawing from over 20 years' experience of computing, he gives examples of management information systems and office automation projects which failed because they did not attend to human needs and weaknesses. In Vallee's view, the real problem is to decide NOW what human qualities are worth fighting for.

Salvaggio (1983) considers the social problems of "information societies." By developing models of the emerging information societies in the USA and Japan, he argues that no two information societies will be alike, as their character will depend on variables such as national ideologies, government policy-making organisations, information policies, technologies, and the market place.

Political issues, raised by the impact of computing, telecommunications, and information technology, include privacy, data protection, freedom of information, and the shadow of "1984." The quarterly journal *Information Age* discusses many of these issues.

Riley (1984) looks at some of the implications of Canada's Access to Information and Privacy Act, which became law on 1 July 1983. As a result, the days of total secrecy between business and government have come to an end in Canada; although trade secrets are protected by an exemption, most information about Canadian companies or other companies operating in Canada is available to Canadian citizens and permanent residents. Frosimi (1982) discusses computers and privacy in general.

Many British citizens have genuine fears about potential threats to liberty that could be brought about by the Data Protection Act and Police and Criminal Evidence Act; in particular, the police could acquire excessive powers to seize data, as a result (Pounder, 1984). The Data Protection Act is controversial and has received much criticism from computer experts, medical professionals, lawyers, and social workers; it is inadequate and needs closer scrutiny (Johnstone, 1984b).

Computing (1984b) reports that British Liberal Party leader, David Steel, introduced a back-bench bill on freedom of information, as an advance on the Data Protection Bill before it became the Data Protection Act. It proposed a total change of attitude from the approach of that Bill, so that all information should be open, unless specific exemptions were made. These exemptions would include: defence and security, relations with foreign governments, law enforcement and legal proceedings, commercial confidences, and individual privacy. Yet the British Conservative Government used outdated official secrets legislation as an excuse not to comment on secret computer networks that were being set up.

One hopeful sign is that concerned British citizens launched the 1984 Campaign for Freedom of Information. While aware of possible uses of information technology against human rights, they also pointed out at least one positive application for computers, their use to make public information more readily available, more quickly, with better accuracy (*Computing*, 1984c).

1984 was the year for many comments about George Orwell's vision of the nightmare of "1984," using two-way TV as a form of telecommunications technology that maintains a horrific totalitarian society. Green's (1984) article is one such commentary that appeared in the literature of information technology; although it acknowledges that there have been some notable misuses of communications technology, such as much of commercial TV and the subtle editing of some broadcast news, he considers that nothing like "1984" has actually occurred.

One reason for this is that many people are not evil. Another is that technologies never end up playing the parts that they were predicted or planned to play; this is especially true of communications technology, which has on the whole had the effect of stimulating, rather than threatening, democratic processes. In the USA, Green considers that it has played a decisive part in helping public opinion, through the widely disseminated media that it has made possible, to stop McCarthyism, end the Vietnam war, and prevent the Nixon Administration from turning the FBI, CIA, and IRS into totalitarian organisations.

NETWORK SECURITY

This section reviews recent discussions of computer security in general, and network security in particular. It then outlines some developments in cryptography and its application, and gives some examples of encryption equipment on the market. It ends by mentioning some problems of data insecurity, including computer crime.

The book by Buck (1982) presents many of the latest security concepts. It assumes that security problems must be approached by applying the same analysis and design tools that are used to develop systems. It considers that risk management techniques are imperative for informed decision making on the potential harmfulness of security risks and the potential effectiveness of security countermeasures. Its Golden State Telephone case study shows how security tools and techniques are applied in practice.

The conference proceedings *Security IFIP/SEC 1983* (Fak, 1983) covers many aspects of computer security, including: security management, data processing security, public concern about security, risk management, education, auditing, computers and the law, access control, and cryptography. It is aimed at security managers, security specialists, auditors, and trainers. Although some of its papers are excellent, others are too brief or academic according to a recent review.

The July 1983 issue of *Computer*, Vol. **16,** No. 7, is an issue on computer security technology—preventing unauthorized access.

The quarterly journal *Information Age* includes papers on security and data protection. A recent article in *Computing* describes the work of the BCS Security Committee and some of its members in these fields (British Computer Society, 1984).

Chapter 9 of the book *Computer Communications, Vol. 1, Principles* (Chou, 1983), discusses security in computer communications systems.

Sidhu (1983) presents a design approach to providing multi-level security in LANs. This design makes maximum use of well-understood security concepts, existing protocols, and readily available hardware. It relies on reliable software to enforce security in LAN interface units.

Kidd and Whitehouse (1983) point out that security control techniques have been studied much less for LANs than for WANs, even though LANs provide a much greater challenge to security, due to their expected proliferation and extensive use of shared resources. They examine the chief threats to security from LANs, based on experience of threats from WANs. They discuss the role of encryption and finally discuss some aspects of TRANSNET, a LAN being designed with special security features.

Menkus (1983) sees many shortcomings and considerable lack of responsibility in the handling of network security. He considers that there are heavy odds against secure transmissions, especially in public WANs covering long distances.

Voydock and Kent (1983) analyse the implications of adding security mechanisms to high level network protocols. They briefly discuss and compare two basic approaches to communications security: link-oriented measures and end-to-end measures. They conclude that end-to-end measures are more appropriate in an open systems environment.

There have been several advances in the application of cryptography to computer network security.

The book *Cryptography and Data Security* (Denning, 1982) presents the principles and concepts of data security and their applications to operating systems, data bases, and computer networks.

Kline et al (1983) discuss the difficulties of constructing reliable digital signatures, then present and analyse a variety of signature protocols. Cheheyl et al (1981) discuss in some detail the verification of security.

Berson and Bauer (1983) describe the end-to-end cryptosystem features of the Sytek LocalNet™ broadband LAN. Kaufman (1983) discusses TRW's approach to upgrading its LAN to include security features, using the Data Encryption Standard (DES) for cryptographic data protection.

Sanders and Varadharajan (1983) describe a security interface that uses the DES to encrypt sensitive data, by means of a 6502 microprocessor that controls encryption, decryption, and communications. It can also store encrypted programs and data files locally on Apple II floppy disks. A communications card, built on these principles, provides secure data storage for the Apple II personal computer, and secure data transmission between the Apple II and any other computer. The interface has been tested extensively, using several DES modes of operation.

Examples of new commercially available equipment for network security include Data Innovation's encryption equipment (Data Innovation, 1983a to 1983c) and Interlekt's INFOSAFE Data Scrambler (Interlekt, 1984).

The fascinating and instructive book *Computer Insecurity* (Norman, 1983) relates a history of computer crimes, frauds, and disasters, both real and imaginary. It is essentially about computer insecurity, the failures of computer systems and of methods designed to safeguard them. It provides a clear account of human errors and ingenuity. As computer fraud is said to cost British industry between £500 million and £2.5 billion a year, and doubtless costs American companies much more, it draws attention to a very serious problem.

NETWORK OWNERSHIP, PLANNING, AND REGULATION

This section is concerned with several aspects of the interfaces between users, network service providers, network product manufacturers and vendors on the one hand, and public authorities on the other. It starts by reporting on currently occurring changes in network ownership, especially those resulting from the breakup of the previous monopolies held by AT&T in the USA and British Telecom in the UK.

It then considers the future of standards and mentions some general policy issues. It finally outlines some contributions to the debate on the regulation of telecommunications.

The report *Communications in Europe—The Changing Environment* (Logica, 1983) provides a comprehensive and up-to-date factual summary of recent changes in network services, network technologies, and the rapidly evolving European political and regulatory environment for telecommunications.

Macdonald (1983) lists six major impacts of AT&T's reorganisation, including its freedom to enter the computer business, and the resulting significant changes in the design of public networks. Weber assesses the causes and effects of this restructuring, and points out some of the problems and opportunities arising as a result; he attempts to identify the most significant contemporary issues for the future of telecommunications in the USA.

Eyeions (1983) discusses the transition from a telecommunications monopoly to an open market now occuring in the UK; he states that these changes are too slow and that British Telecom's own role has aroused considerable controversy. Black (1983) talks about some advantages and disadvantages of government ownership of public packet-switched networks.

Bailey (1983) welcomes new technology and the liberalisation of the British communications market despite the opposition from certain trade unionists. He believes that it will offer users of networks and other communications services a much wider choice, and will help to increase individual freedom of choice and action as well as counter the threat of "1984."

Des Jardins (1983) projects the likely further evolution of Open Systems Interconnection and international network standards. OSI will be achieved gradually by evolution during the next decade. Computer manufacturers and network providers are planning evolutionary growth paths to OSI for their users, and OSI implementations will begin to appear in 1985. By 1990 OSI will be commonplace in North America, Europe, and Japan. Des Jardins gives full details of which international and American network standards are likely to be agreed and approved by the end of 1984.

Williams (1983) reminds us that, before we can achieve optimistic visions of a future where computers and terminals can be connected at will to any other system, we must develop a generally accepted infrastructure of teleprocessing standards. He examines what is being done in this direction, discusses some of the problems to be overcome, and assesses likely future developments.

The Director General of INTELSAT stresses the need for universal standards and compatible transmission technologies (Astrain, 1983). He views ISDN as the planning blueprint for a global information network and urges the achievement of global unity within the framework of transmission diversity.

Riley and Kennett (1983) report the agreement of the European Council of Ministers to a six-point plan drawn up by the European Commission, to combat the divergence and uncertainty of telecommunications development in the EEC (European Economic Community) and fragmentation of its market. The plan's proposals are:

1. Coordination of medium- and long-term planning;

2. Common research and development programs, especially in user interfaces, opto-electronics, and local broadband networks;

3. Agreement on interface standards;

4. Joint development of transnational communications links;

5. Development of the telecommunications infrastructures of poorer European countries;

6. Opening up the communications equipment market.

The Commission will prepare a more detailed programme along these lines. It is aware that a major political effort will be needed to achieve harmonious telecommunications and rapid progress in ISDN.

Probert (1983) discusses how expert systems can complement traditional simulation models in analysing telecommunications policies. He reports on the progress made in this direction by British Telecom policy planners.

Hann (1982) describes and analyses regulatory and technological changes in the computer and telecommunications industries. He explores some implications for the future.

Rutkowski and Marcus (1982) state some of the important business and regulatory issues associated with the development of ISDN.

Fowler (1983) presents a blueprint for regulation-free telecommunications. He explains how "unregulation" and "incrementally freeing-up selected markets" can be used to achieve this goal.

The Director General of INMARSAT outlines some new developments in the work of this international organisation for ship's telecommunications and safety at sea (Lundberg, 1983). Especially important is the Future Global Maritime Distress and Safety System (FGMDSS), which is to replace radiotelegraphy by digital selective calling, radio-telephony, and narrow-band direct printing, using land or satellite communications; its implementation is expected by 1990. Policy issues and regulatory issues will need satisfactory resolution, before INMARSAT and the maritime community can meet the full potentiality of satellite technology.

FUTURE IMPACTS AND POTENTIALITIES OF NETWORKS

This section starts with some projections for British and Japanese network systems and services during the 1980s. It then assesses the effects of World Communications Year (1983) intended especially to promote the spread of telecommunications in the developing countries. After that, an interim report is given on the emergence of London Docklands and Milton Keynes as "wired cities" in the UK. Finally, some examples are given of recently expressed views on the future impacts and potentialities of networking and information technology.

Spencer (1983) outlines current and planned future developments in the data networks, services and products pioneered by British Telecom. He reviews its medium-term and long-term plans, in the context of changes in the market and British Telecom's internal organisation. Telex services are being expanded and enhanced, and many more word processors and computers will be linked directly to it. Full internetworking between PSS, the PSTN, Telex, and Teletex, together with the opening of Satstream, are expected in 1984. The use of ISDN has already started, and it will spread during the 1980s as System X begins to predominate. The prospect of soon being able to use multi-purpose 64 kbits/sec network access for all services is very attractive, and is likely to give good economic benefits to British Telecom and its users especially of PABXs linked to the ISDN by 2 Mbits/ sec channels.

Japan is now developing a new *Information Network System (INS)*, based on digital technology, and making extensive use of optical fibre transmission and high-capacity satellite communications (Kitahara, 1983, 1984). Within about 10 years, it should also be making effective use of fifth generation "intelligent" computers for dialogue with humans. In preparation for INS, the telephone network will be digitised, and the DDX system and a fax network will be developed. All Japanese telecommunications networks and services should have been integrated into INS by 1995.

To prepare for the widespread use of INS, a *Model INS System* is undergoing a five-year trial from 1982 to 1986, mainly in the Musashino and Hitsaka areas but also with some Tokyo users; it uses integrated digital switching systems and serves 10,000 subscribers. Digital telephones, digital fax, digital graphics, and CAPTAIN videotex are being provided, and experiments will be performed on new services. INS will offer users simultaneous communication via several services. At the 1985 Science Exposition at Tsukuba Science City, 50 km North East of Tokyo, INS has been displayed and demonstrated, so that visitors from all over the world are able to look at the INS Model System and comment on it.

Kitahara foresees that INS will become an important part of the infrastructure of the information society now emerging in Japan; it will greatly influence daily life and social activities. The ultimate objective of INS is to contribute to human well-being, and it aims never to threaten it. As one of its planners, Kitahara adopts the excellent philosophy of harmonising natural science, social science, and the humanities.

Lof (1983) describes the work of *World Communications Year (WCY)*, and summarises its principles and objectives. 1983 was dedicated as World Communications Year (WCY) by a unanimous vote of the United Nations General Assembly. The basic objective of WCY was for all countries to look at their communications policies and needs in depth, and to accelerate the development of communications infrastructures. Its programme was coordinated and sponsored by the International Telecommunications Union (ITU).

WCY was a specific set of activities to increase the scope and effectiveness of communications as a force for economic, cultural, and social development. Its principles and objectives were defined by governments and adopted by resolutions of the UN General Assembly, UN Economic and Social Council (ECOSOC), and ITU. WCY emphasised the expansion and refinement of communications infrastructures as a catalyst for development and as an essential part of it. It focussed on the development of these infrastructures at the national level, to meet as rapidly and effectively as possible the communications needs of each country. It devoted special attention to the communications needs of developing countries and to promoting and speeding up the achievement of the objectives of the Transport and Communications Decade in Africa.

Governments and other interested organisations were invited to make voluntary contributions to the special fund for WCY. This money was used essentially to implement specific schemes for the development of infrastructures at national and regional levels. Various UN agencies collaborating with member countries, drew up regularly updated lists of pilot projects relating to communications infrastructures. WCY thus provided a unique opportunity for governments, nongovernmental organisations, manufacturers, and users to work together for the first time in history.

In many ways the actual performance of WCY was a disappointment. Both Lawrence (1983) and Simpson (1983) comment on the lack of publicity it received so that, in the UK at least, there was little awareness of it, and a general failure to communicate its message and its existence. Walton (1984) examines the issues raised at WCY's concluding conference "World Communications—Tomorrow's Trade Routes," which was held in London, and includes summaries of some of its important speeches. He gives examples of several initiatives, associated with WCY, which will hopefully improve world communications in the not too distant future, especially in the developing countries.

Several cities in various parts of the world are already pioneering new computer networks and information technology applications. In the UK, they include London Docklands and Milton Keynes.

London Docklands, an area only a few miles from the City of London, whose former function as a port has ceased, is now undergoing one of the most rapid redevelopments in Britain. At the same time, its application of information technology and telecommunications is proceeding very fast (London Docklands, 1984). British Telecom and Mercury are both building facilities, that are guaranteeing the most modern communications systems in the areas, and providing it with high capacity voice and data lines, both nationally and internationally. Its Enterprise Zone already has sites specifically available for telecommunications and information technology industries and users.

New networking facilities, even better than those provided in the City of London itself, include: two satellite earth stations, fibre optic rings, System X local exchanges, X-Stream private line services, and digital services with integrated voice and data terminals. These services provide high capacity potential for: residential access to unique new services, electronic mail, teleconferencing, cable systems, and new generation cellular radio mobile communications.

Milton Keynes has embarked on an ambitious programme to establish itself as the most advanced city in the UK and in Europe, for the practical application of information technology (Milton Keynes, 1983; Jones, 1984a; de Jonquieres, 1982). Its Information Technology Strategy covers a whole series of related projects, which are designed to provide the best environment for the effective exploitation of information technology. A high-powered IT Policy Advisory Group, together with a leading consultancy firm, Eosys, are advising the Milton Keynes Development Corporation on these projects. A representative IT Users Committee has been formed, to provide a channel for users' views and create a link between the IT Strategy and its application in various sectors.

The existing Milton Keynes coaxial cable system, serving all new homes in the city and operated by British Telecom, is now being upgraded for new services and applications, including interactive services. Milton Keynes now has a public access viewdata system, called "Milton sKreens". The Milton Keynes Energy Park is an urban area, South West of the city centre, where information technology and cable technology will be applied to the saving of energy through innovative energy management services.

One of the most significant aspects will be the development of efficient LANs in Milton Keynes, which plans to become the test-bed for a project to gain practical experience in developing and testing LANs and network standards. The British Department of Industry has chosen to locate its LAN protocol testing centre in the city. It will work with live applications and provide demonstrations of protocols for business applications. It will also have WAN links with other parts of the UK and with Europe.

Several expressions of individual views by leading experts on computer networks have appeared in the recent literature.

Branscomb (1983) sees the 1980s as a decade of office automation where data, text, voice, and image information will be merged into integrated electronic documents. He refers to Carnegie Mellon University, Pittsburgh, as a test-bed for prototypes for LANs and high-performance networks. He mentions some of the new network services now emerging in the USA.

Andrews (1984) considers the future of ISDNs, and predicts that optical fibres and satellites will both play important, largely complementary, parts. However, video distribution, video telephone, and other wide-band services seem unlikely to be launched before the 1990s.

Rankine (1981) reviews the socio-economic consequences of advances in information technology and communications technology. He predicts no significant limits to the future "information society," which could provide significant improvements to quality of life. He also mentions some restraining factors. He advocates a free international flow of information, with appropriate protection of privacy.

Jones (1984b) reports some views recently expressed by James Martin, who predicts an astounding rate of technological change in the next five years. Traditional methods of data processing and programming are on their way out, as they are not productive enough; the process of automation will itself need to be automated!

Cawkell (1984) reviews recent and prospective future developments in information technology and its human aspects, and coins the term "Information Sociotechnology" for this whole area. He foresees really rapid progress in a few parts of this area, and finds that other areas are developing much more slowly. His views on the future of information technology are more cautious than those of many other commentators.

For other expressions of views, see, for example, the books *Communications and the Future* (Didsbury, 1982) and *Telecommunications in the Eighties and Beyond* (Clarke, 1982), Carne's (1982) paper on new dimensions in telecommunications, and the invited addresses at ICCC 82 (*Computer Networks*, 1983).

REFERENCES

M. F. Akhtar (1983) "Evaluating a building-wide local area network," *LocalNet 83 (New York)*, 61–78.

F. T. Andrews, Jr. (Jan 1984) "ISDN '83," *IEEE Communications Magazine*, **22**(1) 6–10.

S. Astrain (Sep 1983) "INTELSAT and the digital communications revolution," *Telecommunications Policy*, **7**(3) 187–189.

S. Bailey (Dec 1983) "The computer revolution is old hat—The challenge is for the management," *Computer Communications*, 38–40.

F. Baylin and A. Toner (1983) *Satellites Today—Microwaves to Movies*, Satellites Today, Boulder, CO.

L. Bernstein (Mar 1982) "A vocabulary for computer communications problems faced in synchronous polled networks," *IEEE Communications Magazine*, **20** (2) 18–22.

T. A. Berson and R. K. Bauer (1983) "Local network cryptosystem architecture," *LocalNet 83 (New York)*, 459–471.

G. S. Bhagri (Jan 1984) "Considerations for ISDN planning and implementation," *IEEE Communications Magazine*, **22**(1) 18–32.

V. K. Bhargava (Jan 1983) "Forward error correction scheme for digital communications," *IEEE Communications Management*, **21**(1) 11–19.

P. Black (Feb 1983) "The state of affairs in worldwide packet networks," *Data Communications*, **12**(2) 97–100.

U. D. Black (1983) *Data Communications, Networks and Distributed Processing*, Reston Publishing Company, Reston, VA.

R. E. Blahut (1983) *Theory and Practice of Error Control Codes*, Addison-Wesley, London and Reading, MA.

S. Bodowski and D. Hanson (Apr 1983) "An award-winning packet-switching selection program," *Data Communications*, **12**(4) 108–116.

L. M. Branscomb (Oct 1983) "Networks for the nineties," IEEE *Communications Magazine*, **21**(7) 38–43.

K. Brayer (Aug 1983) "Routing in a 'mobile' network—Fact or fantasy?," *Data Communications*, **12**(8) 107–109.

British Computer Society (23 Feb 1984) "Society representatives: Security and protection," *Computing*, 35.

British Telecom (1984) *IDA Service Tariffs*, British Telcom, London, Leaflet PH3496 (1/84).

E. R. Buck (1982) *An Introduction to Data Security and Controls*, QED Information Services.

C. Burgess (6 Oct 1983) "US Navy boosts Planet local net," *Computer Weekly*, 8.

E. B. Carne (Jan 1982) "New dimensions in telecommunications," *IEEE Communications Magazine*, **20**(1) 17–25.

A. E. Cawkell (Mar 1984) "Progress in Information Sociotechnology: The ten-year syndrome," *Aslib Proceedings*, **36**(3) 154–162.

M. H. Cheheyl, M. Gasser, G. A. Huff and J. K. Miller (Sep 1981) "Verifying security," *ACM Computing Surveys*, **13**(3) 279–339.

V. E. Cheong and R. A. Hirschheim (1983) *Local Area Networks—Issues, Products, and Developments*, Wiley-Interscience, Chichester and New York.

N. M. Chitre (Spring 1983) "Technology trends in satellite communications," *Journal of Telecommunication Networks*, **2**(1)25–37.

Ed. W. Chou (1983) *Computer Communications, Vol. 1, Principles*, Prentice-Hall, Englewood Cliffs, NJ.

G. C. Clark, Jr. and J. B. Cain (1981) *Error Correction Coding for Digital Communications*, Plenum Press, New York and London.

J. E. Clarke (1982) *Telecommunications in the Eighties and Beyond*, Capel Cure Myers, London.

M. Coffey (4 Feb 1982) "Watching the human factor in office automation," *Computing*, 20.

R. Cole, P. Higginson, P. Lloyd and R. Moulton (Jun 1983) "International net faces problems handling mail and file transfer," *Data Communications*, **12**(6) 175–187.

Computer (Jul 1983) Vol. **16**, No. 7, issue on computer security technology—preventing unwanted access.

Computer Management (1984a) (Feb 1984) "Counting down to digital data," 20–23.

Computer Management (1984b) (Feb 1984) "Finding your way through the maze," 13–16.

Computer Networks (June 1983) Vol. **7**, No. 3, Conference Issue, "Pathways to the Information Society," Invited Addresses to ICCC 82 Conference, London, 7–10 September 1982.

Computing (1984a) (8 Mar 1984) "Report finds an excess of local net products," 3.

Computing (1984b) (15 Mar 1984) "Steel-style stand in the freedom debate," 100.

Computing (1984c) (12 Jan 1984) "Call for freedom of public data," 3.

E. B. Cooper and P. K. Edholm (Feb 1983) "Design issues in broadband local networks," *Data Communications*, **12**(2) 109–122.

K. Custance (Dec 1983) "Home: Where the heart is, but will it become the office of the future?," *Communications Management*, 28–32.

K. Custance (Jan 1984) "A tale of datacomms growth—From Swiss gnomes to US whizz-kids," *Communications Management*, 14–15.

D. Dadzie (1983) "Network management techniques," *dp International 1983*, 153–156.

Data Innovation (1983a) *Introduction to Data Innovation Encryption Equipment*, Data Innovation Ltd., Hemel Hempstead, Herts., England, Leaflet.

Data Innovation (1983b) *ED500 Data Encryption Unit*, Data Innovation Ltd., Hemel Hempstead, Herts., England, Leaflets.

Data Innovation (1983c) *Data Innovation High Speed Encryptors*, Data Innovation Ltd., Hemel Hempstead, Herts., England, Leaflet.

G. De Grandi et al (1983) "HERMES: A research project to implement advanced service on a fibre optic ring," *LocalNet 83 (New York)*, 295–305.

G. de Jonquieres (25 Jun 1982) "Milton Keynes offers itself as a test-bed for the wired of the future," *Financial Times*, 15.

D. E. Denning (1982) *Cryptography and Data Security*, Addison-Wesley, London and Reading, MA.

F. Derfler, Jr. and W. Skillings (1983) *A Manager's Guide to Local Area Networks*, Prentice-Hall, Englewood Cliffs, NJ.

R. Des Jardins (Dec 1983) "Afterword: Evolving Towards OSI," *Proceedings of the IEEE*, **71**(12) 1446–1448.

Ed. H. F. Didsbury, Jr. (1982) *Communications and the Future—Prospects, Promises, and Problems*, World Future Society, Washington, DC.

K. Ditlefsen (1983) "Facilities in the digital PABX—How to avoid opening a new Pandora's box," *Business Telecom 83*, 257–274.

A. Doswell (1983) *Office Automation*, Wiley, Chichester and New York.

T. Durham (23 Feb 1984) "Acorn speeds it up on the Cambridge circuit," *Computing*, 32.

D. Eakin (1985) "A case of mix and match," *Dec User*, 54–57.

G. Ennis (1983) "Design considerations in broadband metropolitan networks," *LocalNet 83 (New York)*, 333–345.

D. A. Eyeions (1983) "Telecommunications in transition," *dp International 1983*, 143–146.

Ed. V. A. Fak (1983) *Security IFIP/SEC 1983*, North-Holland, Amsterdam, Oxford, England, and New York, Proceedings of the First Security Conference, Stockholm, May 1983.

H. Findlow (Mar 1984) "Command control and comms in the commercial world," *Communications Management*, 56–57.

D. C. Flint (1983a) *The Data Ring Main—An Introduction to Local Area Networks*, Wiley Heyden, Chichester and New York.

D. C. Flint (1983b) "The selection of a local communications network," *LocalNet 83* (Europe), 1–12.

M. S. Fowler (Sep 1983) "Regulation-free telecommunications: A blueprint," *Journal of Telecommunication Networks*, **2**(2) 133–137.

R. B. Freeman (Sep 1983) "Control SNA nets by diagnosing problems on-line," *Data Communications*, **12**(9) 145–153.

I. T. Frisch (Spring 1983) "The evolution ot local area networks," *Journal of Telecommunication Networks*, **2**(1) 7–23.

V. Frosimi (1982) "Computers and privacy," *Endeavour*, **6**(3) 119–123.

W. O. Galitz (1980) *Human Factors in Office Automation*, QED/Life Management Associates.

R. Garner (9 Mar 1984) "Light links for Japan's future," *Financial Times*, 12.

K. Gee (Dec 1983) "Choosing a local area network," *Computer Communications*, **6**(6) 313–319.

M. Gerla and R. A. Pazos-Rangel (Feb 1984) "Bandwidth allocation and routing in ISDN's," *IEEE Communications Magazine*, **22**(2) 16–26.

GLEB (1984) *Technology Networks-Science and Technology Serving London's Needs*, Greater London Enterprise Board, London, Report.

R. J. Goldfield (May 1983) "Achieving greater white-collar productivity in the new office," *Byte*, **8**(5) 154–172.

P. E. Green (Feb 1984) "Telecommunications in 1984—What Orwell overlooked," *IEEE Communications Magazine*, **22**(2) 47–50.

W. Günsteide (Mar 1982) "Man and automation in the office," *Information Services & Use*, **1**(5) 263–270.

J. D. Hann (Winter 1982) "Telecommunications developments: Implications for the 80s," *Journal of Telecommunication Networks*, **1**(4) 307–311.

M. Hart (1983) "A migratory path towards voice and data integration," *Business Telecom 83*, 275–281.

K. Hasui, S. Hattori, M. Kato and T. Katsuyama (1983) "Handwritten message switching via an integrated PABX," *LocalNet 83 (New York)*, 19–29.

K. S. Heard (Oct 1983) "Local area networks and the practical aspects of networking," *Computer Networks*, **7**(5) 343–348.

P. Higginson and R. Cole (1983) "Issues in interconnecting local and wide area networks," *Business Telecom 83*, 231–241.

B. Hom (1983) "LAN technologies: One for every application," *LocalNet 83 (New York)*, 41–51.

J. Hooley (Oct 1983) "The PABX—The next mainframe to control distributed processing," *Communications Management*, 50–51.

J. Houldsworth (1983) "Convergence of LAN and digital telephone exchange systems," *LocalNet 83 (Europe)*, 179–194.

C. J. Hughes (May 1983) "Evolution of switched telecommunication networks," *ICL Technical Journal*, **3**(3) 313–329.

IEEE Transactions on Computing, Vol. **C-31**, No. 7 (Jul 1982) special issue on reliable and fault-tolerant computing.

D. Iliffe (16 Feb 1984) "Risks and rewards of the cable era," *Computer Weekly*, 14.

Information Age (ongoing) Butterworth Scientific, Guildford, Surrey, England, Quarterly Journal.

Information Economics and Policy (ongoing) North-Holland, Amsterdam, Oxford, England, and New York, Quarterly Journal.

Interlekt (1984) *Interlekt INFOSAFE Data Scrambler*, Interlekt Electronics Ltd., Reading, England, Leaflet.

B. Jackson (Apr 1983) "Local area networks: How to choose the right one for your organisation," *Communications Management*, 51–59.

H. Jagger (Jan 1984) "Teletex—Electronic mail's great leap forward," *Communications Management*, 32–34.

F. Jennings (13 Oct 1983) "Thinking about the network outside—Introduction to communications networks," *Computer Weekly*, 20.

B. Johnstone (1984a) (13 Mar 1984) "Slice of the action for Third World," *The Times*, 22.

B. Johnstone (1984b) (7 Feb 1984) "The Data Bill: A case for closer scrutiny," *The Times*, 19.

P. Jones (1984a) (22 Mar 1984) "Telecoms: New lengths and widths," *Computing*, 26–27.

R. Jones (1984b) (17 Jan 1984) "The next five years, by James Martin," *The Times*, 17.

L. J. Kaufman (1983) "Application of the DES Standard to the TRW local area network," *LocalNet 83 (New York)*, 473–484.

J. Kavanagh (1 Dec 1983) "GLC puts technology in reach of jobless," *Computer Weekly*, 64.

P. Kelley (1983) "Economics of the networked office," *LocalNet 83 (Europe)*, 25–38.

M. Kenyon (1983) "Management design considerations for local networks," *LocalNet 83 (Europe)*, 13–24.

P. Kidd and P. Whitehouse (1983) "Access control and user authentication on local area networks," *LocalNet 83 (Europe)*, 447–467.

Y. Kitahara (Jan 1983) "Recent developments and the future policy of telecommunications," *Japan Telecommunications Review*, **25**(1) 1–6.

Y. Kitahara (Jan 1984) "Telecommunications for the Advanced Information Society Information Network System (INS)," *Japan Telecommunications Review*, **26** (1)2–7.

C. S. Kline, G. J. Popek, G. Thiel and B. J. Walker (Spring 1983) "Digital signatures: Principles and implementation," *Journal of Telecommunication Networks*, **2**(1) 61–81.

R. D. Klineman (Apr 1983) "Users speak out: The merits of integrating voice and data," *Data Communications*, **12**(4) 189–194.

D. J. Kostas (Jan 1984) "Transition to ISDN—An overview," *IEEE Communications Magazine*, **22**(1) 11–17.

A. Kransdorff (19 Jul 1982) "Why Rank Xerox is sending executives home," *Financial Times*, 10.

G. J. Langford (1983) "Local area network user needs," *LocalNet 83 (New York)*, 31–40.

T. Larsson (1983) "Liberalisation—An alternative approach," *Business Telecom 83*, 109–117.

J. Lawrence (1984a) (1 Mar 1984) "Pull yourselves together . . . ," *Computer News*, 15.

J. Lawrence (1984b) (5 Jan 1984) "All talk—and no communication?," *Computer News*, 11.

F. A. Lefavi (Sep 1983) "Keeping transnational networks clean: The key criteria," *Data Communications*, 12(9) 161–167.

S. H. Leiden (1983) "The geographically distributed local area networks: A case study," *LocalNet 83 (New York)*, 79–89.

J. Leighfield (1983) "Some guidelines for harnessing the new opportunities," *Business Telecom 83*, 163–168.

S. Lin and D. J. Costello, Jr. (1983) *Error Control Coding: Fundamentals and Applications*, Prentice-Hall, Englewood Cliffs, NJ.

J. Locke-Wheaton (Jul 1983) "Choosing a network for in-house development," *Dec User*, 33–35.

C. M. Lof (Nov 1983) "World Communications Year," *IEEE Communications Magazine*, 21 (8) 6–9.

Logica (1981) *The Data Comms Market in Western Europe 1981–87*, Online Publications, Pinner, Middlesex, England, Report.

Logica (1983) *Communications in Europe—The Changing Enviroment*, Logica, London, Report.

London Docklands (1984) *Telecommunications and Information Technology in London Docklands*, London Docklands Development Corporation, London, Leaflet.

O. Lundberg (Sep 1983) "INMARSAT: Looking beyond the maritime community," *Telecommunications Policy*, 2 (3) 192–194.

J. C. Macdonald (May 1983) "The impact of AT&T's reorganization," *Data Communications*, 12 (5) 223–228.

I. Marchbanks (Mar 1984) "Controlling the data network—No longer an optional 'extra,'" *Communications Management*, 54.

R. D. Martin-Royle and G. H. Bennett (Jan 1983) "Optical-fibre transmission systems in the British Telecom network: An overview," *British Telecommunications Engineering*, 1 (4) 190–199.

H. A. Maurer, W. D. Rauch and I. Sebestyén (Sep 1982) "Some remarks on energy and resource consumption of new information technologies," *Information Services & Use*, 2 (2) 73–80.

B. Menkus (Mar 1983) "Long-haul data security: Whose responsibility is it today?," *Data Communications*, 12 (3) 137–144.

Milton Keynes (1983) *Milton Keynes Information Technology Strategy*, Milton Keynes Information Technology Exchange, Milton Keynes, England, Report.

D. Minoli (Feb 1983) "A new design criterion for store-and-forward networks," *Computer Networks*, 7 (1) 9–15.

E. Moura (Jul 1983) "Flow control can optimize a packet switching net's operation," *Data Communications*, 12 (7) 137–142.

T. Murakami (Oct 1982) "Present and future of mobile communication technology," *Japan Telecommunications Review*, 24 (4) 297–306.

A. Newcombe and S. Pasupathy (Aug 1982) "Error rate monitoring for digital communications," *Proceedings of the IEEE*, 70 (8) 805–828.

L. Nirenberg (Jun 1983) "How much should a satellite earth station cost?," *Data Communications*, 12 (6) 99–114.

A. Norman (1983) *Computer Insecurity*, Chapman and Hall, London.

C. Oppenheim (Nov 1981) "Technology and the information professional: Will it make a difference?," *Information Services & Use*, 1 (3) 161–167.

H. J. Otway and M. Peltu (1983) *New Office Technology—Human and Organisational Aspects*, Frances Pinter, London.

R. Perlman (Dec 1983) "Fault-tolerant broadcast of routing information," *Computer Networks*, 2 (6) 395–405.

R. L. Podell (Winter 1982) "A measure of effectiveness for telecommunications," *Journal of Telecommunication Networks*, 1 (4) 371–384.

U. W. Pooch, W. H. Greene and G. G. Moss (1982) *Telecommunications and Networking*, Little, Brown and Company, Bostom, MA and Toronto, Canada.

C. Pounder (9 Feb 1984) "New laws give police powers to seize data," *Computing*, 35.

T. L. Powers and O. P. Mahajan (Spring 1983) "Satellite and lightwave systems for domestic communication," *Journal of Telecommunication Networks*, 2 (1) 39–49.

D. Probert (Apr 1983) "Towards expert systems for telecommunications policy analysis," *Computer Communications*, **6**(2) 58–64.

QED (1982) *Multi-Vendor Data Communications Networks*, QED Information Services.

L. J. Rankine (Aug 1981) "The socio-economic consequences and limitations of the information revolution," *Information Services & Use*, **1**(2) 65–73.

T. Richards Hqeg 1983) "How the network manager keeps the data flowing," *Communications Management*, 22–24.

J. Riley and D. Kennett (6 Oct 1983) "Europe plans harmonious telecomms," *Computer Weekly*, 1.

T. Riley (9 Feb 1984) "Canada opens company files," *Computing*, 34.

E. Rivera and L. Briceño (Winter 1982) "Telematics and unemployment: A survey of an ongoing debate," *Journal of Telecommunication Networks*, **1**(4) 341–347.

R. D. Rosner (1982) *Packet Switching*, Lifetime Learning Publications, Belmont, CA.

A. M. Rutkowski and M. J. Marcus (Jul/Oct 1982) "The Integrated Services Digital Network: Developments and Regulatory Issues," *Computer Communications Review*, **12**(3/4) 68–82.

J. H. Saltzer, K. T. Pogran and D. D. Clark (Aug 1983) "Why a ring?," *Computer Networks*, **7**(4) 223–231.

J. L. Salvaggio (Sep 1983) "Social problems of information societies—The US and Japanese experience," *Telecommunications Policy*, **7**(3) 228–242.

H. Salwen (1983) "Reliability in local area networks," *LocalNet 83 (New York)*, 435–442.

P. W. Sanders and V. Varadharajan (Oct 1983) "Secure communications between microcomputer systems," *Computer Communications*, **6**(5) 245–252.

Ed. R. Sarch (1983) *Data Network Design Strategies*, McGraw Hill, New York and Maidenhead, England.

S. A. Sazegari (May 1983) "Metropolitan networking: Theory and practice," *Data Communications*, **12**(5) 99–113.

P. R. D. Scott (1983) *Reviewing Your Data Transmission Network*, NCC Publications, Manchester, England.

J. Seidler (1983) *Principles of Computer Communication Network Design*, Ellis Horwood, Chichester, England, and Halsted-Wiley, New York.

A. D. Shackman (Apr 1983) "Are satellites in the stars for Europe?," *Data Communications*, **12**(4) 158–163.

D. P. Sidhu (1983) "Multilevel security and local area networks," *LocalNet 83 (New York)*, 443–458.

A. Simpson (Sep 1983) "World Comms Year—Is anybody listening?," *Communications Management*, 28.

G. Spencer (1983) "Inland data services from British Telecom," *Business Telecom 83*, 169–176.

B. W. Stuck (1983a) (Jan 1983) "Which local net bus access is most sensitive to traffic congestion?," *Data Communications*, **12**(1) 107–120.

B. W. Stuck (1983b) "Analyzing congestion in local area networks: IEEE Computer Society Project 802 Local Area Network Standards, *LocalNet 83 (New York)*, 499–512.

J. Taylor (Aug 1982) "Office communications: Reshaping our society?," *Computer Communications*, **5**(4) 176–180.

J. Vallee (1982) *The Network Revolution: Confessions of a Computer Scientist*, And or Press, Berkeley, CA, and (1983) Prism Press, Dorchester, Dorset, England.

V. L. Voydock and S. T. Kent (Jun 1983) "Security mechanisms in high-level network protocols," *ACM Computing Surveys*, **15**(2) 135–171.

G. Walker (Nov/Dec 1983) "Networks make the most of business computers," *Mind Your Own Business*, **6**(10) 74–75.

J. H. Weber (Spring 1983) "AT&T Restructure—1982–1984—Its causes and effects," *Journal of Telecommunication Networks*, **2**(1) 51–59.

Which Computer? (Mar 1984) "Putting you through," 57–68.

P. Whitehouse (Apr 1983) "Know your journey before setting out," *Computer Management*, 32–34.

J. M. Wiley (1983a) (Mar 1983) "Barriers to integrating voice and data," *Data Communications*, **12**(3) 109–113.

J. M. Wiley (1983b) (Mar 1983) "Making DDP and centralized nets compatible," *Data Communications*, **12**(3) 201–210.

D. Williams (1983) "The road to open systems," *dp International 1983*, 147–150.

R. Woolnough (21 Feb 1984) "Data communications the new growth area," *The Times*, 25.

The Yankee Group (1984) *The Report on European Communications*, The Yankee Group, Watford, Herts., England, Report.

Epilogue—The Peace Network

"Computers form networks when they are connected via cables or telephone lines. People form networks when they are connected by sharing the same values and beliefs which are the basis for their relationships. When people who share the same beliefs unite for a common purpose, the process of achieving it becomes more joyful and satisfactory for everybody participating, since a sense of community and togetherness is experienced.... Personal computers are available to many children and adults in industrialised countries. By adding global communication, we are proposing to use them in ways which add value to their applications as well as to the life of their owners and users."

In these words, the small team, which prepared plans for the Peace Network, opened its statement of the essence of its concept for local information processing, combined with global communication. If this initiative succeeds, as it surely deserves to, then indeed a Global Network of Linked Local Area Networks will spread across the world and eventually span the planet, working constructively in the service of mankind.

Sabine Kurjo, the enterprising founder of Peace Network, was born in Silesia, and later worked at CERN near Geneva, to provide a number of user services in its large scientific computer centre. In May 1977, she founded VISION HUMANISTE, a Centre for the Development of Human Potential which had its offices next to the United Nations in Geneva since 1979. She organised four international conferences on humanistic psychology and consciousness, and eventually had a large mailing list, which required the purchase of an Apple II computer.

Late in 1981, she came to London because Bernard Benson, author of *The Peace Book*, needed an assistant with knowledge of word processing. The musical show "Peace Child" was based on his book, and performed at the Royal Albert Hall in London; I watched it and was deeply moved by it. After Bernard Benson had money for a computer donated and received an offer of office space, Sabine Kurjo had an ALTOS-10 computer and an office, with which to design the Peace Network, whose concepts she already had in her mind.

The Peace Network project works with volunteers only. It aims to inform locally and communicate globally. It is felt that local information flow needs to be increased among like-minded people, who live in a society that causes separation and alienation, especially in large cities. Peace Network will attempt to promote the maximum number of contacts and connections locally, between networkers, groups, centres, and events.

It also aims to increase the flow of information between peace-minded and humanitarian "planetary citizens," using global communication, based on personal computers, that will transcend national and geographical barriers. Peace Network will offer services to individuals, groups, organisations, networks, and computer owners. The information that it will handle will cover every subject under the sun!

Individuals will receive an information and referral service by post and telephone. They will be able to subscribe to *The PEACEMIND Bulletin*, providing news from the Peace Network, and to the initial edition and updates of *The Whole Peace Catalogue*. They will be linked to other peaceminded people, especially in their own locality.

Groups, organisations, and networks will be able to announce their events in *The PEACEMIND Bulletin* and have entries in *The Whole Peace Catalogue*. They will be able to obtain advice on how to computerise their own operations, and be put in touch with sympathetic computer owners nearby.

Computer owners will be able to access networks of computers of different types, for: the exchange of electronic mail, conferencing, bulletin board systems, and so on. They will be able to read from and write to a shared data base, containing a directory of resources, mailing lists, and diaries of events. They will be able to meet like-minded groups and organisations in their area.

Since the first edition of this book was published, Peace Network "connecting people and computers to build a more peaceful world" has started operations by using the British public viewdata service Prestel. It can be reached via Prestel page 810272, and provides information under the headings: About Ourselves, Our Activities, Sharing Our Information, Poems & Pictures, Our Contacts, Your Answers to the Peace Question, and About Peace & Computers. You can send messages to it via Prestel Mailbox 017340200.

It is also participating in the "World Peace Network" on EIES, the Electronic Information Exchange System, developed at the New Jersey Institute of Technology, and mentioned in Chapters 14 and 16. Its EIES account number is 620.

The Greater London Council (GLC) is offering its Room 97 for regular use. It is already full of personal computers and Prestel terminals used by GLC. Twice a month, it is the meeting place of Peace Network and associated projects, in particular NetReach, which aims to network computer networks and reach out to people by computers.

Besides using Prestel and the EIES computer network, Peace Network has extensive contacts and collaboration with other social networks like the National Association for the Care and Resettlement of Offenders. Peace Network has also introduced the American Bulletin Board System CommuniTree into the UK, as well as the most recent international computer conferencing system, The META Network, based in Arlington, Virginia. Sabine Kurjo recently said that its members could help local people to use computers to communicate their personal needs. She added that local computers, linked to a global network, would enrich everyone's life, and open up many opportunities for ordinary people.

Peace Network could play a crucial part in transforming human awareness and consciousness towards the positive, creative and constructive frame of mind that will be needed to bring mankind out of its present crisis and conflicts, into its next evolutionary advance towards human fulfilment in a world at peace.

It is vital that Peace Network should succeed, and obtain the support that it so urgently needs for this purpose. It is vital that it should become able to contribute fully to *the healing of mankind* and *the healing of the planet*. IT NEEDS YOUR HELP.

Supplementary Bibliography

The bibliography has three lists. The first list includes several earlier articles and papers on computer networking and allied information technologies, including some discussions of their economic, social and human impacts. It also gives a sample of some recent news items, reports, and comments. The second list gives an extensive selection of additional items, most of them very recent. The third list gives relevant recent books published by Wiley, which are not otherwise mentioned in this book. Those books which are published jointly by Wiley and by the National Computing Centre, Manchester, England, are indicated by "Wiley and NCC". Any chapter(s) to which a reference is specially relevant is (are) listed between brackets after the reference.

First List

ACM Computing Surveys, Vol. **11,** No. 4 (Dec 1979) special issue: cryptology. (Ch 16, Ch 24).

Advisory Council for Applied Reseach and Development (1980) *Information Technology*, HMSO, London.

S. Baker (10 May 1984) "Bell blasts the standards mess," *Computer Weekly*, 33. (Ch 9, Ch 21).

C. Berman (8 Dec 1983) "Midnet strikes for future of bank communications," *Computing*, 24–25. (Ch 11, Ch 22, Ch 23).

R. Bernhard (Sep 1982) "The quandary of office automation," *IEEE Spectrum*, **19**(9) 34–39. (Ch 2, Ch 9, Ch 22).

R. Blom et al (1978) "Encryption methods in data networks," *Ericsson Technics*, **34**(2) 71–105. (Ch 16, Ch 24).

M. Bramer (Nov 1983) "Towards an electronic communications network for education," *Computer Education*, **45,** 25–27. (Ch 14, Ch 22, Ch 23).

Camtec (1983) *Camtec JNT-PAD—Joining Networks Together*, Camtec Electronics Ltd., Leicester, England, Brochure. (Ch 19, Ch 20).

E. B. Carne (Jan 1982) "New dimensions in telecommunications," *IEEE Communications Magazine*, **20**(1) 17–25. (Ch 18, Ch 24).

Ed. G. Carter (1984) *Local Area Networks*, Heinemann Computers in Education and International Computers Limited, London. (Ch 2, Ch 19).

D. Casey (3 May 1984) "Swift network takes off," *Computer Weekly*, 22. (Ch 11, Ch 22, Ch 23).

The CGCT Group (1984) *Private Multiservice Networks: The Integrated Solution*, CGCT, Paris, France, and LCT, Velizy-Villacoublay, France, Brochure. (Ch 19).

G. Charlish (30 Sep 1982) " 'Electronic city' to be networking test bed—Local nets to get state cash," *Financial Times*, 25. (Ch 18, Ch 24).

G. Charlish (11 Sep 1984) "Microfilm fights for a future," *Financial Times*, 12. (Ch 7, Ch 20) (Description of Kodak Image Management System, which includes a LAN).

G. Charlish (3 Oct 1984) "Electronic funds transfer—Who pays for the next stage in cashless shopping?," *Financial Times*, 14. (Ch 11, Ch 22).

G. Charlish (5 Oct 1984) "Value added information—Tailored information for business communications," *Financial Times*, 14. (Ch 11, Ch 22).

D. N. Chorafas (1984) *Designing and Implementing Local Area Networks*, McGraw-Hill, New York.

Communications International (Feb 1982) Focus supplement: data networks, **9**(2) 28–47.

Communications International, Vol. **9**, No. 4 (Apr 1982) USA special report.

Communications Management (Oct 1984) Feature on fibre optics, 47–52. (Ch 8, Ch 20).

Computer Networks (Oct 1983) "PTC '83 Pacific Telecommunications Council" (Conference Report), **7**(5) 359–368.

Computer Networks (Dec 1983) "System Sciences" (Conference Report), **7**(6) 418–423.

Computing (4 Feb 1982) "Highlighting trends in office automation," 18–19 (User survey). (Ch 11, Ch 22).

Computing (12 Jan 1984) Communications supplement.

Computing (31 May 1984) Office automation supplement. (Ch 11, Ch 22).

Ed. I. N. Dallas and E. B. Spratt (1984) *Ring Technology Local Area Networks*, North-Holland, Amsterdam, Oxford, England, and New York.

Data Communications (Dec 1981) Special issue: local networks, Vol. **10**, No. 12. (Ch 2, Ch 19).

Datec (1984) Folder of miscellaneous leaflets on networking, Debenhams Applied Technology Ltd., Taunton, Somerset, England. (Ch 19, Ch 20).

M. Decina (Sep 1982) "Managing ISDN through international standards activities," *IEEE Communications Magazine*, **20**(5) 19–25. (Ch 6, Ch 9, Ch 21).

P. Edwards (21 Jun 1984) "Feeling the way through the mixed maze of telecoms," *Computing*, 40.

H. A. Elion and V. N. Morozov, 1984, *Optoelectronic Switching Systems in Telecommunications and Computers*, Dekker, New York, and Basel, Switzerland.

L. Else (6 Oct 1983) "Life in an electronic village," *Computing*, 23. (Ch 17, Ch 18, Ch 24).

D. Farber and P. Baran (1977) "The convergence of computing and telecommunication systems," *Science*, **195**(4283), 1166–1170.

Financial Times (14 Jul 1982) "US major research to define future of LANs," 10. (Ch 2, Ch 19).

Financial Times (24 and 25 Oct 1983) World telecommunications supplement, Parts 1 and 2.

Financial Times (28 Mar 1984) Electronics in Europe supplement.

Financial Times (16 Apr 1984) The desk top revolution supplement. (Ch 11, Ch 22).

Financial Times (22 Oct 1984) Computers in banking supplement. (Ch 11, Ch 22).

Focom (1984) *Dart System—Fibre Optic Data Communication Network*, Focom Systems Ltd., Leeds, England, Brochure. (Ch 2, Ch 19).

W. R. Franta and J. R. Heath (May 1984) "Hyperchannel local network interconnection through satellite links," *Computer*, **17**(5) 30–39. (Ch 2, Ch 8, Ch 19, Ch 20).

The Futurist (Jun 1984) "Networking; A Global Communications Tool," Special feature on networking, **18**(3) 9–23. (Ch 16, Ch 17, Ch 18, Ch 24).

Ed. F. J. Galland (1982) *Dictionary of Computing—Data Communications, Hardware and Software Basics, Digital Electronics*, Wiley, Chichester, England.

R. Garner (16 Jul 1984) "Toshiba puts networks under foot," *Financial Times*, 14. (Ch 2, ch 21).

A. Goldberger (May 1981) "A designer's review of data communications," *Computer Design*, **20**(5) 103–112.

J. Gowar (1984) *Optical Communication Systems*, Prentice-Hall, Englewood Cliffs, NJ, especially Ch. 16 "Unguided Optical Communication Systems" and Ch. 17 "Optical Fiber Communication Systems."

Gower (1984) *A Planning Guide to Office Automation*, Gower Publishing Company, Aldershot, Hampshire, England. (Ch 11, Ch 22).

A. Hargrave (22 Dec 1980) "Focus on communications technology," *Time*, **116**(25) EB1, EB3, EB5, EB7, EB9, EB11.

Ed. D. A. Hickman (Autumn 1983) *Initial Report of the Distributed Database Working Group of the British Computer Society*, British Computer Society, London. (Ch 13, Ch 22).

C. Hines and G. Searle (1979) *Automatic Unemployment*, Earth Resources Research, London. (Ch 16, Ch 18, Ch 24).

L. J. Hoffman (1977) *Modern Methods for Computer Security and Privacy*, Prentice-Hall, Englewood Cliffs, NJ. (Ch 16, Ch 24).

Ed. L. J. Hoffman (1980) *Computers and Privacy in the Next Decade*, Academic Press, New York and London. (Ch 16, Ch 24).

K. Holder (11 Oct 1984) "IBM is set to win a last ditch battle," *Computer Weekly*, 31. (Ch 9, Ch 21, discusses prospects of SNA as a network standard).

Presented by J. Howlett (Oct 1978) *Report of the National Committee on Computer Networks*, Department of Industry. (Ch 16, Ch 24).

T. Huggins (13 Oct 1983) "ISO puts the ball in suppliers' court," *Computing*, 16. (Ch 9, Ch 21).

T. Huggins (3 Nov 1983) "ISO goes into high gear on open systems," *Computing*, 17. (Ch 9, Ch 21).

Infinet (1983) *Intertel Transmission Control Products-9600 bps Network Control Modem*, Infinet, Inc., Andover, MA, Brochure. (Ch 20).

Infinet (1984) *Infant Network Command Center*, Infinet, Inc., Andover, MA, Leaflet. (Ch 20).

M. R. Irwin and S. C. Johnson (1977) "The information economy and public policy," *Science*, **195**(4283) 1170–1174. (Ch 16, Ch 18, Ch 24).

L. Jennings (Apr 1979) "The human side of tomorrow's communications," *The Futurist*, **12**(3) 104–109. (Ch 18, Ch 24).

H. P. Josephine (Oct 1980) "Electronic mail: The future is now," *Online*, **4**(4) 41–43. (Ch 11, Ch 22).

H. Katzan, Jr. (1979) *Distributed Information Systems*, Petrocelli, New York and Princeton, NJ. (Ch 13, Ch 22).

R. Joyce (Oct 1984) "An all-embracing network?," *Computer Systems*, 85–87.

L. G. Kazovsky (1978) *Transmission of Information in the Optical Waveband*, Wiley, New York and Chichester. (Ch 8, Ch 20).

L. Kehoe (9 Oct 1984) "Brave faces after the software 'quake," *Financial Times*, 14. (Ch 3, Ch 19, includes a table of personal computer networks available now).

J. Kelly (1982) "The demonopolisation of British Telecom," *dp International 1982*, 177–180. (Ch 16, Ch 24).

Y. Kitahara (Jan 1980) "New telecommunications in the information society," *Japan Telecommunications Review*, **22**(1) 3–12. (Ch 16, Ch 18, Ch 24).

L. Kleinrock (Spring 1981) "Packet switching principles," *Journal of Telecommunication Networks*, **2**(1) 1–5.

Ed. A. R. Kmetz and F. K. Von Willisen (1975) *Nonemissive Electrooptic Displays*, Plenum Press. (Ch 7, Ch 20).

J. Kraus (Sep 1982) "Implications of FCC regulation of telecommunications technical standards," *IEEE Communications Magazine*, **20**(5) 28–32. (Ch 9, Ch 16, Ch 21, Ch 24).

R. K. Kwan (Nov 1980) "Electronic message services into the 80's," *IEEE Communications Magazine*, **18**(6) 25–29. (Ch 11, Ch 18, Ch 22, Ch 24).

C. E. Landwehr (Sep 1981) "Formal models for computer security," ACM *Computing Surveys*, **13**(3) 247–278. (Ch 16, Ch 24).

G. Langley (1983) *Telecommunications Primer*, Pitman, London.

A. Lawrence, "IBM widens its net to trap small users," *Computing*, 26. (Ch 9, Ch 21).

J. D. Lenk (1984) *Handbook of Data Communications*, Prentice-Hall, Englewood Cliffs, NJ.

Library Micromation News (Oct 1984) "Online searching with an Apple II micro as a local area network," **6**, 5–8. (Ch 3, Ch 12, Ch 19, Ch 22).

"The Listeners" (1977) "Information technology for the home," *The Information Scientist*, **11**(4) 146–148. (Ch 16, Ch 24).

R. Malik (Jul 1981) "Is the information society different?," *Communications International*, **8**(7) 16, 21. (Ch 16, Ch 24).

P. Manchester (Jun 1984) "Conflict of interests," *Computer Management*, 24–25. (Ch 9, Ch 21) (about network standards).

J. P. Martino (Apr 1979) "Telecommunications in the Year 2000," *The Futurist*, **12**(3) 95–103. (Ch 18, Ch 24).

A. J. Meadows, M. Gordon, and A. Singleton (1984, 2nd. ed.) *Dictionary of Computing and New Information Technology*, Kogan Page, London, and Nichols Publishing Company, New York.

N. D. Meyer (Jun 1980) "Computer-based message systems: A taxonomy," *Telecommunications Policy*, **4**(2) 128–133. (Ch 9, Ch 16, Ch 16, Ch 21, Ch 22, Ch 24).

R. H. Miller and J. F. Vallee (Jun 1980) "Towards a formal representation of EMS," *Telecommunications Policy*, **4**(2) 79–95. (Ch 9, Ch 16, Ch 21, Ch 24).

R. T. Moore, N. F. Gear and H. A. Graf (Apr 1984) "Gridnet: An alternative large distributed network," *Computer*, **17**(4) 57–66. (Ch 2, Ch 3, Ch 21).

J. Newman and S. Harvey (10 May 1984) "The many perils of the post," *Computing*, 41. (Ch 11, Ch 22) (Discusses legal aspects of electronic mail for contracts).

R. R. Panko (Sep 1977) "The outlook for computer mail," *Telecommunications Policy*, **1**(3) 242–253. (Ch 11, Ch 22).

J. N. Pelton (1981) *Global Talk*, Sijthoof and Noordhoff, The Netherlands.

Plessey (1984a) *Plessey IDX—Integrated Digital Exchange*, Plessey Communication Systems Ltd., Beeston, Nottingham, England, Publication No. 8096.

Plessey (1984b) *Plessey Office Automation Systems—IWS.III Workstations*, Plessey Communication Systems Ltd., Beeston, Nottingham, England, Publication No. 8101.

Post Office Engineering Union (Jun 1979) *The Modernisation of Telecommunications*, Report. (Ch 16, Ch 24).

J. A. T. Pritchard (Jun 1984) "Local area networking at NCC—Two years' experience," *Computer Education*, **47**, 14–18. (Ch 2, Ch 21, Ch 23).

R. Ranoulin and C. Fruchard (1984) "Private multiservice networks Carthage and LCT 6500," *Commutation & Transmission*, **1**, 49–60. (Ch 19).

P. Rigg (Apr 1980) "The new networks—Now and in the near future," *Program*, **14**(2) 62–68. (Ch 5, Ch 20).

A. L. Robinson (1977) "Impact of electronics on employment; Productivity and displacement effects," *Science*, **195**(4283) 1179–1184. (Ch 16, Ch 24).

J. Roland (Apr 1979) "The Microelectronic Revolution: How intelligence on a chip will change our lives," *The Futurist*, **13**(2) 81–90. (Ch 16, Ch 18, Ch 24).

J. M. Rosenberg (1984) *Dictionary of Computers, Data Processing & Telecommunications*, Wiley, New York.

M. G. Rowlands (Apr 1983) "Local area networks," *British Telecommunications Engineering*, **2**(1) 6–11. (Ch 2, Ch 19).

Ed. T. A. Rullo (1980) *Advances in Computer Security Management*, Heyden, Philadelphia and London. (Ch 16, Ch 24).

James D. Schaeffler (Feb 1984) "Distributed computer systems for industrial process control," *Computer*, **17**(2) 11–18. (Ch 13, Ch 22).

W. W. Simmons (Apr 1979) "The consensor: A new tool for decision makers," *The Futurist*, **13**(2) 91–94. (Ch 16, Ch 18, Ch 24).

H. A. Simon (1977) "What computers mean for man and society," *Science*, **195**(4283) 1186–1191. (Ch 16, Ch 24).

A. V. Stokes (1984) *Concise Encyclopaedia of Information Technology*, Gower Publishing Company, Aldershot, Hampshire, England.

Strategic Inc. (1982) *Impact of Personal Computer Local Area Networks*, Report. (Ch 2, Ch 3, Ch 11, Ch 16, Ch 19, Ch 24).

F. Taylor (4 Feb 1982) "The systems interconnection standard nears compleion," *Computer Weekly*, 15. (Ch 9, Ch 21).

The Times, Guide to Information Technology (14 Jan 1982).

The Times (21 Oct 1983) Telecommunications special report.

The Times (25 Oct 1984) Office technology special report. (Ch 11, Ch 22).

A. Toffler (1981) *The Third Wave*, Bantam Books, USA. (Ch 16, Ch 18, Ch 24).

A. Tomberg (July 1981) "Key future developments: The role of telecommunications in information retrieval," *Monitor*, **5**, 4–6. (Ch 12, Ch 18, Ch 22, Ch 24).

L. Uhr (1984) *Algorithm-Structured Computer Arrays and Networks*, Academic Press, New York and London. (Ch 13, Ch 22).

D. Von Sanden (Jun 1980) "A public global telecommunication network for voice, text, picture and data transmission," *Telecommunication Journal*, **47**(6) 211–216. (Ch 5, Ch 19).

H. Voysey (6 Oct 1983) "Airing a hybrid of solutions for nets," *Computing*, 24. (Ch 5, Ch 19).

Walmore Communicator (1984) Walmore Electronics Ltd., London. (Ch 8, Ch 19, Ch 20).

Walmore Electronics (1984) *FIBRECOM—Communication in a Flash of Light*, Walmore Electronics Ltd., London, Brochure. (Ch 8, Ch 20).

P. Walton (3 May 1984) "A design for picking up IPA's pieces," *Computing*, 7. (Ch 9, Ch 21).

T. Watanabe (Dec 1980) "Visual communication technology—Priorities for the 1980s," *Telecommunications Policy*, **4**(4), 287–294. (Ch 5, Ch 7, Ch 18, Ch 19, Ch 22, Ch 24).

M. Watson (11 Oct 1984) "Why standards should offer users freedom of choice," *Computer Weekly*, 30. (Ch 9, Ch 21).

E. Williams (27 Jan 1982) "Satellite safety system for ships that pass in the night," *Financial Times*, 12. (Ch 8, Ch 14, Ch 20).

M. B. Williams (Apr 1983) "The Sixth International Conference on Computer Communication: A review, Part 1—the plenary sessions, *British Telecommunications Engineering*, **2**(1) 38–42.

M. B. Williams (Jan 1984) "The Sixth International Conference on Computer Communication: A review, Part 2—The specialist sessions," *British Telecommunications Engineering*, **2**(4) 267–274.

Xtec (1984) *The Problem Solvers—Xtec Serving Your Immediate and Future Data Communications Needs*, Xtec Ltd., Basingstoke, Hampshire, England, Leaflet. (Ch 20).

C. Youett (Oct 1984) "Money down the line," *Communications Management*, 40–44. (Ch 11, Ch 22, about electronic funds transfer).

(1984) *The Principles of Data Communications Series*. Vol. 1, *Basic Concepts of Data Communications*. Vol. 2, *Communications Networks*. Vol. 3, *Techniques in Data Communication*. Vol. 4, *Structure in Data Communications*. Heinemann Computers in Education, London, in conjunction with International Computers Limited, London.

Second List

A. S. Acampora, M. G. Hluchyj and C. D. Tsao (Summer 1984) "A centralized bus architecture for local area networks," *Journal of Telecommunications Networks*, **3** (2) 89–102. (Ch 2, Ch 19).

AES (undated) *AES 7300—Distributed Office Systems—The Real World of Office Automation*, AES Data (UK) Ltd., Sunbury on Thames, Middlesex, England, Brochure. (Ch 11, Ch 22).

Ed. S. R. Ames, Jr. and P. G. Neuman (Jul 1983) *Computer*, **16**(7) Special issue on computer security technology.

T. K. Apostolopoulos and E. N. Protonotarios (Feb 1985) "Queueing analysis of buffered slotted multiple access protocols," *Computer Communications*, **18**(1) 9–21. (Ch 9, Ch 10, Ch 20, Ch 21, mathematical paper).

P. L. Arst and W. Ilie (Mar 1985) "Hybrid satellite networks for distributed data applications," *Data Communications*, **14**(3) 181–188. (Ch 8, Ch 13, Ch 20, Ch 22).

Ed. P. Balaban, K. S. Shanmugan and B. W. Stuck (Jan 1984) *IEEE Journal on Selected Areas of Communication*, **SAC-2**(1) Special issue on computer-aided modeling, analysis, and design of communication system. (Ch 10, Ch 20, mathematical papers).

G. A. Baley (Mar 1985) "One big headache: Incompatible operating systems and file transfer," *Data Communications*, **14**(3) 115–119. (Ch 22).

D. Barlin (Apr 1985) "Buying satellite success is like opening Pandora's bewildering box," *Data Communications*, **14**(4) 165–174. (Ch 8, Ch 17, Ch 20, Ch 24).

J. Bartik (Aug 1984) "IBM's token ring: Have the pieces finally come together?," *Data Commmunications*, **13**(8) 125–139. (Ch 2, Ch 19).

B. Bhusan (Apr 1984) "An architectural solution for voice and data integration," *Data Communications*, **13**(4) 195–203. (Ch 6, Ch 20).

E. J. Blausten (Apr 1984) "Inside ITT's beefed-up design for global packet networking," *Data Communications*, **13**(4) 219–228. (Ch 4, Ch 5, Ch 9, Ch 20, Ch 21).

W. E. Bracker (May 1984) "Sampling the host of new third-party async packages," *Data Communications*, **13**(5) 195–206. (Ch 3, Ch 19).

Ed. S. Brand, B. Robertson and M. McClure (1984) *Whole Earth Software Catalog*, Whole Earth Software Catalog & Review, Sausalito, CA. (Ch 3, Ch 8, Ch 19, Ch 20; the chapter on telecommunicating is especially relevant).

Ed. K. Brayer (Nov 1984) *IEEE Communications Magazine*, **22**(11) Special issue on progress in computer communications. (Ch 10, Ch 20; topics include routing and network performance).

R. D. Bressler and L. T. Piazza (Sep 1984) "When is the private packet net an organization's best solution," *Data Communications*, **13**(9) 215–220. (Ch 17, Ch 24).

British Telecom (1985a) *IDA—Integrated Data Access*, Brochure (new edition). (Ch 5, Ch 19).

British Telecom (1985b) *IDA—A Description of British Telecom's Integrated Services Digital Network*, Brochure. (Ch 5, Ch 19).

British Telecom (1985c) *IDA—IDA Pilot Service Availability*, Leaflet. (Ch 5, Ch 19).

British Telecom (1985d) *IDA—IDA Pilot Service Tariffs*, Leaflet. (Ch 5, Ch 15, Ch 19).

British Telecom International (1985a) *International KiloStream*, Leaflet. (Ch 5, Ch 19).

British Telecom International (1985b) *Satstream*, Leaflet. (Ch 5, Ch 8, Ch 19, Ch 20).

British Telecom Merlin (1984a) *Merlin Data Comms*, Brochure. (Ch 8, Ch 20).

British Telecom Merlin (1984b) *Merlin Tonto—Personal Information Centre*, Leaflet. (Ch 7, Ch 11, Ch 20, Ch 22).

British Telecom Merlin (1985a) *Merlin Datelmux 5100 Range—Statistical Multiplexers*, Leaflet. (Ch 8, Ch 20).

British Telecom Merlin (1985b) *Merlin Datelnet 500—Simultaneous Speech and Data Transmission over Existing PABX Wiring*, Leaflet. (Ch 6, Ch 20).

British Telecom Merlin (1985c) *Merlin Monarch IT440—Voice-Data-Text Communications System,* Brochure. (Ch 6, Ch 7, Ch 11, Ch 20, Ch 22).

British Telecom National Networks (1985) *NetMux Gateway—SNA/X25 Protocol Converter,* Leaflet. (Ch 6, Ch 9, Ch 20, Ch 21).

E. G. Brohm (Jul 1984) "Sampling new technologies of network processors," *Data Communications,* **13**(7) 143–147. (Ch 8, Ch 20).

T. Brooks (Apr 1985) "New technologies and their implications for local area networks," *Computer Communications,* **8**(2) 82–87. (Ch 2, Ch 8, Ch 14, Ch 19, Ch 20, Ch 22).

Business Equipment Digest (Apr 1985) Communications issue. (Ch 7, Ch 8, Ch 20; topics include fax and Telex).

CASE (ongoing) *CASE Direct Sale,* Computer And Systems Engineering plc, Catalogue. (Ch 8, Ch 20).

CASE (1985a) *Data Communications Exhibition Preview—A Guide to New CASE Products,* Computer And Systems Engineering plc, Leaflet. (Ch 8, Ch 20).

CASE (1985b) *Executive 440—Intelligent Error Correcting Modem,* Computer And Systems Engineering plc, Leaflet. (Ch 8, Ch 20).

Case Rixon (1985) *Data Communications Standards Handbook,* Case Rixon Communications, Inc., Silver Spring, MD, Publication 5001. (Ch 9, Ch 21).

D. Casey (Oct 1984) "Keeping a firm's sites in touch," *Management Review Supplement to Computer Weekly,* 36–37. (Ch 13, Ch 22, Ch 23; two case studies of distributed processing).

G. E. Clark and M. K. Wong (Apr 1985) "Verifying conformance to the *X.25* standard," *Data Communications,* **14**(4) 153–161. (Ch 9, Ch 21).

R. T. Clark (Mar 1984) "Electronic funds transfer—The creeping revolution," *Telecommunications Policy,* **8**(1) 29–43. (Ch 11, Ch 22, Ch 24).

Communications International (Sep 1984) **11**(9) 51–86, Special report on PABXs. (Ch 6, Ch 20).

Communications International (Nov 1984) Special report on local area networks, **11**(11) 19–33. (Ch 8, Ch 19).

Communications International (Jan 1985) Special report on modems and multiplexers, **12**(1) 51–56. (Ch 8, Ch 20).

Communications Management (Feb 1985) "PABXs: Making the right choice," 37–46. (Ch 6, Ch 17, Ch 20, Ch 24).

Communications Management (Apr 1985) "Local area networks: Linking the office," 54–65. (Ch 2, Ch 3, Ch 11, Ch 19, Ch 22).

Computer Communication Review, (Jun 1984) *SIGCOMM '84 Tutorials & Symposium. Communication Architectures & Protocols (6-8 Jun 1984, Montreal).* **14**(2). (Ch 9, Ch 21).

Computer Networks (Feb 1984) Special issue on programming languages and open systems interconnection, **8**(1). (Ch 9, Ch 21).

Computer Networks (Aug 1984) Special issue: Selected papers from 1983 Computer Networking Symposium (13 Dec 1983, Silver Spring, MD), **8**(4). (Ch 9, Ch 10, Ch 19, Ch 20).

Computer Weekly (4 Oct 1984) Feature on computers in publishing, 22–30. (Ch 14, Ch 22).

Computer Weekly (10 Jan 1985) Feature on the automated office, 22–30. (Ch 11, Ch 22).

Computing The Magazine (4 Oct 1984) Feature on office automation, 5–14. (Ch 11, Ch 22).

I. Cunningham (May 1984) "Electronic mail standards to get rubber-stamped and go worldwide," *Data Communications,* **13**(5) 159–168. (Ch 9, Ch 11, Ch 21, Ch 22).

Data Communications (1985) *The Executive Guide to Data Communications,* Data Communications, Brooklyn, NY.

Data Communications (Jan 1985) "Data communications glossary," **14**(1) 97–128. (Glossary).

Data Communications (Feb 1985) "User survey exclusive—Terminals hold their own in a rapidly changing market," **14**(2) 97–111. (Ch 7, Ch 20).

Data Communication Extra (Mid-May 1984) "New Product breakthroughs—Update '84". (Ch 20, Ch 21).

Datapro (ongoing) *Reports on Data Communications (International), Reports on Telecommunications, Management of Data Communications, Management of Telecommunications, Directory of Online Services,* Datapro Services sa, CH-1164, Buchillon, Switzerland.

Datec (1985) *Communications—London,* Debenhams Applied Technology Ltd., Taunton, Somerset, England, Folder of Leaflets. (Ch 4, Ch 5, Ch 8, Ch 19, Ch 20, Ch 23).

M. De Brycker (Apr 1985) "LANs in an ISDN: Consistency with the OSI reference model," *Computer Communications,* **8**(2) 74–78 (Apr 1985). (Ch 2, Ch 9, Ch 17, Ch 19, Ch 21, Ch 24).

Ed. G. Deaton (Fall 1984) *Journal of Telecommunication Networks,* **3**(3) Special issue on protocols and standards. (Ch 9, Ch 17, Ch 21, Ch 24).

G. Deaton (Dec 1984) "Multi-access computer nets: Some design decisions," *Data Communications,* **13**(12) 123–136 (Dec 1984). (Ch 9, Ch 17, Ch 21, Ch 24).

DEC (undated) *Towards the Electronic Office—A Guide to Office Systems,* Digital Equipment Corporation, Maynard, MA, Brochure. (Ch 11, Ch 22).

Ed. C. R. Dhas (Mar 1985) *IEEE Communications Magazine,* **23**(3) Special issue on telecommunications protocols. (Ch 9, Ch 21).

R. C. Dixon, N. C. Strole and J. D. Markov (Summer 1984) "A token-ring network for local data communications," *Journal of Telecommunication Networks,* **3**(2) 69–88. (Ch 2, Ch 19).

DTI (1985) *Office Automation Pilot Projects,* Department of Trade and Industry, London, Series of Leaflets. (Ch 11, Ch 22).

R. M. Dudley (Oct 1984) "Evaluating integrated voice/data terminals," *Data Communications,* **13**(10) 118–131. (Ch 7, Ch 20).

S. T. Dufala (Apr 1984) "Microwave nets beam data past crowded routes," *Data Communications,* **13**(4) 211–217. (Ch 8, Ch 20).

S. J. Durham (Apr 1985) "Callback modems mean security and savings," *Data Communications,* **14**(4) 215–219. (Ch 8, Ch 20).

M. Ejiri and T. Endo (Jan 1984) "Facsimile communication in a digital network," *Japan Telecommunications Review,* **26**(1) 19–27. (Ch 7, Ch 20).

G. Evans (Apr 1985) "The U.S. Navy sets new standard for word processing," *Data Communications,* **14**(4) 135–148. (Ch 9, Ch 21, Ch 22).

B. Fadini, A. Marcelli and A. Mazzeo (Apr 1985) "Approach to the performance evaluation and tuning of communication protocol implementation," *Computer Communications,* **8**(2) 59–63. (Ch 9, Ch 21).

FCR (1983) *A Digital Link Service for the 1980s,* France Cables et Radio, Paris, Brochure. (Ch 8, Ch 11, Ch 20, Ch 22).

FCR (undated) *Telecom 1—A Satellite for Digital Business Communications,* France Cables et Radio, Paris, Brochure. (Ch 8, Ch 11, Ch 20, Ch 22).

D. Fidlow (Apr 1985) "A comprehensive approach to network security," *Data Communications,* **14**(4) 195–213. (Ch 17, Ch 24).

R. B. Fish (Dec 1984) "Considerations for picking a corporate backbone network," *Data Communications,* **13**(12) 151–162. (Ch 17, Ch 24).

J. S. Foley (Feb 1985) "The status and direction of open systems interconnection," *Data Communications,* **14**(2) 171–193. (Ch 9, Ch 21).

B. J. Ford (Jan 1985) "Governing by computer," *Communications International,* **12**(1) 24. (Ch 23, Belgian Government's computer communications system).

R. Frankel (Aug 1984) "Tailoring a CSMA local network to research needs," *Data Communications,* **13**(8) 145–154. (Ch 2, Ch 19, Ch 23).

GEC (1984) *GEC 4100 Series Computer Systems—X.25 Packet Switching,* GEC Computer Ltd., Borehamwood, Herts., England. (Ch 9, Ch 21).

J. Geesink (Feb 1985) "Enter babushka—Solve one problem and another emerges," *Management Review Supplement to Computer Weekly,* **16, 18**; reprinted from *Europa,* DEC's management report. (Ch 11, Ch 17, Ch 19, Ch 24, problems of office automation).

V. D. Gligor, G. L. Luckenbaugh (Jan 1984) "Interconnecting heterogeneous data base management systems," *Computer,* **17**(1) 33–43. (Ch 12, Ch 22).

C. Goodwin (10 Jan 1985) "Finding a distributed answer," *Computing The Magazine,* 6–8. (Ch 12, Ch 22, distributed data base).

J. S. Grant (Feb 1985) "Multilink—An open network for personal computers," *Computer Communications,* **8**(1) 27–34. (Ch 3, Ch 19; the "Multilink" described here is *not* the American product of that name).

M. Graube and M. C. Mulder (Oct 1984) "Local area networks," *Computer,* **17**(10) 242–247. (Ch 2, Ch 9, Ch 19, Ch 21).

J. Green-Armytage (25 Oct 1984) "Burroughs listens to its users on the connection question," *Computer Weekly,* 22–23. (Ch 9, Ch 21).

R. M. Groenke and M. Cohen (Dec 1984) "A potpourri of pros and cons on the long haul technologies," *Data Communications,* **13**(12) 113–118. (Ch 17, Ch 24).

A. Gupta (Sep 1984) "Satellite communications; Forward to the brave new world," *IEEE Communications Magazine,* **22**(9) 8–14. (Ch 15, Ch 24).

L. Hart (Sep 1984) "For network managers, finding faults is no easy task," *Data Communications,* **13**(9) 189–192. (Ch 17, Ch 24).

H. M. Heggestad (Apr 1984) "An overview of packet-switching communications," *IEEE Communications Magazine,* **22**(4) 24–31. (Ch 10, Ch 20; partly mathematical paper).

G. Held (Jun 1984) "Expanding the uses of data compression," *Data Communications,* **13**(6) 149–156. (Ch 8, Ch 20).

G. Held (Jul 1984) "Standards would reduce cost of async micro communications," *Data Communications,* **13**(7) 161–168. (Ch 9, Ch 21).

T. Highly (Mar 1985) "Strategies to link mainframes and microcomputers," *Data Communications,* **14**(3) 165–174. (Ch 3, Ch 19).

S. Holmes and M. Fleming (Jun 1984) "Combining the best of SNA and *X.*25 architectures," *Data Communications,* **13**(6) 117–125. (Ch 9, Ch 21; AT&T's XNA (Extended Network Architecture)).

G. J. Holtzman (Apr 1984) "The Pandora System: An interactive system for the design of data communication protocols," *Computer Networks,* **8**(2) 71–79. (Ch 9, Ch 21).

W. N. Hsieh and I. Gitman (May 1984) "How good is your network routing protocol?," *Data Communications,* **13**(5) 231–248. (Ch 9, Ch 10, Ch 21).

W. N. Hsieh and I. Gitman (Jun 1984) "How to prevent congestion in computer networks," *Data Communications,* **13**(6) 209–219. (Ch 10, Ch 17, Ch 20, Ch 24, partly mathematical paper).

W. N. Hsieh and I. Gitman (Jun 1984) "Routing strategies in computer networks," *Computer,* **17**(6) 46–56. (Ch 10, Ch 20).

R. Hunt (Dec 1984) "*X.*25 protocols in the airline industry," *Computer Communications,* **7**(6) 283–288. (Ch 9, Ch 13, Ch 21, Ch 22, Ch 23).

M. Hurst (Sep 1984) "Sharing data between microcomputers on a local host," *Data Communications,* **13**(9) 139–148. (Ch 3, Ch 19).

ICL (1984) *ICL DNX 2000—More Than Just a Telephone System,* International Computer Ltd., London, Brochure. (Ch 6, Ch 20).

M. Ilyas and H. T. Mouffah (Apr 1985) "Performance evaluation of computer networks," *IEEE Communications Magazine,* **23**(4) 18–29. (Ch 10, Ch 20).

Incaa (1983) *The Compatibility Box,* Incaa BV, Apeldoorn, The Netherlands, Leaflet. (Ch 13, Ch 22).

Infa Communications (1985) *INFAPLUG Local Area Networks,* Infa Communications Ltd., Taunton, Somerset, England, Leaflets. (Ch 2, Ch 19).

International Networks (ongoing) Manson, MA, Newsletter on world telecommunications technology and policy.

ITAP (Sep 1983) *Making a Business of Information—A Survey of New Opportunities*, A Report by the Information Technology Advisory Panel, HMSO, London. (Ch 18, Ch 24).

D. Jacobs (Apr 1984) "Breaking the urban data bottlenecks with a private lightwave bypass," *Data Communications*, **13**(4) 119–127. (Ch 8, Ch 20, Ch 23).

Y. Jayachandra (Dec 1984) "Integrating data, voice, and image transmission on a single network," *Data Communications*, **13**(12) 167–178. (Ch 9, Ch 21).

J. T. Johnson (Feb 1985) "Universal flow and capacity index gives picture of network efficiency," *Data Communications*, **14**(2) 171–173. (Ch 10, Ch 20).

S. Joshi and V. Iyer (Jul 1984) "New standards for local networks push upper limits to lightwave data," *Data Communications*, **13**(7) 127–138. (Ch 8, Ch 9, Ch 20, Ch 21).

G. Kasperec (May 1984) "Data analysers are sniffing out network snags," *Data Communications*, **13**(5) 177–186. (Ch 10, Ch 20).

G. Kasperec (1984) *Trouble-shooting the Data Communications Network*, Carnegie Press, Madison, NJ (Ch 10, Ch 17, Ch 20, Ch 24).

D. F. Kerstetter (Sep 1984) "How the State is establishing and all-inclusive net," *Data Communications*, **13**(9) 157–164. (Ch 15, Ch 23, network used by the Commonwealth of Pennsylvania).

N. G. Khabbuz (Sep 1984) "Banks can cut their costs by adding other services to EFT networks," *Data Communications*, **13**(9) 107–114. (Ch 11, Ch 22).

W. Kim (Mar 1984) "Highly available systems for database applications," *ACM Computing Surveys*, **16**(1) 71–98. (Ch 12, Ch 22).

J. F. Kurose, M. Schwartz and Y. Yemini (Mar 1984) "Multiple-access protocols and time-constrained communication," *ACM Computing Surveys*, **16**(1) 43–70. (Ch 9, Ch 21).

T. L. Lenox and R. A. Dean (Jun 1984) "Improve problem management step by step," *Data Communications*, **13**(6) 187–200. (Ch 17, Ch 24).

D. P. Levin (Mar 1985) "Comparing local communications alternatives," *Data Communications*, **14**(3) 243–256. (Ch 2, Ch 19).

Logica (1984) *Clearing House Automated Payments Systems*, Logica UK Ltd., London, Leaflet. (Ch 11, Ch 22).

E. Lucier (Jul 1984) "Putting a Price on File Transfer," *Data Communications*, **13**(7) 177–187. (Ch 3, Ch 19).

K. McDonald (Apr 1985) "A university learns to link computing worlds the hard way," *Data Communications*, **14**(4) 177–184. (Ch 23).

S. L. McGarry (Feb 1985) "Networking has a job to do in the factory," *Data Communications*, **14**(2) 119–128. (Ch 14, Ch 22).

T. Manefield (Aug 1984) "How vendors decide what users need and want," *Data Communications*, **13**(8) 193–201. (Ch 15, Ch 24).

R. Marciniak (Jun 1984) "A message network built to knit the far-flung summer Olympics," *Data Communications*, **13**(6) 177–179. (Ch 23).

D. Matusow (Oct 1984) "Bridging the gap between SNA and other networks," *Data Communications*, **13**(10) 139–144. (Ch 9, Ch 21).

B. Meek (1 Nov 1984) "ISO reshuffles its committee cards," *Computer Weekly*, 28. (Ch 9, Ch 21).

E. E. Mier and J. Bush (Aug 1984) "Rating the long-distance carriers," *Data Communications*, **13**(8) 103–114. (Ch 10, Ch 20).

D. Meucke (May 1984) "Lessons learned in building an international packet network," *Data Communications*, **13**(5) 257–260. (Ch 23).

G. Neri et al. (Apr 1984) "MININET: A local area network for real-time instrumentation applications," *Computer Networks*, **8**(2) 107–131. (Ch 2, Ch 9, Ch 19, Ch 21).

A. Nielsen (Sep 1984) "Danish company links up its army of unlike devices," *Data Communications,* **13**(9) 229–239. (Ch 22, Ch 23).

H. Nobukumi (Oct 1984) "Trends of electronic banking," *Japan Telecommunications Review,* **26**(4) 216–222. (Ch 11, Ch 22).

One-to-One (undated) *One-to-One—Communications for the Computer Age,* One-to-One, London, Brochure and Leaflets. (Ch 11, Ch 22, electronic mail).

L. Orr (Feb 1985) "Gateways to SNA offer mulitivendor network solutions," *Data Communications,* **14**(2) 153–160. (Ch 9, Ch 21).

J. L. Parker (Sep 1984) "Third generation codecs pave way for future digital networks, *Data Communications,* **13**(9) 173–182. (Ch 8, Ch 20).

Ed. F. N. Parr (May 1985) *IEEE Journal on Selected Areas in Communications,* **SAC-3** (3) Issue on communications for personal computers. (Ch 3, Ch 19).

M. W. Patrick (Mar 1985) "The heat is on for phone switches that do a lot of fast shuffling," *Data Communications,* **14**(3) 227–236. (Ch 2, Ch 6, Ch 11, Ch 19, Ch 20, Ch 22, PABXs and LANs in the office).

J. Patterson (25 Apr 1985) "Teletex: What's in it for the user?," *Computer News,* 36–37.

W. Pearson (18 Sep 1984) "VDUs: The crucial questions still to be answered," *Computer News,* 10–11. (Ch 16, Ch 24).

J. S. Petty (Feb 1985) "How to pick your modem: Doing it right means not going by the book," *Data Communications,* **14**(2) 135–146. (Ch 8, Ch 20).

W. G. Phila, D. L. Green and L. J. Cole (May 1984) "Private network integrates data, voice, and video communications," *Data Communications,* **13**(5) 125–135. (Ch 23).

D. Phillips (Mar 1985) "Picking the right strategy for protocol conversion," *Data Communications,* **14**(3) 193–202. (Ch 9, Ch 21, Ch 22).

Ed. R. A. Pickens and D. J. Marsh (Spring 1984) *Journal of Telecommunication Networks,* Special issue on ISDN, **3**(1). (Ch 6, Ch 20).

Ed. R. Pokress (Jan 1984) *IEEE Communications Magazine,* Special issue on integrated services digital networks, **22**(1). (Ch 6, Ch 20).

A. B. Raderman and R. W. Flakes (Mar 1985) "Video and voice communications join Ethernet on a broadband cable," *Data Communications,* **14**(3) 293–303. (Ch 2, Ch 9, Ch 19, Ch 21).

M. Raghupati, K. Ramkumar and M. Satyam (Feb 1985) "Priority-oriented reservation multiple access scheme for data communication through satellites," *Computer Communications,* **8**(1) 22–26. (Ch 9, Ch 10, Ch 20, Ch 21; mathematical paper).

B. Rich (Apr 1985) "Communications and the personal computer," *Computer Communications,* **8**(2) 64–73. (Ch 3, Ch 19, Ch 24; reviews current trends).

T. Richards (2 May 1985) "The spreading net persuades users to concentrate on the future," *Computer News,* 32–33. (Ch 10, Ch 17, Ch 20, Ch 24, problem of effective control and management of mixed networks).

J. P. Roarty and L. A. Marquart (Jan 1985) "Innovations pave the way for growth: A large bank goes distributed," *Data Communications,* **14**(1) 149–157. (Ch 11, Ch 22, Ch 23).

E. S. Rothchild (Oct 1984) "Optical memory: Data storage by laser—Erasable medium may soon be available," *Byte,* **9**(11) 215–224. (Ch 7, Ch 20).

P. Rubenstein and G. Smith (Oct 1984) "The async route—Best suited for a microcomputer's local traffic," *Data Communications,* **13**(10) 177–185. (Ch 3, Ch 9, Ch 19, Ch 21).

Ed. H. Rudin and F. Ricci (Jul 1984) *IEEE Communications Magazine,* **22**(7) Special issue on some users' views of telecommunications needs. (Ch 16, Ch 17, Ch 18, Ch 24).

Ed. J. S. Ryan (Jan 1985) *IEEE Communications Magazine,* **23**(1) Special issue on telecommunications standards. (Ch 9, Ch 21).

W. Sapronov (Jul 1984) "Gateways link long-haul and local networks," *Data Communications,* **13**(7) 111–122. (Ch 9, Ch 21).

W. Sapronov (Jan 1985) "Network users cannot overlook the legal issues," *Data Communications*, **14**(1) 161–166. (Ch 16, Ch 24).

M. D. Sayer (1984) *RS-232 Made Easy (Connecting Computers, Printers, Terminals, and Modems*, Prentice-Hall, Englewood Cliffs, NJ. (Ch 3, Ch 7, Ch 8, Ch 19, Ch 20; useful practical guide).

S. M. Schatz (Jun 1984) "Communication mechanisms for programming distributed systems," *Computer*, **17**(6) 21–28. (Ch 13, Ch 22).

Ed. M. Schwartz (May 1984) *IEEE Communication Magazine*, **22**(5) Special issue on 100 years of communication progress.

Scicon (1984a) *System 34/36/38 ASCII Interface 350/525 Protocol Converter*, Scicon Ltd., Milton Keynes, England, Leaflet. (Ch 11, Ch 20, Ch 21).

Scicon (1984b) *IBM-SNA/SDLC ASCII Interface 350/SNA Protocol Converter*, Scicon Ltd., Milton Keynes, England, Leaflet. (Ch 11, Ch 20, Ch 21).

Scicon (undated) *Draw Your Own Conclusions—Simultaneous Voice and Data Communications over Existing Internal Telephone Lines*, Scicon Ltd., Milton Keynes, England, Leaflet. (Ch 8, Ch 20).

G. Segal, I. Sobkowski and W. De Lorenzo (Oct 1984) "Beyond async—When micros aid in the long haul," *Data Communications*, **13**(10) 191–200. (Ch 9, Ch 13, Ch 19, Ch 22).

S. Serpell (Feb 1985) "Networking secure electronic funds transfer at point of sale," *Computer Communications*, **8**(1) 3–8. (Ch 11, Ch 22).

A. R. Severson (Apr 1984) "AT&T's proposed PBX-to-computer interface standard," *Data Communications*, **13**(4) 157–162. (Ch 6, Ch 9, Ch 20, Ch 21).

A. Simpson (31 Jan 1985) "Electronic mail gets its message across," *Computer News*, 24–25. (Ch 11, Ch 15, Ch 22, Ch 24).

L. B. Sklar (Jun 1984) "Efficiency factors in data communications," *IEEE Communications Magazine*, **22**(6) 33–36. (Ch 10, Ch 20).

W. Stallings (Mar 1984) "Local networks," *ACM Computing Surveys*, **16**(1) 3–41. (Ch 2, Ch 19; with bibliography).

M. Stieglitz (Sep 1984) "Network security: How to get it and keep its costs within reach," *Data Communications*, **13**(9) 245–249. (Ch 16, Ch 24).

A. V. Stokes (Nov 1984) "Commercially available local area networks," *Communicate*, **4**(10) 24. (Ch 2, Ch 3, Ch 19).

A. V. Stokes (Mar 1985) "Further commercially available LANs," *Communicate*, **5**(3) 22. (Ch 2, Ch 3, Ch 19.

B. Struif (Dec 1984) "Transparent LANs and LANs as OSI subnetworks," *Computer Communication*, **7**(6) 296–300. (Ch 2, Ch 9, Ch 19, Ch 20).

Ed. B. W. Stuck and F. A. Tobagi (Nov 1983) *IEEE Journal on Selected Areas of Communications*, SAC-1 (6) Special issue on local area networks. (Ch 2, Ch 19).

H. Sturridge (11 Apr 1985) "Voice meets data: But nothing yet meets needs," *Computer News*, 36–37. (Ch 11, Ch 22).

R. H. Swanson (Jul 1984) "Primer: Satellite communications for managers," *Data Communications*, **13**(7) 151–157. (Ch 8, Ch 17, Ch 20, Ch 24).

K. Taniguchi and S. Ueda (Apr 1984) "New Japanese text communication service—TELETEX in Japan," *Japan Telecommunications Review*, **26**(2) 112–118. (Ch 5, Ch 7, Ch 19, Ch 20).

S. A. Taylor and R. S. Painter (Mar 1985) "Intercampus network chucks point-to-point arrangement," *Data Communications*, **14**(3) 263–271. (Ch 23).

Tekelec (undated) *Tekelec Telecommunications Test Equipment*, Tekelec Ltd., Southend-on-Sea, Essex, England, Brochure. (Ch 10, Ch 20).

Telecommunications Press (1985) *Telecommunications Equipment & Services Directory 1985*, Telecommunications Press, London. (Ch 2 to Ch 8, Ch 10, Ch 19, Ch 20; it also contains much useful information extending the information in both directories of this book).

TeleLink (ongoing) Database Publications Ltd., Stockport, Cheshire, England. (Ch 3, Ch 11, Ch 12,

Ch 14, Ch 19, Ch 22; new periodical covering videotex, personal computer communications, telesoftware, electronic mail, bulletin boards, teleshopping, etc.).

P. Thornton (Apr 1984) "Integrated office networks are on the way—But so are the problems," *Data Communications,* **13**(4) 171–187. (Ch 11, Ch 17, Ch 22, Ch 24).

Ed. C. D. Tsao and F. Ricci (Aug 1984) *IEEE Communications Magazine,* **22**(8) Special issue on architectures of local area networks. (Ch 2, Ch 9, Ch 19, Ch 21).

Ed. S. W. Watkins (Winter 1983) *Journal of Telecommunication Networks,* **2**(4) Special issue on office automation. (Ch 11, Ch 22).

R. W. Webster (Feb 1985) "Building a microcomputer local network," *Data Communications,* **14**(2) 195–203. (Ch 3, Ch 19).

Ed. S. B. Weinstein (May 1984) *IEEE Journal on Selected Areas of Communications,* SAC-2 (3) Special section on communications in the financial industry. (Ch 11, Ch 22).

A. J. Weissberger (Aug 1984) "What's new about IBM's cluster controllers and coax muxes?," *Data Communications,* **13**(8) 161–171. (Ch 6, Ch 20).

T. A. Welch (Jun 1984) "A technique for high-performance data compression," *Computer,* **17**(6) 8–19. (Ch 8, Ch 20).

G. Wheelwright (Apr 1985) "Micro-mainframe links," *Communications International,* **12**(4) 19, 21. (Ch 3, Ch 19).

B. W. Wisser (Mar 1985) "Streamlining communications with network packet switching," *Data Communications,* **14**(3) 309–322. (Ch 4, Ch 19).

B. W. Wuh (Jan 1984) "File placement in distributed computer systems," *Computer,* **17**(1) 23–32. (Ch 13, Ch 22).

S. Yalamanchili, M. Malek and J. K. Aggarwal (Nov 1984) "Workstations in a local area network environment," *Computer,* **17**(11) 74–86. (Ch 2, Ch 7, Ch 19, Ch 20),

P. Yates (Apr 1985) "Factory monitoring the control network," *Computer Communications,* **8**(2) 79–81. (Ch 14, Ch 22, Ch 23).

L. P. Yu (Mar 1985) "The anatomy of a distributed electronic mail network," *Data Communications,* **14**(3) 153–158. (Ch 3, Ch 11, Ch 19, Ch 22).

Ed. P. Zorkoczy (1985) *Oxford Surveys in Information Technology,* vol. 1, Oxford University Press, Oxford, England.

Third List

E. V. Bagshaw (1985) *Networking with Micros,* Wiley and NCC. (Ch 3, Ch 19).

G. B. Bleazard (1982) *Telecommunications in Transition,* Wiley and NCC. (Ch 16, Ch 17, Ch 18, Ch 24).

G. B. Bleazard (1983) *Evaluating Data Transmission Services,* Wiley and NCC. (Ch 5, Ch 19).

Ed. A. Burns (1984) New Information Technology, Ellis Horwood, Chichester, England, and Halsted Press division of Wiley.

D. W. Davies and W. L. Price (1983) *Security for Computer Networks: An Introduction to Data Security in Teleprocessing and Electronic Funds Transfer,* Wiley. (Ch 11, Ch 16, Ch 22, Ch 24).

R. Deasington (1985) *X.25 Explained,* Ellis Horwood, Chichester, England, and Halsted Press division of Wiley.

Ed. P. S. Fisher, J. Slonim and E. A. Unger (1984) *Advances in Distributed Processing Management, Vol. 2,* Wiley. (Ch 10, Ch 13, Ch 20, Ch 22).

P. Hardy (1984) *Digital Private Circuits for Telecommunications,* Wiley and NCC. (Ch 5, Ch 19).

G. Held (1983) *Data Compression: Techniques and Applications: Hardware and Software Considerations,* Wiley. (Ch 8, Ch 20).

J. E. Lane (1983) *Review of British Telecom Services,* Wiley and NCC. (Ch 5, Ch 19).

J. E. Lane (1984) *Corporate Communications Networks,* Wiley and NCC. (Ch 11, Ch 22; with bibliography).

B. E. McMullen and J. F. McMullen (1984) *Micro Computer Communications: A Window on the World,* Wiley. (Ch 3, Ch 12, Ch 19, Ch 22).

P. S. Marcham (1984) *Data Transmission Via PABXs,* Wiley and NCC. (Ch 6, Ch 8, Ch 20).

C. H. Meyer and S. M. Matyas (1982) *Cryptography: A New Dimension in Data Security,* Wiley. (Ch 16, Ch 24).

National Computing Centre (1982) *Handbook of Data Communications* (second edition), Wiley and NCC. (Ch 6, Ch 8, Ch 9, Ch 17, Ch 20, Ch 21, Ch 22; includes glossary and bibliography).

National Computing Centre (1984) *Introducing Computerised Telephone Switchboards,* Wiley and NCC. (Ch 6, Ch 20).

W. E. Perry (1985) *The Micro Mainframe Link,* Wiley.

Ed. J. Slonim, P. S. Fisher and E. A. Unger (1984) *Advances in Data Communications Management, Vol. 2,* Wiley. (Ch 9, Ch 10, Ch 11, Ch 12, Ch 15, Ch 16, Ch 17, Ch 20, Ch 21, Ch 22).

Further relevant books, some very recent, are listed in Wiley's 1985 catalogue: *New and established books from Wiley on Office Automation.*

Glossary

This glossary gives, in alphabetical order, definitions of some of the most important terms and interpretations of commonly used abbreviations arising in connection with computer networks. Although many of these terms are defined elsewhere in the book, where they arise, this glossary allows quick direct reference to their definitions.

Names of specific network systems, services and products are usually excluded from this glossary, but references to their definitions or specifications are given in the Name Index.

Terms relating to allied technologies are mostly omitted, but several of them are introduced elsewhere in the book, especially in Chapters 7 and 8; reference to them can be found via the Subject Index.

Access path   A sequence of functions that allows users and devices of a network to be physically interconnected and to communicate with each other, despite their different characteristics.

Ack   Abbreviation for "Acknowledgment."

Acknowledgment   A control signal confirming safe receipt of a data block.

Acoustic coupler   A modem-like attachment to a telephone, generating and interpreting patterns of sound pulses, that allows a device to communicate via the PSTN.

Adaptive routing   A routing scheme for packets or messages, which adapts to changes in the network and network traffic.

Address   A representation in character(s) of the origin or destination of a packet or message.

Alphabet   An agreed set of characters to represent data.

Analogue   Representing signals, data or information in a transmission medium or device or store in a continuous form.

Anisochronous data channel   A communication channel able to transmit data but not timing information.

Application Layer   Layer or level of application protocols.

Application protocol   Protocol handling data and information for user applications. It handles the communications aspects of a wide range of applications, covering the needs of a variety of users at different sites.

Architecture The "architecture" of a computer network precisely defines the functions of the network and its parts, together with the ways in which the network should be organised. In particular, it specifies the levels of different functions in the network, ranging from data transmission at the lowest levels to user applications at the highest levels.

The Arpanet One of the first large-scale packet-switched networks, which has pioneered many techniques of networking, and links universities and defence establishments on both sides of the Atlantic.

ARQ Abbreviation for "Automatic Repeat Request."

ASCII A character code that is widely used by terminals, computer peripherals and computers.

Asynchronous data channel Alternative term for "anisochronous data channel."

Asynchronous terminal Terminal using start-stop data transmission.

Authentication Technique for ensuring that a received message is known to come from a particular sender, without tampering.

Automated office (Electronic office) An office that at least substantially applies the principles of office automation.

Automatic Repeat Request A technique, used in error control, that requires the receiver to request the retransmission of an incorrectly received message.

Availability The proportion of scheduled operating time, during which a service is ready and working reliably.

Bandwidth of a channel The difference between the highest and lowest frequencies that can be used on the channel. It measures, in Hertz (Hz), the information-carrying capacity of the channel.

Baud The number of data-significant times which a signal may change per second; it is not necessarily the same as bits/sec.

Bibliographic data base A data base that contains information about references to documents, abstracts of documents, and sometimes also contains texts or text extracts of at least some of these documents.

Bit The representation of a single yes-no (binary) choice in a data stream or transmission.

Bits/sec Bits per second, a measure of the data transmission rate of a channel.

Braided ring A form of ring network, where alternative, nonrepeated, links are added, to provide standby for links and nodes that are temporarily not available.

Broadcast network A computer network where each station transmits simultaneously to all other stations in the network; these stations then accept only those received messages that are addressed to them.

Buffer A store in a peripheral device or internal node that temporarily contains packets or messages waiting for the next stage of their journey across the network or into their destination.

Burst A continuous piece of voice or of a data message or of a system command, used in burst switching. It consists of a header, followed by variable length information, followed by an end-of-message byte.

Burst-switched network A switched network using the principle of burst switching.

Burst switching A method of switching, recently developed for use in integrated voice-data networks, where voice and data are divided into bursts, which are typically longer than packets but shorter than messages. Data bursts and voice bursts are treated differently, with the emphasis on reliable transmission of data bursts and rapid transmission of voice bursts.

Bus network A local area network, where the devices are attached to nodes on a single line of cable, or sometimes to a "tree" of such lines.

Byte The representation of a character in a data stream or transmission (usually eight bits).

Cambridge Ring A widely used form of ring network, whose design is based on that of the ring network developed at Cambridge University.

Carrier Sense Multiple Access (CSMA) A class of protocols used to access broadcast networks. It uses the principle of requiring each station to "listen" to the broadcast medium, and not transmit a packet unless it detects no other packet transmissions. Its most important examples are CSMA/CA and CSMA/CD (see separate definitions below).

Carrier Sense Multiple Access with Collision Avoidance (CSMA/CA) A variant of CSMA which avoids "collision" between competing packets from different devices or stations, by sensing the carrier twice before allowing a packet to be transmitted.

Carrier Sense Multiple Access with Collision Detection (CSMA/CD) A variant of CSMA, which applies a special procedure to retransmit packets from different devices or stations that "collide" during the first attempt to transmit them, because they were sent nearly simultaneously. For its operation, it depends on the almost instantaneous detection of a "collision" when it occurs.

CCITT (International Telegraph and Telephone Consultative Committee) An international standards body of PTTs, which decides on standards for telecommunications and computer networks.

Channel A communications path, connecting a transmitter to a receiver.

Channel capacity Maximum data rate that can theoretically be maintained by a communications channel.

Character A single upper or lower case letter or digit or special symbol.

Circuit A physical connection used for communication or telecommunication.

Circuit-switched network A switched network using the principle of circuit switching.

Circuit switching A method of switching, where communication between two users is along a circuit, established for this purpose, for the duration of a call.

Closed User Group (CUG) A group of network users whose members can only receive calls from each other. Usually, they can only make calls to each other, but, in a "closed user group with outgoing access," they may make calls to nonmembers.

Clustered ring A network whose configuration is a star of rings.

Codec Device for conversion between continuous analogue signals and digital bit streams.

Common carrier In North America especially, a company that is licensed by the appropriate government authority to provide basic telecommunications facilities.

Communication net A LAN, whose components are used to interface pieces of equipment to the network's communication mechanisms, so that user devices can exchange information with each other.

Communication network A network using telecommunication to link its users at different locations. For example, a telephone network or data network or computer network.

Communicating word processor A word processor having links with other word processors or devices, often via a computer network.

Compatibility The ability of different parts of a system to work effectively with each other. For example, the ability of different devices to communicate effectively with each other inside a network, and the ability of different networks to use the same or similar protocols when communicating and working with each other.

Computer-communication network Alternative name for "computer network."

Computer network A computing system that uses telecommunications to link together physically separated computers, input/output terminals, and other information-processing devices.

Concentrator A device, with local storage, that multiplexes several inputs on to one output, and vice versa. For example, a node in a packet-switched network.

Configuration Specification of the hardware of a computer network or computer system, in terms of the geometrical arrangement of its components and their interconnections.

Congestion Condition of a network, where the traffic is so heavy that it can no longer handle all of it properly; as a result, the quality of service falls, and the network must restrict incoming traffic to remain effective.

Connection-mode data transmission A mode of data transmission, that involves the establishment and maintenance of a connection, which represents a dynamically negotiated agreement about the transfer of a series of related data units.

Connectionless-mode data transmission A mode of transmission, that allows comparable entities to communicate unrelated data units between each other, without establishing a connection, but relying only on the prior knowledge that these entities have about each other.

Contention Competition between parts of a system for use of a shared resource.

Control signal Signal within a network that is part of its control system.

Cryptography A technique of concealing the content of a message by means of a secret transformation, which only the intended recipient(s) should be able to decode.

CSMA Abbreviation for "Carrier Sense Multiple Access."

CSMA/CA Abbreviation for "Carrier Sense Multiple Access with Collision Avoidance."

CSMA/CD Abbreviation for "Carrier Sense Multiple Access with Collision Detection."

Data Information formally represented, usually in digital form, for processing, storage or transmission. "Information" usually means the significance or meaning that data have for people.

Data base A collection of interrelated data, that are maintained for operational use and that are independent of specific applications and can be used for many of these applications. This collection includes data about things and also about relations between these things. Data bases can range from loose collections of information about a given subject or group of subjects, to very well structured and carefully specified sets of records about the different facets of an organisation's operations.

Data Link Layer Layer or level of Data Link protocols. It specifies how to transfer data along network links, and how to detect and possibly correct any error occurring in the Physical Layer.

Data Link protocol Protocol that handles transmission of data along a single link of a network.

Data network (Digital data network) A telecommunications network, that is specifically designed to carry data traffic as opposed to voice traffic, although it may also carry digitally encoded voice traffic. A computer network is an example of a data network.

Data rate   The rate, in bits/sec, at which a channel carries data.

Datagram   A packet, with source address and destination address, that is transferred by a computer network independently of all other packets.

Deadlock (Lock-up)   An unwanted state of a network or system, from which it cannot escape without special intervention by its operator.

Digital   Representing signals, data or information in a transmission medium or device or store in a discrete form.

Direct access   The process of retrieving information by directly addressing the location in the data base where it occurs. (For example, a user with a clear idea of the subject matter of the enquiry can find the appropriate location from an index, then reach it directly.)

Display   The specific type of formatted image, in colour or black-and-white, that can be displayed on the screen of a visual display terminal television set.

Distributed computing system   A system where computations and data processing operations are carried out over several linked but separate computers or computing devices, usually connected by computer network(s).

ECBDIC   Character code used by IBM computers and equipment.

EFT   Abbreviation for "Electronic funds transfer."

Electronic funds transfer (EFT)   The use of computer networking to allow payments to be made and other financial transactions to be carried out remotely, without the exchange of cheques, documents and physical money.

Electronic mail   Any form of electronic or computerised communication which is an alternative to at least one of the ordinary postal services. It allows users of computer networks to exchange messages.

Electronic office   Alternative term for "automated office."

Electronic publishing   Application of computing, information technology and electronics to the dissemination of information that would previously have been distributed by conventional methods of printing or reproducing paper documents.

Error   Incorrect reception of a bit or byte of transmitted information.

Error burst   Incorrect reception of several successive bits or bytes of transmitted information.

Error detection and correction code   A method of encoding transmitted information, by introducing some redundancy, so that errors in the information, when received, can usually be detected and corrected.

Ethernet   The bus network developed at Xerox PARC, Palo Alto, CA, USA. This has taken two forms, the Experimental Ethernet, originally developed there, and Ethernet Specification, the more or less standard form designed by DEC, Intel and Xerox in collaboration. As this type of design is so prevalent, bus networks that have the same or similar type of design are often, though not quite correctly, called "Ethernets."

Euronet   A European public network service, providing access to large bibliographic data bases situated in EEC countries.

Facsimile   Alternative term for "Telefacsimile."

Fax   Alternative term for "Telefacsimile."

FDM   Abbreviation for "Frequency Division Multiplexing."

Fixed routing A routing scheme where the choice of routes is given, and does not depend on network conditions or traffic.

Flow control Control of data flow, to prevent overfull buffers and loss of data due to receivers unable to accept them.

Forward error correction A technique, used in error control, where redundant information is added to allow the receiver to correct errors.

Frequency Division Multiplexing (FDM) Multiplexing a channel by subdividing its frequency range.

Front end computer A small computer, between a large computer and a computer network, that is used to handle communication between them.

Full duplex channel A channel able to transmit data in both directions at once.

Gateway An interface between two networks, which may seem like one of its own nodes to each of these networks. On the other hand, it may be a special purpose junction node or computer, and it may seem like two nodes, one in each network, connected by a switching link.

GB Abbreviation for "Gigabyte."

Gigabyte About a thousand Megabytes; precisely defined as 1,024 Megabytes.

Half duplex channel A channel able to transmit in either direction, but in only one direction at a time.

Hardware The physical form or configuration of the equipment in a computing system or computer network or telecommunication system or other information system.

Header The first few bytes of a packet, burst, or message, which contain identification, source address, destination address, and other control information, thereby allowing the correct transmission and routing of the packet, burst, or message through the network.

Hertz (Hz) Unit of frequency of a waveform or periodic signal, giving the number of periods per second.

High-level protocol A protocol allowing network users to carry out functions higher than mere transfer of data. For example, application protocols are high level.

Host (Host computer) A user computer that is linked to at least one computer network.

Hz Abbreviation for Hertz.

Information retrieval The process whereby a user extracts required information from a data base.

Information service A possibly computerised service that provides general interest information and also a variety of information for different types of specialist groups, for example business users. (An information service is usually one-way, as it typically sends information only from a data base to a user.)

Integrated information system Information system handling the different information and communication functions and requirements of a given group of users, such as the staff of an office, in a unified way.

Integrated network (Integrated data network) Network that can handle most types of messages, including data, text, graphics, image, and voice, together with mixtures of these types.

Integrated network (special definition) A LAN, which is similar to a local computer network, but handles voice and/or image data, as well as ordinary data.

Intelligent terminal   A terminal that contains some local computing power inside its hardware.

Intercommunication   The transfer of data or information between two communicating users or devices.

Interconnection   The mechanism of providing a channel for data transfer between two communicating users or devices.

Interface   A boundary between two parts of a system, across which their interaction is fully defined.

Interior node   Alternative name for "Switching node."

International Organization for Standardization (ISO)   A leading international standards body.

International Packet-Switched Service (IPSS)   International packet-switched network service provided by British Telecom, to link the UK to computer networks overseas.

IPSS   Abbreviation for "International Packet-Switched Service."

ISO   Abbreviation for "International Organization for Standardization."

ISO Model   Abbreviation for "ISO Reference Model for Open Systems Interconnection".

ISO Reference Model   Abbreviation for "ISO Reference Model for Open Systems Interconnection".

ISOl Reference Model for Open Systems Interconnection (OSI Reference Model, ISO Reference Model, ISO Model)   A specification for network architecture and layers of protocols, that has become so widely adopted that it has become an international standard. It has seven Layers of protocols, which are, from the lowest to the highest: Physical, Data Link, Network, Transport, Session, Presentation, Application.

Isochronous data channel   A communication channel able to transmit timing information as well as data.

KB   Abbreviation for "Kilobyte."

Kbits/sec   Kilobits per second, i.e. a thousand bits per second.

Keyboard   A device with several dozen keys, that is part of a larger device, such as a computer terminal or small computer, that acts as an interface through which users can manually input information to that device. An "alphanumeric keyboard" includes keys for letters of the alphabet and digits and other widely used special symbols.

Keypad   A small (usually hand-held) keyboard, having a limited number of keys, often digits only plus some special symbols.

Keyword   A specific word or phrase, describing an aspect or characteristic or subject matter of an item of information in a data base.

Keyword search   The use of a keyword or a logical combination of keywords to assist a user's information retrieval by narrowing down the extent of the search for the required information.

Kilobyte (KB)   About a thousand bytes; precisely defined as 1,024 bytes.

LAN   Abbreviation for "Local area network."

Leased line (Leased circuit)   A communications channel in a PSTN that is leased from a PTT or common carrier, for exclusive use by the lessee.

Leased network   A data network of leased lines.

Link   A connection between two neighbouring nodes of a network, usually defined in a given direction, though sometimes viewed as the pair of paths, in both directions, between these nodes.

Linked local area network (LLAN) A group of local area networks, that are placed inside a wide area network infrastructure, so that they can communicate with each other effectively, in a well integrated way, over large distances. Thus a linked local area network acts as a single computer network for the communications between the different sites of an organisation. For example, it can be a network configuration that provides communications within and between the different geographically separated premises of a company.

LLAN Abbreviation for "Linked local area network."

Local area network (LAN) A computer network, whose hardware is either contained inside a single building or site or situated within a compact area whose longest dimension is not more than a mile or two.

Local computer access network A LAN, where most of the computer resources reside in relatively few locations, and the requirement is just to provide terminal users with access.

Local computer network (special definition) A LAN, which supports high-speed, high-volume applications, such as large file transfers, distributed processing, and load sharing between closely located devices communicating over a shared medium.

Lock-up Alternative term for "Deadlock."

Logical local area A network configuration, at least 80% of whose traffic is "internal," between nodes in that "area." It differs from a "local area," as usually defined, in that it need not be physically contiguous, so that its nodes could constitute more than one physical cluster.

Loop Alternative term for "ring" or "ring network."

Low-level protocol A protocol concerned with the transfer of data, without reference of their significance.

Mainframe A large or very large computer.

MAN Abbreviation for "Metropolitan area network."

MB Abbreviation for "Megabyte."

Mbits/sec Megabits per second, i.e. a million bits per second.

Medium Physical system or mode by which data and information are transmitted.

Megabyte (MB) About a million bytes; precisely defined as 1,024 KB, i.e. as 1,048,576 bytes.

Menu A set of choices that is presented to the user, inside a single frame, i.e. screenful, of displayed information.

Menu selection The choice of a particular item from a menu, to determine the next stage of an information retrieval or transaction or other response by a user.

Message A block of text or data that the user of a communications network or computer network wishes to have transferred as a whole.

Message service That part of a network service that handles electronic mail.

Message-switched network A communication or computer network, using message switching. Often, such a network operates like a packet-switched network, using the messages as "large packets."

Message switching A method of operating a network, where messages are moved from node to node and can be stored at intermediate nodes during their transfer.

Metropolitan Area Network (MAN) A computer network, typically covering whole or part of a city or conurbation, whose size is larger than that of a local area network, but smaller than that of most wide area networks. Usually it is situated within a compact area, whose largest dimensions range from about a mile to a few dozen miles.

Microcomputer A computing system containing at least one microprocessor; this term is almost equivalent to "personal computer."

Micronet A small local area network, with simpler equipment and lower data transmission rates, that usually links microcomputers.

Microprocessor A very small piece of hardware, usually mounted on a chip, that can act as the central processing unit of a computer.

Minicomputer A computer, intermediate in size and architecture, between a microcomputer and a mainframe.

Mixed-media network Network using more than one transmission medium.

Modem A device allowing data to be translated between the digital form, in which it is held by a set, terminal, or computer, and the analogue form in which it is transmitted along a telephone line. This term is an abbreviation for "modulator-demodulator."

Modulation A technique, used in communications, to adapt an information signal into a signal more suitable for transmission in the communications medium. The reverse process is "demodulation."

Monitor Device for continuously recording the state of affairs in a network, part of a network, or network link. Also, a VDU that is not a TV set.

Multiplexer A device combining the signals from several communication channels into a common channel, of greater bandwidth or data rate, for the purpose of data transmission; for example, a device connecting a single communication channel to a cluster of terminals. At the far end of the channel, a "demultiplexer" extracts each of the original signals and places them into separate channels again.

Multiplexing Technique whereby a communication line or medium can carry several or many channels simultaneously.

Negative acknowledgement A control signal which reports the receipt of a data block with errors; this usually activates the retransmission of the block.

Network access method Protocol or other procedure for allocating network access to different devices or stations competing for its resources.

Network Layer Layer or level of protocol that handles Network Layer protocols. It handles correct routing of messages across a network.

Network Layer protocol Protocol that ensures correct routing of messages across a network to their destinations.

Node A point in a network, through which at least one link passes. Also, a computer in a packet-switched network that does store-and-forward switching.

Noise Extra signals, superimposed on the modulated information signal in a transmission medium, that can cause errors in the received information.

Octet An eight-bit byte.

Office automation The use of technology to enable people working in offices to manage and communicate information more effectively. In practice, it involves some combination of intelligent terminals and work stations, computers, word processing, electronic mail, file stores, telefacsimile, etc., often linked by some sort of local area network, which often has gateways to wide area networks too.

Office of the future General term for more or less automated offices, using the principles of office automation, that will appear at some unspecified time in the future.

Open systems environment An environment that allows network systems, standards, and protocols to evolve continually and become more mutually compatible, as new requirements emerge and technology advances.

Open Systems Interconnection (OSI) An approach to networking that aids the achievement of an open systems environment and, in particular, opens the way to meeting the increasingly urgent requirement for mutual compatibility of different network systems and different devices attached to networks. It provides the basis for the ISO Reference Model for Open Systems Interconnection, which has become the main approach to network architecture, as a result of the work of international and other standards bodies.

OSI Reference Model Preferred abbreviation for "ISO Reference Model for Open Systems Interconnections."

Packet A block of data, handled by a network, that has a well-defined format including a header, and has a maximum size of data field.

Packet radio A form of packet switching, where the transmission paths are ratio links and a transmitted packet may be received by several stations; thus suitable for mobile stations.

Packet-switched network A computer network or data network that uses packet switching.

Packet-Switched Service (PSS) The public packet-switched network in the UK, operated by British Telecom, and providing British users with access to IPSS and thus to overseas packet-switched networks. Also known as Packet SwitchStream.

Packet switching A method of communication inside a switched network, where packkuts are routed to their destination, using address information inside the packets. Packets from different users are interleaved, when transmitted along the network links, and, in this way, all users can share almost all parts of the network almost all of the time.

Parallel data transmission Data transmission one byte at a time, with each bit in the byte being sent along a separate path.

Peripheral node A node acting as origin and/or destination of data messages, and thus a point at the edge of a network.

Permanent virtual circuit A virtual circuit, established for a period by agreement between two users and the network operator; the equivalent of a leased line for a packet-switched network.

Personal computer A computing system, containing at least one microprocessor, that can be used as a self-contained computing system also usually also as an intelligent terminal.

Personal computer network A local area network, similar to a micronet, that links together a set of personal computers, and often also allows them to act as terminals of wide area networks.

Physical Layer Layer or level of protocol that handles Physical Layer protocols. It provides access to the physical communications medium.

Physical Layer protocol Protocol that allows devices to send raw bit streams into and across a computer network.

Port A computer network's or other telecommunication system's access point to a computer.

Positive acknowledgment A control signal which reports the correct receipt of a data block.

Presentation Layer Layer or level of protocol that handles Presentation Layer protocols. It makes application processes independent of differences in data representation, and allows transmitted data to be connected into formats convenient to users.

Presentation Layer protocol Protocol handling basic functions needed to implement user applications, for example a "file transfer protocol" for transferring data files between different devices.

Private circuit A PSTN connection between transmitter and receiver, that bypasses the dialling equipment in the telephone exchange.

Private videotex system A videotex system, whose operator is usually a private enterprise or organisation or specific group of users, and which is not provided as a general public service.

Processing net A LAN, whose components provide an environment for executing user-oriented computing and information processing tasks.

Protocol A well-specified, preferably strictly defined, procedure to control the formatting and exchange of data between different parts of a network, by implementing its functions according to its architecture. Thus each protocol acts at a level, determined by its defined function in relation to the architecture. More generally, a set of rules regulating information flow in a communication or telecommunication system.

PSS Abbreviation for "Packet-Switched Service," or "Packet Switch Stream."

PSTN Abbreviation for "Public-switched telephone network."

PTT A (usually national) public telegraph, telephone, and telecommunications authority. (A PTT is sometimes also responsible for postal services.)

Public switched telephone network (PSTN) A network, provided by a PTT or some other common carrier, to link together a large number of telephones through telephone lines and telephone exchanges. More generally, the world-wide networks of interconnected national PSTNs, provided by PTTs and other common carriers.

Redundancy Extra information added to a message to improve the reliability of its transmission and make it less vulnerable to errors and noise.

Remote job entry (RJE) Submission of a batch computing job to a remote computer via a data link or network.

Response time of network Time between completion of message input at transmitter and start of message output at receiver.

Ring network (Ring) A local area network, all of whose devices are attached to nodes on a loop of cable. In some cases, this loop may be duplicated, or additional links between the nodes may be incorporated.

RJE Abbreviation for "Remote job entry".

Serial data transmission Data transmission one bit at a time over a single path.

Service primitive An abstract element of the interaction between a service user and a service provider, that is independent of implementation.

Session Layer Layer or level of protocol that handles Session Layer protocols. It organises and structures the interactions between application processes, and controls system-dependent aspects of communication sessions between specific end systems.

Session Layer protocol Protocol handling a "session" or series of transactions between devices communicating with each other over a network, for example a "terminal protocol" handling communication between a terminal and a host computer.

Sharing technique Way in which devices and users are allocated bandwidth and other resources in a network.

Signal Waveform or other physical process used to carry data or information.

Snowflake A configuration using stars of stars, so that each node is either a terminal node or the centre of a star of links to more remote nodes.

Software A set of instructions, needed by a computer or other information system, to carry out a specified group of tasks.

Space Division Multiplexing A form of multiplexing, where a data trunk carries its separate messages in separate physical channels.

Standard A generally accepted, or at least widely adopted, formulation, specifying some particular aspect of the operation of a system or network.

Standardisation The process of agreeing standards for protocols, data formats, and other aspects of the operation of a network or system.

Standardised net A LAN, which can provide network services for a wide range of vendor devices which can be attached.

Standards body A representative committee or group of committees, that carries out the process of standardisation on an ongoing basis. In particular, it discusses and proposes the recommendation and negotiates the agreement of standards.

Star network A computer network, linking a cluster of terminals to a central computer or network controller.

Star ring A star network whose central "node" is a ring.

Start-stop Serial data transmission where each byte is sent as a self-contained sequence of bits, without extra timing information.

Station Network node, to which a device is attached, or a combination of network node and attached device.

Statistical multiplexer A multiplexer that can handle variable-length data block transmission and dynamic bandwidth assignment, with the aid of buffer storage to accommodate temporary peak loading on individual channels or groups of channels. It thus allows much better usage of shared data channels.

Statistical Time Division Multiplexing A variant of time division multiplexing, where a time slot is assigned to a channel only when that channel has data to send.

Store-and-forward A technique that stores packets or messages in node memories, while they are waiting for the next stage of their journey across the network.

Structure The "structure" of a network is its general configuration, specifying its components, including nodes and links and attached devices, and the geometrical relations between them.

Subnetwork (Subnet) The communication subsystem of a computer network or data network. For example, a public data communications service.

Switched network A network, which is shared between many users, any one of whom can establish communication with other users when desired.

Switching link A special link inside a gateway between two networks, one end of which is in one network and one end of which is in the other.

Switching node (Switch) A node that routes data messages or packets appropriately, by switching them from the links down which they have just travelled to the correct links for them to enter.

Synchronous data channel Alternative term for "Isochronous data channel."

Synchronous network A network where all channels are synchronised to a common clock.

Synchronous terminal A terminal needing to receive timing information from the transmitter in order to receive data reliably.

TB Abbreviation for "Terabyte."

TDM Abbreviation for "Time Division Multiplexing."

Telefacsimile (Facsimile, Fax) The transmission of information about a document along a telephone line or other communications channel, in such a way that the received signals are reconstructed into a representation of the original page.

Teleprinter A terminal, with an alphanumeric keyboard, that is able to print its input and output.

Telesoftware A facility for distributing and storing computer programs through a teletext and/or viewdata system and/or other computer network.

Teletex A combination of communicating word processing, and telecommunications, which is being developed in accordance with agreed international Teletex standards. In practice, a greatly improved version of Telex.

Teletext The form of videotex where information stored in a computer is broadcast, usually in conjunction with television signals, to the user's TV set or terminal; it is usually one-way, not allowing any feedback from the user.

Telex network A switched public text transmission network, using teleprinters as its terminals.

Terabyte About a million Megabytes; precisely defined as 1,048,576 MB.

Terminal A device, which may or may not contain its own built-in computing facilities, which is able to communicate with a computer, either directly or over at least one computer network. More generally, a device for sending and/or receiving data via a communication channel.

Third party data base A data base, contained in a computer outside a computer network, whose information can be reached by users of that network, by means of a gateway in that network. Third party data bases are used especially by many videotex systems.

Time Division Multiplexing (TDM) Multiplexing a channel by dividing it into (usually equal) slots of time.

Time-out A special action that occurs if an acknowledgment or other required response is not received by a given time.

Time-shared system A computing system, linking clusters of terminals to a mainframe or other central computer, and using the principle of time sharing.

Time sharing A system of sharing computer resources between several users, whereby they access a central computer through terminals and the system allocates their shares of this access.

Topology The "topology" of a network is the geometrical specification of its configuration, showing which connections link which nodes and devices; strictly, this term should not specify the lengths, geography or physical nature of these connections, but it sometimes does so in practice.

Transaction service That part of a videotex or other computer network service that is two-way, as it allows a user to send a specific response that activates particular actions by the system. (For example, a videotex system may be used to order goods or book the travel tickets for a particular journey, or a computer network may be used for electronic funds transfer.)

Transparent A transmission path is "transparent" to some property of the data stream if that stream passes through it without change of that property.

Transport Layer Layer or level of protocol that handles transport protocols. It provides reliable, transparent, cost-effective transfer of data between end systems, together with error recovery and flow control.

Transport protocol (Host-to-host protocol) Protocol that provides reliable end-to-end communication between processes in host computers and other "intelligent" devices.

Transport service of a network Service providing a universal communications interface, offering to implement and operate certain standard facilities, independent of the communications medium below.

Transport technique A method used to establish a channel over a communications link with the aid of multiplexing.

Tree network A bus network whose buses are linked end-to-end and/or end-to-middle.

VDU Abbreviation for "visual display unit" or "visual display terminal."

Video net A network which can carry video and voice as well as text and data.

Videotex The whole class of electronic systems that use a modified television set or visual display terminal to present computer-based information in a user-accessible visual form. (Note that the above definition is my own, corresponding to one of the two widely accepted meanings of the term; unfortunately, the definition of the term is not agreed, as it is often also used as another name for "viewdata.")

Videotex protocol A set of detailed rules and procedures specifying precisely all aspects of the operation of a specified function of a videotex system.

Videotext (Used by some American writers instead of "videotex;" again, it has been applied in either of the two senses indicated above.)

Viewdata A form of videotex that has a two-way connection, usually via telephone or cable, between the user's TV set or terminal and the (usually) remote computer storing information; the user is thus able to interact with and respond to the information so received.

Virtual call A virtual circuit set up by a user when needed and released when no longer required.

Virtual circuit A facility in a packet-switched network that keeps packets between transmitter and receiver in sequence.

Virtual terminal A conceptual terminal, defined as a standard for uniform handling of a variety of actual terminals.

Visual display terminal A terminal that has facilities for visual display that allow it to show a wide variety of images and especially to act as a videotex terminal.

Visual display unit (VDU) A terminal, usually with an alphanumeric keyboard, that is able to display its input and output on a screen.

V-Series Recommendations of CCITT Recommendations for PSTN data transmission, including those dealing with modems.

WAN Abbreviation for "Wide area network."

Wide area network (WAN) A computer network, covering larger regions than those handled by local area networks, typically having distances between its nodes ranging from a few miles to hundreds or even thousands of miles. Thus its coverage is often national, sometimes international and continental, occasionally worldwide.

Word processing   A technique that allows text to be input, edited, and typed or printed electronically, in such a way that, at any time, the current version of the document being written is stored in memory in a named text file.

Word processor   A device, with a keyboard and microprocessor, that is specially designed to perform word processing functions.

Work station   An intelligent terminal especially designed for use in an automated office. It usually combines at least local word processing and computing abilities, with the ability to access information, data base, message and other services via the local area network to which it is attached.

X-Series Recommendations of CCITT   Recommendations for protocols and other specifications for new data networks. For example, the widely used X.25 and its allied protocols.

Directory of Network Services

This Directory gives the names and addresses of several national and international computer network services, together with addressses of a few standards bodies and places where research on networks is being carried out. After the name of each service, the nature of the service is indicated. In order to keep the list short, specialist network services are not included, while most services that offer only videotex are omitted, as they are listed in the Directory of Videotex Services in my book *The Videotex Revolution* (1986), also published by Wiley.

PUBLIC NETWORK SERVICES

Europe

United Kingdom

British Telecom Gold
(Electronic mail and message service)
Capital House, 42 Weston Street, London SE1 3QD
(Tel: 01-403 6777)

British Telecom International Customer Services,
(IPSS packet-switched network)
Gerrard House, 31-45 Gresham Street, London EC2V 7DN
(Tel: 01-606-1489, 01-432 4182)

British Telecom Marketing
(PSS packet-switched network inside UK and access to similar networks overseas, also Datel)
Room 605, Seal House, 1 Swan Lane, London EC4R 3TH
(Tel: 01-357 3288)

British Telecom Packet SwitchStream Customer Service Group
(PSS packet-switched network)
G07, Lutyens House, 1-6 Finsbury Circus, London EC2M 7LY
(Tel: 01-920 0661) Micronet 800
(Personal computer WAN, telesoftware, and videotex)
Telemap Ltd., Durrant House, 8 Herbal Hill, London EC1 5JB
(Tel: 01-278 3143)

Belgium

Régie des Télégraphes et des Téléphones, Departement de la Transmission
(Circuit-switched and packet-switched data networks)
42 rue de Palais, B-1030, Bruxelles
(Tel: +32 2 2217 80 50. Telex: 25351)

Denmark

General Directorate of Posts and Télegraphs, Telecommunications Service, 4th Administration Office
The Datel Service
(Danish part of Nordic Data Network, packet-switched network)
Farvergade 17,2, DK-1007, Koebenhavn K
(Tel: +45 1 116605. Telex: 22999 gentel kh)

Euronet DIANE Information

(Euronet packet-switched information network)
Jean Monnet Building, B4 009, CEC, 1675 Luxembourg
(Tel: (352) 4301 3020 and 4301 2879 (Ansaphone). Telex: 2752 eurdoc lu)

Finland

General Direction of Posts and Telegraphs
Telegraph Division
(Finnish part of Nordic Data Network)
Box 526, SF-0010, Helsinki 10

France

TRANSPAC
(Packet-switched network)
Sous-Direction de la Téléinformatique et des Réseaux Spécialistes, 20 rue les Cases, F-75007, Paris
(Tel: +33 1 551 60 90. Telex: 200124)

Netherlands

PTT Headquarters
Telecommunications Commercial Affairs
(Datanet 1 packet-switched network)
P.O. Box 30000, 2500 GA The Hague
(Tel: +3 70 75 39 08. Telex: 33023)

Norway

Norwegian Telecommunication Administration
(Norwegian part of Nordic Data Network)
Datel Services Office (ATD), P.O. Box 6701 St. Olavspl., N-Oslo 1
(Tel: +47 2 48 89 90. Telex: 11203)

Spain

CTNE
(Various networks)
Direccion Gral. Correos y Telecomunicacion, Conde Penalver, 19, Madrid, 6
(Tel: +34 1 275 36 38. Telex: 42424)

West Germany

Deutsche Bundespost
(Datex data network)
FTZ, B 19, Postfach 50 00, D-6100 Darmstadt
(Tel: +49 6151 83-1. Telex: 419511 ftz)

North America

Canada

Telecom Canada
(Packet-switched network, value added network services)
160 Elgin Street, Room 1150, Ottawa, ON
(Tel: 613-567-3847)

Teleglobe Canada
(Teleconferencing, online data bases, etc.)
680 Ouest Rue Sherbrooke, Montreal, PQ H3A 2S4
(Tel: 514-281-5008)

USA

American Satellite Corp.
(Satellite)
1801 Research Blvd., Rockville, MD 20850
(Tel: 301-251-8333)

Bell System
AT&T Assoc. Telephone Co.
(Telephone, message, and facsimile)
195 Broadway, New York, NY 10002

Communications Satellite Corp.
(Satellite)
950 L'Enfant Plaza, SW, Washington, DC 20024
(Tel: 202-863-6235)

CompuServe
(Home terminal network)
5000 Arlington Center Blvd, PO Box 20212, Columbus, OH 43220
(Tel: 614-457-8600)

CONFER II
(Computer conferencing systtem)
Advertel Communications Systems, Inc., 2067 Ascot, Ann Arbor, MI 48103
(Tel: 313-665-2612)

Dow Jones News Retrieval Service
(Home terminal network)
Dow Jones Co., Inc., PO Box 300, Princeton, NJ 08540
(Tel: 609-452-1511)

Edunet/Educom
(Teleconferencing, educational, and scientific data bases, etc.)
Box 364, Princeton, NJ 08540
(Tel: 609-734-1878, 609-734-1915)

EIES
(Computer conferencing system)
Computerized Conferencing and Communications Center,
New Jersey Institute of Technology, 322 High St., Newark, NJ 07102
(Tel: 201-645-5503, 201-596-EIES)

General Electric Info Services Company
(GEISCO time sharing bureau)
401 N. Washington St., Rockville, MD 20850
(Tel: 301-340-4000)

GTE Satellite Communications and GTE Satellite Corp.
(Satellite)
1 Stamford Forum, Stamford, CT 66904
(Tel: 703-435-7400, 703-442-1000)

GTE Telenet
(Packet-switched network, value added services)
8229 Boone Blvd., Vienna, VA 22180
(Tel: 703-442-1000)

ITT Dialcom
(Electronic mail and message service, teleconferencing, data bases, time sharing)
1109 Spring St., Silver Springs, MD 20910
(Tel: 301-588-1572)

ITT World Communications, Inc.
(Value added network services)
100 Plaza Drive, Secaucus, NJ 07096
(Tel: 800-424-1170)

The META Network
(Computer conferencing system)
Metasystems Design Group, Inc.,
1401 Wilson Blvd., Suite 601, Arlington, VA 22209
(Tel: 703-247-8301)

PCNet
(Personal computer network)
Coordinator, David Caulkins, 340 East Middlefield Avenue, Mountain View, CA 94043

RCA American Communications, Inc.
(Satellite)
400 College Rd., East Princeton, NJ 08540
(Tel: 609-734-4000)

RCA Cylix Communications Network
(Satellite, value added network services)
800 Ridge Lake Blvd., Memphis, TN 38119
(Tel: 901-761-1177)

RCA Global Communications Inc.
(Packet-switched network, facsimile, message, international record)
60 Broad Street, New York, NY 10004
(Tel: 212-248-2121)

Satellite Business Systems
(Satellite, teleconferencing)
8283 Greensboro Drive, McLean, VA 22102
(Tel: 703-442-5000, 703-442-5577)

The Source
(Home terminal network)
Source Telecomputing Corp., 1616 Anderson Road, McLean, VA 22101
(Tel: 703-734-7500)

Tymnet, Inc.
(Packet-switched network, value added services, message service)
2710 Orchard Parkway, San Jose, CA 95134
(Tel: 408-946-4900)

US Satellite Systems, Inc.
(Satellite)
122 East 42nd St., Suite 5000, New York, NY 10168
(Tel: 212-661-4230)

Western Union International Inc.
(Packet-switched network, message, international record, specialised)
One WUI Plaza, New York, NY 10004
(Tel: 212-363 6400)

The Western Union Telegraph Company
(Packet-switched network, satellite, teleconferencing)
One Lake Street, Upper Saddle River, NJ 07458
(Tel: 201-825-5000)

World Net Communications LA
(Value added network services)
9107 Wilshire Blvd., Suite 700, Beverly Hills, CA 90210
(Tel: 213-859-0339)

Rest of World

Australia

Telecom Australia
(Packet-switched network, digital data networks)
8/518 Little Bourke Street, Melbourne, VIC 3000
(Tel: (03) 67 4289. Telex: AA 33998)

STANDARDS BODIES

ANSI (American National Standards Institute)
1430 Broadway, New York, NY 10018
(Tel: 212-354-3330)

CCITT (International Telegraph and Telephone Consultative Committee)
Case Postale 56, 1 rue de Varembe, CH-1211, Genève 20, Switzerland
(Tel: +4122 341240. Telex: 23887 ISO C4)

ISO (International Organization for Standardization)
2 rue de Varembe, CH-1211, Genève 20, Switzerland
(Tel: +4122 346201. Telex: 23000 CH)

NBS (National Bureau of Standards)
Systems and Network Architecture Division
Institute for Computer Sciences and Technology, NBS, Washington, DC 20234

RESEARCH PROJECTS ON COMPUTER NETWORKS

International

The Arpanet
(also a private network service)
Arpanet Network Information Center
Room EJ721, SRI International, Menlo Park, CA 94025, USA
(Tel: 415-859-3695. Telex: 334463)

United Kingdom

British Telecom Research Laboratories
Martlesham Heath, Ipswich, Suffolk IP5 7RE
(Tel: Ipswich (0473) 643242)

INDRA Group
Department of Computer Science
University College London
Gower Street, London WC1E 6BT
(Tel: 01-387 7050×815 or 333)

Rutherford and Appleton Laboratory
Computing Division, Atlas Centre
Chilton, Didcot, Oxfordshire OX11 0QX
(Tel: Abingdon (0235) 21900. Telex: 83159)

France

INRIA (Institut National de Recherche en Informatique et en Automatique)
Domaine de Voluceau, Rocquencourt, B.P. 105-78753 Le Chesnay CEDEX
(Tel: (3) 954 90 20. Telex: 698109)

Directory of Network System Suppliers

North American Suppliers

ADC Magnetics Control Co.

(WAN equipment, WAN management systems)
4900 West 78 St., Bloomington, MN 55435
(Tel: 612-893-3021, 1-800-328-6188)

Advanced Computer Communications

(LAN equipment and software)
720 Santa Barbara St., Santa Barbara, CA 93101
(Tel: 805-963-9431)

Amdahl Communications Systems Division

(WAN equipment, WAN management systems)
2500 Walnut Ave., Marina del Rey, CA 90291
(Tel: 213-822-3202)

Anderson Jacobson, Inc.

(WAN equipment)
521 Charcot Ave., San Jose, CA 95131
(Tel: 408-263-8520)

Apollo Computer, Inc.

(Apollo DOMAIN LAN)
330 Billerica Rd., Chelmsford, MA 01824
(Tel: 617-256-6600)

AT&T Information Systems

(WAN equipment)
One Speedwell Ave., Morristown, NJ 07960
(Tel: 201-898-2000)
also general enquiries for AT&T network products
(Tel: 1-800-222-0400, 1-800-821-2121)

Atlantic Research Corp., Teleproducts Division

(WAN management systems, WAN monitors and testers)
7401 Boston Blvd., Springfield, VA 22153
(Tel: 703-644-9190)

BBN Communications Corp.

(LAN equipment, LAN software, WAN equipment)
33 Moulton St., Cambridge, MA 02238
(Tel: 617-497-2800)

Codex Corp.

(WAN equipment, WAN control systems)
20 Cabot Blvd., Mansfield, MA 02048
(Tel: 617-364-2000)

Compucorp

(OmegaNet® micronet)
2211 Michigan Ave., Santa Monica, CA 90404
(Tel: 213-829-7453)

Contel Information Systems, Inc.

(LANs, LAN software)
130 Steamboat Rd., Great Neck, NY 11024
(Tel: 516-829-5900)

Control Data Corp., Computer Systems Marketing

(LCN LAN)
PO Box 0, Minneapolis, MN 55420
(Tel: 612-853-8100)

Corvus Systems

(Constellation and Omninet personal computer networks, Concept work station)
2029 O'Toole, San Jose, CA 95131
(Tel: 408-946-7700)

Datapoint Corp.

(ARCNET ™ LAN, WAN equipment)
9725 Datapoint Drive, San Antonio, TX 78284
(Tel: 512-699-7059)

Digital Equipment Corp.

(Ethernet equipment, DECnet WAN software)
200 Baker Ave., Concord, MA 01742
(Tel: 617-897-5111)

Dynatech Data Systems

(WAN equipment, WAN analysis and testing equipment)
7644 Dynatech Court, Springfield, VA 22153
(Tel: 703-569-9000)

Dynatech Packet Technology

(LANs, WAN equipment)
6464 General Green Way, Alexandria, VA 22312
(Tel: 703-642-9391)

Ericsson Communications

(LANs, WAN equipment, fiber optic systems, microwave and laser systems)
7465 Lampson Ave., Garden Grove, CA 92461
(Tel: 714-895-3962)

Gandalf Data, Inc.

(PACXNET LAN, WAN equipment)
1019 South Noel Ave., Wheating, IL 60090
(Tel: 312-541-6060)

Gandalf Data Ltd.

(PACXNET LAN, WAN equipment)
100 Colonnade Rd., Ottawa, ON, Canada
(Tel: 613-822-8917)

GTE Business Communications Systems, Inc.

(WAN equipment, satellite earth stations)
12502 Sunrise Valley Drive, Reston, VA 22091
(Tel: 703-435-7400)

Honeywell Information Systems

(WAN equipment)
200 Smith St., Waltham, MA 02154
(Tel: 617-895-6000)

IBM Corp. Direct Response Marketing Dept.

(Modems)
400 Parson's Pond Drive, Franklin Lakes, NJ 07417
(Toll-free tel: 1-800-631-5582 x 84 (most of USA), 1-800-526-2484 x 84 (Alaska and Hawaii))

ICL Computer, Inc.

(LANs, WAN software)
777 Long Ridge Rd., Stamford, CT 06902
(Tel: 203-968-7200)

Infinet, Inc.

(WAN analysis and testing equipment)
Six Shattuck Road, Andover, MA 01810
(Tel: 617-681-0600)

Infotron Systems Corp.

(LANs, WAN equipment, WAN management systems)
Cherry Hill Industrial Center, Cherry Hill, NJ 08003
(Tel: 609-424-9400)

ITT Data Equipment & Systems

(Modems)
One World Trade Center, New York, NY 10048
(Tel: 212-839-0500)

ITT Telecom Network Systems Division

(WAN equipment)
3100 Highwoods Blvd., Raleigh, NC 27604
(Tel: 919-872-3359)

Light Communications

(LANs, optical and infra-red systems)
25 Van Zant St., Norwalk, CT 06855
(Tel: 203-866-6858)

Link Systems

(LAN software, personal computer communications software)
1640 19th St., Santa Monica, CA 90404
(Tel: 213-413-8921)

M/A-COM Linkabit, Inc.

(IDX-300 digital exchange, LAN equipment, WAN equipment)
3033 Science Park Rd., San Diego, CA 92121
(Tel: 714-457-2340)

Micom Systems, Inc.

(INSTANET™ LAN, WAN equipment, WAN management equipment)
20151 Nordhoff St., Chatsworth, CA 91311
(Tel: 213-998-8844)

Microcom, Inc.

(Microcom Network Protocol for microcomputers, LAN software, modems)
1400A Providence Way, Norwood, MA 02062
(Tel: 617-762-9310)

Muirhead, Inc.

(WAN equipment, facsimile equipment)
1101 Bristol Rd., Mountainside, NJ 07092
(Tel: 201-233-6010)

Nestar Systems, Inc.

(Cluster/One, Elf, PLAN 2000 and PLAN 4000 personal computer networks)
2585 East Bayshore Rd., Palo Alto, CA 94303
(Tel: 415-493-2223)

Network Research Group

(LANs, LAN software, personal computer communications software)
1964 Westwood Blvd. 200, Los Angeles, CA 90025
(Tel: 213-474-7717)

Network Systems Corp.

(Hyperbus and Hyperchannel LANs)
7600 Boone Ave. North, Brooklyn Park, MN 55928
(Tel: 612-425-2202)

Nixdorf Computer Corp.

(LANs, WAN software)
300 Third Ave., Waltham, MA 02154
(Tel: 617-890-3600)

Northern Telecom, Inc.

(LAN software, WAN software, office automation systems)
Box 1222, Minneapolis, MN 55440
(Tel: 612-932-8000)

Paradyne Corp.

(LANs, LAN equipment, WAN equipment)
8550 Ulmerston Rd., Largo, FL 33540
(Tel: 813-530-2000)

Philips Information Systems, Inc.

(Office automation systems)
4040 McEwen, Dallas, TX 75234
(Tel: 214-386-5580)

Prime Computer, Inc.

(PRIMENET LAN and WAN equipment and software)
Prime Park, Natick, MA 01760
(Tel: 617-655-8000)

Protean Associates, Inc.

(Pronet LAN)
24 Crescent St., Waltham, MA 02154
(Tel: 617-894-1980)

Racal-Milgo

(WAN equipment)
7800 W. Oakland Park Blvd., Fort Lauderdale, FL 33321
(Tel: 305-591-5212, 305-748-3507)

Racal-Vadic

(WAN equipment)
1525 McCarthy Blvd., Milpilas, CA 95035
(Tel: 408-946-7610)

RCA Service Co. Data Services

(Modems, etc.)
Route 38, Bldg. 204-2, Cherry Hill, NJ 08358
(Tel: 609-338-4375)

Rolm Corp.

(CBX 11 and other PABXs, LANs)
4900 Old Ironsides Drive, Santa Clara, CA 95050
(Tel: 408-986-1000)

Shaffstall Corp.

(Media conversion)
7901 East 88th St., Indianapolis, IN 46256
(Tel: 317-842-2077)

Siemens Communication Systems

(Terminals, teleprinters)
5500 Broken Sound Blvd., Boca Raton, FL 33431
(Tel: 305-994-8100)

STC Systems, Inc.

(WAN equipment, office automation systems)
4 North St., Waldwick, Bergen, NJ 07463
(Tel: 201-445-5050)

Symbiotic Computer Systems, Inc.

(SyMBnet personal computer network)
353 Davis Rd., Fairfield, CT 06430
(Tel: 203-374-5910)

Sytek, Inc.

(LocalNet™ LAN, WAN equipment)
1225 Charleston Rd., Mountain View, CA 94043
(Tel: 415-966-7300)

Tekelec, Inc.

(WAN analysers and simulators)
2932 Wilshire Blvd., Santa Monica, CA 90403
(Tel: 213-829-7305)

Tesdata Systems

(WAN management systems)
7921 Jones Branch Drive, McLean, VA 22102
(Tel: 800-336-0170)

U-Microcomputer, Inc.

(U-NET personal computer network)
300 Broad St., Stamford, CT 06092
(Tel: 203-359-4236)

Ungermann-Bass, Inc.

(Net/One™ LAN)
2560 Mission College Blvd., Santa Clara, CA 95050
(Tel: 408-496-0111)

Vector Graphic, Inc.

(SABER-NET LAN and LINC™ operating system)
500 North Ventu Rd., Thousand Oaks, CA 91320
(Tel: 805-499-5831)

Wang Laboratories, Inc.

(Wangnet LAN, office automation systems)
One Industrial Ave., Lowell, MA 01881
(Tel: 617-459-5000)

Xerox Corp. Office Systems Division

(Ethernet LAN, office automation systems)
1341 W. Mockingbird Lane, Dallas, TX 75247
(Tel: 214-689-6000)

Zilog, Inc.

(Z-Net micronet)
1315 Dell Ave., Campbell, CA 95008
(Tel: 408-370-8000)

Ztel, Inc.

(Private Network Exchange)
181 Ballardvale St., Wilmington, MA 01887
(Tel: 617-657-8730)

For further details of most of these suppliers and of many additional suppliers, see *Data Communications Buyers' Guide 1984*, McGraw-Hill Publications Co., 1221 Avenue of the Americas, New York, NY 10020.

British Suppliers

Acorn Computers Ltd. (Econet Sales Dept.)

(Econet personal computer network)
Fulbourn Road, Cherry Hinton, Cambridge CB1 4JN.
(Tel: 0223-245200)

Altos Computer Systems Ltd.

(Altos TEAMNET LAN)
Suite E, Manhattan House, High St., Crowthorne, Berks RG11 7AT
(Tel: 0344-777991)

Amazon Computers Ltd.

(Semaphore file transfer and media conversion package)
Sunrise Parkway, Linford Wood, Milton Keynes MK14 6LQ
(Tel: 0908-664123)

Amdahl Communication Systems Ltd.

(WAN management equipment)
Amdahl House, 112-118 Cricklade Rd., Swindon, Wiltshire SN2 6AG
(Tel: 0793-45476)

Anderson Jacobson Ltd.

(WAN equipment)
752 Deal Avenue, Slough, Berks SL1 4SJ
(Tel: 0753-821021)

Apollo Computer (UK) Ltd.

(Apollo Domain LAN)
Bulbourne House, Gossoms End, Berkhamsted, Herts HP4 3LP
(Tel: 04427-75026)

British Telecom Merlin

(T-Link WAN software for personal computers)
Anzani House, Trinity Avenue, Felixstowe, Suffolk IP11 8XB
(Tel: 0394-275959)

Camtec Electronics Ltd.

(WAN equipment)
Melton Street, Leicester LE1 3NA
(Tel: 0533-537534)

CAP London Industrial

(X.25 software, mobile work station)
233 High Holborn, London WC1V 7EJ
(Tel: 01-831 6144)

CASE (Computer And Systems Engineering plc)

(BEELINE and GRAPEVINE LANs, WAN equipment)
PO Box 254, Caxton Way, Watford Business Park, Watford, Herts WD1 8XH
(Tel: 0923-33500)

Chernikeeff Telecommunications Ltd.

(Telex management and switching systems)
Church Wharf, Pumping Station Road, Chiswick, London W4 2SN
(Tel: 01-994-6685)

Codex (U.K.) Ltd.

(WAN equipment, WAN control systems)
114/116 Thornton Road, Thornton Heath, Surrey CR4 6XB
(Tel: 01-689-2101)

Compucorp (UK) Ltd.

(OmegaNet® LAN)
Cunningham House, Westfield Lane, Kenton, Middlesex
(Tel: 01-907-0198)

Control Data Ltd.

(LCN LAN)
Control Data House, 179-199 Shaftesbury Ave., London WC2H 8AR
(Tel: 01-240-3400)

Datapoint (U.K.) Ltd.

(ARCNET™ LAN system)
Ventek House, 400 North Circular Road, Neasden, London NW10 0JG
(Tel: 01-459-1222)

Datec (Debenhams Applied Technology Ltd.)

(WAN equipment, WAN service, WAN consultancy)
Bedford House, Park Street, Taunton, Somerset TA1 4DB
(Tel: 0823-87979)
also 500 Chesham House, 150 Regent Street, London W1
(Tel: 01-439 6288)

Digital Equipment Co. Ltd.

(Ethernet equipment, DECnet WAN software)
PO Box 110, Digital Park, Worton Grange, Reading, Berkshire RG2 0TR
(Tel: 0734-868711)

Digital Microsystems Ltd.

(HiNet micronet)
Molly Millars Bridge, Molly Millars Lane, Wokingham, Berkshire RG11 2PQ
(Tel: 0734-793131)

Dynatech Communications (UK) Ltd.

(WAN equipment, WAN analysis and testing equipment)
Fieldings Road, Cheshunt, Herts EN8 9TL
(Tel: 0992-33555)

Fenwood Designs Ltd.

(WAN equipment, telex message switches)
Mill Lane, Godalming, Surrey GU7 1EY
(Tel: 04868-25755)

Ferranti Computer Systems Ltd.

(Broadband LAN, Telex Manager, Teletex Adaptor, Voice Manager)
Simonsway, Wythenshawe, Manchester M22 5LA
(Tel: 061-499-3355)

Focom Systems Ltd.

(Fibre optic LANs)
Unit 10, Hunslet Trading Estate, Severn Road, Hunslet, Leeds LS10 1BL
(Tel: 0532-775757)

Formscan Ltd.

(Media conversion equipment)
Apex House, West End, Frome, Somerset
(Tel: 0373-61446)

Gandalf Digital Communications Ltd.

(PACXNET LAN, WAN equipment)
19 Kingsland Grange, Woolston, Warrington, Cheshire WA1 4RW
(Tel: 0925-818484)

Geac Computers Ltd.

(GEAC LAN)
Unit 2, 1690-1699 Park Ave., Aztec West, Almondsbury, Bristol
(0454-617373, 0454-615215)

GEC Computers Ltd.

(WAN software products)
Elstree Way, Borehamwood, Herts, WD6 1RX
(Tel: 01-953 2030)

Hasler, (GB) Ltd.

(SILK LAN)
Commerce Way, Croydon, CRO 4XA
(Tel: 01-680 6050)

Hawker Siddeley Dynamics Engineering Ltd.

(Multilink micronet)
Bridge Road East, Welwyn Garden City, Herts AL7 1LR
(Tel: 07073-31299)

Hytec Microsystems Ltd.

(TECNET micronet)
Sandy Lane West, Oxford OX4 5JX
(Tel: 0865-714545)

IAL Data Communications

(WAN equipment, WAN network management equipment)
Jays Close, Viables, Basingstoke, Hampshire RG22 4BY
(Tel: 0256-59222)

IBM UK Ltd.

(WAN software)
PO Box 41, North Harbour (Baltic House), Portsmouth, Hampshire PO6 3AU
(Tel: 0705-694941)

ICL Computers Ltd.

(Microlan and OSLAN LANs, WAN software, DRS work stations)
ICL House, Putney, London SW15 1SW.
(Tel: 01-788 7272)

Incaa Computers, UK Branch

(Media conversion)
6 Trinity Close, Felmersham, Bedford MK43 7HW
(Tel: 0234-781300)

Infa Communications Ltd.

(INFAPLUG LAN)
Castle Moat Chambers, Bath Place, Taunton, Somerset TA1 4EP
(Tel: 0823-71128)

Infinet Ltd.

(WAN analysis and testing equipment)
4 First Avenue, Globe Park, Marlow, Bucks. SL7 1YA
(Tel: 06284-75375)

Information Technology Ltd.

(LocalNet™ LAN, WAN equipment and software, IMP office automation systems)
Eaton Rd., Hemel Hempstead, Herts HP2 7LB
(Tel: 0442-3272)
also
Suttons Park Ave., Suttons Industrial Park, Reading, Berkshire RG16 1AZ
(Tel: 0724-664667)
also
Technology House,
Victoria Rd., Winchester, Hampshire SO23 7DU
(Tel: 0962-5444)

Infotron Systems

(LANs, WAN equipment, WAN management systems)
Systems House, Poundbury Rd., Dorchester, Dorset
(Tel: 0305-66016)

Interactive Systems/3M (UK) Ltd.

(Videodata LAN)
PO Box 1, 3M House, Bracknell, Berkshire RG12 1JU
(Tel: 0344-426726)

Interlekt Electronics Ltd.

(WAN analysis and testing equipment)
Interlekt House, 24 Portman Rd., Reading, Berkshire RG3 1LU
(Tel: 0734-589551)

InterMedia Graphic Systems

(Media conversion equipment and software)
MM House, Sebastopol Rd., Aldershot, Hampshire GU11 1UG
(Tel: 0252-313314, 0252-333441)

LDR Systems Ltd.

(Isonet LAN-WAN software)
Balmoral House, Ash Vale, Aldershot, Hampshire GU12 5BB
(Tel: 0252-331666)

Logica UK Ltd.

(Network applications, office automation)
64 Newman St., London W1A 4SE
(Tel: 01-637 9111)

Logica VTS Ltd.

(Polynet LAN, multi-function work stations)
Drakes Way, Greenbridge, Swindon, Wiltshire SN3 3JL
(Tel: 0793-36291)

Logitek Ltd.

(Altos TEAMNET II LAN)
Logitek House, Bradley Lane, Standish, Greater Manchester
(Tel: 0251-426644)

Master Systems (Data Products) Ltd.

(MASTERNET LAN, WAN equipment)
100 Park Street, Camberley, Surrey
(Tel: 0276-685385)

Micom-Borer Ltd.

(INSTANET™ LAN, WAN equipment, WAN network management equipment)
Bel Court, 15 Cradock Rd., Reading, Berkshire RG2 0JT
(Tel: 0734-866801)

Midlectron Ltd.

(V-NET micronet)
Midlectron House, Nottingham Rd., Belper, Derby DE5 1JQ
(Tel: 077382-6811)

Mitel Telecom Ltd.

(PABX products, integrated work stations)
Severnbridge Estate, Portskewett, Newport, Gwent NP6 4YR
(Tel: 0291-423355)

Nestar Systems Ltd.

(Cluster/One, ELF, PLAN personal computer networks)
122-123 High St., Uxbridge, Middlesex UB8 1JT
(Tel: 0895-59831)

Network Systems Corporation Ltd.

(Hyperbus and Hyperchannel LANs)
Kings Ride Court, Ascot, Berkshire SL5 7JR
(Tel: 0990-23399)

Nine Tiles Computer Systems Ltd.

(Multilink micronet, *different* from American product of same name)
25 Greenside, Waterbeach, Cambridge CB5 9HW
(Tel: 0223-862125)

Norsk Data Ltd.

(WAN equipment and WAN software)
Strawberry Hill House, Bath Rd., Newbury, Berkshire RG13 1NU
(Tel: 0635-35544)

Orbis Computers Ltd.

(LANs, LAN equipment)
4a Market Hill, Cambridge CB2 3NJ
(Tel: 0223-312449)

Owl Micro-Communications Ltd.

(Microcomputer communications)
Station Road, Sawbridgeworth, Herts CN21 9LY
(Tel: 0279-723848)

Philips Business Systems

(SOPHO-LAN LAN, SOPHO-NET WAN)
Elektra House, Bergholt Road, Colchester, Essex CO4 5BE
(Tel: 0206-575115)

Plessey Communications Systems Ltd.

(Plessey integrated business information system (IBIS), PABXs, fax)
Beeston, Nottingham NG9 1LA
(Tel: 0602-254822)

Plessey Controls Ltd.

(WAN equipment, WAN control equipment)
Sopers Lane, Poole, Dorset BH1 7ER
(Tel: 0202-675161)

Plessey Office Systems Ltd.

(PABXs)
Beeston, Nottingham NG9 1LA
(Tel: 0602-254831)

Plessey Public Networks Ltd.

(Fibre optic systems, modems, WAN equipment)
Edge Lane, Liverpool L7 9NW
(Tel: 051-228 4830)

Prime Computer (UK) Ltd.

(PRIMENET LAN and WAN equipment and software)
The Hounslow Centre, 1 Lampton Rd., Hounslow, Middlesex TW3 1JB
(Tel: 01-572 7400)

Quorum Computers Ltd.

(Q-LAN)
Polygon House, Commercial Rd., Southampton SO1 0GC
(Tel: 0703-30721)

Racal-Milgo Ltd.

(PLANET LAN, Wan equipment, WAN management equipment)
(UK enquiries) Landata House, Station Rd., Hook, Hampshire RG27 9JF
(Tel: 025672-3911)
also
Crown House, 25 Turners Hill, Cheshunt, Herts EN8 8NJ
(Tel: 0992-33211)
(Overseas enquiries) Richmond Court, 309 Fleet Rd., Fleet, Hampshire GU13 8BU
(Tel: 02514-22144)

Rank Xerox (UK) Ltd.

(Xerox 8000 WAN and office automation equipment)
Bridge House, Oxford Road, Uxbridge UB8 1HS
(Tel: 0895-51133)

Real Time Developments Ltd.

(Clearway micronet)
Lynchford House, Lynchford Lane, Farnborough, Hants GU14 6JA
(Tel: 0252-546213)

Scicon Ltd.

(WAN equipment and software products)
Wavendon Tower, Wavendon, Milton Keynes MK17 8LX
(Tel: 0908-585858)

SEEL (Scientific and Electronic Enterprises Ltd.)

(TRANSRING LAN)
3 Young Square, Brucefield South Industrial Park, Livingston, West Lothian EH54 9BJ, Scotland
(Tel: 0506-411503)

Serious Software

(Media conversion equipment and software)
55 East Rd., London N1 6AH
(Tel: 01-253 2287)

Shaffstall (U.K.) Ltd.

(Media conversion equipment and software)
13-15 Sheet St., Windsor, Berkshire SL4 1AS
(Tel: 07535-55513)

Siemens Ltd.

(Teletex terminals, facsimile equipment)
Siemens House, Windmill Road, Sunbury-on-Thames, Middlesex TW16 7HS
(Tel: 09327 85691)

Sintrom Group

(Ethernet LAN equipment, Micom WAN equipment)
Arkwright Rd., Reading, Berkshire RG2 0LS
(Tel: 0734-85464)

SISCO (Small Information Systems Co. Ltd.)

(LAN, office automation system, computerised telex system)
4 Moorfields, London EC2
(Tel: 01-920 0315)

STC Business Systems Ltd.

(PABX-based systems, WAN equipment)
Crowhurst Rd., Hollingbury, Brighton BN1 8AN
(Tel: 0273-507111)

Symbiotic Computer Systems Ltd.

(SyMBnet personal computer network)
Duroma House, 32 Elmwood Rd., Croydon, Surrey CR9 2TX
(Tel: 01-683 1137)

Symicron Ltd.

(MICROGATE WAN equipment)
36 Westow St., London SE19
(Tel: 01-771 6020)

Systrex Ltd.

(OmegaNet® LAN)
19 Buckingham Gate, London SW1E 6LB
(Tel: 01-630 7675)

Tekelec Ltd.

(WAN analyzers and simulators)
Cumberland House, Baxter Ave., Southend-on-Sea, Essex SS2 6FA
(Tel: 0702-337337)

Tesdata Ltd.

(Hyperbus and Hyperchannel LANs, WAN management systems)
Tesdata House, Hatfield Rd., Slough, Berkshire SL1 1QR
(Tel: 0753-71961)

Thame Systems Ltd.

(Net/One LAN)
Thame Park Road, Thame, Oxon OX9 3XD
(084421-5471)

Torch Computers Ltd.

(TORCHNET personal computer network)
Abberley House, Great Shelford, Cambridge CB2 5LQ
(Tel: 0223-841000)

U-Microcomputers Ltd.

(U-NET personal computer network)
Winstanley Industrial Estate, Long Lane, Warrington, Cheshire WA2 8PR
(Tel: 0925-54117/8)

Userlink Systems Ltd.

(WAN equipment and software, equipment and software for access to online data bases)
Mansion House Chambers, High St., Stockport, Cheshire SK1 1EG
(Tel: 061-429 8232)

Vector Graphic

(SABER-NET LAN and LINC™ operating system)
Vector House, William St., Windsor, Berkshire SL4 1BA
(Tel: 07535-69375)

Walmore Electronics Ltd.

(Fibre optic equipment, modems, WAN equipment)
11/15 Betterton St., London WC2H 9BS
(01-836 1228)

Wang (UK) Ltd.

(WANGNET LAN, office automation systems)
Wang House, 661 London Rd., Isleworth, Middlesex TW7 4EH
(Tel: 01-560 4151)

Xionics Ltd.

(XINET/XIBUS LAN)
Dumbarton House, 68 New Oxford St., London W1N 9LA
(Tel: 01-636-0105)

Xtec Ltd.

(Modems, WAN equipment)
High Street, Hartley Wintney, near Basingstoke, Hampshire RG27 8PB
(Tel: 025126-4222/4233/4344)

Zilog (UK) Ltd.

(Z-Net micronet)
Zilog House, 41-59 Moorbridge Rd., Maidenhead, Berkshire SL6 8PL
(Tel: 0628-39200)

Name Index

Subject Index

Note that a chapter reference, e.g. *"Ch 7"*, is given where whole chapter, or a large part of it, is devoted to the subject in question. A few references are also given to parts of the book. However, for most subjects, references are given only or mainly to specific pages or sequences of pages. Where a subject has several citations, the page numbers of its most important citations are often given in *italics*.